Thematic Prosecution of International Sex Crimes

Morten Bergsmo (editor)

Second Edition

2018
Torkel Opsahl Academic EPublisher
Brussels

Dedicated to the memory of Antonio Cassese

EDITOR'S PREFACE TO THE SECOND EDITION

The first edition was the first book to deal with the topic of thematic prosecution of core international crimes. The subject-matter is equally relevant
today – it remains important to justify the singling out of a narrow range
of criminality for prosecution, whether in internationalized or national
criminal jurisdictions. Thematic prosecutions should be explained to the
public, both when practised by design or less deliberately. Absent proper
justification, the thematic prosecution of core international crimes is likely
to generate increasing controversy.

The favourable reception from critics, including five book reviews,
indicates that the first edition succeeded in its aim of raising awareness
and generating discussion about the possibilities and challenges of the use
of thematic prosecutions. This second edition expands upon the topic,
with the inclusion of three new chapters. The Foreword and Chapter 1
have also been updated. Various editorial changes have been made
throughout the book, including the addition of persistent URLs which
helps users of the e-book version to access all sources concerned online.

I place on record my appreciation for the assistance of Manek Minhas and Gareth Richards in the preparation of this second edition, and of
CHEAH Wui Ling, Audrey WONG Siew Ming, LAU Yu Don, Elaine
LIM Mei Yee, and NG Pei Yi for the first edition. I remain responsible for
imperfections in the book.

Morten Bergsmo

FOREWORD TO THE SECOND EDITION

For three reasons, it is an unusual privilege to write the foreword to this anthology. The first is that it is dedicated to the memory of Antonio Cassese, whose passing in 2011 saddened his family, friends and colleagues. It was my good fortune to work closely with Nino (as he was known to his friends) after I arrived at the United Nations International Criminal Tribunal for the former Yugoslavia ('ICTY') effectively as its first Chief Prosecutor. Nino was then the first President of the Tribunal and his leadership in those early years was crucial to its development. Nino's contribution to the jurisprudence that came from the ICTY is well recognised and highly respected by both academics and practitioners. He will be missed.

The second reason is that the ICTY can be credited with having advanced the modern law regarding gender-related crimes and especially the perpetration of systematic mass rape as a war crime. It was from the ICTY that the first thematic investigation and prosecution of sex crimes came.

The third is being associated again with my friend and colleague, Morten Bergsmo, who provided the inspiration for the conference which gave birth to this anthology and who is also the founder and director of the Centre for International Law Research and Policy, whose department the Forum for International Criminal and Humanitarian Law ('FICHL') has organised the research project.

The ICTY was the first truly international war crimes tribunal. (I exclude the Nuremberg Tribunal of 1945 – it was a multinational tribunal set up by the victorious allies after the Second World War.) Even before the investigations began in The Hague in the middle of 1994, reports proliferated of the rape of many thousands women and girls, especially in Bosnia and Herzegovina. The jurisdiction of the ICTY was limited to the investigation and prosecution of the most serious crimes defined in the Security Council resolution that set up the Tribunal. The only reference to rape as a war crime was to be found in the definition of crimes against humanity. That is a huge crime requiring sufficient evidence to establish that serious crimes were intentionally committed against a "civilian population". The first indictments we were able to issue were against so-called 'small fish' as we were still investigating the more senior leaders under whose command horrific war crimes had been and were then still being perpetrated. With the encouragement, particularly from the two female judges of the Tribunal, we began to charge rape as inhumane treatment, torture and a grave breach of the Geneva Convention, all crimes falling within the jurisdiction of the ICTY.

It is regrettable that the judges and prosecutors of the two United Nations *ad hoc* international war crimes tribunals were not aware of the important deliberations of the United Nations War Crimes Commission ('UNWCC') that sat in London between 1942 and 1948. It comprised leading international law experts from 17 Allied nations, including China and India. The UNWCC preceded and was unrelated to the United Nations that we know today and that was established in 1945. Its remit included the investigation and record of the evidence of war crimes. In effect, it acted as the gatekeeper for the prosecution of war crimes in the domestic military and civil courts of those of the 17 nations that launched prosecutions against alleged war criminals. In consequence of the work of the UNWCC, between 1945 and 1948, over 1,000 trials were held and some 2,700 accused persons faced trial. The vast majority of them were convicted.

The UNWCC gave careful attention to gender-related war crimes, and rape was successfully prosecuted as a war crime in China, Australia, Greece, France and Poland. The deliberations of the UNWCC would have provided strong support for the wider recognition of gender-related crimes in the early days of the Yugoslavia and Rwanda tribunals. Alas, those deliberations were until recently kept secret and classified in the archives of the United Nations in New York. It is to the credit of Dr. Dan Plesch and Ms. Shanti Sattler that the School of Oriental and African Studies ('SOAS'), University of London has successfully made many of those documents publicly available. Their endeavours can be accessed on the web site of the United Nations War Crimes Commission Project that is now part of the Centre for International Studies and Diplomacy at SOAS. Had I been aware of the work of the UNWCC I would not have claimed, as I did in the foreword I wrote for the first edition of this work, that the ICTY can be credited with pioneering the modern law regarding gender-related crimes. I am happy to correct the record.

Because of the neglect of gender-related crimes in humanitarian law, we decided in the Office of the Prosecutor to issue a thematic indictment based on sex crimes that became known as the Foča indictment. (It

iv

was in the town of Foča that the crimes were alleged to have been committed.) This was, I believe, the first-ever thematic prosecution of international sex crimes. It is thus of particular significance and provides a good measure of satisfaction that a conference was held in Cape Town on the topic of the thematic prosecution of sex crimes. It is also fitting that Morten Bergsmo, who played a significant role in putting together that first thematic indictment, played such a leading role. I congratulate CILRAP, Yale University, the University of Cape Town and the Royal Norwegian Government for co-sponsoring this conference. The papers that make up this anthology are of an extremely high standard and make a meaningful contribution to the ever-growing literature on international criminal justice. It remains for me to congratulate all who have been involved in this project.

Richard J. Goldstone
Former Chief Prosecutor of the ICTY and ICTR
Former Justice of the Constitutional Court of South Africa

TABLE OF CONTENTS

1

Towards Rational Thematic Prosecution and the Challenge of International Sex Crimes

Morten Bergsmo[*]

1.1. Understanding and Enhancing Criminal Justice Work Processes: The Concepts of Thematic Prosecution and Criminal Justice Themes

The first judgment of the International Criminal Court ('ICC') – the Lubanga Trial Judgment of 14 March 2012[1] – remains important for several reasons, among which are the following three. First, the obvious, it confirmed that the ICC would be a full-fledged court, not just a court in the making. Since that judgment, the Court has demonstrated its ability to exercise the broad spectrum of powers vested in it by more than 120 States and, consequently, its ability to implement its core mandate: three of its judgments on guilt and punishment, including the Lubanga Appeal Judgment,[2] currently stand final and are being enforced. This is important, as the credibility of the ICC – and of its well-compensated high officials and staff – rests squarely on how its core mandate is implemented.

Secondly, the Lubanga Trial Judgment represented the first affirmation by ICC judges that they believed the Office of the Prosecutor ('ICC-OTP') to be capable of preparing and prosecuting cases that meet the requirements of the Court's legal infrastructure. The OTP has been charged with several key functions, the most important of which are its duties of

---

[*] **Morten Bergsmo** is Director of the Centre for International Law Research and Policy, and a Visiting Professor at Peking University Law School, China. He co-ordinated the preparatory team for the ICC Office of the Prosecutor in 2002–2003, and served as the Office's Senior Legal Adviser and Chief of the Legal Advisory Section until 31 December 2005. The author thanks Manek Minhas for her assistance with reviewing the chapter for the Second Edition.

[1] *Prosecutor v. Thomas Lubanga Dyilo*, Trial Chamber I, Judgment pursuant to Article 74 of the Statute, Case No. ICC-01/04-01/06, 14 March 2012 (http://www.legal-tools.org/doc/677866/).

[2] *Prosecutor v. Thomas Lubanga Dyilo*, Appeals Chamber, Judgment on the appeal of Mr Thomas Lubanga Dyilo against his conviction, Case No. ICC-01/04-01/06, 1 December 2014 (http://www.legal-tools.org/doc/585c75/).

fact-gathering, fact-analysis, and fact-presentation. The Office should serve as the engine of the ICC, by driving the Court's fact-gathering and fact-analysis work processes on behalf of the community of States that has established the Court. It is the force, focus, and precision of the OTP's work on facts, potential evidence, and evidence that defines the factual scope, depth, and quality of cases before the ICC. The OTP's performance of these fact-oriented duties is subject to the scrutiny of ICC judges who determine whether the Office is worthy of the trust placed in it by ICC States Parties. Judgments, such as that by Trial Chamber I in the Lubanga case, serve as touchstones of the OTP's ability in this area.

Thirdly, and most relevant to this anthology's subject matter, the Lubanga Trial Judgment limited itself to the war crimes of conscripting, enlisting, and using child soldiers. Compared with cases before the International Criminal Tribunals for the Former Yugoslavia and Rwanda, the Lubanga Trial Judgment, upheld on appeal, convicted Mr. Lubanga Dyilo of a very narrow range of criminality, which did not include the killings or violations of physical integrity, such as torture or rape, that have characterised the conflict in which he was an actor. It is not easy to argue that Lubanga's conviction is reflective of the overall victimisation in the relevant armed conflict in the Democratic Republic of the Congo ('DRC'). This is not to say that the recruitment and use of child soldiers are not serious international crimes. Their relatively recent criminalisation in international law does not detract from this, but is simply indicative of a slowly changing consensus; from a time when we accepted that children could be war heroes by performing intelligence, communications or other acts of bravery, to our contemporary recognition of the importance of the developmental needs of children and youth.

By singling out the *theme* of recruitment and use of child soldiers in its first case, the ICC legitimised the very idea of *thematic prosecution* at the international and national levels. In doing so, it confirmed the significance of this book's topic and the issues it raises. It also demonstrated the timeliness of an examination of the bases and merits of thematic prosecution, the use of criminal justice themes, and prosecutorial thematisation more generally.

The importance of such examination has been reinforced since the release of the first edition of this book in 2012. Subsequent case-law of the ICC confirms the same practice: in 2016, the Al Mahdi Trial Judgment[3] limited itself to the war crimes of intentionally directing attacks against historic *monuments and buildings* dedicated to religion. Furthermore, there have been growing demands for the theme of *sexual violence* to be prioritised in national accountability processes. In the Democratic Republic of Congo, for example, this has even been reflected in a formal instrument on prioritisation.[4]

This anthology is composed of papers presented at the expert seminar "Thematic Investigation and Prosecution of International Sex Crimes" held in Cape Town on 7-8 March 2011, and co-organised by the Forum for International Criminal and Humanitarian Law ('FICHL'), Yale University, and the University of Cape Town, with financial support from the Norwegian Ministry of Foreign Affairs. It also contains chapters by Roísín Burke, Niamh Hayes, Fletch Williams, Dieneke de Vos, Estelle Zinsstag and Virginie Busck-Nielsen Claeys, all contributions made outside the specific context of the seminar.

Framed on the basis of the first publication on this topic,[5] the FICHL has – through the Cape Town seminar and this anthology – placed the *problématique* of thematic prosecution on the agenda for wide and critical discussion, with the objective of assisting criminal justice actors at the national and international levels to contribute more effectively to the securing of accountability for international sex crimes. Such discussion can generate an increased self-awareness within criminal justice agencies of explicit or implicit institutional practices that may amount to thematic prosecution or criminal justice themes. Incubating self-reflection of this nature can, if the discourse is sufficiently practice-oriented and contains a

---

[3] *Prosecutor v. Ahmad Al Faqi Al Mahdi*, Trial Chamber VIII, Judgment and Sentence, Case No. ICC-01/12-01/15, 27 September 2016 (http://www.legal-tools.org/doc/042397/).

[4] Circulaire No. 02/PCC-PCSM/2018 Relative a la Selection et a la Prioritisation des Affairs de Crimes Contre la Paix et la Securite de l'Humanite, en Particulier Celles Liees aux Violences Sexuelles, au Stade de l'Instruction Prejuridictionnelle [Direction Relating to the Selection and Prioritization of Crimes Against Peace and Security of Humanity, Particularly Those Affected by Sexual Violence, at the Stage of Pre-Jurisdictional Instruction], Democratic Republic of Congo, 19 March 2018.

[5] See Morten Bergsmo, "Tematisk etterforskning og straffeforfølgning av seksualisert vold i konflikt: er det en uproblematisk praksis?" [Thematic investigation and prosecution of sexualised violence in conflict: is that an unproblematic practice?], in Hege Skjeie, Inger Skjelsbæk and Torunn L. Tryggestad (eds.), *Kjønn, Krig, Konflikt* [Gender, War, Conflict], 2008, pp. 79–91.

---

diversity of perspectives, rationalise the institutional practices in question and, by that, increase their quality, cost-efficiency and fairness. Discourse can in this way be a critical component of institutional professionalisation. Facilitating such discourses is one of the main objectives of the Centre for International Law Research and Policy, of which FICHL is a department.

Placing a particular emphasis on international sex crimes or on another similarly narrow range of criminality, such as torture or the destruction of cultural monuments, can turn these crimes into a criminal justice theme within the criminal justice systems in question. Such themes may take the form of focused or thematic investigations and prosecutions of these crimes, or the construction of crime-specific institutional capacity within the criminal justice system.

The authors were invited to address aspects of this thematic emphasis. Their contributions significantly contribute to our awareness and understanding of the practice of thematic prosecution and criminal justice themes, specifically in relation to international sex crimes.

Although some authors focus on international jurisdictions, their ideas can be transposed to national criminal justice systems. It is the latter to which attention is now gradually, and inevitably, shifting. The issue of thematic prosecution of international sex crimes, and other core international crimes, must be addressed by each jurisdiction on its own terms. By analysing thematic prosecution's possibilities, challenges, and consequences, this anthology seeks to equip and empower criminal justice actors. It hopes to assist them in the making of choices that are fully considered and well-reasoned, which will in turn enhance the legitimacy of their decisions.

Crime selection and prioritisation in the field of criminal justice for atrocities primarily takes place in response to the practical challenge of prudently applying limited resources. But examining the concept and practice of prosecutorial thematisation also partially requires the engagement of theoretical questions. Such considerations of principle may only become operational when they are anchored in tools, such as investigation plans and prioritisation criteria. These tools also ensure a measure of transparency and accountability, and can go some way to preventing the politicisation of, or the consideration of irrelevant factors during, the decision-making process. Indeed, jurisdictions should consider making it obligatory for international crimes investigators and prosecutors to justify why an investigation should be initiated in a written investigation plan that places the alleged crimes in a broader context. The institutionalisation of such practical and concrete tools is less susceptible to tokenism, unlike more high-profile implementation measures, such as public announcements of special institutional capacity to deal with international sex crimes.

1.2. Chapter Contributions: Theoretical Perspectives, Case Studies and Critical Analysis

The first part of this anthology comprises two chapters that serve as an introductory stage to the topic of thematic prosecution by providing an overview of issues from two different viewpoints: a theoretical perspective and a prosecutorial-institutional perspective. Margaret M. deGuzman's Chapter 2 sets out and examines how different theoretical bases may inform decisions on whether to give priority to sex crimes. According to deGuzman, while retribution and deterrence bases support selective prosecutions at least some of the time, expressivism and restorative bases provide an even stronger foundation for giving priority to international sex crimes. An argument can be made that at least some perpetrators of sex crimes are more deserving of punishment than some perpetrators of crimes resulting in death. The prosecution of international sex crimes may also provide greater deterrent benefits at least in some circumstances. Most importantly, argues deGuzman in favour of expressivism, there is a significantly greater need for the international community to express its condemnation of international sex crimes than of killings, which are already considered as serious violations of moral norms throughout the world. Victim restorative goals may be more achievable in the context of international sex crimes because, unlike the victims of killing, the immediate victims of sex crimes remain alive and are potentially able to participate in, and benefit from, restorative processes.

While theoretical discussions on the goals of thematic prosecution are important, such prosecutorial decisions are necessarily implemented within specific institutions by real institutional actors who will need to reflexively develop standards and practices that guide such prosecutorial efforts and address their consequences. In Chapter 3, Fabricio Guariglia highlights how the ICC-OTP has developed criteria for situation and case selection, which essentially revolve around the notions of gravity and of the 'most responsible' persons. While the latter's focus on those who hold positions of leadership allows for comprehensive prosecutions which present a broader narrative on the manner in which international sex crimes were committed, the higher we go up the chains of command, the further away we move from the individual victim's episode of sexual violence and his or her suffering. Guariglia highlights how the ICC-OTP may compensate for this, such as by ensuring a representative sample of crimes in its charging, so that victims of uncharged crimes can relate to the victimisation portrayed in the charges; by efficiently utilising the contextual evidence necessary to establish crimes against humanity, and in so doing, portraying the true extent of victimisation; and, in the context of sentencing, leading victim impact evidence that adequately reflects the effects experienced by individual victims of the sexual violence.

The second part of this anthology aims to broaden our understanding of thematic prosecution through a variety of case studies. In Chapter 4, Christopher B. Mahony undertakes a case study of the Special Court of Sierra Leone ('SCSL'). The SCSL, which has often been cited as a "new model" for post-conflict internationalised criminal justice, has been lauded for trying "persons bearing the greatest responsibility" for crimes during Sierra Leone's conflict. By placing the creation of the SCSL in its historical context and by analysing empirical data, Mahony reveals how the Court's designing and co-operating States pursued neo-liberal geopolitical objectives through, *inter alia*, the prioritisation of certain crimes over others. Not only does this pressure to prioritise particular crimes undermine the emergence of case prioritisation norms, it may also end up assisting duplicitous actors who could selectively prefer the thematic prosecution of international sex crimes for political purposes. Homogenising case selection and prioritisation criteria, rather than diversifying it without broad consensus, mitigates the risk of politicisation.

In Chapter 5, Flor de Maria Valdez-Arroyo studies the use of thematic prosecution for sex crimes in Latin America based on the jurisprudence of the Inter-American Court of Human Rights ('IAHRC') and its impact in national prosecutions. She notes that the IAHRC's judgments provide guidance for the prosecution of sex crimes and supports the use of thematic prosecution for expressive objectives. To fully understand the evolving emphasis on international sex crimes, there is a need to study how various practices have developed within their different regional or national contexts. The next chapter by Benson Chinedu Olugbuo examines, among others, the use of mobile courts in the DRC to prosecute serious sex crimes. Susanna Greijer's following chapter brings us beyond jurisdictional case studies to an analysis of the comparable subject of the thematic prosecution of conflict crimes committed against children, whose victimisation and silencing experiences may be said to be similar to that of victims of international sex crimes. Paloma Soria Montañez, who worked as a staff attorney at the NGO, Women's Link Worldwide, offers us a civil society perspective on the prosecution of international sex crimes. While she acknowledges that there is a need to consider whether thematic prosecutions make sense in national courts in light of available material and human resources, she emphasises the need to ensure the integrated prosecution and effective mainstreaming of gender crimes.

The third part of this anthology brings together chapters of a distinct analytical nature. These chapters apply a variety of analytical frameworks and approaches to their subject matter. They challenge assumptions that may underlie thematic prosecution, and explore how social, institutional, and political factors interact in this field. In Chapter 9, Valerie Oosterveld discusses whether the thematic prosecution of international sex crimes to the exclusion of other prohibited acts adequately delivers justice to victims. Such prosecutions fail to capture the crimes' context, nature, and implications. Sexual violence is usually part of a wider picture of victimisation, and often intersects with other seemingly gender-neutral crimes. As well, apparently gender-neutral prohibited acts may have been carried out in gender-specific ways or may have gendered outcomes. By pursuing investigations and prosecutions in which sexual violence is explored within the context of other core international crimes, both the serious nature of the sexual violence and the potentially gendered nature of the other crimes can be highlighted and understood. To achieve this, there is a need for heightened gender competence and expertise among criminal justice actors.

In Chapter 10, Neha Jain applies a pluralistic framework to the international criminal trial that posits the importance of institutional and structural factors that may differ between tribunals, and that have a bearing on the validity of thematic prosecutions, particularly with respect to international sex crimes. She argues that three such factors will be particularly influential when justifying the practice of thematic prosecutions. The first is the status of the court, namely, whether it is a post-conflict tribunal or one that may intervene in situations of on-going conflict. This status will influence what aims the tribunal may legitimately strive towards – retributive, expressive, or deterrent. The second factor is whether an international court can be envisaged as mainly a tool of post-conflict peace building. If it is indeed set up to serve this instrumentalist goal, it may be able to expressly pursue didactic goals and prioritise the investigation and prosecution of international sex crimes. The third factor is the extent of civil party involvement in tribunal proceedings. If victim participation is considered desirable either because it promotes restorative justice or because it assists in the determination of truth by the tribunal, the enhanced role of the victim will influence the extent to which international sex crimes may be prioritised by the court.

In Chapter 11, Olympia Bekou adopts an institutional approach in considering the question of thematic prosecution. She discusses the advantages and disadvantages of creating specialised institutional capacity for the thematic prosecution of international sex crimes. Arguments in favour of specialised units include: long-term commitment; development of knowledge and expertise (training); better resource allocation and mobilisation; better international co-operation; visibility, accountability and outreach; consistency, efficiency, successful prosecutions, and increased capacity. The disadvantages include: added complexity; cost; unit-straddling; rarity of incidence; impact on personnel; impact on victims; potential loss of skill; and marginal influence on case outcomes. The benefits of *ad hoc* arrangements include: mobility and flexibility; lower costs; and the use of existing expertise. Whereas the drawbacks include: increased workload, and the lack of institutional memory, quality control, and sustainability. Bekou advocates for expert training and increasing capacity, regardless of whether this takes place as part of a formal setting.

Drawing on critical legal studies, the next chapter by Alejandra Azuero Quijano explores the potential consequences of how scientific epistemologies of sex difference might provide answers to the following questions: do scientific theories of sex difference serve to explain the channelling of political and economic resources to the investigation of crimes traditionally imagined to be committed by men against women? How is thematic investigation participating in the legal hierarchisation of crimes, and how is scientific knowledge related to this phenomenon? Among others, she highlights the problems associated with binary reasoning and legal categorisation, which has resulted from the feminist advocacy project, and which may have excluded others or damaged the feminist cause.

In the final chapter to part three of this anthology, Kai Ambos studies how thematic investigations and prosecutions, in the sense of focused, but not exclusive, prosecutions of international sex crimes, are a useful tool to increase awareness of and reinforce the prohibition of sexual violence. They may help not only to emphasise sexual violence, but also to clarify the broader context in which the respective crimes occurred. This type of crime requires expert knowledge that may be provided by specialised units or particularly skilled advisers for reasons, *inter alia*, of evidentiary issues or the danger of the re-victimisation of primary victims.

In the last section of this anthology, we have included five invited chapters that were not presented at the seminar. They have been included because their broader subject matter of prosecuting sex crimes is relevant to this anthology's topic of thematic prosecution of international sex crimes. In Chapter 14, Roísín Burke examines the problem of holding United Nations peacekeepers accountable for sexual abuses and proposes different institutional set-ups to facilitate this. In Chapter 15, Niamh Hayes broadly explores the prosecutorial strategy employed by international criminal tribunals to prosecute international sex crimes.

Finally, the three new chapters in this Second Edition examine specific areas of the theme that were not previously covered in detail. In Chapter 16, Fletch Williams focuses on the international law regarding sex crimes against male victims, and the harms suffered in relation to unequal legal protection in this regard. Dieneke de Vos then studies gender dimensions to the interpretation of the ICC's admissibility provisions and how this affects domestic prosecution of sexual and gender-based violence crimes. The last chapter, co-authored by Estelle Zinsstag and Virginie Busck-Nielsen Claeys, explores the restorative paradigm in the context of sexual violence, incuding an examination of the restorative justice mechanisms that may be relevant.

1.3. Further Analysis and Research

In addition to placing the topic of thematic prosecution on the national and international scene, this anthology also highlights the need for further discussion and implicitly identifies a number of directions for future research. Its conceptualisation of this topic and its chapters serve as a suitable starting point for such endeavours, drawing on the seminar concept note and discussions at the FICHL Cape Town seminar referred to above.[6]

First, there needs to be a critical and open-minded consideration of the justifications of thematic prosecution. Mirroring ongoing debates on the objectives of international criminal prosecutions, some authors apply and consider in their chapters below the philosophical justifications of retribution, deterrence, expressivism, and restoration in the context of thematic prosecution. Other authors seek justifications by referring to legal and institutional frameworks, such as the ICC's reference to gravity. In reality, decisions on thematic prosecution are often explained, and at times justified, by pragmatic or political reasons. What is the nature and relationship between these justificatory and explanatory concepts, and how do they contribute to our understanding and implementation of thematic prosecution? More conceptual work should be undertaken, starting with this anthology.

Second, by mapping the various institutional landscapes in which the practice of thematic prosecution has evolved, this anthology's chapters have begun to identify the actors involved in, and impacted by, thematic prosecutorial decisions. It has examined how such prosecutions are often legitimised in terms of victim interests but may not in effect advance such interests. It has explored the perspective of prosecutors afflicted by resource constraints, that of NGOs advocating community empowerment, and that of judges potentially in need of specialist input. There is a need to explore how other actors and stakeholders view and react to thematic prosecution. For example, one reason for giving thematic priority to international sex crimes is arguably the victims' emerging right to the truth. If so, what are the implications of thematic prosecution for victims whose crimes are excluded or de-emphasised as a result? Are international sex crimes qualitatively different from other, otherwise comparable serious international crimes? It would appear that understanding the victimhood of international sex crimes will benefit from further comparison *vis-à-vis* that of other international crimes. There is, therefore, a need to consider how such prosecutions impact accused persons, other conflict victims, affected communities, and even epistemic communities, such as that of international criminal law experts.

---

[6] The seminar interventions by Nobuo Hayashi should be noted in this context.

Last, but not least, this anthology's various chapters warn against an overly enthusiastic or unquestioning acceptance of thematic prosecution. This position goes against that taken by most NGOs, which have widely supported the thematic prosecution of international sex crimes. Given the highly political environment in which the institutions of international criminal justice operate, it would be unwise for them to depart from a well-established and legally secure set of prioritisation criteria, and a widely accepted priority among crimes. Deviating from these standards in favour of thematic prosecution could risk exposing the entire prosecutorial process to manipulation by third-party entities. However, it is often a fact that the administration of criminal justice is susceptible to politics – and *vice versa*. And this is equally, if not more, true of international criminal justice. While this does not require the abandonment of thematic prosecution as a concept or practice, it does require an increased awareness of its associated risks, and the development of appropriate implementation tools that will minimise these risks. Access to such comprehensive knowledge and realistic tools will be particularly important for domestic criminal justice actors whose decisions and justifications will be subject to more rigorous scrutiny by local populations as compared with any decision taken by their international counterparts. Use of thematic prosecution requires clear and public justification to be effective, sustainable and worthy of the trust of victims.

2

An Expressive Rationale
for the Thematic Prosecution of Sex Crimes

Margaret M. deGuzman[*]

2.1. Introduction

Most international criminal courts address situations of mass atrocities with resources that allow them to prosecute only a small fraction of the crimes committed. One of the most critical tasks these courts perform therefore is to decide how to allocate their scarce investigative and prosecutorial resources. A strategy some courts have adopted is to pursue "thematic prosecutions" – that is, to orient cases around particular themes of criminality. This strategy was used in some of the earliest prosecutions for international crimes after the Second World War.[1] More recently, thematic prosecutions have been employed to focus attention on sex crimes.[2] At the International Criminal Tribunal for the former Yugoslavia ('ICTY') teams of investigators have been assigned to uncover evidence

---

[*] **Margaret M. deGuzman** is an Associate Professor of Law at the Beasley School of Law, Temple University, with expertise in criminal law and procedure, and international and comparative law. This essay expands the analysis in my earlier publication entitled "Giving Priority to Sex Crime Prosecutions at International Courts: The Philosophical Foundations of a Feminist Agenda", in *International Criminal Law Review*, 2011, vol. 11, no. 3, p. 515. I am indebted to Marie-Theres DiFillippo and Michael Witsch for excellent research assistance.

[1] See Jonathan A. Bush, "The Prehistory of Corporations and Conspiracy in International Criminal Law: What Nuremberg Really Said", in *Columbia Law Review*, 2009, vol. 109, pp. 1167–73, discussing the history behind prosecutors' decisions to pursue thematic prosecutions at the Nuremberg Military Tribunals. Examples include the trials of industrialists, doctors and judges. Nuremberg Military Tribunal, *United States of America v. Friedrich Flick et al.*, Judgment, 22 December 1947; Nuremberg Military Tribunal, *United States of America v. Carl Krauch et al.*, Judgment, 30 July 1948; Nuremberg Military Tribunal, *United States of America v. Alfried Krupp et al.*, Judgment, 31 July 1948; Nuremberg Military Tribunal, *United States of America v. Karl Brandt et al.*, Judgment, 19 August 1947; Nuremberg Military Tribunal, *United States of America v. Josef Altstötter et al.*, Judgment, 4 December 1947.

[2] John Hagan, *Justice in the Balkans: Prosecuting War Crimes in the Hague Tribunal*, University of Chicago Press, Chicago, 2003, pp. 181–82; Morten Bergsmo, Kjetil Helvig, Ilia Utmelidze and Gorana Žagovec, *The Backlog of Core International Crimes Case Files in Bosnia and Herzegovina*, 2nd ed., Torkel Opsahl Academic EPublisher, Oslo, 2010, p. 109, fn. 46.

---

of sex crimes, and prosecutions have been brought that involve exclusively charges of sex crimes. Thus, for example, the *Foča* case charged a number of former soldiers with crimes related to the infamous "rape camps" in that city.[3]

Even when prosecutors have not pursued thematic sex crime prosecutions, many have articulated an intention to focus special attention on such crimes. For example, the former prosecutor of the International Criminal Court ('ICC'), Luis Moreno-Ocampo, pledged that in selecting cases he would "pay particular attention to [...] sexual and gender-based crimes".[4] The ICTY's first prosecutor, Richard Goldstone, observed that both the ICTY and the International Criminal Tribunal for Rwanda ('ICTR') have shown a unique concern for prosecuting sex crimes.[5] The current prosecutor of the ICTR has also confirmed that sex crime prosecutions are a priority for the tribunal.[6] In fact, in August 2010, a group of current and former international prosecutors issued a declaration drawing attention to the special need for investigation and prosecution of sex crimes.[7]

Despite the increased focus on sex crime prosecutions in recent years, no effort has been made, either at the tribunals or in the scholarship, to provide a philosophical justification for the practice of giving priority to sex crimes. Those who prosecute and write about sex crimes generally

---

[3] International Criminal Tribunal for the Former Yugoslavia ('ICTY'), *Prosecutor v. Kunarać, Zoran Vuković and Radomir Kovač*, Trial Chamber, Judgment, IT-96-23 & 23/1, 22 February 2001 (*Foča* case) (http://www.legal-tools.org/doc/fd881d/); see also ICTY, *Prosecutor v. Anto Furundžija*, Trial Chamber, Judgment, IT-95-17/1, 10 December 1998 (http://www.legal-tools.org/doc/e6081b/) (charging exclusively sex crimes).

[4] International Criminal Court ('ICC'), Office of the Prosecutor, Report on Prosecutorial Strategy, 14 September 2006, p. 7 (https://www.legal-tools.org/doc/6e3bf4/pdf/); see also ICC, Office of the Prosecutor, "Criteria for Selection of Situations and Cases", June 2006, p. 13, unpublished draft document on file with the author: "The Office will pay particular attention to methods of investigations of crimes committed against children, sexual and gender-based crimes"; ICC, Office of the Prosecutor, "Factsheet: Situation in the Central African Republic", p. 3: "The OTP is paying particular attention to the many allegations of sexual crimes".

[5] Richard J. Goldstone, "Prosecuting Rape as a War Crime", in *Case Western Reserve Journal of International Law*, 2002, vol. 34, no. 3, p. 278.

[6] Hassan B. Jallow, "Prosecutorial Discretion and International Criminal Justice", in *Journal of International Criminal Justice*, 2005, vol. 3, no. 1, p. 153.

[7] "The Fourth Chautauqua Declaration: 31 August 2010", in Leila Nadya Sadat (ed.), *Forging a Convention for Crimes against Humanity*, Cambridge University Press, Cambridge, 2011, pp. 545–48.

assume that international courts should increase their focus on such crimes. Commentators sometimes point to the practical and institutional benefits of thematic sex crime prosecutions. Such prosecutions can, for example, increase an institution's capacity to address sex crimes by developing relevant investigative and prosecutorial expertise and expanding the applicable law.[8] But a prior normative question must be addressed: why should international courts give priority to sex crimes when allocating scarce resources? The need for justification stems primarily from the widely accepted maxim that prosecutors should give priority to the most serious crimes. Although sex crimes are considered very serious in most (although not all) parts of the world, they are generally viewed as less serious than crimes resulting in death. At most international courts, the decision to prosecute sex crimes entails a deselection of some crimes involving killing because resources are insufficient to prosecute all rapes and all killings. It is therefore particularly important to understand why sex crimes should be given priority over killing crimes.

The philosophical grounding for thematic sex crime prosecutions must be found in the underlying purposes of international criminal courts. While the moral justifications of international prosecutions are widely disputed, there are four primary contenders: retribution, deterrence, restoration and expression. In the first part of this chapter, I explain why none of the first three theories precludes giving priority to sex crime prosecutions. In fact, each theory supports such prosecutions, at least under some circumstances. I then explain that the strongest justification for giving priority to sex crimes is found in the expressive rationale for international criminal law. In other words, if international criminal law aims to express global norms it should often seek to promote the norms against sex crimes even at the expense of other important norms. The special importance of prosecuting sex crimes lies in their history of underenforcement and in the discrimination that the crimes themselves express.

To be clear, I am not arguing that sex crimes should always be given priority over killing crimes. First, the terms 'sex crimes'[9] and 'killing

---

[8]   Karen Engle, "Feminism and Its (Dis)contents: Criminalizing Wartime Rape in Bosnia and Herzegovina", in *American Journal of International Law*, 2005, vol. 99, no. 4, pp. 781–82 (explaining the ICTY's focus on the development of the law surrounding sex crimes).

[9]   This essay uses the term 'sex crimes' because it provides a clear contrast with crimes involving killing. Nonetheless, many of the arguments made herein also apply to the broader cate-

crimes' encompass a wide array of behaviours and harms. Sex crimes can range in seriousness from non-violent sexual humiliation to sexual slavery and forced pregnancy. Similarly, international crimes involving killing include vastly different crimes from individual unintentional war crimes to genocidal exterminations. In deciding how to allocate resources, prosecutors must consider the nature of the particular crimes committed and the seriousness of the harms inflicted – a task that is outside the scope of this general analysis.

Second, resource allocation decisions involve a host of considerations that cannot be accounted for herein. For example, one of the most important factors in selecting cases for prosecution is the strength of the available evidence.[10] A prosecutor may choose to charge a less serious crime for which he or she is confident of obtaining a conviction rather than a more egregious crime for which the evidence is weaker. Thus, even a prosecutor who accepts the special importance of focusing on sex crimes might avoid charging such crimes when the evidence available to prove other crimes is stronger. Moreover, assuming the strength of the evidence is consistent across crimes, a prosecutor might have other legitimate reasons for not charging sex crimes in a particular case. For example, a witness might have expressed a strong preference for testifying about a killing she observed but not a rape she suffered.[11] More controversially, a prosecutor may decide to drop sex crimes charges in exchange for guilty pleas to other serious crimes.[12]

---

gory of 'gender crimes' – crimes committed on the basis of the victim's (usually female) gender. The choice between sex crimes and crimes involving killing is highlighted herein because the latter are most frequently cited as more serious than sex crimes, and therefore more deserving of prosecution. However, the analysis could be extended to crimes such as torture and slavery that are often placed on a par with sex crimes in terms of seriousness. Such crimes should also sometimes be subordinated to sex crimes for the reasons elucidated herein.

[10] See, for example, Abby Goodnough, "Some Charges May Be Dropped in Bulger Case as Prosecutors Focus on Killings", in *New York Times*, 28 June 2011, citing a US prosecutor as stating: "It is also in the public interest to protect public resources – both executive and judicial – by bringing the defendant to trial on the government's strongest case".

[11] Cf. Bergsmo *et al.*, 2010, p. 122, fn. 80, see *supra* note 2: "Thematic prosecutions should also take the interests of victims duly into account".

[12] Hassan B. Jallow, "Session 5: Debates with Prosecutors at the International Criminal Tribunal for Rwanda: Model or Counter Model for International Criminal Justice? The Perspectives of the Stakeholders", 11 July 2009, p. 8: an ICTR prosecutor explaining the need to

Moreover, the decision whether to engage in thematic prosecutions or otherwise prioritise sex crimes in a particular case must be situated within the broader context of prosecutions undertaken in a given situation.[13] A case selection decision that appears justified in isolation may nonetheless be ill advised when viewed in the context of the other prosecutions in the situation. Thus, for example, while some thematic prosecutions of sex crimes may have been justified in response to the situation in the former Yugoslavia, a decision to focus exclusively on sex crimes despite the prevalence of other serious crimes would have undermined many of the Tribunal's goals. In particular, such a strategy would have detracted from efforts to restore the affected societies by establishing the truth of what happened and building a historical record.

In sum, each case and situation presents unique characteristics, making it unwise to proffer categorical arguments about when prosecutors should give priority to particular crimes. Instead, I make two more modest, but nonetheless important, claims: 1) that each of the philosophical justifications for international criminal prosecutions supports giving priority to sex crimes some of the time; and 2) that the strongest justification for a special focus on sex crimes at international courts lies in the need to express the undervalued norms prohibiting such crimes.

2.2. No Theoretical Argument Precludes Thematic Prosecution of Sex Crimes

The age-old debates about the moral justifications for criminal punishment have begun to find new expression in the context of international criminal law. A small number of scholars have endeavoured to articulate philosophical rationales for international punishment and to question whether such punishment requires different justification from that inflicted at the national level.[14] The most frequently invoked rationales for in-

---

sometimes bargain away sex crimes charges. A judge of the Special Court for Sierra Leone has opined that such plea-bargaining "sends the wrong message to the perpetrator and community": Teresa A. Doherty, Summary of the Second Hague Colloquium, Systematic Sexual Violence and Victims' Rights, The Hague, 7–8 April 2011, p. 7.

13   The term 'situation' in international criminal law refers to the geographic and temporal space in which international crimes have been committed.

14   See, for example, Robert D. Sloane, "The Expressive Capacity of International Punishment: The Limits of the National Law Analogy and the Potential of International Criminal Law", in *Stanford Journal of International Law*, 2006, vol. 43, p. 39; Immi Tallgren, "The Sensibility

ternational criminal adjudication are the familiar ones of retribution, deterrence, restorative justice and expressivism. However, as elaborated below, several of these theories take on a different form when invoked at the international level. Moreover, unlike national theorists, most of whom subscribe to retributivist or deterrent rationales, scholars who have written about criminal law theories at the international level are generally unenthusiastic about retribution,[15] and sceptical about deterrence,[16] but more sanguine about restorative justice[17] and expressivism.[18] In the discussion that follows, I suggest that each of the theories provides at least a partial justification for international criminal prosecution and that none precludes giving priority to sex crimes.

---

and Sense of International Criminal Law", in *European Journal of International Law*, 2002, vol. 13, no. 3, p. 561; David J. Luban, "Fairness to Rightness: Jurisdiction, Legality, and the Legitimacy of International Criminal Law", in Samantha Besson and John Tasioulas (eds.), *The Philosophy of International Law*, Oxford University Press, New York, 2010, p. 569; Mark A. Drumbl, *Atrocity, Punishment, and International Law*, Cambridge University Press, New York, 2007; Stephanos Bibas and William Whitney Burke-White, "International Idealism Meets Domestic-Criminal-Procedure Realism", in *Duke Law Journal*, 2010, vol. 59, no. 4, p. 637; David S. Koller, "The Faith of the International Criminal Lawyer", in *New York University Journal of International Law and Politics*, 2008, vol. 40, p. 1019; Jean Galbraith, "The Pace of International Criminal Justice", in *Michigan Journal of International Law*, 2009, vol. 31, p. 79; Adil Ahmad Haque, "International Crime: In Context and in Contrast", in R.A. Duff, Lindsay Farmer, S.E. Marshall, Massimo Renzo and Victor Tadros (eds.), *Structures of Criminal Law*, Oxford University Press, Oxford, 2011, pp. 17–21.

[15] See, for example, Drumbl, 2007, p. 151, *supra* note 14; Martti Koskenniemi, "Between Impunity and Show Trials", in *Max Planck Yearbook of United Nations Law*, 2002, vol. 6, no. 1, p. 9; Sloane, 2006, p. 67, *supra* note 14.

[16] See, for example, David Wippman, "Atrocities, Deterrence, and the Limits of International Justice", in *Fordham International Law Journal*, 1999, vol. 23, no. 2, p. 473; Jenia Iontcheva Turner, "Nationalizing International Criminal Law: The International Criminal Court as a Roving Mixed Court", in *Stanford Journal of International* Law, 2005, vol. 41, p. 17. See also Payam Akhavan, "Beyond Impunity: Can International Criminal Justice Prevent Future Atrocities?", in *American Journal of International Law*, 2001, vol. 95, no. 1, p. 9, expressing greater optimism about the deterrent effect of international criminal law.

[17] Mark Findlay and Ralph J. Henham, Transforming International Justice: Retributive and Restorative Justice in the Trial Process, Willan Publishing, Portland, 2005; Nancy Combs, *Guilty Pleas in International Criminal Law: Constructing a Restorative Justice Approach*, Stanford University Press, Stanford, 2007, pp. 136–87.

[18] See, for example, Sloane, 2006, p. 39, *supra* note 14; Diane Marie Amann, "Group Mentality, Expressivism, and Genocide", in *International Criminal Law Review*, 2002, vol. 2, no. 2, p. 93; Mirjan Damaška, "What is the Point of International Criminal Justice?", in *Chicago-Kent Law Review*, 2008, vol. 83, no. 1, p. 329.

2.2.1. Retribution

Retributive theories hold that criminal punishment is justified entirely by the moral desert of the perpetrator. While retributivists explain the link between moral desert and punishment in various ways, they share the belief that desert is all that is necessary for the infliction of punishment to be morally right.[19] In fact, many retributivists maintain that criminal punishment is required when moral norms are violated.[20] Retributivism also holds that punishment should be proportionate to the crime committed.[21]

Retribution is one of the most frequently invoked justifications for international criminal punishment.[22] Nonetheless, many scholars reject the idea that retribution should be a central goal of international criminal adjudication.[23] Critics of retributive justifications for international trials tend to focus on the inability of international courts to prosecute all, or even most, of the crimes committed in a given situation, as well as the difficulty of inflicting retributively proportionate punishments for such heinous

---

[19] See, generally, Joshua Dressler, *Cases and Materials on Criminal Law*, 4th ed., West, St Paul, 2007, pp. 38–48, discussing different strands of retributive theory that have developed over time; Paul H. Robinson, "Competing Conceptions of Modern Desert: Vengeful, Deontological, and Empirical", in *Cambridge Law Journal*, 2008, vol. 67, no. 1, p. 145.

[20] Dressler, 2007, p. 39, see *supra* note 19: "For a retributivist, the moral culpability of the offender also gives society the *duty* to punish" (emphasis in original).

[21] *Ibid.*, p. 38.

[22] See, for example, International Criminal Tribunal for Rwanda ('ICTR'), *Prosecutor v. Omar Serushago*, Trial Chamber, Sentence, ICTR-98-39, 5 February 1999, para. 20, noting that retribution and deterrence are the primary objectives of international criminal punishment (http://www.legal-tools.org/doc/e2dddb/); Allison Marston Danner, "Constructing a Hierarchy of Crimes in International Criminal Sentencing", in *Virginia Law Review*, 2001, vol. 87, no. 3, p. 415, fn. 109, citing cases in which the international tribunals considered retribution as a key factor in sentencing.

[23] See, for example, Tallgren, 2002, p. 583, *supra* note 14; Koller, 2008, pp. 1025–26, *supra* note 14; Koskenniemi, 2002, p. 9, *supra* note 15; Drumbl, 2007, p. 151, *supra* note 14; Amann, 2002, p. 116, *supra* note 18. But see Adil Ahmad Haque, "Group Violence and Group Vengeance: Toward a Retributivist Theory of International Criminal Law", in *Buffalo Criminal Law Review*, 2005, vol. 9, no. 1, p. 273, proffering a relational theory of retributive justice in international criminal law; Dan Markel, "The Justice of Amnesty? Towards a Theory of Retributivism in Recovering States", in *University of Toronto Law Journal*, 1999, vol. 49, no. 3, p. 390, arguing that retribution is warranted and required; Larry May, "Defending International Criminal Trials", in Larry May and Jeff Brown (eds.), *Philosophy of Law: Classic and Contemporary Readings*, Oxford University Press, Oxford, 2010, p. 426, espousing retribution as partial justification for international criminal law.

---

crimes as genocide.[24] In these regards, however, international criminal law is not so different from national criminal justice, which is also unable to reach all those who deserve punishment or to inflict proportionate punishment in all cases. Therefore, for those who accept the principle that moral desert justifies punishment, retribution serves as at least a partial justification for international prosecution.

Since retributivists tend to believe that all crimes should be punished, little scholarship exists on how retributive theories should inform crime selection decisions.[25] Without attempting to develop a comprehensive theory here, I propose that retributivism's strong focus on the perpetrator's desert suggests that crimes should be selected, at least in part, according to the relative desert of those who commit them.[26] For present purposes, therefore, the question is whether a person who commits rape is more or less deserving of punishment than one who commits murder when each is committed in a similar context – that is as a war crime, a crime against humanity or with genocidal intent.

In retributive theories, desert is typically considered to be a function of the seriousness of the harm caused and the defendant's culpability as to that harm.[27] Culpability focuses primarily on the defendant's mental state as to the harm inflicted although it may also include factual circumstances bearing on blameworthiness.[28] Scholars have suggested that desert can be measured either empirically – by ascertaining community views – or deontologically, by appealing to moral principles.[29] Empirical studies of desert generally find that people consider killing more serious than rape.[30]

---

[24] See, for example, Drumbl, 2007, pp. 152–56, *supra* note 14; Amann, 2002, p. 117, *supra* note 18.

[25] A notable exception is an article by Michael Cahill, applying retributive principles to develop a theory of resource allocation: Michael T. Cahill, "Retributive Justice in the Real World", in *Washington University Law Review*, 2007, vol. 85, no. 4, p. 815.

[26] See *ibid.*, exploring a threshold model and a consequential model of retribution, each of which requires a focus on relative desert.

[27] Andrew von Hirsch and Nils Jareborg, "Gauging Criminal Harm: A Living Standard Analysis", in *Oxford Journal for Legal Studies*, 1991, vol. 11, no. 1, p. 2.

[28] See *ibid.*, pp. 2–3.

[29] Robinson, 2008, p. 149, see *supra* note 19.

[30] See, for example, Alfred Blumstein and Jacqueline Cohen, "Sentencing of Convicted Offenders: An Analysis of the Public's View", in *Law and Society Review*, 1980, vol. 14, no. 2, p. 231: In a survey of 603 adults from the United States, respondents who were asked to assign the length of a prison sentence in proportion to the seriousness of the crime assigned a

Evidence of such an hierarchy is also found in national sentencing laws, which generally permit greater punishment for murderers than for rapists.[31] For example, the US Supreme Court has ruled that murderers, but

---

shorter mean prison sentence for rape than for first-degree murder, second-degree murder, manslaughter and assault with intent to kill; Jeremy A. Blumenthal, "Perceptions of Crime: A Multidimensional Analysis with Implications for Law and Psychology", in *McGeorge Law Review*, 2007, vol. 38, p. 642: In a study of 42 male and female respondents from the United States, rape was ranked as less serious than murder; Peter H. Rossi *et al.*, "The Seriousness of Crimes: Normative Structure and Individual Differences", in *American Sociological Review*, 1974, vol. 39, no. 2, p. 228: In a study of 200 adults in the United States, forcible rape after breaking into a home was ranked as less serious than the planned killing of a police officer, the planned killing of a person for a fee and the selling of heroin; Mark Warr, Robert F. Meier and Maynard L. Erickson, "Norms, Theories of Punishment, and Publicly Preferred Penalties for Crimes", in *Sociological Quarterly*, 1983, vol. 24, no. 1, p. 82: In a study of 800 adults in the United States, first-degree rape was ranked as less serious than first-degree murder; Ying Keung Kwan *et al.*, "Perceived Crime Seriousness Consensus and Disparity", in *Journal of Criminal Justice*, 2002, vol. 30, no. 6, p. 626: In a study of 846 adults from Hong Kong, rape was ranked as less serious than murder. See also Xabier Agirre Aranburu, "Gravity of Crimes and Responsibility of the Suspect", in Morten Bergsmo (ed.), *Criteria for Prioritizing and Selecting Core International Crimes Cases*, Torkel Opsahl Academic EPublisher, Oslo, 2010, p. 211:

> [A] recent survey conducted in Eastern DRC [Democratic Republic of Congo] confirmed that killing was the highest priority for the local population (92% demanded accountability), followed by rape (69%) and looting (41%).

Citing International Center for Transitional Justice, "Living in Fear: A Population-Based Survey on Attitudes about Peace, Justice, and Social Reconstruction in Eastern Democratic Republic of Congo", August 2008, pp. 40–41.

[31] See, for example, 中华人民共和国刑法 [Criminal Law of the People's Republic of China], 1 July 1979, Chapter IV, Articles 232, 236, providing minimum imprisonment of three to five years for rape, ten years to life for murder (http://www.legal-tools.org/doc/80fc95/); Уголовный Кодекс РФ [Criminal Code of the Russian Federation], 13 June 1996, Articles 105(1), 131(1), providing for imprisonment of three to six years for rape and six to 15 years for murder (http://www.legal-tools.org/doc/8eed35/); Code Pénal [French Penal Code of 1994], Articles 221(1), 222(23), providing 15 years' imprisonment for rape and 30 years' imprisonment for murder (http://www.legal-tools.org/doc/01ab1f/); Kodeks Karny z Dnia 6 Czerwca 1997 r. [Polish Penal Code of 6 June 1997], Articles 148(1), 197(1), providing one to 10 years' imprisonment for rape and eight years to life imprisonment for murder (http://www.legal-tools.org/doc/f6cda6/); Das Deutsche Strafgesetzbuch [German Penal Code], 13 November 1998, Sections 177(1)–(4), 212(1)–(2), providing for a one to five year minimum sentence for rape and five years to life imprisonment for murder (http://www.legal-tools.org/doc/ecd810/); Canada Federal Statutes, Criminal Code, R.S.C. 1985, c. C-46, ss. 235(1), 271(1), providing a maximum of ten years' imprisonment for sexual assault and life imprisonment for first and second degree murder (http://www.legal-tools.org/doc/35111a/);

---

not rapists, can be put to death in part on the grounds that rape is less serious than murder.[32] There is some evidence of the murder/rape hierarchy at the international level as well. For example, the United Nations Special Rapporteur on Extrajudicial, Summary or Arbitrary Executions has concluded that intentional murder is the only crime for which the death penalty is permissible under international law.[33] International courts also sometimes, though not always, impose greater punishment for murder than for rape.[34]

The evidence that many people consider rape less serious than murder does not, however, establish that murderers are more deserving of punishment than rapists as a moral matter. First, social perceptions of the relative seriousness of sex crimes suffer from a discrimination bias. Throughout the world, women's lives and experiences are undervalued. This sexism renders social evaluations of the seriousness of harms typically inflicted on women morally suspect. Paul Robinson, a prominent proponent of empirical measures of desert, argues that criminal law and policy must take community views into account or risk undermining their own authority.[35] While this proposition is difficult to dispute, it is also true that when community views are based on deep-rooted biases, law's moral authority requires the use of law and legal policy to change those

---

Hong Kong Offences Against the Person Ordinance, 30 June 1997, Cap. 200 s. 118, Cap. 212 s. 2, providing life imprisonment for rape and murder.

[32] Supreme Court of the United States, *Coker v. Georgia*, Judgment, 29 June 1977, 433 U.S. 584, p. 598, stating that "in terms of moral depravity and of injury to the person and to the public, [rape] does not compare with murder".

[33] Report of the Special Rapporteur, Philip Alston, United Nations Economic and Social Council, Commission on Human Rights, Civil and Political Rights, Including the Questions of Disappearances and Summary Executions: Extrajudicial, Summary or Arbitrary Executions, UN Doc. E/CN.4/2005/7, 22 December 2004, para. 3.

[34] The judgment in the ICTR's *Semanza* case notes that the jurisprudence of the ICTY and ICTR reflects sentences between 12 and 15 years for rape as a crime against humanity and between 12 and 20 years for murder as a crime against humanity: ICTR, *Prosecutor v. Laurent Semanza*, Trial Chamber, Judgment and Sentence, ICTR-97-20, 15 May 2003, para. 564 (http://www.legal-tools.org/doc/7e668a/). But see Special Court for Sierra Leone, *Prosecutor v. Augustine Gbao et al.*, Trial Chamber, Sentencing Judgment, SCSL-04-15, 8 April 2009, p. 93 ('*RUF* Case Judgment') (http://www.legal-tools.org/doc/f7fbfc/), sentencing Issa Hassan Sesay to 45 years for rape, and another 45 years for sexual enslavement, while his sentences for extermination and murder were 33 years and 40 years, respectively.

[35] Paul H. Robinson and John M. Darley, "Intuitions of Justice: Implications for Criminal Law and Justice Policy", in *Southern California Law Review*, 2007, vol. 81, no. 1, p. 25.

---

views. Crimes that disproportionately affect women are one area where societal views tend to be out of step with moral truths. Until women achieve social equality with men, empirical approaches to measuring desert for such crimes should be treated with suspicion. Moreover, most of the empirical data regarding societal views on the seriousness of crimes has been conducted in developed countries.[36] It remains an open question how those in the developing countries where many international crimes are committed view the relative seriousness of rape and crimes involving killing.

At least for the moment, therefore, it seems more appropriate to ground retributive evaluations of desert for purposes of crime selection in deontological arguments. A deontological approach requires the application of moral principles to assess the harms associated with each type of crime, as well as the levels of culpability of those who perpetrate them.[37] With regard to both harm and culpability, arguments can be made that rape is sometimes more serious than killing in the international context. First, the context of conflict in which many international crimes are committed legitimises killing. Killing one's enemy is the very purpose of war. The laws of war legitimise intentionally killing other people in many circumstances. As such, one who violates those laws by, for example, killing in a manner that is disproportionate to legitimate military objectives may be less culpable for crossing that ill-defined boundary than one who kills intentionally in peacetime. In contrast, sex crimes are never legitimate – the wartime context does nothing to reduce the culpability of those who perpetrate such crimes. Moreover, sex crimes involve discrimination and/or persecution based on gender, which enhances the culpability of their perpetrators.[38] For these reasons, the culpability of a rapist will sometimes be higher than that of a killer in the international context.

---

[36] See, for example, *supra* note 31.

[37] Robinson, 2008, p. 148, *supra* note 19.

[38] Cf. Danner, 2001, p. 481, *supra* note 22, arguing that persecution as a crime against humanity is more serious than non-persecutorial crimes against humanity; Elizabeth A. Pendo, "Recent Developments: Recognizing Violence against Women: Gender and the Hate Crimes Statistics Act", in *Harvard Women's Law Journal*, 1994, vol. 17, p. 157, arguing that violence against women should be recognised as a hate crime; Kathryn Carney, "Rape: The Paradigmatic Hate Crime", in *St. John's Law Review*, 2001, vol. 75, p. 339, arguing that rape is a crime of hate since women are targeted because they are women.

International sex crimes also likely perpetrate greater harm than international killings under some circumstances. The relative harms of crimes are difficult to compare. The concept of harm is undertheorised,[39] and harms against women are particularly poorly understood.[40] Nonetheless, there is reason to suspect that harm against women is especially severe in societies where women's lives are most undervalued, including some of those where many international crimes have been committed in recent years. Where women are marginalised, their experiences of harm may be aggravated.[41] In particular, women who suffer sex crimes may feel shame and humiliation that magnifies the other physical and psychological harms of the crimes. A rape victim in the Democratic Republic of Congo expressed the view that "[i]t is better to die than being raped by [the rebels] and their allies, because such rape is the worst humiliation against a human being".[42] Some international judges have even opined that "[f]or a woman, rape is by far the ultimate offence, sometimes even worse than death because it brings shame on her".[43]

Moreover, some societies react to sex crimes by stigmatising and ostracising the victim and her family.[44] The Special Court for Sierra Leone highlighted this problem as follows:

> As we have found, the victims of sexual violence continue to live their lives in isolation, ostracised from their communities and families, unable to be reintegrated and reunited with their families, and/or in their communities. Many of these victims of sexual violence were ostracised or abandoned by

---

[39] Robin West, *Caring for Justice*, New York University Press, New York, 1997, p. 94.

[40] Fionnuala Ní Aoláin, "Exploring a Feminist Theory of Harm in the Context of Conflicted and Post-Conflict Societies", in *Queen's Law Journal*, 2009, vol. 35, p. 219.

[41] *Ibid.*, pp. 230–31.

[42] "UN: rape being used as weapon of war in DRC", in *Jurist*, 6 July 2011.

[43] ICTY, *Prosecutor v. Milomir Stakić*, Trial Chamber, Judgment, IT-97-24, 31 July 2003, para. 803 (http://www.legal-tools.org/doc/32ecfb/); see also ICTY, *Prosecutor v. Radoslav Brđanin*, Trial Chamber, Judgment, IT-99-36, 1 September 2004, para. 1009 (http://www.legal-tools.org/doc/4c3228/), agreeing with *Stakić* Trial Chamber that "for a woman, rape is by far the ultimate offence" (citation omitted).

[44] Adrien Katherine Wing and Sylke Merchan, "Rape, Ethnicity, and Culture: Spirit Injury from Bosnia to Black America", in *Columbia Human Rights Law Review*, 1993, vol. 25, pp. 4–5:

> The consequences of rape are particularly severe in traditional, patriarchal societies, where the rape victim is often perceived as soiled and unmarriageable, thus, becoming a target of societal ostracism.

> their husbands, and daughters and young girls were unable to
> marry within their community [...]. The Chamber observes
> that the shame and fear experienced by the victims of sexual
> violence, alienated and tore apart communities, creating vac-
> uums where bonds and relations were initially established.[45]

This tendency to blame the victims of sex crimes elevates the harm of sex crimes compared to that of killing crimes. The surviving families of those killed in conflicts, far from being ostracised, often find support in their communities.

Finally, the harm of rape often includes lasting consequences on a community that may not arise from killings. Again, the Special Court for Sierra Leone explained this problem well:

> In the Chamber's view the [defendant groups] inflicted phys-
> ical and psychological pain and harm which transcended the
> individual victim and relatives to an entire society. These
> acts of sexual violence left several women and girls extreme-
> ly traumatised and scarred for life, consequently destroying
> the bearers of future generations. The Chamber infers that
> crimes of sexual violence further erode the moral fibre of so-
> ciety.[46]

Similarly, a representative of civil parties before the Extraordinary Chambers in the Courts of Cambodia opined that the thousands of forced marriages that took place during the Khmer Rouge era in Cambodia "might have seemed less grave in comparison to the thousands killed, [but] the social consequences of this crime might be equally or even more grave".[47]

In sum, despite the evidence that sex crimes are commonly consid-ered less serious in terms of desert than killing crimes, in the context of international crimes the reverse is likely true in some cases. A retributive approach to international justice therefore does not preclude the thematic prosecution of sex crimes and will sometimes support such a strategy.

---

[45] *RUF* Case Judgment, paras. 132–34, see *supra* note 34.

[46] *Ibid.*, para. 135.

[47] Doherty, 2011, see *supra* note 12.

2.2.2. Deterrence

Deterrence theory, a product of utilitarian moral philosophy, justifies criminal punishment not by reference to the perpetrators' moral desert but rather via the claim that punishment persuades perpetrators or potential perpetrators not to commit similar crimes in the future. The dominant model of deterrence maintains that prospective perpetrators engage in a cost/benefit analysis in reaching decisions about whether to commit crimes.[48] Punishment affects that calculus by increasing the cost of crime. While deterrence and prevention are often used interchangeably, deterrence is more accurately viewed as a form of prevention. Crimes can be prevented not only by affecting the calculus of prospective criminals but through various other strategies including promulgating moral norms that inhibit people from even considering committing crimes – the expressive rationale elaborated below.

Deterrence is frequently invoked as a primary justification for the work of international criminal courts. For example, in establishing *ad hoc* criminal tribunals or referring situations to the ICC under Chapter VII, the UN Security Council implicitly proclaims that it believes international prosecutions can deter crimes, thereby helping to restore and maintain international peace and security. International prosecutors invoke deterrence in justifying their work,[49] and judges employ deterrence to validate

---

[48] See Richard A. Posner, "An Economic Theory of the Criminal Law", in *Columbia Law Review*, 1985, vol. 85, no. 6, p. 1221, framing deterrence question as "what criminal penalties are optimal to deter" criminal activity of rational actor.

[49] See, for example, ICC, Office of the Prosecutor, 2006, p. 9, *supra* note 4, stating that the Prosecutor's Office will take steps to reinforce its deterrent impact; Michael P. Scharf, "*The Prosecutor v. Dusko Tadic*: An Appraisal of the First International War Crimes Tribunal since Nuremberg", in *Albany Law Review*, 1997, vol. 60, p. 868, quoting former ICTY prosecutor Richard J. Goldstone as saying: "If people in leadership positions know there's an international court out there, that there's an international prosecutor, and that the international community is going to act as an international police force, I just cannot believe that they aren't going to think twice as to the consequences"; Tia Goldenberg, "'Unfinished Business' Remains at Rwanda Genocide Court", in *Monsters & Critics*, 30 March 2007, citing ICTR Chief Prosecutor, Hassan Jallow, as stating that the certainty of punishment by the ICTR provides deterrence. See also Background Information: Overview, United Nations Conference of Plenipotentiaries on the Establishment of an International Criminal Court at Rome, Italy, 15–17 June 1998: "Effective deterrence is a primary objective of those working to establish the international criminal court".

---

the sentences they impose.[50] Nonetheless, most scholars have expressed scepticism about the ability of international prosecutions to effectuate deterrence.[51] Such authors argue that international criminals are not rational calculators and that the low likelihood of an international conviction would be unlikely to sway even those who engage in the cost/benefit calculus.[52] Some scholars have even suggested that international criminal law is more likely to promote than to deter criminal conduct.[53] A few are more optimistic.[54]

---

[50] See, for example, ICTR, *Prosecutor v. Jean Kambanda*, Trial Chamber, Judgment and Sentence, ICTR-97-23, 4 September 1998, para. 28 ('*Kambanda* Judgment') (http://www.legal-tools.org/doc/49a299/), justifying sentence of life imprisonment in part upon the notion that would-be perpetrators of mass atrocity must be dissuaded by demonstrating that the global community is not prepared to tolerate serious violations of international criminal law); ICTY, *Prosecutor v. Popović et al.*, Trial Chamber, Judgment, 10 June 2010, IT-05-88, para. 228 (http://www.legal-tools.org/doc/481867/), affirming the ICTY's longstanding commitment to deterrence.

[51] See, for example, Findlay and Henham, 2005, see *supra* note 17; Combs, 2007, see *supra* note 17.

[52] See, for example, Sloane, 2006, p. 72, *supra* note 15: "It is doubtful that the average war criminal or *génocidaire* weighs the risk of prosecution, discounted by the likelihood of apprehension, against the perceived benefits of his crimes"; Julian Ku and Jide Nzelibe, "Do International Criminal Tribunals Deter or Exacerbate Humanitarian Atrocities?", in *Washington University Law Quarterly*, 2007, vol. 84, p. 807: "perpetrators of humanitarian atrocities are going to be high-risk individuals who are not likely to be significantly deterred by the prospect of further prosecution by international criminal tribunals"; Wippman, 1999, pp. 477–78, see *supra* note 17, arguing that the conflict mobilised all aspects of society in ways unlikely to be halted for fear of prosecution; James F. Alexander, "The International Criminal Court and the Prevention of Atrocities: Predicting the Court's Impact", in *Villanova Law Review*, 2009, vol. 54, p. 13: "Considering the long odds of prosecution, the numbers are arguably 'too small to make a rational wrongdoer hesitate" (citations omitted).

[53] See, for example, Ku and Nzelibe, 2007, pp. 827–31, *supra* note 52, discussing "political opportunism effects" by which politicians embrace rhetoric of international criminal tribunals to avoid substantive reforms.

[54] See, for example, Akhavan, 2001, p. 10, *supra* note 17, arguing that although immediate deterrence is unlikely once violence has started, prosecutions at international criminal tribunals can deter future acts of mass violence; May, 2010, pp. 426–27, see *supra* note 23, writing that although the fact that not every perpetrator can be prosecuted decreases the deterrent effect of the international criminal tribunals, the punishments handed down by them can provide adequate deterrence; Theodor Meron, "From Nuremberg to The Hague", in *Military Law Review*, 1995, vol. 149, p. 110, suggesting that the "failure of deterrence" is not inevitable; Jonathan I. Charney, "Progress in International Criminal Law?", in *American Journal of International Law*, 1999, vol. 93, no. 2, p. 462, arguing that consistently prosecuting leaders may eventually deter those who provoke the circumstances that encourage international crimes.

The question whether criminal punishment deters – either in international or national law – is notoriously intractable. Proof of a counterfactual – that but for the actions of international courts more crimes would have occurred – is elusive. However, it is equally difficult to demonstrate that deterrence does not work: people rarely admit that they were considering committing crimes but were deterred by the threat of punishment. In the absence of conclusive proof on either side, therefore, it is reasonable to continue to invoke deterrence as at least a partial justification for international adjudication.

Deterrence theories, unlike retributive theories, are inherently concerned with resource allocation – they seek to achieve the greatest amount of deterrent benefit through the lowest expenditure of punishment resources. Economic deterrence theory posits that the rationally calculating potential criminal will decide whether to commit crimes by balancing the likelihood of apprehension against the severity of punishment.[55] Considering these factors in isolation one might be tempted to conclude that killing crimes will be less costly to deter and therefore should be given priority over sex crimes at international courts. Killing crimes are usually easier to prove since witnesses are more reluctant to testify to sex crimes.[56] Moreover, as already discussed, crimes involving killing tend to incur heavier penalties.

There are at least two flaws in this analysis, however. First, it fails to account for the relative value of deterring sex crimes and killing crimes.[57] As Dan Kahan has written, "Unless we know whether and how much we disvalue a particular species of conduct, we can't determine whether the cost of deterring […] it is worth paying".[58] In order to deter-

---

[55] See, for example, Posner, 1985, *supra* note 48.

[56] Institute for War and Peace Reporting ('IWPR') Staff, "International Justice Failing Rape Victims", IWPR, 15 February 2010; Jocelyn Campanaro, "Women, War, and International Law: The Historical Treatment of Gender-Based War Crimes", in *Georgetown Law Journal*, 2001, vol. 89, p. 2575.

[57] Dan M. Kahan, "The Theory of Value Dilemma: A Critique of the Economic Analysis of Criminal Law", in *Ohio State Journal of Criminal Law*, 2004, vol. 1, no. 2, pp. 644–45: "Unless we know whether and how much we disvalue a particular species of conduct, we can't determine whether the cost of deterring any particular amount of it is worth paying."

[58] Cahill, 2007, p. 852, see *supra* note 25. See also Robinson and Darley, 2007, pp. 964–65, *supra* note 35, discussing examples where deterrence-based recidivist statutes may impose heavy punishment without consideration of specific crime's relative harm to society.

---

mine whether to allocate international resources to deterring sex crimes or killing crimes we have to decide how important it is to deter each. I suggest that at least some of the time we should place greater value on deterring sex crimes. As discussed above, some international sex crimes produce greater harms than crimes involving killing. Under those circumstances, a prosecutorial strategy aimed at deterrence should focus on sex crimes.

Furthermore, there are reasons to suspect that deterrence at the international level operates differently from what the economic model posits. International law, unlike national law, does not aim to deter all potential offenders equally but rather sets its sights particularly on leaders. Political and military leaders bear the greatest responsibility for most international crime and deterring them is therefore most important. An economic deterrence analysis is less convincing when applied to such leaders.[59] Leaders are influenced not just by the likelihood of apprehension and severity of punishment, but also by the reputational effects of international indictment. They tend to be motivated by desires for status and power, each of which can be diminished significantly by an international arrest warrant.[60] Moreover, there is evidence that rape charges carry greater reputational costs for international defendants than charges involving killing. International defendants are often more willing to plead guilty to killing crimes than to sex crimes.[61] In fact, the ICTR chief prosecutor Jallow has stated that defendants before that tribunal might be more willing to plead guilty to genocide than to sex crimes.[62]

In sum, when international prosecution aims to deter future criminal conduct, it will sometimes make sense to select sex crimes rather than crimes involving killing.

---

[59] Sloane, 2006, pp. 73–74, see *supra* note 14.

[60] *Ibid.*, p. 74.

[61] Beth van Schaack, "Obstacles on the Road to Gender Justice: The International Criminal Tribunal for Rwanda as Object Lesson", in *American University Journal of Gender, Social Policy and the Law*, 2009, vol. 17, no. 2, p. 395.

[62] Jallow, 2009, p. 8, see *supra* note 12.

2.2.3. Restorative Justice

Restorative justice is a contested concept,[63] but generally seeks to focus society's response to crime on the needs of the affected people. Crime is conceived not merely as an act against the state, but as an offense against a particular victim or victims and relevant communities. Restorative justice therefore seeks to focus society's response to crime on repairing the damage caused to all parties rather than on imposing suffering on the offender.[64] Restorative justice processes typically involve the victim and offender working collaboratively to heal the wounds inflicted by the crime.[65] Such efforts can be alternatives or adjuncts to punishment,[66] and generally require the offender to admit guilt.[67]

Although international criminal trials are not restorative justice processes in the sense typically employed in the national law context, they

---

[63] John Braithwaite, "Narrative and 'Compulsory Compassion'", in *Law and Social Inquiry*, 2006, vol. 31, no. 2, pp. 425–26, noting that restorative justice's "values framework is not settled and clear".

[64] Erik Luna, "Punishment Theory, Holism, and the Procedural Conception of Restorative Justice", in *Utah Law Review*, 2003, vol. 1, pp. 228–29.

[65] *Ibid.*, p. 228. The UN Basic Principles on Use of Restorative Justice Programmes in Criminal Matters defines restorative justice processes thus:

> 'Restorative process' means any process in which the victim and the offender, and, where appropriate, any other individuals or community members affected by a crime, participate together actively in the resolution of matters arising from the crime, generally with the help of a facilitator. Restorative processes may include mediation, conciliation, conferencing and sentencing circles.

UN Economic and Social Council, Resolution 2002/12, UN Doc. E/2002/30, 24 July 2002, Annex para. 2. In the past few decades, such alternative processes as victim–perpetrator conferences and mediation have gained traction in various parts of the world including Canada, New Zealand and Australia: Luna, 2003, p. 229, see *supra* note 64. Moreover, for many years before their adoption in Western countries, restorative justice practices were common in non-Western communities, including those in Rwanda and Uganda. See Carrie Menkel-Meadow, "Restorative Justice: What Is It and Does It Work?", in *Annual Review of Law and Social Science*, 2007, vol. 3, p. 164, describing modern efforts as "variations on" Rwandan and Ugandan restorative processes. Generally, restorative justice practices are limited to crimes that are less serious than those under the ICC's jurisdictions. See *ibid.*, p. 175, noting that in very serious cases (murder, rape, and serious assault) restorative justice is ancillary or supplemental, not substitutionary, to formal adjudication.

[66] Combs, 2007, p. 140, see *supra* note 17.

[67] Kathleen Daly, "The Limits on Restorative Justice", in Dennis Sullivan and Larry Tifft (eds.), *Handbook of Restorative Justice: A Global Perspective*, Routledge, New York, 2006, p. 136.

---

arguably have the potential to implement restorative justice principles. In other words, international courts can structure their work so as to strive to repair the damage caused by the offense rather than merely to punish the offender.[68] In fact, international courts often invoke restorative goals, and some scholars have urged such courts to place greater emphasis on restorative justice.[69]

International trials can be restorative in several ways. First, they can seek to restore the immediate victims of crimes by allowing them to participate in trials[70] and by awarding them reparations.[71] In fact, such efforts may serve not just to restore the victims but also to facilitate reconciliation between victims and offenders.[72] Moreover, beyond the immediate victims, international trials can serve to rehabilitate societies torn apart by conflict or systematic crimes.[73] In particular, international trials are said to promote societal rehabilitation through their truth-telling function and by establishing a historical record of crimes.[74] The suitability of international courts to this function is contested,[75] and the current prosecutor of the ICC has rejected historical record building as a goal of the court.[76] Nonethe-

---

[68] Luna, 2003, pp. 228–29, see *supra* note 64.

[69] See, for example, Findlay and Henham, 2005, *supra* note 17; Combs, 2007, see *supra* note 17.

[70] See Brianne N. McGonigle, "Bridging the Divides in International Criminal Proceedings: An Examination into the Victim Participation Endeavor of the International Criminal Court", in *Florida Journal of International Law*, 2009, vol. 21, no. 1, p. 96: "This participatory regime is an attempt to make a court that punishes individual perpetrators as well as a court that focuses on administering restorative and reparative justice."

[71] Mark Ellis, "The Statute of the International Criminal Court Protects against Sexual Crimes", in *Smart Library on Globalization*, Center on Law and Globalization, 2007.

[72] Some authors have expressed scepticism about this possibility. See, for example, Miriam Aukerman, "Extraordinary Evil, Ordinary Crime: A Framework for Understanding Transitional Justice", in *Harvard Human Rights Journal*, 2002, vol. 15, pp. 80–82.

[73] William A. Schabas, *The UN International Tribunals: The Former Yugoslavia, Rwanda, and Sierra Leone*, Cambridge University Press, Cambridge, 2006, p. 68.

[74] See Danner, 2001, p. 430, *supra* note 22, citing Madeleine Albright's statement that the ICTY's primary purpose was to establish the historical record; Laurel E. Fletcher and Harvey M. Weinstein, "Violence and Social Repair: Rethinking the Contribution of Justice to Reconciliation", in *Human Rights Quarterly*, 2002, vol. 24, no. 3, pp. 586–89, discussing truth-telling function.

[75] Damaška, 2008, see *supra* note 18.

[76] ICC, Office of the Prosecutor, Report on Prosecutorial Strategy: 2009–2012, 1 February 2010, p. 6 (http://www.legal-tools.org/doc/6e3bf4/).

---

less, many writers, including one important judge, cite historical record building as an important purpose of international prosecutions.[77]

Restorative justice goals provide several reasons to give priority to sex crime prosecutions over crimes involving killing. First, with regard to societal restoration, it is important for all major types of criminality in a given conflict to be represented in the prosecutions. Such representation is necessary for the truth of what happened to emerge and for a complete historical record to be created. Representative prosecutions will often require sex crimes to be selected for prosecution over crimes involving killing. Furthermore, prosecutions may be more necessary to restore perpetrators and victims of sex crimes than those affected by killing crimes. In light of the stigma associated with sex crime, they often remain invisible. Without prosecutions, the segments of society that suffered from and perpetrated sex crimes may therefore be left without restorative recourse. Second, individual restoration of the immediate victims of sex crimes is at least possible with regard to victims of sex crimes whereas it is impossible for those who have been killed.

In sum, retribution, deterrence and restorative justice goals not only fail to mitigate against thematic sex crime prosecutions, but even support such resource allocation strategies at least some of the time.

2.3.   The Expressive Rationale for Thematic Sex Crime Prosecutions

While each of the rationales discussed above can serve to justify the work of international criminal courts, such courts are hampered in their ability to achieve these goals by their very limited resources. International courts can only inflict retribution on a small number of those who deserve it and have a limited reach in terms of deterrence and restorative justice. In contrast, international courts are uniquely well-placed to pursue the goal of norm expression.

Expressive theories of law are relatively new and complex,[78] but essentially centre around law's ability to express states of mind – beliefs, attitudes and so on – of the governments or other collectives that promul-

---

[77]   Antonio Cassese, "On the Current Trends towards Criminal Prosecution and Punishment of Breaches of International Humanitarian Law", in *European Journal of International Law*, 1998, vol. 9, no. 1, p. 5.

[78]   Amann, 2002, p. 118, see *supra* note 18.

gate and implement them.[79] The meaning of a legal act need not emanate from the cognitive efforts of any individual or group of individuals, but is instead socially constructed.[80] Law is thus considered to have "social meaning". The social meaning of a legal act depends not on the intention of the actor, but rather on how the act is understood by the relevant audience.[81] An expressivist's normative agenda therefore includes both crafting law to express valued social messages and employing law as a mechanism for altering social norms.[82]

Although all law can be viewed as expression, criminal law is a particularly potent form of expression in light of the severe sanctions it imposes. Moreover, not only is criminal law expressive, so too is the criminal act it addresses.[83] For theorists such as Dan Kahan, therefore, criminal punishment is justified by its ability to counter the wrongful message inherent in the criminal act.[84] In fact, Kahan maintains that punishment is not merely justified but necessary when the relevant community would interpret other forms of expression as inadequate.[85]

---

[79] Elizabeth S. Anderson and Richard H. Pildes, "Expressive Theories of Law: A General Restatement", in *University of Pennsylvania Law Review*, 2000, vol. 148, no. 5, p. 1506; Dan M. Kahan, "What do Alternative Sanctions Mean?", in *University of Chicago Law Review*, 1996, vol. 63, no. 2, p. 597.

[80] Anderson and Pildes, 2000, p. 1525, see *supra* note 79.

[81] Amann, 2002, p. 118, see *supra* note 18. Anderson and Pildes go so far as to say that the social meanings of an act "do not actually have to be recognized by the community, they have to be recognizable by it, if people were to exercise enough interpretive self-scrutiny": Anderson and Pildes, 2000, p. 1525, see *supra* note 79.

[82] Cass R. Sunstein, "On the Expressive Function of Law", in *University of Pennsylvania Law Review*, 1996, vol. 144, no. 5, pp. 2022–24.

[83] See, generally, Dan M. Kahan, "The Secret Ambition of Deterrence", in *Harvard Law Review*, 1999, vol. 113, no. 2, p. 413; Joel Feinberg, "The Expressive Function of Punishment", in *Doing and Deserving: Essays in the Theory of Responsibility*, Princeton University Press, Princeton, 1970, p. 95.

[84] See Dan M. Kahan, "'The Anatomy of Disgust' in Criminal Law", in *Michigan Law Review*, 1998, vol. 96, no. 6, p. 1641, claiming that "an expressively effective punishment must make clear that we are in fact disgusted with what the offender has done".

[85] Kahan, 1996, p. 600, see *supra* note 79; Dan M. Kahan, "What's Really Wrong with Shaming Sanctions", in *Texas Law Review*, 2006, vol. 84, pp. 2075–76, acknowledging that shaming sanctions are an inferior alternative to punishment.

An expressive approach to international criminal law posits that a primary purpose of international trials is to express global norms.[86] The necessary selectivity of international courts does not impede them in pursuing an expressive agenda to the same extent as it does with respect to the other potential goals of such courts. Norm expression does not require that all or even most perpetrators be punished – a small number of symbolic prosecutions can suffice to convey the necessary message. Moreover, international courts are particularly well-suited to expressing global norms. Such courts not only promote norms through their own indictments, investigations, and trials, they also do so by encouraging national prosecutions, which in turn express norms at the local level.

The ICC has the potential to be an especially powerful vehicle for norm expression. When the ICC chooses to prosecute a particular case, it implicitly declares the crimes involved to be among the most serious crimes of concern to the international community as a whole.[87] The ICC's actions are widely covered by the international news media. Furthermore, the ICC operates according to a system of complementarity whereby the Court may not exercise its jurisdiction when national courts are already investigating or prosecuting in good faith.[88] Even the suggestion that the ICC may take action can therefore stimulate national investigations and prosecutions. In addition, the ICC prosecutor has interpreted his mandate to include pursuing 'positive complementarity', that is, the active encouragement and facilitation of national prosecutions.[89] By assisting national prosecutions, the ICC can therefore promote norms even in cases where it takes no active part in prosecuting defendants.

In light of the special ability of international criminal courts to express global norms, it is unsurprising that a growing number of scholars, including this author, have espoused expressive theories as a central purpose – perhaps the central purpose – of international criminal adjudica-

---

[86] Margaret M. deGuzman, "Choosing to Prosecute: Expressive Selection at the International Criminal Court", in *Michigan Journal of International Law*, 2012, vol. 33, no. 2, pp. 265–320.

[87] Rome Statute of the International Criminal Court, Preamble, 17 July 1998, in force 1 July 2002 ('ICC Statute') (http://www.legal-tools.org/doc/7b9af9/).

[88] *Ibid.*, Article 17.

[89] ICC, "Review Conference: ICC President and Prosecutor Participate in Panels on complementarity and co-operation", Press Release, 3 June 2010.

tion.[90] Some international prosecutors have also adopted expressive rationales for their actions. For example, in explaining the decision to bring charges of recruiting child soldiers in the ICC's first case, the Court's prosecutor and deputy prosecutor have highlighted the need to "draw the attention of the world"[91] and "shine a spotlight"[92] on crimes against children. International judges have invoked expressive goals in justifying the sentences they impose. In the sentencing judgment in the ICTY's *Erdemović* case for example, the judges wrote that:

> [T]he International Tribunal sees public reprobation and stigmatisation by the international community, which would thereby express its indignation over heinous crimes and denounce the perpetrators, as one of the essential functions of a prison sentence for a crime against humanity.[93]

Similarly, ICTR judges opined in the *Kambanda* judgment that the sentence would express that "the international community was not ready

---

[90] Amann, 2002, p. 117, see *supra* note 18: "Justification [...] for the larger goal of pursuing international criminal justice may be found, however, in a newer concept, expressivism"; Sloane, 2006, p. 85, see *supra* note 14: "Over time, punishment by international criminal tribunals can shape as well as express social norms"; Damaška, 2008, p. 339, see *supra* note 18: "Among other proclaimed goals specific to international criminal courts, [...] the didactic objective of improving respect for human rights by expressing outrage for their violation are most frequently singled out for emphasis" (citation omitted); Drumbl, 2007, p. 175, see *supra* note 14, noting that "international trials reach a global audience"; Luban, 2010, p. 576, see *supra* note 14: "the most promising justification for international tribunals is their role in *norm projection*: trials are expressive acts broadcasting the news that mass atrocities are, in fact, heinous crimes [...]" (emphasis in original); Gary Jonathan Bass, *Stay the Hand of Vengeance: The Politics of War Crimes Tribunals*, Princeton University Press, Princeton, 2001, p. 13, international criminal law's ability to contribute to the lofty objectives ascribed to it depends far more on enhancing its value as authoritative expression than on ill-fated efforts to identify the 'right' punishment, whatever that could mean, for often unconscionable crimes; deGuzman, 2012, see *supra* note 86 , arguing for an expressive approach to selection decisions. But see Turner, 2005, p. 17, *supra* note 16, arguing that international criminal low does not promote norms, but rather stirs up local backlash.

[91] Luis Moreno Ocampo, "A Word From the Prosecutor", International Criminal Court Newsletter no. 10, November 2006, p. 2.

[92] Fatou Bensouda, Deputy Prosecutor of the International Criminal Court, Statement at the OTP Monthly Media Briefing, 28 August 2006, p. 3.

[93] ICTY, *Prosecutor v. Drazen Erdemović*, Trial Chamber, Sentencing Judgment, IT-96-22, 29 November 1996, para. 65 (http://www.legal-tools.org/doc/eb5c9d/).

---

to tolerate the serious violations of international humanitarian law and human rights".[94]

Although numerous scholars and practitioners have thus endorsed international criminal law expressivism – either explicitly or implicitly – there has been little discussion of an important underlying normative question: Why is it appropriate for the international community – or at least participating states – to employ criminal processes to express norms? There are several plausible answers. First, norm expression can function as a method of crime prevention. Unlike deterrence, which is intended to affect the calculus of individuals disposed to criminal conduct, norm promulgation seeks to ensure that community members never even consider committing crimes. Second, norm expression can serve to restore victims – both the immediate victims of the crimes at issue and victims of similar crimes – by affirming the wrongness of the acts perpetrated against them.[95] Finally, assuming the international community is a 'community' in a meaningful sense – a debate that is beyond the scope of this chapter – that community may have an integrity interest in countering normative expression that conflicts with the community's vision of its identity.[96] Particular kinds of crimes, such as genocide and crimes against humanity, may threaten the international community's identity in a manner that requires contrary expression. The community may therefore wish to engage in such expression even if there is little or no associated utility.[97]

Assuming that international courts should pursue an expressive agenda for one or more these reasons, the question becomes whether such courts should give priority to expressing the norms prohibiting sex crimes at the expense of expressing other important norms such as those against illegal killing. Expressive theories are no more able to provide a definitive guide to case selection than are the other theories discussed above. While expressivism suggests courts should pay attention to the messages their actions send, it does not dictate which messages should be given priority. In the remainder of this essay, I argue that international courts are justified in giving priority to sex crime prosecutions because the norms pro-

---

94   *Kambanda* Judgment, para. 28, see *supra* note 50.
95   I am indebted to Valerie Oosterveld for this observation.
96   Sunstein, 1996, pp. 2026–27, see *supra* note 82.
97   *Ibid.*, p. 2026.

hibiting such crimes are in greater need of expression than the norms against illegal killing. This heightened need for expression has two sources. First, the history of under-enforcement of the norms prohibiting sex crimes has left them weaker than the norms outlawing killing. Second, sex crimes, unlike killing crimes, virtually always convey a message of discrimination that the international community has a particular interest in countering.

2.3.1. Sex Crimes as Underenforced Norms

The prohibitions against sex crimes have a long history of under-enforcement at both the national and international levels.[98] In many, if not most national criminal law systems, sex crimes are given significantly less attention than are crimes involving killing. While all national systems treat murder as a serious crime – probably the most serious – sex crimes are often viewed as unworthy of official or judicial attention.[99] Studies in the United States and Europe, for example, show that impunity for rape is significantly more prevalent than for murder.[100] Catharine MacKinnon,

---

[98] Goldstone, 2002, p. 280, see *supra* note 5: "[F]or many centuries domestic and international legal systems had ignored gender-related crimes."

[99] Sudan provides an extreme example. There, it is more likely for a rape victim to receive lashes or death by stoning than for the rapist to be prosecuted. Amber Henshaw, "Sudan Rape Laws Need Overhaul", in *BBC News*, 29 June 2007.

[100] See, for example, Armen Keteyia, "Rape in America: Justice Denied", in *CBS News*, 9 November 2009: "Rape in this country is surprisingly easy to get away with. The arrest rate last year was just 25 percent – a fraction of the rate for murder – 79 percent, and aggravated assault – 51 percent." Morgan O. Reynolds, "Crime and Punishment in America: 1999", National Center for Policy Analysis, October 1999: "In 1997, the latest year for which prison data are available, the probability of going to prison for murder rose 13 percent from 1996, for rape 1 percent, for robbery 7 percent and for aggravated assault 11 percent"; RTE News, "Conference hears of low rape conviction rate", 16 January 2010: Research revealed that the accused was convicted in just under one third of rape cases; Jo Lovett and Liz Kelly, *Different Systems, Similar Outcomes? Tracking Attrition in Reported Rape Cases across Europe*, Child and Woman Abuse Studies Unit at London Metropolitan University, 2009, p. 111:

> [T]he classic attrition pattern – of increased reporting and falling rates of prosecution and conviction – is now predominant in Europe across both adversarial and investigative legal systems. The range of reporting rates, from a low of 2 per 100,000 to the high of 46, raises questions about the extent to which states have enabled women to report sexual violence [...]. The widespread falling conviction rates also suggest that states are failing the due diligence responsibilities

---

special gender adviser to the ICC prosecutor, cites a "prevalent [...] norm of denying [the] existence [of gender crimes], ignoring them, shaming their victims, and or defining them in legally unprovable ways".[101]

This enforcement failure has long been reflected in the international system as well. First, the law applicable to international courts has long been inadequate with regard to sex crimes. In Richard Goldstone's words, "Men [wrote] the laws of war in an age when rape was regarded as being no more than an inevitable consequence of war".[102] The Geneva Conventions do not list rape as a grave breach subject to criminal sanctions, nor was rape included as a war crime or a crime against humanity in the Charters of the International Military Tribunals at Nuremberg and Tokyo. Second, international prosecutors have often failed to make appropriate use of the law that is available. The Nuremberg prosecutors omitted to charge rape at all, and the Tokyo Tribunal prosecutors only charged sex crimes under such euphemistic rubrics as "inhumane treatment" and "failure to respect family honour and rights".[103] Even modern prosecutors sometimes neglect to allocate sufficient resources to sex crime prosecutions.[104]

Certainly, the advent of the modern international criminal tribunals has brought important advances in the prosecution of sex crimes. When the Statutes of the ICTY and ICTR were drafted in the early 1990s, for example, they included rape as an enumerated crime against humanity. Nonetheless, there was again initial resistance to investigating and prosecuting sex crimes. Investigators at the ICTY and ICTR believed or were instructed that sex crimes were less serious than crimes involving killing and

---

they have under international law, both in protecting women from violence and providing redress and justice if they are a victim of it.

[101] Catharine MacKinnon, Special Gender Adviser to the Prosecutor of the International Criminal Court, "The International Criminal Court and Gender Crimes", presented at the Consultative Conference on International Criminal Justice in New York on 11 September 2009, p. 6.

[102] Goldstone, 2002, p. 279, see *supra* note 5.

[103] See, for example, Anne-Marie L. M. de Brouwer, *Supranational Criminal Prosecution of Sexual Violence: The ICC and the Practice of the ICTY and the ICTR*, Intersentia, Antwerp, 2005, pp. 7–8.

[104] Cf. Tamara F. Lawson, "A Shift Towards Gender Equality in Prosecutions: Realizing Legitimate Enforcement of Crimes Committed Against Women in Municipal and International Criminal Law", in *South Illinois Law Journal*, 2009, vol. 33, no. 2, pp. 188–89, asserting that the prosecution in international cases has "historically neglected the special needs of victimized women and failed to give their cases adequate attention".

should not be pursued.[105] Investigators were heard to make such comments as: "I've got ten dead bodies, how do I have time for rape?" and "So a bunch of guys got riled up after a day of war, what's the big deal?"[106] Defence counsel even questioned the appropriateness of international jurisdiction over sex crimes, arguing that they are insufficiently serious.[107]

Feminists have worked hard to change such attitudes, with some success.[108] In the very first case before the ICTY, feminists filed an *amicus* brief challenging the prosecutor's underemphasis on sex crimes and received a prompt positive response.[109] Similarly, at the ICTR, an early case omitted sex crime charges until an *amicus* brief prompted the prosecution to amend the indictment.[110] The case led to the first international conviction for rape and other forms of sexual violence.[111]

The ICC Statute also made significant strides in ensuring an adequate legal basis for the prosecution of sex crimes. In what several scholars have termed "governance feminism", feminists were again extremely

---

[105] See Peggy Kuo, "Prosecuting Crimes of Sexual Violence in an International Tribunal", in *Case Western Reserve Journal of International Law*, 2002, vol. 35, pp. 310–11; IWPR Staff, 2010, see *supra* note 56, quoting ICTR Judge Navi Pillay as reporting that female investigators told her they were instructed "to just concentrate on the killings, because these were seen as more serious".

[106] Kuo, 2002, pp. 310–11, see *supra* note 104.

[107] Julie Mertus, "When Adding Women Matters: Women's Participation in the International Criminal Tribunal for the Former Yugoslavia", in *Seton Hall Law Review*, 2008, vol. 38, p. 1307, citing interview with former ICTY judge Patricia Wald.

[108] Janet Halley, "Rape at Rome: Feminist Interventions in the Criminalization of Sex-Related Violence in Positive International Criminal Law", in *Michigan Journal of International Law*, 2008, vol. 30, no. 1, pp. 5–6, discussing a feminist agenda in the 1990s to ensure vigorous prosecution of rape.

[109] See *ibid.*, pp. 14–15, discussing feminist advocacy in *Tadić* case. See also Jennifer Green *et al.*, "Affecting the Rules for the Prosecution of Rape and other Gender Based Violence before the International Criminal Tribunal for the former Yugoslavia: A Feminist Proposal and Critique", in *Hastings Women's Law Journal*, 1994, vol. 5, pp. 173–74. The ICTY's first prosecutor, Richard Goldstone, has confirmed that non-governmental organisations were instrumental in ensuring the prosecution of sex crimes at that tribunal in the face of resistant investigators. Goldstone, 2002, p. 280, see *supra* note 5.

[110] For discussion of feminist advocacy in the *Akayesu* case, see Halley, 2008, pp. 15–17, *supra* note 107; Galina Neleava, "The Impact of Transnational Advocacy Networks on the Prosecution of Wartime Rape and Sexual Violence: The Case of the ICTR", in *International Social Science Review*, 2010, vol. 85, pp. 10–11.

[111] ICTR, *Prosecutor v. Jean-Paul Akayesu*, Trial Chamber, Judgment, ICTR-96-4, 2 September 1998 ('*Akayesu* Judgment') (http://www.legal-tools.org/doc/b8d7bd/).

---

active in the Statute's negotiations.[112] Their efforts ensured for example, that despite opposition from the Holy See and the Arab League, among others, the Statute included a broad definition of the term 'gender'.[113] The ICC Statute also mandates that in exercising the prosecutor's duties, he or she must consider "the nature of the crime, in particular where it involves sexual violence, gender violence or violence against children [...]".[114] The Statute further requires that hiring decisions at the court take into account the need to include personnel with expertise in sexual and gender violence.[115]

Despite these successes, many commentators agree that sex crimes remain underenforced at the international level.[116] For example, the

---

[112] Halley, 2008, pp. 101–15, see *supra* note 107.

[113] *Ibid.*, pp. 105–07.

[114] ICC Statute, Article 54(1)(b), see *supra* note 87. While the ICC prosecutor initially justified crime selection in the *Lubanga* case by invoking practical considerations involving timing and evidence availability, more recently he has highlighted the case's role in showcasing the sexual abuse of child soldiers: Luis Moreno-Ocampo, "Keynote Address: Interdisciplinary Colloquium on Sexual Violence as International Crime: Interdisciplinary Approaches to Evidence", in *Law and Social Inquiry*, 2010, vol. 35, pp. 845–46.

[115] ICC Statute, Article 36(8)(b), see *supra* note 87, providing that in selecting judges, "States Parties shall consider the need for legal expertise on violence against women"; Article 42(9), requiring prosecutor to "appoint advisers with legal expertise on [...] sexual and gender violence"; Article 43(6), mandating that the Registrar's Victims and Witness Unit "include staff with expertise in [...] trauma related to sexual violence".

[116] See, for example, Binaifer Nowrojee, "We Can do Better Investigating and Prosecuting International Crimes of Sexual Violence", presented at the Colloquium of Prosecutors of International Criminal Tribunals at Arusha, Tanzania, 25–27 November 2004: "Squandered opportunities, periods of neglect, and repeated mistakes have caused setbacks to effective investigations and prosecutions of sexual violence crimes by international courts"; Brigid Inder, "Statement to the General Debate of the Review Conference of the Rome Statute", presented at the ICC Review Conference, 1 June 2010: "It would appear the strategy underpinning these charges [of gender-based crimes] is still under development and not yet robust enough to sustain the charges and that perhaps modest judicial concepts of gendered violence are being applied in their interpretation"; Uganda Radio Network, "Women Accuse the ICC of Failing Them", 1 June 2010: "A group of activists has accused the International Criminal Court of failing to give prominence to women's issues in conflict...[claiming] the International Criminal Court (ICC) places more emphasis on dialogue with governments than it does in engaging victims of conflict [...] [and that] organizations independent of government and state control are being denied the opportunity to voice concerns of women, who are often the greatest victims of war"; IWPR Staff, 2010, see *supra* note 56, explaining that rape victims from Sierra Leone were largely disappointed that rape was not added to the CDF indictment, since they had taken a big risk to offer evidence in the first place.

Women's Initiative for Gender Justice, the premier advocacy organisation for women in international criminal law, has criticised the ICC for charging its first defendant, a militia leader from the Democratic Republic of Congo, solely with recruiting child soldiers even though the conflict is rife with sex crimes.[117] Even Hassan B. Jallow, chief prosecutor of the ICTR, has admitted that the prosecution of sex crimes at international tribunals could be improved.[118]

International judges have recognised this under-enforcement as a justification for a special focus on sex crimes at international courts. For example, in the ICTR's *Akayesu* judgment the trial chamber stated:

> [T]he Chamber takes note of the interest shown in this issue by non-governmental organizations, which it considers as indicative of public concern over the historical exclusion of rape and other forms of sexual violence from the investigation and prosecution of war crimes. The investigation and presentation of evidence relating to sexual violence is in the interest of justice.[119]

Similarly, judges of the Special Court for Sierra Leone stated:

> The Chamber considers that the specific offences are designed to draw attention to serious crimes that have been historically overlooked and to recognise the particular nature of sexual violence that has been used, often with impunity, as a tactic of war to humiliate, dominate and instil fear in victims, their families and communities during armed conflict.[120]

In contrast to sex crimes, crimes involving killing – even in conflict situations – have a stronger record of enforcement. The laws prohibiting such crimes, including the Geneva Conventions among others, have been in place longer, and their enforcement has not been resisted in the ways elaborated above for sex crimes. This relative under-enforcement of sex crimes thus provides a strong basis to give priority to such crimes in de-

---

[117] Women's Initiative for Gender Justice, "Beni Declaration", in *Making a Statement: A Review of Charges and Prosecutions for Gender-based Crimes before the International Criminal Court*, June 2008, p. 17.

[118] Hassan B. Jallow, "International Criminal Justice, Some Reflections on the Past and the Future", presented at the Fifth Colloquium of Prosecutors of International Criminal Tribunals at Kigali, Rwanda, 11–13 November 2009, p. 8.

[119] *Akayesu* Judgment, para. 417, see *supra* note 111.

[120] *RUF* Case Judgment, para. 156, see *supra* note 34 (citations omitted).

termining which norms international criminal courts should seek to pro-mote. In fact, Richard Goldstone invoked this justification in explaining the thematic *Foča* prosecution, stating: "We have always regarded it as an important part of our mission to redefine and consolidate the place of [sex crimes] in humanitarian law".[121]

2.3.2. The Discriminatory Message of Sex Crimes

The second basis to give priority to sex crimes in setting the expressive agenda of international courts is that, unlike killing crimes, sex crimes virtually always involve the perpetrator's discriminatory valuation of a group – usually women. Although sex crimes against men are more common than frequently believed and are also underprosecuted,[122] most sex crimes are perpetrated against women. Male perpetrators select female victims for harm because they are women. The expression inherent in such crimes is not just that the perpetrator undervalues the particular victim but that he disrespects women in general. As the ICTY judge, Florence Mumba, stated in sentencing one of the defendants in the *Foča* case:

> By the totality of these acts [of sexual violence] you have
> shown the most glaring disrespect for the women's dignity
> and their fundamental human right to sexual self-
> determination [...].[123]

Whether one views the purpose of international criminal law expression as prevention or identity affirmation, it is more important to address crimes motivated by discrimination than comparable crimes committed without discrimination. First, discriminatory crimes are in greater need of prevention because they express the perpetrator's view that not just the victim, but an entire class of people, is less valuable and thus deserving of ill treatment. In explaining the traditional justification for in-

---

[121] ICTR, "Gang Rape, Torture and Enslavement of Muslim Women Charged in ICTY's First Indictment Dealing Specifically with Sexual Offences", Press Release, 27 June 1996. See also Special Court for Sierra Leone, *Prosecutor v. Alex Tamba Brima et al.*, Decision on Prosecution Request for Leave to Amend the Indictment, SCSL-2004-16, 6 May 2004, para. 34, identifying a need to "highlight the high profile nature of the emerging domain of gender offences".

[122] Dustin A. Lewis, "Unrecognized Victims: Sexual Violence against Men in Conflict Settings under International Law", in *Wisconsin International Law Journal*, 2009, vol. 27, pp. 1–4.

[123] ICTY, "Judgment of Trial Chamber II in the *Kunarać, Kovač and Vuković* Case", Press Release, 22 February 2001, p. 5.

---

creased penalties for hate crimes, the US Supreme Court noted that such conduct "is thought to inflict greater individual and societal harm"[124] than crimes committed without such motivation. Left unpunished, the perpetrator and those who agree with his valuation of the victim class are likely to continue harming people belonging to that class. In other words, crimes based on discrimination threaten the security of an entire group.

Imagine for a moment that a soldier uses a weapon incapable of adequately distinguishing combatants from civilians and thus kills several civilians. He then rapes several women. The first crime sends the message: "I am committed to winning the war even if it means violating the rules of armed conflict". This is certainly a dangerous message and countering it through prosecution may help prevent similar rule violations in the future. The rapes, however, send a broader message about the value of women. Prosecuting the rapes not only has the potential to prevent future violations of the rules against rape in armed conflict but also to prevent other crimes that result from the devaluation of women's lives – whether in times of conflict or peace. Thus, an ICTR prosecutor has asserted that:

> [...] the dialogue between international and national prosecutors must include specialized consideration of crimes of sexual violence [because] prosecution of these crimes [is] a key component to stopping the global violence against women.[125]

Furthermore, if the purpose of international prosecution is to reaffirm the values and identity of the international community, that identity is more seriously threatened by crimes involving discrimination than by non-discriminatory crimes. A crime that conveys the perpetrator's devaluation of a particular class of people is more worthy of condemnation than

---

[124] Supreme Court of the United States, *Wisconsin v. Mitchell*, Judgment, 13 June 1993, 508 U.S. 476, pp. 487–88.

[125] Linda Bianchi, "The Investigation and Presentation of Evidence Relating to Sexual Violence", Roundtable on Cooperation between the International Criminal Tribunals and National Prosecuting Authorities Arusha, 26–28 November 2008, paras. 1–2. See also Inder, 2010, *supra* note 116:

> The prosecution of rape and other forms of violence against women by the ICC in these situations would be particularly significant because it would demonstrate that the Court recognises the legal rights of women even when they are denied by the laws and practices of their own country and it would also assist with future domestic prosecutions of non-conflict related rape and other forms of violence.

a comparable act that does not.[126] If our hypothetical war criminal goes unpunished for killing civilians, the international community will have failed to counter his assertion that the rules of armed conflict are optional. If he goes unpunished for the rapes, however, he will not only have successfully expressed disdain for the rules, he will have flouted a norm even more fundamental to the identity of the international community – the fundamental human rights norm of equality between men and women. As such, Catharine MacKinnon has asserted that the ICC's emphasis on sex crimes aims to "signal […] to the world" that the norm of ignoring sex crimes is no longer accepted.[127]

Thus, whether one views the purpose of international criminal law expressivism as prevention or identity affirmation, there will often be compelling reasons to engage in thematic prosecutions or otherwise give priority to sex crimes even at the expense of prosecuting some killings.

2.4. Conclusion

In deciding how to allocate their scarce investigative and prosecutorial resources, some international criminal courts have engaged in thematic prosecutions of sex crimes, and many others have at times chosen to prioritise sex crimes over killing crimes. This chapter has sought to demonstrate that despite the common wisdom that prosecutors should give priority to the most serious crimes and that killing is more serious than rape, thematic sex crime prosecutions are justified by the goals of international criminal adjudication. Sex crimes sometimes inflict greater harms than killing crimes, increasing the value of deterring them as well as the importance of inflicting retribution on their perpetrators. Restorative justice will also sometimes be better promoted by prosecuting sex crimes than killing crimes. Most importantly, the goal of expressing global norms, which some identify as the central task of international criminal law, suggests that sex crimes should often be given priority over other serious crimes when international courts decide whom to prosecute and what charges to bring.

---

[126] Kahan, 1996, p. 598, see *supra* note 79, stating that a racist killing "is more worthy of condemnation" than a mother's revenge killing "because hatred express a more reprehensible valuation"; Pendo, 1994, see *supra* note 38.

[127] MacKinnon, 2009, p. 6, see *supra* note 101.

3

"Those Most Responsible" versus International Sex Crimes: Competing Prosecution Themes?

Fabricio Guariglia[*]

3.1. Introduction

In his provocative play *Death and the Maiden*, the Chilean writer Ariel Dorfman describes the ordeal of Paulina, a former political detainee who recognises her torturer and rapist as the driver that has helped her husband with a flat tire and drove him home. The play poses a number of fundamental questions around the thorny issues of accountability, coming to terms with the past and "own hand justice". For the purposes of this contribution, however, the most important aspects of the play are: first, the shock and trauma of the victim, who suddenly encounters the man who repeatedly raped her to the music of a Schubert string quartet (from which the play borrows its title) during her captivity. Second, the fierce hunger for redress that this encounter triggers: Paulina captures her alleged rapist at gunpoint and submits him to a makeshift "trial", assigning to her shocked husband the task of defending the accused against her charges.

The drama at the centre of the play is a familiar one in the aftermath of mass violations of human rights and international humanitarian law. From Chile and Argentina to South Africa, and from Rwanda to Bosnia, hundreds of victims of sexual offences must have seen their perpetrators walking around in a free and unconcerned manner. Some of these victims may have reacted to that situation by seeking justice through whatever means available, like Paulina in Dorfman's play. Others may have simply walked away in fear and shame. All, I assume, must have been profoundly affected by the encounter and the memories ignited.

---

[*] **Fabricio Guariglia** is the Director of the Prosecution Division at the International Criminal Court. At the time of writing, he was Senior Appeals Counsel. The views expressed herein are solely the author's and should not be attributed to the Office of the Prosecutor or the International Criminal Court. The author thanks Helen Duffy for her helpful comments and suggestions.

What can international justice do for these victims? Is it capable of adequately addressing this human drama? Can it provide meaningful and satisfying answers to them? What would Dorfman's victim have to say about the manner in which international prosecutors have identified, selected and brought to justice sexual violence cases to date? These are all questions that probably we cannot fully answer. But what we can do, and what I intend to do in this chapter, is to explore some of the identifiable tensions between the apparent limitations of international prosecutions and the undeniable right of every victim of rape to have her suffering properly addressed by a court of law, national or international. In particular, I will focus on the International Criminal Court ('ICC') Office of the Prosecutor's formulated policy of focusing its limited resources on the prosecution of those "most responsible" for the commission of crimes within the jurisdiction of the Court, and some of its potential consequences for the prosecution of sexual crimes.

3.2.   Selectivity and International Prosecutions

The complex issue of selectivity in the conduct of criminal prosecutions and in particular the tensions between the exercise of prosecutorial discretion, on the one hand, and the victim's expectations, on the other, are familiar to domestic jurisdictions. All national systems are in one way or another selective, and gate-keeping decisions based on criteria such as strength of the evidence, credibility of the victim's account of events, likelihood of a conviction, and so on are made on a daily basis. This also happens in the particularly sensitive area of sexual violence, and the manner in which these decisions are made has an unavoidable impact on the victims.[1]

In the context of international prosecutorial bodies, which face the challenge of dealing with massive crimes with very limited resources, selectivity has to be assumed as a fact: the question is not whether to select, but *how* to select.[2] As one commentator aptly puts it, the issue is not

---

[1]   See, for instance, Criminal Justice Sexual Offences Taskforce, *Responding to Sexual assault: The Way Forward*, Attorney General's Department, New South Wales, Sydney, 2005, pp. 11–17.

[2]   On the issue of selection generally, see Fabricio Guariglia, "The Selection of Cases by the Office of the Prosecutor of the International Criminal Court", in Carsten Stahn and Göran Sluiter (eds.), *The Emerging Practice of the International Criminal Court*, Martinus Nijhoff

"whether selective prosecution should occur, as it is essentially impossible that it does not, but when selective prosecution is unacceptable".[3] Some interesting developmental stages in this area can be identified: international justice appears to have moved from a rather anarchic approach to selection of cases – at times based on contingent criteria, such as arrest feasibility – to the formulation of some minimal criteria governing selection,[4] and then to the adoption a more defined policy focusing on those persons holding leadership positions.[5] The last step in this development is the adoption, by the ICC's Office of the Prosecutor ('OTP'), of the so-called "most responsible" prosecutorial policy – a policy whereby the OTP focuses "its investigative and prosecutorial efforts and resources on those who bear the greatest responsibility, such as the leaders of the State or organisation allegedly responsible for those crimes".[6] This horizontal cut in the chain of individuals involved in the commission of massive crimes obviously leaves a very high number of alleged perpetrators outside of the scope of international prosecutions. What are then the implications of this policy for the effective prosecution of sexual violence? This issue will be discussed in the following pages.

3.3. Who "Commits" Rape?

One conceivable negative consequence of focusing prosecutorial efforts in those individuals located at the highest echelons of the chain of command would be the effective reduction of the available modes of liability for

---

Publishers, Leiden, 2009, pp. 209 ff. An expert discussion on the criteria for selecting international criminal cases was held by the Forum for International Criminal and Humanitarian Law in 2007. See Morten Bergsmo (ed.), *Criteria for Prioritizing and Selecting Core International Cases*, 2nd ed., Torkel Opsahl Academic EPublisher, Oslo, 2010.

[3] Robert Cryer, *Prosecuting International Crimes: Selectivity and the International Law Regime*, Cambridge University Press, Cambridge, 2005, p. 192.

[4] The October 1995 International Criminal Tribunal for the former Yugoslavia ('ICTY') Office of the Prosecutor criteria provide a first attempt to define at the international level a set of principles governing case selection. See Claudia Angermaier, "Case Selection and Prioritization in the Work of the ICTY", in Morten Bergsmo (ed.), *Criteria for Prioritizing and Selecting Core International Cases*, 2nd ed., Torkel Opsahl Academic EPublisher, Oslo, 2010, p. 31.

[5] A first step in this direction is the 1998 review of cases by the ICTY prosecutor Louise Arbour. See *ibid.*, p. 34.

[6] International Criminal Court ('ICC'), *Paper on Some Policy Issues before the Office of the Prosecutor*, 5 September 2003 (http://www.legal-tools.org/doc/f53870/).

cases of rape and other forms of sexual violence. An interesting example of this is provided by the landmark International Criminal Tribunal for the former Yugoslavia ('ICTY') *Furundžija* case, where the Trial Chamber was faced with the following factual scenario: one accused (Furundžija, a local commander) interrogated the victim (Witness A), while another person (Accused B, Furundžija's subordinate) raped her. As the intensity of the questioning increased, so did that of the rape. This led the Trial Chamber to conclude that the questioning and the rape were part of a single process conducted by both accused.[7] When it came to defining the applicable modes of liability, however, Furundžija was held to be a co-perpetrator of the crime of torture, but only an aider and abettor of the crime of rape. The Chamber concluded that while Furundžija had played a central role in the entire process, he "did not personally rape Witness A, nor can he be considered under the circumstances of this case, to be a co-perpetrator"; however, since his presence and continued interrogation "encouraged Accused B and substantially contributed to the criminal acts committed by him", he did satisfy the requirements of aiding and abetting.[8] Worthy of note is that in an earlier finding made in relation to the crime of torture, the Chamber had concluded that in order to be a co-perpetrator of that crime it was necessary to perform "an integral part" of the torture.[9]

This particular aspect of the *Furundžija* judgment resonates with some rather dated notions of perpetration, whereby the perpetrator (or co-perpetrator) of a crime can only be the person who physically performs at least some of the elements of the crime.[10] It also seems to endorse a view that used to be the prevailing one in civil law jurisdictions whereby even if one accepts a broader concept of perpetration, in the case of rape, only the person who personally rapes the victim can be held liable as a perpetrator. This is because rape belongs to the category of the so-called "own hand crimes", that is, crimes that require a direct personal perpetration by

---

[7] ICTY, *Prosecutor v. Anto Furundžija*, Trial Chamber, Judgment, IT-95-17/1-T, 10 December 1998, paras. 129, 130 and 264 ('*Furundžija* Judgment') (http://www.legal-tools.org/doc/e6081b/).

[8] *Ibid.*, paras. 273–75.

[9] *Ibid.*, para. 257.

[10] Scholars from civil law jurisdictions have referred to this particular approach (now abandoned) as the "formal-objective theory" of modes of liability (*Formal-objektive Theorie*). See Claus Roxin, *Täterschaft und Tatherrschaft*, De Gruyter Recht, Berlin, 1994, pp. 34 ff.

---

the accused.[11] If this position was to be accepted, then focusing on those persons located at the highest echelons of the groups or apparatuses involved in the crimes would have as an indirect and undesirable consequence – that even in situations of mass sexual violence, it would be extremely rare to secure a conviction for "committing" rape, either as a perpetrator or co-perpetrator (direct or indirect), since it is not often the case that leaders get personally involved in the type of crimes that the subordinates commit in the field. A system that is in charge of the prosecution of episodes of massive sexual violence but that does not produce convictions for the actual commission of rape would be, at best, an anomaly. Moreover, in cases where rape is verified as occurring but in relation to which nobody can be clearly identified as being responsible for its commission, such a system could also send a confusing message, whereby rape becomes something closer to a natural catastrophe than to human conduct. This would defeat one of the goals of accountability, which is to decipher and explain the complex network of causation and attribution inherent to the commission of international crimes[12], in the aftermath of mass violations of human rights and international humanitarian law.

Fortunately, post-*Furundžija* developments in this area of the law may avert these fears: first, ICTY jurisprudence has clarified that in order to "commit" a crime as member of a joint criminal enterprise (the theory of liability most frequently used by the ICTY to deal with situations of crimes involving a plurality of persons), the accused's participation need not involve the actual perpetration of a crime, including rape. Rather, that participation "may take the form of assistance in, or contribution to, the execution of the common purpose".[13] This initial expansion would already allow for convictions of high-level accused based on the commission of the crime of rape, even if those accused remained at all times removed

---

[11] See, among others, Juan J. Bustos Ramírez and Hernán Hormazábal Malarée, *Lecciones de Derecho Penal*, vol. 2, Trotta, Madrid, 1999, pp. 293–94; Hans-Heinrich Jesheck and Thomas Weigend, *Lehrbuch des Strafrechts. Allgemeiner Teil*, Duncker & Humblot, Berlin, 1996, pp. 266–67.

[12] Herbert Jäger, "Betrachtungen zum Eichmann-Prozeß", in *Monatschrift für Kriminologie und Strafrechtsreform*, 1962, vol. 45, pp. 73–83.

[13] ICTY, *Prosecutor v. Mitar Vasiljević*, Appeals Chamber, Judgment, IT-98-32-A, 25 February 2004, para. 100 (http://www.legal-tools.org/doc/e35d81/).

from the physical perpetration of the crime.[14] The second important development is represented by the use of theories of indirect perpetration or
indirect co-perpetration (that is (co)perpetration by means) in the ICC pre-
trial decisions that include charges of rape against persons who have not
been personally involved in acts of rape. While these rulings stem from
Pre-Trial Chambers and are by their nature provisional, they do provide
further support to the position that a person removed from the actual perpetration of the acts of rape can be held liable for "committing" the crime
of rape.[15]

3.4.   Bridging the Distance between a "Most Responsible" Policy and the Victim's Individual Story

3.4.1.   The "Notorious Perpetrator"

While the aspects of the *Furundžija* judgments discussed above do not
pose a *legal* problem today, they do remind us of the fact that the higher
up we go in the chain of command, the further away we move from the
individual episode of sexual violence and the particular victim. And as we
venture into a terrain of culpability that is indeed more comprehensive, we
also become less involved with that particular instance of victimisation:
we tell a "broader story" about the decision-making processes that set the

---

[14]   It is worthy of note that even in jurisdictions where the notion that rape is an "own-hand
crime" prevailed there is an increasing resistance to it. For instance, in Argentina, the unit
in the Attorney General's office in charge of co-ordinating the federal prosecutions of past
human rights violations has just issued a legal opinion which states that the notion of rape
as an "own-hand crime" should not be adopted by federal prosecutors. The opinion notes
that the historical rationale behind this restrictive approach to the perpetration of rape,
namely that "rapist" could only be the person who obtains sexual satisfaction through the
act of rape, is a deeply flawed proposition. Rather, the relevant consideration should be:
who exercised control over the act and is therefore responsible for the crime of rape. See Unidad Fiscal de Coordinación y Seguimiento de las Causas por Violaciones a los Derechos
Humanos Cometidas Durante el Terrorismo de Estado, *Consideraciones sobre el Ju-
zagamiento de los Abusos Sexuales Cometidos en el Marco del Terrorismo de Estado*, Procu-
ración General de la Nación, Buenos Aires, 2011, pp. 19–20, quoting further authorities.

[15]   See, for instance, the first Warrant of Arrest issued against the Sudanese President Omar Al
Bashir, stating that there are reasonable grounds to believe that he was responsible, as indirect
perpetrator or as an indirect co-perpetrator of the crime of rape as a crime against humanity,
among other crimes: ICC, Pre-Trial Chamber, Warrant of Arrest for Omar Hassan Ahmad Al
Bashir, ICC-02/05-01/09-1, 4 March 2009 (http://www.legal-tools.org/doc/814cca/).

---

criminal machinery in motion,[16] but we also say less about the human drama lying at the heart of the charges against the accused.

While this limitation is, to some extent, an unavoidable by-product of a prosecutorial policy focused on those persons located at the highest echelons of responsibility, and as such should be addressed as part of the so-called "impunity gap" through resort to other available mechanisms,[17] there are still some things that can be done within a "most responsible" policy to mitigate these concerns. First, it is important to know when to accommodate exceptions to the policy, for instance, in order to deal with the so-called "notorious perpetrators", even if this means going down the chain of command. Let us go back to the *Furundžija* case and put a name to the anonymous "Accused B", the one that physically perpetrates the rape on Witness A: Accused B was called Miroslav Bralo. He was a member of the Jokers, a special unit within the Hrvatsko vijeće obrane ('HVO', Bosnian Defence Council), which was involved in the most serious crimes committed in central Bosnia in 1993. Bralo had a particularly brutal record of violence. He was in prison for the killing of a Muslim man, and while in prison he was allowed to terrorise Muslim fellow inmates at his will.[18] He was released from prison in order to join the attack on the village of Ahmići, where Bosnian Croat forces massacred the Muslim inhabitants. He was convicted of personally committing at least five murders and assisting in the killing of 14 Bosnian Muslim civilians, nine of whom were children. His conviction also covers the brutal rape and torture of Witness A (whom he later imprisoned for two months so she could be further raped by her captors), his involvement in the unlawful confinement and inhuman treatment of Bosnian Muslim civilians, includ-

---

[16] When analysing the so-called "big fish v. small fish" debate in the context of the ICTY, Payam Akhavan notes that "[t]he prosecution of the leader of a particular region promises to tell a more complete story of a conflict than the trial of a low-ranking perpetrator. In other words, the overall contextual facts relevant to establishing the criminal liability of a low-ranking accused such as Tadić or Erdemović are necessarily more limited in scope than the corresponding facts that would establish participation in a widespread or systematic attack on the part of persons in positions of power": Payam Akhavan, "Justice in The Hague, Peace in the Former Yugoslavia? A Commentary on the United Nations War Crimes Tribunal", in *Human Rights Quarterly*, vol. 20, no. 737, 1998, p. 777.

[17] See, *inter alia*, Michael Gibbs, "The ICC Alone Cannot End the Era of Impunity", in *The Guardian*, 12 June 2010.

[18] See ICTY, *Prosecutor v. Zoran Kupreškić et al.*, Trial Chamber, Judgment, IT-95-16-T, 14 January 2000, paras. 77 and 115 (http://www.legal-tools.org/doc/5c6a53/).

ing forced labour and use of civilians as "human shields", setting on fire numerous houses, and blowing up a mosque in Ahmići.[19] Bralo was known and feared.[20] He certainly was a minor player in the persecutory campaign launched in central Bosnia in April 1993, yet his crimes gained prominence in the area.

A prosecutorial strategy focused on those individuals "most responsible" for the crimes should not lose sight of those persons who commit particularly shocking crimes and acquire a level of notoriety that distinguishes their conduct from that of other perpetrators.[21] The ICC Office of the Prosecutor's June 2006 draft Policy Paper on Criteria for Selection of Cases recognised this, and included within the circle of persons who could be singled out for prosecution, "[n]otorious perpetrators who distinguish themselves by their direct responsibility for particularly serious crimes".[22] Including such persons in any prosecutorial programme has clear benefits. First, you prosecute someone whose impunity could seriously disturb the community where the crimes occurred and the victims who suffered them. Second, you simultaneously bring down to earth what has been described as the "abstract narrative" of crimes against humanity and war crimes.[23] You depict the brutality of the crimes committed in the field and you describe how an otherwise normal person – a soldier, a neighbour, a political activist, engaged in this brutality. In the case of Bralo, this exercise meant narrating a particularly shocking story of sexual

---

[19] See ICTY, *Prosecutor v. Miroslav Bralo*, Trial Chamber, Sentencing Judgment, IT-95-17-S, 7 December 2005 ('*Bralo* Sentencing Judgment') (http://www.legal-tools.org/doc/e10281/).

[20] One witness from the Ahmići area whom I met in the context of a separate, but related, ICTY case explained to me the fear with which he received the news that Bralo had been released from prison.

[21] Examples of this category of perpetrators can be Goran Jelisić, who committed shocking atrocities against Bosnian Muslims in the enclave of Brčko, introducing himself to his victims as the "Serbian Adolf". See ICTY, *Prosecutor v. Goran Jelisić*, Trial Chamber, Judgment, IT-95-10-T, 14 December 1999, paras. 102–3 (http://www.legal-tools.org/doc/b3ece5/); and Alfredo Astiz in Argentina, who was responsible for the disappearance of the founder member of Madres de Plaza de Mayo, Azuzena Villaflor, among other crimes.

[22] ICC, Office of the Prosecutor, *Criteria for Selection of Cases (Draft Policy Paper)*, June 2006, para. 38.

[23] Akhavan states that "in their own way, the trials of Tadić, Erdemović, and other small fish may bring home the daily aspect of the abstract narrative of ethnic cleansing, explaining how ordinary people participated in killing and brutalizing their fellow human beings": Akhavan, 1998, p. 780, see *supra* note 16.

---

violence in central Bosnia, which illustrated the scope and impact of such violence in the context of the armed conflict in the former Yugoslavia. The narrative exercise also explains how this type of crimes happened in the field at the "micro" level[24], and enhances the symbolic or expressive function of criminal prosecutions, thereby sending the message that the values harmed by those individual crimes were ones dear to the international community, and which would be upheld and defended at all times.[25]

One difficulty for performing this operation, however, is the scope of the analysis, and in particular, whether the prosecutorial body is using a panoramic lens or a magnifying glass to examine the situation and the actors involved. For example, through a panoramic lens, one can get a wider picture of the victimisation taking place in the field, detect the patterns, the *modus operandi*, the movement of the troops across the territory, and the functional networks that connect all the pieces. However, it is unlikely that one will be able to detect the individual actors that are causing that victimisation at the grassroots level. On the other hand, through a magnifying glass, one loses sight of the wider picture, but may be in a position to put a name to the otherwise anonymous perpetrator that is engaging in sexual violence in the field.

---

[24] To put it in Hannah Arendt's terms, the prosecution of these cases fosters the transformation of a cog in the wheel back into a human being: Hannah Arendt, *Eichmann in Jerusalem*, Penguin, New York, 1992, p. 289.

[25] It is also worthy of note that Bralo not only pleaded guilty, but also expressed genuine remorse for the crimes committed and apologised to the victims, among other efforts to atone for his crimes. In sentencing him, the Trial Chamber stated the following:

> The Trial Chamber further recognises that Bralo's guilty plea, combined with his genuine remorse, is likely to have a positive effect on the rehabilitation of the victims of his crimes, and their communities. As stated by Mehmed Ahmic, the current President of the Ahmići Municipality Council, Bralo is the first person charged by the Tribunal with crimes committed in that area who has admitted his criminal conduct. It accepts his view that this acknowledgement of wrongdoing is extremely important for the entire community in its continuing process of recovery and reconciliation noted.

> (*Bralo* Sentencing Judgment, para. 71, see *supra* note 19.)

Although, as the *Biljana Plavšić* guilty plea before the ICTY shows, leaders can also admit to the crimes charged, this type of episode of remorse and contrition is more likely to take place and have an impact among those who have been personally involved in the commission of the crimes than among leaders who have directed the crimes from the comfortable distance of their offices.

In this sense, it is important to note the differences between the ICC and its predecessors, such as the *ad hoc* tribunals, which were all created to deal with a single situation through a prolonged period of time. For instance, everyone in the ICTY Office of the Prosecutor involved in the investigation and prosecution of the crimes committed by the HVO in central Bosnia in 1993 knew who Bralo was, and what his role in those crimes had been, starting with the sexual violence that he had inflicted on defenceless victims. This is normal: if you have one or more teams that are solely devoted to exploring crimes committed in one confined area during a given period of time, you can put your eye to the microscope and analyse the "grassroots" criminality that forms the fabric of crimes against humanity and war crimes, and in that way learn about the stories of individual victims and perpetrators. However, in the context of the ICC, this type of "micro-analysis" will seldom be possible. This is because the ICC has limited resources to perform the huge task of dealing with multiple situations, each of them comprising hundreds of incidents that may constitute crimes within the jurisdiction of the Court. This does not mean, however, that ICC investigators and prosecutors should give up from the outset, any hope of identifying the Bralos or the Jelisićs or the conflict they are mapping, with a view to selecting the gravest incidents and the groups involved. With the unavoidable limitations that the ICC faces in this respect, efforts should still be made to understand as much as possible, the details of the incidents that have been singled-out as most representative, for in-depth investigation and prosecution. Information about persons involved in them should also be adequately processed and analysed. This is also important for the purposes of making adequately informed decisions on all aspects of the strategy, for the development and presentation of the case: it is not only about not missing Bralo as a potential target; it is also about avoiding the risk of ending up interviewing Bralo as a potential insider witness due to insufficient information about the person and his role in the crimes, a decision that would negatively impact on the credibility and legitimacy of the prosecution in the eyes of the victims and communities affected.[26]

---

[26] To my knowledge, this scenario has not taken place to date.

3.4.2. Other Possible Ways to Bring a "Most Responsible" Policy Closer to the Individual Victims

As mentioned earlier, even though a "leaders only" (or even "mainly") policy will normally lead to the selected cases telling a broader story, such a policy will also move away from the individual episode of victimisation. The questions are then, on the one hand, whether anything can be done to ensure that the story of the individual victim of sexual violence does not disappear within the wave of crimes attributed to the accused, and on the other, whether we can ensure that the individual victim feels a personal connection to the case brought by the prosecution, even if it is not *her* case.[27]

One way to do this is to ensure that the episodes selected for prosecution at trial are clear and illustrative examples of the type of victimisation that has taken place in the field. In this way, the victim of sexual violence, whose individual victimisation has not been included in the prosecution's charges, may still feel that her suffering is nonetheless being addressed, even if in an indirect fashion, through the prosecution of instances of sexual violence similar to the one she suffered. The ICC Office of the Prosecutor has established for these purposes, the notion of "representative sample", whereby incidents are selected "to provide a sample that is reflective of the gravest incidents and the main types of victimization".[28] For instance, in the *Bemba* case, one of the criteria to select the individual incidents of sexual violence that are presented by the prosecution, was the extent to which those incidents were representative of the victimisation inflicted on women, children and men by the militia group involved in the crimes during the rampage of sexual violence in the Central African Republic between October 2002 and March 2003. This poses

---

[27] Connecting the individual victim with the prosecution of the person holding a leadership position is an important challenge for any international tribunal:

> In terms of truth telling and vindicating the suffering of victims, will prosecuting Karadic and Mladic more readily satisfy someone whose neighbor killed members of her family? Can a leader become a symbol for all that happened or do victims of a particular incident need to see someone in the dock with greater proximity to the crime from which they directly suffered? (Akhavan, 1998, p. 779, see *supra* note 16).

[28] ICC, Office of the Prosecutor, Report on Prosecutorial Strategy, 14 September 2006, p. 5 (http://www.legal-tools.org/doc/6e3bf4/).

---

the challenge to identify and collect the evidence that provides for the best sample of the crimes, and to be able to put together a comprehensive sample in instances of extended and multiple forms of victimisation. In the *Bemba* case, there is proximity between the sample and totality, to the extent that the victimisation inflicted was more or less uniform and concentrated in confined areas. However, this will often not be the case. In such situations, resort to other supplementary tools may be needed in order to enhance the representation of the crimes in the prosecution's case.

The use of overview evidence may be one of such tools, that is, the use of evidence that can put the episodes of sexual violence chosen by the prosecution into a wider context (for example, the head of a humanitarian mission which documented cases of sexual violence throughout the territory where the crimes charged took place) and expand the narrative of sexual violence at trial. Another avenue is to use the contextual element of crimes against humanity to narrate the story of uncharged instances of sexual violence that still form part of the widespread or systematic attack on the civilian population. This, again, provides an opportunity to broaden the discussion of sexual violence at trial and to provide further illustration of the true scope of victimisation in the field. Finally, even in cases where the prosecution ultimately decided not to focus on sexual violence for the purposes of the charges, it is still possible to explore instances of such violence during the sentencing stage, as part of the impact of the crimes in the victims and their lives. This is what the ICC Office of the Prosecutor has attempted to do in the *Lubanga* case, where even though the prosecution focused solely on the enlistment, conscription and use in hostilities of child soldiers, instances of sexual violence have been portrayed during the proceedings as part of the children's ordeal once brought into the militia groups.

One final point touches on the rubric under which crimes of sexual violence should be charged, that is, which legal characterisation can best portray the suffering inflicted on the victims? This is a frequent challenge in the context of international criminal jurisdictions, which are equipped with overlapping crimes that at times have uncertain borders for the complex task of putting a legal name to the incidents being prosecuted. In this context, the quest for the most comprehensive legal characterisation can be a particularly hard one, plagued with unpredicted difficulties. For instance, the Special Court for Sierra Leone's choice to prosecute charges of "forced marriage" as "other inhumane acts" under crimes against humanity was, on the one hand, greeted with enthusiasm as a substantial development in the prosecution of gender crimes, and on the other, strongly criticised on the basis that the indicators chosen to distinguish the crime of forced marriage from that of sexual slavery (cooking, cleaning, washing clothes) ultimately reproduced sexist stereotypes of "marriage".[29] At the opposite end of the spectrum we have the overly simplistic – and legally questionable – decision from an ICC Pre-Trial Chamber in the *Bemba* case, rejecting the charge of torture as a crime against humanity brought by the prosecution on the basis that it was cumulative of rape charges.[30] If this decision is followed, then even in situations such as that of the *Furundžija* case, prosecutors would be forced to bring charges that cover only one aspect of the victimisation suffered, depriving the victim of a finding that she was also subject to torture, not only rape, and diminishing the expressive value of a conviction.

---

[29] See the thought-provoking article of Jennifer Gong-Gerschovitz, "Forced Marriage: A "New" Crime Against Humanity?", in *Northwestern Journal of International Human Rights*, 2009, vol. 8, no. 1, pp. 53 ff. The author considers that "[a]lthough the perpetrators of violence used the pretext of marriage quite possibly to avoid charges of rape and sexual slavery, a conviction on these grounds provides the most faithful accounting of the crimes of inflicted against thousands of women and girls in Sierra Leone and in other conflicts throughout the world" (p. 63). The importance of developing an adequate, impartial and objective methodology for the investigation and prosecution of sexual violence, free of any stereotypes or predetermined positions, has been stressed in Xabier Agirre Aranburu, "Sexual Violence beyond Reasonable Doubt: Using Pattern Evidence and Analysis for International Cases", in *Leiden Journal of International Law*, 2010, vol. 23, no. 3, pp. 609–27.

[30] ICC, *Prosecutor v. Jean-Pierre Bemba Gombo*, Pre-Trial Chamber, Decision Pursuant to Article 61(7)(a) of the Rome Statute on the Charges of the Prosecutor against Jean-Pierre Bemba Gombo, ICC-01/05-01/08, 15 June 2009, paras. 307–12 (http://www.legal-tools.org/doc/07965c/). The Pre-Trial Chamber appears to acknowledge that the practice of cumulative charging is allowed in international criminal jurisdictions, and even to endorse the "additional element" test developed by the ICTY Appeals Chamber in the *Čelebići* case. However, it subsequently concludes that the torture charges should be displaced by the rape ones, since the latter crime contains all elements of the former, an assertion that a plain reading of the Elements of Crimes proves to be incorrect. Torture under Article 7(1)(f) of the ICC Statute includes requirements of severe physical or mental pain or suffering and of custody or control over the victim, which are nowhere to be found in relation to the crime of rape under Article 7(1)(g); rape only requires penetration, and force, threat of force or coercion, or taking advantage of coercive circumstances. Thus, and probably inadvertently, by concluding that rape contains all elements of torture plus the distinct element of penetration, the Chamber heightens the legal requirements of the crime of rape, against the express will of the legislator. Rome Statute of the International Criminal Court, Preamble, 17 July 1998, in force 1 July 2002 ('ICC Statute') (http://www.legal-tools.org/doc/7b9af9/).

3.5. Concluding Remarks

At the end of *Death and the Maiden*, Paulina, having obtained a confession from her former captor, has a dialogue with her husband, who has just heard for the first time the full story of his wife's ordeal during captivity. Paulina explains that she wants to exorcise the ghosts from their lives. She tells her husband, among other things, that she wants him to do his work in the truth commission (which she had previously rejected as window-dressing) and that she wants to start listening to Schubert's music again, which her rapist had also taken away from her. Paulina's makeshift trial has resensitised her, restored her autonomy and given her new strength. Could a trial before the ICC produce a similar transformation on the victims of sexual violence in the situation being handled by the Court?

Obviously, this question will not have a single answer. However, in relation to those victims involved in the Court's process, either as witnesses and/or as participants, producing positive effects should be at least one goal that the Court sets for itself. Indeed, restoring the victim's sense of self-respect and producing an authoritative finding that she is not responsible for her own tragedy are aims that should guide any justice initiative after massive violations of human rights law and international humanitarian law.[31] In relation to other victims, the question becomes even more complex and the impact, if it exists, will be very difficult to quantify. But the Court can produce substantial effects in the communities where the crimes occurred, which in turn may provide avenues for the victims to have their suffering addressed. For instance, the Court's intervention may shake the culture of impunity that frequently surrounds the commission of international crimes. It can create momentum for accountability by maximising the symbolic and expressive values of its prosecutions of sexual crimes, and can also support nascent or ongoing national efforts through positive complementarity mechanisms. The rape verdicts of the Fizi mobile court in the Democratic Republic of Congo, a mecha-

---

[31] I borrow these concepts from Jaime Malamud Goti. For a discussion of these notions, see Jaime Malamud Goti, *Game Without End: State Terror and the Politics of Justice*, University of Oklahoma Press, Norman, 1996, pp. 14–17, *inter alia*, with additional references.

---

nism created to complement the work of the ICC, provide a good example of this.[32]

If this happens, if the states of denial[33] accompanying the crimes are perforated by national and international accountability efforts, if the feeling of pervasive impunity starts fading away and a sense of outrage for the crimes committed and a demand for justice takes its place, then perhaps by the next encounter, the one that walks away in fear and shame is the rapist, not the victim.

---

[32] See Kelly Askin, "Fizi mobile court: rape verdicts", in *International Justice Tribune*, no. 123, March 2011.

[33] The term belongs to Stanley Cohen, *States of Denial: Knowing about Atrocities and Suffering*, Polity Press, Cambridge, 2001, ch. 1 ("The Elementary Forms of Denial"), discussing collective defence mechanisms created to cope with guilt through the negation of the very existence of the crimes.

4

Prioritising International Sex Crimes before the Special Court for Sierra Leone: One More Instrument of Political Manipulation?

Christopher B. Mahony[*]

4.1. Introduction

Over the past two decades the prosecution of international crimes[1] has become increasingly common, with international organisations and individual states taking political positions over their legitimacy and conduct. Efforts to ensure impartiality and independence in the selection of cases prosecuted, however, have largely failed. Independent case selection has been compromised because states have sought to impede prosecution where they view doing so as antithetical to their interests. Unsurprisingly, states have been happy to allow prosecutions where they view them as furthering their interests. The power to impede, to allow and to shape case selection has therefore become a useful instrument of foreign policy for states.

Historically, prosecution of international crimes has not provided proportionate case selection attention to sex crimes. Advocacy groups have rightly sought to ensure that sex crimes are represented among cases selected for prosecution. However, the prioritisation of sex crimes cases

---

[*] **Christopher B. Mahony** is a Research Fellow at the Centre for International Law Research and Policy; a Visiting Research Fellow at the Georgetown University Law Center; and a Political Economy Adviser with the Independent Evaluation Group, World Bank. At the time of writing, he was serving as Deputy Director of the New Zealand Centre for Human Rights Law, Policy and Practice, Faculty of Law, University of Auckland.

[1] International crimes include crimes against the peace (the 'crime of aggression'), genocide, war crimes, crimes against humanity and other serious violations of international humanitarian law. International crimes are generally considered under customary international law to be those for which individual criminal responsibility may be applied. For an examination of these crimes, see Antonio Cassese, *International Criminal Law*, 2nd ed., Oxford University Press, New York, 2008; Dapo Akande, "Sources of International Criminal Law", in Antonio Cassese (ed.), *The Oxford Companion to International Criminal Justice*, Oxford University Press, New York, 2009, pp. 41–53; M. Cherif Bassiouni, *Introduction to International Criminal Law*, Transnational Publishers, New York, 2003.

for prosecution is a step further still and confronts an emerging norm of case selection prioritisation that applies greater gravity to murder than sex crimes or torture.[2]

This chapter employs the case of the Special Court for Sierra Leone to examine the efficacy of prioritising sex crimes in selection of international crimes cases. The empirical data supporting this material is drawn from over 100 interviews dating from April 2003 to January 2011 and experience working at both the Special Court and the Truth and Reconciliation Commission. The interviewees include Sierra Leonean victims, perpetrators, lawyers, politicians, civil society activists and of course practitioners working at the Special Court. Perhaps more important for the theme of this chapter, interviewees also included defence and prosecution counsel and investigators at the Special Court, a former British high commissioner, state delegates to the United Nations Security Council, US diplomats as well as senators and representatives, their staffers working on US policy in West Africa and key personnel at the US State Department working on transitional initiatives and US policy in the region.

The chapter seeks to examine Special Court case selection and the nature of investigative practices within the context of the politics of the conflict's conclusion. I argue that the Court's creation was driven more by a politically expedient British narrative and a partisan shift in US policy than by independent intent to address impunity. I also argue that pressure created by advocacy groups for prosecution of international crimes in the region was employed more because of its political utility rather than its perceived merit. In short, actors who designed the Court and controlled critical elements of its function, cherry-picked and manipulated transitional justice discourse for their own interests. In the process of doing so, they undermined an authentic pursuit of justice for the victims of Sierra Leone's conflict. This chapter cautions against diversion from an emerging norm of case prioritisation criteria (that places murder as the most serious of crimes). To do so suggests that those creating and designing internationalised courts, and those creating local frameworks for prosecution of international crimes, would not employ or refuse to employ this policy based on political consideration, rather than a case's merit. It also suggests that prosecution personnel at the local and international levels

---

[2]   Morten Bergsmo, Chapter 1 above.

would not selectively employ thematic criteria based on considerations relating to current and future state co-operation. Circumstances lending greater scope for selective prosecution, I argue, undermine rather than further the need to ensure independent prosecution of sex crimes.

My argument is premised by the assumption that states, particularly powerful states best placed to affect negotiation of Court creation and design, employ a constructivist approach to courts trying international crimes. In order to interpret a constructivist approach in international law, we must employ "practical reason" in understanding the human agency's power in building social structures.[3] Jutta Brunnée and Stephen Toope argue:

> Law is persuasive when it is viewed as legitimate, largely in terms of internal process values, and when, as a result of the existence of basic social understandings, it can call upon reasoned argument, particularly analogy, to justify its processes and its broad substantive ends, thereby creating shared rhetorical knowledge.[4]

Furthermore, the authors argue that legitimacy is derived from rules and norms created by mutual construction via a wide range of participants.[5]

I argue that rules and norms relating to case selection bear little resemblance to those that might derive legitimacy according to Brunnee and Toope. I employ the succinctly stated summary of the constructivist explanation of international relations:

> Rules and norms constitute the international game by determining who the actors are, what rules they must follow if they wish to ensure that particular consequences follow from specific acts, and how titles to possessions can be established and transferred. In other words, norms do not cause a state to act in a particular way, but rather provide reasons for a state to do so.[6]

---

[3] Jutta Brunnée and Stephen J. Toope, "International Law and Constructivism: Elements of an Interactional Theory of International Law", in *Columbia Journal of Transnational Law*, vol. 39, 2000, p. 27.

[4] *Ibid.*, p. 72.

[5] *Ibid.*, 2000, p. 74.

[6] Ngaire Woods, *Explaining International Relations since 1945*, Oxford University Press, Oxford, 1996, p. 26.

I start off by examining the conflict, particularly its conclusion, before addressing the design of the court and the nature and impact of state co-operation on case selection. I conclude by considering the nature and effect of key case selection norms inherent in court design and function – what would a departure from an emerging norm that places murder as the most serious crime before torture and sex crimes mean for retributive, deterrent and expressivist goals?[7]

Sierra Leone is a small coastal West African country and a former British colony. It is bordered by Guinea to the north and East and Liberia to the south. The causes and motivations behind the conflict are a point of scholarly contention. West African, American, British and French interests have commonly been aligned in attempting to solicit external commercial penetration and diplomatic and security influence. However, these states have historically competed among one another for the fruits external hegemony bear. This competition has been pursued through the development of regional allies such as Libya for the French and Nigeria for Britain and the United States. These two regional powers have often supported friendly parties in conflicts in the region in furtherance of their patron's interests. The Sierra Leonean civil conflict is a case study in the theory of external leveraging of regional power politics.

In March 1991, an armed insurgency called the Revolutionary United Front ('RUF') led by Foday Sankoh and supported by Charles Taylor's Liberian National Patriotic Front ('NPFL') entered eastern Sierra Leone from Liberia to try to overthrow the government of Joseph Momoh. Both the RUF and the NPFL leadership had received training and financial support from Libya and, according to Western intelligence, held French third party tacit support via Burkina Faso and Côte d'Ivoire from which Taylor launched his Liberian rebellion.[8]

The war would cause tens of thousands of deaths, over a million displacements, and upwards of 400,000 amputations of one or more limbs. The number of victims of sex crimes is unknown. They constituted just 3.3 per cent of total crimes reported to the Truth and Reconciliation

---

[7] Morten Bergsmo, Chapter 1 above.

[8] Special Court for Sierra Leone ('SCSL'), *Prosecutor v. Charles Taylor*, Trial Chamber, Transcript, SCSL-2003-01-T, 9 November 2009, p. 31441 ('*Taylor* Transcript').

Commission.[9] Low reporting of sex crimes suggests more about the stigma experienced by victims than its prevalence during the conflict. The commission did not attempt to estimate the totality of these crimes. However, it is commonly recognised that rape is widespread in Sierra Leone, particularly so during the conflict.[10] The UN special rapporteur on the elimination of violence against women, Radhika Coomaraswamy, estimated that more than 50 per cent of Sierra Leonean women and girls were victims of sexual violence.[11]

In 1992 a group of Sierra Leone Army ('SLA') soldiers venting discontent at poor treatment by the government conducted a coup, establishing the National Provisional Ruling Council ('NPRC'). In power, the army were ineffective in countering the RUF. As a consequence, many rural communities formed local civil defence forces ('CDFs') to defend themselves from both the RUF and an increasingly ill-disciplined army. The CDFs would also end up committing numerous and egregious violations during the conflict but comparatively few crimes sexually orientated in nature.

In 1995 the NPRC's then greatest source of revenue, the SIERMCO and Sierra Rutile mines, were captured. With British personnel and commercial interests threatened, the British government helped secure a deal that provided diamond-mining concessions worth \$2 billion and interests in Sierra Rutile to a British firm. In return for these commercial interests, the firm organised a mercenary force to capture the two sites, defend Freetown and engage the RUF.[12]

---

[9] Truth and Reconciliation Commission, Sierra Leone, *Witness to Truth: Report of the Sierra Leone Truth and Reconciliation Commission*, vol. 2, 2004, GPL Press, Accra, p. 35 ('TRC Report, vol. 2').

[10] Amnesty International, "Sierra Leone: Rape and Other Forms of Violence against Girls and Women", 29 June 2000, AI Index: AFR 51/35/00.

[11] "Violence Against Women Rife During Sierra Leonean War", in *Agence France-Presse*, 20 March 2002, cited in Stephanie H. Bald, "Searching for a Lost Childhood: Will the Special Court of Sierra Leone Find Justice for Its Children?", in *American University International Law Review*, 2002, vol. 18, no. 2, p. 546.

[12] Ian Douglas, "Fighting for Diamonds: Private Military Companies in Sierra Leone", in Jakkie Cilliers and Peggy Mason (eds.), *Peace, Profit or Plunder? The Privatisation of Security in War-Torn African Societies*, Institute for Security Studies, Pretoria, 1999, pp. 179–80; EO deployed 150 to 200 men and a helicopter gunship: P.W. Singer, *Corporate Warriors: The Rise of the Privatized Military Industry*, Cornell University Press, Ithaca, NY, 2003, p. 104; David Keen, *Conflict and Collusion in Sierra Leone*, James Currey, London, 2005, p. 151;

In 1996 dubious elections were held bringing the NPRC adviser Ahmed Tejan Kabbah to the presidency.[13] A failed attempt at peace led Kabbah to depend more heavily on the CDFs for support. The SLA was viewed by the Kabbah government as commonly operating alongside the RUF.

Kabbah's perceived hostility towards the army prompted it to conduct a coup in May 1997.[14] At the army's request, the RUF leader Foday Sankoh, then in detention in Nigeria, ordered the RUF to join the SLA in the government.[15] Kabbah fled to Guinea where, in close counsel with Britain, he established a government in exile. Britain then procured a large Nigerian force under the banner of regional peacekeeping to assist CDF efforts to force Kabbah's return.[16] The SLA marginalised the RUF from peace talks, fermenting distrust between the SLA and the RUF – something that Kabbah, by then no longer president, would later exploit.[17]

In neighbouring Liberia, Charles Taylor comprehensively won the Liberian presidency. The United States, having previously viewed Taylor as an agent of Francophone encroachment in a historically US sphere of influence, actively engaged the RUF's Liberian supporter in diplomacy.

David J. Francis, "Mercenary Intervention in Sierra Leone: Providing National Security or International Exploitation", in *Third World Quarterly*, 1999, vol. 20, no. 2, pp. 319–38; Truth and Reconciliation Commission, Sierra Leone, *Witness to Truth: Report of the Sierra Leone Truth and Reconciliation Commission*, vol. 3B, 2004, GSL Press, Accra, p. 68; Eeben Barlow, *Executive Outcomes: Against All Odds*, Galago Publishing, Alberton, 1999, p. 325; Deborah D. Avant, *The Market of Force: the Consequences of Privatizing Security*, Cambridge University Press, Cambridge, 2005, p. 86; David Shearer, *Private Armies and Military Intervention*, Adelphi Paper 316 IISS, Oxford University Press, Oxford, 1998, p. 49; Sandline International, "Comment on Book Entitled 'Mercenaries – an African Security Dilemma'", 14 March 2000.

[13] Southern irregularities included 345 per cent turnout in Pujehun, 155 per cent in Bonthe, 139 per cent in Kailahun, 117 per cent in Kenema and 90 per cent in Bo: Jimmy D. Kandeh, "Transition without Rupture: Sierra Leone's Transfer Election of 1996", in *African Studies Review*, 1998, vol. 41, no. 2, pp. 98, 105.

[14] Keen, 2005, pp. 197–201, see *supra* note 12; Truth and Reconciliation Commission, Sierra Leone, *Witness to Truth: Report of the Sierra Leone Truth and Reconciliation Commission*, vol. 3A, 2004, pp. 234–36 ('TRC Report, vol. 3A').

[15] *Ibid.*, pp. 245–46.

[16] Interview with former Tunisian delegate to the UN Security Council, The Hague, 11 June 2009.

[17] Economic Community of West African States Six-Month Peace Plans for Sierra Leone, 23 October 1997.

Taylor's strongest US relationships were developed with the US special envoy for human rights and democracy in Africa, Jesse Jackson, and the Black Congressional Caucus leader Donald Payne.[18] Despite rapprochement with the United States, Taylor maintained close ties to France, visiting Paris in 1998 to declare Liberian plans for privatisation and for French business to spearhead the process.[19] French encroachment into the historically British sphere of influence in Sierra Leone posed a tremendous threat to British commercial, diplomatic and security interests.

The Kabbah government was returned to power by an Economic Community of West African States Monitoring Group ('ECOMOG') and CDF attack planned and co-ordinated by the British mercenary group Sandline. British support of the CDF violated UN sanctions that Britain had proposed and lead.[20]

In March 1999 circumstances demanded a conciliatory British stance. At the time Nigeria sought to draw down ECOMOG forces in Sierra Leone[21] while the United States and France continued to support Taylor and the RUF. The British foreign minister, Robin Cook, met with his French counterpart Hubert Védrine in Abuja from where he instructed a reluctant Kabbah to pursue dialogue with the RUF.[22] Jackson confronted Kabbah at a conference in Ghana and brought him to Togo to negotiate the Lomé Peace Accord with the RUF.[23] Kabbah and Sankoh eventually agreed a power-sharing peace deal, amnesty for crimes committed and the replacement of ECOMOG with a UN force. Britain was isolated in its support for Kabbah and antipathy towards Taylor and the RUF. Two key dynamics changed in Britain's favour in 1999 and 2000.

---

[18]　Kenneth R. Timmerman, "Jesse, Liberia and Blood Diamonds", in *Insight Magazine*, 25 July 2003; Ismail Rashid, "The Lomé Peace Negotiations", in *Conciliation Resources*, September 2000.

[19]　Star Radio, "Liberian Daily News Bulletin", in *All Africa.com*, 30 September 1998.

[20]　Lansana Gberie, "War and State Collapse: The Case of Sierra Leone", M.A. Thesis, Wilfrid Laurier University, 1997, p. 166; "Britain's Role in Sierra Leone", in *BBC News*, 10 September 2000; Interview, Tunisian delegate, see *supra* note 16.

[21]　"IRIN Update 420 for 11 March 1999", University of Pennsylvania, African Studies Center, 11 March 1999.

[22]　Keen, 2005, p. 250, see *supra* note 12.

[23]　Rashid, 2000, see *supra* note 18.

4.2. Local Security and External Politics Shift in Favour of Kabbah and Britain

The first change to occur in favour of Britain was the Kabbah government's rapprochement with the SLA. The SLA/RUF alliance had been undermined by the SLA's exclusion from the Lomé negotiations and agreement by the RUF. This tension was exacerbated when the RUF field commander Sam Bockarie briefly took captive the SLA leader, Johnny Paul Koroma.[24] These events pushed the SLA away from the RUF and towards Kabbah. This changed the security dynamics dramatically in favour of Kabbah and his British supporters. Kabbah now had the majority of the SLA (some SLA elements remained aligned to the RUF), a large ECOMOG force, and of course the CDFs at his disposal.

Perhaps the most important swing of support came from the Republican-controlled US Senate that sought to change the Clinton administration's policy in the region against the Liberian president Charles Taylor and the RUF. The foreign affairs appropriations committee chairman has the power to block money for foreign policy without hearings, debate or votes.[25] Then Republican chairman, Senator Judd Gregg, used that power to block funding of $96 million for the UN's Sierra Leone mission – money required for education and vocational programmes promised to combatants under the Lomé Accord. Gregg, a fiscal conservative, was also impeding payment of $1.77 billion owed to the UN by the United States.[26] Gregg had argued that US finance would be better spent domestically than on policy he viewed as ill-informed and unethical, citing Liberia and Sierra Leone.[27] The Sierra Leone UN funding represented the only real incentives for ordinary RUF combatants to disarm. Emboldened by his emerging local security strength and by Republican support in the United States, Kabbah refused to grant many allocated RUF positions in

---

[24] TRC Report, vol. 3A, pp. 343–44, see *supra* note 14; Sierra Leone Web Archives, "Sierra Leone News", October 1999.

[25] Tim Weiner, "Solitary Republican Senator Blocks Peacekeeping Funds", in *New York Times*, 19 May 2000.

[26] *Ibid.*

[27] Interview with former staffer to United States Ambassador to the United Nations, Richard Holbrooke, 13 January 2011; see also *ibid.*

government.[28] In congruence with the British government, Kabbah continued to cite RUF reluctance to disarm as the sole driver of post-Lomé instability. This narrative was adopted by the mass media. Little attention was drawn to the non-disarmament of the CDFs or the refusal of the Kabbah government to fulfil its obligations under the peace agreement.

The pressure on combatants to disarm without any incentive to do so culminated in their May 2000 seizure of over 550 United Nations Mission in Sierra Leone ('UNAMSIL') peacekeepers. Four peacekeepers were killed and three injured.[29] In response, Kabbah deployed the SLA alongside the CDFs to arrest senior RUF figures in Freetown. This included a CDF and SLA attack, under cover of protest, on Sankoh's house.[30] The government described the fracas as hostile RUF action against a democratic government, a narrative actively deployed by the British government and adopted by the mass media.[31] In response, the RUF marched on Freetown but were met and repelled by a coalition of SLA, CDF, ECOMOG and British troops (co-ordinated, armed and trained by the British).[32] The RUF had been effectively labelled the aggressors as Britain began to act without Security Council approval but with moral legitimacy derived from the narrative it had manufactured.

The British government was now working with Gregg to change US policy against Taylor. In response to the hostage taking, Gregg stated he would continue to block US peacekeeping funds until Lomé was abandoned and all feasible efforts were used to undermine Taylor's rule in Liberia.[33] Gregg also called for "an international war crimes tribunal" to "investigate and punish atrocities committed by the RUF", the first time such a tribunal had been publicly proposed.[34]

---

[28] United Nations Security Council, Fourth Report of the Secretary-General on the United Nations Mission in Sierra Leone, UN Doc. S/2000/455, 19 May 2000, p. 3; TRC Report, vol. 3A, p. 249, see *supra* note 14.

[29] TRC Report, vol. 3A, p. 358, see *supra* note 14.

[30] *Ibid.*, pp. 245–49, 415–21.

[31] *Ibid.*, pp. 233, 245–49, 393, 377, 405–06, 415–21.

[32] *Ibid.*, pp. 331, 457–58; International Crisis Group ('ICG'), "Liberia: The Key to Ending Regional Instability", in *Africa Report*, no. 43, 24 April 2002, p. 4.

[33] Judd Gregg, "A Graveyard Peace", in *Washington Post*, 9 May 2000.

[34] *Ibid.*

Gregg and his staffers had met with then US ambassador to the UN, Richard Holbrooke, and his staffers to discuss US policy towards Sierra Leone and Liberia.[35] Gregg made the case that the United States was using taxpayer dollars for ill-informed policy and that $368 million of overdue US peacekeeping funding would remain withheld until US policy changed.[36]

4.3. The Clinton Administration Concede

Indications of an Anglo-American compromise could be seen in a statement from the Kabbah government that private security firms from either the United States or Britain would be contracted to provide security in the diamond-mining areas. Taylor's pledge of 3,000 Liberian troops to an Economic Community of West African States ('ECOWAS') peacekeeping contingent in Sierra Leone, and his call for Sankoh to be moved to a third country, indicated his acknowledgement of a change in Clinton administration policy.[37] Holbrooke and Gregg had agreed on a shift in policy against Taylor, directed at the removal of his regime using a diversity of instruments.[38] These would include sponsoring an armed rebellion against Taylor's government, establishing a tribunal that would indict him, placing sanctions on his government that would weaken his ability to repel a rebel force, and provide support to local political opponents.[39] Holbrooke and Gregg intended that one or a combination of these methods would force Taylor from power.[40]

On 5 June 2000 the US State Department announced it was in consultation with the UN and Britain to bring perpetrators of crimes in Sierra Leone to justice, indicating that crimes committed since the Lomé amnesty were not covered by it.[41] This implied that the United States considered

---

[35] Interview, Holbrooke staffer, 2011, see *supra* note 27; Interview with former staffer to Senator Judd Gregg, 13 December 2010, Washington, D.C.

[36] Interview, Holbrooke staffer, 2011, see *supra* note 27; Interview, Gregg staffer, 2010, see *supra* note 35; Weiner, 2000, see *supra* note 25.

[37] Sierra Leone Web Archive, "Sierra Leone News", June 2000.

[38] Interview, Holbrooke staffer, 2011, see *supra* note 27; Interview, Gregg staffer, 2010, see *supra* note 35.

[39] Interview, Gregg staffer, 2010, see *supra* note 35.

[40] *Ibid.*

[41] Sierra Leone Web Archive, 2000, see *supra* note 37.

that crimes committed prior to Lomé were. Jackson was fired as special envoy. The next day Gregg released $368 million in peacekeeping funds ($96 million for Sierra Leone) that he had been blocking.[42] Until this time, the Clinton administration had termed Gregg's blockage of the funds "a grave mistake".[43] The Clinton administration had officially indicated its shift in policy in a letter to Gregg from Holbrooke. The letter, the contents of which the two had negotiated, stated that Sankoh should have no political future, that the UN should try to disrupt the RUF's hold on diamonds, and that the United States should come up with a strategy to deal with Taylor.[44] On June 6 Gregg made the following statement:

> The United States will not turn a blind eye to the rape of the people and of the land of Sierra Leone. We will demand that brutal thugs are held accountable for their atrocities and regional troublemakers must look with fear to their own future.[45]

4.4. Negotiating a Tribunal

The United States and Britain began to negotiate the possibility of a tribunal at the Security Council. However, France, Russia and China viewed this move as an attempt to deal with Liberia through the back door.[46] The three permanent members of the Security Council concluded that any tribunal should be funded by the United States and Britain themselves unlike the tribunals for the former Yugoslavia and Rwanda.[47] The United States and Britain also favoured a hybrid model funded by voluntary donations. They viewed the Court's hybridity as less costly than its predecessors while granting donor states greater fiscal control over the selection and behaviour of key court personnel.[48] The British UN representative,

---

[42] *Ibid.*; Weiner, 2000, see *supra* note 25.

[43] Tim Weiner, "G.O.P. Senator Frees Millions for U.N. Mission in Sierra Leone", in *New York Times*, 7 June 2000.

[44] *Ibid.*

[45] Sierra Leone Web Archive, 2000, see *supra* note 37.

[46] Interview, Tunisian delegate, 2009, see *supra* note 16.

[47] *Ibid.*; Interview with former US Department of State, Deputy Ambassador at Large for War Crimes Issues, Michael Miklaucic, via telephone, 20 September 2011.

[48] Interview, Tunisian delegate, 2009, see *supra* note 16; Interview, Holbrooke staffer, 2011, see *supra* note 27; Interview, Gregg staffer, 2010, see *supra* note 35.

Jeremy Greenstock, stated a comprehensive resolution was being proposed to expand the UNAMSIL force, to bring to justice those that had attacked peacekeepers and committed violations of international law, and to address the illegal RUF trade of diamonds for arms.[49]

4.5. The Emergence of Regime Change Strategy for Liberia

Within a month of the meeting between Holbrooke and Gregg, the proposed US strategy was materialising for Taylor's government in Liberia. The British government asked Kabbah to write a letter to the Security Council requesting it to establish an international criminal tribunal.[50] After a closed session, the Security Council found that the RUF had violated the Lomé Agreement and that those responsible for taking UN peacekeepers hostage should be "brought to justice".[51] An armed militia called Liberians United for Reconciliation and Democracy ('LURD') that was in contact with military officers from both the United States and Britain, attacked north-western Liberia from Guinea.[52] The Guinean leader Lansana Conté had been a strong US ally in the region. His forces were provided with increased US military training and ammunition for their offensive against Taylor.[53]

The Liberian government, with support from ECOWAS, France, China and Russia, appealed to the Security Council to lift sanctions placed on it. However, Britain and the United States remained steadfastly opposed.[54] In the face of Anglo-American hostility, Taylor attempted to appease the United States through diplomatic patrons in both the Democrat and Republican parties. However, all arms, as well as both parties of the US government now appeared unified in their opposition to Taylor's

---

[49] Sierra Leone Web Archive, 2000, see *supra* note 37; Interview, Holbrooke staffer, 2011, see *supra* note 27; Interview, Gregg staffer, 2010, see *supra* note 35.

[50] Interview, Tunisian delegate, 2009, see *supra* note 16.

[51] United Nations Security Council, Official Communiqué of the 4163rd meeting of the Security Council, UN Doc. S/PV.4163, 21 June 2000.

[52] ICG, 2002, p. 4, see *supra* note 32.

[53] *Ibid.*, p. 5; *Taylor* Transcript, 9 November 2009, pp. 31332–33, see *supra* note 8; Interview, Gregg staffer, 2010, see *supra* note 35; United States House of Representatives, Hearing before Subcommittee on Africa, Global Human Rights and International Operations, The Impact of Liberia's Election on West Africa, 8 February 2006, pp. 61–62.

[54] *Taylor* Transcript, pp. 31338–39, see *supra* note 8; Interview, Tunisian delegate, 2009, see *supra* note 16.

Liberian regime. In October 2000 the Clinton administration banned entry to the United States to Taylor and other senior Liberian officials.[55] In 2001, after meeting with George Bush on Taylor's behalf, the prominent Republican evangelist Pat Robertson told Taylor:

> [T]he only thing I can advise you to do, Mr President, is appeal to God, because what I'm hearing from George Bush, there's nothing that you can do about what America intends to do.[56]

4.6. Creating a Special Court as a Part of Strategy Aimed to Affect Liberian Regime Change

On 14 August 2000 the UN Security Council requested the UN secretary-general to create a "Special Court" for Sierra Leone by negotiating an agreement with the government of Sierra Leone.[57] Taylor hoped France would be able to push through sanctions on Guinea for its support of the LURD, since Liberia was under sanctions for supporting the RUF.[58] He had overestimated French clout.

The initial leanings of the Special Court were inherent in the empowering resolution that commended the efforts of the government of Sierra Leone and ECOWAS for bringing lasting peace to Sierra Leone.[59] In August 2001 the Security Council passed a resolution to create the Special Court and the White House asked the Department of Defense lawyer David Crane to "help set up an experiment in West Africa".[60] Crane began utilising Department of Defense intelligence information to formulate

---

55 White House Office of the Press Secretary (Philadelphia, Pennsylvania), Proclamation 7359: Suspension of Entry as Immigrants and Nonimmigrants of persons impeding the peace process in Sierra Leone, 10 October 2000.

56 *Taylor* Transcript, p. 31335, see *supra* note 8.

56 Interview, Tunisian delegate, 2009, see *supra* note 16.

57 United Nations Security Council, Resolution 1315 (2000), UN Doc. S/RES/1315, 14 August 2000 ('UNSC Resolution 1315') (http://www.legal-tools.org/doc/95897f/); United Nations Security Council, Liberia Diamond Ban and Travel Ban come into Force, Press Release, UN Doc. SC/7058, 7 May 2001.

58 ICG, 2002, p. 25, see *supra* note 32.

59 UNSC Resolution 1315, see *supra* note 57.

60 David M. Crane, "The Triumph of Good over Evil ... The Investigation, Indictment, and Arrest of Charles Taylor: A Regional Approach to Justice", Speech at the Baldy Centre for Law and Social Policy, University of Buffalo, 17 February 2010.

---

who he believed was most responsible for crimes committed during the conflict.[61]

The Security Council resolution made ambitious claims as to the impact a "Special Court" might have for Sierra Leone. It states:

> In the particular circumstances of Sierra Leone, a credible system of justice and accountability for the very serious crimes committed there would end impunity and would contribute to the process of national reconciliation and to the restoration and maintenance of peace [...].[62]

Once Security Council consensus had been reached on the Court's creation and financial independence from UN coffers, Britain and the United States largely controlled the Security Council's position towards the Court.[63]

Resolution 1314 proposed a tribunal which had, based upon conclusions it had already made, assumed non-culpability for crimes by the leadership of one party to the conflict. Further, in drafting and negotiating the resolution, permanent Security Council members either assumed non-culpability for their own financial, political or military role, or sought to impede investigation of that role. Resolution 1314 was widely lauded by rights groups as evidence of the international community's intent to address impunity no matter what office perpetrators hold.

4.7. The Statute

The Special Court Statute provides *ad hoc* amnesty to peacekeepers and government-aligned private military contractors. It places those persons within the primary jurisdiction of their state and requires Security Council approval for the Court to investigate them.[64] This puts ECOMOG soldiers or British military officers beyond the reach of the Court. It may also have excluded from prosecution British diplomats and servicemen co-ordinating the military support of the CDFs. British support for the CDFs,

---

[61] *Ibid.*; Interview with David Crane, Former Chief Prosecutor, Special Court for Sierra Leone, via telephone, 17 August 2010.

[62] UNSC Resolution 1315, see *supra* note 57.

[63] Interview, Tunisian delegate, 2009.

[64] Statute of the Special Court for Sierra Leone, created 14 August 2000, entry into force 16 January 2002, Article 1(2)–(3) ('SCSL Statute') (http://www.legal-tools.org/doc/aa0e20/).

in spite of sanctions, was documented by a British parliamentary inquiry which found that the British high commissioner had co-ordinated armaments supply and had briefed the Foreign Office of his doing so.[65] Whether or not the article provides immunity to the CDFs is an argument its counsel did not raise.

But the Statute left Kabbah's government open to indictment. The Kabbah government had made clear to the secretary-general's office its reluctance to agree to co-operate with a Special Court until the Court was established and the prosecutor had been appointed.[66] Article 2 of the agreement between the UN and the Sierra Leonean government stipulates that the secretary-general and the president of Sierra Leone will appoint key Court personnel.[67]

4.8. Prosecution Case Selection

In the years within the jurisdiction of the Court (30 November 1996 onwards), the Truth and Reconciliation Commission attributed 57 per cent of abuses to the RUF, 30 per cent to the SLA and 12 per cent to the CDFs, with a negligible percentage committed by ECOMOG forces.[68] Prosecution of ECOMOG personnel was, therefore, unwarranted, under the exercise of numeric gravity. Nonetheless, ECOMOG abuses were brought to the attention of prosecution personnel by investigators. They were not pursued because of the amnesty, not because of the comparatively lesser scale of ECOMOG offending.[69] More importantly, the *ad hoc* amnesty protects any personnel in a peacekeeping role in an agreement with the government. This meant that British or British-procured advisers co-ordinating pro-Kabbah forces against the RUF could not be held accountable.

Because the British and United States governments were responsible for funding the Court, they also recommended Court appointments

---

[65] Sir Thomas Legg and Sir Robin Ibbs, *Report of* the Sierra Leone Arms Investigation, House of Commons Paper 1016, 27 July 1998, p. 28; Keen, 2005, p. 218, see *supra* note 12.

[66] United Nations, Report of the Secretary-General on the Establishment of a Special Court for Sierra Leone, UN Doc. S/2000/915, 4 October 2000, para. 8 (http://www.legal-tools.org/doc/4af5d2/).

[67] SCSL Statute, see *supra* note 64.

[68] TRC Report, vol. 2, p. 39, see *supra* note 9.

[69] Interview with former prosecution investigator for the SCSL, via telephone, 26 August 2010.

---

critical to case selection and could withhold funding where case selection fell or threatened to fall outside expectation.[70] The United States recommended Crane to be the Court's first chief prosecutor. The government of Sierra Leone appointed Desmond De Silva, a former colleague of Kabbah's, as Crane's deputy.[71]

Prosecutorial policy, empowered to target "those who bear the greatest responsibility", bore the hallmarks of preferring British and US interests from the outset.[72] The original prosecutor, Crane, admits available intelligence at the Department of Defense was critically instructive in formulating whom to target.[73] Since being informed he was likely to be appointed as prosecutor in September 2001, he had had almost a year to examine Department of Defense information. He also stated that after seeking non-governmental organisation corroboration of Department of Defense information, he held "a four corners idea as to who bore the greatest responsibility" before going to Sierra Leone to begin investigations.[74]

In exercising his prosecutorial discretion, the Security Council had directed the prosecutor to use "those leaders who, in committing such crimes, have threatened the establishment of and implementation of the peace process in Sierra Leone" as a guiding philosophy.[75]

One investigator noted that upon the arrival of the prosecutor in Sierra Leone, it was already clear which persons were going to be investigated.[76] The prosecution's confidence in its case selection appeared to draw upon rigid, yet commonly adopted narratives that failed to reflect the offending of one party to the conflict. Crane viewed the conflict as beginning because of individual criminal gain.[77] He viewed his case against the RUF as the "blood diamond story" – "the movie for real" – in which the

---

[70] Interview with Robin Vincent, former Registrar, Special Court for Sierra Leone, Cheltenham, United Kingdom, 19 April 2007.

[71] United Kingdom Parliament, Select Committee on Standards and Privileges, Minutes of Evidence, 19 July 2005.

[72] Interview, Crane, 2010, *supra* note 61.

[73] *Ibid.*

[74] *Ibid.*; Interview, Miklaucic, 2011, *supra* note 47.

[75] UNSC Resolution 1315, p. 2, see *supra* note 57.

[76] Interview, former prosecution investigator for SCSL, 2010, see *supra* note 69.

[77] Crane, 2010, see *supra* note 60.

motives for the RUF insurgency "all boiled down to a commodity, generally diamonds" and the personal criminal gain of the RUF leadership.[78] He also viewed the conflict as "a good news story" because "the good guys (Kabbah and the British government) won".[79]

British intelligence officers from MI6 who met with Crane in Europe and West Africa reinforced Crane's Department of Defense analysis.[80] British and American intelligence officers were sharing intelligence on RUF procurement of financial, military and logistical support that was passed to the prosecution.[81] Kabbah had directed the British-provided inspector-general of police, Keith Biddle, to co-operate with the Special Court. Biddle co-operated by providing Sierra Leonean police investigators who were prominent in the investigation of the CDFs.[82]

Between a month and 45 days after the prosecutor's arrival in Sierra Leone, the crimes and who were to be prosecuted for them were sufficiently clear to allow indictments to be drafted.[83] Every major appointing authority and, as a consequence, key prosecution appointees, excluding the Human Rights Watch-seconded advisers, had a historical or institutional conflict of interest stemming from professional experience aligned to a party to the conflict. These professional allegiances were exaggerated by reliance on information from interested institutions, and by functional impediments of state co-operation provided by the Kabbah government.

The prosecutor indicted the RUF leadership and Taylor but neglected to pursue foreign supporters such as Ibrahim Bah the arms dealer, Blaise Compaoré, the president of Burkina Faso, and Libyan leader Muammar Gaddafi. The former registrar, Robin Vincent, cites political pressure on Crane not to indict Gaddafi, despite his culpability, due to the appearance of a Gaddafi indictment by a US-funded tribunal.[84] Crane ad-

---

[78] *Ibid.*; House of Representatives Committee on the Judiciary, Subcommittee on Crime, Terrorism, and Homeland Security, Prosecuting the Use of Children in Times of Conflict: The Lost Generation of Sierra Leone, Testimony of David M. Crane, 8 April 2008, p. 40.

[79] Crane, 2010, see *supra* note 60.

[80] Interview, Crane, 2010, see *supra* note 61.

[81] *Taylor* Transcript, p. 31446, see *supra* note 8.

[82] Interview, Crane, 2010, see *supra* note 61; Interview, former prosecution investigator for SCSL, 2010, see *supra* note 69.

[83] Interview, Crane, 2010, see *supra* note 61.

[84] Interview, Vincent, 2007, see *supra* note 70.

mits he "found Gaddafi to bear the greatest responsibility", but viewed his indictment as too politically sensitive.[85] The Court's dependence on voluntary contributions from the United States and Britain was also critically instructive. Explaining his non-indictment as "a political decision", Crane stated: "If I had indicted Gaddafi and Compaoré then we would have been shut down".[86] Crane visited the US State Department approximately four times annually where he sought the War Crimes Office view as to who was to be prosecuted.[87] Crane has cited Gaddafi's oil-orientated clout at the Security Council, particularly with Britain, as driving the sensitivity surrounding his potential indictment.[88] In response, the British foreign secretary, Jack Straw, stated he "had no recollection of knowing any involvement by the U.K. in influencing investigations".[89] The British Foreign Office stated that "the issue of indictments is a matter for the Prosecutor" and that "it is committed to ensuring there is no impunity for those alleged to have committed the most serious crimes".[90] In November 2002 a decision was therefore taken to pursue only one of the three heads of state allegedly involved in the RUF joint criminal enterprise.[91]

Compaoré and the weapons trader, Ibrahim Bah, who organised the facilitation of arms through Burkina Faso to the RUF, were originally thought to be within the political parameters of indictment. Their cooperation with the US government on terrorism (Bah was on the payroll of US intelligence), as well as the anticipated political and diplomatic fallout of indicting more than one head of state, outweighed the good of holding them accountable.[92]

The original list of potential accused was larger than the final number prosecuted. It did include Compaoré, but on the side of the CDFs,

---

[85] Interview with David Crane, former Chief Prosecutor, Special Court for Sierra Leone, via telephone, 17 May 2007.

[86] *Ibid.*; Interview, Crane, 2010, see *supra* note 61.

[87] Interview, Miklaucic, 2011, see *supra* note 47.

[88] David Crane, "Gaddafi Instrumental in Sierra Leone Conflict", in *Awoko*, 6 March 2011.

[89] *Ibid.*

[90] *Ibid.*

[91] Interview, Crane, 2010, see *supra* note 61.

[92] Interview, former prosecution investigator for SCSL, 2010, *supra* note 69. According to intelligence reports, Bah had been given $10,000 by US officials who also bought him a plane ticket to Abidjan where he spoke to US officials in January 2002 as well as in Ouagadougou in February. See *Taylor* Transcript, pp. 31451–53, *supra* note 8.

Hinga Norman was as high as the chain of command went. However, Norman's position as deputy minister of defence meant he reported to the defence minister, a position also held by Kabbah.[93] The Court and many of its proponents have cited the prosecution of the CDF accused as demonstrating Kabbah's willingness to allow impartial investigation of all parties. Since 1997, however, the relationship between Norman and Kabbah had been one of deep mistrust.[94] Many observers believed Norman sought to usurp Kabbah as leader of the Sierra Leone People's Party and that Kabbah and those close to him, particularly Vice President Solomon Berewa, viewed Norman as a political threat.[95]

The security threat the CDFs posed was also diminished through the stigmatisation associated with the prosecution's labelling of the organisation as criminal.[96] From the time of the prosecution's arrival in October 2002, there was no suggestion of investigating anyone in the CDF chain of command higher than Norman. Some elements of the prosecution provided leads for investigation of the political and military supporters of the CDFs. Those sources did not believe the information was actively pursued.[97]

The first apparent impediment to the pursuit of Kabbah appeared to be Court dependency upon local co-operation with security forces. Prosecution personnel were conscious that the investigation and prosecution of accused depended on Sierra Leonean state co-operation. They were particularly cognisant of the experience of Carla Del Ponte at the International Criminal Tribunal for Rwanda ('ICTR'), who was forced from her post

---

[93] Interview, former prosecution investigator for SCSL, 2010, see *supra* note 69.

[94] TRC Report, vol. 3A, see *supra* note 14.

[95] Interview with Sierra Leone Law Reform Commissioner, Peter Tucker, 5 April 2007, Freetown; Interview with Campaign for Good Governance director, Olayinka Creighton-Randall, Freetown, 3 April 2007; Interview with Truth and Reconciliation Commission "Military and Political History of the Conflict" chapter author, Gavin Simpson, Freetown, 30 March 2007; Interview with Alhaji Ibrahim Ben Kargbo, President of the Sierra Leone Association of Journalists, Freetown, 4 April 2007.

[96] Danny Hoffman, "Citizens and Soldiers: Community Defence in Sierra Leone before and after the Special Court", in Lansana Gberie (ed.), *Rescuing a Fragile State: Sierra Leone 2002–2008*, Wilfrid Laurier University Press, Ontario, 2009, pp. 119–27.

[97] Interview, former prosecution investigator for SCSL, 2010, see *supra* note 69.

after investigating elements of the Rwandan government's culpability.[98] Attempts to vigorously pursue incriminating information relating to Kabbah, other senior elements of the Sierra Leone People's Party or elements of the British government, may have caused a cessation of co-operation similar to that experienced at the ICTR. However, Crane insists there was no evidence available to the prosecution implicating either Kabbah or Berewa.[99] To what extent British, American or Sierra Leonean intelligence would or did make such information available is unclear.

The government's posturing towards potential deviation from politically expedient case selection was evident when Sierra Leone's attorney general responded to a defence request to subpoena Kabbah to appear as a witness. The attorney general told the Court it should not act "in vain" because the non-enforcement of the subpoena by the Sierra Leonean government would "diminish" the Court's authority.[100] The Court ate humble pie and refused to subpoena Kabbah.[101]

In his concurring but separate opinion, Justice Itoe exuded the kind of judicial subordination to politics that fed discontent among many combatants who took up arms against the state. Itoe stated that the president's position as one of "the princes who govern us" requires

> an environment, an atmosphere, and an institutional framework for them to perform their duties in all tranquillity and without any unnecessary interferences which could result from the issuance of a Subpoena.[102]

---

[98] Interview with former adviser to the prosecutor, Special Court for Sierra Leone, Washington, D.C., 23 July 2010.

[99] Interview, Crane, 2010, see *supra* note 61.

[100] SCSL, *Prosecutor v. Moinina Fofana, Allieu Kondewa and Sam Hinga Norman*, Trial Chamber, Transcript, SCSL-2004-14-T, 14 February 2006, p. 74.

[101] SCSL, *Prosecutor v. Moinina Fofana, Allieu Kondewa and Sam Hinga Norman*, Trial Chamber, Decision on motions by Moinina Fofana and Sam Hinga Norman for the issuance of a subpoena ad testificandum to H.E. Alhaji Dr. Ahmed Tejan Kabbah, President of the Republic of Sierra Leone, SCSL-04-14-T, 13 June 2006, Justice Thompson dissenting ('*Fofana* Decision') (http://www.legal-tools.org/doc/80d460/); SCSL, *Prosecutor v. Moinina Fofana, Allieu Kondewa and Sam Hinga Norman*, Appeals Chamber, Dissenting Opinion of Honorable Justice Robertson on decision on interlocutory appeals against Trial Chamber decision refusing to subpoena the President of Sierra Leone, SCSL-2004-14-T, 11 September 2006 (http://www.legal-tools.org/doc/2c9bb2/).

[102] *Fofana* Decision, p. 42, see *supra* note 101.

Prosecution case selection was also reinforced by the Court's functional characteristics that severely compromised the right to a fair trial. Because donors had a vested interest in successful prosecutions, the prosecutor's office was provided totally disproportionate funding. The prosecutor was able to appeal directly to donors for funding, but the defence was reliant upon the Registrar to make its case.

The most prominent compromise of the defendants' rights was the prosecution's jurisdiction over witness protection. The location of the Special Court's Witness and Victims Section, in the secure prosecution area, is inaccessible to other court organs including the defence. Further, the prosecution had its own witness protection programme supplementary to the Court programme.[103] Egregious prosecution practices such as leisure trips for insider witnesses to one of Sierra Leone's premier beach resorts severely undermined witness legitimacy.[104]

Prosecution witness engagement, finance and jurisdiction create a conflict of interest and potential witness inducement. The Trial Chamber refused to examine these practices – citing the need for an expedient trial.[105] Tim Kelsall best describes the impact of inauthentic and evasive witness narratives in his book *Culture under Cross-examination*. Kelsall describes the SCSL counsel's difficulties in extrapolating truth from witness testimony and the tendency of some members of the bench to extract selectively.[106]

4.9. Conclusion

The Special Court's design and function had serious consequences for case selection and for the Sierra Leonean transitional justice experience. The Security Council, referring to a potential special court, described how "a credible system of justice and accountability would end impunity and

---

[103] Christopher B. Mahony, *The Justice Sector Afterthought: Witness Protection in Africa*, Institute for Security Studies, Pretoria, 2010, pp. 84–86.

[104] *Ibid.*; SCSL, *Prosecutor v. Issa Hassan Sesay, Morris Kallon and Augustine Gbao*, Trial Chamber, Transcript, Trial Chamber I, SCSL-2004-15-T, 20 June 2007, pp. 48–52 ('*Gbao Transcript*').

[105] *Gbao* Transcript, pp. 52–59, 61.

[106] Tim Kelsall, Culture under Cross-examination: International Justice and the Special Court for Sierra Leone, Cambridge University Press, Cambridge, 2009.

---

contribute to the process of national reconciliation and to the restoration and maintenance of peace".[107]

A credible system of justice might have contributed to addressing impunity in Sierra Leone, and the region. However, my findings indicate that the Special Court was more about prosecuting victor's justice and administering Liberian regime change than conducting an impartial investigation of all parties to the conflict. The absence of quantitative or qualitative criteria instructing case selection reinforced this. The primary concerns behind the Court's creation were to assist regime change in Liberia and regime consolidation in Sierra Leone. Mitigating the threat the CDFs posed to Kabbah, by prosecuting its military leadership, served the latter of these concerns. Case selection criteria that prioritise sexually orientated offending may have justified non-prosecution of CDF crimes because CDF offending in this area was particularly reduced.

If preference for thematic prioritisation of sex crimes were employed in the future, it would serve to deconstruct the emerging norm of prioritising murder first.[108] A constructivist perspective argues: "norms do not cause a state to act in a particular way, but rather provide reasons for a state to do so".[109] This tells us that *Realpolitik* would first instruct who was to be prosecuted and who was not. Thematic prioritisation criteria reinforcing expedient case selection would then be selected. In the case of the Special Court, thematic prioritisation of murder, particularly where cannibalism was employed, would promote CDF prosecution. Cannibalism was committed by the CDF at a similar rate to the RUF.[110] It formed a prominent part of CDF member initiation, an element brought to the attention of Kabbah without response.[111] Spiritual and moral undertakings not to commit rape also formed a prominent part of CDF initiation. The CDF believed pre-battle sexual relations or sexual contact would diminish their powers of immunity to withstand attacks or wounds. According to the Truth and Reconciliation Commission database, the CDFs committed only 6 per cent of sexually orientated violations during the conflict.[112]

---

[107] UNSC Resolution 1315, see *supra* note 57.

[108] Bergsmo, 2011, Chapter 1 above.

[109] Woods, 1996, p. 26, see *supra* note 6.

[110] TRC Report, vol. 3A, pp. 478, 496, *supra* note 14.

[111] *Ibid.*, p. 479.

[112] *Ibid.*, p. 176.

This statistic could have justified non-selection of the CDFs for prosecution under a policy of thematic prioritisation of sex crimes. In future prosecution of international crimes, it is important that genuine proponents of international criminal justice recognise and act to mitigate selective use of thematic prosecution. Consolidating adoption of contemporary norms is critical. Continuing to place decisive emphasis on gravity and prioritising murder, followed by sex crimes and torture, may go some way toward preventing politically expedient preferencing of thematic prosecution.

States have clearly developed and employed methods of shaping prosecution case selection in cases involving international crimes. These methods include designing tribunal jurisdiction, structure and dependence on external actors as well as methods of co-operation including, funding, seconding of personnel, provision of information, granting of access to witnesses and territory, arrest and provision of suspects, and co-operation on witness protection and investigation.

Academia and interest groups need to better assess the need not only to prioritise sex crimes but also to prioritise other themes of offending, as well as thematic prioritisation against other modes of prioritisation such as temporal prioritisation or prioritisation of intent. The merits of all potential avenues of prioritisation need to be weighed individually and against each other in order to warrant adjustment of the emerging norm (prioritising murder first). To focus attention on justification for prioritising one theme without weighing it against others and without forming broad consensus as to how emerging norms should be changed undermines the legitimacy of thematic prioritisation.

Structural and functional independence, as well as a certain level of familiarity, are required for punitive justice processes to hold legitimacy. A critical component of independence is clear criteria instructing case selection. The ICC has a role to play in providing more specific guidance as to what criteria should be employed in order for states to meet the complementarity threshold of 'capacity' and 'willingness'. The scope for interpretation of those two words leaves too much discretion in the prosecutor's hands. It also leaves too much discretion in the hands of states constructing extraordinary criminal justice processes to prosecute international crimes. States are arguably better positioned to shape domestic criminal justice processes for politically expedient outcomes than international criminal tribunals, where design is negotiated with other states. Co-operative methods employed by states to shape case selection may, where states wield inadequate clout, be overcome by a savvy prosecutor cognisant of the nuances of state/court interaction and diplomatic sensitivities. However, a savvy prosecutor may not simply overcome specific case prioritisation criteria, such as the Special Court's instructed focus on crimes undermining the peace process, or temporal or territorial limitations on jurisdiction, with a deft strategic diplomatic touch. Equitable and entrenched norms that bind states and other actors designing the jurisdiction and structure of courts prosecuting international crimes provide the only impediment to design-orientated manipulation.

I now turn to how a diffuse norm might affect retributive, deterrent and expressive goals of prosecution. Where shifting normative case selection to prioritise sex crimes over murder facilitates selective prosecution, retributive, deterrent and expressive goals of prosecution are undermined. Selective prosecution undermines retributive goals because retributive outcomes are provided to victims of politically expedient offending parties or individuals, but not victims of those wielding clout with designing and co-operating actors.[113]

Similarly, deterrent goals may be undermined because offending parties may not be deterred from engaging in sex crimes by selective prosecution. Instead, they may be deterred from losing a conflict, failing to ensure sufficient external patronage, or from negotiating sufficiently robust terms of amnesty or a manipulable transitional justice process.

Despite selective prosecution, expressivist goals may be retained where a culture is convinced of the stigma of engaging in sex crimes and the merit of prosecuting that form of criminality, despite the selectivity of prosecution. Selective prosecution may, however, lend manipulating actors a low-cost expression of support for a co-operative international endeavour.[114] The Special Court's prosecution of "forced marriage", a criminal creation itself viewed by Tim Kelsall as culturally contentious,[115] I

---

[113] Selective retribution is not an unfamiliar phenomenon for Sierra Leoneans. They have witnessed before the trials and commissions of enquiry established by incoming regimes with expressive intent to justify themselves and discredit their predecessors. Upon examining Sierra Leone's history of regime change, be it the regimes of Juxton-Smith, Siaka Stevens or Valentine Strasser, one observes these processes.

[114] Oona Hathaway, "Do Human Rights Treaties Make a Difference?", in *Yale Law Journal*, 2002, vol. 111, p. 111.

[115] Kelsall, 2009, pp. 243–55, see *supra* note 106. Kelsall also argues that expressivist goals of engineering social change should not be pursued through international law with its notions of

---

argue, presented a low-cost affirmation of an international endeavour, unlikely to cause Sierra Leone's government to affect cessation of the practice.

A citizenry and international community sceptical of an institution pursuing selective prosecution may nonetheless acknowledge the criminality of sexually related offending and the legitimacy of its prosecution. However, it remains untenable that positive expressivist outcomes are achieved at the expense of retribution and deterrence. Where courts prosecuting international crimes are created and design by external actors with disparate cultural backgrounds, the expressivist impact of the institution may be impeded by perceptions of cultural hegemony and an absence of legitimacy.

States wield ever more discreet and sophisticated techniques to affect case selection that serves their interests. The neoliberal rhetoric so often accompanying prosecution of international crimes, and in some cases underpinning scholarly consideration of case selection criteria, requires a more constructivist lens. Diversifying rather than homogenising case selection criteria provides one more manipulative tool to those seeking to shape case selection for duplicitous purposes. As international criminal justice shifts towards pressurising states to carry out prosecutions domestically, preferencing thematic prosecution of sex crimes against the grain of consolidating emerging norms lends greater manipulative discretion to duplicitous actors.

---

individual autonomy, self determination and sexual freedom (p. 255). This argument might be reinforced by the absence of consultation with Sierra Leoneans, other than elites, during the Court's design.

5

Prospects for Thematic Prosecution
of International Sex Crimes in Latin America

Flor de Maria Valdez-Arroyo[*]

In the particular case of Latin America, where no international criminal tribunal exists, human rights violations that may constitute international crimes like genocide, crimes against humanity and war crimes[1] have to be prosecuted in national tribunals. Sexual violence, one of the most common aggressions in armed conflicts and dictatorships that took place in the region in the past half century, was documented as a systematic and widespread practice by truth commissions and civil society organisations only in the past two decades. Despite these efforts to give visibility to this scourge, at that time no trials were started in domestic jurisdictions for a number of reasons. Among them is the existence of amnesty laws applicable to the perpetrators of crimes committed during dictatorships or armed conflict, criminal codes that did not address international crimes,[2] the reluctance of the victims to give their account of the violence they endured due to fear or shame or mistrust to the judicial system, and the lack of awareness in general that sexual violence is a violation of human rights that could constitute a war crime or a crime against humanity.[3] Therefore, thematic prosecution of sex crimes has not been raised as an issue nor expressly established by national courts.

---

[*] **Flor de Maria Valdez-Arroyo** is a consultant of the Inter-American Commission of Women at the Organization of American States.

[1] For the purposes of this chapter, 'international crimes' will be used interchangeably with 'genocide, crimes against humanity and war crimes'.

[2] For the purposes of this chapter, 'thematic prosecution of sex crimes' will mean the prosecutorial prioritisation, at least initially, of international sex crimes over other crimes, including arguably more serious crimes as killings. The definition was provided in the Concept Note of the Seminar "Thematic Investigation and Prosecution of International Sex Crimes" organised by the Forum for International Criminal and Humanitarian Law, Yale University and the University of Cape Town, and held in Cape Town, South Africa, 7–8 March 2011.

[3] For more information on the legal framework of international crimes in the region, see Kai Ambos, "Latin American and International Criminal Law: Introduction and General Overview", in *International Criminal Law Review*, vol. 10, no. 4, 2010, pp. 39–43.

However, in recent years the region has witnessed indictments and judgments stating that rape and other forms of sexual violence were perpetrated as crimes against humanity. This is due to two main reasons. First, the ratification of the Statute that created the International Criminal Court ('ICC'), which led to the enactment of implementing legislation that typified international crimes in the national criminal codes. Second, the influence of the inter-American system of protection of human rights in national courts. The reports and decisions of the Inter-American Commission on Human Rights ('IACHR') as well as the jurisprudence of the Inter-American Court of Human Rights ('the Court') reaffirmed the obligation of states to investigate and punish gross violations of human rights in general, and sexual violence in particular. The said jurisprudence was produced while analysing the violations of the American Convention on Human Rights ('ACHR') and most importantly, the Inter-American Convention on the Prevention, Punishment and Eradication of Violence against Women or Convention of Belém do Pará. The Convention of Belém do Pará, the first international treaty in the world focused on violence against women and the most ratified inter-American human rights treaty in the Americas,[4] enshrines in Article 7 the state's duty of due diligence in the investigation, prosecution and punishment of said violence, as well as the provision of reparations for the victims.

In light of these developments, would thematic prosecution be eventually used by national courts? The prioritisation of cases is a practice that originated in most international tribunals due to budget constraints that would make it impossible to prosecute all crimes that come to their knowledge. Political reasons for the prioritisation of certain cases are not excluded since these tribunals were created by states who tailored their objectives and rules in the tribunal's statute. National courts, on the contrary, have a different origin and approach compared with international tribunals. In theory, national courts in the region prosecute all cases supported with enough evidence in order to fulfil the state's international obligations, as contained in the ACHR and the Convention of Belém do Pará, to ensure men and women's right of access to justice. Furthermore,

---

[4] Organization of American States, Inter-American Convention on the Prevention, Punishment and Eradication of Violence against Women ('Convention of Belém do Pará'), 9 June 1994 (http://www.legal-tools.org/doc/7784cf/) has been ratified by 32 states from Latin America and the Caribbean at the time of writing.

national courts are regarded as less susceptible to political influence,[5] since in Latin America the judiciary is, at least on paper, an independent power and no influence can divert them from their duty to provide justice for all.

Since the inter-American system is focused on the enforcement of inter-American human rights law in national courts, and the Court addresses the responsibility of the state's human rights obligations rather than the responsibility of individual perpetrators, thematic prosecution of sex crimes is not addressed *per se*. Nevertheless, the Court's assessment of the expressivist value of the law, which is one of the foundations of thematic prosecution, would support the said practice especially in crimes as invisible, underprosecuted, and unpunished in the region as sex crimes. In that regard, the Court showcases its expressivist spirit by condemning the historically unequal power relations between men and women, and the consequent deep-rooted patterns of discrimination against women and girls in the region which was also stated in the Convention of Belém do Pará, and ensuring visibility of sexual violence as a weapon of war. This would confirm Robert Sloane's statement that the expressive capacity of punishment best accommodates the confluence of international criminal law and international human rights law.[6]

Another justification of thematic prosecution, namely the gravity of sex crimes in contexts of gross violations of human rights, is assessed by the Court especially when these crimes are perpetrated by state agents or non-state actors with the instigation, tolerance, or acquiescence of the state, as part of the state's policy. This analysis is usually done by contextualising sex crimes, which would require the identification of most actors and patterns of violence involved, as well as the acknowledgement of all the facts possible. Prosecuting sex crimes does not only ensure access to justice for the victims, it would ensure that their experiences are given visibility within a context as well as a place in their society's history.

Bearing this context in mind, this chapter explores possible grounds for the use of thematic prosecution in Latin America based on two indicators: the jurisprudence of the Court regarding sex crimes and its impact in

---

[5] For more information, see Robert D. Sloane, "The Expressive Capacity on International Punishment: The Limits of the National Law Analogy and the Potential of International Criminal Law", in *Stanford Journal of International Law*, 2007, vol. 43, pp. 40 and 55.

[6] *Ibid.*, p. 44.

national prosecutions. In section 5.1. we examine the mandates of the Convention of Belém do Pará and explore some judgments of the Inter-American Court of Human Rights, especially five that address violations to the Convention: *Castro Castro Prison v. Peru* (2006),[7] *González et al. ('Cotton Field') v. Mexico* (2009),[8] *'Dos Erres' Massacre v. Guatemala* (2009),[9] *Rosendo Cantú et al. v. Mexico* (2010)[10] and *Fernández Ortega et al. v. Mexico* (2010).[11] Other judgments assessing the prohibition of amnesties, statutes of limitation, and other mechanisms that ensure impunity for gross violation of human rights; and the right to truth as both an individual and collective right are also reviewed. In section 5.2., we examine three cases from Argentina and Peru, whose domestic tribunals have already indicted or judged sexual violence as a war crime, crimes against humanity or crime amounting to genocide; we will note the influence of the Court's jurisprudence in achieving that goal.

5.1. The Framework: The Convention of Belém do Pará and the Court's Jurisprudence Related to the Violation of its Dispositions

5.1.1. The Mandates of the Convention of Belém do Pará

Among the contributions of the Convention of Belém do Pará is its ample definition of violence against women, understanding it as "any act or conduct, based on gender, which causes death or physical, sexual or psychological harm or suffering to women, whether in the public or private

---

[7]   Inter-American Court of Human Rights, *Case of the Miguel Castro Castro Prison v. Peru*, Judgment (Merits, Reparations and Costs), 25 November 2006, Series C, no. 160 (http://www.legal-tools.org/doc/7d2681/).

[8]   Inter-American Court of Human Rights, *Case of González et al. ('Cotton Field') v. Mexico*, Judgment (Preliminary Objection, Merits, Reparations and Costs), 16 November 2009, Series C, no. 205 (http://www.legal-tools.org/doc/f142b2/).

[9]   Inter-American Court of Human Rights, *Case of the 'Las Dos Erres' Massacre v. Guatemala* Judgment (Preliminary Objection, Merits, Reparations and Costs), 24 November 2009, Series C, no. 211 (http://www.legal-tools.org/doc/81b0e7/).

[10] Inter-American Court of Human Rights, *Case of Rosendo Cantú et al. v. Mexico*, Judgment (Preliminary Objection, Merits, Reparations, and Costs), 31 August 2010, Series C, no. 216 (http://www.legal-tools.org/doc/8f4223/).

[11] Inter-American Court of Human Rights, *Case of Fernández Ortega et al. v. Mexico*, Judgment (Preliminary Objections, Merits, Reparations, and Costs), 30 August 2010, Series C, no. 215 (http://www.legal-tools.org/doc/0732b7/).

sphere". Article 2 expands the scope of perpetrators by stating that the said violence can occur within the family or domestic unit, or within any other interpersonal relationship in the community, and that it can be perpetrated or condoned by the state or its agents. It is particularly important that, in Article 9, the Convention asks the states parties to take special account of the situation of vulnerability of women when they are affected by armed conflict or deprived of their freedom, among other circumstances.

Another milestone of the Convention is the recognition, in Article 3, of the right of women and girls to a life free from violence in public and private spheres. The said right shall be understood, according to Article 6, as the right of women to be free from all forms of discrimination, and the right to be valued and educated free of stereotyped patterns of behaviour, social, and cultural practices based on concepts of inferiority or subordination. In order to ensure the full exercise and enjoyment of this right, Article 7 of the Convention lists a number of obligations of the state to prevent, investigate, punish, and eradicate violence against women,[12]

---

[12] Convention of Belém do Pará, Article 7, see *supra* note 4: The States Parties condemn all forms of violence against women and agree to pursue, by all appropriate means and without delay, policies to prevent, punish and eradicate such violence and undertake to:

a. refrain from engaging in any act or practice of violence against women and to ensure that their authorities, officials, personnel, agents, and institutions act in conformity with this obligation;

b. apply due diligence to prevent, investigate and impose penalties for violence against women;

c. include in their domestic legislation penal, civil, administrative and any other type of provisions that may be needed to prevent, punish and eradicate violence against women and to adopt appropriate administrative measures where necessary;

d. adopt legal measures to require the perpetrator to refrain from harassing, intimidating or threatening the woman or using any method that harms or endangers her life or integrity, or damages her property;

e. take all appropriate measures, including legislative measures, to amend or repeal existing laws and regulations or to modify legal or customary practices which sustain the persistence and tolerance of violence against women;

f. establish fair and effective legal procedures for women who have been subjected to violence which include, among others, protective measures, a timely hearing and effective access to such procedures;

g. establish the necessary legal and administrative mechanisms to ensure that women subjected to violence have effective access to restitution, reparations or other just and effective remedies; and

h. adopt such legislative or other measures as may be necessary to give effect to this Convention.

among which stands the obligation to apply due diligence to prevent, investigate, and impose penalties for violence against women.

Furthermore, the Convention allows the lodging of petitions with the IACHR regarding violations to Article 7, which among them is the obligation of due diligence. Therefore when states, via their domestic tribunals, do not fulfil this obligation and perpetrators of sex crimes are not indicted or are acquitted, victims can file a petition to the IACHR. This organ will analyse the matter and further issue a report with recommendations to the denounced state. If these recommendations are not complied with, the Commission will submit the case to the Court.

In the five cases where sexual violence was involved,[13] the Commission usually requests the Court to pronounce on the violation of the obligation of the state to ensure to all persons, subject to their jurisdiction, the free and full exercise of those rights and freedoms as established in Article 1(1) of the ACHR. Moreover, it was also demanded that the duty of due diligence established in Article 7 of the Convention of Belém do Pará. The judgments of the Court in the said cases have been critical not only in developing the contents of the duty of due diligence in the prevention, investigation, and punishment of violence against women, but also in analysing the existence of sex crimes in both contexts of armed conflict and times of peace.

Perhaps the main contribution of the Convention is that its mere existence showcases that violence against women is indeed a serious violation of human rights and that states have the political will to recognise it as such and act accordingly. During the debate of the draft text of the Convention launched by the Inter-American Commission of Women ('CIM') of the Organization of American States, Jorge Seall-Sasiain favoured the adoption of a Convention on the subject because:

> An international convention of the requisite specificity could make violence against women the gravest and most extreme form of discrimination against them, and a violation of human rights with specific features. Indeed, the complex difficulties of the phenomenon: its occurrence within the privacy of the home, its misperception as a private conjugal matter, the reluctance of authorities and individuals to intervene, the lack or fewness of shelters for women, their fear of retalia-

---

[13] See p. 90.

tion, loss of property rights or loss of custody of the children, and the whole backdrop of a patriarchal society, must be taken into account in defining the problem.[14]

The Court summarised this view in *González et al. ('Cotton Field') v. Mexico* when remarking that the Convention:

> reflects a uniform concern throughout the hemisphere about the severity of the problem of violence against women, its relationship to the discrimination traditionally suffered by women, and the need to adopt comprehensive strategies to prevent, punish and eliminate it.[15]

5.1.2. The Court's Jurisprudence

As stated in *González et al. ('Cotton Field') v. Mexico*, the purpose of the existence of a system of individual petitions within the Convention of Belém do Pará is to achieve the greatest right to judicial protection possible in those states that have accepted judicial control by the Court.[16] In order to enhance this protection, through its jurisprudence the Court has been developing arguments and standards that give content to the obligations established by the Convention related to the prevention, investigation and punishment of violence against women.

In this sub-section, some of these arguments are examined: the gravity of sexual violence, the prohibition of amnesties and statutes of limitation and its relation to the 'interests of justice', and the right to truth in its individual and collective dimensions.

---

[14] Jorge Seall-Sasiain, "Preparation and Viability of a Convention on Violence against Women", in Inter-American Commission of Women, *Proceedings: Inter-American Consultation on Women and Violence*, Organization of American States, Inter-American Commission of Women, Washington, D.C., 1990, p. 141.

[15] *González et al. ('Cotton Field') v. Mexico*, para. 61, see *supra* note 8.

[16] *Ibid.*

5.1.2.1. Gravity of Sexual Violence in the Jurisprudence of the Court

5.1.2.1.1. Participation of State Agents in the Perpetration of the Crime or Existence of a State's Policy

In the jurisprudence of the Court, the participation of states agents have always been regarded as an indicator of gravity, since violence is exercised by the same officers in charge of protecting the population and ensuring the free and full exercise of all rights and freedoms by all persons subject to their jurisdiction. In the gender-pioneering sentence *Castro Castro Prison v. Peru* (2006), where violations to Article 7 of the Convention of Belém do Pará were addressed by the Court for the first time, the Court acknowledges that the rape of a detainee by a state agent is an especially gross and reprehensible act, taking into account the victim's vulnerability and the abuse of power displayed by the agent.[17] In addition, in the judgments of *Rosendo Cantú et al. v. Mexico* and *Fernández Ortega et al. v. Mexico* which related to the rape of indigenous women by state agents, the Commission sustained to the Court the demand against Mexico by concluding that rape perpetrated by the members of any state's security forces against civil population constitutes a grave violation of human rights, especially the right to personal integrity (Article 5 ACHR) and the right to have the honour and dignity protected (Article 11 ACHR).[18]

Sexual violence is considered grave when committed as part of a state policy. In both *'Dos Erres' Massacre v. Guatemala* and *Plan de Sánchez Massacre v. Guatemala* (2004),[19] where sexual violence was committed against women and girls was held before their killing along with other members of the communities of Dos Erres and Plan de Sanchez, the Court determined that the "rape of women was a state practice, executed in the context of massacres, directed to destroying the dig-

---

[17] *Castro Castro Prison v. Peru*, para 311, see *supra* note 7.

[18] *Rosendo Cantú et al. v. Mexico*, para. 80, see *supra* note 10; *Fernández Ortega et al. v. Mexico*, para. 90, see *supra* note 11.

[19] Inter-American Court of Human Rights, *Case of the Plan de Sánchez Massacre v. Guatemala*, Judgment (Reparations and Costs), 19 November 2004, Series C, no. 116 (http://www.legal-tools.org/doc/e8533d/).

nity of women at a cultural, social, family, and individual level"[20] and that the "lack of investigation of grave facts against human treatment such as torture and sexual violence in armed conflicts and/or systematic patterns, constitutes a breach of the state's obligations in relation to grave human rights violations".[21]

5.1.2.1.2. Context of Discrimination and Patterns of Gender-Related Violence

The biggest breakthrough of the system was when sexual violence was considered as a grave violation of human rights when fuelled by a context of discrimination or patterns of gender-related violence. The judgment *González et al. ('Cotton Field') v. Mexico* recalls the several reports and the government of Mexico's acknowledgement of responsibility in which the high rates of violent deaths of women in Ciudad Juarez were due to a "culture of discrimination" and a pattern of gender-related violence that influenced these murders.[22]

In fact, the Court's jurisprudence in general notes the importance of analysing patterns of violence when investigating and punishing a specific type of violation of human rights.[23] This analysis is applicable regardless of the context of armed conflict or internal strife. In the particular case of *González et al. ('Cotton Field') v. Mexico*, the Court stated that Mexico failed to consider the brutal murder of women in Ciudad Juarez as part of a generalised phenomenon of gender-based violence. In the case *Castro Castro Prison v. Peru*, the Court verified that the sexual crimes committed against the female inmates of the Castro Castro prison responded to a pattern of violence against women in armed conflict already documented by the Peruvian Truth and Reconciliation Commission. That pattern implied the use of sexual violence as means to punish, intimidate, pressure, humiliate and degrade the population.[24]

---

[20] *'Dos Erres' Massacre v. Guatemala*, para. 139, see *supra* note 9; *Plan de Sánchez Massacre v. Guatemala*, paras. 19, 49, see *supra* note 19.

[21] *'Dos Erres' Massacre v. Guatemala*, para. 140, see *supra* note 9.

[22] *González et al. ('Cotton Field') v. Mexico*, para. 399, see *supra* note 8.

[23] *Ibid.*, para. 366.

[24] *Castro Castro Prison v. Peru*, para. 226, see *supra* note 7.

In this context, the assessment of discrimination and inequalities, their causes and consequences, remain essential. The Convention of Belém do Pará had already established in its Preamble that violence against women constituted a manifestation of the historically unequal power relations between women and men and that it strikes society at its very foundations. In fact, one of the arguments used to promote the adoption of a regional convention on violence against women was that despite the existence of national legislation and international treaties on human rights, the phenomenon of violence against women did not diminished but increased, and that an explicit legal prohibition was needed to create awareness of the problem.[25]

5.1.2.1.3. Impunity

Another indicator of gravity of cases of violence against women considered by the Court was the impunity surrounding these cases. Most of the gross violations of human rights that included sexual violence were not properly investigated and did not have a sentence, or had concluded with an exoneration of the accused due to lack of proof or the statutes of limitation. As the Court established in *González et al. ('Cotton Field') v. Mexico*, the impunity of the crimes committed sends the message that:

> violence against women is tolerated; this leads to their perpetuation, together with social acceptance of the phenomenon, the feeling women have that they are not safe, and their persistent mistrust in the system of administration of justice.[26]

In the assessment of gravity due to impunity, time is a critical factor. In earlier jurisprudence the Court considered the right of access to justice, whose objective was to ensure, within a reasonable time, the right of the alleged victims or their next of kin to have everything necessary done to uncover the truth of the events and to punish those responsible.[27]

---

[25] Seall-Sasiain, 1990, p. 141, see *supra* note 14.

[26] *González et al. ('Cotton Field') v. Mexico*, para. 400, see *supra* note 8.

[27] Inter-American Court of Human Rights, *Case of Bulacio v. Argentina*, Judgment (Merits, Reparations, and Costs), 18 September 2003, Series C, no. 100, para. 114 (http://www.legal-tools.org/doc/19d7a7/); Inter-American Court of Human Rights, *Case of Zambrano Vélez et al. v. Ecuador*, Judgment (Merits, Reparations, and Costs), 4 July 2007, Series C, no. 166, para. 115; and Inter-American Court of Human Rights, *Case of Kawas Fernández v. Honduras*, Judgment (Merits, Reparations and Costs), 3 April 2009, Series C, no. 196, para. 112.

In *González et al. ('Cotton Field') v. Mexico*, the Court linked the increase of violence against women in Ciudad Juarez with the lack of investigation to establish the truth by stating that, up until 2005, most of the crimes had not been resolved, and murders with characteristics of sexual violence involved higher levels of impunity.[28]

5.1.2.1.4. Objective and/or Impact of Sexual Violence in the Victims' Lives

Another element considered when gravity is assessed is the objective or impact of sexual violence against women. In *Castro Castro Prison v. Peru*, the Court described the gravity of rape as:

> [an] extremely traumatic experience that may have serious consequences and it causes great physical and psychological damage that leaves the victim "physically and emotionally humiliated".

Furthermore, following the reasoning of the European Court of Human Rights ('ECtHR')'s *Aydin v. Turkey* (1997), it settles that the inflicted damage is a "situation difficult to overcome with time, contrary to what happens with other traumatic experiences".[29]

One of the contributions of the Court is that it analysed the impact by taking into account the personal, familiar, and communitarian spheres of the victims. In both *Rosendo-Cantú et al. v. Mexico* and *Fernández Ortega et al. v. Mexico* the Court determined that rape was a paradigmatic form of violence against women that had consequences that go beyond the victim.[30] In *González et al. ('Cotton Field') v. Mexico*, the message sent with the sexually-connoted torture or mutilation of women before their murder is that of hate because of their gender, which led several researchers and activists to call this phenomenon femicide (*feminicidio*).[31] In '*Dos*

---

[28] *González et al. ('Cotton Field') v. Mexico*, para. 164, see *supra* note 8.

[29] *Castro Castro Prison v. Peru*, para. 311, see *supra* note 7.

[30] *Fernández Ortega et al. v. Mexico*, para. 119, see *supra* note 11; *Rosendo Cantú et al. v. Mexico*, para. 109, see *supra* note 10.

[31] For more information on femicide, see Ana Carcedo, *No Olvidamos ni Aceptamos: Femicidio en Centroamérica 2000–2006* [We Neither Forget nor Accept: Femicides in Central America 2000–2006], CEFEMINA, San José, 2010; Patsili Toledo Vásques, *Feminicidio* [Femicide], UN High Commissioner for Human Rights, Mexico DF, 2009; Latin American and Caribbean Committee for the Defense of Women's Rights (CLADEM), *Monitoreo sobre el Feminicidio/Femicidio en Bolivia, Ecuador, Paraguay, Peru y Republica Dominicana* [Monitoring

---

Erres' Massacre v. Guatemala, the sexual violence perpetrated within the massacre had the objective to terrorise the community prior to their collective murder; while in *Plan de Sánchez Massacre v. Guatemala*, the impact of the violence on women was assessed from an intercultural perspective, debating the impact of violence on the role of women as transmitters of culture, spirituality and memory of the Maya-Achí community.[32]

The above analysis is essential to support the notion of violence against women as a grave violation of human rights. Common factors analysed in the cases include: the participation of the state through the action of state actors or through its failure to prevent and prosecute the activities of non-states actors; the existence of a structured policy or a pattern based on omissions; the social context of discrimination and an acceptance of violence against women due to prejudice and stereotypes that regard women as inferior to men; the impunity surrounding the cases and the deep impact of sexual violence in the victim, their families and communities have been the common factors in the cases analysed.

5.1.2.2. The "Interests of Justice" and Prohibition of Amnesties in the Jurisprudence of the Court

The Statute that created the International Criminal Court (1998) establishes in Article 53 that the prosecutor may in some circumstances decline to prosecute on grounds that it would not serve the interests of justice. Since no consensus as to its meaning was reached at the Rome Conference, this Article has been understood to function as an open door for amnesties or other non-prosecutorial alternatives.[33] It has also been regarded to mean: "so that justice may be administered in an orderly way", or "the good administration of justice", or "advancing the trial process".[34]

Femicide in Bolivia, Ecuador, Paraguay, Peru and Dominican Republic], CLADEM, Lima, 2008; and also from CLADEM, *Monitoreo sobre el Feminicidio/Femicidio en El Salvador, Guatemala, Honduras, Mexico, Nicaragua y Panama* [Monitoring Femicide in El Salvador, Guatemala, Honduras, Mexico, Nicaragua and Panama], CLADEM, Lima, 2007.

[32] Expert report of Augusto Willemsen–Diaz before the Court, in *Plan de Sánchez Massacre v. Guatemala*, p. 20, and also paras. 49(12) and 85, see *supra* note 19.

[33] Human Rights Watch, "The Meaning of 'the Interests of Justice' in Article 53 of the Rome Statute", 1 June 2005, p. 4.

[34] *Ibid.*, p. 6.

As for Latin America and the Caribbean, only Article 8(5) of the AHCR regarding the right to a fair trial deals with the subject. It mentions that criminal proceedings shall be public, except insofar as may be necessary to protect the interests of justice. The Court has yet to develop the notion, while the Commission has used it in some cases, determining that the "higher interests of justice" implied the right to the truth.[35] The "interests of justice" are also taken into account by the Court when ensuring that the acts of acquiescence by the state are acceptable for the purposes of the inter-American system of protection of human rights.[36] So far no mention of "interests of justice" has been undertaken when analysing cases of sexual violence that reached the inter-American system; however, the aforementioned elements would suggest that the Court would understand that "interests of justice" implies the protection of the interests of the victim. That is the reason why the right to truth is protected and the acquiescence of the state does not jeopardise the rights of the petitioner, especially to access and obtain justice and reparations.

As to the possibility of considering the notion of "interests of justice" as an open door for amnesties, the application of statutes of limitation or any other form of exoneration of responsibility for the perpetration of human rights abuses, the Court has already settled that these measures are prohibited by the inter-American system. In *Chumbipuma Aguirre et al. ('Barrios Altos') v. Peru* (2001) the Court referred to the so-called self-amnesties are manifestly incompatible with the objectives of the Conven-

---

[35] Inter-American Court of Human Rights, *Case of Myrna Mack Chang v. Guatemala*, Judgment (Merits, Reparations and Costs), Reasoned Opinion of Judge Antonio Cançado-Trindade, 25 November 2003, Series C, no. 101, para. 17 (http://www.legal-tools.org/doc/48eac7/).

[36] In *Kawas Fernández v. Honduras*, see *supra* note 27, the Court indicates that:

> [it] does not limit itself to merely verifying the formal conditions of the said acts, but relates them to the nature and gravity of the alleged violations, the requirements and interests of justice, the particular circumstances of each case, and the attitude and position of the parties.

It was also stated, among others, in the case of *Myrna Mack-Chang v. Guatemala*, paras. 106–108, see *supra* note 35; and Inter-American Court of Human Rights, *Kimel v. Argentina*, Judgment (Merits, Reparations and Costs), 2 May 2008, Series C, no. 177, para. 24.

tion[37] and "an inadmissible offence against the right to truth and the right to justice".[38] The Court added:

> This Court considers that all amnesty provisions, provisions on prescription and the establishment of measures designed to eliminate responsibility are inadmissible, because they are intended to prevent the investigation and punishment of those responsible for serious human rights violations such as torture, extrajudicial, summary or arbitrary execution and forced disappearance, all of them prohibited because they violate non-derogable rights recognized by international human rights law.[39]

The judgment in *Almonacid-Arellano v. Chile* (2006) goes further on the prohibition of amnesties and focuses on the issue of the statutes of limitation, remarking that the time passed cannot pose as an obstacle for the victims seeking to obtain justice, due to the gravity of the crime and the longstanding duration of the harm produced. They further added:

> [that] the damage caused by these crimes still prevails in the national society and the international community, both of which demand that those responsible be investigated and punished.[40]

Both *Chumbipuma Aguirre et al. ('Barrios Altos') v. Peru* (2001) and *Almonacid-Arellano v. Chile* (2006) have been crucial to starting the debate and the eventual overturning of amnesty laws that prevented the prosecution of international crimes, as well as the rejection of statutes of limitation for crimes that constituted gross violations of human rights in the region. National courts judging sexual violence as a crime against humanity are now relying on these rulings to reject exceptions related to the application of statutes of limitations.[41]

Furthermore, while the Court's rulings did not address the issue of sexual violence, it established a standard for these cases when they fall

---

[37] Inter-American Court of Human Rights, *Case of Barrios Altos v. Peru*, Judgment (Merits), 14 March 2001, Series C, no. 75, para. 43 (http://www.legal-tools.org/doc/f1439e/).

[38] *Ibid.*, para. 5.

[39] *Ibid.*, para. 41.

[40] Inter-American Court of Human Rights, *Case of Almonacid-Arellano et al. v. Chile*, Judgment (Preliminary Objections, Merits, Reparations and Costs), 26 September 2006, Series C, no.154, para. 152 (http://www.legal-tools.org/doc/3543c4/).

[41] See *infra* section 5.2.

within the indicators of gravity referred to in the previous section. As a result, they will be included as the "serious human rights violations" as stated in *Chumbipuma Aguirre et al. ('Barrios Altos') v. Peru* (2001) and therefore amnesties, statutes of limitation and other provisions of exoneration of responsibility will not be applicable. In *Castro Castro Prison v. Peru, Rosendo-Cantú v. Mexico* and *Fernández Ortega et al. v. Mexico*, the Court agreed that the sexual violence endured by the victims met the three elements required for it to be considered torture: 1) it is intentionally inflicted; 2) it causes severe physical or mental suffering; and 3) it is perpetrated with a certain aim or objective.[42] For that reason, rape can amount to torture even when it occurred only once and outside an establishment controlled by the state[43] In fact, the Court recognised that rape, as well as torture, aims at intimidating, degrading, humiliating, punishing and controlling the victim.[44]

On the subject of sexual violence and torture, however, it is interesting to note the position of the Court in *'Dos Erres' Massacre v. Guatemala*. In that judgment, the Court undertakes analysis of torture and sexual violence as if they were two separate issues. At one point the Court assesses the lack of investigation of the massacre at the domestic level, criticising that it focused on murder and not "on alleged torture against members of the community *and other* alleged acts of violence against the children and female population".[45] Then, while quoting the report of the Comisión de Esclarecimiento Histórico ('CEH'), establishes that:

> [t]he State had official knowledge of alleged acts of torture against the population and children of the community, *as well as* abortions and other types of sexual violence against girls and women (emphasis added).

The separation, however, seems to blur when the Court determined that the government of Guatemala should effectively "investigate all facts of the massacre [...] particularly the alleged acts of torture, in light of the

---

[42] Standard followed by the Court since *Case of Bueno-Alves v. Argentina*, Judgment (Merits, Reparations and Costs), 11 May 2007, Series C, no. 164 (http://www.legal-tools.org/doc/0888d1/).

[43] *Rosendo Cantú et al. v. Mexico*, para. 118, see *supra* note 10.

[44] *Ibid.*, para. 117.

[45] *'Dos Erres' Massacre v. Guatemala*, para. 136, see *supra* note 9 (emphasis added).

differentiated impact of the alleged violence against girls and women".[46] This resolution would not only acknowledge that the sexual violence found in the case was indeed torture, but also demand a gender-sensitive analysis, which is the only way to assess the different impact of violence in both women and men.

5.1.2.3. The Right to Truth in the Jurisprudence of the Court

While the right to truth is still in emergence, the inter-American system of protection of human rights has promoted and ensured it since the establishment of the Court. As an individual right, the Court has recognised, since *Velásquez Rodríguez v. Honduras* (1988), the state's general duty of due diligence to investigate the violations of the rights enshrined in the AHCR, and the "search for the truth by the government". This search had to be effective and must be assumed by the state as its own legal duty.[47] The prohibition of amnesties, statutes of limitation and other means of exonerating of criminal responsibility also intends to guarantee the exercise of this right and to avoid putting it into jeopardy, as seen in section 5.1.2.2.

The search for the historical truth has become the pillar of the right to a domestic remedy and access to justice, and the fact that the state's duty of due diligence in the prevention, investigation, and punishment of violence against women is consecrated in the Convention of Belém do Pará makes it an obligation of states to fulfil in the benefit of women.

The Court has been vocal and consistent throughout the years on the development of the individual right to truth. However, it has just started to address the collective right to truth. In its jurisprudence the Court has established that not only the victim is entitled to the right to truth, but also the next-of-kin[48] and society.[49] It is noteworthy that in *González et al.*

---

[46] *Ibid.*, para. 233.

[47] Inter-American Court of Human Rights, *Case of Velásquez-Rodríguez v. Honduras*, Judgment (Merits), 29 July 1988, Series C, no. 4, para. 177 (http://www.legal-tools.org/doc/18607f/).

[48] *Plan de Sánchez Massacre v. Guatemala*, para. 97, see *supra* note 19; *Castro Castro Prison v. Peru*, para. 382, see *supra* note 7.

[49] *González et al. ('Cotton Field') v. Mexico*, para. 388, see *supra* note 8; Inter-American Court of Human Rights, *Case of Gomes-Lund et al. (Guerrilha do Araguaia) v. Brazil*, Judgment

('Cotton Field') v. Mexico – a landmark case regarding gender crimes, the Court had elaborated on the requirement of the right to truth:

> the determination of the most complete historical truth possible, which includes determination of the collective patterns of action, and of all those who, in different ways, took part in said violations.[50]

This jurisprudence favouring the right to truth would also encourage the prosecution of sex crimes in the region. One of the contributions of the Court is to require the state, based on the duty of due diligence, to establish the historical truth and all the facts of the crimes, taking into account the different impact of the crimes in women (as stated in *'Dos Erres' Massacre v. Guatemala*[51] and in *Castro Castro Prison v. Peru*[52]); the patterns of violence especially when more than one factor of discrimination is present (which were crucial in *González et al. ('Cotton Field') v. Mexico,* when the victims were discriminated for their being women and poor, or in *'Dos Erres' Massacre v. Guatemala*, where the victims were women, indigenous and poor) and the role of women in her family and community (reparations in *Plan de Sánchez Massacre v. Guatemala* were determined to try to fix the damage caused by the rape and death of women as keepers and transmitters of the culture).

Regarding thematic prosecution, the emergence of the right to truth as a collective right would better support the thematic prosecution of sex crimes. The individual's right to truth belongs to all men and women, and is usually individually exercised and adjudicated. This loses the perspective on the context that framed the crimes. Sexual violence as war crimes, crimes against humanity or crimes amounting to genocide usually have a collectivity of perpetrators, perhaps with different backgrounds but with the same motivation: target and harm a collectivity of victims who perhaps shared no more bonds than being targeted by these perpetrators. The establishing of collective truth, therefore, would require a more complete assessment of the victims' suffering; their relationships among themselves; the previous relationships with the perpetrators, if any; and the re-

---

(Preliminary Objections, Merits, Reparations, and Costs), Judgment, 24 November 2010, Series C, no. 219, para. 200 (http://www.legal-tools.org/doc/a66e9e/).

[50] *González et al. ('Cotton Field') v. Mexico*, para. 454, see *supra* note 8.

[51] *'Dos Erres' Massacre v. Guatemala*, para. 233, see *supra* note 9.

[52] *Castro Castro Prison v. Peru*, para. 223, see *supra* note 7.

lationships with their state and other groups. The context is of critical importance, since it frames (in)equality and power relations, among others relevant. The characteristics, relationships and experiences of all actors are crucial to depict a story as complete and as inclusive as possible, in which society can identify the causes of violence, the patterns it took and its consequences.

The experiences of women were mostly absent either in these cases or as individual ones, in national courts and truth commissions in the region until 1998 when Guatemala's Memory of Silence report was released; and in the very Court's jurisprudence until 2006 with the case of *Castro Castro Prison v. Peru*. For that reason, prioritising cases of sexual violence would fill the void by including women's experiences in the general narrative and, by making them visible and public, this will send the message that the said crimes cannot be committed and society must address their causes in order to prevent these facts from happening again. In that way, the collective truth would therefore be more inclusive, with women and all actors involved. It would not be narrowed to a men-only experience or a women-only experience.

5.2. National Cases on International Sex Crimes

The jurisprudence of the Court addressing sexual violence as international crimes has impacted in domestic tribunals in Latin America in recent years, encouraging more domestic trials on international sex crimes. Before that, either the said cases remained unpunished or the victims of human rights abuses and their advocates opted for the universal jurisdiction in order to achieve justice denied by national courts. Due to the successful use of universal jurisdiction in the extradition request of Chile's former president Augusto Pinochet, victims preferred to file their complaints before Spain's Audiencia Nacional (National Court).[53]

In this section we have selected three cases from Argentina and Peru: two with judgments and one with an indictment and a court order starting prosecution. These cases are interesting comparisons because the three

---

[53] One of the most emblematic cases filed before the Audiencia Nacional is the Mayan genocide perpetrated by the Guatemalan army and the paramilitary Patrullas de Autodefensa Civil ('PAC') from 1979 to 1986. The case was filed by the Rigoberta Menchu Tum Foundation and other organisations in 1999 against Efrain Rios-Montt, *de facto* president of Guatemala (1982–1983) and seven other high-ranking Guatemalan officials, and is still ongoing.

of them have used different strategies. In Argentina, rape and other sexual violence crimes were prosecuted as collective cases, and alongside other serious crimes like murder and torture. In Peru, on the contrary, there is one indictment on sexual crimes only.

5.2.1. Argentina: Case of *Gregorio Rafael Molina*[54]

Gregorio Rafael Molina was an officer serving at the Military Air Force Base of Mar del Plata, also known as La Cueva (the Cave) Detention Centre, between 1974 and 1982. He was accused of and condemned by the Oral Tribunal of Mar del Plata in June 2010 to life imprisonment for several crimes against humanity, among them a number of counts of rape and counts of attempted rape of two women.

This case is an important jurisprudence for several reasons. It is the first one in which sexual violence was considered as a crime against humanity by itself and not subsumed under part of other crimes such as torture. In that regard it went further than the *Horacio Américo Barcos*[55] and *Miara et al.*[56] judgments in which rape and other forms of sexual violence were declared a form of torment or torture. While rape is considered a form of torture in the Court's jurisprudence, the *Molina* judgment contributes to increasing the visibility of rape and sexual violence in general as a specific crime systematically perpetrated against detainees, especially women.

Second, it expressly followed the jurisprudence of the Court as well as the ACHR and the Convention of Belém do Pará. This is relevant since most national jurisprudence dealing with international crimes usually quote jurisprudence from international criminal tribunals rather than the Court's jurisprudence or human rights treaties. Interestingly enough, the *Molina* judgment relies on the Court's reasoning in *Castro Castro Prison v. Peru* which was based on the rulings of the International Criminal Tribunal for Rwanda's *Akayesu* judgment, and the International Criminal for

---

[54] Federal Criminal Oral Tribunal of Mar del Plata, Argentina, File no. 2086 and accumulated no. 2277 against Gregorio Rafael Molina, Judgment, 11 June 2010 ('*Molina*').

[55] Federal Criminal Oral Tribunal of Santa Fe, Argentina, *Cause Horacio Américo Barcos*, Judgment 08/10, 19 April 2010.

[56] Federal Criminal Oral Tribunal No. 2 of the Autonomous City of Buenos Aires, Argentina; File no. 1668, *Miara et al.*; and File 1673, *Tepedino, Carlos Alberto Roque*, Judgment, 22 March 2011.

the former Yugoslavia's *Kunarać et al.* Hence the Court translates the developments in international criminal courts into guidelines and mandates for the national courts to follow.

As for thematic prosecution of international sex crimes, no evident criteria are identified. However, it appears that the existence of survivors willing to tell their stories in court was the main factor that influenced the going forward of their prosecution. In the *Molina* case, the testimonies of two victims and other witnesses were the main and only evidence produced by the prosecution to prove the counts on sexual violence and establish a pattern of violence against detained women. This is of utmost relevance considering that in the 2008 judgment of *Santiago Omar Riveros et al.*, due to the low number of testimonies related to rape, the Court dismissed, for lack of merit, the rape counts against Riveros, asserting that the said cases were isolated and therefore did not constitute a pattern or systematic practice and were therefore not a crime against humanity.[57]

In any case, rape and sexual violence carry less jail time than murder, even if prosecuted as a crime against humanity. Jail time was used as a criterion to assess the veracity of the victims' testimonies, since the Tribunal established that it is not likely that the victims have any interest in making up a story about being raped provided that the maximum prison time for those crimes is minimum compared to those for the other international crimes in the same case.[58]

5.2.2. Argentina: *Miara et al.*[59] (Cases Atlético, Banco and Olimpo)

In this case, Samuel Miara and other 16 co-defendants were condemned to life imprisonment for a number of crimes against humanity perpetrated in the Club Atlético, Banco and El Olimpo detention centres, and unlike the *Molina* judgment in which there were counts of rape as crime against hu-

---

[57] Federal Court in Criminal and Correctional Matters no. 2 of San Martín, Argentina; File 4012, *Santiago Omar Riveros et al.*, Judgment, 19 December 2008.

[58] Federal Criminal Oral Tribunal of Mar del Plata, Argentina, *Gregorio Rafael Molina* case, p. 110.

[59] In the cause 1668, the co-defendants were Samuel Miara, Raúl González, Juan Carlos Avena, Eduardo Emilio Kalinec, Juan Carlos Falcón, Eufemio Jorge Uballes, Luís Juan Donocik, Oscar Augusto Isidro Rolón, Julio Héctor Simón, Roberto Antonio Rosa, Guillermo Víctor Cardozo, Eugenio Pereyra Apestegui, Raúl Antonio Guglielminetti, Ricardo Taddei and Enrique José Del Pino. In cause 1673, the co-defendants were Carlos Alberto Roque Tepedino, Mario Alberto Gómez Arenas, Enrique José Del Pino and Juan Carlos Avena.

manity *per se,* in *Miara et al.* sexual violence was subsumed into the figure of torment (*tormento*), so there were no specific counts of rape or sexual abuse. This is so because the subjective element, according to the Tribunal, fits better with the criminal type of torment rather than aggression to the sexual integrity.[60]

The judgment establishes that sexual violence was part of a core of degrading practices, not only in the aforementioned detention centres aforementioned, but also in all centres that carried out the systematic plan imposed by the *de facto* regime in power between 1976 and 1983. Following *Castro Castro Prison v. Peru*, the judgment asserted that the cases of enforced nudity constituted sexual violence, while the same crime together with sexualised verbal abuse against the detainees was considered "sexual torture" in accordance with the Istanbul Protocol.[61]

As for thematic prosecution, again, no criterion has been put in evidence, but this judgment suggests a different approach from that of the *Molina* judgment. Both of them based their cases of sexual violence mostly on the testimony of victims and witnesses, which happened to be key in the prosecution of these crimes. However, in *Miara et al.* the witnesses, all of them survivors of the detention centres, provided most of the testimonies related to sexual violence, since a large number of victims did not come forward or were among the murdered or disappeared.

From both judgments it could be inferred that the statement of the victim herself could give the prosecution a greater chance to present counts of rape or other forms of sexual violence as crimes against humanity, without subsuming it as torment. If there are more witnesses than victims, the prosecution will optimise their accounts to establish a pattern of torture and inhumane treatment in the detention centres, and provide an engendered content to the "imposition of torment" crime.

---

[60]   Federal Criminal Oral Tribunal no. 2 of the Autonomous City of Buenos Aires, Argentina, *Miara et al.*, p. 862.

[61]   *Ibid.*, pp. 858–59.

5.2.3. Peru: Case of *Manta and Vilca*[62]

Manta and Vilca are two villages in Huancavelica, Peru. In accordance with the Peruvian Comisión de la Verdad y Reconciliación ('CVR', Truth and Reconciliation Commission), they were both reported to have endured sexual violence as a systematic or widespread practice during the 1980–2000 internal armed conflict in Peru. Overall the CVR identified a total of 538 cases of sexual violence in the country in the same period, from which 13 are currently being reviewed by prosecutors and only three have indictments and/or are in the commencement of trial stage (*apertura de instruccion*). *Manta and Vilca* is one of the cases with a court order opening prosecution.

Manta and Vilca, similarly to *Molina*, is addressing rape as a crime against humanity *per se*. The reason, however, is mostly formal: at the time of the commission of the crimes the Peruvian Criminal Code did not typify torture, only rape.[63] The judge did not elaborate on the crimes against humanity in the court order opening prosecution. The latter only develops the subject of crimes against humanity in order to support the non-applicability of the statutes of limitation for said crimes.[64]

This case differs from both Argentinian cases because the indictment contemplates the counts of rape only, whereas *Molina* and *Miara et al.* consisted of complex cases with a number of crimes against humanity involved.

In terms of thematic prosecution, there appears to be two main reasons for going forward with the prosecution of this case: the evidence (in this case the testimony of the victim and the forensic psychological examination), and the fact that the case was highlighted by the CVR final report. It is interesting to see how the CVR and civil society cooperating in the disseminating of the findings of the final report can influence public prosecutors in their work of strengthening their cases for indictment. On the other hand, from the court order opening prosecution, the lack of fa-

---

62 Fourth Supraprovincial Criminal Court, Peru, File 2007-00899-0 (against Rufino Donato Rivera Quispe, Vicente Yance Collahuacho, Epifanio Delfin Quiñones Loyola, Sabino Rodrigo Valentin Rutti, Amador Gutierrez Lisarbe, Julio Julian Meza Garcia, Pedro Chanel Perez Lopez and Martin Sierra Gabriel), Court order opening prosecution, 3 April 2009.

63 *Ibid.*, pp. 9–10.

64 *Ibid.*, pp. 23–26.

---

miliarity of the judiciary with sexual crimes as war crimes and crimes against humanity is worrisome. The judge remains mostly silent when sustaining that rape was a widespread and/or systematic practice, and that the use of the principle of legality and non-retroactivity of the law goes against the core notion of crimes against humanity, which can be prosecuted at any time. As the process develops it might pose an obstacle in the prosecution of these crimes.

5.3. Conclusion

The Convention of Belém do Pará and the Court have already given sufficient guidelines through its jurisprudence to assess the gravity of sex crimes perpetrated in the region. The Court found that these crimes are generally committed by state agents or as part of a state's policy; that they correspond with a generalised discrimination against women that allows for extreme forms of violence against them in the public and private spheres; and that they usually go unpunished and have a more devastating impact in the victim and her community compared to other human rights abuses. In cases of massive gross violations of human rights, contextualising the violence endured by women will give a better insight not only of their own suffering, but also that of each of the members of her community and the community as a whole.

Therefore, national courts have an obligation to prosecute human rights abuses and, if there is a backlog of cases, the aforementioned criteria could prove useful in supporting the case to prioritise the prosecution of sex crimes. The Court's rulings would also support the use of thematic prosecution in its expressivist sense since the inter-American system of protection of human rights aims to eradicate violence against women, give visibility to the said crimes in broader contexts as conflicts or massacres, and ensuring women's right to justice regardless of the time that has passed. The strong ties between the inter-American system of protection of human rights and domestic tribunals in the region would guarantee the application of the said guidelines and the introduction of new ones as the Court's jurisprudence develops, for example, in the case of the right to truth. *Castro Castro Prison v. Peru* is the most quoted judgment, but it looks like it will only be a matter of time before the national courts to use the other judgments analysed in this chapter, which were ruled on during or after the national judgments or opening of prosecution.

This favourable context is enhanced by recently enacted legislation punishing international crimes, and the progressive removal of amnesties and statutes of limitations that prevent the prosecution of gross violations of human rights. Still, national courts in the region still face two main challenges while prosecuting sexual violence configured as international crimes. Since an important number of sex crimes were committed during the dictatorships and internal armed conflicts that took place three to four decades ago, a first challenge will be the time that has passed between the perpetration of the crime and its prosecution, which will endanger the collection of evidence and the location of victims and witnesses. The second challenge is the reluctance of the victims to come forward and tell their stories of violence. The higher visibility of sexual violence as a gross violation of human rights has encouraged more and more women to talk; however, due to the time that has passed, a large number of victims have rebuilt their lives and do not feel the need to come back to that memory again. Feelings of fear, angst and shame will also prevent the victims from filing a case. As long as the account from the victim is still seen as the main piece of evidence in the prosecution of sex crimes that have been committed far in the past, the number of indictments and trials will be low. The lower the numbers, the less the backlogs of cases in that matter, and hence the less likelihood that national courts will find it necessary to establish public criteria for the prioritising of cases of international sex crimes.

6

Thematic Prosecution of International Sex Crimes and Stigmatisation of Victims and Survivors: Two Sides of the Same Coin?

Benson Chinedu Olugbuo[*]

Witness: My body was affected. [...] I was very ashamed. Now I have become useless. That is something that I do not believe anyone could be subjected to in life, that is to totally destroy someone's body. You become totally useless. You no longer have any value. When somebody sees you, they do not value you any longer, and they look down on you. God forgive me.[1]

Judge: [W]hat you have said, that a woman who is raped is a woman who has no value, she has to be ashamed, she is totally useless, that is not true. [...] [T]he shame here is the shame of the entire world. This is dishonour for humanity. You should not be ashamed. You are brave. You are courageous. What you are doing today is going to help society to realise that they are not doing their job correctly. Please do not consider yourself as useless. You are not. You are respectable. Generally speaking, I respect women. After my mother, you are the woman that I respect most in this world. Thank you.[2]

---

[*] **Benson Chinedu Olugbuo** is Programmes Manager at the Centre for Democracy and Development, Nigeria. He holds a doctorate from the University of Cape Town. Earlier drafts of this chapter were presented at the "Thematic Investigation and Prosecution of International Sex Crimes" conference organised by the Forum for International Criminal and Humanitarian Law in Cape Town on 7–8 March 2011 and the Emerging Researchers' Breakaway of the Faculty of Law, University of Cape Town at Mount Fleur Estate, Stellenbosch on 13–15 June 2011. I am grateful to participants at the two workshops for their comments and to Oluwatoyin Badejogbin for his invaluable suggestions.

[1] International Criminal Court ('ICC'), *Prosecutor v. Germain Katanga and Mathieu Ngudjolo Chui*, Trial Chamber, Court Proceedings, ICC-01/04-01/07, 14 May 2010, p. 39 (http://www.legal-tools.org/doc/bb0444/).

[2] *Ibid.*

Thematic prosecution of international sex crimes involves the selection and prioritisation of sexual crimes over and above other crimes for investigation and prosecution at national or international judicial institutions. Despite arguments objecting to this process due to competing prosecutorial demands, lack of resources and trained personnel, proponents are of the opinion that it is an effective way of dealing with the recurring phenomenon of sexual violence during armed conflicts. This chapter argues that the solution to sexual violence may not lie with targeted prosecution of international sex crimes. Rather, efforts should be made to address the underlying factors that result in the stigmatisation of victims and survivors of sexual violence. This chapter further argues that these underlying factors also lead to the exacerbation of international sex crimes during armed conflicts and, if not addressed, will further stigmatise victims and survivors through targeted investigations and prosecutions.

6.1. Introduction

Thematic prosecution of international sex crimes is the process by which prosecutors and investigators focus on the selection and prioritisation of sex crimes for prosecution either at national or international criminal justice institutions.[3] It may involve exclusive focus on sex crimes to the exclusion of other crimes of concern to the international community. It may also involve prioritisation of the prosecution of sex crimes but not to the exclusion of other crimes. The appropriateness of focusing on the prosecution of sex-based crimes has been questioned because of empirical evidence indicating that many people consider sex crimes to be less serious than crimes resulting in death.[4] Furthermore, there are issues of inadequate resources and lack of effective capacity to deal with thematic prosecution of international sex crimes.

International sex crimes can be prosecuted either as genocide,[5] crimes against humanity[6] or war crimes.[7] In relation to genocide, the acts[8]

---

[3] Morten Bergsmo, "International Sex Crimes as a Criminal Justice Theme", FICHL Policy Brief Series No. 4 (2011), Torkel Opsahl Academic EPublisher, Brussels, 2011, p. 1.

[4] *Ibid.*, p. 2.

[5] United Nations General Assembly, Convention on the Prevention and Punishment of the Crime of Genocide adopted by resolution 260(III)A, 9 December 1948, entry into force 12 January 1951, Article 2 (http://www.legal-tools.org/doc/498c38/); United Nations, Statute of the International Criminal Tribunal for the former Yugoslavia, adopted 25 May 1993 by reso-

must be committed with the intent to destroy, in whole or in part, a national, ethnical, racial or religious group. Sexual crimes that fall under crimes against humanity are rape, sexual slavery, enforced prostitution, forced pregnancy, enforced sterilisation, or any other form of sexual violence of comparable gravity.[9] For sex crimes to be classified as war crimes, the acts must be committed as part of a plan or policy or as part of a large scale commission of such crimes during international[10] or non-international armed conflicts.[11]

Rape and sexual violence have been systematically used as weapons of war, military strategy and in some instances to change the ethnic compositions of communities.[12] We are confronted daily with stories of inter-

---

lution 827, amended 7 July 2009, Article 4 ('ICTY Statute') (http://www.legal-tools.org/doc/b4f63b/); United Nations, Statute of the International Criminal Tribunal for Rwanda, adopted 8 November 1994 by resolution 955, Article 2 ('ICTR Statute') (http://www.legal-tools.org/doc/8732d6/); Rome Statute of the International Criminal Court, 17 July 1998, in force 1 July 2002, Article 7 ('ICC Statute') (http://www.legal-tools.org/doc/7b9af9/).

[6] To meet the threshold of culpability, the crimes must be committed as part of a widespread or systematic attack directed against any civilian population, with knowledge of the attack.

[7] Acts like rape, sexual slavery, enforced prostitution, forced pregnancy, enforced sterilisation, and any other form of sexual violence also constituting a serious violation of Article 3 common to the Four Geneva Conventions; Article 8 of the ICC Statute, see *supra* note 5.

[8] Killing members of the group, causing serious bodily or mental harm to members of the group, deliberately inflicting on the group conditions of life calculated to bring about its physical destruction in whole or in part, imposing measures intended to prevent births within the group, and forcibly transferring children of the group to another group.

[9] ICC Statute, Article 7(g), see *supra* note 5.

[10] *Ibid.*, Article 8(2)(b)(xxii).

[11] *Ibid.*, Article 8(2)(c)(vi).

[12] "War's Overlooked Victims: Rape is Horrifyingly Widespread in Conflicts All Around the World", in *The Economist*, 13 January 2011; Alexis Arieff, "Sexual Violence in African Conflicts", in *Congressional Research Service Report*, 30 November 2010, p. 8; Michele Leiby, "Wartime Sexual Violence in Guatemala and Peru", in *International Studies Quarterly*, 2009, vol. 53, p. 449; Nancy Farwell, "War Rape: New Conceptualizations and Responses", in *Affilia*, 2004, vol. 19, no. 4, pp. 389–403; Jeanne Ward and Mendy Marsh, "Sexual Violence Against Women and Girls in War and Its Aftermath: Realities, Responses, and Required Resources", Briefing Paper Prepared for Symposium on Sexual Violence in Conflict, Brussels, 21–23 June 2006; Manuela Melandri, "Gender and Reconciliation in Post-Conflict Societies: The dilemmas of Responding to Large Scale Violence", in *International Public Policy Review*, 2009, vol. 5, no. 1, p. 9.

---

national sex crimes that still shock the conscience of humanity.[13] Most victims and survivors[14] of international sex crimes suffer in silence while some live with fear and regret.[15] A good number are blamed by the society for what befell them and are subjected to various forms of discrimination.[16] Some of them are rejected by their families while many who are predominantly women are left by their husbands.[17] The problem is exacerbated by the trauma of their experiences and the inability to relate it to family members because of stigmatisation.[18] Many suffer multiple medical conditions as a result of sexual violence perpetrated against them.[19] Despite this gloomy picture, the international community has tried to punish those who commit crimes of sexual violence and international sex crimes.

The Nuremberg and Tokyo Tribunals have been criticised for low-level prosecution of international sex crimes notwithstanding the level of atrocities committed during the Second World War.[20] There was considerable improvement in the treatment of victims of international sex crimes at the International Criminal Tribunal for the former Yugoslavia ('ICTY') and the International Criminal Tribunal for Rwanda ('ICTR') set up by the United Nations ('UN'). However, their rights were limited as they par-

---

[13] Eve Ayiera, "Sexual Violence in Conflict: A Problematic International Discourse", in *Feminist Africa*, 2010, vol. 14, p. 13.

[14] I have decided to use the terms 'victims and survivors' together. Megan Mullet, "Fulfilling the Promise of Payne: Creating Participatory Opportunities for Survivors in Capital Cases", in *Indiana Law Journal*, 2011, vol. 86, pp. 1617–47. For a critique of the use of 'victims', see Martha Minow, "Surviving Victim Talk", in *University of California Los Angeles Law Review*, 1993, vol. 40, pp. 1411–45.

[15] Evelyne Josse, "'They came with two guns': The Consequences of Sexual Violence for the Mental Health of Women in Armed Conflicts", in *International Review of the Red Cross*, 2010, vol. 92, no. 887, p. 184.

[16] *Ibid.*

[17] *Ibid.*, p. 179.

[18] John Ehrenreich, "Coping with Disasters: A Guidebook to Psychological Intervention", October 2001.

[19] Human Rights Watch, "My Heart is Cut: Sexual Violence by Rebels and Pro-Government Forces in Côte d'Ivoire", 2007, vol. 19, no. 11(A), p. 86.

[20] Theodor Meron, "Reflections on the Prosecution of War Crimes by International Tribunals", in *American Journal of International Law*, 2006, vol. 100, no. 3, p. 567.

ticipated in the trials only as witnesses.[21] The advent of the International
Criminal Court ('ICC') and its promotion and protection of the rights of
victims of international sex crimes is seen as a positive development.[22]

The chapter seeks to answer the question whether the prioritisation
of prosecuting international sex crimes will ultimately eliminate or reduce
the incidences of sexual violence. It will also investigate whether targeted
prosecution will result in further stigmatisation or labelling of victims and
survivors of international sex crimes. In addressing the above question,
the chapter is divided into four broad sections. Section 6.2. addresses the
theoretical and conceptual framework of the chapter by analysing the
prevalence of international sex crimes and stigmatisation of sexual violence. Section 6.3. discusses the intervention of the ICTY and the ICTR.
Section 6.4. looks at the UN Security Council interventions through the
resolutions adopted to fight sexual violence during armed conflicts. Section 6.5. draws attention to emerging scenarios in the Democratic Republic of Congo ('DRC') and its impact on the prosecution of international
sex crimes at the national level. Section 6.6. concludes the chapter. The
chapter concentrates on international sex crimes[23] committed during international and non-international armed conflicts although the arguments
could be relevant for judicial systems seeking ways and means to contain
sex crimes committed at the national level.

6.2. Conceptual and Theoretical Framework of Sexual Violence

In conceptualising the definition of rape, Susan Brownmiller states that
"[m]an's discovery that his genitalia could serve as a weapon to generate
fear must rank as one of the most important discoveries of prehistoric
time, along with the use of fire and first crude stone axe".[24] She further
argues that rape is "a conscious process of intimidation by which *all* men

---

[21] Anne-Marie de Brouwer and Marc Groenhuijsen, "The Role of Victims in International
Criminal Proceedings", in Göran Sluiter and Sergey Vasiliev (eds.), *International Criminal
Procedure: Towards Coherent Body of Law*, CMP Publishing, London, 2009, p. 149.

[22] Cherie Booth and Max du Plessis, "The International Criminal Court and Victims of Sexual
Violence", in *South African Journal of Criminal Justice*, 2005, vol. 18, no. 3, p. 252.

[23] The terms 'international sex crimes', 'sexual violence' and 'sex crimes' are used interchangeably.

[24] Susan Brownmiller, *Against Our Will: Men, Women and Rape*, Simon and Schuster, New
York, 1975, p. 14.

---

keep *all* women in a state of fear".[25] For Brownmiller, rape is the earliest expression of an intent by men to control women through fear and intimidation and this process has succeeded in changing women's perception and their social status. This definition indicts all men as capable of committing rape. However, the definition does not take into consideration the fact that men and boys are at times victims of rape though probably on a smaller scale compared to women.[26]

Regarding rape during armed conflicts, Christine Chinkin states:

> Women are raped in all forms of armed conflict, international and internal, whether the conflict is fought primarily on religious, ethnic, political or nationalist grounds, or a combination of all these. They are raped by men from all sides – both enemy and "friendly" forces.[27]

Chinkin believes women are targeted by soldiers as part of a war strategy whether they are winning or losing the war. Women lose out in the process as they are neither protected by the victorious soldiers nor by the defeated armed forces.

Ann Cahill explores the physical and emotional challenges of sexual violence on women. She states that rape is "a pervasive, sustained, and repetitive, but not ultimately defining, element of the development of women's experience".[28] She further argues that sex crimes are experienced differently by different women with some common features shared by them.[29] Rape marks women as different from men and the experience of sexual violence for women begins with the body and the significance does not end there.[30] Cahill's definition goes beyond the physical by connecting the emotionally and psychologically debilitating effects of rape on women.

---

25 *Ibid.*, p. 15 (emphasis in original).

26 Dustin Lewis, "Unrecognised Victims: Sexual Violence against Men in Conflict Settings Under International Law", in *Wisconsin International Law Journal*, 2009, vol. 27, no. 1, pp. 1–49; Gertie Pretorius and Richard Hull, "The Experience of Male Rape in Non-Institutionalised Settings", in *Indo-Pacific Journal of Phenomenology*, 2005, vol. 5, no. 2, pp. 1–11.

27 Christine Chinkin, "Rape and Sexual Abuse of Women in International Law", in *European Journal of International Law*, 1994, vol. 5, no. 1, p. 326.

28 Ann Cahill, *Rethinking Rape*, Cornell University Press, Ithaca, NY, 2001, p. 4.

29 *Ibid.*, p. 5.

30 *Ibid.*, p. 5.

The definition of rape in international law has not been consistent.[31] International law has developed at a snail's pace in relation to the crime of rape and sexual violence committed during armed conflicts. Until very recently, the specific elements of the crime of rape were not clearly set out. However, based on the decisions of the ICTY and ICTR, there is an emerging consensus on the definition of rape, both in terms of the *actus reus* and the *mens rea*, although some differences still persist.[32]

In the *Prosecutor v. Tadić* case,[33] the accused person was charged with crimes under grave breaches of the Geneva Conventions of 1949; violations of the laws and customs of war; and crimes against humanity. Although there was insufficient evidence to convict Tadić for all the crimes he was accused of, the ICTY found that he aided and abetted sexual violence crimes.[34]

In *Prosecutor v. Akayesu*,[35] the ICTR found that rape and sexual violence constituted an act of genocide when committed with specific intent to destroy a group in whole or in part.[36] The ICTR made an unprecedented legal decision by finding that rape and sexual violence underpinning crimes against humanity also constituted the crime of genocide.[37] The Trial Chamber defined rape as:

> a physical invasion of a sexual nature, committed on a person under circumstances which are coercive. Sexual violence which includes rape is considered to be any act of a sexual

---

[31] UN Economic and Social Council, Contemporary Forms of Slavery: Systematic Rape, Sexual Slavery and Slavery-like Practices during Armed Conflict, Final Report Submitted by Gay J. McDougall, UN Doc. E/CN.4/Sub.2/1998/13, 22 June 1998.

[32] Mark Ellis, "Breaking the Silence: Rape as an International Crime", in *Case Western Reserve Journal of International Law*, 2007, vol. 38, no. 2, p. 229.

[33] ICTY, *Prosecutor v. Duško Tadić*, Trial Chamber, Opinion and Judgment, IT-94-1-T, 7 May 1997 (http://www.legal-tools.org/doc/0a90ae/).

[34] *Ibid.*, para. 726; Ellis, 2004, p. 226, see *supra* note 32.

[35] ICTR, *Prosecutor v. Akayesu*, Trial Chamber, Judgment, ICTR-96-4-T, 2 September 1998 ('*Akayesu* Judgment') (http://www.legal-tools.org/doc/b8d7bd/).

[36] *Ibid.*, para 71.

[37] George Mugwanya, "The Contribution of the International Criminal Tribunal for Rwanda to the Development of the International Criminal Law", in Chacha Murungu and Japhet Biegon (eds.), *Prosecution of International Crimes in Africa*, Pretoria University Law Press, Pretoria, 2011, p. 68.

nature which is committed on a person under circumstances which are coercive.[38]

The ICTY in *Prosecutor v. Furundžija*[39] defines rape as:

> [...] sexual penetration, however slight, either of the vagina or anus of the victim by the penis of the perpetrator, or any other object used by the perpetrator, or of the mouth of the victim by the penis of the perpetrator, where such penetration is effected by coercion or force or threat of force against the victim or a third person.[40]

Furthermore, in *Prosecutor v. Kunarać, Kovač and Vuković* the ICTY held that:

> [r]ape is the sexual penetration, however slight: (a) of a vagina or anus of the victim by the penis of the perpetrator or any other object used by the perpetrator; or (b) the mouth of the victim by the penis of the perpetrator; where such sexual penetration occurs without the consent of the victim. Consent for this purpose must be consent given voluntarily, as a result of the victim's free will, assessed in the context of the surrounding circumstances. The *mens rea* is the intention to effect this sexual penetration, and the knowledge that it occurs without the consent of the victim.[41]

This definition has been endorsed by subsequent cases decided by the ICTR.[42] The Elements of Crimes of the ICC provides that there is a crime of rape if:

> [...] invasion was committed by force, or by threat of force or coercion, such as that caused by fear of violence, duress, detention, psychological oppression or abuse of power,

---

[38] *Akayesu* Judgment, para. 598, see *supra* note 35; Diane Amann, "Prosecutor v. Akayesu. Case ICTR-96-4-T", in *American Journal of International Law*, 1999, vol. 93, no. 1, p. 197.

[39] ICTY, *Prosecutor v. Anto Furundžija*, Trial Chamber, Judgment, IT-95-17/1-T, 10 December 1998 (http://www.legal-tools.org/doc/e6081b/).

[40] *Ibid.*, para. 185.

[41] ICTY, *Prosecutor v. Dragoljub Kunarać, Radomir Kovač and Zoran Vuković*, Trial Chamber, Judgment, IT-96-23 & 23/1, 22 February 2001, para 460 (http://www.legal-tools.org/doc/fd881d/).

[42] ICTR, *Prosecutor v. Sylvestre Gacumbitsi*, Appeals Chamber, Judgment, ICTR-01-64-A, 7 July 2006, paras. 147–57 (http://www.legal-tools.org/doc/aa51a3/); ICTR, *Prosecutor v. Mikaeli Muhimana*, Trial Chamber, Judgment, ICTR-95-1B-T, 28 April 2005, paras. 550–51 (http://www.legal-tools.org/doc/87fe83/); Mugwanya, 2011, p. 72, see *supra* note 37.

against such person or another person, or by taking advantage of a coercive environment, or the invasion was
committed against a person incapable of giving genuine consent.[43]

The UN has defined violence against women as any act of gender-
based violence that results in, or is likely to result in, physical, sexual or
mental harm or suffering to women, including threats of such acts, coercion or arbitrary deprivation of liberty, whether occurring in public or in
private life.[44] Among several forms of violence against women identified
by the UN, systematic sexual abuses including international sex crimes
that occur during international and non-international armed conflicts are
glaring forms of violence against women.

Sexual violence against women during armed conflicts has a long
history and its effect on women is devastating.[45] According to Amnesty
International,

[r]ape constitutes an especially humiliating assault. Consequently, it often carries traumatic social repercussions, which
may be affected by a woman's cultural origins or social status. Such factors may affect her ability to bear the trauma of
rape, let alone the time it may take for her to come to terms
with the emotional distress and physical effects of rape.[46]

6.3. International Criminal Justice and Sexual Violence

Despite the incidents of rape and sexual violence that has dogged the international community during several conflicts throughout the world, their
prosecution has not been as effective as expected. This is due to several
reasons. One is the lack of political will by those responsible to take action. Another reason is the tendency not to recognise rape and sexual vio-

---

[43] ICC, Elements of Crimes, 11 June 2010, Article 7(1)(g)-1 (http://www.legal-
tools.org/doc/3c0e2d/).

[44] World Health Organisation, "Violence against Women", Fact Sheet No. 239, November
2009.

[45] Chinkin, 1994, p. 327, see *supra* note 27; Rosalind Dixon, "Rape as a Crime in International
Humanitarian Law: Where to from Here", in *European Journal of International Law*, 2002,
vol. 13, no. 3, p. 700.

[46] Amnesty International, "Bosnia-Herzegovina: Rape and Sexual Abuse by Armed Forces",
1993, EUR 63/01/93, p. 1.

lence as specific crimes but ancillary to other crimes of concern to the international community.

After the First World War, the War Crimes Commission was set up in 1919 to examine the atrocities committed by Germany and other Axis powers during the war, as it was evident that rape and other forms of sexual violence had been used by the German army against citizens of Belgium and France.[47] Though the prosecutions did not succeed, rape and enforced prostitution were recognised as violations of the laws and customs of war.[48]

During the Second World War, several incidents of rape and sexual violence also took place, but during Nuremberg trials there was no political will to prosecute these crimes.[49] A major deficiency of the Nuremberg trials was the absolute neglect of international sex crimes against women.[50] The Tokyo Tribunal was more effective in prosecuting international sex crimes compared with the Nuremberg Tribunal. This is because rape was prosecuted as a war crime, under "inhumane treatment", "ill-treatment" and "failure to respect family honour and rights".[51]

International sex crimes occur regularly during armed conflicts and most times perpetrators are not held accountable.[52] Few examples in Sudan and Libya are discussed. In Darfur, Sudan, the Janjaweed militias have been accused of complicity with the government forces to commit international sex crimes of mass rape and other sexual crimes against Darfuris. The International Commission of Inquiry found several incidents of mass rape and sexual crimes committed against women and girls in Darfur and stated:

> [...] deliberate aggressions against women and girls, including gang rapes, occurred during the attacks on the villages [...] women and girls were abducted, held in confinement for

---

47 Kelly Askin, War Crimes against Women: Prosecution in International War Crimes Tribunal, Martinus Nijhoff Publishers, Dordrecht, 1997, p. 42.

48 *Ibid.*

49 De Brouwer and Groenhuijsen, 2009, p. 7, see *supra* note 21.

50 Askin, 1997, p. 97, see *supra* note 47.

51 *Ibid.*

52 Kim Thuy Seelinger, Helene Silverberg and Robin Mejia "The Investigation and Prosecution of Sexual Violence", Sexual Violence and Accountability Project Working Paper Series, Human Rights Center University of California, Berkeley, May 2011.

several days and repeatedly raped during that time [...] rape
and other forms of sexual violence continued during flight
and further displacement, including when women left towns
and IDP sites to collect wood or water. In certain areas, rapes
also occurred inside towns. Some women and girls became
pregnant as a result of rape.[53]

The International Commission of Inquiry further stated that international
sex crimes committed in Darfur may have been under-reported "due to the
sensitivity of the issue and the stigma associated with rape".[54] Its report
provided a springboard for the referral of the Darfur conflict to the ICC in
2005 by the Security Council acting under Chapter VII of the UN Charter.[55]

In Libya, it was alleged that children as young at eight years old
were sexually assaulted during the conflict between Libyan National
Transitional Council ('NTC') fighters and Muammar Gaddafi-led soldiers.[56] Furthermore, there were allegations that Gaddafi-led soldiers were
given Viagra to aid them in sexual violence during the conflict with the
NTC forces.[57]

Though it is desirable to prosecute perpetrators of sexual violence,
the impact of sexual violence on victims and survivors at times is not mitigated by prosecution of perpetrators. Some authors have argued that there
are limitations to what criminal justice institutions can achieve in relation
to victims and survivors of sexual crimes.[58] Nicola Henry is of the view
that international criminal justice does not always provide satisfaction and
closure to victims and survivors.[59] Efforts should be made at the national

---

[53] United Nations, Report of the International Commission of Inquiry on Darfur to the United
Nations Secretary-General, pursuant to the Security Council Resolution 1564 of 18 September 2004, Geneva, 25 January 2005.

[54] *Ibid.*, para. 336.

[55] United Nations Security Council, Resolution 1593, UN Doc. S/RES/1593 (2005), 31
March 2005 (http://www.legal-tools.org/doc/4b208f/).

[56] Save the Children, "Save the Children Receives Reports of Child Rape in Libya", 26 April
2011.

[57] "Libya Troops 'Given Viagra to Rape'", in *Herald Sun*, 29 April 2011.

[58] Dianne Martin, "Retribution Revisited: A Reconsideration of Feminist Criminal Law Reform
Strategies", in *Osgoode Hall Law Journal*, 1998, vol. 36, no. 1, p. 155.

[59] Nicola Henry, "Witness to Rape: The Limits and Potentials of International War Crimes
Trials for Victims of Wartime Sexual Violence", in *International Journal of Transitional
Justice*, 2009, vol. 3, no. 1, p. 130.

level to provide accountability mechanisms for international sex crimes. These mechanisms should complement both national and international criminal justice systems aimed at alleviating the immediate impact of sexual violence on victims and survivors.

6.3.1. The International Criminal Tribunal for the Former Yugoslavia

The events in the former Yugoslavia that led to the establishment of the ICTY are documented.[60] Elisabeth Wood has argued that the sexual abuse of Bosnian Muslim women by Bosnian Serb forces was so systematic and widespread that it was a crime against humanity under international law.[61] All parties to the conflict in Bosnia and Herzegovina committed abuses, including rape and sexual violence. While Muslim women were the chief victims, the main perpetrators were members of Serbian armed forces.[62] There is consensus amongst some scholars that rape and sexual violence were used as strategies and weapons of war especially against Muslim women by Bosnian Serbs.[63]

The Serbian forces carried out unprecedented ethnic cleansing, targeting women and girls while holding several of them captive as sexual slaves. Women were repeatedly raped to make them pregnant and held in captivity to ensure that they did not terminate the pregnancy. This was to make them have non-Muslim children thereby changing the composition of the families. This confirms the argument by Dianna Marder of the philosophy and thought process of the perpetrator that, "[w]hen I rape your

---

[60] Bert Swart, Alexander Zahar and Göran Sluiter (eds.), *The Legacy of the International Criminal Tribunal for the Former Yugoslavia*, Oxford University Press, New York, 2011; Askin, 1997, see *supra* note 47; Ivan Simonovic, "The Role of the ICTY in the Development of International Criminal Adjudication", in *Fordham International Law Journal*, 1999, vol. 23, no. 2 pp. 440–59; Lilian Barria and Steven Roper, "How Effective are International Criminal Tribunals? An Analysis of the ICTY and ICTR", in *International Journal of Human Rights*, 2005, vol. 9, no. 3, pp. 349–68.

[61] Elisabeth Wood, "Variation in Sexual Violence during War", in *Politics and Society*, 2006, vol. 34, no. 3, p. 307.

[62] Amnesty International, 1993, p. 3, see *supra* note 46.

[63] Danise Aydelott, "Mass Rape during War: Prosecuting Bosnian Rapists under International Law", in *Emory International Law Review*, 1993, vol. 7, p. 600; Theodor Meron, "Rape as a Crime under International Humanitarian Law", in *American Journal of International Law*, 1993, vol. 87, no. 3, p. 425; Theodor Meron, "The Case for War Crimes Trials in Yugoslavia", in *Foreign Affairs*, 1993, vol. 72, no. 3, p. 125.

woman, [...] I destroy your property. I insult you. I humiliate you. If I rape all your women, I defile an entire generation. And if I force your women to bear my children, I pollute your race".[64] These heinous crimes are not targeted only at the women but the family, society and community at large.

Rape during armed conflicts is also used as a bonding process and as initiation rites for soldiers.[65] According to Radhika Coomaraswamy:

> During wartime, sexual violence is not usually a private crime. It is often committed in public, in front of fellow soldiers and the family of the victim. This public spectacle is aimed at instilling terror among the population, but it also strengthens bonds and comradeship among fellow soldiers or militias. The public acts are meant to harden the warrior and to create shared experiences among the men. Studies into the lives of perpetrators have clearly shown that this element of male bonding is an essential aspect of rapes during wartime.[66]

Perpetrators of rape and sexual violence see the society, community and future generations through the body of the woman and her violation is the ultimate conquest.[67] It is these mindsets, thought processes, and false assumptions about military strategies of rape and sexual violence during armed conflicts that has fuelled the unprecedented international sex crimes against women despite laws enacted to prohibit the crimes.[68] These false assumptions may have also resulted in the low reportage of rape of men and boys during war as they do not fall into the "war booty" narra-

---

[64] Dianna Marder, "Once Again, Rape Becomes a Weapon of War", in *Atlanta Journal and Constitution*, 17 February 1993, p. 111, quoted in Danise Aydelott, 1993, p. 587, see *supra* note 63.

[65] Jelke Boesten, "Analysing Rape Regimes at the Interface of War and Peace in Peru", in *International Journal of Transitional Justice*, 2010, vol. 4, no. 1, p. 117.

[66] Radhika Coomaraswamy, "Sexual Violence during Wartime", in Helen Durham and Tracy Gurd (eds.), *Listening to the Silences: Women and War*, Martinus Nijhoff Publishers, Leiden, 2005, p. 55.

[67] Simon Chesterman, "Never Again ... and Again: Law, Order and the Gender of War Crimes in Bosnia and Beyond", in *Yale Journal of International Law*, 1991, vol. 22, no. 2, pp. 325–28.

[68] Carrie Sperline, "Mother of Atrocities: Pauline Nyiramasuhuko's Role in Rwanda Genocide", in *Fordham Urban Law Journal*, 2006, vol. 33, p. 662.

---

tives.[69] The stigma attached to rape and sexual violence by the society has also made it difficult for victims and survivors to relate their experiences because of the fear of stigmatisation and loss of social status in the community.

Not all victims and survivors subscribe to criminal processes because of its negative effects. While some find succour and relief in giving evidence during criminal proceedings, others find it difficult and traumatising.[70] The cross-examinations by defence counsel that take place during criminal trials also contribute to the stress and discomfort of victims and survivors who elect to become witnesses. Some of them are forced to relive traumatic experiences while giving evidence in criminal proceedings and may become retraumatised in the process.

6.3.2. International Criminal Tribunal for Rwanda

Between April and July 1994 about 500,000 to one million Tutsis and moderate Hutus were killed in a planned genocide orchestrated by political leaders, threatened with the loss of political power.[71] The UN Security Council set up the ICTR to hold leaders of the genocide accountable. The ICTR has been credited with making advances in the protection of victims and survivors of sexual crime. The widespread and systematic rape of Tutsi women that occurred in Rwanda, according to the ICTR, amounted to genocide.[72] Despite the advances made by the ICTR, it has also been argued by some scholars that the establishment of the ICTR was an afterthought as the international community failed to protect those killed during the genocide.[73] The ICTR has tried several individuals accused of

---

[69] Sandesh Sivakuraman, "Lost in Translation: UN responses to sexual violence against men and boys in situations of armed conflict", in *International Review of the Red Cross 201*, vol. 92, no. 877 pp. 259–77; Will Storr, "The Rape of Men", in *The Observer*, 17 July 2011; Lara Stemple, "Male Rape and Human Rights", in *Hastings Law Journal*, 2009, vol. 60, pp. 605–47.

[70] Alexandra Miller, "From the International Criminal Tribunal for Rwanda to the International Criminal Court: Expanding the Definition of Genocide to Include Rape", in *Penn State Law Review*, 2003, vol. 108, no. 1, p. 357.

[71] Human Rights Watch, Shattered Lives: Sexual Violence During the Rwandan Genocide and Its Aftermath, Human Rights Watch, New York, 1999.

[72] *Akayesu* Judgment, paras. 732–34, see *supra* note 35.

---

complicity in the genocide that took place in Rwanda. However, one case
that stands out in relation to rape and sexual violence after the case of
Akayesu is *Prosecutor v. Nyiramasuhuko*.[74]

Pauline Nyiramasuhuko is from the region of Butare in Rwanda and
was an administrator, lawyer and politician. She was a member of the in-
ner circle of the Hutu government in Kigali. She was a close friend of
Agathe Habyarimana, the wife of the former president of Rwanda, Juvénal Habyarimana, whose death triggered the genocide in 1994.[75] Initially,
Butare was immune to the slaughter that was going on around Rwanda for
several reasons. It had a concentration of both Tutsis and Hutus. The National University of Rwanda was based there, including the Research Institute. Furthermore, Jean Baptiste Habyarimana of, the *préfet* of Butare
préfecture refused to be drawn into the Hutu power ideology of the extermination of Tutsis.[76]

However, things changed when Nyiramasuhuko arrived from Kigali
to "cleanse" Butare of Tutsi elements and to carry out the plan of killing
Tutsis and moderate Hutus in collaboration with the Interahamwe militia
imported from other regions of Rwanda.[77] What makes Nyiramasuhuko's
case very interesting is the fact that she was the minister of family and
women's development. Furthermore, it is also said that she has a Tutsi
background and therefore can be classified as a Tutsi.[78]

Nyiramasuhuko encouraged the Interahamwe to rape their victims
before killing them.[79] She may have been under pressure to maintain po-

---

[73] Alison Hopkins, "Defining the Protected Groups in the Law of Genocide: Learning from the
Experience of the International Criminal Tribunal for Rwanda", in *InfraRead: Dalhousie
Journal of Legal Studies Online Supplement*, 2010, vol. 1, p. 27; Brent Beardsley, "The End-
less Debate over the 'G Word'", in *Genocide Studies and Prevention*, 2006, vol. 1, no. 1, pp.
79–82; A. Walter Dorn, Jonathan Matloff and Jennifer Matthews, "Preventing The Blood-
bath: Could the UN have Predicted and Prevented the Rwanda Genocide?", in *Journal of
Conflict Studies*, 2000, vol. 20, no. 1, pp. 9–52.

[74] ICTR, *Prosecutor v. Pauline Nyiramasuhuko et al.*, Trial Chamber, Judgment and Sentence,
ICTR-98-42-T, 24 June 2011 ('*Nyiramasuhuko* Judgment') (http://www.legal-
tools.org/doc/e2c881/). Other accused persons are Arsène Shalom Ntahobali, Sylvain Nsabi-
mana, Alphonse Nteziryayo, Joseph Kanyabashi and Élie Ndayambaje.

[75] Peter Landesman, "A Woman's Work", in *New York Times*, 15 September 2002.

[76] *Nyiramasuhuko* Judgment, para. 637, see *supra* note 74.

[77] *Ibid.*, paras. 926–33.

[78] Landesman, 2002, see *supra* note 75.

[79] *Nyiramasuhuko* Judgment, para. 5938, see *supra* note 74.

litical favour with the Hutu government and in that process proceeded to act with murderous intent while encouraging the Interahamwe to rape and kill Tutsi elements that stood against her political future and power base. Nyiramasuhuko was convicted of rape as a crime against humanity. The Trial Chamber was disappointed with the prosecution for omitting the crime of rape as genocide in the charges against her.[80]

Nyiramasuhuko's conviction was based on the massive support and encouragement she gave to the Interahamwe militias to rape and kill Tutsi women.[81] The Trial Chamber stated that Nyiramasuhuko had a superior–subordinate relationship with the Interahamwe. Her effective control over them was evidenced by the fact that her orders to rape Tutsi women were obeyed. She knew of, and failed to prevent or punish the rapes and was held responsible as a superior for the international sex crimes perpetrated by the Interahamwe.[82]

Nyiramasuhuko's involvement in the rape and killings committed against the Tutsi in Butare bring to question the argument by Brownmiller that women are raped by men to keep them in perpetual state of fear. Nyiramasuhuko is a woman. She did not commit the rapes herself. But she aided and abetted those who did and encouraged them to rape their victims before killing them.[83] The ICTR found her guilty of rape as a crime against humanity and stated that she bears responsibility as a superior for the rapes perpetrated by the Interahamwe.[84]

It seems from the discussions above that rape is no longer gender specific and can be employed by both men and women. According to Sam Sasan Shoamanesh:

> The Nyiramasuhuko case and its horrendous facts have demonstrated that rape as a tool of war is not gender specific and can be employed with severe cruelty by men and women alike; indeed, that women can be ruthless agents of egregious

---

[80]   *Ibid.*, para. 6087.
[81]   *Ibid.*, para. 6087.
[82]   *Ibid.*, para. 6088.
[83]   *Ibid.*, para. 6014.
[84]   *Ibid.*, para. 6088.

violations of human rights on a par with their male counter-parts.[85]

Carrie Sperling supports this view and argues that there is nothing special in the way and manner Nyiramasuhuko acted. She believes that expressing outrage about Nyiramasuhuko's behaviour reinforces the same prejudices and patriarchal ideologies that perpetuate rape and sexual violence against women.[86] The general belief that it is only men that have monopoly of power to commit atrocities should be discountenanced as there have been instances where women have facilitated and contributed not only to the rape and abuse of fellow women but also to the overall strategy of conquering the enemy.[87] The conviction of Pauline Nyiramasuhuko for rape and sexual violence reinforces the argument that men as well as women were complicit in the genocide in Rwanda.

6.3.3. The International Criminal Court

The Rome Statute entered into force on 1 July 2002 enabling the establishment of the ICC.[88] The Court has achieved modest successes coupled with complimentary controversies.[89] The practical application of the ICC Statute in relation to victims generally has not been without shortcomings as the ICC tries to assert its existence and relevance. Victims of crimes are allowed to participate actively during trials. Alex Little argues that this will likely limit the rights of defendants.[90] The activation of cases by the ICC has also brought to the fore the need for national judicial systems to promote the rights of victims of international sex crimes under the princi-

---

[85] Sam Shoamanesh, "Nyiramasuhuko: The Mother Who Awarded Rape For Murder", in *The Huffpost World*, 9 August 2011.

[86] Carrie Sperling, "Mother of Atrocities: Pauline Nyiramasuhuko's Role in the Rwanda Genocide", in *Fordham Urban Law Journal*, 2006, vol. 33, p. 658.

[87] Nicole Hogg, "Women's Participation in the Rwanda Genocide: Mothers or Monsters?", in *International Committee of the Red Cross*, 2010, vol. 92, no. 877, p. 92.

[88] ICC Statute, see *supra* note 5.

[89] Nick Grono, "The International Criminal Court: Success or Failure?", in *Open Democracy*, 9 June 2008; Mitja Mertens, "The International Criminal Court: A European Success Story?", in *EU Diplomacy Papers*, 2011, vol. 1, pp. 1–22.

[90] Alex Little, "Balancing Accountability and Victim Autonomy at the International Criminal Court", in *Georgetown Journal of International Law*, 2007, vol. 38, no. 2, p. 378.

ple of complementarity.[91] This is because the ICC Statute provides that, "it is the primary responsibility of states to hold accountable its nationals accused of international crimes".[92]

Supporters of the Court argue that its success can be seen not only in the cases currently before the court but also in its deterrent effect on potential criminals.[93] However, critics like Mahmood Mamdani argue that the Court is neither free nor independent from the politicisation of the UN Security Council.[94] Some of those indicted by the Court are yet to be arrested and there have been arguments about the need for the court not to give the impression that it is a Western tool targeting weak African states.[95]

The ICC lacks enforcement officers like the police and military. It depends heavily on the co-operation and goodwill of states parties and non-state parties. The ICC has also been dogged by the peace and justice debate.[96] Zachary Lomo has called on the ICC to withdraw its indictments in Uganda and allow local means of dispute resolution to be implemented.[97] Another issue confronting the ICC is that some of the superpowers

---

[91] Benson Olugbuo, "Positive Complementarity and the Fight Against Impunity in Africa", in Chacha Murungu and Japhet Biegon (eds.), *Prosecution of International Crimes in Africa*, Pretoria University Law Press, Pretoria, 2011, p. 251.

[92] ICC Statute, Preamble, see *supra* note 88; Open Society Foundations, "Putting Complementarity into Practice: Domestic Justice for International Crimes in DRC, Uganda, and Kenya", Open Society Foundations, New York, 2011; Markus Benzing, "The Complementarity Regime of the International Criminal Court: International Criminal Justice between State Sovereignty and the Fight Against Impunity", in Armin von Bogdandy and Rüdiger Wolfrum (eds.), *Max Planck Yearbook of United Nations Law*, 2003, vol. 7, p. 592.

[93] Payam Akhavan, "Are International Criminal Tribunal a Disincentive to Peace? Reconciling Judicial Romanticism with Political Realism", in *Human Rights Quarterly*, 2009, vol. 31, no. 3, p. 636; Payam Akhavan, "Beyond Impunity: Can International Criminal Justice Prevent Future Atrocities?", in *American Journal of International Law*, 2001, vol. 95, no. 7, p. 12.

[94] Mahmood Mamdani, Saviours and Survivors: Darfur, Politics and the War on Terror, HSRC Press, Cape Town, 2009, p. 287.

[95] Charles Jalloh, "Regionalizing International Criminal Law?", in *International Criminal Law Review*, 2009, vol. 9, no. 3, p. 499.

[96] Julie Flint and Alex de Waal, "To Put Justice before Peace Spells Disaster for Sudan", in *The Guardian*, 6 March 2009; Alex de Waal and Julie Flint, "ICC Approach Risks Peacemaking in Darfur", in *The Guardian*, 10 June 2008; Julie Flint and Alex De Waal, "Justice off Course in Darfur", in *Washington Post*, 28 June 2008.

[97] Zachary Lomo, "Why the International Criminal Court must withdraw Indictments against the Top LRA Leaders: A Legal Perspective", in *The Sunday Monitor*, 20 August 2006; Zachary Lomo and Lucy Hovil, "Behind the Violence: Causes, Consequences and the Search for

---

like the United States and Russia are not state parties to the ICC Statute. However, as permanent members of the UN Security Council they have participated in referring the conflicts in Sudan and Libya to the ICC.[98] Despite these challenges, the ICC has continued to investigate and prosecute cases relating to international sex crimes in its docket.[99]

The progress achieved by the ICC in prosecuting international sex crimes is not a result of the Office of the Prosecutor's initiative. It is a civil society-driven campaign that has criticised the way investigations in DRC are handled.[100] In fact, when the Office of the Prosecutor issued the first arrest warrant against Thomas Lubanga for conscription of child soldiers, there was outrage in DRC as activists contended that there were cases of sexual crimes that the prosecutor had ignored. It was argued that the prosecutor was insensitive to the plight of the women who faced several challenges daily due to sexual crimes committed against them by warring parties in the conflict.[101]

In the *Germain Katanga and Mathieu Ngudjolo Chui* case,[102] the defendants' indictments include rape and sexual slavery as war crimes[103] and crimes against humanity.[104] In the *Callixte Mbarushimana* case,[105] the accused person was charged with acts of rape constituting war crimes[106] and crimes against humanity.[107] The Women's Initiative for Gender Jus-

---

Solutions to the War in Northern Uganda", Refugee Law Project Working Paper 11, 2004, p. 48.

[98] UN Security Council, Resolution 1593, see *supra* note 55; United Nations Security Council, Resolution 1970, UN Doc. S/RES/1970 (2011), 26 February 2011 (http://www.legal-tools.org/doc/00a45e/).

[99] Patricia Viseur Sellers, "Gender Strategy Is Not a Luxury for International Courts", in *American University Journal of Gender, Social Policy and the Law*, 2009, vol. 17, no. 2, p. 322.

[100] Meredith Tax, "The ICC's Failure to Prosecute Gender Violence Is Symptomatic of the Way Human Rights Advocacy Has Come to Overlook Women", in *Womensphere*, 29 December 2010 .

[101] Susana SáCouto and Katherine Cleary, "Investigation of sexual violence and gender-based crimes at the International Criminal Court", in *American University Journal of Gender, Social Policy and the Law*, 2009, vol. 17, no. 2, p. 341.

[102] ICC, *Prosecutor v. Germain Katanga and Mathieu Ngudjolo Chui*, ICC-01/04-01/07.

[103] ICC Statute, Article 8(2)(b)(xxii), see *supra* note 88.

[104] *Ibid.*, Article 7(1)(g).

[105] ICC, *Prosecutor v. Callixte Mbarushimana*, ICC-01/04-01/10.

[106] ICC Statute, Articles 8(2)(b)(xxii) and 8(2)(e)(vi), see *supra* note 88.

[107] *Ibid.*, Article 7(1)(g).

tice argues that "charges brought against Mbarushimana reflect a new effort by the OTP to charging a wider range of gender-based crimes at the arrest warrant proceedings".[108]

The Office of the Prosecutor opened an investigation on the crimes committed in the Central African Republic in 2007 and singled out mass rape and international sex crimes for prosecution. According to the Office of the Prosecutor,

> [t]he allegations of sexual crimes are detailed and substantiated. The information we have now suggests that the rape of civilians was committed in numbers that cannot be ignored under international law.[109]

In the confirmation hearing by the ICC on the charges of war crimes and crimes against humanity against Jean-Pierre Bemba Gombo, Pre-Trial Chamber II stated that acts of rape were committed as part of the widespread attack directed against the Central African Republic population and that rapes occurred when civilians resisted the looting of their goods by soldiers.[110]

6.4. National Response to International Sex Crimes in the DRC

The rate at which international sex crimes are committed in the DRC is alarming.[111] The number of the people alleged to have been raped is higher than the available data because of the stigmatisation and social exclusion suffered by women who have been experienced sexual violence.[112] An average of 48 women and girls are raped every hour in the DRC. Furthermore, 400,000 females aged 15 to 49 were raped over a 12-month pe-

---

[108] Women's Initiative for Gender Justice, "Gender Report Card of the International Criminal Court 2010", The Hague, November 2010.

[109] ICC, "Prosecutor Opens Investigation in the Central African Republic", 22 May 2007.

[110] ICC, *Prosecutor v. Jean-Pierre Bemba Gombo*, Pre-Trial Chamber, Decision Pursuant to Article 61(7)(a) and (b) of the Rome Statute on the Charges of the Prosecutor Against Jean-Pierre Bemba Gombo, ICC-01/05-01/08, 15 June 2009, para. 188 (http://www.legal-tools.org/doc/07965c/).

[111] Gregory Gordon, "An African Marshall Plan: Changing U.S. Policy to Promote the Rule of Law and Prevent Mass Atrocity in the Democratic Republic of the Congo", in *Fordham International Law Journal*, 2008, vol. 32, no. 5, p. 1362.

[112] Amber Peterman, Tia Palermo and Caryn Bredenkamp, "Estimates and Determinants of Sexual Violence Against Women in the Democratic Republic of Congo", in *American Journal of Public Health*, 2011, vol. 101, no. 6, p. 1060.

riod in 2006 and 2007.[113] The former UN special representative on sexual
violence in conflict, Margot Wallström, believes that the DRC is "the rape
capital of the world".[114] Things are so bad that women are escorted to the
market by UN troops to avoid being raped while on their way there.[115]
The head of the United Nations Stabilisation Mission in the DRC
('MONUSCO'), Roger Meece, stated that about 15,000 women were
raped in 2010 in the country.[116]

To counter this worrisome development, mobile courts have been
established to deal with mass rapes and crimes against civilians committed by soldiers and it has been argued that these courts are having minimum desired impacts.[117] In February 2011, a mobile court in eastern DRC
investigating a case of mass rape and sexual violence sentenced a military
commanding officer, Daniel Kibibi Mutware, to 20 years in jail for crimes
against humanity.[118] He was accused of sending his troops to rape and
loot from a civilian population in eastern DRC. About 49 women testified
against the officer and those indicted with him. The defendants were
charged with crimes against humanity involving rape, false imprisonment,
terrorism and other inhuman acts in violation of the ICC Statute. These
allegations were based on the activities of the accused persons in January
2011 in Fizi, South Kivu.

According to the Avocats Sans Frontières, 89 victims of mass rape
and sexual violence demanded redress before the military court. Furthermore, 58 of the 89 victims who testified also stated that they had been
subjected to arbitrary confinement, the looting of their property and other
forms of inhuman and degrading treatment.[119] Despite the success record-

---

[113] *Ibid.*, pp.1064–65.

[114] "UN Official Calls DR Congo 'rape capital of the world'", in *BBC*, 28 April 2010.

[115] *Ibid.*

[116] "15,000 Rapes in War-torn DR Congo", in *Aljazeera*, 16 October 2010.

[117] Tessa Khan and Jim Wormington, "Mobile Courts in the DRC: Lessons from Development
for International Criminal Justice", Oxford Transitional Justice Research Working Paper Series, 2011; Kelly Askin, "Fizi Diary: Finally, Justice For All?", in *Open Society Foundation
Blog*, 18 February 2011; International Bar Association, "Rebuilding Courts and Trust: An
Assessment of the Needs of the Justice System in the Democratic Republic of Congo", August 2009, p. 37.

[118] "DR Congo Colonel Kibibi Mutware Jailed for Mass Rape", in *BBC*, 21 February 2011.

[119] Avocats Sans Frontières, "Lieutenant-Colonel Mutware (DRC) Sentenced to 20 Years Imprisonment", 27 April 2011.

ed by the mobile courts in the Fizi trial, a word of caution is necessary here. This is not the first time that mobile courts have convicted soldiers on sex-related crimes in the DRC. Some of those who were convicted escaped from prison and no compensation was paid to the victims of the crimes.[120]

International instruments ratified by the DRC apply directly in the country as long as these are not contrary to law and custom.[121] While the Preamble to the revised Constitution acknowledges that the DRC had ratified the ICC Statute, it did not adopt the Statute's definitions of genocide, war crimes and crimes against humanity. Instead the Constitution proposed alternate, unclear definitions.[122] Military courts in DRC have exclusive jurisdiction over genocide, war crimes and crimes against humanity even if the perpetrator is a civilian.[123]

There have been concerns about the military courts and their jurisdiction over civilians as it violates the Principles and Guidelines on the Right to a Fair Trial and Legal Assistance in Africa.[124] Though international treaties ratified by the DRC apply directly, it should be stated that some provisions of the ICC Statute are not self-executing and will require some form of implementation. For example, there is a need to specify which government agency will be responsible for co-operation between the ICC and the DRC government.[125]

---

[120] Avocats Sans Frontières, "Case Study: The Application of the Rome Statute of the International Criminal Court by the Courts of the Democratic Republic of Congo", 2009.

[121] Constitution de la République Démocratique du Congo, 18 February 2006, Articles 153 and 215 (http://www.legal-tools.org/doc/c9a8c6/).

[122] Mima Adjami and Guy Mushiata, "Democratic Republic of Congo: Impact of the Rome Statute and the International Criminal Court", International Center for Transitional Justice Briefing Paper, The Rome Statute Review Conference, Kampala, June 2010.

[123] International Center for Transitional Justice, "The Democratic Republic of Congo Must Adopt the Rome Statute Implementation Law", April 2010.

[124] African Union, Principles and Guidelines on the Right to a Fair Trial and Legal Assistance in Africa, adopted 29 May 2003, Principle L(c); Marcel Koso, "The Democratic Republic of Congo: Military Justice and Human Rights: An Urgent Need to Complete Reforms", Open Society Initiative for Southern Africa, 2009.

[125] ICC Statute, Part 9, "International Cooperation and Judicial Assistance", see *supra* note 88.

6.5. The Impact of the United Nations Security Council Resolutions

The UN Security Council has tried to assert its relevance in combating international crimes and sexual violence during conflicts. Its intervention is not limited to the establishment of the international tribunals. In relation to the protection of women during armed conflicts, the Security Council has helped to strengthen international humanitarian law. It has also promoted women as stakeholders in conflict prevention and resolution efforts.[126] The Security Council had adopted several resolutions aimed at protecting the rights of women during armed conflicts. Resolutions 1325 (2000), 1820 (2008) and 1888 (2009) are discussed to highlight the experiences of women during armed conflicts and how the resolutions have been used to combat international sex crimes.

Security Council resolution 1325 was adopted in 2000 to empower women in relation to issues of conflict prevention, resolution and reducing gender-based violence through mainstreaming gender-specific concerns in peace and security policy considerations.[127] In furtherance of its intended objectives, the resolution "[r]ecognize[d] that an understanding of the impact of armed conflict on women and girls, effective institutional arrangements to guarantee their protection and full participation in the peace process can significantly contribute to the maintenance and promotion of international peace and security".[128] The resolution also called on all parties to armed conflicts to take special measures to protect women and girls from gender-based violence, particularly rape and other forms of sexual abuse, and all other forms of violence in situations of armed conflict.[129] The resolution emphasised the responsibility of all states to put an end to impunity and to prosecute those responsible for genocide, crimes against humanity, war crimes including those relating to sexual violence against

---

[126] Alain Guy Tachou-Sipowo, "The Security Council on Women in War: Between Peacebuilding and Humanitarian Protection", in *International Review of the Red Cross*, 2010, vol. 92, no. 877, p. 207.

[127] Amy Barrow, "UN Security Council Resolutions 1325 and 1820: Constructing Gender in Armed Conflict and International Humanitarian Law", in *International Review of the Red Cross*, 2010, vol. 92, no. 877, p. 229.

[128] United Nations Security Council, Resolution 1325, UN Doc. S/RES/1325 (2000), 31 October 2000, Preamble (http://www.legal-tools.org/doc/ce43ee/).

[129] *Ibid.*, Para 10.

women and girls. It therefore stressed the need to exclude these crimes, where feasible from amnesty provisions.[130]

There have been criticisms of the Security Council resolutions regarding their content in relation to international sex crimes. Maria Butler argues that most times, Security Council resolutions address issues relating to protection and prosecution while neglecting prevention strategies, which should be a major component of any Security Council intervention to maintain international peace and security.[131]

Resolution 1820 of 2008 is focused principally on sexual violence in armed conflicts.[132] It strengthens the understanding of international sex crimes beyond the existing provisions of the Geneva Conventions.[133] The resolution acknowledges that sexual violence can be used as "a tactic of war in order to deliberately target civilians or as a part of a widespread or systematic attack against civilian populations".[134] It states that sexual violence can significantly exacerbate situations of armed conflict and may impede the restoration of international peace and security.[135] The Security Council also states that it would take effective steps to prevent and respond to acts of sexual violence by adopting appropriate steps to address widespread or systematic sexual violence.[136]

Resolution 1820 also notes that rape and other forms of sexual violence can constitute war crime, crime against humanity, or genocide.[137] The resolution calls on member states of the UN to exclude sexual violence crimes from amnesty provisions during conflict resolution processes.[138] The resolution reiterates the obligations of UN member states in

---

[130] *Ibid.*, Para 11.

[131] Maria Butler *et al.*, "Women, Peace and Security Handbook: Compilation and Analysis of United Nations Security Council Resolution Language 2000–2010" in *Peace Women Project of Women's International League for Peace and Freedom*, available at http://www.peacewomen.org/assets/file/peacewomen_schandbook_2010.pdf, last accessed on 6 October 2011.

[132] Barrow, 2010, p. 232, *supra* note 127.

[133] *Ibid.*

[134] United Nations Security Council, Resolution 1820, UN Doc. S/RES/1820 (2008), 19 June 2008, para. 1 (http://www.legal-tools.org/doc/298f16/).

[135] *Ibid.*

[136] *Ibid.*

[137] *Ibid.*, para. 4.

[138] *Ibid.*

prosecuting persons responsible for international sex crimes.[139] In addition, resolution 1820 mandates member states to ensure that all victims of sexual violence, particularly women and girls, have equal protection under the law and equal access to justice.[140]

Resolution 1888 (2009) on Women and Peace and Security[141] mandates peacekeeping missions to protect women and girls from sexual violence during armed conflict. In the Preamble of the resolution, the Security Council acknowledges the ineffective resolutions it had passed in the past demanding a cessation of sexual violence against women during armed conflict.[142]

Despite the resolutions adopted by the Security Council to end international sex crimes during armed conflicts, it appears that there is no dramatic decrease in the prevalence of sexual crimes committed during armed conflicts. This may be as a result of lack of enforcement mechanisms. Alain-Guy Tachou Sipowo argues that the Security Council has gone beyond the bounds of Chapter VII of the UN Charter and adopted resolutions declaratory of international law.[143] He further states that the impact of the resolutions will be limited because thematic resolutions do not impose the same binding obligations as those of decisions made in response to a threat to peace or international security.[144]

6.6. Conclusion

This chapter has shown that women bear the brunt of armed conflicts whether international or non-international most of the time, and are subjected to untold hardships. Some victims and survivors of international sex crimes will no doubt insist on the thematic investigation and prosecution of perpetrators for sexual violence. However, this process may only be effective if the underlying causes of rape and sexual violence during conflicts are addressed and adequately dealt with.

---

[139] *Ibid.*

[140] *Ibid.*

[141] United Nations Security Council, Resolution 1888, UN Doc. S/RES/1888 (2009), 30 September 2009 (http://www.legal-tools.org/doc/874a1a/).

[142] *Ibid.*, Preamble.

[143] Tachou-Sipowo, 2010, p. 217, *supra* note 126.

[144] *Ibid.*

Victims of rape are generally traumatised. Furthermore, they may display some medical conditions such as social withdrawal, uncertainty, anxieties, depression, tensions, anorexia, suicidal moods, or simple disorientation in space and time.[145] The psychological and emotional problems suffered by victims of sexual violence notwithstanding, most of the time, the society sees them as the guilty ones and the perpetrators as the victims. In some instances, the body of the victim or survivor is used to celebrate victory and the subjugation of the enemy.[146]

Addressing the causes of sexual violence will involve confronting stigma and the social exclusion experienced by victims and survivors of international sex crimes. This will be in line with the resolution adopted during the Review Conference of the ICC on the impact of the ICC Statute system on victims and affected communities. The resolution encourages governments, communities and civil organisations at the national and local levels to play an active role in sensitising communities on the rights of victims especially victims of sexual violence in accordance with the ICC Statute.[147] Furthermore the populace is required to speak out against the marginalisation and stigmatisation of victims and survivors by assisting them in their social reintegration process and by their participation in consultations, and to combat a culture of impunity for these crimes.[148]

Care should also be taken to avoid the further stigmatisation of victims and survivors of sexual crimes through thematic prosecution as it may reinforce existing prejudices and limitations placed on women if we see sexual violence as purely a women's tragedy. The need for accountability for international sex crimes should be pursued with vigour, but

---

[145] Martina Belić and Vesna Kesić, "Interim Report No. 2", Center for Women War Victims, Zagreb, August 1993–February 1994.

[146] Amanda Beltz, "Prosecuting Rape in International Criminal Trials: The Need to Balance Victims' Rights with the Rights of the Accused", in *St. John's Journal of Legal Commentary*, 2008, vol. 23, no. 1, p. 172.

[147] ICC, Assembly of States Parties, Resolution RC/Res.2: The Impact of the Rome Statute System on Victims and Affected Communities, Official Records of the Review Conference of the Rome Statute of the International Criminal Court, Kampala, 31 May–11 June 2010 (http://www.legal-tools.org/doc/de6c31/).

[148] *Ibid.*

women's perception and immediate needs should not be sacrificed on the altar of targeted prosecution of international sex crimes.[149]

During conflicts, women's bodies are seen as strategic battle-grounds.[150] As long as the root causes of these perceptions are not dealt with, thematic prosecution of international sex crimes will likely restigmatise victims and survivors. This is because the underlying causes of international sex crimes will be glossed over in the bid to achieve targeted investigation and prosecution. The reduction and subsequent elimination of incidences of sexual violence should involve the community shifting the blame and stigma from the victim and survivor to the perpetrator of the crime.[151] This will ensure that victims and survivors are given opportunities to regain their lives by reducing their sufferings that are made worse by stigmatisation. Victims and survivors should be consulted in making decisions that affect them directly. It is also important for the UN Security Council to ensure the enforcement of its resolutions and sanctions on sexual violence during conflicts.

Education, empowerment and the opportunity to contribute their own quota to the development of the society should be seen as a good way to help victims and survivors achieve their goals in life. There is a need for the reorientation of the armies and militaries, including those who use private military units. The notion that the body of women can used to celebrate victory or punish those defeated has to be changed. This will require concerted efforts of all involved. Research has shown that not all military units engage in international sex crimes as a reward for soldiers. According to Elisabeth Wood:

> Rape during war is not inevitable. When it occurs, rape is not an unavoidable collateral damage of war. Its victims – men and women of all ages – were not brought down by cross-fire or errant missile. They were intentionally violated; the question then is: Is anyone beyond the immediate perpetrator responsible for the crime? Armed groups – non-state actors

---

[149] Clare McGlynn, "Feminism, Rape and the Search for Justice", in *Oxford Journal of Legal Studies*, 2011, vol. 31, no. 4, p. 13.

[150] UN Office for the Coordination of Humanitarian Affairs, "Our Bodies – Their Battle Ground: Gender-based Violence in Conflict Zones", September 2004.

[151] Judith Lewis Herman, "Justice from the Victim's Perspective", in *Violence Against Women*, 2005, vol. 11, no. 5, p. 585.

as well as state militaries – often effectively limit sexual violence by their members, to exclude sexual violence from their repertoire. The fact that many armed groups do not engage in sexual violence should help to put the stigma of sexual violence on the perpetrators rather than the victims of sexual violence and strengthen accountability for sexual violence.[152]

Reversing the current tide of stigma associated with international sex crimes on victims and survivors, adequate enlightenment, education, empowerment and cultural mobilisation will provide positive developments. According to Susan Brownmiller:

> Rape can be eradicated, not merely controlled or avoided on an individual basis, but the approach must be long-range and cooperative, and must have the understanding and good will of many men as well as women.[153]

This will include mobilisation for attitudinal changes on ideas that reinforce the stigma that victims are responsible for the crimes and women's bodies are battlegrounds to celebrate the conquest of the enemy.

---

[152] Elizabeth Wood, "Sexual Violence during War: Variation and Accountability", in Alette Smeulers and Elies van Sliedregt (eds.), *Collective Crimes and International Criminal Justice: An Interdisciplinary Approach*, Intersentia, Antwerp, 2010, p. 322; Elizabeth Wood, "Armed Groups and Sexual Violence: When Is Wartime Rape Rare?", in *Politics and Society*, 2009, vol. 37, no. 1, p. 153; Wood, 2006, pp. 307–41, see *supra* note 61.

[153] Brownmiller, 1975, p. 404, see *supra* note 24.

7

Thematic Prosecution of Crimes against Children

Susanna Greijer[*]

7.1. Introduction

International criminal justice aims at ending impunity for those who
commit the most serious crimes, but due to factors such as limited resources (both temporal and infrastructural), an important choice must be
made: who should be prosecuted? It is unrealistic to hope or expect (and
perhaps it is even undesirable) that all authors of international crimes be
held accountable in an international court or tribunal. This chapter looks
at the specific choice of the International Criminal Court ('ICC') to try, in
its very first cases, persons for the crimes of recruiting and using children
in armed conflict.

The aim of the chapter is threefold. First, the intention is to shed
light on the reasons that lie behind the prosecutor's choice to prosecute
thematically – that is, to grant particular attention to crimes against children – in the Court's initial case law. It starts by offering a brief overview
of the crimes as such, before raising the question as to whether a specific,
and thus deliberate, strategy lies behind the choice to prosecute thematically, or whether the reasons are merely coincidental.

Second, an important question arises when considering thematic
prosecutions, namely, whether the underlying reasons for choosing to
prosecute thematically are always the same, regardless of whether the focus is on sex crimes or on child recruitment. Part of the chapter therefore
aims at discerning eventual common features that could explain why these
two typologies of crimes have gained such an increased attention within
international judicial bodies.

In conclusion, the chapter seeks to identify eventual reasons that
could justify the choice to prosecute thematically, taking into account the

---

[*] **Susanna Greijer** is a Consultant with ECPAT International and the Council of Europe; and a
Legal Expert on Fundamental Rights and Children's Rights with Brainiact. Since the time of
writing, the author has received a Ph.D. from the Department of Law, European University
Institute, Italy.

potential impact that such prosecutions may have on international justice as a whole.

7.2. Reasons Behind the Choice to Prosecute Crimes against Children

When the decision to prosecute international crimes is taken, some criteria for the selection of cases must necessarily be found. "Sometimes these criteria are legal, rational, regulated and follow elaborated strategies. Other times, they obey no rational rules".[1] Do the selection criteria used to prosecute for crimes against children belong to the first or second of these two assumptions? This section starts with looking at the inclusion of the acts of conscripting, enlisting and using children in armed conflict as war crimes under the ICC Statute, and then move on to examine the reasons to thematically prosecute such crimes in the initial case law of the ICC.

7.2.1. The War Crimes of Conscripting, Enlisting and Using Children under 15 in an Armed Conflict

The ICC Statute represents the first international instrument in which the acts of recruiting and using children in armed conflict are explicitly classified as international crimes and, more precisely, as war crimes.[2] According to Article 8(2)(b), applicable in international armed conflicts, the acts of "[c]onscripting or enlisting children under the age of fifteen years into the national armed forces or using them to participate actively in hostilities" constitute war crimes. Article 8(2)(e), applicable in non-international armed conflicts, contains a prohibition adapted to that context, setting forth that "[c]onscripting or enlisting children under the age of fifteen years into armed forces or groups or using them to participate actively in hostilities" constitute war crimes. Whether carried out in an international armed conflict or in a non-international one, the above-mentioned acts are included as war crimes by the ICC Statute under the category "other seri-

---

[1] Mirna Goransky and Maria Luisa Piqué, "(The Lack of) Criteria for the Selection of Crimes against Humanity Cases: The Experience of Argentina", in Morten Bergsmo (ed.), *Criteria for Prioritizing and Selecting Core International Crimes Cases*, 2nd ed., Torkel Opsahl Academic EPublisher, 2010, p. 91.

[2] Rome Statute of the International Criminal Court, 17 July 1998, in force 1 July 2002, ('ICC Statute') (http://www.legal-tools.org/doc/7b9af9/).

ous violations of the laws and customs" applicable to armed conflict.[3] But, if they had not previously been codified as such, where exactly do these war crimes come from? Did the inclusion of the above-mentioned acts in the ICC Statute represent, as has been suggested, an innovation, and thus a step away from the codification process that the ICC Statute is often identified with?

7.2.1.1. Crimes against Children as War Crimes

The four 1949 Geneva Conventions are silent with regard to the direct involvement of children in armed conflict, but Geneva Convention IV on the protection of civilians makes a number of important references to children and their protection.[4] On the other hand, the two 1977 Additional Protocols I and II to the Geneva Conventions are perfectly explicit in their prohibition of the acts of recruiting or using children under the age of 15 in armed conflict.[5] Such acts are not, however, considered by these instruments as "grave breaches".

Nevertheless, while it is true that the Geneva Conventions and Additional Protocol I make a distinction between grave breaches and "other" violations, and that only grave breaches are considered as war crimes,[6] it is important to recall that "grave beaches of those instruments are war crimes of gravity, but do not exhaust that concept".[7] Moreover, in 1977,

---

[3] *Ibid.*, Article 8(2)(b) and (e).

[4] Geneva Convention IV Relative to the Protection of Civilian Persons in Time of War, 12 August 1949, Articles 14, 17, 23, 24, 38(5), 50, 68, 82, 94, and 132 (http://www.legal-tools.org/doc/d5e260/). Moreover, Geneva Convention IV, Article 51 states: "The Occupying Power may not compel protected persons to serve in its armed or auxiliary forces. No pressure or propaganda which aims at securing voluntary enlistment is permitted".

[5] Protocol Additional to the Geneva Conventions of 12 August 1949, and relating to the Protection of Victims of International Armed Conflicts ('Additional Protocol I'), 8 June 1977, Article 77(2) on the Protection of Children (http://www.legal-tools.org/doc/d9328a/); and Protocol Additional to the Geneva Conventions of 12 August 1949, and relating to the Protection of Victims of Non-International Armed Conflicts ('Additional Protocol II'), 7 December 1978, Article 4(3) on Fundamental Guarantees (http://www.legal-tools.org/doc/fd14c4/).

[6] Additional Protocol I, Article 85(5), see *supra* note 5.

[7] G.I.A.D. Draper, *The Implementation and Enforcement of the Geneva Conventions of 1949 and of the two Additional Protocols of 1978*, The Hague Academy of International Law, Sijthoff & Noordhoff, Alphen aan den Rijn, 1980, p. 33.

---

an explicit obligation already existed upon states to react against *all* breaches. Indeed, Article 86(1) of Additional Protocol I sets forth that:

> [t]he High Contracting Parties and the Parties to the conflict shall repress grave breaches, and take measures necessary to suppress all other breaches, of the Conventions or of this Protocol [...].

Nothing thus prevents a state from enacting penal measures against breaches of Additional Protocol I, whether these are of a grave nature or not.

Additional Protocol II does not make any distinction between grave or "other" breaches. Furthermore, it remains less detailed with regard to the repression of breaches. Nevertheless, considering the existence of an apposite Article regarding penal prosecutions[8] does, at the very least, not exclude such action.

Between the Additional Protocols and the adoption of the ICC Statute in 1998, one major international law instrument containing provisions relative to children and armed conflict was adopted. The 1989 Convention on the Rights of the Child,[9] the most comprehensive international instrument on children's rights, repeats almost to the letter what Additional Protocol I had already established, illustrating the close relationship between international humanitarian law and international human rights law.[10] In its Article 38, the Convention on the Rights of the Child prohibits the recruitment and use of children under the age of 15 in armed conflict[11] and recalls the obligations of states to comply with their obligations under international humanitarian law relative to children. This Article should also be read in the light of Article 4 of the Convention on the Rights of the Child, which sets forth that "States Parties shall undertake all appropriate legislative, administrative, and other measures for the implementation of

---

8   Additional Protocol II, Article 6 on penal prosecutions, see *supra* note 5.

9   United Nations General Assembly, Convention on the Rights of the Child, UN Doc. A/RES/44/25, 20 November 1989 (http://www.legal-tools.org/doc/f48f9e/).

10   United Nations General Assembly, Promotion and Protection of the Rights of Children: Impact of Armed Conflict on Children, Note by the Secretary-General, , UN Doc. A/51/306, 26 August 1996, para. 228; Ann Sheppard, "Child Soldiers: Is the Optional Protocol Evidence of an Emerging 'Straight-18' Consensus?", in *International Journal of Children's Rights*, 2000, vol. 8, p. 42.

11   The Convention on the Rights of the Child makes no distinction between armed conflicts of an international or non-international nature.

---

the rights recognized in the present Convention". The Convention on the Rights of the Child is the most ratified human rights treaty in the world, and the overwhelming support for its provisions as well as the extended practice of state reporting and monitoring on children's rights indicate that this instrument today belongs to customary international law.

In addition to this quasi-universal instrument, an important regional treaty was adopted in 1990 with regard to children. The African Charter on the Rights and the Welfare of the Child establishes, first of all, that a child is any human being under the age of 18 years.[12] Furthermore, the Charter sets forth that states shall "take all necessary measures to ensure that no child shall take a direct part in hostilities and refrain in particular, from recruiting any child".[13]

A practical example of actions aimed at implementing the prohibition to recruit and use children in armed conflict can be taken from the United Nations Security Council that, in 1998, decided to include this issue on its agenda.[14] The issue was soon considered a threat against international peace and security, and eight binding resolutions and several presidential statements have so far been adopted, condemning the practice and calling for a stronger international response against it.[15] Moreover, a

---

[12] Organisation of African Unity, African Charter on the Rights and Welfare of the Child, doc. CAB/LEG/249/49, 1 July 1990, Article 2 (http://www.legal-tools.org/doc/be2c54/).

[13] *Ibid.*, Article 22(2).

[14] The first step in the United Nations Security Council's involvement in the issue of children and armed conflict came as a Presidential Statement condemning the targeting of children in armed conflict, UN Doc. S/PRST/1998/18, 29 June 1998.

[15] United Nations Security Council, Resolution 1261, UN Doc. S/RES/1261 (1999), 25 August 1999 (http://www.legal-tools.org/doc/47dd5d/); United Nations Security Council, Resolution 1314, UN Doc. S/RES/1314 (2000), 11 August 2000 (http://www.legal-tools.org/doc/b9f3e1/); United Nations Security Council, Resolution 1379, UN Doc. S/RES/1379 (2001), 20 November 2001 (http://www.legal-tools.org/doc/316310/); United Nations Security Council, Resolution 1460, UN Doc. S/RES/1460 (2003) (http://www.legal-tools.org/doc/e1d228/); United Nations Security Council, Resolution 1539, UN Doc. S/RES/1539 (2004), 22 April 2004 (http://www.legal-tools.org/doc/bc52a5/); United Nations Security Council, Resolution 1612, UN Doc. S/RES/1612 (2005), 26 July 2005 (http://www.legal-tools.org/doc/807dd5/); United Nations Security Council, Resolution 1882, UN Doc. S/RES/1882 (2009), 4 August 2009 (http://www.legal-tools.org/doc/e6a8db/); United Nations Security Council, Resolution 1998, UN Doc. S/RES/1998 (2011), 12 July 2011 (http://www.legal-tools.org/doc/948257/); and Presidential Statements: UN Doc. S/PRST/1998/18, UN Doc. S/PRST/2006/33, UN Doc. S/PRST/2008/6, UN Doc. S/PRST/2008/28, UN Doc. S/PRST/2009/9, and UN Doc. S/PRST/2010/10.

---

specific Working Group on Children and Armed Conflict has been created under the Security Council.[16]

The Convention on the Rights of the Child only refers to state actors, and leaves the issue of non-state actors recruiting children into armed groups outside of the scope of the Convention. This is troubling because, as knowledge has grown stronger regarding the plight of children in war, it has become clear that child recruitment is much more frequent in non-state armed groups than in the armed forces. In the Optional Protocol to the Convention on the Rights of the Child on the Involvement of Children in Armed Conflict ('OPAC'),[17] adopted in 2000, this issue was addressed by imposing an explicit obligation on the states party to the Protocol to take measures against non-state actors who use such practices:

> Armed groups that are distinct from the armed forces of a State should not, under any circumstances, recruit or use in hostilities persons under the age of 18 years.
>
> States Parties shall take all feasible measures to prevent such recruitment and use, including the adoption of legal measures necessary to prohibit and criminalize such practices.[18]

As this article illustrates, the OPAC also raises the age limit for the recruitment and use of persons in armed hostilities. For armed conflicts not of an international character, the prohibition to recruit persons under 18 years of age became absolute with this Protocol. For international armed conflicts, instead, the prohibition is somewhat limited. Articles 1 to 3 of the Protocol establish that children under the age of 18 must not be "compulsorily" recruited into the armed forces of a state, nor take a "direct" part in hostilities. Nevertheless, with regard to voluntary recruitment, the OPAC only requires that states increase the minimum age for voluntary recruitment. The Committee on the Rights of the Child has interpreted this raise in the minimum age for voluntary recruitment as a requirement to be expressed in "years", which results in the new minimum age for

---

[16] UN Security Council, Resolution 1612 (2005), para. 8, see *supra* note 15.

[17] United Nations General Assembly, Optional Protocol to the Convention on the Rights of the Child on the Involvement of Children in Armed Conflict, UN Doc. A/RES/54.263, adopted 25 May 2000, entry into force 12 February 2002 (http://www.legal-tools.org/doc/669fb1/).

[18] *Ibid.*, Articles 4(1)–(2).

voluntary recruitment being that of 16 years of age.[19] States are, however, encouraged to increase the age limit to 18 years for all types of recruitment.[20]

The OPAC was adopted after the ICC Statute, and may perhaps seem of little relevance to the latter. Nevertheless, negotiations had been ongoing for years before the OPAC was finally adopted in 2000. It may therefore serve as an element in arguing that the prohibition of recruitment and use of children under the age of 15 was a customary rule already before the adoption of the ICC Statute, and that such acts were considered crimes for which penal actions should be undertaken. Had that not been the understanding of many states, it seems doubtful that the OPAC, and Article 4 in particular, would have been adopted and supported by 142 states.[21]

Turning instead to international judicial practice, the creation and case law of the International Criminal Tribunals for the former Yugoslavia ('ICTY') and Rwanda ('ICTR') have contributed in a fundamental way to the development of international criminal law. The jurisprudence of these two *ad hoc* tribunals has also contributed to the evolution of customary international law relative to war crimes. One important example is that of sex crimes, such as rape and sexual slavery, which through these two tribunals have been given increased attention and have been treated as crimes of the maximum gravity.

These two tribunals did not, however, have jurisdiction over the crimes of recruiting and using children in armed hostilities.[22] Indeed, the

---

[19] Laura Theytaz Bergman, *Reporting on the OPSC and OPAC: A Guide for Non-Governmental Organizations*, Geneva, NGO Group for the Convention on the Rights of the Child , 2010, p. 2.

[20] The United Nations Committee on the Rights of the Child has recommended that the minimum age for recruitment and use of children in armed conflict be raised to 18 years since the beginning of the 1990s. See for instance 2nd Session, UN Doc. CRC/C/10, 5 October 1992, paras. 68, 77.

[21] The number of states party to the OPAC as of 1 September 2011.

[22] Thus although the abuse of and negative impact on children was massive and widespread in both conflicts. In Rwanda many children under the age of 15 also fought in the war. For more information with regard to children's involvement in the Rwandan genocide, see for instance Roméo Dallaire, *They Fight Like Children, They Die Like Soldiers*, Hutchinson, London, 2010. On the impact of the conflict in former Yugoslavia see for example Council of Europe Resolution 1011 (1993) on the situation of women and children in the former Yugoslavia.

only international court with jurisdiction over the crimes of recruiting and using children in armed conflict, besides the ICC, is the Special Court for Sierra Leone ('SCSL'). The Statute of this hybrid court, which establishes a mixed jurisdiction of both international law applicable in non-international armed conflicts and of Sierra Leonean law, was adopted sub-sequent to the ICC Statute in 2000. The SCSL was created through an agreement between the United Nations and the government of Sierra Leo-ne, in order to grant accountability for those carrying the greatest respon-sibility for the atrocious crimes committed in the country's 11-year civil war – a war largely fought by children. The armed conflict in Sierra Leo-ne counted tens of thousands of children actively involved in the hostili-ties, many of whom were as young as seven at the time of their recruit-ment. Surveys have shown that 70 per cent of ex-combatants were chil-dren at the start of the war, and 72 per cent of all ex-combatants claim to have been forcibly conscripted.[23] The decision to include the crimes of recruiting and using children in armed hostilities in the jurisdiction of the Court was therefore a natural step in the accountability process.

In its May 2004 Decision on Preliminary Motion Based on Lack of Jurisdiction in the case against Hinga Norman,[24] the Appeals Chamber of the SCSL held that the prohibition of the recruitment and use of children in armed conflict was already part of international customary law before 1996, and that these acts constituted an international crime for which in-dividual criminal responsibility should be established.[25] To support this

---

See also Jenny Kuper, *Military Training and Children in Armed Conflict: Law, Policy and Practice*, Martinus Nijhoff Publishers, Leiden, 2005.

[23] Survey by the Post-conflict Reintegration Initiative for Development and Empowerment (PRIDE), a Sierra Leonean non-governmental organisation, assisted by the International Cen-ter for Transitional Justice, cited in Elizabeth M. Evenson, "Truth and Justice in Sierra Leo-ne: Coordination between Commission and Court", in *Columbia Law Review*, 2004, vol. 104, no. 3, p. 762.

[24] Sam Hinga Norman was one of the leaders of the former Civil Defence Forces. He was in-dicted, among other charges, for the crimes of conscripting or enlisting children under the age of 15 years into armed forces or groups or using them to participate actively in hostilities. The case against Hinga Norman was closed before a sentence had been pronounced, due to the death of the accused.

[25] Special Court for Sierra Leone ('SCSL'), *Prosecutor v. Moinina Fofana, Allieu Kondewa and Sam Hinga Norman*, Appeals Chamber, Decision on Preliminary Motion Based on Lack of Jurisdiction (Child Recruitment), SCSL-2004-14-AR72(E), 31 May 2004 ('*Norman* Deci-sion') (http://www.legal-tools.org/doc/28cc4d/ and http://www.legal-tools.org/doc/e0e77c/).

---

position, the Appeals Chamber offered an extensive explanation, basing itself to a great extent on the test established by the ICTY in *Tadić*, to determine whether a breach of international humanitarian law is subject to prosecution and punishment.[26] According to this test, the rule must be part of customary or conventional law and the violation must constitute an infringement of international humanitarian law. The violation must also be serious; that is, breaching a rule that both protects fundamental values and involves serious consequences for the victim. Finally, the violation must entail individual criminal responsibility, under customary or conventional law, of the person committing it. The Court also recalled, again with reference to the ICTY case law,[27] the general principles of *nullum crimen sine lege* and *nulla poena sine lege* as essential elements of all legal systems.[28]

The first part of the challenge, namely whether or not the rule prohibiting child recruitment existed in international (customary) law by 1996 and whether a violation of the rule constituted an infringement of international humanitarian law, could be addressed without much difficulty, and the Appeals Chamber replied to this part rather swiftly. Instead, a much more detailed response was required for the second part, namely whether the violation was of a serious character and entailed individual criminal responsibility at the time of the indictments. In this respect, the Appeals Chamber relied heavily on the *amicus curiae* letters from various human rights organisations, which strongly emphasised the fundamental value of the prohibition to recruit and use children in armed conflict.[29] The Appeals Chamber also recalled:

> [T]he rejection of the use of child soldiers by the international community was widespread by 1994. [...] Citizens of Sierra Leone, and even less, persons in leadership roles, cannot possibly argue that they did not know that recruiting children was a criminal act in violation of international humanitarian law. Child recruitment was criminalized before it was explicitly set out as a criminal prohibition in treaty law and certain-

---

26   *Ibid.*

27   Specifically ICTY, *Prosecutor v. Enver Hadžihasanović et al.*, IT-01-47.

28   *Norman* Decision, para. 25, see *supra* note 25.

29   *Ibid.*

ly by November 1996, the starting point of the time frame relevant to the indictments.[30]

According to the Appeals Chamber, the principles of legality and specificity were upheld.[31] The position that the recruitment and use of children in armed conflict was a crime by the time of the SCSL indictments has also been supported by the UN secretary-general who, in his report on the establishment of the Special Court, emphasised that

> [v]iolations of common article 3 of the Geneva Conventions and of article 4 of Additional Protocol II thereto committed in an armed conflict not of an international character have long been considered customary international law, and in particular since the establishment of the two International Tribunals, have been recognized as customarily entailing the individual criminal responsibility of the accused.[32]

Although the textual definition of recruitment and use of children under 15 in armed conflict as war crimes had not been used prior to the adoption of the ICC Statute, it can be argued that those acts were indeed already considered as crimes under international law, and that their inclusion in the ICC Statute as war crimes was neither a surprise nor a novelty.[33]

7.2.2. The Choice of the Prosecutor of the ICC to Prosecute for War Crimes against Children

The choice of a case can, arguably, be divided into two different phases. The first phase is represented by the choice of a situation; that is, a country in which international crimes have been committed. This choice needs to be made on the basis of factors such as security on the ground, possibilities of witness and victim protection, chances of arrest warrants being carried out, and other practical issues which will determine whether an investigation should be initiated. The prosecutor also has to evaluate the

---

[30] *Ibid.*, paras. 52–53.

[31] *Ibid.*, para. 53.

[32] UN Security Council, Report of the Secretary-General on the Establishment of a Special Court for Sierra Leone, UN Doc. S/2000/915, 4 October 2000, para. 14.

[33] This is also clear from the negotiation process of the ICC Statute, in which states agreed immediately that the crime of recruiting and using children in armed conflict should be included. There was, however, some discussion on the exact wording of the relevant provisions.

"interests of justice" of initiating an investigation in a certain country.[34] The second phase relates to the choice of cases; that is, of which persons to indict and for which crimes. This chapter addresses only the second phase of the choice.

Thematic investigations for the crimes of recruiting and using children in armed conflict have been used by the ICC in the situations of Uganda and the Democratic Republic of Congo ('DRC'), and the two first trials to initiate before the ICC both concern those crimes.[35] What were the reasons or criteria used by the prosecutor to select these particular crimes in the situations of the DRC and Uganda, and to perhaps *not* choose to prosecute for other crimes (equally or more serious, depending on the position one takes)?

The Office of the Prosecutor of the ICC has published certain criteria that it claims to follow in its case selection procedure. First of all, in its policy paper from 2003, the Office declared that it would follow a "two-tiered approach". According to this approach, the prosecutor would choose to prosecute "leaders who bear most responsibility for the crimes", whereas national prosecutions or other means of justice would be encouraged for lower-ranking perpetrators.[36]

7.2.2.1. Assessing Gravity

In its Report on Prosecutorial Strategy from 2006, the Office of the Prosecutor presented a so-called "sequenced approach to selection".[37] This approach meant, according to the prosecutor, that cases would be selected on the basis of gravity. Support for such a strategy can be found in the ICC Statute, in the articles relative to the admissibility of a case, and the initiation of an investigation.[38] The Office of the Prosecutor introduced four criteria which, considered together, would serve to determine the gravity of a case: 1) the scale of the crime; 2) the nature of the crime; 3)

---

[34] ICC Statute, Article 53, see *supra* note 2.

[35] ICC, *Prosecutor v. Thomas Lubanga Dyilo*, ICC-01/04-01/06; and ICC, *Prosecutor v. Germain Katanga and Mathieu Ngudjolo Chui*, ICC-01/04-01/07.

[36] ICC, Office of the Prosecutor, Paper on Some Policy Issues before the Office of the Prosecutor, September 2003 (https://www.legal-tools.org/doc/f53870/pdf/).

[37] ICC, Office of the Prosecutor, Report on Prosecutorial Strategy, 14 September 2006 (https://www.legal-tools.org/doc/6e3bf4/pdf/).

[38] ICC Statute, Articles 17 and 53, see *supra* note 2.

the manner of the crime; and 4) the impact of the crime. These criteria have thereafter been inserted in the Regulations of the Office of the Prosecutor, which entered into force in 2009.[39]

The gravity element in the selection of international court cases has been criticised as subjective and it has been suggested that it should not be used to select cases for prosecution. While there may be some truth in that, it cannot be ignored that this element, and the criteria of which it is composed, has played a determinant role in the case selection of the ICC Prosecutor. Therefore, instead of dismissing this element, it ought to be carefully considered to – if anything – determine its correct interpretation and use.

The first criterion, the scale of the crime, is the most straight-forward one. It requires that numbers of both direct and indirect victims be taken into account, and that temporal and geographical intensity be considered.[40] This criterion, because it looks at time, area, and numbers, represents the most objective of the four.

In the ICC prosecutor's selection of the crimes of recruiting and using children in armed conflict, this criterion undoubtedly played an important role. Both in the conflicts in DRC and in Uganda, the practices of recruiting and using children have been widespread and have involved tens of thousands of children, both boys and girls, some as young as seven years old.[41] The massive scale of these acts shocked the Office of the Prosecutor in its first two investigations, and there was a strong agreement that something had to be done about the rampant impunity that was connected to the crimes.

In the case of Uganda, the Lord's Resistance Army ('LRA') has been active since 1987 and has systematically recruited children, often with the help of heinous rituals,[42] since the beginning of its existence.

---

[39] ICC, Regulations of the Office of the Prosecutor, ICC-BD/05-01-09, entry into force 23 April 2009, Regulation 29(2) (http://www.legal-tools.org/doc/a97226/).

[40] ICC, Policy Paper on Preliminary Examinations, 1 November 2013, para. 62 (http://www.legal-tools.org/doc/acb906/).

[41] See Coalition to Stop the Use of Child Soldiers, *Child Soldiers: Global Report 2004*, Coalition to Stop the Use of Child Soldiers, London, 2004.

[42] Pictures of Ugandan children with lips, noses and ears cut off are not unusual, and the initiation rituals that recruited children had to go through are among the most chocking and repulsive that one can imagine. For more on children in the Ugandan armed groups and forces,

This is a typical pattern in many places where children are involved in armed conflict; their recruitment and use is often large-scale, long-lasting, and systematic.[43] The ICC does not have jurisdiction over crimes occurring before 2002. Nevertheless, if the prosecutor is to take into account the temporal element as an indicator of the gravity of the crimes committed, he should, arguably, look at the entire time span during which the crimes have occurred.

In the DRC, all parties to the armed conflict, including the government armed forces, have been involved in recruiting thousands of children for combat and support roles, as well as for sexual slavery. Following the opening of the ICC investigation in 2004, a number of legislative changes have been made in the DRC in order to increase the protection of children and prevent their recruitment.

The second criterion, the nature of the crime, refers to the specific elements of each offence,[44] and is more complicated to interpret. Based on the argument that most national legal systems prioritise certain kinds of crimes, which involve loss of life or serious violation of physical integrity, it was held that this criterion should be considered in the selection of cases.[45] Such an approach will often result in the automatic prioritisation of crimes involving the victim's death.

In light of the objectives of modern international criminal justice, which seems to have moved away from the classical "punishment as retribution" discourse to endorse a vision that is more directed toward the future, and to deterrent and restorative elements, this implicit hierarchy can be questioned. In a world where contemporary armed conflicts increasingly involve the civilian population, and where the crimes committed are often strategically targeted against vulnerable groups and intended to de-

---

see, for instance, Peter Eichstaedt, *First Kill Your Family: Child Soldiers of Uganda and the Lord's Resistance Army*, Lawrence Hill Books, Chicago, 2009.

[43] See for example, beside Uganda, the conflicts in Sierra Leone, Colombia, Sri Lanka and Myanmar.

[44] ICC, Policy Paper on Preliminary Examinations, see *supra* note 40.

[45] Paul Seils, "The Selection and Prioritization of Cases by the Office of the Prosecutor of the International Criminal Court", in Morten Bergsmo (ed.), *Criteria for Prioritizing and Selecting Core International Crimes Cases*, 2nd ed., Torkel Opsahl Academic EPublisher, 2010, p. 73, *supra* note 1.

prive victims of all human dignity, the gravity criteria of crimes may need to be re-evaluated.

The selection of crimes in international courts should reflect the reality in which sexual slavery and the transformation of young children into slaughter machines – that is, crimes involving a complete deprivation of the victims' value as human beings, or "murder of the soul"[46] – can, depending on the situation, be of greater gravity than the deprivation of lives on a battlefield. This issue seems, at least, worthy of discussion as it raises some important questions as to the objectives of international criminal justice, which are relevant for the interpretation of the gravity element in ICC case selection.

The manner of the crime represents the third criterion of the Office of the Prosecutor to determine gravity. It is intended to encompass especially aggravating factors such as particular cruelty, targeting of especially vulnerable victims, and abuse of authority.[47] Like the first criterion relative to the scale of the crime, it can be applied in a more objective way. Although it may be argued that all of the crimes that are included in the ICC Statute are of particular cruelty, and that this is the very reason why they have been included therein and categorised as international crimes, not all such crimes are committed with the intention to touch the harmless and the vulnerable. To deliberately target those individuals who, in their initial position, could pose no threat to their aggressors indeed seems like an aggravating factor of an act that would already represent a very serious crime had it been committed against enemy combatants.

For what concerns children recruited into armed groups or forces, it seems obvious that this crime is targeting an especially vulnerable group, namely children under the age of 15 years. Furthermore, the exercise of recruiting and using these children, forcing them through military training and to commit crimes – often under life threat and through various forms of physical and sexual abuse – is also a clear case of abuse of authority.

---

46   Binaifer Nowrojee, "'Your Justice is Too Slow': Will the ICTR Fail Rwanda's Rape Victims?", United Nations Research Institute for Social Development, Occasional Paper 10, November 2005, p. 1.

47   ICC, Policy Paper on Preliminary Examinations, see *supra* note 40.

Whether particular cruelty is used is, arguably, a more subjective matter, which necessitates a case-to-case evaluation.[48]

Lastly, the fourth criterion for gravity is the impact of the crime. Impact can arguably be seen in two ways in this context. First, impact can be seen as the deterrent effect that the prosecution of certain crimes may have.[49] However, one of the main purposes of international prosecutions in general is to deter would-be perpetrators from committing international crimes.[50] Second, certain crimes can cause an extremely widespread and profound negative impact on the civilian population and/or on a society at large,[51] and may therefore be granted priority in the crime selection process. Again, this criterion is subjective and depends, for instance, on whether short-term or long-term impact is considered. If impact is seen as something immediate, the loss of life may seem of the utmost gravity. However, if long-term impact is favoured, such impact will depend on its effects on the post-conflict situation of a country and that country's chances to peace and reconciliation.

Certainly, transforming tens of thousands of children into weapons of war instead of sending them to school has anything but a positive long-term impact on a (post-conflict) society that needs to get back on its feet and create a lasting peace.

The Office of the Prosecutor's criteria for assessing gravity could open up a new way of crime selection, which, if rightly used, may better reflect the reality of armed conflicts and mass atrocities of today. Combined with a gender-sensitive and child-friendly structure and *modus operandi*, the potential of the ICC to represent a new international criminal justice, which contributes to ending impunity and empowers women and children to take the future in their hands, is huge.

---

[48] There is, in my view, no doubt that abducting a child and forcing him or her to kill and commit other heinous crimes, as well as subjecting him or her to physical and/or sexual abuse, sometimes for years, is beyond cruel treatment; it is denying that child to be human.

[49] Seils, 2010, p. 75, see *supra* note 45.

[50] Andrew Altman and Christopher Heath Wellman, *A Liberal Theory of International Justice*, Oxford University Press, Oxford, 2009, p. 90. The importance of deterrence has also been noted by the *ad hoc* tribunals for the former Yugoslavia and Rwanda, which in several cases highlighted this factor.

[51] ICC, Policy Paper on Preliminary Examinations, para. 70(d), see *supra* note 40.

7.2.2.2. The Case of *Prosecutor v. Thomas Lubanga Dyilo*

At the beginning of 2006, the Office of the Prosecutor decided to issue a warrant of arrest for Thomas Lubanga Dyilo – leader of the rebel group Union des patriotes congolais ('UPC', Union of Congolese Patriots) – for the war crimes of conscripting, enlisting and using children in armed conflict,[52] and brought no charges in relation to other crimes that were allegedly committed in the region and by Lubanga himself, such as killings or rapes. At that time, the two prosecutorial strategies referred to above had not yet been issued and only the 2003 policy paper, in which no particular interest in crimes for children was manifested and no reference to gravity was made, existed. To what extent did the course of events influence the Office of the Prosecutor's prosecutorial strategy and not *vice versa*?

While the arrest warrants against five members of the LRA in Uganda that were issued in 2005 contained several charges of crimes against humanity and war crimes, the warrant against Lubanga brought only three charges, related to the enlistment, conscription and use of children in armed conflict. The LRA charges also included, but were not limited to, the forced enlisting of children. Indeed, they reflected a broader picture of the conflict in which a series of crimes, such as sexual slavery and rape, attacks on the civilian population, murder and pillaging, and recruitment and use of children, were committed. The prosecutorial "thematisation" in the Ugandan situation could be seen as a choice to focus on a selection of serious crimes committed in the country, not granting exclusivity to one crime only.

The decision to charge Lubanga only for crimes against children provoked a lot of criticism among civil society organisations, and there was a strong opinion that allegations of killings and sexual violence should have been reflected in the charges.[53] The Office of the Prosecutor has explained its choice by emphasising, first, the seriousness of the crimes contained in the Lubanga indictment. Second, in its application for

---

[52] ICC, *Prosecutor v. Thomas Lubanga Dyilo*, Warrant of Arrest, ICC-01/04-01/06, 10 February 2006 (http://www.legal-tools.org/doc/59846f/).

[53] See for instance Human Rights Watch, who wrote a letter to the ICC prosecutor lamenting the narrow charges. For a short account on the criticism relative to the Lubanga case, see Shiela Vélez, "Victims Raise Their Voice in the Lubanga Case", Aegis Trust, 23 October 2009.

an arrest warrant for Lubanga, the prosecutor asked to leave open the possibility of bringing further charges against the accused.

While the seriousness of such crimes was not discussed, a few points can be made in favour of the decision. As illustrated in section 7.2.1., the history of the approach towards the acts of recruiting and using children in armed conflict shows an increasing determination to put an end to these practices. From their prohibition in the Additional Protocols to the four Geneva Conventions in 1977, to their proscription through the 1989 Convention on the Rights of the Child, and all the way to their inclusion as war crimes in the ICC Statute in 1998, as well as the obligation on states to criminalise such acts in the 2000 Optional Protocol to the Convention on the Rights of the Child, the acts of recruiting and using children in armed conflict have, relatively quickly, gone from being a widespread but little-known practice to representing one of the most serious international crimes. The horrific impact of these acts on hundreds of thousands of children is today widely known.

According to the reports of the Office of the Prosecutor, the decision to focus only on crimes against children was also triggered by another factor; namely, the possible imminent release of Lubanga from DRC custody. At that time of the investigation, the prosecutor was not able to bring charges for other crimes and, instead of risking Lubanga's release, decided to demand his arrest on the basis of the evidence that already existed. The prosecutor thus introduced the concept of the so-called "principle of opportunity".[54]

In addition to this, it has been argued that the prosecutor had to avoid charging Lubanga for the same acts that had led to his arrest in the DRC. This was in order not to violate the complementarity rule, according to which the ICC has jurisdiction only in cases where the state has taken no action or, in case of action, where it has proven unwilling or unable to carry out the investigation/prosecution.[55] In the *Lubanga* case, however, it is doubtful whether this reasoning was necessary. First, the DRC had already made a self-referral to the ICC of its situation,[56] thus granting the

---

[54] Seils, 2010, p. 75, see *supra* note 45.

[55] ICC Statute, Article 17, see *supra* note 2.

[56] See ICC, "Prosecutor Receives Referral of the Situation in the Democratic Republic of Congo", Press Release, ICC-OTP-20040419-50, 19 April 2004.

Court admission to investigate international crimes on its territory. Second, the fact that Lubanga had been held in custody for charges of crimes against humanity for nearly 12 months with no further action taken – and the high possibility that he would have been released without trial at the fulfilment of 12 months in custody – seem to indicate a failure, whether on the grounds of inability or unwillingness, on behalf of the DRC authorities to carry out the investigation on its own. Since no trial was being carried out, or had even been planned, against Lubanga, it seems far-fetched to exclude the Court's jurisdiction for crimes that he had been indicted for in the DRC. Nevertheless, at the time of the ICC arrest of Lubanga, the prosecutor estimated that he had sufficient grounds to indict him for child recruitment only.

Regarding the possibility of bringing further charges against the accused, it is unclear how much effort was made by the Office of the Prosecutor to actually do so. The Office did indicate in its application for an arrest warrant that it wanted to leave open the possibility of bringing further charges.[57] Nevertheless, at a later stage, the Office stated that it would not continue the investigation due to security risks. The chance to bring further charges to the case was thus excluded and, indeed, at the time of the initiation of the trial against Lubanga in 2009, no such amendments had been done.

This leads to a question regarding international criminal proceedings: Can additional charges be brought against a person who has already been indicted for other crimes and, if so, when? The ICC Statute clearly sets forth that the possibility exists for the prosecutor to add or withdraw charges to a case as the investigation process in a country situation advances, as long as this is done prior to the Pre-trial Chamber's hearing on the confirmation of charges.[58] Between this hearing and the commencement of the trial, the prosecutor may also, with the permission of the Pre-trial Chamber, amend the charges, but if the amendment seeks to add further charges a new hearing on the confirmation of those charges must be held.[59] In the Lubanga case, the Pre-Trial Chamber held that the investiga-

---

[57] Seils, 2010, p. 74, see *supra* note 46.
[58] ICC Statute, Article 61(4), see *supra* note 2.
[59] *Ibid.*, Article 61(9).

tion must be completed by the time the confirmation hearing starts, unless there are exceptional circumstances.[60]

Once the trial has commenced, the prosecutor can no longer amend the existing charges or add new ones.[61] This can be done, on the other hand, by the Trial Chamber. Court Regulation 55 entitles, in accordance with the *iura novit curia* principle,[62] the Trial Chamber to change the legal characterisation of facts as long as it does not exceed the facts and circumstances described in the charges and any amendments to the charges. In order to ensure that the rights of the accused are respected, the Trial Chamber may suspend the hearing to allow for an effective preparation of the defence.[63]

Despite the theoretical grounds for an amendment of charges during the trial phase, this possibility was rejected in the case of *Prosecutor v. Lubanga*. The ICC Appeals Chamber reversed a decision by the Trial Chamber to consider amendments of the charges to include crimes of sexual slavery and inhuman or cruel treatment.[64] The victims' representatives had asked for this in view of the massive witness testimony of rape and sexual abuse in Lubanga's militia that was presented before the Trial Chamber. Although the Appeals Chamber recognised that a modification of the legal characterisation of the facts is not necessarily incompatible with general principles of international law (or with the ICC Statute for that matter), it held that the Trial Chamber's reasoning in the Lubanga case was flawed and reversed the decision. The Appeals Chamber held that Regulation 55, and the requirement that the facts and circumstances

---

[60] ICC, *Prosecutor v. Thomas Lubanga Dyilo*, Decision on the Final System of Disclosure and the Establishment of a Timetable, ICC-01/04-01/06-102, 15 May 2006, paras. 130–131 (http://www.legal-tools.org/doc/052848/), cited in Kai Ambos and Dennis Miller, "Structure and Function of the Confirmation Procedure before the ICC from a Comparative Perspective", in *International Criminal Law Review*, 2007, vol. 7, p. 339.

[61] Ambos and Miller, 2007, p. 347, see *supra* note 60.

[62] *Ibid.*, p. 359.

[63] ICC, Regulations of the Court, ICC-BD/01-02-07, 18 December 2007, Regulation 55 on the Authority of the Chamber to modify the legal characterisation of facts (http://www.legal-tools.org/doc/ca2089/). See also ICC Statute, Article 74(2), see *supra* note 2, which sets forth that, in its decisions, the Trial Chamber "shall not exceed the facts and circumstances described in the charges and any amendment to the charges".

[64] See "Lubanga Case: ICC Appeals Chamber Reverses Decision on the Legal Characterisation of the Facts", in *The Hague Justice Portal*, 8 December 2009.

---

described in the charges and any amendments thereto must not be exceed-
ed, had been wrongly interpreted by the Trial Chamber. A wrongful application of this Regulation would risk compromising its compliance with
internationally recognised human rights, as set forth by Article 21(3) of
the ICC Statute.[65]

A similar issue was addressed by the SCSL, which, in the case of
Prosecutor v. Sesay, Kallon and Gbao (the 'RUF case'), allowed for two
instances of amendments of charges. The first was made in February
2004, before the trial commenced, and therefore leaves little to discuss in
terms of procedural issues. Nevertheless, the amended indictment is
noteworthy because it included, for the first time under international law,
the charge of forced marriage as a crime against humanity under the category "other inhumane acts".[66] The opinions among gender advocates regarding this 'new' crime differ widely, and the decision has been seen by
some to stigmatise women instead of achieving the opposite.[67] The accused in the RUF case were found guilty of forced marriage by the Trial
Chamber in its 2009 judgment.[68]

The joint trial against three RUF members commenced in July 2004
and in 2006 a new amendment was made following the Trial Chamber's
decision to partially grant a motion by the prosecutor to do so.[69] However,
the approved amendment was merely a matter of form, and the Chamber
instead rejected what would have been a substantial change. The prosecutor's request was to amend the indictment by changing not the counts
themselves, but the time frame within which the crimes contained in the
charges had been committed. The defence opposed the amendment, hold-

---

[65] ICC, *Prosecutor v. Thomas Lubanga Dyilo*, Appeals Chamber, Judgment on the appeals of
Mr Lubanga Dyilo and the Prosecutor against the Decision of Trial Chamber I of 14 July
2009, ICC-01/04-01/06-T-219-ENG, 8 December 2009 (http://www.legal-
tools.org/doc/40d015/).

[66] Micaela Frulli, "Advancing International Criminal Law: The Special Court for Sierra Leone
Recognizes Forced Marriage as a 'New Crime against Humanity'", in *Journal of International Criminal Justice*, 2008, vol. 6, no. 5, pp. 1012–33.

[67] Tom Perriello and Marieke Wierda, *The Special Court for Sierra Leone under Scrutiny*,
International Center for Transitional Justice, New York, 2006, p. 27.

[68] SCSL, *Prosecutor v. Issa Hassan Sesay, Morris Kallon, Augustine Gbao*, Trial Chamber,
Judgment, SCSL-04-15-T, 2 March 2009 (http://www.legal-tools.org/doc/7f05b7/).

[69] SCSL, 4th Annual Report of the President of the Special Court for Sierra Leone, January
2006 to May 2007, p. 17 (http://www.legal-tools.org/doc/b9d1d2/).

---

ing that it would be prejudicial to the rights of the accused, since it would allow for the introduction of a large number of factual allegations of the crimes.[70]

Like in the Lubanga case before the ICC, the SCSL rejected the possibility of substantially amending the indictment during trial, due to risk of compromising the rights of the accused. In another case, the SCSL Trial Chamber also rejected a motion of amendment of charges before the commencement of the trial. In the case of *Prosecutor v. Hinga Norman, Fofana and Kondewa* ('CDF case'), the prosecution filed a motion asking to add four new counts to the already existing ones. While the Court had already allowed for such amendments in the RUF and the Armed Forces Revolutionary Council ('AFRC') cases, this time it took the opposite decision. According to the Chamber, the request was filed too late, not respecting the imperative of due diligence, and would therefore result in a violation of the defendant's right to a fair and expeditious trial.[71]

If the ICC were to categorically reject all motions for amendments of charges, this would risk putting an extremely high pressure on the Office of the Prosecutor. The prosecutor is supposed to start his cases as soon as possible after an investigation has been initiated, and the expeditious conduct of the proceedings shall be guaranteed. However, there may be situations in which, in the interests of justice, amendments of the legal characterisation of the facts should be seriously considered and permitted. Making it impossible, in practice, to make such amendments once the trial has commenced may increase the risk that very serious crimes go unpunished and that victims are deprived of their right to justice. While the rights of the accused should always be guaranteed in international criminal proceedings, the Court should also, within the framework of the law, carefully evaluate this risk. Depending on the case, it may serve justice better to amend the legal characterisation of facts, temporarily halting the

---

[70] SCSL, *Prosecutor v. Issa Hassan Sesay, Morris Kallon, Augustine Gbao*, Trial Chamber, Decision on Prosecution Application for Leave to Amend the Indictment, SCSL-2004-15, 31 July 2006 (http://www.legal-tools.org/doc/f7ab29/).

[71] SCSL, *Prosecutor v. Sam Hinga Norman, Moinina Fofana, Allieu Kondewa*, Trial Chamber, Decision on Prosecution Request for Leave to Amend the Indictment, SCSL-04-14-PT, 20 May 2004 (http://www.legal-tools.org/doc/41f3b3/ and http://www.legal-tools.org/doc/15ca04/).

hearings in order for the accused to have an adequate chance to prepare his or her defence.

In the case of *Prosecutor v. Lubanga*, the many girls who were abducted both for purposes of use in the armed conflict and of sexual slavery will never get any recognition (at least not through the ICC) of the atrocious sex crimes that Lubanga and his men committed against them, but 'only' for the crimes of which both boys and girls fell victims; that is, the recruitment and use of children in armed conflict.[72] Nevertheless, if the rights of the accused could not be guaranteed, the Appeals Chamber took the right decision to reject the amendment of charges. Considering the particularities relative to the Lubanga case, and the prosecutorial strategy that is reflected in the other cases of the ICC, it seems fair to say that the choice to focus exclusively on crimes against children is not a deliberate strategy of the Office of the Prosecutor. Rather, the circumstances surrounding the case were determinant for the way it was shaped. The Office indicated, in its prosecutorial strategy of both 2006 and 2009, that it would pay particular attention to crimes against children, without further specifying what this means.[73] Nevertheless, at no point has the Office of the Prosecutor manifested the intention to focus exclusively on those crimes, while leaving other serious crimes unpunished. Indeed, the indictments of the other cases of the ICC that involve crimes against children also contain several other charges.

7.3. Thematic Prosecution of Sex Crimes and Crimes against Children: Two Crimes, One Approach?

At the ICC, both crimes against children and sex crimes are given special importance. But the thematic investigation and prosecution of sex crimes started much earlier through the case law of the ICTY and ICTR, which were created in 1993 and 1994 respectively.[74] This section discusses the

---

[72] It should be noted that, although to a lesser extent, boys also fall victim of sex crimes.

[73] ICC, Office of the Prosecutor, Report on Prosecutorial Strategy, see *supra* note 37; and ICC, Office of the Prosecutor, Prosecutorial Strategy 2009–2012, 1 February 2010 (http://www.legal-tools.org/doc/6ed914/).

[74] The ICTY was established by the UN Security Council, Resolution 827, UN Doc. S/RES/827 (1993), 25 May 1993 (http://www.legal-tools.org/doc/dc079b/); the ICTR by UN Security Council, Resolution 955, UN Doc. S/RES/955 (1994), 8 November 1994 (http://www.legal-tools.org/doc/f5ef47/).

attention paid to these two types of crimes in international criminal justice and examine whether there are (or should be) similarities in the approach toward them.

7.3.1. Evolution of the Crimes

Child recruitment and sexual violence have been frequent in armed conflicts since far back in history, but these practices have been considered differently in different time periods. Rape, for instance, was seen both as a property crime and as a crime against the honour of the husband or the family before being considered as a crime against women or a 'gender crime'.

The reactions against these practices have evolved gradually during the twentieth century, with the rise of human rights law and the adoption of international (legal) instruments aiming at protecting women and children.[75] In international humanitarian law, the Geneva Conventions and their Additional Protocols establish a special protection for women and children, defining them as protected persons. These instruments also prohibit (some forms of) sexual violence and child recruitment. Geneva Convention IV and the Additional Protocols set forth that women shall be the object of special respect and shall be protected in particular against rape, enforced prostitution and any other form of indecent assault.[76] Such acts are not defined by these instruments as "grave breaches" (although inhuman treatment is, which could arguably include sexual violence), but states nevertheless had the obligation to take measures to end such viola-

---

[75] Examples of such instruments are: United Nations General Assembly, Universal Declaration for Human Rights, 10 December 1948 (http://www.legal-tools.org/doc/de5d83/); UN General Assembly, International Covenant on Civil and Political Rights, 16 December 1966 (http://www.legal-tools.org/doc/2838f3/); United Nations General Assembly, International Covenant on Economic, Social and Cultural Rights, 16 December 1966 (http://www.legal-tools.org/doc/06b87e/); United Nations General Assembly, Resolution 3318, Declaration on the Protection of Women and Children in Emergency and Armed Conflict, UN Doc. A/RES/3314(XXIX), 14 December 1974 (http://www.legal-tools.org/doc/752c30/); United Nations General Assembly, Convention for the Elimination of the Discrimination against Women ('CEDAW'), 18 December 1979 (http://www.legal-tools.org/doc/6dc4e4/); Convention on the Rights of the Child, see *supra* note 9; Optional Protocol on the Involvement of Children in Armed Conflict, see *supra* note 17.

[76] Geneva Convention IV, Article 27, see *supra* note 4; Additional Protocol I, Article 76, see *supra* note 5; and Additional Protocol II, Article 4(2), see *supra* note 5.

tions.[77] As mentioned above, Geneva Convention IV also establishes special protection for children under 15, and the Additional Protocols explicitly prohibit the recruitment and use of children under the age of 15 in both international and non-international armed conflicts.[78] Again, such acts are not defined by these instruments as "grave breaches".

From the adoption of the Additional Protocols, international criminal law has developed greatly and today sexual violence and child recruitment are international crimes under international law. Rape and sexual violence were codified as international crimes much earlier than child recruitment, although initially in a limited manner. The wars in the former Yugoslavia and in Rwanda were shocking in terms of the atrocities committed against women and girls of all ages and this was one of the reasons why the UN Security Council decided to establish the tribunals for these two countries. The ICTY had, explicitly, jurisdiction only over the crime of rape.[79] Nevertheless, the term 'rape' has been broadly interpreted to encompass other forms of sexual assault such as enforced prostitution.[80] The ICTR followed in the footsteps of the ICTY, and was granted jurisdiction over the same types of crimes as the former. Based upon the evidence of widespread and systematic rape and other sexual violence that emerged throughout the investigations of the Office of the Prosecutor, the prosecutor decided to consider this specific category of crimes for prosecution. The first international case regarding sex crimes, in which rape was defined, comes from the ICTR: the *Akayesu* case.

In the ICC Statute, sex crimes are defined in a far more detailed way, which better reflects the many facets of sexual violence. These crimes are constituted by acts of rape, sexual slavery, enforced prostitu-

---

[77] Geneva Convention IV, Article 146, see *supra* note 4, establishes that "[e]ach High Contracting Party shall take measures necessary for the suppression of all acts contrary to the provisions of the present Convention other than the grave breaches defined in the following Article".

[78] Additional Protocol I, Article 77, see *supra* note 5, and Additional Protocol II, Article 4(3), see *supra* note 5.

[79] United Nations, Statute of the International Criminal Tribunal for the former Yugoslavia, adopted 25 May 1993 by resolution 827, amended 7 July 2009, Article 5(g) ('ICTY Statute') (http://www.legal-tools.org/doc/b4f63b/).

[80] See, for example, UN Security Council, Report of the Secretary-General pursuant to Paragraph 2 of Security Council Resolution 808 (1993), UN Doc. S/25704 and Add. 1, 3 May 1993 (http://www.legal-tools.org/doc/c2640a/).

tion, forced pregnancy, enforced sterilisation, or any other form of sexual violence of comparable gravity or which constitutes a serious violation of the Geneva Conventions.[81] The SCSL also had jurisdiction over sex crimes and, to a great extent, copied its definition of such crimes from the ICC Statute.

With the label 'crimes against children' I refer to the acts of conscripting or enlisting children under 15 years of age into armed groups or forces and/or using them to participate actively in hostilities, whether in an armed conflict of an international or non-international character.[82] In international human rights law, and for those states that have ratified the OPAC, there is a (partial) prohibition to recruit and/or use children under the age of 18 years.[83]

While sex crimes can be committed both as crimes against humanity and as war crimes, depending on how they are carried out and the circumstances in which they take place, crimes against children can only amount to war crimes. Thus, to qualify as international crimes these acts must always take place within the context of an armed conflict. As can be seen from the definition of sex crimes – for example, forced pregnancy – sex crimes cover acts that are mainly carried out against women, but there are of course cases in which men, although in a much smaller number, fall victim of, for instance, rape.[84] Obviously, the victim of a sex crime can be a child and, to a striking extent, victims of child recruitment are also victims of sex crimes within those crimes.

This creates a complex picture, in which the sufferer of the crimes is, very often, repeatedly victimised. First, this revictimisation can present itself as a situation in which an individual is subject to several acts of violence, spread out in time, constituting different (international) crimes. Examples of this type of revictimisation can be that of women who have been sexually abused by members of an armed group and flee their home villages, only to be (apart from displaced) sexually abused again, either by members of the same or of another armed group. The frequent destiny of

---

[81] ICC Statute, Article 7(1)(g) relative to crimes against humanity, Article 8(2)(b)(xxii) and 8(2)(e)(vi) relative to war crimes, see *supra* note 2.

[82] *Ibid.*, Article 8(2)(b)(xxvi) and 8(2)(e)(vii) relative to war crimes.

[83] Optional Protocol to the CRC, see *supra* note 17.

[84] See, for example, Christine Chinkin, "Rape and Sexual Abuse of Women in International Law", in *European Journal of International Law*, 1994, vol. 5, no. 1, pp. 326–41.

children who – after having escaped or been demobilised from one armed group – are forced into the armed forces or into an enemy group, or even re-recruited into the same group they had first ran away from, represent another such example.

Second, women and children who have been victims of sexual violence or who have been recruited and forced to commit atrocious acts in the context of an armed conflict are often vulnerable to further exploitation in post-conflict settings, deriving from, for instance, the rejection from their husbands or families in the home community.

Third, and most important for the purposes of this chapter, there is often a revictimisation that derives from the very efforts to respond to these crimes. In criminal proceedings, such revictimisation can be found, for instance, when hearings and interrogations are carried out by personnel that do not have any knowledge in gender sensitivity. This was, reportedly, the case in some of the ICTY and ICTR cases.[85]

'Double victimisation' can, arguably, occur for many different crimes and is not necessarily limited to the two types of crimes discussed here. So why is it that a special attention is needed for sex crimes and crimes against children, and how is it justified?[86] First of all, 'classic' wars, that is, military combat between the armed forces of two or more states, have been almost completely supplanted by civil wars, which involve the civilian population to a much larger extent than before.[87] This makes women and children especially vulnerable to victimisation. It is, furthermore, recognised that certain crimes – which strongly undermine the sense of dignity of the victim and include strong elements of shame and humiliation – are particularly hard to have to talk about and to recover from. Indeed, it is no coincidence that rape has been called "murder of the

---

[85] One example of this can be found in Anne-Marie de Brouwer, "Gacumbitsi Judgment", in Göran Sluiter and André Klip (eds.), *Annotated Leading Cases of International Criminal Tribunals: The International Criminal Tribunal for Rwanda 2005–2006*, Intersentia, Antwerp, 2009, pp. 583–94.

[86] Despite the fact that the special focus on sex crimes and on crimes against children surely has a wide range of reasons, for reasons of time and space, only a few of them are discussed here.

[87] Estimates show that up to 75 per cent of victims of today's conflicts are civilians, as opposed to 5 per cent at the beginning of the twentieth century. See Jeanne Ward and Mendy Marsh, "Sexual Violence Against Women and Girls in War and Its Aftermath: Realities, Responses, and Required Resources", Briefing Paper Prepared for the Symposium on Sexual Violence in Conflict and Beyond, Brussels, 21–23 June 2006.

---

soul".[88] As mentioned above, women and children who fall victim of sexual violence and/or recruitment are often vulnerable to further exploitation in post-conflict settings. They are often rejected by their families and home communities, and seen as "tainted" or "haunted by bad spirits", because of what they have been put through or forced to do.[89] Raped women may be abandoned by their husbands and children may be pushed away by families who are ashamed or afraid of them. For those women and children, the only way to survive may be to turn to prostitution or criminal activities.

Even where justice mechanisms are established in a post-conflict setting, women and children are particularly vulnerable to revictimisation. One typical example can be found in the worrying number of accounts of peace keeping officers who have committed rape and other sex crimes against women they were supposedly there to protect,[90] or of security or government officers who have used demobilised children for intelligence purposes or for favours that risk putting them in danger and/or that constitute some form of abuse.[91] But it is not always necessary for a crime to be committed in the post-conflict phase; sometimes the very justice system as such is simply not sufficiently sensitive to protect victims of crimes that involve a strong sense of humiliation. Since the mechanisms to reach justice – whether truth and reconciliation commissions, courts or rehabilitation or reparations programmes – tend to include testimony, witnesses and victims will generally have to tell what they have seen or suffered. For many victims this means reliving their atrocious experiences a second time, and for reasons of shame, traumatisation and fear of reprisals they may be reluctant to talk.[92] In order to attenuate this 'double victimisation', which often involves a strong feeling of degradation and risks further undermining the victim's self-esteem, certain thematic considerations can be made.

---

[88] Nowrojee, 2005, see *supra* note 46.

[89] Eichstaedt, 2009, p. 24, see *supra* note 42.

[90] See, for example, Chinkin, 1994, *supra* note 84.

[91] On the use of child recruits for intelligence purposes, see Coalition to Stop the Use of Child Soldiers, *Child Soldiers Global Report 2008 – Colombia*, Coalition to Stop the Use of Child Soldiers, London, 2008.

[92] UN Commission on Human Rights, Rape and Abuse of Women in the Territory of the Former Yugoslavia, Report of the Secretary-General, UN Doc. E/CN.4/1994/5, 30 June 1993, para. 13.

To thematically prosecute certain crimes does not necessarily mean that such crimes are prioritised over other crimes, which will be left unaddressed, but rather that such crimes are investigated and prosecuted in a thematic way, meaning that methods specific to the acts and the victims are employed. Such specific, or thematic, methods increasingly involve gender aspects – like having female personnel interrogate female victims and ensuring that all personnel working with victims of sex crimes receive training in gender sensitivity and other specifically relevant skills. The same goes for child victims, for whom child friendly procedures are needed. These include having as small a number as possible of persons interrogate a child victim, having child psychologists present, shortening the length of each interrogation, and so on. Special units, with thematic expertise, may be created for these purposes.

The ICC is the first of its kind to have incorporated gender-sensitive and child-friendly considerations in its structure. The Court currently has more than 60 per cent female judges, and many of the judges have experience and/or expertise in gender issues.[93] Moreover, special advisers on gender issues have been appointed, and the Court also envisages work with external experts.[94] The prosecutor has adopted a prosecutorial strategy that involves paying special attention to gender crimes and crimes against children, as well as to investigative methods for such crimes.

A further consideration that has to be made when addressing situations in which the victims of the crimes are, to a high degree, still alive, is the repercussions that they can have on post-conflict societies in the long run. The recovery from these types of crimes is a difficult and lengthy procedure, which does not always result in a full rehabilitation of the victim. Many victims of sex crimes have to live the rest of their lives with irreparable physical damage, or with sexually transmittable diseases that may even kill them. Moreover, the feelings of fear and degradation may persist throughout the women's whole lives and, where rape has been widespread, risk undermining the sense of security and well-being of a whole community.[95] Children who have been forced or convinced to commit atrocities may, depending on the legal system they belong to, be

---

[93] Louise Chappell, "Gender and Judging at the International Criminal Court", in *Politics and Gender*, 2010, vol. 6, no. 3, pp. 484–95.

[94] ICC, Office of the Prosecutor, Prosecutorial Strategy 2009–2012, see *supra* note 73.

[95] Chinkin, 1994, see *supra* note 84.

held accountable for war crimes and imprisoned. Other times they are abandoned by the system and never have the chance to go back to school or to reintegrate into society. Those children know nothing but violence and crime, and the repercussions that this will have on post-conflict societies with high rates of child participation in the armed conflict, risk being massive in the long run.

Finally, the systematic nature characterising sex crimes in recent conflicts has made it imperative to address those crimes firmly. This was the case in the conflict of the former Yugoslavia where the massive, organised and systematic committing of sex crimes became, at least in some parts, an instrument of warfare.[96] Those acts were so obviously targeted against one group of people, that is, women, that they constituted an unacceptable discrimination on the basis of sex, widely banned by both customary and conventional human rights law.[97] Still, in the words of Theodor Meron,

> [i]ndescribable abuse of thousands of women in the territory of former Yugoslavia was needed to shock the international community into re-thinking the prohibition of rape as a crime under the laws of war.[98]

A similar type of pattern, relative to both women and children, could be seen in the civil war of Sierra Leone. This decade-long armed conflict saw tens of thousands of children involved in the fighting, and a huge majority of the children recruited into the RUF were abducted.[99] This group was composed of up to 80 per cent children under the age of 15. In the other factions the percentage of abductions was lower, but the voluntary recruitment of children in those groups seems to correlate with

---

[96] United Nations Security Council, Resolution 820, UN Doc. S/RES/820 (1993), 17 April 1993 (http://www.legal-tools.org/doc/8119b2/).

[97] See, for example, Universal Declaration for Human Rights, see *supra* note 75; International Covenant on Civil and Political Rights, especially Article 4, see *supra* note 75; and CEDAW, Article 1, see *supra* note 75.

[98] Theodor Meron, "Rape as a Crime under International Humanitarian Law", in *American Journal of International Law*, 1994, vol. 87, no. 3, p. 425.

[99] Myriam Denov, *Child Soldiers: Sierra Leone's Revolutionary United Front*, Cambridge University Press, Cambridge, 2010, p. 63.

the higher percentage of displaced children.[100] Thousands of girls were abducted and forced to become 'bush wives' to the soldiers.

This armed conflict – based on power battles that took place far above the heads of the children who were forced to fight it – has resulted in Sierra Leone still being, more than 15 years after the end of the war, one of the least developed countries in the world[101] with a population of a median age of 19 years,[102] and where only about 40 per cent of the population above 15 years of age is literate.[103] We are again in front of a situation in which one group of individuals, more vulnerable than the average population, was directly targeted. This time, however, we are not only in front of a systematic violation used as an instrument of war, but of a systematic violation which involves transforming the victims themselves into weapons of the continued warfare. The distinction may seem irrelevant but can be of great importance in terms of accountability issues. Facing these and other situations of wide-scale abuses, which particularly targeted women and/or children, the international community was forced to react. The reaction has many facets, and ranges from socio-political and humanitarian steps to legal and enforcement measures.

For what concerns sex crimes, the Convention on the Elimination of All Forms of Discrimination against Women, adopted in 1979, brought women into the focus of human rights concerns and prohibits discrimination against women. Furthermore, the United Nations High Commissioner for Refugees has advocated for the needs of women affected by armed conflict, and has developed programmes that especially target women.[104] In 1994, a UN special rapporteur on violence against women was appointed, with the mandate to work for the elimination of all forms of gender-

---

[100] Macartan Humphreys and Jeremy M. Weinstein, "What the Fighters Say: A Survey of Ex-Combatants in Sierra Leone", Center on Globalization and Sustainable Development, Working Paper no. 20, 2004.

[101] Sierra Leone was listed as number 158 out of 169 states in United Nations Development Programme ('UNDP'), *Human Development Report 2010: The Real Wealth of Nations: Pathways to Human Development*, United Nations Development Programme, New York, 2010, pp. 142 ff.

[102] See Central Intelligence Agency, "The World Factbook", 1 May 2017 (https://www.cia.gov/library/publications/the-world-factbook/geos/sl.html).

[103] UNDP, 2010, *supra* note 101.

[104] See, for example, Ward and Marsh, 2006, *supra* note 87.

based violence.[105] UN Security Council resolution 1325, adopted in 2000, addresses the impact of armed conflict on women and calls for – among other things – an increased participation and representation of women in decision-making, an increased attention to the needs of women and girls in armed conflict, and gender perspectives to be taken into account in post-conflict processes and operations.[106]

With regard to the recruitment and use of children in armed conflict, the 1989 adoption of the Convention on the Rights of the Child was a turning point. The decade that followed was filled with initiatives to strengthen the rights and protection of the child, especially in times of armed conflict. A UN special representative for children and armed conflict was appointed, the issue was put on the permanent agenda of the UN Security Council and regarded as a threat to international peace and security, and the OPAC was negotiated and, finally, adopted in 2000. Moreover, the Statutes for the ICC and the SCSL were adopted in 1998 and 2000 respectively, both containing provisions defining the recruitment and use of children in armed conflict as international crimes for which they had the jurisdiction to establish individual criminal responsibility.

7.3.2. International Criminal Law Responses

On the level of international criminal law, the response to the above-mentioned situations resulted in the creation of two *ad hoc* tribunals, ICTY and the ICTR, and one hybrid tribunal, the SCSL. These judicial institutions initiated a path toward international criminal justice for the crimes here discussed, and were soon followed by the first permanent international criminal tribunal, the ICC, which began its activity in 2002.

The ICTY has, throughout its case law, given increasing priority to sex crimes.[107] The ICTY Statute and Rules do not contain a list of case

---

[105] The first special rapporteur was Radhika Coomaraswamy, and she was the UN special representative for children and armed conflict until 2012.

[106] United Nations Security Council, Resolution 1325, UN Doc. S/RES/1325 (2000), 31 October 2000, Preamble (http://www.legal-tools.org/doc/ce43ee/).

[107] Especially noteworthy are the so-called *Foča* cases:

> In June 1996, the first indictment which deal[t] exclusively with sexual violence was issued in relation to events that took place in the municipality of Foca, to the south east of Sarajevo. This indictment allege[d] that when the area was taken over by Serb forces in April

selection criteria and, in the beginning, availability of evidence was a strong factor in deciding who was to be indicted.[108] This, coupled with the fact that the mandate of the Tribunal was very broad,[109] led to many cases against 'low-level' perpetrators – something that several of the judges of the ICTY have strongly criticised. By the end of 1995, certain selection criteria were elaborated by the Office of the Prosecutor and one of them was to take into account the level of responsibility of the accused.[110] After this, a statement by then chief prosecutor Louise Arbour followed, indicating a shift towards a more accused-based prosecutorial strategy. A Presidential Statement from the UN Security Council in 2002 indicated its agreement that the ICTY should focus on individuals in leading positions rather than on low-level perpetrators, whose cases could be transferred to domestic courts.[111] In 2004, this strategy became binding on the tribunal as UN Security Council resolution 1534 established that the prosecutor were to select only such cases for prosecution that targeted persons of the most senior level.[112]

The Statute of the ICTR established the tribunal's jurisdiction over persons responsible for serious violations of international humanitarian law committed in Rwanda and surrounding states in 1994.[113] The prosecutor decided to focus on the most serious violations, and took as a starting

---

1992, many Muslim women were detained in houses, apartments, schools and other buildings, and were subjected to repeated rape by soldiers. [...] women and girls were enslaved in houses run like brothels, where they were also forced to perform domestic work [...].

Extract from Women 2000, "Sexual Violence and Armed Conflict: United Nations Response", United Nations, Division for the Advancement of Women, Department of Economic and Social Affairs, April 1998.

[108] Claudia Angermaier, "Case Selection and Prioritization Criteria in the Work of the International Criminal Tribunal for the Former Yugoslavia", in Morten Bergsmo (ed.), *Criteria for Prioritizing and Selecting Core International Crimes Cases*, 2nd ed., Torkel Opsahl Academic EPublisher, 2010, p. 30.

[109] UN Security Council, Resolution 827, see *supra* note 74, sets forth that the Tribunal shall prosecute persons responsible for serious violations of international humanitarian law committed in the territory of the former Yugoslavia.

[110] Angermaier, 2010, *supra* note 108.

[111] *Ibid.*

[112] UN Security Council, Resolution 1534, UN Doc. S/RES/1534 (2004), 26 May 2004 (http://www.legal-tools.org/doc/4e06ee/).

[113] The ICTR was established by UN Security Council, Resolution 955, see *supra* note 74.

point "the fact that the genocide in Rwanda was a result of a well-planned conspiracy by members of the government in power, the ruling party, the MRND [National Republican Movement for Democracy and Development] and the senior military leadership".[114] Included in the violations under the jurisdiction of the ICTR is the crime of rape[115] and – based upon the evidence of widespread and systematic rape and other sexual violence that emerged throughout the investigations of the Office of the Prosecutor – the prosecutor decided to consider this specific category of crimes for prosecution.[116]

The SCSL is, instead, a court with the mandate to prosecute a very limited number of persons and its statute sets forth that the Special Court shall prosecute "persons who bear the greatest responsibility for serious violations of international humanitarian law".[117] The cases of the special court all contain long lists of crimes covering the atrocities committed during the civil war, but the crimes that drew most attention were the cruel and widespread practices of sexual violence and child recruitment.

The widespread practice to recruit and use children in the Sierra Leonean conflict resulted in a situation where every single case of the Special Court involved those crimes. Thus, in the cases against three leaders of the AFRC, three leaders of the RUF and three leaders of the CDF,[118] the charges included these (and other) crimes. The same was true for the final case before the SCSL, that against Charles Taylor, the former president of Liberia.

The SCSL was the first international court to convict persons for the crimes of recruiting and using children in armed conflict. As illustrated above, the jurisprudence of the SCSL was highly controversial for concluding in 1996 that the acts of recruiting and using children in armed

---

[114] Alex Obote-Odora, "Case Selection and Prioritization Criteria at the International Criminal Tribunal for Rwanda", in Morten Bergsmo (ed.), *Criteria for Prioritizing and Selecting Core International Crimes Cases*, 2nd ed., Torkel Opsahl Academic EPublisher, 2010, p. 56.

[115] United Nations, Statute of the International Criminal Tribunal for Rwanda, adopted 8 November 1994 by resolution 955, Articles 3(g) and 4(e) ('ICTR Statute') (http://www.legal-tools.org/doc/8732d6/).

[116] Obote-Odora, 2010, p. 59, see *supra* note 114.

[117] Statute of the Special Court for Sierra Leone, created 14 August 2000, entry into force 16 January 2002, Article 1 ('SCSL Statute') (http://www.legal-tools.org/doc/aa0e20/).

[118] One of the accused, Sam Hinga Norman, died before the end of the trial.

conflict were crimes entailing individual criminal responsibility under customary international law, when the court's temporal jurisdiction began.

The SCSL was, moreover, the first court to consider "forced marriage" a crime against humanity. This crime is not explicitly included in its statute, but in the AFRC case (*Brima, Kamara, and Kanu*), the Appeals Chamber reversed the Trial Chamber's decision to consider forced marriage only as a form of sexual slavery, and defined it as a separate crime against humanity, punishable under the statute as "other inhumane acts".[119]

The Statute of the SCSL contains a somewhat worrying provision, namely Article 7, which grants the court jurisdiction over persons above the age of 15 years. However, the chief prosecutor of the Special Court stated already at an early stage that he had no intention to indict anyone under the age of eighteen years.[120] Moreover, if read in combination with Article 1 of the Statute, it seems highly unlikely that an indictment of anyone under the age of eighteen would have been possible.[121]

Sex crimes are codified in the ICC Statute both as war crimes and as crimes against humanity, depending on the context in which they take place. They include acts of rape, sexual slavery, enforced prostitution, forced pregnancy, enforced sterilisation, or any other form of sexual violence of comparable gravity (in the case of crimes against humanity) or any other form of sexual violence also constituting a grave breach of the Geneva Conventions (in the case of war crimes committed in an international armed conflict), or any other form of sexual violence also constituting a serious violation of Article 3 common to the four Geneva Conventions (in the case of war crimes committed in a non-international armed conflict).[122]

Crimes against children are, as illustrated in the first part of this section, defined in the ICC Statute as war crimes. Such crimes consist of the acts of conscripting or enlisting children under the age of 15 years into the

---

[119] Frulli, 2008, see *supra* note 66.

[120] Despite the high number of children participating in the Sierra Leone civil war, it is still unlikely that a person of such young age vested a role of supreme command or responsibility.

[121] The restrictive language of the SCSL Statute to prosecute only those "carrying the greatest responsibility" would have made it difficult to include charges against children. Moreover, the Court adopted a very restrictive interpretation of this article.

[122] ICC Statute, Articles 7(1)(g), 8(2)(b)(xxii) and 8(2)(e)(vi), see *supra* note 2.

national armed forces or using them to participate actively in hostilities (in the case of war crimes committed in the context of an international armed conflict) or conscripting or enlisting children under the age of 15 years into armed forces or groups or using them to participate actively in hostilities (in the case of war crimes committed in the context of a non-international armed conflict).[123]

The ICC is the first institution to integrate child and gender considerations within the institutional framework of the Court. Moreover, of the three cases that have so far been initiated before the Court, it is interesting to note that one case focuses exclusively on conscription, enlistment and use of children in armed conflict;[124] one case focuses, to a high degree, on sex crimes;[125] and one case contains charges of both these crimes.[126] Moreover, the case of *Prosecutor v. Bemba* has drawn a lot of attention, because it represents the first international trial in which the sitting judges are all women.

7.3.2.1.   Added Value of Thematic Prosecutions

What is the interest in devoting special attention to sex crimes and crimes against children in international courts? In the jurisprudence of the ICTY and ICTR, the attention granted to sex crimes served the purpose of showing the extreme gravity of such crimes. Before the creation of those two tribunals, rape had been a frequent – but frequently ignored – practice in armed conflict, both as a strategy of ethnic cleansing and to undermine the strength of the men in a community (who would feel that they could not protect their women), and as an easy way of affecting the civilian population in civil wars and causing the greatest harm possible.

---

[123]   *Ibid.*, Articles 8(2)(b)(xxvi) and (vii).

[124]   ICC, *Prosecutor v. Thomas Lubanga Dyilo*, see *supra* note 35.

[125]   International Criminal Court, *Prosecutor v. Jean-Pierre Bemba Gombo*, ICC-01/05-01/08. The charges against Bemba, who is the former vice president of the DRC, indicted by the ICC for crimes committed in the Central African Republic, consist of sex crimes, murder and pillaging.

[126]   ICC, *Prosecutor v. Germain Katanga and Mathieu Ngudjolo Chui*, see *supra* note 35. The charges in this case consist of: using children to participate actively in hostilities, sexual slavery and rape, inhuman treatment, outrages upon personal dignity, directing an attack against the civilian population, wilful killing, pillaging, and destruction of property.

Looking at the case law of the SCSL, it can only be hoped that it too will have served, in the long run, to emphasise the extreme gravity of turning children into weapons of war. The example of Sierra Leone is certainly there to show what a vast destruction a country suffers when such a huge part of its younger generation are actively involved in war, and how long the road to reconstruction is. Hopefully, however, the Court is also there to show that international criminal justice offers a way to fight such violence and that the most important thing is to hold those who recruit children accountable, while the children themselves must be treated mainly as victims in need of help to recover and reintegrate into society.[127]

Today the ICC is up and working and is, it seems, here to stay. Its Statute grants it jurisdiction over the worst forms of sex crimes and over certain forms of recruitment and use of children in armed conflict. As has been illustrated in this chapter, many signs exist to indicate that the Court is taking gender and child issues seriously, and that the Office of the Prosecutor intends to give special attention to crimes against women and children. Indeed, the initial case law of the Court also confirms this.

For the first time, we have an international criminal institution of a permanent character, which is construed in a way as to take into consideration the most vulnerable members of society. Moreover, a fair attempt is made to empower women and to grant gender equality within the functions of the Court. It is easy to imagine that the more women's roles in society are strengthened, the rarer the systematic attacks against women that we have seen – for example, in the former Yugoslavia and in the DRC – will be. This may be especially true for international crimes, which often see high public officials as responsible for the systematic and massive commission of such crimes.

For what concerns children, the importance of rehabilitation and education is fundamental to avoid perpetuating the violence they have suffered and learned how to use. If many children are recruited and taught to fight and use arms and violence, while no sufficient efforts are made to

---

[127] This does not mean that the victims of the crimes that children have committed during an armed conflict should not have a chance to seek reparations for what they have suffered, but rather that such reparations should follow a pattern in which those victims are, just as the child recruits, seen as victims of those persons who are responsible for the war crimes of recruiting and using children in armed conflict (and any eventual other crimes such persons may have committed or ordered).

turn them back into children again, the risks that those kids grow up to become warlords and/or criminals seem infinitely higher. In the clear-sighted words of a Haitian boy: "People see violence, they grow up with it, and they know it. They repeat it".[128] In this sense, the preventative impact that prosecutions can have may be much more important for these types of crimes than for other crimes that are often considered more serious, such as killings.

As this chapter has shown, sexual violence was defined as an international crime several years before child recruitment was. Several examples of this pattern, in which the protection of children follows in the footprints of the protection of women, can be found also in human rights law. The CEDAW, for instance, was adopted in 1979, 10 years before the adoption of the Convention on the Rights of the Child. Before 1998, no international court had ever had jurisdiction over the crimes of recruiting and using children in armed conflict. Thus, the definition of these crimes in the Statutes of the SCSL and ICC reflects customary international law at the time representing the beginning of their temporal jurisdiction (in the case of the SCSL) or at the time of their adoption (the case of the ICC Statute). Since then, the Optional Protocol to the Convention on the Rights of the Child on the involvement of children in armed conflict has been adopted, prohibiting compulsory recruitment and direct participation in hostilities of all children under the age of 18 years. Perhaps with time, just as sex crimes were developed between the creation of the ICTY and the ICC, the definition of crimes against children will develop and protect all children – not only those under the age of 15 – from having to fight the wars of adults.

A difficulty present in the debate on child recruitment, which is non-existent with regard to sex crimes, is the eventual responsibility of the child. Very often, children involved in armed conflicts are seen as perpetrators who should be punished for their acts. This severely undermines the gravity of the crimes committed against those children in the first place, and risks undermining the importance of rehabilitative mechanisms for children who have fallen victims of recruitment. A somewhat far-fetched but interesting comparison in the domain of sex crimes is the

---

[128] Quoted in United Nations General Assembly, Report of the Special Representative of the Secretary-General for Children and Armed Conflict: The Machel Study and the 10-year Strategic Review, UN Doc. A/62/228, 13 August 2007.

discourse on consent. This discourse has for many years undermined the gravity of sex crimes, somehow insinuating that the victims could have consented to the abuse.[129] The same type of questions is asked when facing children who have been used as combatants: what if they volunteered? Does that not change things? What if they were not really forced to commit some of those atrocious acts? What if they even enjoyed it?

This is not the right place to answer these questions. However, a few brief remarks can be made. Indeed, this kind of reasoning exists and is not uncommon. But it is superfluous, and sometimes perhaps even counterproductive, in terms of international peace and justice. It moves the focus away from what is really important and places the emphasis on a secondary issue (how destroyed are these children?) In doing so, it represents yet another example of the revictimisation of a certain group of members of society. By seeking to punish children who have been illegally included in armed groups or forces, we risk diminishing their already thin chances of ever finding their way back to a normal life. It causes their stigmatisation and further alienation from a society that has already let them down once: by not respecting its legal (and moral) obligations and ensuring that those children received the protection they were entitled by law.

7.4. Conclusion: Justifications for Thematic Prosecutions and Their Eventual Impact on Justice

Thematic prosecutions may be a positive step in the evolution of international criminal justice, but the meaning attributed to 'thematic' must be carefully reflected upon. In the case of *Prosecutor v. Lubanga*, a form of 'thematicity' that risks limiting the overall potential of international criminal justice was adopted. Crimes against children were prosecuted, while other equally serious crimes were left unpunished. Nevertheless, as this chapter has attempted to highlight, the exclusive prosecution of Lubanga for the crimes of recruiting and using children in armed conflict did not represent a deliberate strategy of the Office of the Prosecutor. Rather, the context in which the Lubanga investigation unfolded strongly influenced the case against him. Two arguments seem to have influenced the choice to try him solely for crimes against children. First, it is hard to deny that

---

[129] For an interesting article on this, see de Brouwer, 2009, *supra* note 85.

the overwhelming evidence of massive, and often brutal, child recruitment and the gravity of that crime played a role in selecting it for prosecution. Second, there was an important element related to the Court as such and its credibility. Failing to arrest the LRA members indicted in the situation of Uganda, Lubanga needed to be held accountable, even if that would mean prosecuting him for only a fraction of the crimes he may have been responsible for. Risking the disappearance of Lubanga and a possible subsequent failure to arrest him simply was not an option. In this sense, the principle of opportunity was used to its maximum. Although this may not represent an ideal prosecutorial strategy, the fact that it is a unique situation in the Court's developing case law thus far tells us that we should not be too hard on this relatively new and inexperienced institution.

Thematic investigation and prosecution for the crimes of recruiting and using children may increase the focus on children and the gravity of these crimes. This is a positive step towards the establishment of a strong deterrent power, which can contribute to the prevention of this practice. Nevertheless, if prosecuted exclusively, there is a risk of not showing the whole picture of abuses that children often fall victim to while associated with armed groups or forces. If the crimes are not properly contextualised, they risk not being properly understood and therefore not properly addressed by the Court.

Thematic prosecutions should only exceptionally imply that one or only a few crimes are prosecuted, with the remaining crimes granted impunity. In the interest of truth and justice, criminal proceedings should aim at reflecting the reality on the ground. This almost always means considering a range of serious crimes for prosecution. The thematicity should then lie not in the prosecution of some crimes to the exclusion of others but in the development of appropriate institutional capacities to address specific types of crimes properly. Sex crimes and crimes against children are both types of crimes that require a special knowledge and format to ensure that the goals of international criminal justice can be reached. Developing such capacities and efficiently prosecuting those crimes can reinforce the sense of importance accorded to them. This positive effect may spill over into the domestic legal systems of countries in which international crimes take place, and ensure that victims of sex crimes and child recruitment are not subject to revictimisation.

When faced with a situation in which a great number of the victims are survivors, special attention needs to be paid to the restorative potential of international criminal justice. The goal of restorative justice may in some cases justify the choice to prosecute sex crimes and crimes against children, and to invest the necessary resources in order to do so in a way that is sensitive to the particularities of those crimes. While crimes involving killings are universally recognised as crimes of the most serious nature, it seems important to work for an equal recognition of the gravity of sex crimes and crimes against children, which severely affect the future of an already war-torn society and its members. International criminal justice, with the ICC as a main actor, is perhaps the best forum to achieve this.

8

Looking Forward: The Prosecution of
Sex Crimes in National Courts

Paloma Soria Montañez[*]

8.1. Introduction

Historically, rape and other sexual offenses were considered violations of
family honour or male honour. They were seen as private offences and/or
as collateral damage in conflict situations rather than as felonies, such as
murder. Furthermore, depending on the context, gender crimes may lead
to a breakdown or severe trauma not only for the victim but for the whole
community. Such an environment makes it more difficult for victims or
witnesses to talk about these crimes. These and other reasons have contributed to a lack of investigation and prosecution of those felonies, including under international criminal law. As a consequence, they are often
committed with total impunity.[1]

Since the 1990s we have witnessed incredible efforts to increase
awareness about gender crimes and to develop strategies to investigate
and prosecute them in the international arena.[2] These efforts have led to

---

[*] **Paloma Soria Montañez** is an Associate Investigator with the Office of the Prosecutor, International Criminal Court. At the time of writing, she was a staff attorney at Women's Link
Worldwide's Madrid office, specialising in human trafficking, migrant women's rights, intersectional discrimination and international gender crimes. She holds a law degree from the
University of Málaga, Spain, and a Masters degree in International Solidarity Action in Europe from the Carlos III University in Madrid, Spain). She has given several lectures related
to gender and international criminal law, human trafficking and intersectional discrimination,
and authored various essays related to these issues. In 2009, she was a visiting attorney at the
Center for Justice and Accountability in San Francisco, USA, where she worked on integrating a gender perspective into the Center's litigation projects.

[1] Kristen Boon, "Rape and Forced Pregnancy under the ICC Statute: Human Dignity, Autonomy, and Consent", in *Columbia Human Rights Law Review*, 2001, vol. 32, pp. 627–28, stating that despite the prohibition of rape and other acts of sexual violence as international
crimes and their "extensive documentation", these crimes "were designated as moral crimes
and outrages on honor, a classification that tended to focus on perceived violations of the victim's honor or dignity, rather than physical and mental trauma brought about by an assault".

[2] Rhonda Copelon, "Gender Crimes as War Crimes: Integrating Crimes against Women into
International Criminal Law", in *McGill Law Journal*, 2000, vol. 46, no. 3, p. 219; Kelly D.

---

the development of ground-breaking jurisprudence on gender crimes by the international tribunals of the former Yugoslavia and Rwanda. These courts, for the first time, held individuals responsible for gender-based violence and sexual acts – leading to unique progress in the fight against impunity. International criminal tribunals investigated and prosecuted the crimes of rape as torture, rape as a crime against humanity, rape as genocide and rape as a war crime, as well as other gender-based crimes.[3] Furthermore, the prosecution of these crimes in both tribunals led to the inclusion of several gender crimes in the International Criminal Court ('ICC') Statute and the Statute of the Special Court of Sierra Leone ('SCSL'). Such provisions opened the door to the investigation of these crimes by the ICC[4] and some international and hybrid courts, such as the SCSL and the Extraordinary Chambers in the Courts of Cambodia ('ECCC').[5]

Askin, "Prosecuting Wartime Rape and other Gender-related Crimes under International Law: Extraordinary Advances, Enduring Obstacles", in *Berkeley Journal of International Law*, 2003, vol. 21, no. 2, p. 288.

[3] For further acknowledgement in the development of the above-mentioned jurisprudence, see Askin, 2003, *supra* note 2; Anne-Marie L.M. de Brouwer, *Supranational Criminal Prosecution of Sexual Violence: The ICC and the Practice of the ICTY and the ICTR*, Intersentia, Antwerp, 2005, pp. 9–19; Angela M. Banks, *Sexual Violence and International Criminal Law: An Analysis of the Ad Hoc Tribunal's Jurisprudence & the International Criminal Court's Elements of Crimes*, College of William and Mary Law School, 2005.

[4] Dianne Luping, "Investigation and Prosecution of Sexual and Gender-based Crimes before the International Criminal Court", in *Journal of Gender, Social Policy and the Law*, 2009, vol. 17, no. 2, p. 452, stating "the impetus to effectively deal" with gender based crimes and advancements in the relevant law are reflected under the ICC Statute, the Rules of Procedure and Evidence of the Court, Elements of the Crimes, and the work of the Office of the Prosecutor of the ICC in this field.

[5] The Statute of the Special Court for Sierra Leone, created 14 August 2000, entry into force 16 January 2002 ('SCSL Statute') (http://www.legal-tools.org/doc/aa0e20/) includes the crimes of rape, sexual slavery, enforced prostitution, forced pregnancy and any other form of sexual violence as crimes against humanity under Article 2(g). Several gender-based crimes were also included as violations of Article 3 common to the Geneva Conventions and of Additional Protocol II under Article 3(e). The SCSL has ruled in different decisions on the crime of rape as a crime against humanity. In *Prosecutor v. Issa Sesay, Morris Kallon and Augustine Gbao*, the Trial Chamber set an important precedent condemning for the first time in an internationalized Court the crime of forced marriage as a crime against humanity: SCSL, *Prosecutor v. Issa Sesay, Morris Kallon and Augustine Gbao*, Trial Chamber, Judgment, SCSL-04-15, 2 March 2009, paras. 1297, 1301, 1473, 1582 ('*RUF* case') (http://www.legal-tools.org/doc/7f05b7/). The Extraordinary Chambers in the Courts of Cambodia ('ECCC'), created by the Law on the Establishment of the Extraordinary Chambers in the Courts of

---

Importantly, alongside this rising awareness about sex crimes in the international criminal law field, we have also witnessed the development of International human rights Law as well as important jurisprudence from regional courts that enforce the obligation of states to investigate and prosecute these crimes.[6]

As such, we can affirm that states have the obligation to investigate and prosecute sex crimes that constitute genocide, crimes against humanity, war crimes, torture, or other international crimes. This is true for national courts undertaking this type of litigation where crimes that occurred within their own jurisdiction are being prosecuted, as well as for national courts investigating and prosecuting international crimes using the principle of universal jurisdiction.

It is also true that Article 1 of the Statute affirms that the ICC's efforts are to be complementary to the work of national courts, which means that national jurisdictions have priority over international jurisdictions in the fight against impunity. For all of these reasons it is imperative that the international community now focuses on national courts as the logical jurisdictions for prosecuting sex crimes. The international community must

---

Cambodia, 12 February 2001 (http://www.legal-tools.org/doc/b1caed/) for the prosecution of crimes committed during the period of Democratic Kampuchea, includes the crime of rape as Crime against Humanity under Article 5. In 2010 the ECCC convicted in Case 001 the head of the Khmer Rouge for the offence of torture, including one instance of rape as crimes against humanity. ECCC, Trial Chamber, *Prosecutor v. Kaing Guek Eav*, 001-18-07-2007, 26 July 2010 (http://www.legal-tools.org/doc/dbdb62/). In Case 002, *Prosecutor v. Nuon Chea, Khieu Samphan, Ieng Thirith and Ieng Sary*, 002/19-09-2007/ECCC/TC, the co-investigating justice determined that the defendants should be prosecuted for crimes against humanity, including rape. The rape charges stem from the arrangement of forced marriages and forced sexual relations, which are also charged as other inhumane acts.

[6] United Nations ('UN') Security Council resolutions on women, peace and security are examples of the commitment of states to prevent, prosecute and condemn the commission of sex crimes in conflict situations. Thus, United Nations Security Council, Resolution 1325, UN Doc. S/RES/1325 (2000), 31 October 2000, Preamble para. 11 (http://www.legal-tools.org/doc/ce43ee/): "[...] emphasizes the responsibility of all States to put an end to impunity and to prosecute those responsible for genocide, crimes against humanity, war crimes including those relating to sexual violence against women and girls". Further, UN Security Council, Resolution 1820, UN Doc. S/RES/1820 (2008), 19 June 2008, para. 4 (http://www.legal-tools.org/doc/298f16/) and UN Security Council, Resolution 1889,UN Doc. S/RES/1889 (2009), 5 October 2009, para. 3 (http://www.legal-tools.org/doc/d208d7/) stress the need to prosecute those responsible for crimes of rape and other forms of sexual violence which can constitute war crimes, crimes against humanity or constitutive acts with respect to genocide.

rise to the challenge of playing a prominent role in fostering mechanisms to assist states to strengthen their capacities to combat impunity. Meanwhile, states face the challenge of restoring confidence in the rule of law.

Some states are currently litigating human rights violations in national courts. This is an extremely important development in international criminal law as these national prosecutions open this arena for more investigations and prosecutions of international crimes, including gender crimes. On top of that, national courts do not have limited mandates, which allow more people to access justice and provide a unique opportunity to develop new jurisprudence in different countries that can contribute to the punishment of different human rights violations that occur in each context. The work of national courts also allows the prosecution of these crimes in states that have not ratified the ICC Statute, or do not accept the use of universal jurisdiction against them.

Taking all the above-mentioned factors into account, this chapter considers the thematic investigation and prosecution of international sex crimes in national courts from the point of view of a practitioner. In the first part, I present two case studies, on Argentina and Guatemala, focusing on the prosecution of sex crimes in national courts in both countries. I also discuss the option of prosecuting gender-based crimes under the universal jurisdiction principle in Spain. Finally, the chapter presents some proposals and ideas about thematic prosecutions in national courts with the intention of continuing the debate.

8.2. Prosecution of Sex Crimes in National Courts: Cases in Argentina and Guatemala

International courts have promoted and enabled the prosecution of gender crimes and developed important jurisprudence and guidelines regarding how to prosecute these crimes. More importantly, this has allowed for increasing awareness about the importance of considering gender when investigating human rights violations. Furthermore, international human rights law has reinforced the obligation of states to investigate and prosecute gender crimes. Now these efforts must be continued in national courts. Working with national courts will help to consolidate the efforts made in the international arena. It will lead to an increased awareness of the importance of including gender crimes, and it will foster new strategies and jurisprudence to investigate and prosecute sex crimes.

As part of my work as staff attorney at Women's Link Worldwide, an international organisation working to promote gender equality in courts through the use of legal strategies, I have had the opportunity to develop and co-ordinate our work focused on international gender crimes. For a better understanding of the arguments I present here, it is important to offer the definition that we use of international gender crimes. In situations of conflict, detention or any other situations of imprisonment, men and women, girls and boys, may suffer sexual violence. When using the term sexual violence, including rape, we may consider how it was interpreted by the International Criminal Tribunal for Rwanda ('ICTR') in the *Akayesu* case:

> Any act of a sexual nature which is committed on a person under circumstances which are coercive. Sexual violence is not limited to physical invasion of the human body and may include acts which do not involve penetration or even physical contact.[7]

An analysis with a gender perspective of sexual violence requires the consideration of different forms of such violence, the aims with which that violence is used against men and women according to gender roles attributed to them in each context and society, and the person that perpetrates that violence, among other factors. Given all of this, when we talk about international gender crimes we are not referring to a new type of crime, but rather to the manner in which international crimes are interpreted with a gender perspective.

In our work focusing on international gender crimes, Women's Link aims to promote the investigation and prosecution of international gender crimes with a special focus on national courts litigating human rights violations. We also advocate for the consideration of the jurisprudence and legal strategies developed in international courts as examples and tools to promote the prosecution of gender crimes in national courts.

Our work has allowed us to participate in litigation for human rights violations in Argentina, Guatemala and Spain – in this last case through the use of the principle of universal jurisdiction. Based on our experience we can affirm that in most countries litigating human rights violations that

---

[7] International Criminal Tribunal of Rwanda ('ICTR'), *Prosecutor v. Jean-Paul Akayesu*, Trial Chamber, Judgment, ICTR-96-4-T, 2 September 1998, para. 688 (http://www.legal-tools.org/doc/b8d7bd/).

---

occurred in a conflict situation, gender crimes are never or almost never investigated or tried. Yet the importance and interest in the consideration of these crimes is growing and finding its way onto the agenda of the human rights community in national contexts.

8.2.1. Case Study of Argentina: Undertaking the Prosecution of International Sex Crimes in National Courts

In the period from 1976 to 1983 an estimated 30,000 persons "disappeared" under the military dictatorship in Argentina in what is known as the Dirty War. In 2005, more than 20 years after the end of state terrorism, the Supreme Court of Argentina definitively held that the amnesty laws, known as the '*obediencia debida*' and '*punto final*', were unconstitutional and therefore null and void.[8] Today Argentina is one of the few countries in the world that is holding perpetrators of torture and crimes against humanity to account in its own judicial system, in large part due to the efforts of civil society.

As of December 2010, 820 people are being prosecuted, meaning that there is a court order opening a judicial process against a concrete individual. Another 212 people have been prosecuted, and of those 196 have been convicted and 21 acquitted.[9]

---

[8] On 24 August 2004, the Supreme Court of Argentina stated in the case of *Arancibia Clavel, Enrique* that crimes against humanity do not have a statute of limitations. After this decision, the Court stated in the case of *Simón, Julio Héctor* that amnesty laws were unconstitutional, and further denied the effect of any rules that could oppose the advance of processes or the prosecution and conviction of those responsible, or impede ongoing investigations. For detailed information on these processes and the actual prosecution of international crimes in Argentinian courts, see Mirna Goransky and María Luisa Piqué, "(The Lack of) Criteria for the Selection of Crimes Against Humanity Cases: The Case of Argentina", in Morten Bergsmo (ed.), *Criteria for Prioritizing and Selecting Core International Crimes Cases*, Torkel Opsahl Academic EPublisher, Oslo, 2010, pp. 91–105.

[9] Unidad Fiscal de Coordinación y Seguimiento de las causas por violaciones a los Derechos Humanos cometidas durante el terrorismo de Estado, "Informe sobre el estado de las causas por violaciones a los derechos humanos cometidas durante el terrorismo de Estado" Buenos Aires, 2010. With regard to statistics, it is worth noting data from a report analysing the sexual violence elements of the judgments from different international tribunals, with information up to 9 March 2009, stated that of 75 completed cases prosecuted by the International Criminal Tribunal for the former Yugoslavia ('ICTY'), there were 24 in which judgments contain sexual violence findings and/or agreed facts. With regard to the ICTR, of 24 completed cases, there are 13 in which judgments contain sexual violence findings and/or agreed facts. Gabriël H Oosthuizen, *Review of the Sexual Violence Elements of the Judgments of the International*

In 2009, Women's Link had the opportunity to travel to Argentina and meet with attorneys, prosecutors and judges who participate in human rights cases. We found a high interest in the consideration of gender crimes, but a lack of 'visibilisation' and investigation of those crimes in existing litigation.

Nevertheless, in April 2010 the Tribunal Oral en lo Criminal Federal de Santa Fé (Federal Criminal Court of Santa Fé) issued the first decision for the crime of rape constituting torture as a crime against humanity.[10] Two months later, the Tribunal Oral en lo Criminal Federal de Mar del Plata (Federal Criminal Court of Mar del Plata) issued another decision, stating the rapes suffered by women in different detention centres in Argentina during the state terrorism were not isolated or occasional occurrences but systematic practices executed as part of the clandestine plan of repression and extermination, and thus constituted crimes against humanity.[11]

We began to work with some civil society organisations and with the Human Rights Unit of the Prosecutor's Office in Argentina to increase awareness about the occurrence of gender crimes, as well as the mechanisms available in international law for prosecuting them. One of the results of that joint work was the organisation in August of 2010, together with the Center of Legal and Social Studies, and with the support of the Human Rights Unit, of the Seminar "International Criminal Law and Gender in the Context of the Process of Justice for Human Rights Violations Committed during the Military Dictatorship in Argentina". Federal judges, prosecutors and attorneys from different regions of the country attended this seminar that had an important impact both in legal circles and in the media. Since then, Argentinian courts have continued issuing more decisions condemning the crimes of rape as torture and rape as a crime against humanity.[12]

Criminal Tribunal for the Former Yugoslavia, the International Criminal Tribunal for Rwanda, and the Special Court for Sierra Leone in the Light of Security Council Resolution 1820, United Nations, Department of Peacekeeping Operations, New York, 2010.

[10] Tribunal Oral en lo Criminal Federal de Santa Fé, *Barcos, Horacio Américo*, case no. 43/08, Judgment, 19 April 2010, p. 99.

[11] Tribunal Oral en lo Criminal Federal de Mar del Plata, *Molina, Gregorio Rafael*, case no. 2086, Judgment, July 2010, pp. 19–20.

[12] Juzgado Federal no. 1 de Miguel de Tucumán, *Arsenales, Miguel de Azcuénaga CCD*, case no. 443/84, Judgment, 27 December 2010, pp. 171–78; Tribunal Oral en lo Criminal Federal no. 2 de la Ciudad Autónoma de Buenos Aires, *Miara et al.*, case no. 1668 and *Tepedino et*

We continue to work together with the Human Rights Unit and with the Center of Legal and Social Studies, to support the prosecution of gender crimes. One of our collaborations was the creation of a memorandum about the crime of forced abortion, a crime that has never been investigated by international courts.[13]

8.2.2. Case Study of Guatemala: From the Comisión de Esclarecimiento Histórico to the Prosecution of International Crimes

From 1960 to 1996 Guatemala suffered an internal armed conflict that led to the killing, torture and other human rights violations of thousands of people, primarily indigenous Mayans, amounting to genocide. With the signing of the peace agreements in 1996, Guatemala established the Comisión de Esclarecimiento Histórico (Commission for Historical Clarification) sponsored by the United Nations, with the objectives of investigating the facts and human rights violations that took place during the armed conflict, issuing a report, and making recommendations to promote "peace and national harmony in Guatemala".[14] The Commission, while investigating human rights violations, had the opportunity to document many facts of gender violence during the conflict. In the final report one of the chapters focused on sexual violence against women.

Some human rights violations committed during the internal armed conflict have been denounced in the Inter-American system. The Inter-American Court of Human Rights has condemned Guatemala in different cases. In a decision issued on 27 January 2009 in the cases of Myrna Mack Chang, Maritza Urrutia, Masacre Plan de Sánchez, Molina Theissen and Tiu Tojín, all related to human rights violations that occurred during the internal armed conflict, the Court reaffirmed the state's obligation to

---

al., case no. 1673, Judgment, 22 March 2011, pp. 858–69; Juzgado Federal no. 1 de Miguel de Tucumán, *Fernandez Juarez, María Lilia y Herrera, Gustavo Enrique*, case no. 133/05, Judgment, 19 May 2011, pp. 53–68.

[13] For further information on our work, see Women's Link Worldwide (http://www.womenslinkworldwide.org).

[14] Comisión de Esclarecimiento Histórico, *Guatemala: Memoria del silencio*, United Nations Office for Project Services, 1999.

investigate and put an end to the impunity and found that Guatemala still had not satisfied its obligations.[15]

In addition to the regional cases, a few proceedings are taking place in national courts denouncing the crimes committed. Landmark decisions include the 2009 conviction of Felipe Cusanero Coj for the crime of forced disappearance committed against six people, and the 2011 decision convicting four military officers for the crime of genocide involving the massacre in Las Dos Erres. In this last decision, the Court considered that the gender violence committed against women during the massacre caused grave pain and suffering for the victims to this day.

At the moment, some non-governmental organisations litigating before national courts are considering the inclusion of the investigation and prosecution of sex crimes in genocide cases. To this end, Women's Link has filed an expert report in the case against Héctor Mario López Fuentes, recently detained and awaiting trial in Guatemala.

8.2.3. Investigation and Prosecution of Sex Crimes under the Principle of Universal Jurisdiction: Litigation in Spain

States are historically reluctant to prosecute international crimes in national courts and to prosecute their own nationals. This is the reason why, together with international and hybrid courts, some states use the principle of universal jurisdiction to develop a national legal and institutional capacity to investigate and prosecute international crimes committed by foreign citizens in foreign countries in their national courts.[16] Under the principle of universal jurisdiction, any state is empowered to bring to trial persons accused of international crimes, regardless of the place of commission of the crime or the nationality of the author or of the victim.[17]

On 25 January 2008, Women's Link filed the first complaint denouncing a gender-based crime under the principle of universal jurisdic-

---

[15] Inter-American Court of Human Rights, *Bámaca Velásquez v. Guatemala*, Monitoring compliance of provisional measures, Judgment, Series C no. 70, 27 January 2009, para. 23.

[16] Morten Bergsmo, "The Theme of Selection and Prioritization Criteria and Why It Is Relevant", in Morten Bergsmo (ed.), *Criteria for Prioritizing and Selecting Core International Crimes Cases*, Torkel Opsahl Academic EPublisher, Oslo, 2010, pp. 7–8.

[17] Antonio Cassese, *International Criminal Law*, 2nd ed., Oxford University Press, New York, 2008, p. 338.

tion in Spain's Audiencia Nacional (National Court).[18] The National Court is the tribunal that has jurisdiction to investigate and try international crimes that occurred outside Spain. The complaint denounced the crime of rape as torture at the hands of state agents suffered by a Spanish citizen in San Salvador Atenco, Mexico, in 2006. It is known as the 'Atenco case'.

Currently continuing our work with universal jurisdiction cases in Spain, Women's Link is leading a legal strategy to make further progress in the investigation and prosecution of sex crimes in the Guatemala case that is being investigated by Judge Santiago Pedraz Gómez at the Spanish National Court for the crimes of genocide, torture and terrorism.[19] In June 2011, Women's Link filed, for the first time in a universal jurisdiction case pending before the Spanish National Court, an amended complaint in the Guatemala case asking for the investigation and prosecution of gender crimes that took place in Guatemala during the conflict, specifically the crime of rape as torture, and the acts of rape, measures intended to prevent births within the group, and forced displacement as genocide. Furthermore, and also for the first time before the National Court, two expert witnesses testified about gender crimes.[20]

In July 2011, Judge Pedraz issued a historic resolution asking for the prosecution of gender crimes as genocide in order to satisfactorily perform the tribunal's duty to investigate, prosecute and punish international crimes. The judge also stated that the facts regarding the gender crimes

---

[18] Until very recently, the law regulating universal jurisdiction in Spain was one of the most progressive in the world, allowing a very wide interpretation of the concept of universal jurisdiction. Many cases were filed at the Spanish National Court, beginning in 1998. The best known was the arrest of General Augusto Pinochet ordered by Judge Baltasar Garzón. In 2005, the Constitutional Court in Spain interpreted the national law on universal jurisdiction to be "absolute" and thus not requiring any link to Spain in order to file at the Court in that country. There are currently cases before the Spanish National Court regarding Guatemala, Rwanda, Tibet, Israel, El Salvador, and more. Despite all of these prosecutions, before we filed the Atenco complaint, a gender crime had never been brought before this court.

[19] The present project is being implemented together with the Center for Justice and Accountability, USA.

[20] Patricia Viseur Sellers testified about states' responsibility to prosecute gender crimes under international legal norms and according to the relevant international jurisprudence; and María Eugenia Solís, a Guatemalan lawyer expert on gender violence, bore witness to the concrete phenomenon of gender violence against Mayan women during the armed conflict in Guatemala.

---

included in the amended complaint are now integrated into the general facts relating to the crimes of genocide, but nevertheless, it is necessary to charge them as their own crimes so that they do not remain unpunished.[21]

8.2.4. Thematic Investigation and Prosecution of Sex Crimes in National Courts: Some Thoughts to Continue the Debate

As mentioned at the beginning of this chapter, states have a responsibility to prevent, investigate and prosecute perpetrators of international crimes. This mandate includes the prevention, investigation and prosecution of sex crimes, meaning that courts must take into account what happened both to men and women during a particular conflict, how violence was executed in a different way taking into account the role of men and women in the context and society where the crimes occurred, and never assuming that sex crimes or gender crimes only happen to women.

An overview of the situation in national courts shows us that sex crimes are almost never investigated under international criminal law, although increasingly there are these sorts of initiatives. The work in Argentina, Guatemala and Spain allows us to make some observations regarding the thematic investigation and prosecution of international sex crimes in national courts.

The first consideration we must take into account is that the lack of efforts to include sex crimes in existing human rights trials is a missed opportunity. As we all know, the investigation and prosecution of human rights violations requires huge effort, resources, trained judges, prosecutors and attorneys, and viable jurisdictions. Once all these factors are in place allowing for such prosecutions, to exclude gender crimes is, without a doubt, a lost chance.

Taking into account the material and human resources that must be invested in the litigation of human rights violations, we must consider if thematic prosecutions make sense in the context of national courts. Instigating a thematic prosecution in a national court would mean that the investigation and prosecution of other serious crimes may be set aside. Furthermore, in order to justify the legal strategy of thematic prosecution, it would be necessary to be able to explain why some crimes are considered

---

21. Audiencia Nacional de España, *Efrain Rios Montt et al.*, Auto Diligencias Previas 331/1999, Juzgado de Instrucción No. 1, 26 July 2011.

more serious than others. While it is true that in some conflicts there may be evidence that one crime has been committed more commonly that others, it is not productive to rate human rights violations. Thus, justifying investigating some crimes and not others may prove to be highly controversial, including among civil society.

Importantly, integrated prosecution of gender crimes can help raise public awareness not only regarding sex crimes under international law, but also about gender violence in general. Thus, it is desirable that gender crimes be prosecuted at the same time as all other crimes, so that the investigation of these crimes become an integral part of the prosecution of human rights violations in general.

One way to ensure integrated prosecution would be to have gender advisers in each tribunal or prosecutor's office. Gender advisers would allow for the secure compilation of evidence and the development of gender inclusive policies, protocols or practices. It would also permit the appropriate consideration of the facts in each context, helping to determine correctly what crimes should be treated as genocide, crimes against humanity, torture or war crimes. On top of this, special measures relating to security and protection would apply for victims and witnesses of these crimes. It would also help to expand the kind of evidence that could be admitted and considered to prove these crimes and the implementation of best practices with regard to the evaluation of the evidence in gender crimes in general.

An alternative option for the effective mainstreaming of gender crimes is to have trained prosecutors and judges, so that the above-mentioned skills can be developed and implemented by the members of the tribunal or the prosecutor's office. Also, it is important that practitioners have knowledge regarding gender roles in a given context in order to adequately charge crimes.

Another important consideration is the impact of including gender crimes in all national reparations processes. If sex crimes are not included in the prosecution of international crimes, it is impossible for reparations to be for all of the victims, since the specific crimes targeting women and men based on gender would be left out of the reparation process.

In conclusion, we can affirm that the investigation and prosecution of international sex crimes is an increasing reality today. The ideas outlined here must be analysed in context, attending to the needs of every country litigating human rights violations. The most important point is that once a country assumes the challenge of prosecuting those who have committed international crimes, gender crimes must be considered so as to combat the culture of impunity and seek justice and reparations for all of society.

9

Contextualising Sexual Violence in the Prosecution of International Crimes

Valerie Oosterveld[*]

Sexual violence taking place during conflict or mass atrocities is usually part of a wider picture of complex victimisation. Rape, sexual slavery, sexual mutilation and other similar acts are often accompanied by, or intersect with, other prohibited acts. For example, sexual violence crimes may have occurred alongside or be used to facilitate the crime against humanity of murder, enslavement, torture or persecution. Further, seemingly gender-neutral prohibited acts may have been carried out in gender-specific ways or may have gendered outcomes. For these reasons, conscious contextualisation of sexual violence within international criminal prosecutions is crucial: by pursuing investigations and prosecutions in which sexual violence is explored within the context of other genocidal acts, crimes against humanity or war crimes, both the serious nature of sexual violence and the potentially gendered nature of other crimes can be highlighted and understood.

This chapter explores the value of pursuing the prosecution of sexual violence within the context of related charges of genocide, crimes against humanity or war crimes. It begins by arguing that there may be specific factual circumstances in which exclusive, or nearly exclusive, prosecutorial focus on sexual violence charges may be valuable. However, generally, sexual violence charges should be situated within a narrative explaining the multitude of violations in a given atrocity scenario. This approach is more reflective of the realities of those who suffered the sexual violence crimes: they are not only, for instance, survivors of rape, but

---

[*] **Valerie Oosterveld** is a Professor at the University of Western Ontario, Canada, where she serves as the Deputy Director of the Center for Transitional Justice and Post-Conflict Reconstruction. She previously served in the Legal Affairs Bureau of Canada's Department of Foreign Affairs and International Trade, and was a member of the Canadian delegation to the International Criminal Court negotiations and subsequent Assembly States Parties. She teaches international criminal law, international human rights law, international organisations and public international law. She specialises on gender issues within international criminal justice.

also usually simultaneous victims of other serious acts such as pillage, cruel treatment or enslavement. Each violation has a place within the narrative. A comprehensive understanding of the violations helps to explain the depth of harm caused to the victims and, in turn, can and should inform sentencing. This chapter then turns to an exploration of two recent positive examples, within international and internationalised tribunals, of nuanced contextualisation of sexual violence crimes. It concludes by discussing the need for heightened gender competence and gender expertise within all offices, whether international or domestic, focused on the investigation and prosecution of genocide, crimes against humanity and war crimes, as well as among counsel for victims and within judiciaries.

9.1. Prosecution and Contextualisation of Sexual Violence Crimes

When faced with a multitude of violations of international criminal law, there are a number of interrelated reasons for selecting acts of sexual violence for prosecution. First, these acts are serious violations of physical and/or psychological integrity and are therefore similar in harm and effect to other prohibited acts of genocide, crimes against humanity and war crimes involving grave personal injury.[1] Prosecuting them assists in exposing the depth of harm to victims, their families and their communities.[2] Second, historically, sexual violence offences directed against girls and women were ignored, mislabelled as an inevitable consequence of war, or deemed as less important than other forms of violence.[3] Sexual violence

---

[1] International Criminal Tribunal for Rwanda ('ICTR'), *Prosecutor v. Emmanuel Rukundo*, Appeals Chamber, Judgment (Judge Pocar's Partially Dissenting Opinion), ICTR-01-70, 20 October 2010, paras. 4, 9 (*'Rukundo* Appeals Judgment') (http://www.legal-tools.org/doc/d5b969/).

[2] On harms to families and communities, see Special Court for Sierra Leone ('SCSL'), *Prosecutor v. Issa Hassan Sesay, Morris Kallon and Augustine Gbao*, Trial Chamber, Judgment, SCSL-04-15, 2 March 2009, para. 1349 (*'RUF* Judgment') (http://www.legal-tools.org/doc/7f05b7/). On emotional harms to victims, harms to the victim's home and personal spaces, harms to the victim's children and to those to whom female victims are intimately connected, see Fionnuala Ní Aoláin, Dina Francesca Haynes and Naomi Cahn, "Criminal Justice for Gendered Violence and Beyond", in *International Criminal Law Review*, 2011, vol. 11, no. 3, p. 426.

[3] Kelly D. Askin, *War Crimes against Women: Prosecution in International War Crimes Tribunals*, Martinus Nijhoff Publishers, The Hague, 1997, p. 377.

---

directed against men and boys was similarly silenced.[4] More recently, these views of sexual violence have been demonstrated to be not only the result of discriminatory and incorrect assumptions, but also harmful to the discovery of the truth of what actually happened in any given conflict or atrocity scenario.[5] In other words, the discrimination inherent in the perpetration of acts of sexual violence was compounded by discriminatory lack of recognition of these acts within international and domestic criminal prosecutions. Thus, the prosecution of sexual violence crimes today demonstrates a break with these past mistakes and therefore a break in this discriminatory chain. Prosecution publicly 'surfaces'[6] sexual violence and its harm and denotes how conflict has gender-specific impacts upon individuals, communities and nations.[7]

The third justification for the prosecution of sexual violence crimes occurring within genocide, war or other situations of atrocity is explored by Margaret deGuzman in this volume: there is an important expressive function inherent in the prosecution of sexual violence crimes. The prosecution of sexual violence crimes serves to express to the international community generally that these acts are illegal and those who committed or permitted them are to be held accountable and condemned.[8] As Doris Buss explains:

> In international criminal prosecutions, rape and other forms
> of sexual harm are identified *as harms*, they are prosecuted

---

[4] Sandesh Sivakumaran, "Sexual Violence Against Men in Armed Conflict", in *European Journal of International Law*, 2007, vol. 18, no. 2, pp. 255–56.

[5] Hilary Charlesworth and Christine Chinkin, *The Boundaries of International Law: A Feminist Analysis*, Manchester University Press, Manchester, 2000, pp. 251–52, 328, 334. See also Kelly D. Askin, "The Jurisprudence of the International War Crimes Tribunals: Securing Gender Justice for Some Survivors", in Helen Durham and Tracey Gurd (eds.), *Listening to the Silences: Women and War*, Martinus Nijhoff Publishers, New York, 2005, pp. 126, 152–53.

[6] This important notion of 'surfacing' gender-based violence in conflict was introduced by Rhonda Copelon in "Surfacing Gender: Re-engraving Crimes Against Women in Humanitarian Law", in *Hastings Women's Law Journal*, 1994, vol. 5, pp. 243–65.

[7] Doris Buss, "Performing Legal Order: Some Feminist Thoughts on International Criminal Law", in *International Criminal Law Review*, 2011, vol. 11, no. 3, p. 412.

[8] Buss describes this as "social meanings communicated and interpreted through legal processes": *Ibid.*, p. 411.

> *as crimes*, and they result in punishment through years of in-
> carceration for those found guilty.[9]

Critically, prosecution of these acts also illustrates to the victims and their communities that their suffering was the result of illegal activity.[10] This naming is an important step in the dismantling of discriminatory stereotypes – and stigma – that surround raped women, girls, men and boys in many societies.[11] Fair and accurate labelling of crimes is one of the underlying goals of international criminal law,[12] and this labelling must include the public labelling of sexual violence crimes.

These justifications can support the choice of prosecuting sexual violence crimes among charges for other acts or on their own. There are very strong justifications for the prosecution, in a contextual manner, of sexual violence crimes among charges for other acts. Thus, this choice will be explored first. One reason for choosing to prosecute sexual violence crimes among other charges is that individuals who suffer sexual violence crimes often also suffer other forms of violation. These other forms of harm may have facilitated the carrying out of the sexual violence (for example, illegal detention), may have accompanied the sexual violence (for example, torture or murder), may have surrounded the sexual violence (for example, sexual violence occurring amid pillage), or may have preceded or followed the sexual violence.

Second, sexual violence crimes may have been just one aspect of the larger gendered nature or outcomes of a particular episode in a conflict or mass violation. When determining or telling the story of a particular episode in a conflict or mass atrocity and the role of the accused in that episode, it is important to be aware of the intersection of gender, rather than just sexual violence, with that scenario. Gender is a complex and multi-layered concept, involving socially constructed ideas of 'maleness' and 'femaleness' that can vary across cultures and over time.[13] If investi-

---

9   *Ibid.*, p. 414.

10   Buss notes that this may also be seen as "political recognition": *Ibid.*, p. 414.

11   This stigma was described by the *RUF* Judgment, para. 1349, see *supra* note 2.

12   Darryl Robinson, "The Identity Crisis of International Criminal Law", in *Leiden Journal of International Law*, 2008, vol. 21, no. 4, p. 942.

13   See United Nations Entity for Gender Equality and the Empowerment of Women, "Gender Mainstreaming: Concepts and Definitions", which defines the term 'gender' as:

gators and prosecutors are sensitive to how assumptions about gender underlie the choice of crime or explain targeting, then they will better understand both the role of sexual violence crimes and the role of seemingly gender-neutral crimes within a conflict or mass violation. For example, men and boys may be targeted for certain forms of violence for reasons related either to overarching assumptions about 'maleness' – for example, an assumption by the perpetrators that all males are inclined to pick up weapons and fight if given the opportunity – and/or assumptions about how the means of targeting will affect the victims and be received by males and females in the victims' communities. Similarly, women and girls are also targeted on the basis of assumptions about 'femaleness', usually related to the subordinate position of women and girls, and/or because of how such victimisation will be received in the victims' communities.[14]

Some examples might be helpful here. In some cases before the International Criminal Tribunal for Rwanda ('ICTR'), the evidence demonstrated that men and boys were killed in different ways than women and girls, with men being targeted for direct machete attacks and women and

---

the social attributes and opportunities associated with being male and female and the relationships between women and men and girls and boys, as well as the relations between women and those between men. These attributes, opportunities and relationships are socially constructed and are learned through socialization processes. They are context/ time-specific and changeable. Gender determines what is expected, allowed and valued in a women or a man in a given context. In most societies there are differences and inequalities between women and men in responsibilities assigned, activities undertaken, access to and control over resources, as well as decision-making opportunities. Gender is part of the broader socio-cultural context. Other important criteria for socio-cultural analysis include class, race, poverty level, ethnic group and age.

[14] Ní Aoláin *et al.*, 2011, p. 429, see *supra* note 2:

[...] the horrors that many women experienced during conflict are augmented by the insight that their cultural and social mores were as much the target of sexual violation as their physical bodies. Men do not generally experience systematic sexual violation in this way, and the cultural constructs of harm to men's bodies have differing social meanings in the theatre of war. Not only do combatants target a women's body but, equally, in the fray is the body politic she represents.

girls for rape or sexual mutilation leading to death.[15] In the International Criminal Tribunal for the former Yugoslavia ('ICTY'), some cases illustrate different treatment for detained men and women,[16] or different acts being directed against men and against women in order to eliminate a cultural community.[17] That said, different outcomes are not necessary for the identification of the gendered nature of crimes. The exploration of forced marriage by the Extraordinary Chambers in the Courts of Cambodia is a good example. The Khmer Rouge believed that marriage was a necessary precursor to procreation and thus forced individuals to marry in order to increase the population of ideal citizens.[18] The negative effects experienced by both male and female victims of this act were sometimes gender differentiated, but often were similar.[19] And yet the act of forced marriage is a gendered act because it is based on societal norms of 'femaleness' and 'maleness'.

Third, harms are connected.[20] Therefore, the victim of sexual violence is often also a victim of a number of other violations, and she or he often feels that all of these wrongs should be addressed in some manner.[21] The victim's subjective experiences are multifaceted: harms are not easily

---

[15] See, for example, ICTR, *Prosecutor v. Théoneste Bagosora et al.*, Trial Chamber, Transcript, ICTR-98-41, 3 February 2004, pp. 51–52 (Examination-in-Chief of Major Brent Beardsley).

[16] For example, in the Čelebići prison camp in Bosnia and Herzegovina, male and female detainees were mistreated and sometimes that mistreatment took gender-specific forms such as rape of women and suffocation of men: International Criminal Tribunal for the former Yugoslavia ('ICTY'), *Prosecutor v. Zdravko Mucić et al.*, Trial Chamber, Judgment, IT-96-21, 16 November 1998, paras. 936–37, 957–62, 970–77 (http://www.legal-tools.org/doc/6b4a33/).

[17] For example, in eastern Bosnia, able-bodied Bosnian Muslim men and boys between the ages of 15 and 65 were targeted for death, while Muslim women and girls, as well as young Muslim boys and senior males, were targeted for forcible transfer away from their homes. This differential treatment had profound implications, both for those murdered and for the survivors: ICTY, *Prosecutor v. Vujadin Popović et al.*, Trial Chamber, Judgment, IT-05-88, 10 June 2010, paras. 779, 841, 844, 846–47, 856–62, 883–86 (http://www.legal-tools.org/doc/481867/).

[18] Extraordinary Chambers in the Courts of Cambodia ('ECCC'), *Prosecutor v. Nuon Chea, Ieng Sary, Khieu Samphan and Ieng Thirith* (Case 002), Closing Order, 002/19-09-2007/ECCC, 15 September 2011, paras. 216–20, 1442–47.

[19] *Ibid.*

[20] Ní Aoláin *et al.*, 2011, p. 426, see *supra* note 2.

[21] *Ibid.*, pp. 430–32, 442.

---

divided into pieces that can be measured independently.[22] Prosecutions in international criminal tribunals have, for the most part, been broadly contextual insofar as they have tended to focus on a representative sampling of serious violations[23] in a particular geographic area within a specific time period.[24] However, these prosecutions have not always placed the sexual violence crimes in nuanced context (when sexual violence has actually been reflected in indictments or arrest warrants)[25] by examining the interrelationships between the sexual violence and the other violations, nor have they always explored how the harms caused by sexual violence can be compounded by other violations, and vice versa.

It is important to note that nuanced contextualisation as advocated in this chapter, while providing definite advantages in explaining the gendered nature of violations and better telling the victims' stories, has its inherent limits. Feminist theory highlights that violence against women and girls happens in a larger social and global context underpinned by

---

[22] This was the experience of female victims and witnesses of sexual violence in the SCSL trial in *Prosecutor v. Moinina Fofana and Allieu Kondewa*, SCSL-2004-14 (commonly referred to as the Civil Defence Forces ('CDF') case). As a result of a series of questionable motions decisions by the majority judges, these victim-witnesses were asked to bifurcate their evidence into non-sexual violence and sexual violence evidence, with the latter evidence excluded from the proceedings. These women suffered psychological distress as a result of being unable to describe the full nature of the harms done to them. See Michelle Staggs Kelsall and Shanee Stepakoff, "'When We Wanted to Talk About Rape': Silencing Sexual Violence at the Special Court for Sierra Leone", in *International Journal of Transitional Justice*, 2007, vol. 1, no. 3, pp. 355–74. It is also crucial to note here that not all of the wrongs experienced by victims may qualify as international crimes; addressing the totality of harms therefore requires multifaceted responses beyond the criminal trial: Ní Aoláin *et al.*, 2011, p. 426, see *supra* note 2.

[23] This is reflected by the use of gravity criteria by the ICC Office of the Prosecutor. See Paul Seils, "The Selection and Prioritization of Cases by the Office of the Prosecutor of the International Criminal Court", in Morten Bergsmo (ed.), *Criteria for Prioritizing and Selecting Core International Crimes Cases*, Torkel Opsahl Academic EPublisher, Oslo, 2010, p. 72.

[24] On the use of geographic sampling by the ICTR, see Alex Obote-Odora, "Case Selection and Prioritization Criteria at the International Criminal Tribunal for Rwanda", in Morten Bergsmo (ed.), *Criteria for Prioritizing and Selecting Core International Crimes Cases*, Torkel Opsahl Academic EPublisher, Oslo, 2010, pp. 59–60.

[25] Sexual violence has not always been charged even when it forms an important part of the context, or it has been charged but the charges have not been (effectively) pursued: Ní Aoláin *et al.*, 2011, pp. 437–40, see *supra* note 2. See also Beth van Schaack, "Obstacles on the Road to Gender Justice: The International Criminal Tribunal for Rwanda as Object Lesson", in *American University Journal of Gender, Social Policy and the Law*, 2009, vol. 17, no. 2, pp. 375, 381–82.

---

gender, and other, inequality.[26] The individualised international criminal trial tends not to address this overarching context.[27] This means that the role of such discrimination in creating the room for sexual violence during conflict is largely left unexplored. Thus, individualised international criminal justice "can also dangerously distract international attention from the large-scale, systemic failures that underpin conflict".[28] In addition, some of the violations suffered by victims may not qualify as international crimes, and yet may be felt just as keenly by those victims. While harms to the body may be recognised as crimes, "emotional harms, harms to the home and personal spaces, harms to children and to those with whom women are intimately connected" may not be.[29] Addressing the entirety of the harms therefore requires multifaceted responses beyond the criminal trial.[30]

Having made the argument for a nuanced contextualisation of sexual violence charges, there are times when a particular prosecution may usefully focus exclusively, or nearly exclusively, on sexual violence. To date, such thematic prosecutions have been relatively rare.[31] Of the concluded proceedings for 126 accused,[32] the ICTY has focused only two trials exclusively on acts of sexual and gender-based violence.[33] At the International Criminal Court ('ICC'), two cases focus predominately on crimes of sexual and gender-based violence.[34] The experiences of the ICC and ICTY to date illustrate that a sexual violence-specific thematic prose-

---

[26] Charlesworth and Chinkin, 2000, pp. 4, 12–14, see *supra* note 5.

[27] Buss, 2011, p. 416, see *supra* note 7.

[28] *Ibid.*, p. 419.

[29] Ní Aoláin *et al.*, 2011, p. 426, see *supra* note 2.

[30] *Ibid.*

[31] It may therefore be premature to analyse the merits or demerits of sexual violence-only prosecutions.

[32] ICTY, "Key Figures of the Cases" (http://www.icty.org/en/cases/key-figures-cases).

[33] ICTY, *Prosecutor v. Anto Furundžija*, Trial Chamber, Judgment, IT-95-17/1, 21 July 2000 and 10 December 1998 (http://www.legal-tools.org/doc/e6081b/); ICTY, *Prosecutor v. Dragoljub Kunarac, Zoran Vuković and Radomir Kovač*, Trial Chamber, Judgment, IT-96-23 & 23/1, 12 June 2002 and 22 February 2001 (http://www.legal-tools.org/doc/fd881d/).

[34] ICC, *Prosecutor v. Jean-Pierre Bemba Gombo*, Pre-Trial Chamber, Warrant of Arrest, ICC-01/05-01/08, 23 March 2008, para. 21 (http://www.legal-tools.org/doc/1b66ef/); ICC, Pre-Trial Chamber, *Prosecutor v. Callixte Mbarushimana*, Warrant of Arrest, ICC-01/04-01/10, 9 April 2012, paras. 7(iii), 10(vii), 10 (viii) ('*Mbarushimana* Arrest Warrant') (http://www.legal-tools.org/doc/27b448/).

---

cution may make sense in certain factual circumstances: for example, when the aspect of the conflict being investigated demonstrates that a representative sample of the most serious crimes will naturally focus on a range of sexual violence crimes; where the best evidence for a particular accused bearing the greatest responsibility is focused on sexual violence; or where there are a number of prosecutions focused on a particular attack or geographic time period and these prosecutions are chosen to highlight a diversity of experiences, including those of sexual violence.

In sum, while there are times when a prosecution focused largely or exclusively on sexual violence is useful or necessary, at other times it is helpful to integrate sexual violence charges among charges for other violations occurring in the same attack or geographical area, in order to place the sexual violence crimes and, indeed, all of the violations, in context, to best explain the cumulative harms faced by victims.

9.2. Contextualisation of Sexual Violence Crimes: A Method

Contextualisation of sexual violence crimes helps to explain the serious nature of sexual violence and the potentially gendered nature of other crimes. Such contextualisation makes sense, given the practice often followed within international criminal tribunals of prosecuting a representative sample of serious incidents. For example, the ICC's Office of the Prosecutor has indicated that its goal is "to provide a sample that reflects the gravest incidents and the main types of victimization" in selecting incidents for trial.[35] As established above, sexual violence is serious and is often present alongside other forms of victimisation. It therefore follows that sexual violence crimes should be included in the sample of grave incidents in a given crime scenario, such as an attack on civilians.

Contextualisation is important and necessary, but there are not many good examples to date of nuanced contextualisation within international criminal law. One exception can be found in the ICC's *Mbarushimana* indictment. Callixte Mbarushimana is alleged to have been a very senior member of Forces démocratiques pour la libération du Rwanda (Democratic Forces for the Liberation of Rwanda), "the most recent incarnation of Rwandan rebel groups established by former *génocidaires*

---

[35] ICC, Office of the Prosecutor, Report of Prosecutorial Strategy: 2009–2012, 1 February 2010, para. 20 (http://www.legal-tools.org/doc/6e3bf4/).

who fled Rwanda after the 1994 genocide", and therefore accused of contributing to the implementation of a common plan to carry out the group's atrocities.[36] The group is accused of carrying out a series of attacks in the Kivu provinces of the Democratic Republic of the Congo in 2009 involving murders, rapes, gender-based persecution, torture, other inhumane acts, inhuman treatment and destruction of property.[37] The prosecutor has placed the sexual violence crimes – rape, sexual torture and sexual mutilation – within the context of other acts, showing how they are interlinked.[38] At the same time, he also intends to demonstrate the role of mass sexual violence in the group's strategic aims to gain political power.[39] In other words, he plans to look at sexual violence up close, through witness testimony of specific acts, and from afar, by examining the effect of sexual violence crimes in subjugating the civilian population.

Another helpful example of contextualisation can be found in the judgment of the Trial Chamber of the Special Court for Sierra Leone in *Prosecutor v. Sesay and Others*.[40] In that judgment, the judges examined the evidence of sexual violence and concluded that this violence was "not intended merely for personal satisfaction or a means of sexual gratification for the fighter".[41] Rather, the Revolutionary United Front adopted a "calculated and concerted pattern […] to use sexual violence as a weapon of terror" against civilians, resulting in an "atmosphere in which violence, oppression and lawlessness prevailed".[42] The Revolutionary United Front used "perverse methods of sexual violence against women and men of all ages", including "brutal gang rapes, the insertion of various objects into victims' genitalia, the raping of pregnant women and forced sexual intercourse between male and female civilian abductees".[43] These methods also involved the routine capture and abduction of women and girls, who

---

[36] ICC, Office of the Prosecutor, "New ICC Arrest: Leader of Movement Involved in Massive Rapes in the DRC is Apprehended in Paris", Press Release, 11 October 2010.

[37] *Mbarushimana* Arrest Warrant, paras. 2, 7, 10, see supra note 34.

[38] ICC, *Prosecutor v. Callixte Mbarushimana*, Pre-Trial Chamber, Transcript, ICC-01/04-01/10, 19 September 2011, pp. 17–18, 22, 25 (http://www.legal-tools.org/doc/3bc3bf/).

[39] ICC, Office of the Prosecutor, 2010, see *supra* note 36.

[40] *RUF* Judgment, see *supra* note 2.

[41] *Ibid.*, para. 1348.

[42] *Ibid.*, para. 1347.

[43] *Ibid.* (footnotes in original not included).

were then forced into prolonged exclusive conjugal relationships with rebels as so-called "wives".[44] The Trial Chamber further argued:

> [T]he savage nature [of the sexual violence] demonstrates
> that these acts were committed with the specific intent of
> spreading fear amongst the civilian population as a whole, in
> order to break the will of the population and ensure their
> submission to AFRC/RUF control.[45]

Combined with other forms of violence by the Revolutionary United Front, the sexual violence "effectively disempowered the civilian
population and had a direct effect of instilling fear on entire communities".[46] The Revolutionary United Front relied on the cascading effect of
their sexual and non-sexual violations: their crimes not only "abused, de-
based and isolated the individual victim", but also demonstrated that the
male members of the civilian community "were unable to protect their
own wives, daughters, mothers and sisters", and "deliberately destroyed
the existing family nucleus" by relying upon the societal stigma associated with sexual violence to ensure that "[v]ictims of sexual violence were
ostracised, husbands left their wives, and daughters and young girls were
unable to marry within their community".[47] In turn, these effects undermined "the cultural values and relationships which held the [Sierra Le-
onean] societies together".[48] The Trial Chamber concluded that "rape,
sexual slavery, 'forced marriages' and outrages upon personal dignity,
when committed against a civilian population with the specific intent to
terrorise, amount to acts of terror".[49]

Through this reasoning, the Trial Chamber placed the sexual violence in context by examining: who were the targeted victims (largely ci-

---

[44] *Ibid.*, para. 1351.

[45] *Ibid.*, para. 1348.

[46] *Ibid.* See also para. 1351, which refers to the pattern of sexual enslavement as a "deliberate system intended to spread terror".

[47] *Ibid.*, paras. 1349–50. See also the reference in para. 1349 to the Revolutionary United Front's "calculated consequences" of sexual violence.

[48] *Ibid.*, para. 1349.

[49] *Ibid.*, para. 1352. This holding was upheld by SCSL, *Prosecutor v. Issa Hassan Sesay, Morris Kallon and Augustine Gbao*, Appeals Chamber, Judgment, SCSL-04-15, 26 October 2009, para. 990 (http://www.legal-tools.org/doc/133b48/).

vilian women and girls, but also men and boys);[50] what other acts often took place alongside the sexual violence; how these victims were affected by the sexual violence and how that victimisation was compounded by pre-existing societal discrimination; how the experience of these victims was also compounded by other violations; and how the perpetrators relied on the compounding effects of sexual violence combined with other violence and discrimination. In order to do this, the Trial Chamber had to look at sexual violence up close, by examining witness testimony of specific acts, and from afar, by examining the terrorising effect of those crimes on the entire civilian population. By looking closely at individual acts and looking more widely at patterns and overarching effects, the actual role and consequences of gender-based violence were more deeply explained than if only the individual acts were examined.[51]

There may be a concern that contextualisation of sexual violence crimes could result in trivialising or otherwise losing sight of them among the other violations. However, the type of nuanced and gender-sensitive contextualisation advocated in this chapter is meant to avoid such a scenario. If good contextualisation practices are followed, then the correct questions are asked and answered by investigators, prosecutors, victims counsel and judges to not only reveal the sexual violence crimes, but also the connection between these crimes and the other indicted violations, as well as the cumulative harm.

9.3. Enhanced Gender Competence and Gender Expertise

The type of gender-sensitive contextualisation advocated in this chapter has rarely been achieved within international and internationalised tribunals. Simply investigating and including sexual violence charges in an indictment is not enough. Bringing evidence of sexual violence is also not enough. A clear example of this unfortunately occurred in the appeals judgment of the ICTR in *Prosecutor v. Emmanuel Rukundo*. In that judgment, it appears that the majority judges failed to understand a particular sexual assault in context and ended up relying on a regressive, decontex-

---

[50] *RUF* Judgment, paras. 1207–1208, 1304–1305, see *supra* note 2, on the sexual mutilation of male genitals and forced sex by male civilians.

[51] Valerie Oosterveld, "The Gender Jurisprudence of the Special Court for Sierra Leone: Progress in the Revolutionary United Front Judgments", in *Cornell International Law Journal*, 2011, vol. 44, no. 1, p. 70.

tualised characterisation of the sexual violence. Rukundo, an ordained priest and military chaplain for the Rwandan armed forces, had been convicted at trial of committing genocide by causing serious mental harm to a young Tutsi woman when he sexually assaulted her in May 1994 at a seminary in Gitarama prefecture.[52] The victim had testified that, when he arrived at the seminary, she had asked Rukundo to hide her in his room as she feared for her life.[53] He told that he could not help her as her entire family had to be killed.[54] She helped him carry some items to his room, in the hope that he would change his mind. Once in the room, he locked the door, placed his pistol on the table, forced the victim onto his bed, opened the zipper to his trousers, and tried to spread her legs and have sexual intercourse. She resisted and instead he rubbed himself against her until he ejaculated. She testified that she felt that she could not escape because he had physically pinned her down and because he was "in a position of authority and had a gun".[55] A majority of the Trial Chamber interpreted this evidence in light of the "highly charged, oppressive and other circumstances surrounding the sexual assault", especially the context of mass violence directed against Tutsis in the area and the specifics of Rukundo's words prior to the assault, and entered a conviction.[56]

A majority of the Appeals Chamber overturned this conviction, finding the "general context of mass violence" against Tutsis to be irrelevant to genocidal intent with respect to this incident.[57] The majority judges characterised Rukundo's actions against the young woman as "unplanned and spontaneous": "an opportunistic crime that was not accompanied by the specific intent to commit genocide".[58] In doing so, the judges in effect placed a higher burden of proof on the linkage of sexual violence to genocidal intent than they had for other types of prohibited genocidal acts. They found that the sexual assault was "qualitatively different"

---

[52] *Rukundo* Appeals Judgment, para. 227, *supra* note 1. See also ICTR, *Prosecutor v. Emmanuel Rukundo*, Trial Chamber, Judgment, ICTR-01-70, 27 February 2009, paras. 4, 574–576 ('*Rukundo* Trial Judgment') (http://www.legal-tools.org/doc/1c7819/).

[53] *Rukundo* Trial Judgment, paras. 373, 384, see *supra* note 52.

[54] *Ibid.*, para. 373.

[55] *Ibid.*

[56] *Ibid.*, paras. 388, 576.

[57] *Rukundo* Appeals Judgment, para. 236, see *supra* note 1.

[58] *Ibid.*

from Rukundo's other acts of genocide (such as the search for, and subsequent assault or murder of, Tutsis) and therefore separate from and unlinked to those other acts.[59] In other words, the majority appeals judges succumbed to a time-worn but incorrect view of sexual violence as somehow "private" (because it deals with "intimate aspects of our bodies and minds"[60]) and therefore distinguishable from and unlinked to other forms of violence. They decontextualised the sexual violence. Unfortunately, this is not the first time decontextualisation of sexual violence has happened at the ICTR as this was also an issue in *Prosecutor v. Juvénal Kajelijeli*.[61]

Judge Pocar issued a strong and convincing partially dissenting opinion in *Prosecutor v. Emmanuel Rukundo* that illustrated a gender-sensitive contextual understanding of the situation. In his view, Rukundo's words "clearly conveyed Rukundo's knowledge that his victim was Tutsi and that she and the other members of her family should be killed for this reason alone".[62] These words were to be considered in the context of: 1) violence in the surrounding area in which Tutsis were being hunted down; 2) the victim's state (she was "dirty and hungry and her place of refuge was not safe"); 3) her previous knowledge of and trust in Rukundo; 4) the fact that Rukundo was armed; and 5) the use of force by Rukundo against her to commit a sexual act.[63] Judge Pocar felt that the majority's classification of the assault as an opportunistic crime indicated that the majority "does not fully appreciate the seriousness of the crime" and misunderstands the distinction between motive and intent: even if the perpetrator's motivation is entirely sexual, it does not follow that the perpetra-

---

[59] *Ibid.*

[60] Xabier Agirre Aranburu, "Sexual Violence beyond Reasonable Doubt: Using Pattern Evidence and Analysis for International Cases", in *Leiden Journal of International Law*, 2010, vol. 23, no. 3, p. 612.

[61] Compare the consideration and interpretation of the evidence by a majority of the Trial Chamber with that of dissenting Judge Ramaroson: ICTR, *Prosecutor v. Juvénal Kajelijeli*, Trial Chamber, Judgment and Sentence, ICTR-98-44A, 1 December 2003, paras. 679–83, 917–25 (http://www.legal-tools.org/doc/afa827/); and ICTR, *Prosecutor v. Juvénal Kajelijeli*, Trial Chamber, Dissenting Opinion of Judge Arlette Ramaroson, ICTR-98-44A, 1 December 2003 (http://www.legal-tools.org/doc/e4797f/), in its entirety, including the discussion in para. 99 of the context of the sexual violence.

[62] *Rukundo* Appeals Judgment, para. 3 of Judge Pocar's Partially Dissenting Opinion, see *supra* note 1.

[63] *Ibid.*, paras. 5–8.

tor does not have the requisite intent or that his conduct does not cause severe pain and suffering.[64] While Judge Pocar's analysis did not undo the damage, caused by the majority judges, to the analysis of harm by Rukundo, to the victim whose evidence (and violation) was deemed unrelated to the genocide, and to international criminal law's understanding of gender, it does provide a model for gender-sensitive contextual analysis. Judge Pocar answered these key questions. What does the evidence show happened to the victim? What was the effect? What was the situation of the victim at the time of the violation? Was the victim's vulnerability to the sexual violence linked to the overarching context? Are there linkages between the sexual violence and other prohibited acts? Was the perpetrator acting with intent linked to that overarching context?

To be clear, to argue for a gender-sensitive contextual analysis of sexual violence during genocide, crimes against humanity or war crimes is not to somehow argue for an easing of the standards of proof for these acts: in fact, in cases of sexual violence, the international tribunals have often required more (rather than less) evidence than is actually required, particularly when it comes to an analysis of the evidence for purposes of individual or superior criminal responsibility.[65] Rather, the argument for contextual analysis is an argument for a better, deeper, more nuanced understanding of when, why and how sexual violence takes place during genocide, war or other forms of atrocity. Investigations, prosecutions and judicial deliberations should examine *actus reus* and *mens rea* through the lens of the questions inherently asked by Judge Pocar. This requires increased gender competence and gender expertise within investigators, prosecutors, victims' counsel and judges tasked at the international, regional and domestic levels with examining international crimes. The term 'gender competence' refers to "the capacity to identify where difference on the basis of gender is significant, and act in ways that produce more equitable outcomes for men and women".[66] Gender competence should be present in all investigators, prosecutors, victims' counsel and judges. In-

---

[64] *Ibid.*, para. 10.

[65] Susana SáCouto and Katherine Cleary, "The Importance of Effective Investigation of Sexual Violence and Gender-Based Crimes at the International Criminal Court", in *American University Journal of Gender, Social Policy and the Law*, 2009, vol. 17, no. 2, pp. 353–58.

[66] Monash University Medicine, Nursing and Health Sciences, "Gender Competence" (http://www.med.monash.edu.au/gendermed/competence.html).

---

deed, this competence should be present at the hiring or appointment stage, at least for some positions.[67] Since this is not presently the case at the international tribunals,[68] increased training is urgently needed and must be maintained over time and despite staff turnover. Gender competence increases the capacity of investigators and prosecutors to uncover how gender-based violence is part of a continuum of violence. Gender expertise is also needed, in addition to institution-wide gender competence. That is, there should be at least some investigators, prosecutors, victims' counsel and judges who have experience and applied knowledge that goes much deeper than gender competence, in order to put into place a workable "gender strategy".[69] For example, Xabier Agirre Aranburu has outlined the importance of having, on staff, investigators trained in gathering and analysing pattern evidence of sexual violence.[70]

The benefits of increased gender competence and deeper gender expertise are clear: the presence of both are likely to lead to a better and more nuanced understanding of when, why and how sexual violence takes place during genocide, war or other forms of atrocity. This fuller understanding helps to explain the interconnected and cumulative nature of harms in any given conflict or scenario of mass violation, and therefore allows for a better evaluation of appropriate sentencing. It also creates a more accurate portrayal of what occurred in a particular situation, explaining not only the effect on the victim(s) but also the intent of the perpetrator(s). The stronger this capacity, the more we will understand that gender-based violence is not only about violence directed toward women: it is about why and how men, women, girls and boys are targeted for different crimes.

---

[67] "Awareness of the seriousness of sexual violence should be a precondition of work in the investigation of international crimes"; see Agirre Aranburu, 2010, p. 627, *supra* note 60.

[68] Women's Initiative for Gender Justice, "Gender Report Card on the International Criminal Court 2010", The Hague, November 2010, pp. 50–51, 62–64. See also van Schaack, 2009, pp. 367, 375, 385 and 406, see *supra* note 25.

[69] On the necessity for gender strategies within international criminal tribunals, see Patricia Viseur Sellers, "Gender Strategy is Not a Luxury for International Courts", in *American University Journal of Gender, Social Policy and the Law*, 2009, vol. 17, no. 2, pp. 303–25. On the necessity of gender competence and gender expertise among investigative and prosecutorial staff, see ICTR, Office of the Prosecutor, "Best Practices Manual for the Investigation and Prosecution of Sexual Violence Crimes in Situations of Armed Conflict: Lessons from the International Criminal Tribunal for Rwanda", 2008, paras. 17–30, 36, 47.

[70] Agirre Aranburu, 2010, p. 627, see *supra* note 60.

9.4. Conclusion

Janet Halley has argued that an emphasis on the prosecution of rape during conflict

> can background other bad things: to import the idea that 'rape is a fate worse than death' into the setting of armed conflict - for example, to declare that the panoramic violence of the Yugoslav conflict was a 'war against women' - is to background the death that armed conflict brings to people generally, and specifically to the death it brings to men.[71]

While this assumption can be both questioned and decisively countered,[72] it is also true that nuanced and gender-specific contextualisation directly addresses this concern by foregrounding both murder and rape. Indeed, such contextualisation explores the linkages between murder and rape, the harms stemming from each, and the compounded harms coming from both together. In so doing, it addresses victimisation from the point of view of the perpetrator by asking whether and how these forms of violation fit together, and from the point of view of the victim by examining the place of each crime in the individual and overall victimisation.

Sexual violence is a crime rooted in a specific social construction of gender roles and in discrimination, especially the social, economic and political subordination of women and girls. It is therefore a specific expression of gender-based discrimination. There may be situations in which a prosecution focused only on sexual violence crimes may be useful or natural: for example, when prosecuting an attack in which sexual violence was the dominant form of violation. At other times, however, the placement of sexual violence crimes within a larger context of other genocidal acts, crimes against humanity or war crimes, better explains the sexual violence. It may also better explain the other forms of violence, which may also similarly be expressions of gender-based discrimination while appearing on their surface to be gender neutral. By exploring the linkages between the crimes, the gendered nature of these crimes (and not only of

---

[71] Janet Halley, "Rape in Berlin: Reconsidering the Criminalization of Rape in the International Law of Armed Conflict", in *Melbourne Journal of International Law*, 2008, vol. 9, no. 1, p. 80.

[72] See, for example, a critique by Maria Grahn-Farley, "The Politics of Inevitability", in Sari Kouvo and Zoe Pearson (eds.), *Feminist Perspectives on Contemporary International Law: Between Resistance and Compliance?*, Hart Publishing, Oxford, 2011, pp. 109–29.

the sexual violence) may become clearer. Undertaking a truly gender-sensitive form of contextualisation requires improved gender competence and deeper gender expertise within all tribunals and courts tasked with prosecuting genocide, crimes against humanity and war crimes. Gender competence and expertise must be present from the point of the initial investigations through to the phases of judgment and sentencing, so as to better uncover and explain the role of gender in serious crimes today.

10

Going Beyond Prosecutorial Discretion: Institutional Factors Influencing Thematic Prosecution

Neha Jain[*]

10.1. Introduction

International criminal courts are charged with a singular task: establishing accountability for crimes that far exceed routine instances of criminal conduct in their horrific nature and brutality that involve participation by thousands of persons spread over large geographical regions and long time periods. Given that these courts operate within significant pressures of time, personnel and budgets, they cannot be expected to pursue each and every incidence of violence that would fall within their jurisdiction. Some element of selection and prioritisation, which is not uncommon even for most domestic criminal courts, is thus rather inevitable in the practice of international criminal courts. There has been little discussion however of how this selectivity may be justified. Can international courts legitimately prioritise offences such as international sex crimes, or the recruitment of child soldiers, if this may mean that crimes such as mass killings go unpunished?

In this chapter, I offer a pluralistic account of the international criminal trial that posits the importance of institutional and structural factors that may differ between tribunals and that have a bearing on the validity of thematic prosecutions, particularly investigations and prosecutions of international sex crimes. I argue that three such factors will be particularly influential in seeking justifications for the practice of thematic prosecutions. The first is the status of the court – whether it is a post-conflict tribunal or one that may intervene in situations of ongoing conflict. This status will influence what aims the tribunal may legitimately strive towards –

---

[*] **Neha Jain** is Associate Professor and McKnight Land-Grant Professor at the University of Minnesota Law School. At the time of writing, she was a Georgetown University Law Research Fellow and Adjunct Professor.

retributive, expressive or deterrent. The second factor is the court's role in post-conflict peacebuilding and the establishment of the rule of law. If the court is primarily set up to serve this instrumental goal, it may be able to expressly pursue didactic goals and prioritise investigation and prosecution of sex crimes. The third factor is the extent of civil party involvement in the tribunal proceedings. If victim participation can be considered desirable either because it promotes restorative justice or assists in the determination of truth by the tribunal, the enhanced role of the victim will influence the extent to which sex crimes will be prioritised by the court.

I address each of these arguments by focusing on the rather unique scenario presented by the charge of forced marriages before the Extraordinary Chambers in the Courts of Cambodia ('ECCC'). The procedural history of the crime of forced marriages before the ECCC presents an interesting case study for several reasons. First, the crime was not included in the first introductory submission filed by the co-prosecutors before the Office of the Co-Investigating Judges ('OCIJ'). It is only after the lawyers acting for civil parties filed applications that specifically alleged the commission of forced marriages and other sexual crimes by the Khmer Rouge that the charge was seriously taken up by the tribunal.[1] Second, the scarce investigative, prosecutorial and judicial resources that would be need to be devoted to prosecuting forced marriages before the ECCC echo concerns similar to those that any debate on thematic prosecutions must address.

10.2. Forced Marriages at the ECCC

10.2.1. Background to the Proceedings on Forced Marriages

To properly appreciate the relevance of the charge of forced marriages to the issue of thematic prosecutions, it is useful to have some background on the Khmer Rouge regime and the kinds of crimes that the ECCC has to consider. The victory of the forces of the Communist Party of Kampuchea (popularly known as the 'Khmer Rouge') over Phnom Penh on 17 April 1975 marked the establishment of a four-year-long reign of terror over

---

[1]   See Civil Parties' Co-Lawyers' Request for Supplementary Preliminary Investigations, 001/18-07-2007-ECCC/TC, 9 February 2009 ('First Request') (http://www.eccc.gov.kh/sites/default/files/documents/courtdoc/E11_EN.pdf).

Cambodia.[2] The Khmer Rouge came to power with the aim of establishing a socialist, fully independent and socially and ethnically homogeneous Cambodia. In its ruthless pursuit of this mission, it attempted to abolish all pre-existing economic, social and cultural institutions, transform the Cambodian population into a collective workforce, and suppress all elements that were perceived as a threat to the new order.[3] Purges were carried out against ethnic minorities, intellectuals, Buddhists, foreigners, supporters of the former prime minister Lon Nol, and the urban 'capitalist' class dubbed the "new people".[4] The regime evacuated cities; abolished money, private property and religion; and set up rural collectives in which thousands died of disease, starvation and overwork. Estimates of the dead range from 1.7 million to 3 million, out of a 1975 population estimated at 7.3 million.[5] Vietnam's invasion of Cambodia in late December 1978 signalled the end of the regime, and Heng Samrin was installed as head of state in the new People's Republic of Kampuchea ('PRK'). The Khmer Rouge and the Vietnamese continued to clash throughout the 1980s, and a comprehensive settlement was achieved only in October 1991 with the signing of the Paris Agreements.[6]

The initial impetus for the ECCC came in the form of a letter addressed by the two co-prime ministers of Cambodia to the United Nations ('UN') secretary-general, requesting the international community's assistance in establishing the truth about, and accountability for, the crimes

---

[2] Group of Experts for Cambodia, Report of the Group of Experts for Cambodia Established Pursuant to General Assembly Resolution 52/135, UN Doc. S/1999/231, A/53/850, 16 March 1999, paras. 14–15 ('Report of the Group of Experts') (http://www.legal-tools.org/doc/3da509/).

[3] David P. Chandler, *Brother Number One: A Political Biography of Pol Pot*, Westview Press, Boulder, 1999, p. 3; Serge Thion, "The Cambodian Idea of Revolution", in David P. Chandler and Ben Kiernan (eds.), *Revolution and Its Aftermath in Kampuchea: Eight Essays*, Yale University Southeast Asia Studies, New Haven, 1983, p. 10; Time Magazine, "Cambodia: Long March from Phnom Penh", 19 May 1975.

[4] Ben Kiernan, "External and Indigenous Sources of Khmer Rouge Ideology", in Odd Arne Westad and Sophie Quinn-Judge (eds.), *The Third Indochina War: Conflict Between China, Vietnam and Cambodia 1972–79*, Routledge, London, 2006, pp. 187, 192–93; Dan Fletcher, "A Brief History of the Khmer Rouge", in *Time Magazine*, 17 February 2009; Ben Kiernan, *The Pol Pot Regime: Race, Power, and Genocide in Cambodia under the Khmer Rouge, 1975-79*, Yale University Press, New Haven, 2002, pp. 251–309.

[5] United States Department of State, "Background Note: Cambodia", 2009.

[6] *Ibid.*; Report of the Group of Experts, 1999, paras. 36–40, see *supra* note 2.

---

committed during the Khmer Rouge regime.[7] In response, a committee of a Group of Experts was formed to look into the nature of the crimes and explore options for prosecution. The report of the Group of Experts acknowledged that though the Khmer Rouge could no longer be considered a fighting force, it still retained a key position in domestic politics with several of its former members occupying important positions in Cambodia's two major political parties.[8] It therefore emphasised the twin goals of individual accountability and national reconciliation in its choice of the category of persons who should be targeted for investigation as well as the modalities of bringing them to justice. The report recommended that the proposed tribunal focus on those most responsible for the atrocities committed during the regime and envisaged about twenty to thirty persons being indicted by the prosecutor.[9] It also recommended that the trials should take place before an international tribunal, similar to the International Criminal Tribunal for the former Yugoslavia ('ICTY') and International Criminal Tribunal for Rwanda ('ICTR').[10] While it did not disfavour the possibility of a truth and reconciliation commission that would operate parallel to the tribunal, it clearly prioritised the latter, which it hoped would in any event bring to light the range of atrocities perpetrated by the Khmer Rouge and contribute to knowledge and reconciliation through the trial process.[11]

The Cambodian government rejected the recommendation to establish an international tribunal but, after prolonged negotiations,[12] a compromise was reached whereby the ECCC would be set up as a tribunal within the Cambodian system and controlled by Cambodians, but involving significant UN participation.[13] The ECCC has been established as an

---

[7] Report of the Group of Experts, 1999, para. 5, see *supra* note 2.

[8] *Ibid.*, paras. 95–98.

[9] *Ibid.*, paras. 102–11.

[10] *Ibid.*, paras. 122–84.

[11] *Ibid.*, paras. 199–209.

[12] George Chigas, "The Politics of Defining Justice After the Cambodian Genocide", in *Journal of Genocide Research*, 2000, vol. 2, no. 2, pp. 245, 256–57.

[13] Suzannah Linton, "Cambodia, East Timor and Sierra Leone: Experiments in International Justice", in *Criminal Law Forum*, 2001, vol. 12, pp. 185, 188–90.

independent institution within the Cambodian judiciary[14] by a statute passed by the government of Cambodia,[15] which incorporates the provisions of the 2003 Agreement between Cambodia and the UN.[16] It has a majority of national judges both at the Trial Chamber (three Cambodian and two foreign) and the Supreme Court Chamber (four Cambodian and three foreign) levels.[17] Decisions have to be adopted as far as possible, by unanimity, and in the absence of that, by a 'super-majority rule', that is, at least four out of the five Trial Chamber judges and five out of the seven Supreme Court Chamber judges must have voted in favour of the decision.[18] The prosecution team is headed by co-equal Cambodian and international prosecutors.[19] All judicial investigations are the responsibility of two co-investigating judges: one Cambodian and one international.[20] All disputes between the national and international co-prosecutors and co-investigating judges are settled by a Pre-Trial Chamber that has a majority of national judges and must adopt decisions in accordance with the super-majority rule.[21]

The ECCC Trial Chamber rendered its first judgment in July 2010 against Duch,[22] who was deputy chairman and then chairman of S-21, an infamous Khmer Rouge security centre that conducted interrogations and executions of perceived enemies of the regime from 1975 to 1979.[23] For

---

[14] ECCC, *Prosecutor v. Kaing Guek Eav*, Pre-Trial Chamber, Decision on Appeal Against Provisional Detention Order of Kang Guek Eav alias "Duch", 001/18-07-2007, 3 December 2007, para. 19 (http://www.legal-tools.org/doc/fe0ba1/).

[15] Agreement Between the United Nations and the Royal Government of Cambodia Concerning the Prosecution under Cambodian Law of Crimes Committed During the Period of Democratic Kampuchea, 6 June 2003, Article 2 (https://www.legal-tools.org/doc/3a33d3/pdf/).

[16] Sarah M. H. Nouwen, "'Hybrid courts': The Hybrid Category of a New Type of International Crimes Courts", in *Utrecht Law Review*, 2006, vol. 2, no. 2, pp. 190, 200.

[17] Cambodia, National Assembly, Law on the Establishment of Extraordinary Chambers in the Courts of Cambodia for the Prosecution of Crimes Committed during the Period of Democratic Kampuchea, Article 9, NS/RKM/1004/006, 27 October 2004 (http://www.legal-tools.org/doc/88d544/).

[18] *Ibid.*, Article 14.

[19] *Ibid.*, Article 16.

[20] *Ibid.*, Article 23.

[21] *Ibid.*, Articles 20 and 23.

[22] ECCC, *Prosecutor v. Kaing Guek Eav alias Duch*, Trial Chamber, Judgment, 001/18-07-2007, 26 July 2010 (http://www.legal-tools.org/doc/dbdb62/).

[23] *Ibid.*, p. 111.

---

his role as commandant of S-21, the Trial Chamber found Duch guilty of crimes against humanity (including murder, extermination, enslavement, imprisonment, torture, persecution on political grounds and other inhumane acts) and grave breaches of the 1949 Geneva Conventions (including wilful killing, torture and inhumane treatment, wilfully causing great suffering or serious injury to body or health, wilfully depriving a prisoner of war or civilian of the rights of fair and regular trial, and unlawful confinement of civilians).[24] The ECCC has indicted four other suspects, all of whom were high-ranking members in the Democratic Kampuchea government.[25]

10.2.2. Litigating Forced Marriages before the ECCC

In order to understand how the charge of forced marriages came to be included in the proceedings before the ECCC, it is important to appreciate the largely civil law-influenced trial process at the court. The Internal Rules of the ECCC specify that all prosecutions are the responsibility of the ECCC co-prosecutors. Once the co-prosecutors have reason to believe that crimes within the ECCC's jurisdiction have been committed, they set the stage for a judicial investigation by forwarding an introductory submission to the OCIJ.[26] This statement must contain the relevant facts, offences and legal provisions, and the names of the accused, as applicable. It is accompanied by evidentiary material in support of its claims.[27] The OCIJ conducts a judicial investigation on the basis of this introductory submission and other supplementary submissions filed by the co-prosecutors.[28] The issuance of a closing order concludes the investigation, and either dismisses the case against the charged person, or indicts him and forwards the case to trial.[29] As mentioned earlier, the first introducto-

---

[24] *Ibid.*, p. 567.

[25] The other four indicted persons are: Khieu Samphan, the Democratic Kampuchea regime's former head of state; Ieng Sary, the former deputy prime minister and minister for foreign affairs; Sary's wife, Ieng Thirith, the former minister for social affairs; and Nuon Chea, the former deputy secretary of the Communist Party of Kampuchea. See further, ECCC, Case 002 (http://www.eccc.gov.kh/en/case/topic/2).

[26] ECCC, Internal Rules, Rev. 9, Rule 53(1), 16 January 2015 ('ECCC Internal Rules') (http://www.legal-tools.org/doc/b8838e/).

[27] *Ibid.*, Rule 53(1)–(2).

[28] *Ibid.*, Rule 55(2).

[29] *Ibid.*, Rule 67(1).

ry submission by the co-prosecutors did not contain any mention of the crime of forced marriages. Forced marriage charges were first introduced in the proceedings by the lawyers for civil parties who filed a request for supplementary preliminary investigations[30] under Rule 49 of the Internal Rules.[31]

In this request, the civil parties' lawyers argued that the Khmer Rouge followed a policy of conducting mass forced marriages in Cambodia between persons who were mostly strangers, with a view to controlling the reproductive capacity and the birth of children who would support the revolution.[32] These marriages eschewed traditional Khmer rituals associated with the wedding ceremony and individuals were coerced into marrying persons of the Khmer Rouge's choosing on pain of punishment, or even death.[33] The marriages had elements of the crimes of rape, enslavement, forced pregnancy and forced marriages as "other inhumane acts" already recognised in international law.[34] While the practice of such

---

[30] First Request, 2009, see *supra* note 1.

[31] ECCC Internal Rules, Rule 49: Exercising Public Action, see *supra* note 26:

　1. Prosecution of crimes within the jurisdiction of the ECCC may be initiated only by the Co-Prosecutors, whether at their own discretion or on the basis of a complaint.

　2. The Co-Prosecutors shall receive and consider all written complaints or information alleging commission of crimes within the jurisdiction of the ECCC. Such complaints or information may be lodged with the Co-Prosecutors by any person, organisation or other source who witnessed or was a victim of such alleged crimes, or who has knowledge of such alleged crimes.

　3. A complaint referred to in this Rule may also be prepared and/or lodged on behalf of a Victim by a lawyer or Victims' Association. Copies of all such written complaints shall be kept with the Office of Administration and may be translated into the working languages of the ECCC, as needed.

　4. Such complaints shall not automatically initiate criminal prosecution, and the Co-Prosecutors shall decide, at their discretion, whether to reject the complaint, include the complaint in an ongoing preliminary investigation, conduct a new preliminary investigation or forward the complaint directly to the Co-Investigating Judges. The Co-Prosecutors shall inform the complainant of the decision as soon as possible and in any case not more than 60 (sixty) days after registration of the complaint.

　5. A decision not to pursue a complaint shall not have the effect of *res judicata*. The Co-Prosecutors may change their decision at any time in which case the complainant shall be so informed as soon as possible and in any case not more than 30 (thirty) days from the decision.

[32] First Request, 2009, pp. 4, 7, 29, see *supra* note 1.

[33] *Ibid.*, pp. 4, 38.

[34] *Ibid.*, pp. 6, 20–32.

---

marriages was widespread during the Democratic Kampuchea regime and the evidence on the case file corroborated this finding, they had not been properly investigated by the ECCC and did not form part of the introductory submission.[35] The civil parties' lawyers thus urged that witnesses should be interviewed and a supplementary submission filed so that new charges could be brought against the accused for forced marriages and related sexual crimes. This would fulfil the ECCC's mandate of ascertaining the truth and bringing justice to the victims, especially given the large number of the victims of this crime and its negative effect on Cambodian society. It would also be in keeping with the recognition of gender crimes and their devastating impact on societies by other international tribunals.[36]

This request led to a flurry of activity by the ECCC. On 17 March 2009, the OCIJ forwarded the case file of the judicial investigation to the Office of the Co-Prosecutors for its opinion on the need for a supplementary submission concerning the civil parties' claims of forced marriages.[37] On 30 April 2009, the co-prosecutors filed a supplementary submission requesting and authorising further investigations by the OCIJ into four civil party complaints that alleged victimisation on account of forced marriages and other non-consensual sexual relations. They also authorised investigation into any other facts referencing forced marriages that would facilitate proving the ECCC's jurisdiction or the mode of the liability of the four accused (Duch's case file had been separated from the other accused earlier and labelled Case File 001.)[38] Shortly after, on 15 July 2009, the civil parties' lawyers filed their second request for investigative actions[39] under Rule 55(10) of the Internal Rules[40] concerning the existence

---

[35] *Ibid.*, pp. 1–3.

[36] *Ibid.*, pp. 42–45.

[37] ECCC, Civil Parties' Co-Lawyers' Second Request for Investigative Actions Concerning Forced Marriages and Forced Sexual Relations, 002/19-09-2007-ECCC/OCIJ, 15 July 2009, p. 3 ('Second Request') (http://www.eccc.gov.kh/en/documents/court/civil-parties39-co-lawyers39-request-investigative-actions-concerning-forced-marriage).

[38] *Ibid.*, p. 3.

[39] *Ibid.*

[40] At any time during an investigation, the co-prosecutors, a charged person or a civil party may request the co-investigating judges to make such orders or undertake such investigative action as they consider useful for the conduct of the investigation. If the co-investigating judges do not agree with the request, they shall issue a rejection order as soon as possible and, in any event, before the end of the judicial investigation. The order, which shall set out the reasons for the rejection, shall be notified to the parties and shall be subject to appeal.

of forced marriages under the Khmer Rouge and their appropriate legal classification, arguing that given the gravity of these crimes immediate investigation was required.[41] The civil parties outlined the legal elements of the crime of forced marriages, noted that they are as grave as enumerated crimes against humanity and may indeed include some of them such as enslavement, rape and torture, and that they have been recognised as a crime against humanity of "other inhumane acts" by international tribunals.[42] They reiterated and expanded upon the factual evidence pointing to the occurrence of widespread forced marriages under the Khmer Rouge as a matter of state policy.[43] The request urged that the OCIJ has discretion to determine the scope of judicial investigations. If they have knowledge of conduct that could constitute a crime under the ECCC's jurisdiction, the duty to investigate such conduct is also inherent in civil law systems of criminal law such as the Cambodian criminal law system on which the procedural law of the ECCC is based.[44]

The OCIJ's public statement on the scope of the judicial investigations in Case File 002 against the four accused issued on 5 November 2009 marked the first significant victory for the civil parties.[45] In this statement, the OCIJ included "forced marriage throughout Democratic Kampuchea" within the scope of its investigations.[46] Emboldened by this acknowledgement, the lawyers for civil parties filed a fourth investigative request on 4 December 2009,[47] identifying and requesting the investigation of particular witnesses in specific locations, obtaining expert advice on the crime of forced marriages by named expert witnesses, and that interviews be conducted by gender-trained female staff.[48] The OCIJ issued its Order on the Request for Investigative Action Concerning Forced Mar-

---

[41] Second Request, 2009, p. 1, see *supra* note 37.

[42] *Ibid.*, pp. 5–8.

[43] *Ibid.*, pp. 9–14, 16–17

[44] *Ibid.*, p. 30.

[45] ECCC, Office of the Co-Investigating Judges, Statement from the Co-Investigating Judges, Judicial Investigation of Case 002/19-09-2007 and Civil Party Applications, 002/19-09-2007-ECCC-OCIJ, 5 November 2009.

[46] *Ibid.*, p. 5.

[47] ECCC, Co-Lawyers' for the Civil Parties' Fourth Investigative Request Concerning Forced Marriages and Sexually Related Crimes, 002/19-09-2007-ECCC/OCIJ, 4 December 2009 (http://www.legal-tools.org/doc/93980e-1/).

[48] *Ibid.*

riages and Forced Sexual Relations[49] granting the request to conduct investigations into forced marriages throughout Cambodia and inviting *amici curiae* briefs on the subject, while declining to appoint experts or only female investigators.[50] On 15 September 2010, the OCIJ issued its closing order in Case 002[51] indicting the four accused for violations of the 1956 Cambodian Penal Code, genocide, grave breaches of the Geneva Conventions, and crimes against humanity including rape and other inhumane acts (stemming from the allegations of forced marriage and forced sexual relations).[52]

The proceedings on forced marriages before the ECCC raise questions similar to those that any international tribunal pursuing a policy of thematic prosecutions will confront. The ECCC is an *ad hoc* tribunal that has been plagued by political problems, lack of co-operation from the Cambodian government, limited resources and ongoing budgetary woes. Operating within these constraints, it has been tasked with establishing accountability for a panoply of extremely serious international crimes, including the "crime of crimes" of genocide. Given its precarious position and the burden it has to discharge of prosecuting what would without doubt be considered some of the most horrendous crimes ever litigated before an international tribunal – including widespread murders, acts of torture and genocide – what lessons can we learn from the prominent position that the crime of forced marriages, which some would consider a 'less serious offence', now occupies in the proceedings?

I argue that the charge of forced marriages before the Khmer Rouge tribunal points to important institutional and structural factors that constrain or encourage the prosecution of sex crimes, or indeed other crimes that would be deemed 'less serious' before international tribunals. These factors, moreover, have deeper implications for the project of international criminal justice. What is the primary purpose of criminal tribunals in a

---

[49] ECCC, Office of the Co-Investigating Judges, Order on Request for Investigative Action Concerning Forced Marriages and Forced Sexual Relations, 002/19-09-2007-ECCC/ OCIJ, 18 December 2009.

[50] *Ibid.*, pp. 12–15, 18.

[51] ECCC, Office of the Co-Investigating Judges, Closing Order, Case no. 002/19-09-2007-ECCC/OCIJ, 15 September 2010 ('Closing Order') (http://www.legal-tools.org/doc/25a2d0/).

[52] *Ibid.*, p. 1613.

---

particular situation of mass atrocity? How should tribunal justice accommodate the interests of various affected actors in the aftermath of mass atrocity? And what role can legal institutions have in societal change, especially in post-conflict societies? I will address each of these in turn.

10.3. The Differing Challenges of *Ex Post* and *Ex Ante* Tribunals

10.3.1. Different Goals of International Courts

At first glance, the statement that the goal of international criminal tribunals is to achieve accountability for international crimes appears a truism. Once one examines this claim a little more closely, the cracks beneath the surface become apparent. While bringing to justice alleged perpetrators of international crimes is undoubtedly a mandate of all international tribunals,[53] it applies with more force in the case of *ex post* tribunals such as the ECCC. These are courts that are set up in the aftermath of conflict to establish accountability for the crimes that were committed in a particular region,[54] and while they may have other objectives, such as preventing a recurrence of violence or helping achieve political and social stability[55] – the goal of accountability introduces a strong 'backward-looking' element into the tribunal proceedings. In contrast, tribunals such as the ICC are also *ex ante* courts[56] – the situations referred to the ICC may be situations of on-going violence; violence that occurred in the very recent past; or

---

[53] See, for example, UN Security Council, Resolution 827, UN Doc. S/RES/827 (1993), 25 May 1993 (http://www.legal-tools.org/doc/dc079b/); UN Security Council, Resolution 955, UN Doc. S/RES/955 (1994), 8 November 1994 (http://www.legal-tools.org/doc/f5ef47/); UN Security Council, Report of the Secretary-General pursuant to Paragraph 2 of Security Council Resolution 808 (1993), UN Doc. S/25704 and Add. 1, 3 May 1993, para. 26 (http://www.legal-tools.org/doc/c2640a/); Report of the Group of Experts, paras. 102–6, see *supra* note 2; Rome Statute of the International Criminal Court, 17 July 1998, in force 1 July 2002, Preamble (http://www.legal-tools.org/doc/7b9af9/).

[54] On the distinction between *ex post* and *ex ante* tribunals, see Mahnoush A. Arsanjani and W. Michael Reisman, "The Law-in-Action of the International Criminal Court", in *American Journal of International Law*, 2005, vol. 99, no. 2, p. 385.

[55] On the various goals put forward by international tribunals and their advocates, see Minna Schrag, "Lessons Learned from ICTY Experience", in *Journal of International Criminal Justice*, 2004, vol. 2, no. 2, pp. 427–28; Justin Levit, "Developments in the Law: International Criminal Law", in *Harvard Law Review*, 2001, vol. 114, no. 7, pp. 1961–74.

[56] Arsanjani and Reisman, 2005, p. 385, see *supra* note 54.

---

conflict that took place some years ago.[57] The reasons for referral to the ICC may also differ greatly. For instance, even though the deterrent capacity of international criminal tribunals has been called into question,[58] there is at least a plausible argument to be made that ICC referrals can have deterrent effects in situations of ongoing conflict where the perpetrators of atrocities continue to wield political power and the ICC must strike a delicate balance between the demands of retributive justice on the one hand and peace and stability on the other.[59] Payam Akhavan gives the examples of three recent interventions by the ICC, in the situations in Côte d'Ivoire, Uganda and Darfur. In Côte d'Ivoire, the threat of ICC prosecution for incitement of violence against civilians and ethnic, religious or racial communities[60] was touted as a significant factor in stopping the government-controlled media's radio and television broadcasts of messages of hate, and potentially preventing the mob violence from escalating into genocide.[61] In the case of Uganda, referral of the situation concerning atrocities perpetrated by the Lord's Resistance Army ('LRA') to the ICC is considered a crucial factor in Sudan ceasing to harbour the LRA. This deprived the LRA of important bases in southern Sudan, resulting in a rapid de-escalation of violence in northern Uganda and ultimately forcing its leader, Joseph Kony, to come to the negotiating table.[62] Even in Sudan, the Security Council's referral of the situation in Darfur to the ICC has strained the relationship between the government and the Janjaweed mili-

---

[57] See, for instance, the different stages at which ICC referrals have been invoked in the situations in Kenya and Libya: UN Security Council, Resolution 1970, UN Doc. S/RES/1970 (2011), 26 February 2011 (http://www.legal-tools.org/doc/00a45e/) referring the situation in Libya to the ICC; ICC, Pre-Trial Chamber II, Decision Pursuant to Article 15 of the Rome Statute on the Authorization of an Investigation into the Situation in the Republic of Kenya, ICC-01/09, 31 March 2010 (http://www.legal-tools.org/doc/338a6f/).

[58] See, for example, Robert D. Sloane, "The Expressive Capacity of International Punishment: The Limits of the National Law Analogy and the Potential of International Criminal Law", in *Stanford Journal of International Law*, 2007, vol. 43, no. 1, pp. 39, 72; Mirjan Damaška, "What is the Point of International Criminal Justice?", in *Chicago Kent Law Review*, 2008, vol. 83, no. 1, pp. 329, 344–45; Levit, 2001, pp. 1963–66, see *supra* note 55.

[59] Payam Akhavan, "Are International Criminal Tribunals a Disincentive to Peace?: Reconciling Judicial Romanticism with Political Realism", in *Human Rights Quarterly*, 2009, vol. 31, no. 3, pp. 624, 627.

[60] Juan E. Méndez, Statement of the Special Adviser on the Prevention of Genocide, United Nations News Centre, 15 November 2004.

[61] Akhavan, 2009, pp. 639–40, see *supra* note 59.

[62] *Ibid.*, pp. 641–44.

---

tia and forced the Sudanese authorities to include the issue of accountability for the crimes committed in Darfur into the political calculus.[63] This ability of a tribunal such as the ICC to intervene in situations of impending or prevailing conflict inevitably means that the proceedings before the tribunals can be relatively forward looking in their aims – that is, while retributive justice as an end in itself may be one of the aims, and an important one at that, other demands such as deterrence or even communication of condemnation may take precedence.

This difference in prioritisation of aims would have important consequences for which crimes take precedence when making decisions on the allocation of limited resources for investigation and prosecution. In tribunals such as the ECCC, it could well be argued that, if the tribunal is essentially seeking retributive justice as a primary goal of the trial, the crime of forced marriages could be more readily relegated to nearer the bottom of the prioritisation hierarchy. Retributivism holds "not only that we must not punish the innocent, or punish the guilty more than they deserve, but that we should punish the guilty to the extent that they deserve".[64] While there are several versions of retributive justice extant – the absolutist, the threshold and the consequentialist[65] – by almost any of these measures, some of the other crimes before the ECCC would take priority. For the absolutist retributivist, since limited resources would make punishment of all criminals impractical, his compromise would be to punish the maximum number of offenders regardless of the seriousness of the crime.[66] In the case of international tribunals like the ECCC, this consideration is to some extent already foreclosed by their jurisdictional mandate to focus on senior leaders and those most responsible for the crimes in question. For the consequentialist retributivist who wants to maximise the total amount of deserved punishment, the decisive factor would be the per-unit cost of the deserved punishment.[67] This cost is, however, difficult to calculate in the concrete circumstances of the

---

[63] *Ibid.*, pp. 649–50.

[64] "Legal Punishment", in Stanford Encyclopaedia of Philosophy.

[65] See Michael T. Cahill, "Retributive Justice in the Real World", in *Washington University Law Review*, 2007, vol. 85, no. 4, pp. 815, 848–53.

[66] *Ibid.*, p. 849.

[67] *Ibid.*, p. 851.

crime.[68] For the threshold retributivist, it would be important to establish a ranking of crimes according to their seriousness and punish them in sequence, departing from this hierarchy only in limited cases.[69] According to the dessert-based approach to retribution, the seriousness of the harm is calculated based on the conduct's degree of harmfulness and the actor's culpability.[70] In the case of crimes before the ECCC, given that the accused have been charged with genocide,[71] which requires conduct carried out with the specific intent of destroying an enumerated group,[72] the crimes that form part of the genocide charge (and of which forced marriage does not form part) could arguably be considered more serious. This criterion would moreover not be particularly helpful in prioritisation decisions involving crimes within the same category of crimes – say murder and rape as instruments of genocide, such as in the case of the prosecution of rape by the ICTR.[73] Similarly, while quantification of the quality and extent of harm suffered is a task fraught with perils, especially in the context of international crimes where there is a minimum threshold of gravity and suffering implied in the very nature of the crime, it would not be difficult to construct an argument that loss of life on a genocidal scale is more harmful than forced marriages, despite their widespread nature. Thus, while courts have refrained from constructing a hierarchy of crimes,[74] given the status of genocide as the "crime of crimes" and the

---

[68] *Ibid.*, pp. 851–52.

[69] *Ibid.*, p. 850.

[70] See, for example, Andrew von Hirsch and Nils Jareborg, "Gauging Criminal Harm: A Living Standard Analysis", in *Oxford Journal of Legal Studies*, 1991, vol. 11, no. 1, pp. 1–38.

[71] Closing Order, 2010, p. 1613, see *supra* note 51.

[72] On genocide and the requirement of specific intent, see William A. Schabas, *Genocide in International Law: The Crime of Crimes*, Cambridge University Press, Cambridge, 2000, pp. 217–25; Antonio Cassese, *International Criminal Law*, Oxford University Press, Oxford, 2008, p. 137. This has been challenged in recent literature, in for example, Claus Kress, "The Darfur Report and Genocidal Intent", in *Journal of International Criminal Justice*, 2005, vol. 3, no. 3, pp. 562–78 (https://www.legal-tools.org/doc/84fec6/pdf/).

[73] On rape being prosecuted as genocide, see ICTR, *Prosecutor v. Jean-Paul Akayesu*, Trial Chamber, Judgment, ICTR-96-4, 2 September 1998, pp. 732–73 (http://www.legal-tools.org/doc/b8d7bd/). For a thoughtful analysis of this practice at the ICTR, see Doris E. Buss, "Rethinking 'Rape as a Weapon of War'", in *Feminist Legal Studies*, 2009, vol. 17, no. 2, p. 145.

[74] See Jennifer J. Clark, "Zero to Life: Sentencing Appeals at the International Criminal Tribunals for the Former Yugoslavia and Rwanda", in *Georgetown Law Journal*, 2008, vol. 96, no. 5, pp. 1685, 1697, referring to the jurisprudence of the ICTY and the ICTR rejecting a hierar-

moral weight such a label carries,[75] the retributivist approach may favour prioritisation of all crimes that occur within a certain context – such as intent to destroy the group (genocide) rather than as a widespread attack against a civilian population (crimes against humanity). The concerns of feminists that the recognition of rape as an independent sexual crime that harms all women in times of conflict as well as in peacetime would be subsumed by its prosecution as an instrument of genocide[76] should at least make us cautious towards advocating such a solution. Moreover, if the contextual element for the crimes remains the same – that is, all the individual crimes occur as crimes against humanity – a retributive posture may rarely prioritise sex crimes, or indeed any other crimes, over those that involve loss of life.

In the case of a tribunal such as the ICC, since the pursuit of aims other than retributive justice may take precedence, the prosecution's decision to prioritise the attack by Sudanese rebels on African Union peacekeeping troops, resulting in the deaths of 12 peacekeepers and serious injuries to eight others,[77] can be seen as serving the objectives of the ICC. While this decision cannot perhaps be justified on a strict retributivist basis given the sheer scale of atrocities allegedly committed by government

---

chy of crimes: ICTR, *Prosecutor v. Clément Kayishema et al.*, Appeals Chamber, Judgment (reasons), ICTR-95-1, 1 June 2001, p. 367 (http://www.legal-tools.org/doc/9ea5f4/); ICTY, *Prosecutor v. Anto Furundžija*, Appeals Chamber, Judgment, IT-95-17/1, 21 July 2000, p. 246 (http://www.legal-tools.org/doc/660d3f/); ICTY, *Prosecutor v. Milomir Stakić*, Appeals Chamber, Judgment, IT-97-24, 22 March 2006, p. 375 (http://www.legal-tools.org/doc/09f75f/).

[75] See, for instance, the ICC prosecutor's attempts to add genocide to the charges against Omar Al-Bashir: ICC, *Prosecutor v. Omar Hassan Ahmad Al Bashir*, Prosecution's Application for Leave to Appeal the "Decision on the Prosecution's Application for a Warrant of Arrest against Omar Hassan Ahmad Al Bashir", ICC-02/05-01/09, 10 March 2009 (http://www.legal-tools.org/doc/b30a0d/).

[76] For an excellent account of this debate, see Karen Engle, "Feminism and its (Dis)contents: Criminalizing Wartime Rape in Bosnia and Herzegovina", in *American Journal of International Law*, 2005, vol. 99, no. 4, pp. 778, 785–87, referring especially to Rhonda Copelon, "Surfacing Gender: Reconceptualizing Crimes against Women in Time of War", in Alexandra Stiglmayer (ed.), *Mass Rape: The War against Women in Bosnia-Herzegovina*, University of Nebraska Press, Lincoln, 1994, pp. 198, 205, 207.

[77] For details of the procedural history, see ICC, *Prosecutor v. Bahar Idriss Abu Garda*, Pre-Trial Chamber, Decision on Confirmation of Charges, ICC-02/05-02/09, 8 February 2010 ('*Abu Garda* Decision') (http://www.legal-tools.org/doc/cb3614/).

forces in Sudan,[78] it furthers other important aims including potentially deterring further such attacks by the rebels, demonstrating impartiality, and facilitating the crucial peacekeeping function of such forces in conflict zones.[79] As the ICC Pre-Trial Chamber stated in its decision on confirmation of charges, the attack on peacekeepers not only had a grave impact on the immediate victims of the attack and their families, but the suspension and disruption of their activities had severe consequences for the local civilian population which relied on them for protection and humanitarian assistance.[80] Similar justifications could be used in the case of prosecuting sexual crimes, especially in societies where an attack on the female population is widely considered an attack on the entire community for diverse reasons – because of the image of women in a particular society, due to its effect on the reproductive function, and because of the message of impotence it sends to the male population.[81]

10.3.2. Pragmatic Factors Affecting Investigations and Prosecutions

Another more pragmatic factor that may have a stronger influence on the investigative and prosecution efforts of *ex ante* tribunals when contrasted with their post-conflict counterparts is the political, resource and information constraints that the former must operate within. For instance, it is suggested that in the context of the DRC, while there were reports of serious crimes having been committed in the provinces of Ituri, North Kivu and South Kivu, the ICC's initial investigations targeted the crimes in Ituri. This was a strategic decision keeping in mind the better security for conducting investigations as a result of the presence of UN peacekeepers in the region and also the fact that the rebels in Ituri did not enjoy the support of the DRC government on which the ICC relied for support.[82] There are also other limitations that any evidence gathering exercise will en-

---

[78] See Human Rights Watch, "ICC/Darfur: Court Acts to Protect African Peacekeepers", 17 May 2009, noting the difference in the scale of atrocities committed by rebels as contrasted with government forces; Amy Stillman, "Prosecutors Hit Back at Rebel Case Criticism", in *ACR*, no. 210, Institute for War and Peace Reporting, 24 April 2009.

[79] See Human Rights Watch, "ICC Hearing on Darfuri Rebel Leader", 14 October 2009.

[80] *Abu Garda* Decision, para. 33, see *supra* note 77.

[81] See, for example, Christine Chinkin, "Rape and Sexual Abuse of Women in International Law", in *European Journal of International Law*, 1995, vol. 5, no. 1, pp. 3–5; Buss, 2009, pp. 148–49 and references therein, *supra* note 73.

[82] Akhavan, 2009, pp. 631–32, see *supra* note 59.

counter in situations of conflict: 1) the territory where alleged crimes are taking place may be inaccessible or only partially accessible; 2) reaching and interviewing witnesses may be difficult; and 3) the collapse of state and civil society institutions could severely limit access to assistance in terms of information, personnel and resources.[83] This may make the investigation and prosecution of sex crimes in particular quite challenging. Sex crimes are considered to be especially prone to the problem of underreporting, even in times of peace, due to factors such the victim's feelings of guilt, shame or even fear.[84] This under-reporting is only exacerbated in times of conflict for several reasons: 1) victims may not be able to reach any state or non-state agency to report the incident to; 2) the alleged perpetrators of rape may be agents of the state; and 3) the perpetrator may kill the victim after.[85] An international tribunal that is reliant on domestic authorities and civil society institutions to conduct investigations may thus find it much harder to do so for sexual offences as compared to crimes such as murder.

The experience of the charge of forced marriages before the ECCC, a post-conflict tribunal, presents an interesting contrast. As one of the lawyers for civil parties, Silke Studzinsky, recalls:

> The prosecution and the co-investigating judges did not independently investigate sexual crimes initially both because they were heavily reliant on documentary evidence compiled by the Documentation Center for Cambodia, an independent NGO based, which did not specifically mention these crimes, and because they operated under the widely held assumption that the Khmer Rouge had followed a strict policy of severely punishing any sexual crimes, which resulted in their near absolute prevention.[86]

---

[83] See "Pursuing Justice in Ongoing Conflict: Examining the Challenges", Report on Wilton Park Conference, WPSO8/7, para. 4, 7–10 December 2008.

[84] Jennifer L. Green, "Uncovering Collective Rape: A Comparative Study of Political Sexual Violence" in *International Journal of Sociology*, 2004, vol. 34, no. 1, pp. 97, 104; Elisabeth J. Wood, "Variation in Sexual Violence During War", in *Politics and Society*, 2006, vol. 34, no. 3, pp. 307, 318–19.

[85] Green, 2004, p. 105, see *supra* note 84; Wood, 2006, pp. 318–19, see *supra* note 84.

[86] Silke Studzinsky, "Die Roten Khmer befahlen Zwangsheiraten und Vergewaltigungen", in *Streit*, 2009, vol. 2, p. 59.

All this changed with the press conference by Studzinsky and the lawyers for civil parties, where they made public the sexual crimes committed against their client, a transsexual who was forced to behave and dress as a man under the Khmer Rouge.[87] In the days following the conference, several calls came in through the radio, alleging victimisation on account of sexual crimes under the Khmer Rouge. The lawyers for civil parties were also able to unearth literature and studies by academics written in the aftermath of the regime, documenting instances of sexual assault and forced marriages.[88] Thus, a significant factor in being able to bring charges of forced marriages and related sexual offences before the tribunal was the ability of victims to report the allegations and pre-existing studies corroborating their existence. Neither may have been feasible in the context of a pre-conflict tribunal.

I now want to move on to my second factor on the institutional and structural elements influencing the prosecution of sexual crimes, which is quite closely related to the discussion on the aims of the tribunal. This is the vision of the tribunal as one of the tools of post-conflict transitional peace building and establishment of the rule of law.

10.4. The International Tribunal as an Instrument of Post-Conflict Rule of Law Development

There has been a recent trend in academic literature discussing the long-term impact of international and hybrid criminal tribunals on the societies in which they operate – that is, apart from the limited, albeit integral, aim of bringing perpetrators of atrocities to justice, whether such interventions can be meaningful in promoting the rule of law in transitional polities.[89] For instance, Jane Stromseth argues that at least part of the assessment of

---

[87] *Ibid.*

[88] *Ibid.*

[89] See, for example, Jane Stromseth, "Justice on the Ground: Can International Criminal Courts Strengthen Domestic Rule of Law in Post Conflict Societies?", in *Hague Journal of the Rule of Law*, 2009, vol. 1, no. 1, pp. 87–88; see, generally, Hideaki Shinoda, "Peace-Building by the Rule of Law: A Examination of Intervention in the Form of International Tribunals", in *International Journal of Peace Studies*, 2002, vol. 7, no. 1, p. 41; "Outreach of International Justice: How Can the Work of an International Criminal Tribunal Foster the Rule of Law in National Jurisdictions?", in *Symposium on the Legacy of International Criminal Courts and Tribunals in Africa*, ICTR and International Center for Ethics, Justice, and Public Life, Brandeis University, 2010, p. 34.

the record of an international or hybrid court must depend on whether the court is able to induce confidence about fair justice in the people affected by the conflict and to rebuild and strengthen collapsed judicial institutions in such societies.[90] She claims that trials for mass atrocity have an inevitable communicative effect, which influences the confidence of affected parties about fair justice. The trials must therefore aim to demonstrate that certain conduct is impermissible, that persons will be held accountable for it; and that justice can be substantively and procedurally fair.[91]

If an international trial is envisaged mainly as a crucial appliance in the toolbox of measures seeking to promote the rule of law in a post conflict society, it would justify prioritising the investigation and prosecution of crimes that are deemed to contribute more directly to this purpose. This is arguably a different calculus from that undertaken by tribunals such as the International Military Tribunal at Nuremberg, where the main focus of the tribunal, at least in the initial stages, was to condemn Nazi aggression and the law of atrocity only acquired prominence subsequently.[92]

Scholars have argued that the traumatic past of societies that experienced periods of severe violations of human rights and violence tends to recur in different forms,[93] and while there is no concrete evidence to indicate that trials or other reconciliation measures can truly break this cycle of violence and trauma,[94] the international trial as an instrument for the establishment of the rule of law at least attempts to pave the way to belief in and support for fundamental human rights principles. This norm-creating function of the international trial is inevitably reflected through the persons and crimes it chooses to prosecute. Sex crimes could justifiably be considered an appropriate category for prioritisation for prosecution under this rubric for several reasons.

While it should be obvious that prevention of impunity for crimes such as killings, torture and other forms of harm resulting in severe suffer-

---

[90] Stromseth, 2009, pp. 89–91, see *supra* note 89.

[91] *Ibid.*, p. 92.

[92] See Mark A. Drumbl, "Pluralizing International Criminal Justice", in *Michigan Law Review*, 2005, vol. 103, no. 6, pp. 1295, 1299.

[93] See Alexander Wilde, "Irruptions of Memory: Expressive Politics in Chile's Transition to Democracy", in *Journal of Latin American Studies*, 1999, vol. 31, no. 2, pp. 473–74.

[94] See Laurel E. Fletcher, Harvey M. Weinstein with Jamie Rowen, "Context, Timing and the Dynamics of Transitional Justice", in *Human Rights Quarterly*, 2009, vol. 31, pp. 163, 169.

ing should feature prominently on the communicative agenda of international trials, perhaps a special case can be made for focusing on crimes that are less universally regarded, at least in practice, as equally deserving of condemnation.[95] In other words, in a world of scarce resources, the norm-creating and enforcing function of international tribunals can arguably be better directed to sending a clear message that sex crimes are considered equally egregious violations of human dignity as any of the crimes that are more traditionally accepted as such.[96]

This argument has particular force in countries where gender relations have been historically unequal and harmful to women, both in times of peace as well as in times of war. In the case of Cambodia, the government followed an official policy of amnesiac silence about the atrocities during the Khmer Rouge, which was only reluctantly discarded with the establishment of the ECCC.[97] As proceedings before the ECCC gathered momentum, the outreach activities carried out by ECCC officials combined with vigorous information and outreach campaigns by non-governmental organisations and civil society groups active in Cambodia introduced an entire generation of Cambodians, some for the very first time, to the horrific nature of the crimes committed by the Khmer Rouge.[98] However, this resurgence of interest in Cambodia's past left untouched the issue of sexual crimes during the Khmer Rouge regime. As the interview with Studzinsky reminds us, this was due to the common assumption that such crimes did not occur during the Democratic Kampuchea regime and the otherwise extensive documentation on Khmer Rouge

---

[95] See Margaret M. deGuzman, "Giving Priority to Sex Crime Prosecutions: The Philosophical Foundations of a Feminist Agenda", in *International Criminal Law Review*, 2011, vol. 11, no. 3, pp. 515, 521–22.

[96] *Ibid.*, pp. 525–26.

[97] See David Chandler, "Cambodia Deals with its Past: Collective Memory, Demonisation and Induced Amnesia", in *Totalitarian Movements and Political Religions*, 2008, vol. 9, no. 2, pp. 355–56.

[98] Alex Bates, *Transitional Justice in Cambodia: Analytical Report*, British Institute of International and Comparative Law, London, 2010, pp. 69–70. On the level of knowledge about the Khmer Rouge regime in Cambodian society, see also Phuong Pham, Patrick Vinck and Mychelle Balthazard, *So We Will Never Forget: A Population-Based Survey on Attitudes About Social Reconstruction and the Extraordinary Chambers in the Courts of Cambodia*, Human Rights Center, University of California Berkeley, January 2009, pp. 25–27.

atrocities by Documentation Center of Cambodia ('DCCAM') did not single them out.[99]

This lack of attention to sexual crimes must be seen in the context of current Cambodian society, which is characterised by severe gender disparities. Despite the fact that women are heads of over a quarter of Cambodian households, women continue to be regarded as occupying a lower status in the social hierarchy.[100] Laws prohibiting violence against women, including domestic violence, rape, crimes against sex workers, also suffer from problems of underenforcement, contributing to a culture of impunity.[101]

Highlighting investigation and prosecution of sex crimes in post-conflict societies can have far-reaching expressive and didactic effects.[102] Not only can international tribunals establish accountability for crimes, the recognition of which at the international criminal law level is relatively recent and fragile, but also contribute to establishing societal norms that proscribe violence against women, even in times of peace. This potential would also be in line with the position taken by feminist scholars who argue that crimes against women in wartime are made more acceptable by the everyday underprosecution of violent crimes routinely committed against women, with which they have more in common than is apparent at first glance.[103]

10.5. The Role of Civil Parties in International Criminal Trials

Discussions on the history of prosecution of sex crimes by international tribunals readily acknowledge that sex crimes were included within the jurisdiction of the ICTY and the ICTR at least in part due to extensive ad-

---

[99] Studzinsky, 2009, see *supra* note 86.

[100] "A Fair Share for Women: Cambodia Gender Assessment", United Nations Development Fund for Women, World Bank, Asian Development Bank, the United Nations Development Programme and Department for International Development of the United Kingdom, 2004, p. 3.

[101] *Ibid.*, pp. 10–11.

[102] See deGuzman, 2011, pp. 525–26, *supra* note 95.

[103] See Rhonda Copelon, "Surfacing Gender: Reconceptualizing Crimes Against Women in Times of War", in Lois Ann Lorentzen and Jennifer Turpin (eds.), *The Women and War Reader*, New York University Press, New York, 1998, pp. 64, 75; Carolyn Nordstrom, "Girls Behind the (Front) Lines", in Lois Ann Lorentzen and Jennifer Turpin (eds.), *The Women and War Reader*, New York University Press, New York, 1998, p. 86.

vocacy by women's organisations.[104] The ICTY Statute specifically enumerates rape as a crime against humanity; the ICTY's Victims and Witnesses Unit must provide support particularly in cases of sexual offences and has been encouraged to appoint qualified women on its staff; the ICTY's Rules of Evidence contain special provisions for sexual offences; and the position of a legal adviser for gender-related crimes has been created for the ICTY and the ICTR.[105]

Despite the pioneering work of the ICTY and the ICTY in respect of support for victims of sex crimes and acknowledgement of their suffering, it would not be unfair to suggest that these earlier international courts were not as 'victim-centric' as their more recent counterparts. Much has been made of the far greater participatory role according to victims in the process of the ICC and the ECCC.[106] The general perception is that the ECCC provides for the most robust mechanism for participation by victims acting as civil parties.[107] According to the ECCC Internal Rules, victims can participate in proceedings before the ECCC by "supporting the prosecution" and seek collective and moral reparations.[108] The exact

---

[104] Hilary Charlesworth, "Feminist Methods in International Law", in *American Journal of International Law*, 1999, vol. 93, no. 2, pp. 379, 387; Richard Goldstone, "The United Nations' War Crimes Tribunals: An Assessment", in *Connecticut Journal of International Law*, 1997, vol. 12, pp. 227, 231.

[105] Karen Engle, "Feminism and Its (Dis)contents: Criminalizing Wartime Rape in Bosnia and Herzegovina", in *American Journal of International Law*, 2005, vol. 99, no. 4, pp. 778, 781.

[106] On victim participation at the ICC, see generally T. Markus Funk, *Victims' Rights and Advocacy at the International Criminal Court*, Oxford University Press, Oxford, 2010; Carsten Stahn, Héctor Olásolo and Kate Gibson, "Participation of Victims in Pre-trial Proceedings of the ICC", in *Journal of International Criminal Law*, 2006, vol. 4, no. 2, p. 219; Håkan Friman, "The International Criminal Court and Participation of Victims: A Third Party to the Proceedings?", in *Leiden Journal of International Law*, 2009, vol. 22, no. 3, p. 485. On victim participation at the ECCC, see Robert Petit and Anees Ahmed, "A Review of the Jurisprudence of the Khmer Rouge Tribunal", in *Northwestern Journal of International Human Rights*, 2010, vol. 8, pp. 165, 173–74; David Boyle, "The Rights of Victims: Participation, Representation, Protection, Reparation", in *Journal of International Criminal Justice*, 2006, vol. 4, no. 2, p. 307.

[107] See, for example, Brianne N. McGonigle, "Two for the Price of One: Attempts by the Extraordinary Chambers in the Courts of Cambodia to Combine Retributive and Restorative Justice Principles", in *Leiden Journal of International Law*, 2009, vol. 22, no. 1, pp. 127, 142–45; see also Mahdev Mohan, "The Paradox of Victim-Centrism: Victim Participation at the Khmer Rouge Tribunal", in *International Criminal Law Review*, 2009, vol. 9, no. 5, pp. 733, 735–36.

[108] ECCC Internal Rules, Rule 23(1), see *supra* note 26.

---

scope of victim participation in trial proceedings is still in a state of flux, and after an initial expansive understanding of victims' rights, the Trial Chamber has been slowly limiting their participation.[109] For instance, the Chamber has held that civil parties do not have a general right of equal participation with the co-prosecutors and cannot make submissions on issues of sentencing or pose questions pertaining to the accused's character.[110] The Internal Rules have also been revised and while the civil parties may participate individually at the pre-trial stage, they must comprise a single consolidated group at the trial stage and be represented by lead co-lawyers who file a single claim for reparations.[111] Leaving aside the exact restrictions on participation contemplated and their potential repercussions, it bears noting that the charge of forced marriages may well never have been litigated before the ECCC if the civil parties were not permitted to play a crucial participatory role in the pre-trial stage.

One can, of course, question whether such a prominent role for victims in the trial proceedings such that it enables them to influence the charges filed against the accused is in fact a positive development. Advocates of a victim-centric approach in international trials argue that participation enables the victim to regain agency and control over his life, restores his dignity, affirms and validates his experience and contributes to truth-telling and healing.[112] This approach borrows from the restorative

---

[109] See Alain Werner and Daniella Rudy, "Civil Party Representation at the ECCC: Sounding the Retreat in International Criminal Law?", in *Northwestern Journal of International Human Rights*, 2010, vol. 8, no. 3, pp. 301–02.

[110] ECCC, *Prosecutor v. Kaing Guek Eav*, Trial Chamber, Decision on Civil Parties' Co-Lawyers' Joint Request for a Ruling on the Standing of Civil Parties' Lawyers to make Submissions on Sentencing and Directions Concerning the Questioning of the Accused, Experts and Witnesses Testifying on Character, 001/18-07-2007/ECCC/TC, 12 October 2009, paras. 25 and 46 (http://www.legal-tools.org/doc/657eb2/). See further Werner and Rudy, 2010, p. 303, see *supra* note 109.

[111] ECCC Internal Rules, Rule 23(3), see *supra* note 26; Werner and Rudy, 2010, p. 303, see *supra* note 109.

[112] See the discussion in Mohan, 2009, pp. 736–37, *supra* note 107; Naomi Roht-Arriaza, "Impunity and Human Rights", in Naomi Roht-Arriaza (ed.), *Impunity and Human Rights in International Law and Practice*, Oxford University Press, Oxford, 1995, p. 21; Raquel Aldana-Pindell, "An Emerging Universality of Justiciable Victims' Rights in the Criminal Process to Curtail Impunity for State-Sponsored Crimes", in *Human Rights Quarterly*, 2005, vol. 26, no. 3, pp. 607, 675; Jamie O'Connell, "Gambling with the Psyche: Does Prosecuting Human Rights Violators Console Their Victims?", in *Harvard International Law Journal*, 2005, vol. 46, no. 2, pp. 295, 337.

justice paradigm that has recently gained popularity in domestic criminal law circles. Restorative justice views crime as conduct that violates people and relationships resulting in an obligation to make reparations and conceives of justice as a purpose driven process bringing together the actors affected by the crime with a view to achieving reconciliation.[113] As one of its most influential proponents, John Braithwaite states that this primary focus on the crime's consequences and the needs this generates for the affected community makes restorative justice "more act focused and less focused on the offender as a person; more victim-focused and less offender-focused".[114]

While the restorative justice focus on victims and affected communities is undoubtedly appealing, caution must be exercised before adopting it uncritically at the international criminal law level for several reasons. First, some variants of the model have invited criticism at the domestic level for their vagueness in defining key terms, their potential inconsistency with the demands of impartiality in sentencing, and for altogether overly expansive substantive and procedural rights granted to victims, especially as concerns sentencing.[115] Second, the claim that granting participatory rights to victims in international trials actually achieves the objectives of healing and reconciliation is not always supported by empirical evidence. In the context of the ECCC, some of the research actually points to a contrary result: the disjunction between the experiences and expectations of victims and the manner in which they get interpreted through the lens of the legal process at the ECCC has actually left many who did participate in the process embittered, disillusioned, and frustrated.[116]

Enhanced victim participation may nonetheless form an important structural feature of international tribunals if it is considered useful for different consequentialist reasons: the obligation of the tribunal to establish the 'truth' about the crimes that occurred during the events under its

---

[113] David Dolinko, "Restorative Justice and the Justification of Punishment", in *Utah Law Review*, 2003, vol. 319, pp. 319–320.

[114] John Braithwaite, *Restorative Justice and Responsive Regulation*, Oxford University Press, Oxford, 2002, p. 96.

[115] For a detailed critique, see Andrew Ashworth, "Responsibilities, Rights and Restorative Justice", in *British Journal of Criminology*, 2002, vol. 42, no. 3, pp. 578–95; Andrew von Hirsch and Andrew Ashworth, *Proportionate Sentencing: Exploring the Principles*, Oxford University Press, Oxford, 2005, pp. 110–30.

[116] Mohan, 2009, pp. 737–38, see *supra* note 107.

consideration. If the objective of the tribunal is indeed to paint as accurate and complete a portrait as it can of the atrocities committed by the accused before it, then the more opportunities that are accorded to parties to assist the court in this goal, the better. This is in fact one of the arguments used by the lawyers for civil parties for including the crime of forced marriages in the list of charges against the accused.[117] This rationale may apply even more strongly in the case of tribunals similar to the ECCC which are oriented quite strongly towards the civil law model[118] where one of the primary purposes of the criminal trial, at least in principle, is to establish the truth.

10.6. Conclusion

The prosecutions for forced marriages before the ECCC do not strictly mirror the dilemmas that a pure case of thematic prosecutions may have to face. Controversial as the charge of forced marriages may be in the context of the ECCC, due to its relatively late addition to the other charges against the accused, it does not pose the more pressing concern that its pursuit would jeopardise any prospects of investigating and prosecuting other offences. Nonetheless, a close study of the case assists us in conducting a mapping exercise which identifies factors – normative, pragmatic and institutional – that would be relevant in the justification of the practice of thematic prosecutions. This exercise, as the chapter demonstrates, is, however, merely a first and fairly modest step in addressing the challenge of thematic prosecutions. Any further examination of the rationale behind thematic prosecutions must go deeper and unravel the knotty issues that lie at the heart of these factors and which remain unresolved in international criminal justice – what should be the ultimate goal of prosecutions for mass atrocity and how can this best be achieved through the design and structure of international criminal tribunals.

---

[117] ECCC, First Request, p. 43, *supra* note 1.

[118] For the ECCC's civil law orientation, see generally Kate Gibson and Daniella Rudy, "A New Model of International Criminal Procedure?: The Progress of the *Duch* Trial at the ECCC", in *Journal of International Criminal Justice*, 2009, vol. 7, no. 5, p. 1005.

11

Special Mechanisms to Investigate
and Prosecute International Sex Crimes:
Pro and Contra Arguments

Olympia Bekou[*]

11.1. Introduction

Thematic prosecutions cannot take place in a vacuum. They require an institutional framework in which to occur. When contemplating thematic prosecutions at the national level, one cannot fail to notice that they are inextricably linked to issues of institutional capacity. Investigating and prosecuting core international crimes at the domestic level is not an easy task. The principle of complementarity ensures that national jurisdictions, alongside the International Criminal Court ('ICC'), share the burden of putting an end to impunity for core international crimes.[1] International sex crimes share with the rest of the core international crimes, both the element of gravity as well as the complexity in terms of investigations and prosecutions. However, what sets them apart is perhaps the fact that they are emotive and political.

In this chapter, international sex crimes will not be examined *per se*. Rather, the emphasis will be on the national level and the institutional capacity needed in order to investigate and prosecute core international crimes at the national level, including international sex crimes.[2] In par-

---

[*] **Olympia Bekou** is a Professor of Public International Law at the University of Nottingham, where she serves as Head of the International Criminal Justice Unit, Human Rights Law Centre; and a Deputy Director of the Case Matrix Network. I am indebted to Hilary Peden and Yusuke Hara for collating some materials for me. All errors or omissions remain mine alone.

[1] See Rome Statute of the International Criminal Court, 17 July 1998, in force 1 July 2002, Preamble para. 10, Articles 1 and 17 ('ICC Statute') (http://www.legal-tools.org/doc/7b9af9/).

[2] On the significance of national capacity for the investigation and prosecution of international crimes, see generally Morten Bergsmo, Olympia Bekou and Annika Jones, "Complementarity and the Construction of National Ability", in Carsten Stahn and Mohamed M. El Zeidy (eds.), *The International Criminal Court and Complementarity: From Theory to Practice*, vol. II, Cambridge University Press, Cambridge, 2011, pp. 1052–70.

---

ticular, the chapter will explore the advantages and disadvantages associated with having special mechanisms, in the form of specialised units, for such crimes. The necessity, or not, for specialised units goes beyond sex crimes. Arguments for or against specialised mechanisms apply irrespective of the types of crimes involved.

Besides examining the desirability of having specialised units, the chapter will also discuss whether national prosecutions of core international crimes may be better served by *ad hoc* arrangements. The purpose of this juxtaposition is to present a balanced overview of the key options available when considering whether or not to invest in the creation of specialised units at the national level. The chapter concludes with the acknowledgement that given that both options have considerable advantages and disadvantages, it is difficult to propose a single solution that would be suitable for all national jurisdictions at all times. However, it is clear that a degree of specialisation, whether in the form of specialised mechanisms or particular expertise that could be resorted to, would be of benefit for the effective investigation or prosecution of core international crimes, thematic or otherwise.

11.2. Specialised Units: Some Preliminary Observations

The proliferation of specialised units at the national level is a relatively recent phenomenon. Specialised units dealing with terrorism, organised crime, crimes against children, public health offences and so on have mushroomed among the judicial systems of the most developed nations.

Specialised units for the investigation and prosecution of core international crimes first appeared to deal with Second World War criminals who had fled the *loci commissi delicti* and settled in other countries. Australia, Austria, Canada, France, Poland, Spain, the Netherlands, the United Kingdom and the United States all conducted trials involving Nazi war criminals.[3] With the completion of those cases, most of such units were dismantled to be replaced in the modern post-*ad hoc* tribunal and ICC establishment era with specialised units ready to make the complementarity promise a reality, with infrastructure being put in place in order to deal with core international crimes, if and when these arise. The fact that such

---

[3]   See, generally, Timothy L.H. McCormack and Gerry J. Simpson (eds.), *The Law of War Crimes: National and International Approaches*, Kluwer, The Hague, 1997.

units, with their current post-Second World War mandate, have only been in existence for a short period to date, makes it difficult to discern any patterns. Currently, there is not much research or statistics available on the issue. Assessing the performance of such efforts will require a few more years and hard empirical data, before any comparative statistical analysis may be undertaken. At the time of writing, any examination of such units can only be made on the basis of some general arguments and through the lens of experience from other areas of specialisation, such as the investigation and prosecution of ordinary sex crimes nationally.

Specialisation may occur at a number of different levels: immigration, investigation (policing), prosecution and adjudication.

When discussing specialisation in the investigation and prosecution of international sex crimes, one needs to focus not just on investigation and prosecutions *per se*, but also on how such perpetrators enter into the system and whether the trial itself, if that stage is reached, should also be conducted by specialised units. Although this chapter is primarily concerned with investigation and prosecution, attention ought to be drawn to issues of immigration first.

Even without delving into the complex area of asylum and immigration law, which falls outside the remit of this chapter, it is clear that a number of perpetrators of core international crimes, including international sex crimes, will be picked up at the moment when they are trying to enter a country other than their country of origin, or when they apply for asylum, visas or naturalisation in a new country. This is why a number of states, particularly in Europe, have created specialised units within their border agencies and immigration authorities to deal with such influx. Examples would include the Netherlands[4] or the United Kingdom.[5] Specialisation therefore occurs even at the stage prior to the actual investigation of a crime.

Besides immigration, the thrust of the debate on the merits or demerits of specialised units can be found in the investigation and prosecution of such crimes. Although variations on the ground regarding the manner of investigation and prosecution of international sex crimes would largely depend on a state's belonging to the inquisitorial or adversarial

---

[4] See *infra* note 10.

[5] See *infra* note 12.

tradition, arguments relating to specialisation would be the same, with perhaps some differences in the modalities of implementing the scheme.

The next preliminary issue that needs to be considered is what drives the move towards having special mechanisms. The answer is not immediately obvious. Specialisation cannot be grounded in a legal obligation nor can it be found in a uniform political reality that warrants the creation of such units.

With that in mind, a quick look at the world map reveals that with the exception of Canada,[6] which has a long-standing presence and commitment in human rights and international criminal justice issues, the concentration of formalised special units for core international crimes is found primarily on the European continent. Denmark,[7] Germany,[8] Sweden,[9] the Netherlands,[10] Norway[11] and the United Kingdom to some extent[12] have gone down the route of specialisation. It is therefore worth ex-

---

[6] The Public Prosecution Service of Canada ('PPSC') is responsible for prosecuting offences under the Crimes Against Humanity and War Crimes Act. The PPSC's first prosecution under the Act resulted in the conviction to life imprisonment of Désiré Munyaneza for genocide, crimes against humanity and war crimes in relation to the Rwandan genocide. This case is on appeal at the time of writing. A second case, that of *R. v. Mungwarere*, who was charged in 2009 with genocide, is currently ongoing with the additional charges of war crimes and crimes against humanity made against him in 2010, a trial date set for 2012. See Public Prosecution Service of Canada, "Annual Report 2010–2011", November 2010.

[7] Pursuant to the Ministerial Order No.1146/2002, the Special International Crimes Office ('SICO') of the Danish Prosecution Service was created with a special mandate for legal proceedings in relation to international crimes, including genocide, crimes against humanity, war crimes, acts of terrorism and other serious crimes committed abroad. Other serious crimes include homicide, torture, deprivation of liberty, rape, bombing and arson.

[8] In Germany, a Special Unit for the Fight against War Crimes was created in 2003 and in 2009 it was renamed the Central Unit for the Fight against War Crimes and further offences pursuant to the Code of Crimes against International Law (Zentralstelle für die Bekämpfung von Kriegsverbrechen und weiteren Straftaten nach dem Völkerstrafgesetzbuch ('ZBKV').

[9] Following a decision of the National Police Board on 5 September 2007, the National Criminal Police's War Crimes Unit in Sweden has operated since March 2008. It is responsible for investigation and prosecution of war crimes, crimes against humanity and genocide.

[10] The Dutch War Crimes unit is located within the Immigration and Naturalisation service.

[11] The National Authority for Prosecution of Organised and Other Serious Crime in Norway was created in 2005, bearing a special responsibility for investigating and prosecuting cases concerning organised crimes, high-tech crime and international crimes, including genocide, crimes against humanity and war crimes.

---

amining what makes the European continent more open to the establishment of specialised units.

For countries belonging to the European Union ('EU'), the impact that European integration has had on the issue of specialisation needs to be examined. In recent years, the EU has been a staunch supporter of the ICC and has taken considerable steps in support of the Court.[13] Among the various instruments that have been promulgated by the EU,[14] European Council Decision 2003/335/JH[15] fosters closer co-operation in the investigation and prosecution of core international crimes, by setting up a European network of contact points and by inviting member states to "consider the need to set up or designate specialist units within the competent law enforcement authorities with particular responsibility for investigating and, as appropriate, prosecuting the crimes in question".[16] However, despite the influential role that EU law has played in that field more generally, it does not account for notable aberrations in the European continent. Out of all EU member states, the ones that have specialised units remain the exception. Among the larger EU member states, France,[17] and also Spain, do not have operational specialised investigative and prosecu-

---

[12] Although the United Kingdom does not have a special unit within its prosecution service, it does, however, have a war crimes team within the UK Border Agency. Moreover, the counter-terrorism unit of the Metropolitan Police provides assistance with investigation on an *ad hoc* basis.

[13] See Antonis Antoniadis and Olympia Bekou, "The European Union and the International Criminal Court: An Awkward Symbiosis in Interesting Times", in *International Criminal Law Review*, 2007, vol. 7, no. 4, pp. 621–55.

[14] Council Decision 2011/168/CFSP, 21 March 2011, on the International Criminal Court and repealing Common Position 2003/444/CFSP and Action Plan to follow-up on the Decision on the International Criminal Court, Council of the European Union, 12080/11, 12 July 2011.

[15] Council of the European Union, Council Decision 2003/335/JHA, 8 May 2003, on the investigation and prosecution of genocide, crimes against humanity and war, official journal L 118/12, 14 May 2003.

[16] *Ibid.*, Article 4.

[17] Although a draft for the creation has gone before the French Senate, the unit is not operational at the time of writing. See France, Sénat, "Projet de loi relatif à la repartition du contentieux et creation d'un pole specialise dans les crimes contre l'humanité au TGI de Paris", Session ordinaire de 2009–2010, 3 March 2010. See also the recommendations on the draft submitted by Amnesty International, International Federation for Human Rights ('FIDH'), Human Rights Watch ('HRW'), Ligue des Droits de l'Homme and Redress, entitled "Recommandations relatives a l'etablissement d'un pole specialisé dans les crimes de guerre et contre l'humanité au Tribunal de Grande Instance de Paris", March 2011.

---

torial units despite the fact that they have both been involved in the prosecution of core international crimes. And while France is in the process of establishing such a unit, hopefully before not too long, no such unit exists in Spain, which is interesting given the latter's position on universal jurisdiction as developed over the years.[18]

Despite the absence for a firm legal basis requiring the establishment of specialised units, such units have made their appearance on the legal stage. Whether they are here or not to stay depends largely on their efficiency, their ability to bring about successful convictions, and perhaps most importantly their cost-effectiveness.

11.2.1. The Advantages of Special Mechanisms

Having examined some preliminary issues, let us now turn to the advantages specialisation offers, which may explain why states have begun to invest in creating specialised units. Given the absence of empirical data to prove or disprove the perceived advantages, what is presented below are some advantages that would apply generally where specialised units exist, irrespective of the type of crime targeted.

11.2.1.1. Long-Term Commitment

The first advantage is perhaps the most symbolic one: the mere existence of a specialised unit indicates that a long-term commitment to investigating and prosecuting these specific crimes exists.[19] It emphasises that impunity for these crimes will not be tolerated.[20] That is not to say that the existence of the unit, if not coupled with relevant action, would suffice. However, it can be safely assumed that states which have committed the resources required for the establishment of such units would be prepared

---

[18] See Enrique Carnero Rojo, "National Legislation Providing for the Prosecution and Punishment of International Crimes in Spain", in *Journal of International Criminal Justice,* 2011, vol. 9, no. 3, pp. 699–728; Ignacio de la Rasilla del Moral, "The Swan Song of Universal Jurisdiction in Spain", in *International Criminal Law Review,* 2009, vol. 9, no. 5, pp. 777–808.

[19] See Redress and FIDH, "Strategies for the Effective Investigation and Prosecution of Serious International Crimes: The Practice of Specialised War Crimes Units", 9 December 2010.

[20] Canada's Crimes against Humanity and War Crimes Program (http://justice.gc.ca/eng/cj-jp/wc-cdg/index.html).

to put them to good use. Building capacity on a longer term basis ensures better long-term planning and the ability to deal with cases as they arise.

11.2.1.2. Development of Knowledge and Expertise (Training)

An advantage closely linked to what the existence of special mechanisms signals is the development of expertise and knowledge within the unit and how this will enable the unit to better perform its duties in the future.[21] A specialised unit is able to bring together experts from more than one field, such as judges, prosecutors, interpreters and researchers, to deal with certain crimes that may be complex and sensitive.[22]

11.2.1.3. Better Resource Allocation and Mobilisation

Having one unit respond to all crimes in a certain field concentrates the information and resources needed for these crimes in one department. This allows for the better mobilisation of resources to prosecute international crimes in particular.[23] This, in turn, would have the positive result of reducing any overlap in prosecution and investigation activities.[24]

11.2.1.4. Better International Co-operation

The next advantage relates to co-operation. Given that the ICC system relies heavily on state authorities to provide all aspects of co-operation,[25] and given the prominent extra-territorial element in the investigation and prosecution of core international crimes, the existence of such units also

---

[21] Redress and FIDH, 2010, p. 9, see *supra* note 19.

[22] Michèle Alliot-Marie and Bernard Kouchner, "Pour la création d'un pôle 'génocides et crimes contre l'humanité' au TGI de Paris,", in *Le Monde*, 6 January 2010.

[23] Diane Orentlicher, Independent Study on Best Practices, including Recommendations, to Assist States in Strengthening their Domestic Capacity to Combat all Aspects of Impunity, UN Economic and Social Council, UN Doc. E/CN.4/2004/88, 27 February 2004, para. 41.

[24] Redress and FIDH, 2010, p. 9, see *supra* note 19.

[25] See ICC Statute, Article 86, *supra* note 1. A statement made by the late Antonio Cassese with regard to the ICTY was that the tribunal "remains very much like a giant without arms and legs – it needs artificial limbs to walk and work. And these artificial limbs are state authorities. If the cooperation of states is not forthcoming, the ICTY cannot fulfil its functions". This rings true of the ICC as well: Antonio Cassese, "On Current Trends towards Criminal Prosecution and Punishment of Breaches of International Humanitarian Law", in *European Journal of International Law*, 1998, vol. 9, no. 1, p. 9.

---

facilitates communication with similar units in other countries when it is easy to identify who is responsible for certain crimes.[26]

Besides the formal/institutional aspect of co-operation there is also a human dimension associated with the existence of specialised units. The professional contacts that key personnel employed by such units are likely to develop with colleagues from other such units operating in other countries should not be underestimated. Although formal routes will always have to be followed for the execution of a co-operation request, there is anecdotal evidence to suggest that peer-to-peer communication greatly facilitates the progress of a case, particularly when the request involves co-operation from abroad. Inevitably, colleagues across countries who share the same work pressures and expertise can develop a *lingua franca* when dealing with colleagues from other countries. This dual aspect of co-operation, both formal and informal, can be better served through the existence of specialised units.

11.2.1.5. Visibility, Accountability and Outreach

The next benefit of having specialised units relates to externalising the work that the unit undertakes and making it accessible for the wider public, and thus increasing its societal impact. When a single unit is responsible for a certain type of crime, it is in a position to better ensure external visibility of its work and accountability of the investigation and prosecution of these crimes in the eyes of the public.[27] Furthermore, a specialised unit creates better awareness of the issues with which it engages and can also more effectively facilitate the development of outreach and awareness programmes.[28]

---

[26] Within the EU, cooperation is facilitated through Council Decision 2002/494/JHA of 13 June 2002 – which set up a European network of contract points in respect of persons responsible for genocide, crimes against humanity and war crimes – and Council Decision 2003/335/JHA of 8 May 2003, on the investigation and prosecution of genocide, crimes against humanity and war crimes, see *supra* note 15.

[27] Redress and FIDH, 2010, p. 9, see *supra* note 19.

[28] *Ibid*, p. 25.

11.2.1.6. Consistency, Efficiency, Successful Prosecutions

When these national units are created and are reasonably mobile, they could ensure consistency in the investigation and prosecution of a certain type of crime throughout one jurisdiction.[29] This is particularly relevant to crimes like core international crimes which have a low instance of occurrence, but which are very serious offences that require specialised knowledge and, owing to their nature, increased sensitivity.

Assuming that the personnel in these units are given special training, they would most likely be able to more effectively and efficiently investigate and prosecute the specialised crimes concerned as compared to ordinary personnel who would have to pick up a highly complex new area of the law for the purposes of dealing with a rather limited number of specialised cases. For instance, a specialised lawyer would be in a better position to assess the strengths and weaknesses of a case and would therefore have higher chances of success in court.[30]

11.2.1.7. Increased Capacity

Finally, in countries where universal jurisdiction is applied, often personnel with experience only in domestic crimes are involved in international crimes. However, if there is a specialised unit for core international crimes this would lead to increased capacity to properly investigate and prosecute these crimes both abroad and at home.[31]

The creation and operation of specialised units offers distinct advantages. These can be classed as predominantly structural, that is, such advantages are associated with the increased institutional capacity that the creation of such special mechanisms entails. But the human dimension associated with sustainable training, as well as cross-border co-operation, contributes significantly to the desirability of specialised units for the investigation and prosecution of core international crimes, including sex crimes.

---

[29] Dawn Beichner and Cassia Spohn, "Prosecutorial Charging Decisions in Sexual Assault Cases: Examining the Impact of a Specialized Prosecution Unit", in *Criminal Justice Policy Review*, 2005, vol. 16, no. 4, p. 462.

[30] *Ibid.*

[31] Track Impunity Always ('TRIAL'), "Une unité pour crimes de guerre: en Suisse aussi?", in *Bulletin d'information*, no. 12, 2007.

11.2.2. The Disadvantages of Special Mechanisms

Every effort where major structural change is required within established and functioning judicial systems is likely to be tainted by the realisation that a number of disadvantages can also be discerned. The creation of special mechanisms for thematic prosecutions is no exception.

11.2.2.1. Added complexity

First and foremost, the very creation of specialised units introduces an added layer of complexity. If each type of crime were to be assigned a special unit, this would create an unnecessarily complex system, not least in terms of policing. It is, therefore, important to consider which types of crime merit special units.[32] Associated with this is the issue of prioritisation *ratione materiae*. The following dilemma therefore ensues: why sex crimes and not child soldiers for instance? In other words, specialisation may require a justification as to why a certain category of crimes is prioritised over another. The criteria for such prioritisation, and the legal framework under which such units would need to operate at the national level, are a matter that has to be left to each individual state to decide as this would impinge on questions of national policy.

Complexity is likely to be present not only at the initial stages of the establishment of special mechanisms, but also throughout the operation of the system. Even when the initial start-up cost is overcome, the additional steps that a specialised unit adds to the normal criminal justice process may jeopardise the smooth investigation or prosecution of a case. If, however, specialised units are likely to provide better justice in the long run, then the initial start up cost and added complexity is counterbalanced by the long-term gains.

The fact remains that the complexity that the creation of specialised units brings both in terms of how the new unit would fit in the existing criminal justice system, but also in terms of the ensuing prioritisation dilemmas, is a real issue that needs to be seriously considered prior to advocating in favour of such units.

---

[32] John P. Crank and Robert Langworthy, "An Institutional Perspective of Policing", in *Journal of Criminal Law and Criminology*, 1993, vol. 83, no. 2, p. 343.

11.2.2.2. Cost

Closely linked to the issue of added complexity discussed above is the question of cost. Creating specialised units comes at a premium and this is likely to be the key practical argument against such unit creation. Besides the expense required for the initial stage of creation, the cost of running such units is likely to be higher than that of dealing with core international crimes within the normal criminal justice system. A more complex system and special training also requires a larger budget, which may not be feasible in all national jurisdictions, particularly in relation to those of less well-resourced states or states in transition.

11.2.2.3. Unit-Straddling

A further downside associated with specialised units can be observed when crimes falling under the remit of the special unit are interconnected with other crimes or regimes. What this author calls 'unit-straddling' could potentially occur. For instance, if a peacekeeper commits a sex crime abroad, then jurisdiction would have to be accrued potentially to more than one conflicting agency: 1) the specialised unit entrusted with the investigation and prosecution of core international crimes; and 2) the military system of justice (which, owing to the alleged perpetrator and his membership of the state's armed forces could also have jurisdiction). The example above is one of many possible combinations.[33] It would not be wise to try and delimitate each unit's remit prior to a conflict among units arising. If anything, it might be difficult to predict where the unit-straddling is likely to occur or where potential conflicts are likely to arise as the constituent elements of each case may differ. Each case should therefore be dealt with *in concreto*. In any case, unit-straddling may result in unnecessary overlap of personnel and duplication of effort and should be avoided to the extent that it is possible.

11.2.2.4. Rarity of Incidence

The next disadvantage that can be identified is linked to resource allocation, based on the rarity of incidence of core international crimes. Core

---

[33] Consider also the possibility of specialisation within a specialised system, that is, whether a specialised unit for the prosecution of sex crimes is needed within a state's military justice.

international crimes do not routinely occur. Whether a specialised unit will be extensively used or not depends on the position of a state as a post-conflict country or country in transition, the presence of perpetrators or victims on its territory or the exercise of universal jurisdiction. A specialised unit can be underused at best, redundant and even a waste of resources at worst, if the number of reported cases is low.[34] This point serves as a useful reminder that not all countries and jurisdictions would warrant specialised units because of the rarity of incidence of certain international crimes. In such instances, resources could be better used if allocated on other parts of the criminal justice system.

11.2.2.5. Impact on Personnel

On the other hand, it is possible that the reverse can happen. In jurisdictions with high incidence of crimes that would come under the remit of specialised units, special unit personnel could be overworked and experience burn-out. In other words, getting the balance right between numbers of predicted cases and actual personnel will be crucial for resources to be allocated as efficiently as possible. The human factor and the impact that a low or high number of cases would have on key personnel should not be underestimated.

11.2.2.6. Impact on Victims

The impact such units may have on the victims and their perception of justice should also be taken into consideration. Specialised units could potentially marginalise victims because these crimes are separate from mainstream judicial processes and may therefore be perceived as a 'special crime'. This might be the case with regard to special sex crimes units where victims may be particularly vulnerable.[35] How victims perceive the justice process is an important aspect of any judicial system; this is more so when victims of core international crimes are concerned.

---

[34] Redress and FIDH, 2010, p. 27, see *supra* note 19.

[35] Saferworld, "Addressing Violence against Women in Security and Justice Programmes", 11 March 2010, p. 9.

11.2.2.7. De-skilling

A rather important disadvantage of having specialised units is so-called de-skilling. What is meant by de-skilling is that, as a result of specialisation, few people possess the necessary knowledge and expertise to process a case falling under the remit of the special unit. For example, in an ordinary rape case, when a victim presents himself or herself at a police station, if specially trained personnel are away attending to another case, the remaining police staff would not be as competent in the collecting of primary forensic evidence from the victim, because they would not feel competent or able to do so. This leads to potential loss of valuable primary evidence in the absence of skilled personnel. The same could be said for specialised units regarding core international crimes. The complexity of such cases inevitably leads to high levels of specialisation among staff who develop particular expertise in a relatively narrow field. Their less skilled counterparts would inevitably lag so far behind that it would make it impossible to fill in their shoes when needed. Depending on the system as a whole and how the specialised unit operates within it, the specialised unit could thus be rendered inaccessible to victims. If specialised personnel are unavailable at the time of reporting the crime or if there are too many bureaucratic procedures in place, access to justice may be delayed or even seriously jeopardised. This could cause delays, affect evidence collection, further impacting the outcome of the case, as well as the victim's perception of justice.

11.2.2.8. Marginal Influence on Case Outcomes

Finally, and while extrapolating from specialisation in the case of ordinary crimes, and though mindful of the fact that no empirical research is currently available on specialised units pertaining to international crimes, the actual influence that such units have on case outcomes would have to be considered. If the prosecution of domestic sex crimes by special units are anything to go by, some studies have revealed that specialised prosecution units do not influence the end result of cases.[36] Whether this would transpose also to the investigation or prosecution of core international crimes cases remains to be seen and cannot currently be firmly established based on the data available to date.

---

[36] Beichner and Spohn, 2005, p. 490, see *supra* note 29.

11.3. *'Jura novit curia'* or *'Jura novit curia specialis'*?

Having examined the pro and contra arguments on the creation and operation of specialised units for investigation and prosecution of core international crimes, it is worth considering, for a more complete overview,
whether there might also be a need to have specialised judges who would
be able to undertake thematic prosecution. Should specialisation at the
national level end before entering the courtroom or should a case be made
in favour of specialised courts as well?

Although the idea of specialised courts to deal with core international crimes is not new, specialised chambers have been created as a
measure of responding to specific post-conflict settings, either to deal
with large numbers of cases (see, for example, the special war crimes
chamber in Bosnia and Herzegovina),[37] in anticipation of numerous such
cases (see the example of Uganda),[38] or have been proposed to deal with
ongoing conflicts such as the situation of the Democratic Republic of
Congo.[39] Some of the advantages and disadvantages, discussed above,
would equally apply to the establishment of a specialised court system as
well. However, there might be less of an incentive to formally establish
such special chambers if a state is not likely to be faced with large numbers of cases. Judges of states that have joined the ICC Statute would, in
any case, benefit from receiving international criminal law training, which
could be put to good use when faced with core international crimes cases,
as these may be brought before them. With that in mind, although specialised knowledge would be welcome, advocating the creation of special
chambers in all instances may not be justified.

11.4. *Ad hoc* Arrangements

An alternative to having specialised units is to deal with thematic prosecutions using *ad hoc* arrangements. Having examined the advantages and

---

[37] On the Court of Bosnia and Herzegovina see http://www.sudbih.gov.ba/?jezik=e.

[38] The division of the Judiciary, Republic of Uganda, has been renamed the International
Crimes Division (http://www.judiciary.go.ug/).

[39] In the context of the workshop that gave rise to this book, a presentation was made on the
possibility of creating a mixed chamber in the Democratic Republic of Congo, which was
published as Club des Amis du Droit du Congo, "The Mixed Specialized Court as a Mechanism of Repression of International Crime in the Democratic Republic of the Congo: Lessons
Learned from Cambodia, East Timor, Kosovo, and Bosnia", October 2011.

disadvantages associated with the creation of specialised units, the benefits and drawbacks of *ad hoc* arrangements for the investigation and prosecution of core international crimes, including international sex crimes, should therefore also be considered.

11.4.1. The Advantages of *ad hoc* Arrangements

11.4.1.1. Mobility and Flexibility

The first advantage associated with *ad hoc* arrangements relates to the mobility and flexibility that non-formalised arrangements offer. Specialised units are ordinarily concentrated in the capital of the state in question. However, in most systems, investigation and prosecution as well as adjudication are decentralised. It would not be feasible to create specialised units in each location where prosecutorial capacity exists, nor would it always be desirable. This is because it depends on the circumstances of the case in question, to move all cases to a single location. The use of *ad hoc* experts on international crimes within a country would, therefore, allow for mobility and flexibility. It would not restrict the investigation and prosecution to large urban areas alone, thus bringing justice closer to the people it concerns.[40]

11.4.1.2. Lower Cost

One of the key disadvantages of having specialised units is, as discussed above, the issue of cost.[41] Conversely, this is perhaps the most prominent advantage of *ad hoc* arrangements. When only a limited number of special advisers are working on specific issues within the entire national jurisdiction, this would lower the cost in the budget associated with their engagement in the process. Such savings would be particularly efficient if there is a lower incidence of core international crimes in that particular jurisdiction. In such an instance, it might not be prudent to proceed with creating a unit whose staff are employed only on a part-time basis and might be better to resort to *ad hoc* arrangements.

---

[40] See Chandra Lekha Sriram, "Revolutions in Accountability: New Approaches to Past Abuses", in *American University International Law Review*, 2003, vol. 19, no. 2, p. 383.

[41] See section 11.2.2. *supra.*

11.4.1.3. Use of Existing Expertise

Some of the criticism of having special units is that despite their existence, the training level is still not high enough to effectively combat international crimes. Employing special advisers in an *ad hoc* capacity would enable a government to choose a specific individual based on qualifications and expertise they already possess, rather than having to provide on-the-job training. As no start-up costs would be involved in such an instance, employing individuals who are established in their field would come at a reduced cost, whilst a high level of expertise to deal with core international crimes would, at the same time, be maintained.

The above advantages presuppose that either some competency is already present in a given jurisdiction or that it can be imported relatively easily from abroad. Mobility and flexibility, as well as reduced costs, are certainly compelling reasons in favour of *ad hoc* arrangements. However, as with specialised units, the case for such arrangements is not so clear-cut so as to suggest that this would apply to each and every case before thematic prosecutions can take place.

11.4.2. The Disadvantages of *ad hoc* Arrangements

Besides the advantages described in the section above, *ad hoc* arrangements also carry certain disadvantages, which are examined briefly in the next section.

11.4.2.1. Workload

The first disadvantage relates to the issue of workload. *ad hoc* advisors could become overworked if there are too many cases. While the issue of workload was dealt with regard to the special units above, finding the right balance would be key to the success of either option. Maintaining a roster of experts who can be called upon at the point of need might be a workable solution. Inevitably, however, the adviser who would have to juggle the *ad hoc* appointment alongside possibly a full-time job may not be able to give a high level of attention to each case which he or she handles. The quality therefore of the case may suffer as a result.

11.4.2.2. Lack of Institutional Memory, Quality Control and Sustainability

Perhaps the greatest drawback of *ad hoc* arrangements is that advisers would not be a consistent part of the system. In any case, the *ad hoc* advisers would not be able to carry out all stages of the investigation and prosecution by themselves. They would still have to rely on police and prosecutors, who will work according to the normal operational protocols and procedures. Advisers moving in and out of cases may lose the overview of each case and not provide a sustainable basis on which to proceed. Moreover, such an arrangement does not encourage the building of capacity for future cases. Police and prosecution teams would still have to be trained alongside the adviser on how to conduct processes of investigation and prosecution correctly, counterbalancing some of the advantages.

The temporality of advisers would have an impact on the institutional culture. There will not necessarily be any institutional memory, particularly if: 1) advisers are only employed for a fraction of the time; 2) there are a large number of them; or 3) they are frequently replaced. Moreover, in developmental terms, employing *ad hoc* advisers does not foster the development of long-term in-house capacity, nor does it facilitate accountability in case there are problems with the adviser's work. The latter point is quite important for quality control purposes.

From the above, it is clear that *ad hoc* arrangements, while offering more mobility and flexibility, equally carry drawbacks that would affect their effectiveness. Robust mechanisms of quality control procedures would have to be instituted in order to guarantee sustainability of the process in the absence of a permanent system in place. While no solution is risk free, meticulous planning and selection of the right people for the job might counterbalance the disadvantages associated with the use of *ad hoc* arrangements.

11.5. Concluding Observations

It is hoped that the preceding exposition has provided a balanced overview of the main pro and contra arguments of both specialised mechanisms and *ad hoc* arrangements. The question whether to specialise or not to specialise can be answered neither in the affirmative nor in the negative. Despite the distinct advantages that specialisation offers, there are equally significant disadvantages, with de-skilling and unit-straddling constituting very serious reasons to revisit the issue of specialised units. Although there is a clear need for expert knowledge, such compartmental-isation may prove to be detrimental to the overall functioning of the criminal justice process in a core crimes case.

What is clear from the above discussion is that a 'one-size-fits-all' approach cannot possibly work for thematic prosecutions, including the prosecution of international sex crimes. Although special mechanisms offer significant advantages, it has to be acknowledged that it is neither feasible nor desirable to insist that each and every state must create specialised units. If such specialisation is alien to the legal system in question, it is likely to be riddled with more problems than it can potentially manage to solve. However, a strong case for expert training and an increase in capacity could be advocated for the investigation and prosecution of core international crimes, sex crimes included, regardless of whether this forms a permanent part of the established system or is the result of *ad hoc* arrangements.

12

Science and International Thematic Prosecution of Sex Crimes: A Tale of Re-essentialisation

Alejandra Azuero Quijano[*]

12.1. Introduction

International thematic prosecution of sex crimes is a model for criminal investigation that emerged as the result of successful Western feminist advocacy efforts dating back to the early 1990s.[1] This article demonstrates that, as a feminist project, thematic prosecution has undergone three clearly identifiable phases. The first period began in 1993, when feminists negotiated the inclusion of rape as an international crime under the jurisdiction of the International Criminal Tribunal for the Former Yugoslavia ('ICTY') and the International Criminal Tribunal for Rwanda ('ICTR'). The following year, the ICTY prosecutor Richard Goldstone appointed Patricia Viseur Sellers, a prominent feminist internationalist, as legal adviser on gender for the ICTY. It took feminists less than five years to crystallise this first phase, with the result that "gender strategising" could

---

[*]   **Alejandra Azuero Quijano** is an SJD Candidate at Harvard Law School. I would like to thank Morten Bergsmo and the rest of the organisers of the FICHL Cape Town Seminar. I owe much to Sarah Richardson, whose forthcoming book inspired the presentation I gave at Cape Town in March 2011. Our conversations about genetics and gender have fed my growing interest for the place of science in legal discourse. I would also like to thank Lucie White for her invaluable mentoring during the past years. Her comments to a previous draft of this chapter were essential to this project. Finally, I would like to thank Amelia J. Evans, for encouraging me to write, and selflessly reading and commenting on previous drafts.

[1]   Although feminism is not the only force behind the rise of thematic prosecution it is definitely the most significant. This volume and the conference that preceded its publication attest to the fact that today international prosecution of sex crimes is an issue that appeals to a broader community of scholars and practitioners from within and without the legal field. For a summary of feminist efforts to reverse the under-prosecution of sex crimes by giving priority to thematic sex crime prosecutions see Margaret M. deGuzman, "Giving Priority to Sex Crime Prosecutions at International Courts: The Philosophical Foundations of a Feminist Agenda", in *International Criminal Law Review*, vol. 11, pp. 516–19. See also Margaret M. deGuzman, "An Expressive Rationale for the Thematic Prosecution of Sex Crimes", in this volume; and Valerie Oosterveld, "Contextualising Sexual Violence in the Prosecution of International Crimes", also in this volume.

no longer be considered a luxury for international criminal courts.[2] During the second phase, feminists successfully pushed for prioritising and isolating the prosecution of sex crimes at the ICTY.[3] This occurred between 1995 and 2001 when the ICTY issued the first indictments and verdicts *exclusively* for counts of rape and sexual slavery in *Kunarać et al.*[4] – also known as the Foča cases. Such cases became the first thematic prosecution of sex crimes in the history of international criminal courts. Finally, the third phase began in 2006 when, after a thematic prosecution approach prioritised the unlawful enlistment of children, the ICC excluded charges of sexual violence in the case against Thomas Lubanga Dyilo.[5] Despite this decision being considered a reversal of feminists' advocacy achievements, in little more than 20 years, the thematic prosecution of sex crimes became part of mainstream international criminal law practice.

The parallelism between the international legal feminist project in international criminal law – which had the notorious participation of American feminists[6] – and the US women's health movement project for the development of sex-specific biomedicine is the departing point of this

---

[2] I am referencing here the title of a keynote address by Patricia Viseur Sellers entitled "Gender Strategy Is Not a Luxury for International Courts", in *American University Journal of Gender, Social Policy and the Law*, 2009, vol. 17, no. 2, p. 301.

[3] For a discussion of feminist engagement with international criminal law in the mid-late 1990s, see Doris Buss, "Performing Legal Order: Some Feminist Thoughts on International Criminal Law", in *International Criminal Law Review*, 2011, vol. 11, no. 3, pp. 412–13.

[4] International Criminal Tribunal for the former Yugoslavia ('ICTY'), *Prosecutor v. Dragoljub Kunarać, Radomir Kovač and Zoran Vuković*, Trial Chamber, Judgment, IT-96-23-T and IT-96-23/1-T, 22 February 2001 ('*Kunarać et al.* Judgment') (http://www.legal-tools.org/doc/fd881d/).

[5] For a feminist critique of the *Lubanga* case, see Valentina Spiga, "Indirect Victims' Participation in the Lubanga Trial", in *Journal of International Criminal Justice*, 2010, vol. 8, no. 1, pp. 183–98, discussing the Court's decision to deny sexual violence survivors the status of indirect victims; Sienna Merope, "Recharacterizing the Lubanga Case: Regulation 55 and the Consequences for Gender Justice at the ICC", in *Criminal Law Forum*, 2011, vol. 22, no. 3, pp. 1–36, discussing the Court's decision to omit any charges of sexual violence against the accused.

[6] For a critical discussion of the role of American feminists in setting the agenda during the 1990s to ensure the criminalisation of rape at the ICTY and the International Criminal Court see, for example, Janet Halley, "Rape at Rome: Feminist Interventions in the Criminalization of Sex-Related Violence in Positive International Criminal Law", in *Michigan Journal of International Law*, 2008, vol. 30, no. 1, pp. 1–123; Janet Halley, "Rape in Berlin: Reconsidering the Criminalisation of Rape in the International Law of Armed Conflict", in *Melbourne Journal of International Law*, 2008, vol. 9, no. 1, p. 114.

---

chapter. During the last two decades, health feminists in the United States have endorsed scientific theories of essential biological differences between the sexes and used them to justify the need to isolate medical research to focus uniquely on women and girls, and to ultimately create separate specialised institutions for women's health.[7]

First, between 1990 and 1995, health feminists ardently lobbied before Congress for the creation of separate offices within the Department of Health to address women's health concerns; while also pushing for the mandatory inclusion of women in clinical trials and the subsequent analysis of data separately according to sex. As a result, "gender strategising" ceased to be considered a luxury for American biomedical institutions. Second, between 1995 and 2004, women's health advocates championed sex-specific research agendas.[8] They also expanded their argument about essential biological differences between men and women beyond disease and health concerns, sustaining that sexual difference could also explain female behaviour.[9] It became the first time feminists countered their own project – longstanding since the 1970s – to dissociate gender from nature (the latter in turn is associated with sex), and instead argued in favour of gender being determined by differences at the biological level.[10] Finally,

---

[7] Steven Epstein, *Inclusion: The Politics in Medical Research*, University of Chicago Press, Chicago, 2007, pp. 233–57; Sarah S. Richardson, *Sex Itself: Male and Female in the Human Genome*, University of Chicago Press, 2013.

[8] Richardson, 2013, see *supra* note 7.

[9] This expansion was partly subsequent to the publication of a report by the Institute of Medicine and sponsored by the Society for Women's Health Research. See Institute of Medicine, *Exploring the Biological Contributions to Human Health: Does Sex Matter?*, National Academies Press, Washington DC, 2001:

> Sex differences in health throughout the lifespan have been documented. Exploring the Biological Contributions to Human Health begins to snap the pieces of the puzzle into place so that this knowledge can be used to improve health for both sexes. From behaviour and cognition to metabolism and response to chemicals and infectious organisms, this book explores the health impact of sex (being male or female, according to reproductive organs and chromosomes) and gender (one's sense of self as male or female in society).

[10] Anne Fausto-Sterling, *Sexing the Body: Gender Politics and the Construction of Sexuality*, Basic Books, New York, 2000, pp. 3–4:

> In 1972 the sexologists John Money and Anke Ehrhardt popularized the idea that sex and gender are separate categories. Sex, they ar-

---

starting in 2005, feminists enlisted genomic findings about sexual differ-ence[11] to champion the idea that all biomedical research ought to be con-ducted and designed to take into account genomics' assertion that men and women should be considered different species. In little more than 20 years health feminists made a remarkable turn to arguments of essential differences between the sexes.

The alignment between the two feminist projects over the past two decades is nothing less than astounding. What we are witnessing is a re-essentialisation of feminist advocacy in law and science in ways that are as surprising as the fact that the phenomenon has remained largely unex-plored by theorists of science[12] and legal academics alike. However, it is not in my interest to argue this is a case of 'bad science'. Nor am I claim-ing that science is being distorted and captured by politics, or arguing for the need to establish sociological explanations and causal links. What cap-tivates me about the matching moves of both projects and their almost

---

gued refers to physical attributes and is anatomically and physiolog-ically determined. Gender they saw as a psychological transfor-mation of the self – the internal conviction that one is either male or female (gender identity) and the behavioural expressions of that conviction […]. Meanwhile, the second-wave feminists of the 1970s also argued that sex is distinct from gender – that social institutions, themselves designed to perpetuate gender inequality, produce most of the differences between men and women […]. Money, Ehrhardt, and feminists set the terms so that sex represented the body's anat-omy and physiological workings and gender represented social forc-es that molded behaviour. Feminists did not question physical sex; it was the psychological and cultural meanings of these differences – gender – that was at issue.

11   My analysis of the rise of genomic models of sexual difference is based on the work of Sarah Richardson. See Sarah S. Richardson, "Sexes, Species, and Genomes: Why Males and Fe-males are not Like Humans and Chimpanzees", in *Biology and Philosophy,* 2010, vol. 25, no. 5, pp. 823–41.

12   See, for example, Carla Fehr, "The Evolution of Sex: Domains and Explanatory Pluralism", in *Biology and Philosophy,* 2001, vol. 16, no. 2, pp. 145–70; Richardson, 2010, p. 837, see *supra* note 11: "Despite its ubiquity in biological explanation, the foundations of the concept of sex (unlike that of species and population, for instance) in biology have gone largely unex-amined"; Epstein, 2007, p. 254, see *supra* note 7:

[V]arious authorities perform the social control function of fitting individuals into categories. Yet the active labor that goes into mak-ing sex appear dichotomous is generally invisible to the broader so-ciety, or at least, rarely remarked upon.

---

perfect correspondence in time is how it points in the direction of the complex relationship between feminists and scientists when it comes to shaping the meaning(s) of sexual difference(s).[13] I reinterpret the emergence and proliferation of thematic prosecutions as a scenario where international legal feminists have explicitly and implicitly engaged with essentialist biological ideas about sexual difference.[14] This is a tale of re-essentialisation that does not end with a lesson about how, when and why feminists should engage, reject or ignore biological explanations of sexual difference. Instead, it ends by raising questions about the ways in which both projects might be gesturing towards the emergence of a novel regime of ideological governance of sexual difference.

The chapter is structured in three parts. I tell the parallel histories of both projects articulated in three successive periods in order to track the different phases of re-essentialisation of advocacy in both spheres. I have given each period a title that speaks commonly to the science and the law. Section 12.2. tells about the "era of gender strategising"; section 12.3. outlines the rise of sex-specific research agendas in biomedicine and international criminal law; and section 12.4. describes the emergence of a post-genomic age. The purpose of what follows is to dislodge the familiarity with the virtues of thematic prosecution. Putting the arguments in their historical context and allowing the reader to see them afresh would

---

[13] Fausto-Sterling, 2000, p. 4, see *supra* note 10. Fausto-Sterling poignantly discusses how feminists have constantly oscillated between endorsing and rejecting scientific explanations of sexual difference, while also influencing the production of scientific knowledge. Often, this coming and going has been justified by the need to dislocate long-standing cultural associations between sex, nature, and femalehood. Other times, feminists have opted to ignore science altogether. However, for Fausto-Sterling argues that:

> [F]eminists definitions of sex and gender left open the possibility that male/female differences in cognitive function and behaviour could result from sex differences [...] in ceding territories of physical sex, feminists left themselves open to renewed attack on the grounds of biological difference. Indeed, feminism has encountered massive resistance from the domains of biology, medicine, and significant components of social science.

See also, Anne Fausto-Sterling, *Myths of Gender: Biological Theories about Women and Men*, Basic Books, New York, 1992, p. 162; here the author discusses the influence of feminist advocacy in science.

[14] Fausto-Sterling, 2000, p. 8, see *supra* note 10: "Feminists, too, have used scientific arguments to bolster their cause".

render visible the part of the process that led to their familiarity and "ring of truth".[15]

12.2. The Era of Gender Strategising: 1990–1995

> It is readily understood that gender is a code word. Gender strategy, especially if gleaned from court decisions, case law, press releases, or public pronouncements of international courts or tribunals, is frequently reduced to: "Oh, were the female sexual assault charges (read rape) included in the indictment?"[16]

Early in the 1990s feminists championed gender-based analysis of disease and violence to reverse the invisibility of women's experience[17] in health policies and criminal law.[18] Women's health advocates asserted that breast cancer – among several other illnesses and conditions – should be seen as a woman's disease,[19] despite the fact it also occurred in men. At approximately the same time, legal feminists used international treaty negotiations to push for the international recognition of rape against women.

---

[15] Evelyn F. Keller, *Refiguring Life: Metaphors of Twentieth-Century Biology*, New York University Press, New York, 1995, p. 9.

[16] Sellers, 2009, p. 303, see *supra* note 2.

[17] Buss, 2011, p. 413, see *supra* note 3:

> The fact that women *experience* wartime violence in ways particular to them as women was largely disregarded in the post–1945 period. Feminist activists thus needed to address an immediate gap in knowledge about, and political commitment to addressing, sexual violence in conflict situations (emphasis added).

[18] See, for example, Sellers, 2009, pp. 301–26, *supra* note 2, discussing the history of gender strategising between 1990 and 2009; Dianne Luping, "Investigation and Prosecution of Sexual and Gender-Based Crimes before the International Criminal Court", in *American University Journal of Gender, Social Policy and the Law*, 2009, vol. 17, no. 2, p. 431, discussing the history of feminist advocacy in international criminal courts up to the adoption of the ICC Statute. Buss, 2011, p. 413, see *supra* note 3:

> The fact that women experience wartime violence in ways particular to them as women was largely disregarded in the post–1945 period. Feminist activists thus needed to address an immediate gap in knowledge about, and political commitment to addressing, sexual violence in conflict situations.

[19] Carole S. Weisman, "Breast Cancer Policy-Making", in Anne S. Kasper and Susan J. Ferguson (eds.), *Breast Cancer: Society Shapes an Epidemic*, Palgrave, New York, 2002, p. 213: "[…] because breast cancer is primarily an illness of women, gender issues have been central to its politics".

The conclusion was the same: breast cancer and rape need to be seen as gender-coded phenomena.[20] Although in their campaigning efforts neither group of feminists expressly denied that men could get breast cancer, that men are raped, or that women can and do rape, they did imply, and sometimes even publicly stated, that these gender-coded phenomena occurred uniquely against women.[21]

Consequently, under the banner of gender-based disease and crime, feminist organisations for women's health and rights' pushed for the establishment of what they foresaw as gender-competent institutional formations. Such institutions would be able to address the overlooked needs of women and girls. Gender-coded analysis of disease and criminal violence set the stage for a whole architecture of gender-coded institutional formations and protocols. I will call this first period of health and legal advocacy, the "era of gender strategising".

12.2.1. Gender Strategising at the *ad hoc* Tribunals

Stemming from feminist anti-rape campaigning during the 1970s and 1980s in the United States,[22] feminist activists moved outside the domestic arena and began to push for the international recognition of sexual vio-

---

[20] See, for example, Buss, 2011, p. 413, *supra* note 3. In Buss's words, one of the goals of 1990s feminist activism "was to ensure that rape remains visible as a gendered crime, not just or only a crime against an ethnic/ racial/religious community. The concern here was (and is) that sexual violence against women might grab international attention only when it can be seen as part of an attack on a community; as 'the dishonoring of the nation'. The task then was and is to ensure the ongoing visibility of the gendered nature of the harms women face in conflict, while maintaining recognition of the political, social and economic complexity of violence and conflict" (emphasis added).

[21] Former legal adviser for the ICTY and ICTR, Patricia Viseur Sellers addressed this issue and characterised as unfortunate the reduction of gender to sexual violence against women and girls in the field of international criminal law: "*Gender* in the popular sense – not necessarily in the academic sense, and I am quite aware that I am in a university – *is shorthand for women and girls*. The word evokes comments, such as, 'Oh, I read an article on gender', or 'Oh, they've got a new gender thing coming out, right?' [...] Gender depends on the meaning given en males and females in the context of a society. So we often speak in 'reductionist' terms, *reducing gender to women*, and when we refer to gender strategy we tend to reduce it to sexual violence committed *against women and girls*. This is unfortunate. There is room for growth" (emphasis added). See Sellers, 2011, p. 303–04, see *supra* note 2.

[22] *Ibid.*: "Remember the gender strategy at the International Criminal Tribunal for the former Yugoslavia (ICTY) directly descends from the Western feminist banners that led the domestic campaigns against rape in the 1970s and 80s".

---

lence.[23] The efforts for international recognition fell into two components. One was the negotiation by international legal feminists for the recognition of sexual violence as a breach of women's human rights.[24] The second was advocacy for the international criminalisation of sexual violence in armed conflict.[25] Due in part to specialisation of feminism at large,[26] and to divisions within the international legal feminist movement,[27] the two agendas of legal reform have followed different trajectories.

The history of gender strategising in international criminal law begins a few years before the UN Security Council established the *ad hoc* tribunals in Yugoslavia and Rwanda. By 1993, reports of sexual violence in the Bosnia and Herzegovina conflicts had reached the international media.[28] Perhaps conscious of this attention, the Security Council quickly

---

[23] See, for example, Hilary Charlesworth, Christine Chinkin, and Shelley Wright, "Feminist Approaches to International Law", in *American Journal of International Law,* 1991, vol. 85, no. 4, pp. 613–45, narrating the emergence of this feminist-activist push; see also Janet Halley *et al.*, "From the International to the Local in Feminist Legal Responses to Rape, Prostitution/Sex Work, and Sex Trafficking: Four Studies in Contemporary Governance Feminism", in *Harvard Journal of Law and Gender*, 2006, vol. 29, no. 2, p. 342, for a discussion of the internationalisation of the turn in American feminism to criminal/social control visions of law.

[24] Rhonda Copelon, "Toward Accountability for Violence Against Women in War: Progress and Challenges", in Elizabeth D. Heineman (ed.), *Sexual Violence in Conflict Zones: From the Ancient World to the Era of Human Rights*, University of Pennsylvania Press, Philadelphia, 2011, pp. 232–56, describing the process of changing the status of sexual violence in international human rights law.

[25] For a general discussion of feminist involvement in the international criminalisation of sexual violence in war, see Barbara Bedont and Katherine Hall Martinez, "Ending Impunity for Gender Crimes under the International Criminal Court", in *Brown Journal of World Affairs*, 1999, vol. 6, pp. 65–85; Rhonda Copelon, "Integrating Crimes against Women into International Criminal Law", in *McGill Law Journal,* 2000, vol. 46, no. 3, pp. 217–40; Karen Engle, "Feminism and Its (Dis)contents: Criminalizing Wartime Rape in Bosnia and Herzegovina", in *American Journal of International Law*, 2005, vol. 99, no. 4, pp. 778–816.

[26] Ellen Messer-Davidow, *Disciplining Feminism: From Social Activism to Academic Discourse*, Duke University Press, Durham, 2002, p. 207. Specialisation is part of the trajectory of disciplinary growth of feminism, one that tends to intensify the production of differences within feminist discourses.

[27] Engle, 2005, pp. 778–816, see *supra* note 25, for an illuminating account of divisions within international legal feminism.

[28] Alexandra Stiglmayer's journalistic account, first published in German and later translated to English, was one of the first documents to set off the alarms: Alexandra Stiglmayer (ed.), *Mass Rape: The War Against Women in Bosnia-Herzegovina,* University of Nebraska Press, Lincoln, 1994.

---

established a commission of experts to verify the situation in the Balkans. The report produced by the Commission of Experts,[29] led by M. Cherif Bassiouni, became both the basis for the establishment of the Yugoslavia tribunal in 1993 and a milestone in the campaigning for criminalisation of rape insofar as it established patterns of sexual violence.[30] Indeed, the documentation of sexual violence in Annex IX of the Commission's report is still considered by legal practitioners and scholars to be a landmark in terms of the documentation and legal analysis of sexual violence against women and men in war.[31]

The first step of the gender strategy meant including sexual violence as a constituent act of the crimes that fell under the jurisdiction of the ICTY. Thus, the era of gender strategising begins following the publication of the Commission of Expert's report, as feminists successfully influenced the inclusion of rape as a crime against humanity under the

---

[29] The report includes documentation of thousands of cases of crimes and abuses, including information ensuing from over 200 interviews with survivors and witnesses to sexual violence committed against civilians. United Nations Security Council, Final Report of the United Nations Commission of Experts Established Pursuant to Security Council Resolution 780, Annex IX: Rape and Sexual Assault, UN Doc. S/1994/674, 27 May 1994 ('Commission of Experts, Final Report') (http://www.legal-tools.org/doc/4eb957/). An official letter dated 24 May 1994 from the secretary-general of the United Nations, Kofi Annan, presents the report of the Commission of Experts to the UN Security Council, UN Doc. S/1994/674 (http://www.legal-tools.org/doc/3a3ae2/).

[30] Commission of Experts, Final Report, see *supra* note 29: "Five patterns emerge from the reported cases, regardless of the ethnicity of the perpetrators or the victims". The Commission also included a medical team sent by the UN "to investigate rape in the former Yugoslavia". The rationale behind this decision was that medical data could be a method for verifying claims of widespread rape in Bosnia:

> Using a public health approach, medical personnel can help provide evidence of the scale of these abuses. An illustration of this kind of documentation is provided by the international team of four physicians (which included one of us [Shana Swiss] sent by the UN to investigate reports sent by the UN to investigate reports of rape in the former Yugoslavia in January 1993.

Shana Swiss and Joan E. Giller, "Rape as a Crime of War: A Medical Perspective", in *Journal of American Medical Association*, 1993, vol. 270, no. 5, p. 613.

[31] Commission of Experts, Final Report, see *supra* note 29:

> There have also been instances of sexual abuse of *men* as well as castration and mutilation of *male sexual organs* [...]. *Men* are also subject to sexual assault. They are forced to rape women and to perform sex acts on guards or each other. They have also been subjected to castration, circumcision or other sexual mutilation.

---

jurisdiction of an international tribunal for the first time. These developments first occurred through Article 5 of the ICTY Statute,[32] and one year later through Article 3 of the ICTR Statute.[33] Once reform had taken place at the statutory level, the next step was the transformation of institutional arrangements and prosecutorial practices. International legal feminists aimed to create separate units of investigation for gender-related crimes.[34] They saw this institutional arrangement as a necessary precondition to infuse with gender expertise the production of evidence and the interpretation of procedural rules during the investigations. However, partly due to lack of political will, and partly because of budget constraints, the so-called sex crime units were not created. Instead, in 1994 Richard Goldstone appointed a full-time legal adviser for gender, and made her responsible for the implementation of the tribunal's gender strategy.[35] This mod-

---

[32] United Nations, Statute of the International Criminal Tribunal for the former Yugoslavia, adopted 25 May 1993 by resolution 827, amended 7 July 2009 ('ICTY Statute') (http://www.legal-tools.org/doc/b4f63b/). Article 5 on Crimes against humanity states: "The International Tribunal shall have the power to prosecute persons responsible for the following crimes when committed in armed conflict, whether international or internal in character, and directed against any civilian population: (a) murder; (b) extermination; (c) enslavement; (d) deportation; (e) imprisonment; (f) torture; (g) rape; (h) persecutions on political, racial and religious grounds; (i) other inhumane acts".

[33] United Nations, Statute of the International Criminal Tribunal for Rwanda, adopted 8 November 1994 by resolution 955 ('ICTR Statute') (http://www.legal-tools.org/doc/8732d6/). Article 3 on Crimes against humanity states: "The International Tribunal for Rwanda shall have the power to prosecute persons responsible for the following crimes when committed as part of a widespread or systematic attack against any civilian population on national, political, ethnic, racial or religious grounds: (a) murder; (b) extermination; (c) enslavement; (d) deportation; (e) imprisonment; (f) torture; (g) rape; (h) persecutions on political, racial and religious grounds; (i) Other inhumane acts".

[34] Sellers, 2009, p. 307, see *supra* note 2:

> In 1994, after the naming of a Prosecutor, women's groups, especially European and American groups (both North and South Americans) pursued their discussions with both the Prosecutor and the Deputy Prosecutor at the ICTY. They urged the establishment of a separate prosecution unit for sexual assault investigations. Women's groups wanted to ensure that sexual assault investigations were a forethought, and not an afterthought. The vigilant contributors reiterated that the investigation and prosecution of sexual assault crimes were integral to the Tribunal's mandate.

[35] Sellers occupied the same position at the ICTR from 1995 until 1999.

> In order conscientiously to address the prevalence of sexual assault allegations committed in the former Yugoslavia and Rwanda, a legal

---

el of gender expertise, aimed at coordinating, supervising and educating teams of well-trained court personnel, has remained instrumental to the international legal feminist agenda for gender-competent international courts.[36]

Interestingly, the vocabulary that emerged from this period involved an intricate system of gender-coding aimed at making visible the harmful experiences of women and girls in war.[37] In a nutshell, the system was grounded on the use of the word 'gender' as, effectively, a synonym for "women and girls".[38] In Sellers' own words, gender became a "code" to refer to women and girls.[39] This move transformed the interpretation of other expressions and international criminal law categories. Gender

---

adviser for gender-related crimes has been appointed. The adviser, as a member of the Prosecutor's secretariat, reports directly to the Prosecutor and the two Deputy Prosecutors and has three major areas of responsibility: to provide advice on gender-related crimes and women's policy issues, including internal gender issues such as hiring and promotion; to work with the Prosecution Section to formulate the legal strategy and the development of international criminal law jurisprudence for sexual assaults; and to assist the Investigations Unit in developing an investigative strategy to pursue evidence of sexual assaults.

United Nations, Second Annual Report of the International Tribunal for the Prosecution of Persons Responsible for Serious Violations of International Humanitarian Law Committed in the Territory of the Former Yugoslavia Since 1991, UN Doc. A/50/365-S/1995/728, 23 August 1995 (http://www.legal-tools.org/doc/9a66a1/).

[36] Bedont and Hall Martinez, 1999, p. 76, see *supra* note 25: "The Gender Legal Advisor has been instrumental in ensuring the investigation and prosecution of sexual violence crimes".

[37] See, for example, Buss, 2011, p. 413, *supra* note 17; Engle, 2005, p. 814, *supra* note 25: "for the most part, feminists in both camps emphazised male-on-female sexual violence as the harm that needed to be addressed by the ICTY."

[38] Sellers, 2009, p. 303, see *supra* note 2. For other examples, see Kelly D. Askin, "Prosecuting Wartime Rape and Other Gender-Related Crimes Under International Law: Extraordinary Advances, Enduring Obstacles", in *Berkeley Journal of International Law*, 2003, vol. 21, no. 2, p. 317, for an instance of the interchangeable use of the words 'gender', and the expression 'women and girls'; Jennifer Green *et al.*, "Affecting the Rules for the Prosecution of Rape and Other Gender-Based Violence before the International Criminal Tribunal for the Former Yugoslavia: A Feminist Proposal and Critique", in *Hastings Women's Law Journal*, 1994, vol. 5, no. 2, p. 173, using the expression gender-based crimes while referring to increased international attention to violence against women.

[39] Sellers, 2009, see *supra* note 17.

crimes stood for rape against women and girls,[40] while gender strategies were defined as the "legal ability to prosecute crimes committed against women and girls under humanitarian law [...]";[41] and gender-competent tribunals defined as those that successfully addressed the sexual assaults under their jurisdiction.[42] Gender justice required the arrest of suspects, the adjudication on individual responsibility and the delivery of jurisprudence aimed at countering impunity of sexual assaults against women and girls,[43] while gender injustice became the mishandling of sexual assault charges against women by prosecutors.[44] In this coding system, gender ended up simultaneously equated to sex,[45] while embodied by women and girls.[46] Tellingly, by the end of her genealogy of international legal feminist advocacy, Sellers had replaced the use of the expression 'gender-based crimes' for 'sex-based crimes'.[47]

---

[40] Sellers, 2009, p. 305, see *supra* note 2: "Even though the reduction of gender strategy to sexual violence is too simplistic, there exists a basis of truth. However, there is an emerging, hopefully prevailing, norm that gender crimes under international criminal law and under humanitarian law should not be limited to prosecution of sexual violence. Gender crimes should not be limited, to what I call the 'R word': rape. Rape was just the beachhead; the proverbial landing at Normandy, so that we could wade ashore at Kigali. It was the enumerated provisional place where we chose to disembark while under fire and while behind enemy lines." See also Askin, 2003, pp. 288–349, *supra* note 38, using throughout the article the expression 'gender-related crimes' to refer to rape against women and girls; Engle, 2005, p. 801, *supra* note 25, noting how Sellers suggests 'gender crimes' and 'sexual assault' were considered as one and the same from the early 1990s.

[41] Sellers, 2009, p. 305, see *supra* note 2.

[42] *Ibid.*

[43] *Ibid.*

[44] *Ibid.*, p. 316.

[45] "An unintended consequence of the jurisprudence might well be that the primary harm to be addressed becomes one of sex, not of violence or gender oppression": Engle, 2005, pp. 801, 815, see *supra* note 25, poignantly discussing the "replacement of a focus on gender with a focus on sex" as one of the unintended consequences of the gender strategy at the ICTY.

[46] Sellers, 2009, p. 316, see *supra* note 17: "Repeatedly the raped female, the sexual assault victim/survivor, has become unforgivably reduced to embody gender strategy. This is reasonable to a certain extent."

[47] *Ibid.*: "The successes of the ICTY and the ICTR – meaning the arrest of suspects, the adjudication of crimes based on individual responsibility, and the delivery of jurisprudence that countered impunity including impunity for sex-based crimes – are great."

12.2.2. Gender Strategising in Biomedical Research

While legal feminists called for gender strategising at the *ad hoc* tribunals, a sector of the US women's health movement pushed for their own version of gender strategies by denouncing the lack of sex and gender-specific research.[48] They called for the inclusion of women in clinical trials and the regulation of biomedical research so that it would include analysis of results according to the sex of the participants. Underlying this feminist strategy was the idea of "illnesses and disorders that affect women predominantly or differently than men"[49] needed to be addressed by producing more data on women. In 1990, under the leadership of Florence Haseltine and Joanne Howes, a coalition that included feminist activists and people from scientific and medical establishments created the Society for Women's Health Research ('SWHR').[50] This non-profit organisation became the steering wheel of advocacy efforts against the lack of clinical investigations on "disease and conditions that affect women *uniquely*".[51] Their first big success was to get Congress's General Accountability Office ('GAO') to evaluate the policies and practices related to the application of the National Institutes of Health ('NIH').[52]

The next strategic step of the SWHR was to push for the creation of separate offices for sex and gender-specific research within the department of health.[53] As a result of this successful advocacy effort, GAO created the Office for Research on Women's Health ('ORWH'). But health

---

[48] See, for example, Tracy L. Johnson and Elizabeth Fee, "Introduction to Women's Health Research", in Florence P. Haseltine (ed.), *Women's Health Research: A Medical and Policy Primer*, Society for the Advancement of Women's Health Research, Washington, DC, 1997, recounting how women have been excluded from medical research for decades.

[49] Society for Women's Health Research (http://swhr.org/about/).

[50] See, for example, Karen L. Baird, "Beyond Reproduction: The Women's Health Movement in the 1990s", in Karen L. Baird, with Dana-Ain Davis and Kimberly Christensen (eds.), *Beyond Reproduction: Women's Health, Activism, and Public Policy*, Associated University Press, Cranburry, 2009, p. 9, for a broad history of the movement during this first period of advocacy; Karen L. Baird, "Protecting the Fetus: The NIH and FDA Medical Research Policies", in Karen L. Baird, Dana-Ain Davis and Kimberly Christensen (eds.), *Beyond Reproduction: Women's Health, Activism, and Public Policy*, Associated University Press, Cranbury, 2009, for an account of the role of SWHR in this process.

[51] Society for Women's Health Research, see *supra* note 49.

[52] Epstein, 2007, p. 303, see *supra* note 7.

[53] *Ibid.*, pp. 233–57.

---

feminists, in the same fashion as international legal feminists, believed it was necessary to create separate institutional formations exclusively dedicated to research on women's biomedical issues.[54] By 1993, they succeeded in getting the NIH Revitalization Act passed in Congress, making it mandatory to include women in all clinical trials. After this decision the FDA issued a guideline on "calling analysis of data by *gender*".[55]

The push for legal reform was expected to transform scientific and medical practices in two fundamental ways. On the one hand, it would make the inclusion of women in medical trials a legal obligation; and second, it would mandate the analysis of medical trial results by sex. This second objective is also linked to a third and more ambitious project health feminists already had in mind: setting up clinical research trials in order to carry out biomedical research specifically aimed at measuring differences between males and females. Despite the fact that the whole point of their effort was to promote biomedical research practice grounded on biological sexual difference, they referred to it as "sex and gender differences research", while using both terms interchangeably.[56]

The push for the establishment of institutions with expertise on women's issues both in biomedicine and international criminal law was

---

[54] I thank Sarah Richardson for pointing out to me this trend in the women's health movement. According to Richardson, health feminists aimed, first, for the establishment of offices within institutions and later for the creation of permanent specialised units and institutions to carry out sex-difference research. See Richardson, 2013, *supra* note 7. See also Epstein, 2007, pp. 233–57, *supra* note 7.

[55] The NIH Revitalization Act ordered the inclusion of women in trials combined with the analysis of results by sex. Furthermore it made the ORWH a permanent entity. See, for example, Society for Women's Health Research, "SWHR Timeline" (http://swhr.org/about/swhr-timeline/); Epstein, 2007, p. 304, see *supra* note 7. See also, J. Claude Bennet, "Inclusion of Women in Clinical Trials: Policies for Population Subgroups", in *New England Journal of Medicine*, 1993, vol. 329, pp. 288–92, discussing the pros and cons of the inclusion of women in clinical trials.

[56] Altogether it remains unclear whether or not health feminists were sustaining the idea of gender being grounded in biology, nor if biological sexual differences were being deployed to analyse female social behaviour. For an example of the interchangeable use of sex and gender in this type of research see, A. Parekh, W. Sanhai, S. Marts and K. Uhl, "Advancing women's health *via* FDA Critical Path Initiative", in *Drug Discovery Today: Technologies*, 2007, vol. 4, no. 2, p. 69: "Studying sex and gender differences is critical to understanding diseases that affect women solely, disproportionately or differently from men."

---

the result of a successful shift in their advocacy strategies.[57] The shift was grounded on the assumption that men and women were the two relevant groups to compare.[58] Steven Epstein has criticised this trend in women's health advocacy and framed it as partaking in what he calls the "inclusion and difference paradigm", which is a "set of changes in research policies, ideologies, and practices, and the accompanying creation of bureaucratic offices, procedures, and monitoring systems".[59] The turn towards differences between the sexes in feminist advocacy, argues Epstein, is part of a tendency to dethrone the standard human and replace it with group-specific approaches.[60] He argues that in doing so, the women's health

---

[57] I thank Sarah Richardson for pointing out to me the relation between institution building and changes in advocacy strategies in the field of sex-based biology.

[58] Epstein, 2007, p. 250, see *supra* note 7:

> As Judith Lorber has argued, the overriding mistake of so many 'epistemologically spurious' studies of sex differences in both the biological and the social sciences is that they begin simply by assuming that 'men' and 'women' are the relevant groups to compare, look for the differences between them, and then attribute whatever they find to the underlying sex difference.

See also Judith Lorber, "Believing Is Seeing: Biology as Ideology", in *Gender and Society*, December 1993, vol. 7, no. 4, p. 571.

[59] According to Epstein, this biopolitical paradigm refers to "the research and policy focus on including diverse groups as participants in medical studies and in measuring differences across those groups". Epstein, 2007, pp. 6, 17, see *supra* note 7:

> [It is biopolitical because] it reflects the presumption that health research is an appropriate an important site for state intervention and regulation and because it infuses the life sciences with new political import. [...] It hybridizes scientific and state policies and categories. Specifically, it takes two different areas of concern – the meaning of biological difference and the status of socially subordinated groups – and weaves them together by articulating a distinctive way of asking and answering questions about the demarcating of subpopulations of patients and citizens.

[60] *Ibid.*, pp. 233–57:

> There has been almost no scholarly attention to the broad-scale attempt to dethrone the "standard human" and mandate a group-specific approach to biomedical knowledge production – an identity-centered redefinition of U.S. biomedical research practice that encompasses multiple social categories.

movement has participated in the creation of equivalence across two pre-viously distinguishable forms of difference – gender and sex.[61]

The parallel between the gender strategising of health feminists and international legal feminists between 1990 and 1995 shows a shared move towards re-essentialisation of advocacy efforts already underway. The first step in that direction was the flattening of gender and sex either by reducing gender to refer to women and girls, interchangeably using both categories, or implicitly and explicitly suggesting that gender is deter-mined by biological differences.[62] Interestingly, feminists' use of gender and sex coding in both spheres appears as an invitation for sex-based in-stitutional formations. However, these institutional projects are not pre-sented to the public as sex-coded but gender-coded initiatives. By 1995 each group of advocates had succeeded in influencing the creation of new institutions, the renovation of old ones, and the transformation of institu-tional practices within their own spheres of action.

12.3. The Rise of Sex-Specific Agendas: 1996–2001

> The very fact of dividing subjects into male and female cate-gories for research purposes may serve to reify and perpetu-ate a socially created dichotomy. The search for differences can help to create the differences, if you are looking for something you are likely to find it.[63]

In the previous section I described how feminists' gender-coded analysis of both female disease and criminal violence against women set the stage for a whole architecture of sex-based institutional formations and proto-cols. This era of female inclusive institution building under the banner of gender strategising was succeeded by a period of advocacy aimed at fur-ther differentiating men and women on the basis of sexual difference.[64]

---

[61] *Ibid.*, p. 142: "[S]ex/gender, race/ethnicity, and age are all treated as formally equivalent modes of difference to be 'handled' administratively in similar ways."

[62] For a discussion on how this shift counters the feminist project – longstanding since the 1970s – to dissociate gender from nature, and instead supports the idea of gender being de-termined by differences at the biological level, see Fausto-Sterling, 2000, *supra* note 10.

[63] Susan Star Leigh, "Sex Differences and the Dichotomization of the Brain: Methods, Limits and Problems in Research on Consciousness", in R. Hubbard and M. Lowe (eds.), *Genes and Gender II*, Gordian Press, New York, 1979, cited in Epstein, 2007, p. 251, see *supra* note 7.

[64] During the early 1990s advocates for change used early reports of such differences as a ra-tionale for inclusionary reform, during this second period, inclusionary policies and proce-

Successful feminist advocacy during the second half of the 1990s led to the implementation of methods and institutional practices that separated, and often isolated the analysis of illness, health conditions or criminal conduct, on the basis that it affected women predominantly, or differently than men. Between 1996 and 2001 feminist advocacy thus moved into another era, which geared away from inclusion and pushed for institutions to develop sex-specific agendas.[65]

During this period, thematic prosecutions became the prime focus of international feminists' sex-specific agenda. Under this prosecutorial model, sexual crimes committed by men against women[66] were prioritised, grouped and investigated in isolation from other acts that also fell under the jurisdiction of the ICTY. Health feminists' own version of a sex-specific agenda led to the emergence of sex-based biology, which is explained in further detail in section 12.3.2.[67] Dichotomist sexual coding, along with the flattening of gender and sex, remained two key underpinnings of this period. However, in this period feminists appear to go one step further in their embrace of essentialist notions of sexual difference, by claiming or assuming the overriding significance of biology and genetics in understanding the behaviour of males and females. In this way these two feminist projects inadvertently make their projects increasingly dependent on the possibility of containing reality in mutually exclusive categories like males and females, or victims and perpetrators. I will call this era "the rise of sex-specific agendas".

12.3.1. The Birth of Sex-Specific Prosecutions

Between 1996 and 2001, international legal feminists successfully completed the second phase of their project for redefining the status of sex

---

dures for subgroup comparisons resulted in proliferation of difference findings. Epstein, 2007, p. 235, see *supra* note 7.

[65] I borrow this category from Sarah Richardson's analysis of sex-specific research agendas in a post-genomic context. See Richardson, 2013, *supra* note 7.

[66] Karen Engle has pointed our how the ICTY's prosecutorial strategy has functioned "to see all sexual assault as reproducing the dynamics of male-on-female (sexual) violence": Engle, 2005, p. 815, see *supra* note 25.

[67] Epstein, 2007, pp. 233–57, see *supra* note 7:

> [E]mphasis on sex differences in medicine is part of a larger trend toward claiming or assuming the overriding significance of biology and genetics in understanding the behaviour of males and females.

---

crimes in international humanitarian law. Two major events mark this period. The first are the landmark *Foča* cases which involve the indictments and verdicts against Kunarać, Kovač and Vuković.[68] The *Foča* cases refer to the prosecution and conviction of three middle-ranking Bosnian police officers for their individual responsibility in the rapes and sexual enslavement of Muslim women from the municipality of Foča in the early 1990s. The second event is the adoption of the ICC Statute in 1998.

Foča is the ICTY case that has received the most media attention, following the Milošević trial.[69] It was the first time in history that an international tribunal convicted an accused solely on counts of sexual violence.[70] Even more significant is the fact that the convictions were the result of a prosecutorial strategy designed to prioritise, group and isolate sexual crimes committed against women from a broader repertoire of criminal acts that occurred in *Foča* around the same time.[71] The convictions against Kunarać, Kovač and Vuković constitute the first example of international thematic prosecutions of sexual violence in armed conflict.[72]

It was not mere coincidence that in *Foča* the ICTY grouped sexual crimes committed predominantly against women and simultaneously isolated their prosecution from the investigation of other offences under its jurisdiction. International legal feminists, together with non-governmental organisations and university-based institutes, lobbied and campaigned for

---

[68] *Kunarać et al.* Judgment, see *supra* note 4.

[69] Minna Schrag, "Lessons Learned from ICTY Experience", in *Journal of International Criminal Justice*, 2004, vol. 2, no. 2, p. 427–43.

[70] Institute for War and Peace Reporting, "*Foca* Rape Case", 22 February 2005:

> This trial and verdicts have two very important aspects for international law. This is the first conviction by an international court for sexual enslavement and the first trial to deal exclusively with sexual crimes per se rather than grouping such offences with killings and similar war crimes as the "accompanying phenomena" of war.

[71] See, for example, Doris Buss, "Rethinking 'Rape as a Weapon of War'", in *Feminist Legal Studies*, 2009, vol. 17, no. 2, pp. 145–63, discussing the importance this case played in shifting the understanding of sexual violence against women as simply accompanying phenomena to other crimes.

[72] See Schrag, 2004, pp. 427–43, *supra* note 69, discussing how the thematic approach to prosecution in Foča countered the initial internal decision at the ICTY Office of the Prosecutor not to pursue 'theme cases'.

---

the prioritisation of cases of systematic rape against women.[73] In response, as the press release following the indictment reveals, the Office of the Prosecutor had decided to "pay specific attention to gender-related crimes".[74] The head prosecutor at the ICTY, Richard Goldstone, placed the prioritisation of sex crimes against women at the core of the tribunal's mission.[75] The prosecutor himself portrayed the separate prosecution of sex crimes committed by men against women as the core of the gender strategy of the court.

The prosecution strategy in *Foča* was designed to meet two objectives. First, it was intended to focus exclusively on sexual crimes against women; and second, it was meant to bring attention to the systematic nature of rapes of Bosnian Muslim women.[76] By having the first successful thematic prosecution of rape also become the first ICTY prosecution for rape as an autonomous act that constituted a crime against humanity, *Foča* created a link between the isolation of sex crimes and proving the system-

---

[73] For detailed analyses of feminist campaigning at the ICTY, see Janet Halley *et al.*, "From the International to the Local in Feminist Legal Responses to Rape, Prostitution/Sex Work, and Sex Trafficking: Four Studies in Contemporary Governance Feminism", in *Harvard Journal of Law and Gender*, 2006, vol. 29, pp. 342–47; Kelly D. Askin, "A Decade of the Development of Gender Crimes in International Courts and Tribunals: 1993–2003", in *Human Rights Brief*, 2004, vol. 11, no. 3, p. 16; Engle, 2005, p. 778, see *supra* note 25, for an account of feminist activists' concerted effort to affect the prosecutorial strategies at the ICTY; Joanne Barkan, "As Old as War Itself: Rape in Foca", in *Dissent*, Winter 2002, p. 63–64, for a detailed account of feminist campaigning in Foča.

[74] ICTY, "Gang Rape, Torture and Enslavement of Muslim Women Charged in ICTY's First Indictment Dealing Specifically with Sexual Offences", Press Release, CC/PIO/093-E, 27 June 1996:

> The indictment made public today is the result of an investigation which commenced in late 1994. This indictment fully illustrates the OTP's strategy [...] to investigate the operation of detention facilities in connection with the takeover of parts of Bosnia and Herzegovina by the Bosnian Serb forces [...] *to pay specific attention to gender-related crimes*" [emphasis added].

[75] *Ibid.*: "We have always regarded it as an important part of our mission to redefine and consolidate the place of these offences in humanitarian law."

[76] During the seminar that preceded this volume, Morten Bergsmo pointed out that "international sex crimes were first investigated and prosecuted in a systematic manner by the ICTY through the so-called Foča cases". See Engle, 2005, p. 798, *supra* note 25, discussing how the exclusive focus on rape was widely acknowledged and seen as precedent.

---

atic nature of sexual violence against women in war.[77] Despite having resulted in some disappointment for feminists, it became the iconic "rape case", and demonstrated the potential of a sex-specific thematic prosecution for the advancement of feminist goals.[78]

Unfortunately, *Foča*'s symbolic power in shaping the legal consciousness of its time also legitimised the need to strategically isolate cases of sexual violence against women in order to make them successful. This legitimised the practice of sex-specific prosecution at a time when it was still hard to appreciate some of its unintended consequences.[79] Neither was it easy to appreciate amid the success of feminist campaigning how slowly but steadily a context of heightened reductionism of gender to sex was unfolding.

The adoption of the ICC Statute clearly illustrates how the success of international feminist campaigning was fraught with a strong taint of re-essentialisation. Three years before the final verdicts in *Foča*, Article

---

[77] The front page of the *New York Times* quoted a court spokesman, who called it a "landmark indictment because it focuses exclusively on sexual assaults, without including any other charges [...]. There is no precedent for this. It is of major legal significance because it illustrates the court's strategy to focus on gender-related crimes and give them their proper place in the prosecution of war crimes": Engle, 2005, p. 798, see *supra* note 25.

[78] Barkan, 2002, see *supra* note 73:

> History – in so far as it will deal with human rights for women – will likely judge one strategic decision made by the ICTY as invaluable: the decision to put together "the rape case". Even in the early stages of the tribunal's work, the lobbying to get prosecutors to pay attention to sexual offenses paid off. Before long, more than 20 percent of the charges filed at the ICTY involved allegations of sexual assault – an extraordinarily high percentage in light of the past record. But in any individual case, the rape of women was only one crime among many being prosecuted. If rape were overshadowed in most trials by other crimes, the possibility of breaking new legal ground for women's rights decreased. But, hypothetically, a case devoted to just one type of crime, just one category of victim, and just one place might have significant impact on the law and on public opinion. In late 1994, the ICTY office of the prosecutor, supported by women's rights advocates, began the investigation for a rape case. The prosecutors would investigate only sexual crimes and only those committed against women. The place they chose to investigate was Foca.

[79] See Engle, 2005, *supra* note 25, for a discussion of some of the unintended consequences of feminist advocacy at the ICTY.

7(3) of the ICC Statute defined gender as referring only to the "two sex-es".[80] Despite containing the most comprehensive enumeration of sex crimes in international criminal law to date, and incorporating several structural provisions designed to facilitate the effective investigation and prosecution of sex crimes,[81] the equation of gender to sex had become embedded in the future statutory and regulatory framework of the ICC.[82]

12.3.2. The Birth of Sex-Based Biology

Sex-based biology is a term coined by Florence Haseltine[83] – founder of the Society for Women's Health Research ('SWHR')[84] – referring to "the study of sex differences in health and disease".[85] Substantively, sex-based

---

[80] Rome Statute of the International Criminal Court, 17 July 1998, in force 1 July 2002, Article 7(3) ('ICC Statute') (http://www.legal-tools.org/doc/7b9af9/) provides in full:

> For the purpose of this Statute, it is understood that the term 'gen-der' refers to the two sexes, male and female, within the context of society. The term 'gender' does not indicate any meaning different from the above.

[81] See, for example, Merope, 2011, p. 2, *supra* note 5. For a discussion of these provisions as the result of over a decade of feminist advocacy see, for example, Susana SáCouto and Katherine Cleary, "The Importance of Effective Investigation of Sexual Violence and Gender-Based Crimes at the International Criminal Court", in *American University Journal of Gender, Social Policy and the Law*, 2009, vol. 17, no. 2, pp. 337, 339.

[82] For a thorough and balanced analysis of the downside of the definition of gender in the ICC Statute, see Valerie Oosterveld, "The Definition of 'Gender' in the Rome Statute of the International Criminal Court: A Step Forward or Back for International Criminal Justice", in *Harvard Human Rights Journal*, 2005, vol. 18, p. 55.

[83] Haseltine has published extensively on the topic of women's health research, and specifically in the field of sex-based biology. See, for example, Florence P. Haseltine, "Formula for Change: Examining the Glass Ceiling", in Florence P. Haseltine (ed.), 1997, p. 255, *supra* note 48; Florence P. Haseltine, "Gender Differences in Addiction and Recovery", in *Journal of Women's Health & Gender-Based Medicine*, July 2000, vol. 9, no. 6, pp. 579–83.

[84] Steven Epstein, "Beyond Inclusion, Beyond Difference: The Biopolitics of Health", in Ian Whitmarsh and David S. Jones (eds.), *What's the Use of Race: Modern Governance and the Biology of Difference*, Massachusetts Institute of Technology, 2010, pp. 62–87:

> In the early 1990s, the SWHR had coalesced around the goal of in-clusion of women in research and had campaigned for the NIH Re-vitalization Act. By the late 1990s, the Society's raison d'etre was the furtherance of research on differences between men and women that bore medical significance.

[85] SWHR appears to be the most salient organisation in accounts that retrace the emergence and development of sex-based biology. In some of these accounts Haseltine appears as also having coined the term gender-specific biology. It remains unclear whether or not SBB is differ-

---

biology involves both increased research on women's health, and sex-based analysis of data.[86] Methodologically, it entails the push for the establishment of institutions specialised in doing research about diseases and conditions that affect women uniquely.[87] The rise of sex-based biology is the result of a conscious and certainly successful transformation in feminist women's health advocacy strategies from sameness as inclusion to sameness as difference.[88] The movement towards difference was marked by a strong activist return to arguments that highlight the biological differences between males and females, accompanied by growing funding of research that reflects this shift.

As a social movement that has "swum in feminist currents", sex-based biology distinguishes itself from feminist health movements of the 1970s and 1980s by showing eagerness to embrace assertions of biological differences by sex.[89] This has remained the core of health feminist ad-

---

ent from gender-specific biology. However, they both appear to rely heavily on notions of sexual difference to *explain* gender attributes. See, for example, Steven Epstein, "Bodily Differences and Collective Identities: The Politics of Gender and Race in Biomedical Research in the United States", in *Body & Society*, 2004, vol. 10, nos. 2/3, p. 194:

> In recent years, the emphasis on biological difference has also been promoted by advocacy groups such as the Society for the Advancement of Women's Health Research, which heralds the new field of 'gender-specific biology' – a term invented by Florence Haseltine and defined as 'the field of scientific inquiry committed to identifying the biological and physiological differences between men and women.

[86] Epstein, 2007, p. 243, see *supra* note 7.

[87] Society for Women's Health Research, see *supra* note 49.

[88] Early in the 1990s feminist health activism made a significant move from arguing fundamental sameness towards arguing fundamental differences between the sexes – what Steve Epstein has called the inclusion and exclusion paradigm. During the 1970s and 80s, American women's health activism focused on the inclusion of women's health needs and concerns in public policy and scientific research agendas. However, by the early 1990s the inclusionary policies and procedures achieved had resulted in the proliferation of scientific findings reinforcing the idea of difference between the sexes. As a result of this process, a strand of the feminist movement began pushing for "the emphasis on sex differences in medicine". See Epstein, 2007, p. 236, *supra* note 7; Richardson, 2013, *supra* note 7, for detailed discussions of this move from sameness to difference and the complex web of implications for scientific practices.

[89] Epstein, 2007, p. 244, 247, see *supra* note 7:

> The strategic moves in the construction and public representation of sex-based biology raise important questions about the politics of

vocacy strategies for over more than a decade.[90] Sex-based biology is grounded on a conception of the sexes as dramatically different, and claims to have "revolutionized the way that the scientific community views the sexes".[91] If not a revolution, a major transformation took place between 1995 and 2001. While in the 1970s the term 'gender' was absent from biomedical writing and research, today the words 'sex' and 'gender' are everywhere in biomedical literature.[92] What we observe in their usage starting in the mid-1990s is a trend to interchange them without any explanation. Contrary to the trend from the 1970s, when the use of the term 'gender' expanded while that of 'sex' contracted in biomedical writing. From the 1990s onwards, the usage of 'sex' has expanded while that of 'gender' has contracted to the point that today 'gender' appears to have been reduced to 'sex'.

---

women's health and about the broader feminist currents within which the women's health movement has swum.

Drawing from the work of Hara Estroff Marano, Epstein catalogues it as post-feminism, ("the fruits of previous feminist struggles are now being reaped [...] it's safe to talk about sex differences again"). However, sex-based biology proponents locate it "broadly within the legacy of feminism", despite ideological divides within the women's health movement. Others like Bernadine Healy call it the "third stage of feminism" or even "post-feminism". See, for example, Epstein, 2007, p. 248, *supra* note 7; Marianne Legato, "Gender-Specific Physiology: How Real is it? How Important is it?", in *International Journal of Fertility and Women's Medicine,* 1997, vol. 42, no. 1, p. 26.

90   Epstein, 2007, p. 241, see *supra* note 7:

> [Sex-based biology] emphasize[s] fundamental, thoroughgoing, biological differences between men's and women's bodies [...] those who subscribe this movement believe that women – and men – deserve separated medical scrutiny because they are biologically different at the level of the cell, the organ, the system, the organism.

91   Society for Women's Health Research, "Before the Senate Appropriations Subcommittee on Labor, Health and Human Services, Education, and Other Related Agencies", 15 March 2010.

92   Nancy Krieger, "Genders, Sexes, and Health: What Are the Connections – and Why Does It Matter?", in *International Journal of Epidemiology,* 2003, vol. 32, no. 4, p. 652:

> Open up any biomedical or public health journal prior to the 1970s, and one term will be glaringly absent: gender. Open up any recent biomedical or public health journal, and two terms will be used either: (1) interchangeably, or (2) as distinct constructs: gender and sex.

The term 'sex-based biology' was well established by the end of the 1990s.[93] In 2001, the Institute of Medicine published a report sponsored by SWHR entitled "Exploring the Biological Contributions to Human Health: Does Sex Matter?".[94] This publication is considered to signal the naissance of sex-based biology as a field of biomedical study. The report, which concluded with a recommendation for scientists to investigate sex "from womb to tomb",[95] became a powerful advocacy tool used by the SWHR and its allies to advocate for major funding for sex-specific research before Congress.[96] It became the banner under which sex-based biology expanded the use of sex-difference research from its initial priority – studying women's responses to medication – towards its application in interdisciplinary studies of female behaviour.[97]

The rise of sex-based biology, starting in 1995, and the subsequent development of sex-specific research agendas with their heightened emphasis on sex differences, occurred in a context of ever-growing claims and assumptions of the "overriding significance of biology and genetics in understanding the behaviour of males and females".[98] As Anne Fausto-Sterling announced back in 1985: "[t]he popular press and scientists alike have apparently fallen in love with the gene".[99] As explanations of sexual difference move from human anatomy and chromosomes towards genetic expression, the enlistment of sex-specific research to explain and understand male and female behaviour augmented rapidly. The public and sci-

---

[93] In 1995, the SWHR held its first national meeting focused on sex-based biology. Phyllis Greenberger and Sherry Marts, "News from the Society of Women's Health Research: Hormones, Chromosomes and the Future of Sex-Based Biology", in *Journal of Women's Health and Gender-Based Medicine*, 2000, vol. 9, no. 9, p. 937:

> The intriguing notion – that sex differences could be found at a level as basic as the control of gene expression – led the Society to begin planning a series of conferences with a focus on basic research in sex-based biology.

[94] Institute of Medicine, *Exploring the Biological Contributions to Human Health: Does Sex Matter?*, National Academy Press, Washington DC, 2001.

[95] *Ibid.*, p. 5.

[96] Thanks to SWHR post-report advocacy strategies in 2001 Congress passed a new funding initiative aimed at the creation of specialised centers of research on sex and gender factors affecting women's lives. See Epstein, 2007, p. 242, *supra* note 7.

[97] See, for example, Greenberger and Marts, 2000, pp. 93–938, *supra* note 93.

[98] Epstein, 2007, p. 236, see *supra* note 7.

[99] Fausto-Sterling, 1985, p. 62, see *supra* note 13 (first edition).

---

entists alike seemed increasingly interested in proving or disproving how much of our social behaviour can be explained through genetic mapping.

The rise of sex-specific agendas in international criminal law and biomedicine is characterised by an increasing turn towards notions of fundamental difference between the sexes. Of course, in each sphere these notions tend to manifest themselves quite differently. This turn towards difference echoed both during the *Foča* case, and the birth of sex-based biology. Choosing to isolate the prosecution of crimes against women and biomedical investigations of female reactions to medicine produced more data on sexual difference, and this data was used to further assert differences among men and women. The criticism of sex-specific agendas in biomedicine by authors like Epstein and Richardson[100] illuminate some of the unintended consequences of these practices, including on international legal feminists' agendas. For instance, we could examine the ways in which the practice of sex-specific prosecutions obscure commonalities across males and females (that is, when females are perpetrators or male are victims of sexual violence); and occludes differences within each sex (that is, the rape of indigenous women or women with disabilities). However, despite the pressing need to formulate these questions – and many others – to ensure that the gender strategising remained true to its goals of reversing the invisibility of harmful experiences of women and girls, by the beginning of the twenty-first century sex-specific prosecution and biomedical research were so well meaning and seen as such advancements for women that it was hard to argue they could be reinforcing gender stereotypes[101] or disguising problems of categorisation of the two sexes as unambiguously divided.[102]

12.4. The Post-Genomic Age: 2002–2010

> [Today] contrary to politically correct visions of a shared, universal human genome, males and females are more genetically different than ever conceived.[103]

---

[100] See Epstein 2007, *supra* note 7; Richardson, 2013, *supra* note 7.

[101] Richardson, 2013, *supra* note 7, for the analysis of this phenomenon in sex-specific biomedical research.

[102] See Epstein, 2007, p. 253, *supra* note 7, arguing "there is no unambiguous divide between the two sexes".

[103] Richardson, 2010, p. 824, see *supra* note 11.

Between 2005 and 2010 international legal feminists have dealt with the paradoxical effects of advocating for sex-specific agendas. While sex-based biology advocates joyfully enlisted recent findings in genomic science, placing sexual differences at the level of genetic expression, international legal feminists saw the ICC to be turning gender strategising on its head when trying to prioritise the prosecution of war crimes constituted by the unlawful enlistment of children. As biological explanations of sexual difference shift from the anatomic and chromosomal towards locating the essence of sex at the level of genetic expression, it becomes harder for feminists to contain the expansive quality of binary thinking embedded in sex-specific agendas. This is the case especially when the "labors involved in making sex appear dichotomous"[104] in feminist advocacy remain largely unexplored.[105]

The classification of individuals into mutually exclusive categories that apparently have nothing to do with sex – that is, victims and perpetrators – is inevitably infused with social constructions about men and women. When gender is reduced, confused, or replaced by sex, and sex is thought to be determined by genes, assertions about stereotypical gender differences (that is, women are victims and men are perpetrators of sexual violence in war) gain an apparent truth-value. Consequently, gender attributes – even stereotypical ones – end up associated to notions of nature and essence. The challenge of feminist projects in the face of such scenarios is not the facticity of biological sexes, but the unintended consequences of binary thinking for their own political agendas.

12.4.1. Investigating Sex Crimes in a Post-Genomic Age

In 2006, the ICC issued a warrant of arrest against Thomas Lubanga, former commander-in-chief of Forces Patriotiques pour la Libération du Congo ('FPLC').[106] After his arrest and the confirmation of charges by a

---

[104] Epstein, 2007, see *supra* note 7.

[105] See Lynda Birke, "Sitting on the Fence: Biology, Feminism and Gender-Bending Environments", in *Women's Studies International Forum,* 2000, vol. 23, no. 5, p. 587–99, discussing the challenges of examining feminist advocates' use of categories such as sex and gender due to the "schism between feminist theorists and feminist activists".

[106] ICC, "Issuance of a Warrant of Arrest against Thomas Lubanga Dyilo", ICC-OTP-20060302-126, Press Release, 14 March 2006:

Pre-Trial Chamber, Lubanga became the first person to be tried under the ICC Statute.[107] This case signals the beginning of a new phase in the development of thematic prosecutions for two reasons. On the one hand, the case inaugurates the practice of thematic prosecution at the ICC, having progressed from its use in special tribunals; and on the other hand, it is the first time an international court explicitly alludes to a thematic prioritisation strategy not centered on gender-based crimes. Instead, Lubanga's trial focuses solely on his responsibility as co-perpetrator of war crimes consisting of enlisting and conscripting children under the age of 15.[108]

The principle of selective prosecution broadly defines the practice of criminal investigations at the ICC. In order to select the crimes the court first goes through several "screening decisions".[109] First, the focus is on crimes committed by "those persons who bear the greatest responsibility".[110] Second, the investigation focuses on those crimes of the accused that "show a sample [...] reflective of the gravest incidents".[111] Third, when it comes to choosing which group of crimes will be part of the sample the court must identify and prioritise the main types of victimisa-

---

> Thomas Lubanga Dyilo founded the UPC in September 2000 and became its president. In September 2002, he set up the FPLC as the military wing of the UPC and became its commander-in-chief. During the fighting in Ituri, more than 8,000 civilians have died and in excess of 600,000 others have been displaced. In 2002, the FPLC seized control of Bunia and parts of Ituri in Orientale Province.

[107] International Justice Monitor, "Thomas Lubanga", available on the website of the International Justice Monitor.

[108] Valentina Spiga, "Indirect Victims' Participation in the *Lubanga* Trial", in *Journal of International Criminal Justice*, 2010, vol. 8, no. 1, p. 191, see *supra* note 5: "analyzing the criminal charge that results from the breach to the prohibition of using persons under the age of 15 to participate actively in hostilities."

[109] On the notion "screening decisions" as the ICC Office of the Prosecutor's prerogative of selecting which situations to investigate and deciding how to prioritise, see Allison Marston Danner, "Prosecutorial Discretion and Legitimacy", in Guest Lecture Series of the Office of the Prosecutor, The Hague, 13 June 2005.

[110] ICC, Press Release, see *supra* note 106.

[111] ICC, Office of the Prosecutor, Report on Prosecutorial Strategy, 14 September 2006 (https://www.legal-tools.org/doc/6e3bf4/pdf/). See, for example, Sienna Merope, "Recharacterizing the Lubanga Case: Regulation 55 and the Consequences for Gender Justice at the ICC", in *Criminal Law Forum*, 2011, vol. 22, no. 3, pp. 311–46, discussing the Office of the Prosecutor's screening decisions in *Lubanga*.

---

tion.[112] The ICC has deployed the notion of gravity to identify such types, when they are considered grave on the basis of their quantitative or qualitative salience. In other words, they have to be frequent, egregious or both. In *Lubanga*, the Office of the Prosecutor prioritised child enlisting on the basis that it was both quantitatively[113] and qualitatively[114] salient. In deciding to prosecute solely on the basis of child enlistment, the Office of the Prosecutor was also making a political decision to use the *Lubanga* case to send a message about the status of child enlistment as an international crime.[115]

International legal feminist advocates and scholars,[116] together with internationalist commentators and human rights organisations,[117] de-

---

[112] Merope, 2011, see *supra* note 111.

[113] International Criminal Court, *Prosecutor v. Thomas Lubanga Dyilo,* Confirmation Hearing: Introductory Comments of Senior Trial Attorney Ekkehard Withopf, 9 November 2006 (*'Lubanga* Confirmation Hearing'):

> [T]he Prosecution will show the face of a military commander who for the sake of that war, together with others, conscripted and enlisted children under the age of fifteen years into the FPLC. Thomas Lubanga Dyilo made the children get military training. Thomas Lubanga Dyilo made them train to kill. Thomas Lubanga Dyilo made the children kill. And Thomas Lubanga Dyilo let the children die. Die in hostilities. *Many, many children.* (emphasis added)

[114] ICC, Press Release, see *supra* note 106:

> Young children – boys and girls alike – were taken from their families and forced to join the FPLC. They were taken away and trained in camps set up for this purpose. As president of the UPC and commander-in-chief of the FPLC, Thomas Lubanga Dyilo exercised de facto authority. He had ultimate control over the adoption and implementation of the UPC's and FPLC's policies and practices, which consisted, amongst other things, of enlisting and conscripting children under the age of fifteen years into the FPLC and using them to participate actively in hostilities.

[115] *Lubanga* Confirmation Hearing, see *supra* note 113:

> This Confirmation Hearing will give the world a picture, an idea about the brutality of the life of child soldiers. And it will give the world a picture about people who are responsible for it. Criminally responsible. In this case: Thomas Lubanga Dyilo.

[116] See, for example, SáCouto and Cleary, 2009, p. 337–59, *supra* note 81, for a detailed recount of reactions to exclusion of charges for sexual violence in *Lubanga*; Merope, 2011, *supra* note 111, analysing the consequences for gender justice of the Trial Chamber decision not to recharacterise the facts; Suzan M. Pritchett, "Entrenched Hegemony, Efficient Procedure, or Selective Justice?: An Inquiry into Charges for Gender-Based Violence at the International

---

nounced the decision to exclude charges of sexual violence from the investigation against Lubanga and the refusal to let the victims of sexual assaults committed by child soldiers participate in the proceedings. They read this as turning the principle of gender strategising on its head. Feminists' criticisms seem legitimate, insofar as the Court's decision meant that acts of sexual violence by child soldiers against women, and against child soldiers themselves, should not be prioritised despite evidence of their high frequency and egregiousness.[118] However, in asserting this view, international legal feminists failed to appreciate that the reasoning behind this exclusion is the same type of reasoning that underpins sex-specific prosecutions: successful international prosecution of gender crimes requires isolating the investigation from other criminal acts.

As it is clear from feminist reactions to *Lubanga*, the problem is not that the Office of the Prosecutor chose to prosecute child enlistment, but that it found this strategy irreconcilable with the formulation of charges on sexual violence despite the evidence.[119] Given the long-standing history of associating women and children in both feminist and child advocacy strategies, it appears surprising that the Trial Chamber refused to include women as indirect victims.[120] One possible explanation for this phenome-

---

Criminal Court", in *Transnational Law and Contemporary Problems*, 2008, vol. 17, no. 1, pp. 265–305, case note applying "critical feminist jurisprudential analysis to the application of the Rome Statute in the ICC case of *Prosecutor v. Thomas Lubanga*"; deGuzman, 2011, p. 518, *supra* note 1, discussing feminist organisations' reaction to *Lubanga*.

[117] Women's Initiative for Gender Justice, "Letter from Women's Initiatives for Gender Justice to Mr. Luis Moreno Ocampo", 20 September 2006; see also Human Rights Watch, "Joint Letter to the Chief Prosecutor of the International Criminal Court", 31 July 2006; Avocats Sans Frontières *et al.*, "Joint Letter from Avocats Sans Frontières *et al.* to the Chief Prosecutor of the International Criminal Court, D.R. Congo: ICC Charges Raise Concern", 31 July 2006.

[118] See, for example, Avocats Sans Frontières *et al.*, 2006, *supra* note 117; SáCouto and Cleary, 2009, see *supra* note 81, discussing the existence of evidence supporting allegations that girls had been kidnapped into Lubanga's militia and were often raped and/or kept as sex slaves; Pritchett, 2008, p. 267, see *supra* note 116, noting how it is "virtually undoubted that violence against women in the DRC conflict has been systematic and widespread".

[119] Despite vocal criticisms against the omission of charges in the Lubanga case, feminists have qualified as "positive developments" for gender strategising the fact that subsequent ICC decisions have included charges for sexual violence: See SáCouto and Cleary, 2009, p. 342, *supra* note 81.

[120] The Office of the Prosecutor's draft policy on victim participation attests of the existence of a difference in views between the Trial Chamber and the Office in respect to making the victims of rape by child soldiers into indirect victims of Lubanga. Despite the Office's view, the

---

non is to read *Lubanga* as a sex-specific prosecution. To exclude women as victims of child soldiers is the only way to salvage the sexual difference that underpins the binary of victims and perpetrators. In other words, to see child soldiers as victims of Lubanga and perpetrators of sexual assaults at the same time is an impossible move under a sex-difference approach to prosecution. Children could not be considered victims and perpetrators insofar as one cannot be female and male at the same time.[121]

This statement by Catharine MacKinnon, special gender adviser to the ICC and vocal feminist advocate of thematic prosecutions, brings to the foreground how the coupling of female (victim) and the male (perpetrator) is reproduced over and over. Interestingly, MacKinnon is using it to differentiate between boy and girls within the category of child soldiers: "Lubanga made boys into rapists and girls into sex slaves in order to make them into soldiers he could command and use at will".[122]

The coupling of female/victims and male/perpetrators and the treatment of both couples as dichotomous categories, thus mutually exclusive, might help understand what prevented the ICC from including women as indirect victims, nor formulating charges against Lubanga for sexual

---

Trial Chamber concluded in favour of the exclusion of victims of child soldier rape from the category of victims. Sexual violence was left out of the charges against Lubanga. Despite its efforts, the Office of the Prosecutor failed to convince the Court of its theory of indirect victimhood:

> The Office concurs that "victims" under rule 85(a) can be persons who were not the direct targets of a crime, but who suffered indirect harm as a result of the commission of a crime. The Office supports a broad characterization of "indirect victims". In Lubanga, the Office expressed its views that those who have suffered harm as a result of crimes committed by child soldiers, *i.e.* as a consequence of the crimes charged, are also entitled to participate.

See ICC, Policy Paper on Victims' Participation, 12 April 2010 (http://www.legal-tools.org/doc/3c204f/).

[121] See, for example, Spiga, 2010, p. 184, *supra* note 5, for a meditation on the question "when the direct victims are at the same time perpetrators, as in the case of child soldiers, who may inflict harm upon others.

[122] For a note on the role of gender advisers at international courts *vis-à-vis* instance of sexual violence involving child soldiers, see Sellers, 2009, p. 301, *supra* note 2:

> The Legal Advisor should also address the sexual assaults committed upon boy soldiers and sexual assaults boy soldiers are ordered to commit as part of their training or in order to "carry out" their military missions.

---

assaults committed by children.[123] Furthermore, it could even illuminate the exclusion of sexual violence charges against Lubanga, including his responsibility for sexual assaults perpetrated against male and female child soldiers.[124]

12.4.2. Investigating Sexual Difference in a Post-Genomic Age

In March 2005, the Duke Institute for Genome Sciences and Policy ('IGSP') issued a press release announcing "the first comprehensive survey of gene activity has revealed an unexpected level of variation among individuals".[125] The results were described as potentially having major implications for "understanding the differences in traits among women and between males and females, in terms of both health, disease [...] as well as normal gender differences".[126] In essence, said Huntington

---

[123] For discussion of the tensions of showcasing the prosecution against Lubanga as a case dealing with the sexual abuse of child soldiers given the decision not to include counts of sexual violence, see Margaret M. deGuzman, "Choosing to Prosecute: Expressive Selection at the International Criminal Court", in *Michigan Journal of International Law*, forthcoming 2012, p. 26, noting how, "[w]hile the ICC prosecutor initially justified crime selection in the Lubanga case by invoking practical considerations involving timing and evidence availability", he later highlighted "the case's role in showcasing the sexual abuse of child soldiers". See also Luis Moreno-Ocampo, "Keynote Address: Interdisciplinary Colloquium on Sexual Violence as International Crime: Interdisciplinary Approaches to Evidence", in *Law and Social Inquiry*, 2010, vol. 15, no. 4, pp. 845–46.

[124] The male child (child soldier) is the victim, and the male adult (Lubanga) is the perpetrator. The male child is read as the female in the victim–perpetrator scheme. Thus, it excludes the possibility of including women as victims, much less of charging Lubanga of rapes of the child soldiers. In both hypotheses, the female/victim male-child would be considered a male/perpetrator male-child. Following binary reasoning under which male and female are mutually exclusive categories the required move would be against the goal of the court, since it would entail the impossibility of making the male/child a victim of unlawful enlistment.

[125] The NIH supported their findings as published in the March 2005 edition of the journal *Nature*. Laura Carrel and Huntington Willard, "X-Inactivation Profile Reveals Extensive Variability in X-Linked Gene Expression in Females", in *Nature*, vol. 434, no. 7031, pp. 400–04.

[126] From the outset, the authors of the investigation used the words *sex* and *gender* to suggest that their findings would have bearings for the study of sex and gender. See Duke Medicine News and Communications, "X Chromosome Variation May Explain Differences Among Women, Between Sexes", 16 March 2005:

> Such characteristic genomic differences should be recognized as a potential factor to explain sex-specific traits both in complex disease, as well as normal gender differences.

Willard, one of the authors of the report, "there is not one human genome, but two – male and female".[127]

Following the announcement, several news outlets published their takes on the report.[128] While most writers focused on the difference between men and women, others, like Maureen Dowd from the *New York Times*, chose to focus on what the findings said about difference among women: "[w]omen are not only more different from men than we knew. Women are more different from each other than we knew – creatures of 'infinite variety', as Shakespeare wrote".[129] Indeed, as Willard stated to the press:

> [t]he findings suggest a remarkable and previously unsuspected degree of expression heterogeneity among females in the population [and] further work is required to explore potential consequences of that variation.[130]

Despite divergent emphasis in reporting, the remarkable fascination these findings generated serves as a reminder of the preoccupation that scientists and popular press had with the gene.[131]

But what does it mean to say – quoting the *New York Times* – "that, women are, indeed, 'a different species'"?[132] The historian of science, Sarah Richardson, interprets the finding in the following way.[133] Based on

---

[127] *Ibid.* See also Richardson, 2010, p. 823, *supra* note 11, discussing the way the findings by Willard and Carrel were presented to the public.

[128] Fred Guterl, "The Truth About Gender", in *Newsweek*, 2005, vol. 145, no. 13, pp. 38–39:

> [A] new study has found that women and men differ genetically almost as much as humans differ from chimpanzees [...]. [The] study published last week in the journal Nature puts this difference at about 1 percent. Considering that the genetic makeup of chimpanzees and humans differs by only 1.5 percent, this is significant. "You could say that there are two human genomes, one for men and one for women", says Huntington Willard, a geneticist at Duke University and coauthor of the article.

See also Richardson, 2010, p. 823, *supra* note 11, for a detailed discussion of media reporting of the findings.

[129] Maureen Dowd, "X-Celling over Men", in *New York Times*, 20 March 2005.

[130] Duke Medicine News and Communications, 2005, see *supra* note 126.

[131] Fausto-Sterling, 1992, p. 62, see *supra* note 13: "The popular press and scientists alike have apparently fallen in love with the gene".

[132] Dowd, 2005, see *supra* note 129.

[133] Richardson, 2010, p. 823, see *supra* note 11.

differences between their DNA maps – also known as genomes – men and women ought to be considered members of different animal species.[134] Richardson points out two discursive moves that ensue from this assertion. On the one hand, arguing that males and females have different genomes entails an analogy between sex and species; and on the other hand, this formulation carries along a reversal – if not a contradiction – *vis-à-vis* the single genome paradigm dominant during the 1990s.[135] Furthermore, she observes:

> Willard's construction argues this shift is part of a broader move in human genomics – a subfield within molecular biology that studies human DNA maps – toward studies of human diversity, focusing on the differences between different populations.[136]

The findings by Willard and Carrel signal the emergence of a "genomic concept of sex"[137] and a "genomic model of biological sex differences".[138] The uncritical embrace by genetic researchers of the newly found variations between male and female genes[139] – considered nothing less than astounding[140] – set up the stage for the breadth and scope of a discursive

---

[134] *Ibid.* In comparative genomic research about sex differences males are considered different species, based on the differences between their DNA maps.

[135] "Part of what gives Willard's statement [...] its effect and significance is its startling reversal of the mantra of the 1990s Human Genome Project (HGP) – that there is a single human genome and humans are 99.9% identical". See *ibid.*, p. 827, *supra* note 11, discussing how the existence of two different human genomes can be read as a reversal – if not a contradiction – of the 1990s *single human genome* mantra widely publicised by the Human Genome Project.

[136] *Ibid.*

[137] "Recent genetic research on human sex differences evidences the emergence of a 'genomic' concept of sex, analogizing sexes to 'species' and 'genetic populations". *Ibid.*

[138] *Ibid.*

[139] *Ibid.*, pp. 827, 837–39:

> I find that there are not strong, empirical, explanatory, social, or ethical reasons for genomicizing sex differences. For these reasons, it is more advisable to refer to 'sex differences in the human genome' than to 'male genome' and 'female genome' [...]. [T]here are not strong empirical, explanatory, social, or ethical reasons for genomicizing sex differences.

[140] Lauren A. Weiss *et al.*, "The Sex-Specific Genetic Architecture of Quantitative Traits in Humans", in *Nature Genetics*, 2006, vol. 38, no. 2, pp. 218–22.

shift that has considerably transformed "in an often invisible way", think-ing about genetic differences between the sexes.[141]

Richardson poignantly illustrates this point. First, she observes how the "genomic construction of biological sex differences"[142] inaccurately implies far greater variation between males and females than understand-ings of sexual difference still dominant in the 1990s. In doing so, she ar-gues, they play "into traditional gender-ideological views of sex differ-ences".[143] Second, she points out how seeing males and females as differ-ent species is influenced by phylogenetics, a subfield of genomics that uses, and is criticised for using, population-based genetic variation (also known as profiling) to explain differences in health and disease between racial and ethnic groups.[144] Third, since this scientific model stems from the assertion that male and female genes differ systematically from each other, Richardson argues that it tends to discard altogether the idea of a single human genome – at least in the context of sex research. Thus, doing so implicitly legitimises the scientific analysis of "males and females in-dependently of the other".[145]

What Richardson describes is an extraordinary shift towards binary thinking about sex in biology that has largely gone unnoticed in other realms of knowledge, including feminist legal theory and practice.[146] Thus, the "methodological consequences [of this discursive move] for the study of the social dynamics of gender"[147] have been denounced by only a few voices in academia. Nonetheless, the fact that this is happening pre-cisely at a time when sex-specific agendas proliferate in international le-

---

[141] See Richardson, 2010, pp. 830–31, *supra* note 11.

[142] *Ibid.*, p. 828.

[143] *Ibid.*: "Thinking of males and females as having different genomes exaggerates the amount of difference between them [...] playing into traditional gender-ideological views of sex differ-ences."

[144] *Ibid.*

[145] This is the case despite the fact that sexes do not meet any of the criteria required to be cate-gorised as a species interbreeding, shared common ancestry, morphology, spatial and tem-poral boundaries. See *ibid.*, pp. 831–32.

[146] Despite its ubiquity in biological explanation, the foundations of the concept of sex (unlike that of species and population) in biology have gone largely unexamined. *Ibid.*, p. 837. See also Fehr, 2001, *supra* note 12: "Indeed, binary thinking underpins 'genomic thinking' about sex difference in biology".

[147] See Richardson, 2010, p. 837, *supra* note 11.

gal feminist projects is of particular interest; chiefly, given the well-documented tendency in biology to "expand the relevance of explanatory categories beyond their empirically warranted limits".[148] Since there is evidence of the importance of the single human genome paradigm both for late twentieth-century science, liberal social discourse, and feminist agendas,[149] the emergence of a two-human-genome paradigm merits – at least – that we raise some questions about the unintended consequence of prosecutorial practices that either assume or foster binary thinking about the sexes.

12.5. Some Questions about the Future of Thematic Prosecution

In this chapter, I have offered a reinterpretation of the emergence of international thematic prosecutions of sex crimes and the rise of sex-specific biomedical research as parallel tales of re-essentialisation. I argue it is a scenario where international legal feminists have explicitly and implicitly engaged with biologically grounded notions of essential differences between men and women. Nonetheless, this tale of re-essentialisation does not end with a lesson about how, when and why feminists should engage, reject or simply ignore biological explanations of sexual difference. Instead, it ends by raising questions about the ways in which these two feminist projects might be gesturing towards the emergence of a novel regime of ideological governance of sexual difference.

In this final section, I will step back from the parallel I have just presented in order to ask some questions that might help make sense of the ways in which two apparently very successful feminist projects have produced results that are gender essentialising. After all, is it not surprising that gender-coding disease and crime has led to gender essentialising? I invite future exploration of these questions.

Questions about binary reasoning. This chapter raises a series of questions regarding the vices and virtues of binary thinking for feminist agendas, in general, and for international legal feminism in particular.

---

[148] John Dupré, *The Disorder of Things: Metaphysical Foundations of the Disunity of Science*, Harvard University Press, Cambridge, MA, 1993, p. 79.

[149] See Richardson, 2010, p. 827, *supra* note 11:

> The power and importance of this idea of a single, shared human genome in the late twentieth century science and liberal social discourse should not be underestimated.

Why is binary thinking problematic? The problem with binary thinking derives from its potential to disguise problems of categorisation.[150] The unjustified use of sex as an organising category for analysing disease or crime, combined with the interchangeable use of sex and gender as categories of analysis and the reduction of gender to sex, are all different manifestations of binary thinking. As I discussed in sections 12.2., 12.3. and 12.4., these moves have had tangible effects for feminist advocacy projects (that is, obscuring commonalities across men and women, obscuring differences within each sex). I would add that ignoring binary thinking also dismisses feminist critiques of scientific categories of sexual difference.

Questions about categorisation. What is the relation, if any, between mutually exclusive categorisation associated with binary thinking and subordination? I maintain that the story I have told in these pages is not simply a story about re-essentialisation. It is also a story about a shift from a regime of epistemic subordination to a regime of oppression through categorisation. When asking these questions it should not be forgotten that the two feminist projects that are the subject of my argument are part of a broader governance trend that gives overriding significance to sex and gender for understanding and managing male and female behaviour.

Questions about governance. The account I gave here has an institutional focus. It derives from an interest in understanding the conflicts and compromises that shape how international thematic prosecution of sex crimes becomes policy, practice, and institutional formations. Questions about governance are thus read as ways to better understand the processes by which social and legal changes take institutionalised forms. There are questions about the institutional formations that have followed the move towards re-essentialisation in feminist advocacy agendas. What would it look like to create institutional formations that respond to sexual

---

[150] "It is not the facticity of the two biological sexes that is problematic from the perspective of critical gender theory [search Fausto and Google "the construction of sex"]; rather, it is *binary thinking* that carries the epistemic failure and leads to shaky reasoning about sex in biology [...]. As gender theorists have observed, binaries invite dualistic, dichotomous thinking, so that it becomes difficult to think of two without subsuming one in to the other, ranking them, implying polarity or complementarity, or posing them as opposites" (see books cited by Richardson, 2010, p. 838, *supra* note 11) Binaries tend to imply exhaustive categories and to drive reasoning toward the detection of difference as fixed polarity". See *ibid.*

difference as variation instead of seeing it as dichotomous? Is there a way of ensuring that institutions do not get entrapped in the practice of governance I have presented in these pages?

Questions about governance also offer the possibility to engage with the place of governance *in* feminist projects. For example, the two feminist agendas I have analysed here can be read as manifestations of governance feminism. As such, they show the "incremental but by now quite noticeable installation of feminists and feminist ideas in actual legal-institutional power".[151]

Questions about feminism. Last and surely not least, this chapter raises a series of important questions about feminist theory and practice. How does the phenomenon described here relate to the professionalisation of feminists? How does it relate to the specialisation of feminism? As Ellen Messer-Davidow has pointed out, specialisation is part of the trajectory of disciplinary growth of feminism, one that tends to intensify the production of differences within feminist discourses.[152] However, commonalities between health and international legal feminists' activist strategies during the past two decades defy the tendency of feminism to grow towards difference within its own ranks. All the more relevant is that we consider how and when these two particular spheres of feminist advocacy align. Finally, there is the issue of professionalisation, and how experts trained in gender within their own fields have become key players for the development of new prosecutorial and biomedical knowledge.[153]

---

[151] See Halley *et al.*, 2006, *supra* note 23.

[152] Messer-Davidow, 2002, p. 207, see *supra* note 26.

[153] Epstein, 2007, see *supra* note 7:

> While an insistence on equality as sameness was a typical strategy of feminist movement in past decades, in more recent years notions of essential difference appear to provide strategic wedge specially to certain sectors of the women's health movement [...] this wave [...] reflects the professionalization of the women's health movement and the concomitant rise of some women (often white and middle-class) to positions of authority and influence [...].

See also Richardson, 2013, *supra* note 7, discussing how the women's health movement is about professional women's activism, professional women advocating for women's issues). What Epstein and Richardson have identified as the professionalisation of women's health activism is illustrative of a well-documented global phenomenon since the 1980s: the professionalisation of feminism altogether. See Sabine Langa, "The NGO-Ization of Feminism: In-

---

Questions about genetics. Amid this landscape of "geneticisa-tion",[154] is it possible to ignore the impact of genetics for international legal feminist advocacy agendas? After all, there are some serious feminist critiques of this tendency.[155] It is precisely in the context of evaluating thematic prosecution as institutional design and feminist practice as it is today, where there is space for thinking how we ought to engage with the science in thematic prosecution tomorrow.

---

stitutionalization and Institution Building within the German Women's Movement", in Bonnie G. Smith (ed.), *Global Feminisms Since 1945*, Routledge, London, 2000, p. 290:

> Globalization has changed the nature of women's activism [...]. The reality of a visible women's movement is replaced by the professionalization of feminism, resting in the policy decisions of a few individuals.

[154] Antoinette Rouvroy, *Human Genes and Neoliberal Governance: A Foucauldian Critique,* Routledge-Cavendish, London, 2008, p. 124, discussing the concept as the ever growing tendency to distinguish people one from another on the basis of genetics.

[155] This question is inspired by the work of Anne K. Eckman: See Anne K. Eckman, "Beyond the Yentl Syndrome: Making Women Visible in Post 1990 Women's Health Discourse, in Paula A. Treichler, Lisa Cartwright and Constance Penley (eds.), *The Visible Woman: Imaging Technologies, Gender, and Science*, New York University Press, New York, p. 145.

13

Thematic Investigations and Prosecution of International Sex Crimes: Some Critical Comments from a Theoretical and Comparative Perspective

Kai Ambos[*]

The increasing awareness with regard to sexual violence in situations of armed conflict brings up several challenges and questions on best investigative practices. Thematic investigations may offer a suitable approach, but they have to be refined taking into account theoretical considerations and comparative experiences. With this aim in mind, the present chapter proceeds in a threefold manner. In the introduction, three points are set out regarding what we know for sure amounts to sex crimes. In the second part, the possibly still existing disproportion between the number of sex crimes and investigations is addressed and explanations attempted. In the third and last part, the concept of thematic investigations/prosecutions is defined and justifications for a so defined concept are presented.

13.1. Introduction: The Existing State of Our Knowledge of Sex Crimes and Their Prosecution (What We Know for Sure)

There is no longer an issue of definition. While at the beginning of their work the *ad hoc* tribunals were confronted with an absence of a definition of sexual violence under international law,[1] this gap was later remedied.[2]

---

[*] **Kai Ambos** is Chair of Criminal Law, Criminal Procedure, Comparative Law and International Criminal Law at the Georg-August-Universität Göttingen. He is also judge at the District Court in Göttingen. I am grateful to my doctoral student Assessorin Sabine Klein for her most valuable assistance and to Ousman Njikam, LL.M. and doctoral candidate GAU for language revision.

[1] International Criminal Tribunal for Rwanda ('ICTR'), *Prosecutor v. Jean-Paul Akayesu*, Trial Chamber, Judgment, ICTR-96-4-T, 2 September 1998, para. 686 ('*Akayesu* Trial Judgment') (http://www.legal-tools.org/doc/b8d7bd/):

> In considering the extent to which acts of sexual violence constitute crimes against humanity under Article 3(g) of its Statute, the Tribu-

---

In any case, the prosecution of sex crimes did not fail because of the absence of a legal definition but for procedural reasons. For example, it could not be proven that the crimes had happened in the first place, or that the accused was involved.[3]

Also, a second problem of a procedural nature, namely the systematic underinvestigation and underprosecution of sex crimes, although certainly a fact in the (missing) history of sex crimes prosecutions,[4] seems to disappear slowly but steadily, with the increasing awareness and media

---

nal must define rape, as there is no commonly accepted definition of the term in international law.

International Criminal Tribunal for the former Yugoslavia ('ICTY'), *Prosecutor v. Anto Furundžija,* Trial Chamber, Judgment, IT-95-17/1-T, 10 December 1998, para. 175 ('*Furundžija* Trial Judgment') (http://www.legal-tools.org/doc/e6081b/): "No definition of rape can be found in international law." See also Dianne Luping, "Investigation and Prosecution of Sexual and Gender-Based Crimes before the International Criminal Court", in *American University Journal of Gender, Social Policy & the Law,* 2009, vol. 17, no. 2, p. 448.

[2] See my chapter on the criminalisation of sex crimes, "Sexual Offences in International Criminal Law, with a Special Focus on the Rome Statute of the International Criminal Court", in Morten Bergsmo, Alf Butenschøn Skre and Elisabeth J. Wood (eds.), *Understanding and Proving International Sex Crimes,* Torkel Opsahl Academic EPublisher, Oslo, 2012, pp. 143–74.

[3] Cf. Daniel J. Franklin, "Failed Rape Prosecutions at the International Criminal Tribunal for Rwanda", in *Georgetown Journal of Gender and the Law,* 2008, vol. 9, pp. 181–208.

[4] See, for example, Tamara F. Lawson, "A Shift Towards Gender Equality in Prosecutions: Realizing Legitimate Enforcement of Crimes Committed Against Women in Municipal and International Criminal Law", in *Southern Illinois University Law Journal,* 2009, vol. 33, pp. 204 ff., arguing that sexual violence was routinely ignored as a crime; it was considered an inevitable consequence of the nature of war and the sexual urges or needs of men; its prosecution before the war crimes tribunals of Nuremberg and Tokyo was largely neglected. See also the statement of Fatou Bensouda, ICC Deputy Prosecutor, who, according to Luping, 2009, p. 433, see *supra* note 1, said: "It was high time that such crimes cease to be regarded as 'inevitable-by-products' of war and receive the serious attention that they deserve". See also Luping, *ibid.,* pp. 436, quoting, *inter alia,* Kelly D. Askin, *War Crimes against Women: Prosecution in International War Crimes Tribunals,* Kluwer Law International, The Hague 1997, p. 19:

> [s]exual assault has been increasingly outlawed through the years, but this prohibition has rarely been enforced. Consequently, rape and other forms of sexual assault have thrived in wartime, progressing from a perceived incidental act of the conqueror, to a reward of the victor, to a discernable mighty weapon of war.

---

coverage of sex crimes.[5] Today, it is widely recognised that there is an urgent need to address sexual violence in armed conflict and to combat the policy of using sexual violence as a "weapon of war". An increase in prosecutions and trials dealing with sex crimes has followed suit.[6] However, this does not mean that everything is fine. An understanding of the extent and meaning of sexual violence still needs to be further developed.[7] There may still be a disproportion between the number of prosecutions

---

[5]   See, for example, Lawson, 2009, p. 205, *supra* note 4: Modern "on-the-scene" media coverage of the Yugoslav conflict exposed the crimes as they were happening causing public outrage and changing the position towards sex crimes.

[6]   See as the first relevant judgment, *Akayesu* Trial Judgment, para. 731, *supra* note 1:

> Indeed, rape and sexual violence certainly constitute infliction of serious bodily and mental harm on the victims and are even, according to the Chamber, one of the worst ways of [inflicting] harm on the victim as he or she suffers both bodily and mental harm. [...] These rapes resulted in physical and psychological destruction of Tutsi women, their families and their communities.

See also Susana SáCouto and Katherine Cleary, "The Importance of Effective Investigation of Sexual Violence and Gender-Based Crimes at the ICC", in *American University Journal of Gender, Social Policy & the Law,* 2009, vol. 17, no. 2, pp. 348 ff., arguing that since the creation of the *ad hoc* Tribunals there have been significant improvements in the prosecution of such crimes; Lawson, 2009, pp. 208 ff., see *supra* note 4, referring to *Akayesu* as the first convicted by an international court for sexual violence in a civil war. For a summary of the development of legal sanctions, see Fionnuala Ní Aoláin, Dina Francesca Haynes and Naomi Cahn, "Criminal Justice for Gendered Violence and Beyond", in *International Criminal Law Review,* 2011, vol. 11, no. 3, pp. 432 ff. Patricia M. Wald, "Women on International Courts: Some Lessons Learned", in *International Criminal Law Review*, 2011, vol. 11, no. 3, pp. 401 ff. still complains about significant crimes against women even in peacetime:

> I continue to be perplexed by the irony that crimes against women and children committed in wartime – rape, cruel treatment, sexual slavery, and forced marriages – go unrecognised and accepted as part of normal life in peacetime in many parts of the world.

For a critique of the International Criminal Court's ('ICC') refusal to accept cumulative charges for sexual crimes in *Bemba Gombo,* see Laurie Green, "First-Class Crimes, Second-Class Justice: Cumulative Charges for Gender-Based Crimes at the International Criminal Court", in *International Criminal Law Review,* 2011, vol. 11, no. 3, pp. 529 ff., claiming sexual crimes at the ICC being "still under-investigated, under-prosecuted and remain the least condemned crime"; Solange Mouthaan, "The Prosecution of Gender-based Crimes at the ICC: Challenges and Opportunities", in *International Criminal Law Review,* 2011, vol. 11, no. 3, p. 775.

[7]   Cf. for a good critique pointing to open questions despite legal reforms and existing accountability, Ní Aoláin *et al.*, 2011, p. 428, see *supra* note 6.

---

and the actual extent, severity and number of sex crimes. We shall return to this question below.

   Criminal justice, whether international or not, is always and necessarily selective.[8] In the case of the international criminal justice system, this selectivity is intrinsic, since the jurisdiction of international criminal tribunals is always limited in various ways (*ratione materiae, ratione temporis, ratione personae*). Limitations also result from the specific goals of international criminal justice, the necessary discretion of the international prosecutors (who may formulate 'streamlined' indictments, or none at all, in a given situation), and limited personal and financial recourses.[9] All these factors make it necessary to develop rational criteria for the prioritisation and selection of cases.[10]

---

[8]   For a good definition see, for example, Kenneth Culp Davis, *Discretionary Justice: A Preliminary Inquiry*, Louisiana State University Press, Baton Rouge, 1969, p. 163:

> When an enforcement agency or officer has discretionary power to do nothing about a case in which enforcement would be clearly justified, the result is power of selective enforcement […]. Selective enforcement may also mean selection of the law that will be enforced; an officer may enforce one statute fully, never enforce another and pick and choose in enforcing a third.

On the necessary selectivity, Kai Ambos, "Comparative Summary of the National Reports", in Louise Arbour *et al.* (eds.), *The Prosecutor of a Permanent International Criminal Court*, Max-Planck Institute for Foreign and International Criminal Law, Freiburg, 2000, p. 525: "[e]ven if a strict mandatory prosecution is called for there are mechanisms of factual discretion since no criminal justice system has nowadays the capacity to prosecute all offences no matter how serious they are". On the international criminal justice see Robert Cryer, *Prosecuting International Crimes: Selectivity and the International Criminal Regime*, Cambridge University Press, Cambridge, 2005, p. 192.

[9]   See, for example, Louise Arbour, "Stefan A. Riesenfeld Award Lecture – Crimes Against Women under International Law", in *Berkeley Journal of International Law*, 2003, vol. 21, no. 2, p. 203: "The offenses in the former Yugoslavia and Rwanda that fell within our jurisdiction were so numerous and deserving of prosecution that we had to be very strict about how we prioritised cases. In general terms, we determined that we had to concentrate on the most serious offenses that could bring us to the highest possible echelons of command".

[10]   See Morten Bergsmo (ed.), *Criteria for Prioritizing and Selecting Core International Crimes Cases*, Torkel Opsahl Academic EPublisher, Oslo, 2009 (http://www.fichl.org/fileadmin/fichl/documents/FICHL_4_Second_Edition_web.pdf); see also Kai Ambos (ed.), *Selección y priorización como estrategia de persecución en los casos de crímenes internacionales*, Deutsche Gesellschaft für Internationale Zusammenarbeit ('GIZ') proyecto ProFis, Bogotá, 2011.

13.2. Uncharted Territory: Too Little or Disproportionate Investigation/Prosecution? Possible Explanations

13.2.1. Is There Still a Disproportion between the Number of Sex Crimes and the Number of Investigations/Prosecutions?

The disproportionately low level of international prosecutions of sex crimes has been bewailed.[11] Empirical assessments of this issue are not known and, to be sure, would come along with obvious methodological problems. As for the national level, an examination of crime statistics as well as studies on the estimated numbers of unrecorded cases and their relation to prosecutorial statistics may be a helpful approach, although the outcome will not be certain and will probably differ significantly depending on the country, the particular circumstances of each country (for example, its ability to record prosecutorial statistics), and the respective data assessment practices. As for the international level, an analysis of crimes prosecuted by international tribunals appears possible,[12] but the gathering and assessment of data regarding (gender) crimes in the respective conflict situations proves to be difficult[13] and differs from situation to situation.[14] Moreover, it should be noted that the recognition of large-scale sexual crimes in conflict situations is of recent date,[15] and we are only beginning to understand the impact of such crimes on the conflicts and the persons affected. This entails an uncertainty, which may also influence empirical assessment.

---

[11]   Ní Aoláin et al., 2011, pp. 439–40, see *supra* note 6, with further references.

[12]   For example, at the ICTY, as of mid-2011, 78 of the 161 accused (48.4 per cent) had been charged with acts of sexual violence. Twenty-eight of them have been convicted, 13 indictments were withdrawn or the accused deceased before the trial, 11 accused were acquitted of the sexual violence charges. Nineteen of the proceedings are still ongoing, six cases have been referred to a national jurisdiction, and one accused is still a fugitive.

[13]   Circumstances in conflict situations often entail that atrocities remain unrecorded – given the general reluctance to report widespread crimes to the authorities and the death of possible witnesses.

[14]   The problems of date on sexual violence became apparent in different studies on sexual violence in the Democratic Republic of Congo ('DRC'): whereas an UN report estimated the number of rapes as about 16.000 in one year, another study subsequently concluded that the number was about 25 times higher (400,000). Cf. BBC News Africa, "DR Congo: 48 Rapes Every Hour, US Study Finds", 12 May 2011.

[15]   Ambos, 2011, p. 145, fn. 6 and 7 (with text), see *supra* note 2.

Apart from the question of proportionality between the number of crimes and the number of prosecutions, one may need to further explore whether the existing prosecutions properly reflect the harm caused in the respective situations of violence. Thus, it has been claimed that violence against women is accompanied by other significant harms not captured by sex crimes prosecutions.[16] Another explanation of disproportion could be the fact that the prosecution of sexual violence is not part and parcel of the ordinary investigatory activities of the international tribunals, but presupposes significant external lobbying and advocacy.[17]

13.2.2. Factors Explaining Investigative Disproportions

If, *arguendo*, we assume that the discussed disproportion exists, the question arises as to how it can be explained. One explanation refers to the above-mentioned selectivity of international criminal justice. Does it not affect the investigation of sex crimes too? Indeed, streamlined indictments necessarily entail the leaving out of potential charges for which enough evidence may exist to satisfy the means of proof, albeit not as much as for other potential charges that become part of the indictment.[18] Yet, more importantly, the disproportion can be explained by factors that are peculiar to sex crimes.

13.2.2.1. Sex Crimes: Difficulties of Proof

First, there is the problem that sex crimes are particularly difficult to prove. As forensic evidence will rarely be available, the prosecution's case depends heavily on witness testimony.[19] Although the international

---

[16] Ní Aoláin *et al.*, 2011, pp. 426, 428 ff., 439–40, see *supra* note 6, mentioning "emotional harms, harms to the home, harms to children and to those with whom women are intimately connected" (p. 426); see also Jaya Ramji-Nogales, "Questioning Hierarchies of Harm: Women, Forced Migration, and International Criminal Law", in *International Criminal Law Review*, 2011, vol. 11, no. 3, pp. 463 ff., pointing to "private and opportunistic harms" (p. 463) and to a lack of accountability in connection with forced migrations.

[17] Ní Aoláin *et al.*, 2011, pp. 437 ff., see *supra* note 6, referring to the ICTR *Akayesu* case and the ICC *Lubanga* proceedings.

[18] Critique with regard to sex crimes, see Suzan M. Pritchett, "Entrenched Hegemony, Efficient Procedure, or Selective Justice?: An Enquiry into Charges for Gender-based Violence at the International Criminal Court", in *Transnational Law & Contemporary Problems,* 2008, vol. 17, no. 1, pp. 292–93.

[19] Cf. ICTY, Office of the Prosecutor, "Reliving the Past: The Challenges of Testifying".

---

tribunals' procedural rules provide for some flexibility as to the burden of evidence,[20] it remains highly difficult to obtain reliable witness testimony. There are either no direct eyewitnesses because victims are killed after the act, or potential witnesses are killed before or after the act.[21] It is also possible that the sexual violence occurs in private places and is informed by discriminatory gender relations.[22] Existing witnesses are reluctant to testify for reasons of traumatisation, fear and/or mistrust.[23] A related problem is that sex crimes are not easily identifiable since "these crimes inflict physical and psychological wounds, which women can conceal to avoid further emotional anguish, ostracism, and retaliation from perpetrators who may live nearby".[24] As a result, investigation and prosecution depends on the reliance on hearsay and circumstantial evidence.

Apart from these issues relating to the means of proof, it has also been criticised that the 'standard of proof' required in cases of sexual violence is higher than in other cases.[25] While in ordinary cases, so it is ar-

---

[20] ICC, Rules of Procedure and Evidence ('RPE'), adopted 9 September 2002, ICC-ASP/1/3 (http://www.legal-tools.org/doc/8bcf6f/), provides that "a Chamber shall not impose a legal requirement that corroboration is required in order to prove any crime within the jurisdiction of the Court, in particular, crimes of sexual violence". See also ICTY, Rules of Procedure and Evidence, adopted 11 February 1994, as amended 8 December 2010, IT/32/Rev. 45, Rule 96 (http://www.legal-tools.org/doc/950cb6/), and ICTR, Rules of Procedure and Evidence, adopted 29 June 1995, as amended 1 October 2009, Rule 96 (http://www.legal-tools.org/doc/c6a7c6/). Both provisions contain evidential eases (for example, a corroboration of the victim's testimony is not required). ICTY Rule 96 was the first rule of this kind at an international tribunal. Therefore, Patricia V. Sellers, "The 'Appeal' of Sexual Violence: The *Akayesu/Gacumbitsi* Cases", in Elize Delport (ed.), *Gender-based Violence in Africa: Perspectives from the Continent*, Centre for Human Rights, University of Pretoria, 2009, p. 306, describes it as "groundbreaking". On evidentiary rules, see also Luping, 2009, pp. 482–83, *supra* note 1.

[21] Franklin, 2008, pp. 209 ff., see *supra* note 3.

[22] Pritchett, 2008, p. 293, see *supra* note 18.

[23] As described by the ICTY, Office of the Prosecutor, see *supra* note 19:

> Victims of sexual violence face various social, psychological and sometimes even physical impediments to coming forward and testifying. Some of the potential witnesses feel that their security may be jeopardised should they come to testify. In addition, identifying oneself as a victim of sexual violence may lead to stigmatisation within one's society, making return to normal life even more difficult.

[24] Beth van Schaack, "Obstacles on the Road to Gender Justice", in *American University Journal of Gender, Social Policy & the Law*, 2009, vol. 17, no. 2, p. 369.

[25] SáCouto and Cleary, 2009, pp. 353 ff., see *supra* note 6, with further references.

---

gued, circumstantial evidence to prove a certain mode of liability is, as a rule, considered to be sufficient, the case law dealing with sexual violence is more reluctant as regards a specific connection between an accused's conduct and acts of sexual violence.[26]

13.2.2.2. Technical Pitfalls

Even if sex crimes cases are investigated and prosecuted, this may, given the complexity of the surrounding factual, cultural and other circumstances, not be done properly. A particularly challenging problem is the treatment of victim witnesses, that is, witnesses who, at the same time, have been the victims of sexual violence. These often-traumatised victims may find some relief after participating in the trial proceedings through testify-

---

[26] *Ibid.*, who point to several decisions where more evidence has been required to proof sex crimes as for other crimes committed by the same perpetrator in the same context. Distinguishing between different modes of liability, SáCouto and Cleary are referring to ICTY *Prosecutor v. Stanislav Galić*, Trial Chamber, Judgment, IT-98-29-T, 5 December 2003, paras. 729–40 (http://www.legal-tools.org/doc/eb6006/); ICTY, *Prosecutor v. Stanislav Galić*, Appeals Chamber, Judgment, IT-98-29-A, 30 November 2006, paras. 177, 178, 389 (http://www.legal-tools.org/doc/c81a32/); ICTR, *Prosecutor v. Juvénal Kajelijeli*, Trial Chamber, Judgment and Sentence, ICTR-98-44A-T, 1 December 2003, para. 681, 683, 780, 923 ('Kajelijeli Trial Judgment') (http://www.legal-tools.org/doc/afa827/), where an order to commit rapes has not been found; while it was proven that the accused knew of and authorised sexual assaults in general, evidence for a specific order was missing; ICTY, *Prosecutor v. Dario Kordić and Mario Čerkez*, Appeals Chamber, Judgment, IT-95-14/2-A, 17 December 2004, para. 27 (on instigation) (http://www.legal-tools.org/doc/738211/); ICTY, *Prosecutor v. Radoslav Brđanin*, Trial Chamber, Judgment, IT-99-36-T, 1 September 2004, paras. 577, 1054 (http://www.legal-tools.org/doc/4c3228/); ICTR, *Prosecutor v. Sylvestre Gacumbitsi*, Appeals Chamber, Judgment, ICTR-2001-64-A, 7 July 2006, paras. 133, 135, 137, 138 (http://www.legal-tools.org/doc/aa51a3/), dismissing instigation due to a lack of evidence that the accused's activities [instigation to rape via megaphone] substantially contributed to the commission of rapes. SáCouto and Cleary, 2009, pp. 358 ff., see *supra* note 6, are concluding on the basis of this case law:

> In sum, the jurisprudence of the *ad hoc* tribunals suggests that, in cases of sexual violence and gender-based crimes, international tribunals may be reluctant to draw meaningful inferences from circumstantial evidence and appear to prefer direct or more specific evidence as to knowledge or causality, even when such evidence is not required as a matter of law. Thus, without a thorough investigation, significant expertise, and intensive analysis of evidence relating to these crimes-including the broader context which makes clear that the sexual violence is an integral part of the organized war effort rather than mere 'incidental' or 'opportunistic' incidents – these cases are unlikely to be pursued or successfully prosecuted.

ing.[27] Yet, they normally find the act of giving testimony particularly challenging, given their personal situation as a victim witness and the general sensitivity surrounding issues of sexual violence, for example, cultural taboos with regard to the precise description of the sexual acts. In addition, cross-examination may, for these witnesses, be particularly stressful.[28] Thus, the whole exercise of testifying may lead to a secondary victimisation (re-victimisation) of the primary victims, it may reinforce "the invisibility of the crimes and the invisibility of the mainly female victims or survivors of the sexual violence".[29] The latter has also been recognised by the Trial Chamber of the International Criminal Tribunal for the former Yugoslavia ('ICTY') in the *Tadić* case:

> [T]raditional court practice and procedure has been known to exacerbate the victim's ordeal during trial. Women who have been raped and have sought justice in the legal system commonly compare the experience to being raped a second time.[30]

From the prosecution's perspective, the inappropriate handling of sexual violence cases may deter potential witnesses from testifying[31] or may have unpredictable implications on the behaviour of a witness in

---

[27]   Hereto Wendy Lobwein, former witness support officer at the ICTY: "For some [victims of sexual violence who testified at the ICTY], I've letters, even from their medical practitioners saying it was a 'groundbreaking moment in their life' and that their psychological and physical health has improved with their testimony"; cited according to ICTY, Office of the Prosecutor, see *supra* note 19.

[28]   On encumbrances and risks of victim witnesses of sexual violence (danger of life, distressful memories, lacking information and contact, gaps in terms of time, humiliations while testifying – especially in cross-examination, lacking feedback after trial and so on.) see Karin Griese, *Folgen sexueller Kriegsgewalt*, 2nd ed., Mabuse-Verlag, Frankfurt, 2006, pp. 417 ff.

[29]   Sellers, 2009, see *supra* note 20. Similar also Karen Engle and Annelies Lottmann, "The Force of Shame", in Clare McGlynn and Vanessa E. Munro (eds.), *Rethinking Rape Law: International and Comparative Perspectives*, Routledge, London, 2010, pp. 81–82 with further references. For a thorough assessment of secondary victimisation, see Stefanie Bock, *Das Opfer vor dem Internationalen Strafgerichtshof*, Duncker and Humblot, Berlin, 2010, pp. 70 ff. (general), 403 ff. (on protection against secondary victimisation), and pp. 422 ff. (on sexual crimes).

[30]   ICTY, *Prosecutor v. Duško Tadić*, Trial Chamber, Decision on the Prosecutor's Motion Requesting Protective Measures for Victims and Witnesses, IT-94-1-T, 10 August 1995, para. 46 (http://www.legal-tools.org/doc/ff53bf/).

[31]   Similarly linking 'procedural safeguards' for victims and witnesses to their likeliness to report or testify about a crime, Mouthaan, 2011, pp. 788–98, see *supra* note 6.

court. On a more general level, it has been argued that, without a specific unit or body handling gender issues within the Office of the Prosecutor, gender related issues may not be represented properly during the trial and appeals proceedings.[32]

13.2.2.3. The 'Strong Case Problem'

This all leads, in turn, to something that we could call the 'satisfactory evidence' or 'strong case problem'. The argumentative syllogism goes as follows:

1. The provability of charges is the decisive factor for a prosecutor in favour or against prosecution.[33]

2. Sex crimes are generally considered more difficult to prove.

3. Thus, they tend to be avoided and other charges relating to concurrent cases, which are easier to prove, are selected.[34]

---

[32] Sellers, 2009, pp. 14 ff., see *supra* note 20, speaks of "gender injustice" in relation to a "mishandling of sexual assaults" at the ICTR in times where no legal adviser on gender within the Office of the Prosecutor has been appointed. As an example, she refers to Kajelijeli Trial Judgment, see *supra* note 26. Cf. Doris Buss, "Learning our Lessons? The Rwanda Tribunal Record on Prosecuting Rape", in Clare McGlynn and Vanessa E. Munro (eds.), *Rethinking Rape Law: International and Comparative Perspectives*, Routledge, London, 2010, pp. 61 ff., especially p. 64, arguing that the ICTR failed to hold promises made with the Akayesu Judgment and linking this, partly, to the decision to discharge gender advisers. Buss, *ibid.*, p. 64, furthermore draws attention to the case of ICTR, *Prosecutor v. Emmanuel Bagambiki et al.*, Trial Chamber, Judgment, ICTR-99-46-T, 25 February 2004 (http://www.legal-tools.org/doc/60036f/), where the Office of the Prosecutor did not pursue charges of sexual violence although evidence on such crimes was available, due to "personnel problems".

[33] Lawson, 2009, p. 187, see *supra* note 4: "Prosecutors are typically motivated only to pursue cases they can win, and arguably those are the cases which contain the most legitimate evidence of guilt. Additionally, prosecutors are ethically bound to only file a case when there is sufficient admissible evidence to support the charge". Against this tendency the American Bar Association's Standards for Criminal Justice: The Prosecution Function 3–3.9(e), 3rd ed., 1993, cited in Lawson, *ibid.*:

> In cases which involve a serious threat to the community, the prosecutor should not be deterred from prosecution by the fact that in the jurisdiction juries have tended to acquit persons accused of the particular kind of criminal act in question.

[34] See also ICC, Office of the Prosecutor, Paper on Some Policy Issues before the Office of the Prosecutor: Annex: Referrals and Communications, 5 September 2003, p. 3 (http://www.legal-tools.org/doc/f53870/): "the Prosecutor has to take into account [...] the likelihood of any effective investigation being possible". With regard to sex crimes, Lawson,

---

As Binaifer Nowrojee puts it: "[i]n a bid to comply with pressure to speed up the trials, prosecuting teams were encouraged to cut unnecessary charges. Sexual violence charges were seen to be in that category".[35]

13.3. Thematic Investigations and Prosecution

The question remains as to whether (and if so, to what extent) the issues presented above can be addressed by 'thematic' investigations and prosecutions. First, thematic prosecution must be defined and examples given, before the possible justifications are discussed.

13.3.1. Definition and Examples

According to the convenors of our seminar, thematic prosecutions are to be understood as:

> [P]rosecutorial prioritization [...] of [...] sex crimes over other crimes [...] sometimes [...] necessary in order to focus adequate resources to build complex and time-consuming cases when there is a large backlog of cases.[36]

This is in contrast to the standard approach, according to which the totality of crimes – including possible sex crimes – is to be considered first. Only after that has been done, can or should one proceed to prioritise those crimes that are most serious overall. On the other hand, so the seminar convenors continue, thematic prosecution:

> [...] entails that these crimes are singled out and prioritized for investigation and prosecution, even if that means that there may not be enough resources to investigate murders or other serious crimes that do not involve sexual violence.[37]

It is my understanding that thematic investigations and prosecutions cannot operate at the expense of other important investigations. The con-

---

2009, p. 193, see *supra* note 4, on the difficulty in the setting up 'the strong case' and resulting in urge to avoid pursuing less 'winnable' sexual violence cases.

[35] Binaifer Nowrojee, *'Your Justice Is Too Slow'*: Will the ICTR Fail Rwanda's Rape Victims?, United Nations Research Institute for Social Development, Occasional Paper 10, November 2005, p. 10.

[36] Forum for International and Humanitarian Law, Seminar on "Thematic Investigation and Prosecution of International Sex Crimes", Concept and Programme, Cape Town, 7–8 March 2011.

[37] *Ibid.*

---

cept can only mean that a given criminal justice system, international or national, puts a special emphasis on certain areas of criminality to increase the efficiency of investigations and prosecutions in these areas. Understood in this way, thematic prosecutions are nothing unique or new to national criminal justice systems. In fact, they are quite common in established special fields of criminal law and criminality, for example, in economic criminal law (including fraud offences), corruption, drugs law and tax law. Many national jurisdictions also consider the prosecution of international crimes on the basis of international criminal law as a special field of criminal law. Thus, national systems set up specialised units or branches of their national prosecution authorities to deal with these offences.[38] On a supranational level, European Union law provides for such units.[39]

Following this practice, it seems perfectly possible to also set up special units for the prosecution of sexual violence. Such units already exist in some jurisdictions or sub-jurisdictions, where sexual violence is recognised as a major social problem and the political will and resources to set up a specialised infrastructure exists.[40] In fact, such a unit exists on the international level within the ICC Office of the Prosecutor (the Gender

---

[38] For example, European countries like Belgium, Denmark, Germany, Sweden, the Netherlands, Norway and the United Kingdom; moreover, Canada and the United States. See the overview in Jürgen Schurr, "Strategies for the Effective Investigation and Prosecution of Serious International Crimes: The Practice of Specialised War Crimes Units", in Redress and International Federation for Human Rights, December 2010 (overview list on p. 31). As an example of one of the ICC situation countries, Uganda is currently establishing an International Crimes Division at its High Court with corresponding units within the prosecution and police authorities; see the Ugandan Judiciary's website. Schurr, *ibid.*, p. 18, even doubts whether national jurisdictional bodies could, at all, be efficiently able to prosecute international crimes if they are not equipped with special arrangements; see also Olympia Bekou's chapter on specialised units in this volume, Chapter 11.

[39] Thus, the Council of the European Union, with Decision 2002/494/JHA, 13 June 2002, set up a European network of contact points in respect of international crimes to facilitate cooperation between the competent international authorities (Article 1). Then, with Decision 2003/335/JHA, 8 May 2003, it called its members to "consider the need to set up or designate specialist units within the competent law enforcement authorities with particular responsibility for investigating and, as appropriate, prosecuting the crimes in question". See Article 4 (2003) of the Council Decision.

[40] This is, for example, the case in Germany. On special police and judicial divisions to deal with sexual and gender-based violence cases in Liberia, see Laura Golakeh, "Liberia Becoming Leader in Eradicating Sexual and Gender-Based Violence", in *Global Press Institute*, 14 June 2011.

---

and Children's Unit, 'GCU')[41] and within other international/mixed tribunals as well.[42] Such specialised units within the Office of the Prosecutor are to be distinguished from specialised victims support units, which belong, in organisational terms, to the registries of the international tribunals.[43] These units have, rather, a supporting function and are in charge of

---

[41] Cf. Luping, 2009, pp. 434, 489, see *supra* note 1. Moreover, Luis Moreno-Ocampo appointed in November 2008, to counter mounting criticism; Sellers, 2009, p. 330, fn. 81, see *supra* note 20; Catharine MacKinnon as special gender adviser, see ICC "ICC Prosecutor Appoints Prof. Catharine A. MacKinnon as Special Adviser on Gender Crimes", Press Release, 26 November 2008 (http://www.legal-tools.org/doc/866eda/). Rome Statute of the International Criminal Court, 17 July 1998, in force 1 July 2002, Article 42(9) ('ICC Statute') (http://www.legal-tools.org/doc/7b9af9/) provides that the prosecutor "shall appoint advisers with legal expertise on specific issues, including, but not limited to, sexual and gender violence and violence against children".

[42] At the ICTY, already as early as October 1994, Patricia Viseur Sellers had been appointed as a legal adviser for gender at the Office of the Prosecutor; cf. Sellers, 2009, p. 307, see *supra* note 20. According to Michelle Jarvis, senior legal adviser to the prosecutor, e-mail of 13 September 2011 to the author, a "sexual assault and rape investigation team" has been created in the Office of the Prosecutor in 1995, and in the subsequent years, specific female investigators were hired. Currently, a Prosecuting Sexual Violence Working Group within the Office of the Prosecutor has the mandate to strengthen the Office's work on gender issues, and a senior legal adviser with special knowledge on gender issues has been appointed. Sellers has subsequently (1995–1999) also been appointed as a legal adviser for gender at the ICTR's Office of the Prosecutor where, after her departure, there were two gender advisers (Sellers, *ibid.*, p. 307). Nevertheless, since the millennium's turn the ICTR Office of the Prosecutor was no longer equipped with such an adviser (Sellers, *ibid.*, pp. 314–15, criticising prosecution's mishandling of sexual violence case but also seeing improvement in the recent jurisprudence). At the Special Court for Sierra Leone ('SCSL'), the chief prosecutor, David Crane, "incorporated policies and modalities to investigations of crimes committed against women", but did not appoint an adviser for gender; see Sellers, *ibid*, p. 316. At the Extraordinary Chambers in the Courts of Cambodia ('ECCC'), no special units for gender crimes are in place (Sellers, *ibid.*, p. 316), but when in 2009 a request for the investigation of gender related crimes were brought before the ECCC, those granted these applications stating:

> With respect to the request that gender trained female investigators and interpreters be assigned to conduct interviews relating to forced marriage allegations, the Co-Investigating Judges affirm the need for gender sensitive techniques in cases concerning sexual and gender-based violence testimony. Although the current staffing of OCIJ does not include female investigators, all efforts are being made to ensure best practices are fully implemented.

See ECCC, Office of the Co-Investigating Judges, Order on Request for Investigative Action Concerning Forced Marriages and Forced Sexual Relations, 002/19-09-2007-ECC-OCIJ, D268/2, 18 December 2009, para. 15.

[43] For example, at the ICC, a Victims and Witnesses Unit has been established pursuant to ICC Statute, Article 43(6), see *supra* note 41. According to this Article, measures of the Victims

---

measures of witness/victims protection. In contrast, specialised units within the Office of the Prosecutor such as the GCU are part of the investigation and prosecution machinery and thus see victims as potential witnesses for the prosecution's case. Yet, given the ICC prosecutor's obligation to protect victims and witnesses during the investigative stage (pursuant to Article 68(1) of the ICC Statute),[44] specialised units within the Office of the Prosecutor and gender advisers may also help to comply with this obligation and react to the specific circumstances linked to cases of sexual violence. The specialised units assigned to the Registry can assist the prosecutor in this task.[45]

Still, this does not deny the fact that sex crimes are normally not committed in isolation but together with ordinary offences (for example, unlawful deprivation of liberty, bodily injury, manslaughter) or even, at the level of international criminal law, as part of a broader campaign against the civilian population. Then the question arises as to whether the sexual offences can be properly isolated or taken out from the broader criminal conduct. Even if this were possible, it may not always be reasonable to do so, for example, in a case where the sex crimes are intimately

---

and Witnesses Unit are to be provided "in consultation with the Office of the Prosecutor". Here, "[p]articular attention is given to vulnerable groups, such as victims of sexual or gender violence, children, the elderly and persons with disabilities. The VWU [Victims and Witnesses Unit] support services promote gender-sensitive measures to facilitate the testimony of victims of sexual violence". At the ICTR, pursuant to ICTR, Rules of Procedure and Evidence, Rule 34, see *supra* note 20, a Witness and Victims Support Section exists under the authority of the Registrar. The ICTY has a similar unit. Warning of dangerous overlaps between units located at the Registry and the Office of the Prosecutor, see Mouthaan, 2011, p. 788, *supra* note 6.

[44] ICC Statute, Article 68(1), see *supra* note 41 reads:

> The Court shall take appropriate measures to protect the safety, physical and psychological well-being, dignity and privacy of victims and witnesses. In so doing, the Court shall have regard to all relevant factors, including age, gender as defined in article 7, paragraph 3, and health, and the nature of the crime, in particular, but not limited to, where the crime involves sexual or gender violence or violence against children. The Prosecutor shall take such measures particularly during the investigation and prosecution of such crimes.

See also Luping, 2009, pp. 479 ff., *supra* note 1.

[45] Seeing "specialized support services [...] [as] vital to the successful prosecution of gendered violence"; Ní Aoláin *et al.*, 2011, p. 436, see *supra* note 6.

---

linked or overlapping with the other crimes; otherwise one would lose sight of the broader context.[46]

From a practical prosecutorial perspective, the question arises at what point thematic prosecutions are possible at all. An investigator or a prosecutor normally does not dissect the criminal events to be investigated and prosecuted in fine pieces. They take a look at the crime scene and the criminal results as a whole, at least at the beginning of the investigation, and this very practical approach is difficult to reconcile with a thematic one.[47] In the words of an experienced international prosecutor: "The prosecution works with big lamps, not magnifying glasses".[48] Consequently, sexual violence will always be investigated and prosecuted together with other crimes, while special attention may be paid to acts of sexual violence. As stated by the ICC Office of the Prosecutor, the Office is committed "to do a selection of cases that represent the entire criminality and modes of victimisation. The Office will pay particular attention to methods of investigations of crimes committed against children, sexual and gender-based crimes".[49] In fact, the Office of the Prosecutor has already set up special mechanisms and organisational approaches to better assess sexual crimes that may have occurred in a situation under investigation. Thus, for example, in Uganda, the Office's investigators working on the ground were all trained in the handling of sexual and gender-based crimes.[50] In any case, this is still a work in progress and constant improvement is necessary: "The Office will work with external actors, *inter alia*, with regard to sexual and gender crimes to constantly update prosecutorial techniques".[51]

Up to now, the only exclusive or focused sex investigation – regarding a situation of sexual slavery and forced prostitution – was carried out

---

[46] As argued by Valerie Oosterveld in Chapter 9 of this volume.

[47] The point was convincingly made by prosecutor Herminia T. Angeles from the Philippine Ministry of Justice, who participated most actively in the seminar.

[48] Fabricio Guariglia, a senior appeals counsel at the ICC Office of the Prosecutor, statement at the seminar on "Thematic Investigation and Prosecution of International Sex Crimes", Cape Town, 7–8 March 2011.

[49] ICC, Office of the Prosecutor, Report on Prosecutorial Strategy, 14 September 2006 (https://www.legal-tools.org/doc/6e3bf4/pdf/).

[50] Luping, 2009, p. 48, see *supra* note 1.

[51] ICC, Office of the Prosecutor, ICC Prosecutorial Strategy 2009–2012, 1 February 2010, para. 29 (http://www.legal-tools.org/doc/6ed914/).

in the ICTY's *Foča* case.[52] This is the exception that confirms the rule, since, in this case, the sex crimes offered such a pattern of widespread and systematic crimes that it was worthwhile to be investigated and prosecuted for its own sake. In any case, the ICC, despite having a special gender adviser since November 2008[53] focusing specifically on sex crimes,[54] has so far not grounded a prosecution exclusively on international sex offences. In *Lubanga*, the prosecution abstained from charging sex crimes[55] and this decision was not remedied until the trial judgment of 14 March 2012.[56] In *Katanga*, four out of 10 charges (three of crimes against hu-

---

[52] ICTY, *Prosecutor v. Dragoljub Kunarać, Zoran Vuković and Radomir Kovać*, Trial Chamber, Judgment, IT-96-23-T and IT-96-23/1-T, 22 February 2001, especially pp. 217 ff. (http://www.legal-tools.org/doc/fd881d/); and ICTY, *Prosecutor v. Dragoljub Kunarać, Zoran Vuković and Radomir Kovać*, Appeals Chamber, Judgment, IT-96-23 and IT-23/1-A, 12 June 2002 (http://www.legal-tools.org/doc/029a09/). The three defendants were convicted for rape, torture and enslavement as crimes against humanity. For a critical analysis see James McHenry, "Justice for FOCA: The International Criminal Tribunal for Yugoslavia's Prosecution of Rape and Enslavement as Crimes Against Humanity", in *Tulsa Journal of Comparative and International Law*, 2002, vol. 10, no. 1, pp. 183 ff., especially pp. 218 ff. on the judgment's significance; Doris Buss, "Prosecuting Mass Rape: *Prosecutor v. Dragoljub Kunarać, Radomir Kovać and Zoran Vuković*", in *Feminist Legal Studies*, 2002, vol. 10, no. 1, pp. 91 ff. For statistics concerning the coverage of sexual crimes at the ICTY, see *supra* note 12. On policy considerations how to better emphasise sexual crimes in international proceedings, see Nowrojee, 2005, p. 3, fn. 4, *supra* note 35; and Arbour, 2003, p. 203, *supra* note 9, saying on the issue of thematic investigations and prosecutions the following: "One of the debates that we had constantly in the office of the prosecutor was: should we "normalise" the prosecution of sexual violence, or should we keep nurturing it as separate issue? The debate was whether we should just announce that a sexual offence was like any other offence that all investigators must be attentive to and must prosecute as part of any investigation".

[53] See *supra* note 42.

[54] See ICC, Office of the Prosecutor, Fatou Bensouda, "Update on Judicial Proceedings: A Focus on Charging and Prosecuting Sexual and Gender Crimes", Speech, 30 September 2008.

[55] For a critical analysis see SáCouto and Clearly, 2009, p. 341, *supra* note 6, arguing that Lubanga was charged only with recruiting and using child soldiers, although the evidence of sexual violence was present. See also Pritchett, 2008, p. 293, *supra* note 18, according to which the prosecution could not establish a link between individual rapists and Lubanga himself.

[56] ICC, *Prosecutor v. Thomas Lubanga Dyilo*, Trial Chamber I, Judgment pursuant to Article 74 of the Statute, ICC-01/04-01/06, 14 March 2012, paras. 16, 630 (http://www.legal-tools.org/doc/677866/). This procedural decision cannot be remedied by reading 'sexual violence' into the conduct of the war crime of recruiting children pursuant to Article 8(2)(e)(vii) of the ICC Statute (but see Judge Odio Benito's Dissent, paras. 15–21) since this violates the strict construction requirement and amounts to a prohibited analogy (Article 22(2) of the ICC

---

manity and seven of war crimes) referred to sexual violence (sexual slavery under Articles 7(1)(g), 8(2)(b)(xxii)) and rape under Articles 7(1)(g), 8(2)(b)(xxii)).[57] Even in the *Bemba* case, which is generally considered as a case about rape as a weapon of war,[58] rape was only one, albeit highly significant,[59] count among three, namely, in addition to rape, murder as a crimes against humanity (Article 7(1)(a)) and a war crime (Article 8(2)(c)(i)) and pillaging as a war crime (Article 8(2)(e)(v)). Finally, the Forces démocratiques de libération du Rwanda leader, Callixte Mbarushimana, has been charged, *inter alia*, with rape as crime against humanity and war crime.[60] Also, other IC investigations in Uganda,[61] Su-

---

Statute). Regrettably, the prosecutor and his deputy (Fatou Bensouda) omitted to mention the procedural side of this issue in their press conference the day after the judgment where they criticised the majority decision. See for a comprehensive analysis of the judgment and this issue, Kai Ambos, "The First Judgment of the International Criminal Court (Prosecutor v. Lubanga): A Comprehensive Analysis of the Legal Issues", in *International Criminal Law Review*, 2012, vol. 12, no. 2, pp. 137–38, fn. 156.

[57] ICC *Prosecutor v. Germain Katanga and Mathieu Ngudjolo Chui*, Pre-Trial Chamber, Warrant of Arrest for Germain Katanga, ICC-01/04-01/07, 3 July 2007, pp. 4–5 (http://www.legal-tools.org/doc/4a8301/); ICC, *Prosecutor v. Germain Katanga and Mathieu Ngudjolo Chui*, Pre-Trial Chamber, Decision on the Confirmation of the Charges, ICC-01/04-01/07, 30 September 2008, paras. 354, 436, 444 ('*Katanga* Confirmation of Charges') (http://www.legal-tools.org/doc/67a9ec/) .

[58] According to Sudan Vision, "Africa in Focus: Prosecutor: Ex-Congo VP Used Rape as Weapon", 13 January 2011, Fatou Bensouda has said that "rape outnumbered killings, and the prosecution intended to focus its case on sexual violence as a weapon of war". See also Maggie Fick, "Bemba at The Hague: A Focus on Sexual Violence", in *Enough*, 15 January 2009.

[59] See ICC, *Prosecutor v. Jean-Pierre Bemba Gombo*, Pre-Trial Chamber, Decision Pursuant to Article 61(7)(a) and (b) on the Charges against Jean-Pierre Bemba Gombo, 01/05–01/08, 15 June 2009, paras. 171–85 ('*Bemba* Confirmation Decision') (http://www.legal-tools.org/doc/07965c/) enumerating various acts of rape and witnesses; also in para. 186 referring to "indirect evidence, such as hearsay evidence and several NGO and UN reports, is of a corroborating nature and reflects the large number of acts of rape which occurred in the same locations referred to by direct witnesses during the same period, namely from on or about 26 October 2002 to 15 March 2003" (fn. omitted).

[60] ICC, *Prosecutor v. Callixte Mbarushimana*, Pre-Trial Chamber, Warrant of Arrest for Callixte Mbarushimana, ICC-01/04-01/10, 9 April 2012, para. 10 (vii) and (viii) (http://www.legal-tools.org/doc/27b448/).

[61] Charges of *rape and sexual slavery* are part of warrants of arrests in the Ugandan situation; see ICC, *Prosecutor v. Joseph Kony, Vincent Otti and Okot Odhiambo*, Pre-Trial Chamber, Warrant of Arrest for Joseph Kony issued on 8 July 2005 as amended on 27 September 2005, Public redacted version, ICC-02/04-01/05-53 (http://www.legal-tools.org/doc/db11ef/): sexual slavery: count 1 (p. 12), rape: counts 2, 3 (pp. 12–13); ICC, *Prosecutor v. Joseph Kony,*

---

dan,[62] Kenya[63] and Libya[64] are targeting, but never exclusively, alleged acts of sexual violence.

13.3.2. Justifications

There are essentially four justifications for thematic prosecutions in the sense explained above.

13.3.2.1. The Sensitivity and Complexity of International Sex Crimes

As already mentioned above, international sex crimes are of an extraordinarily sensitive nature. The prosecution will often have to deal with traumatised witnesses/victims to obtain the necessary evidence. Depending on the cultural context, it may be taboo to speak of any sexual behaviour at

---

Vincent Otti and Okot Odhiambo, Pre-Trial Chamber, Warrant of Arrest for Vincent Otti, Public redacted version, ICC-02/04-01/05-54, 8 July 2005, (http://www.legal-tools.org/doc/f7c78c/): sexual slavery: count 1 (p. 12), rape: count 3 (p. 13). See also Luping, 2009, pp. 493, 495, *supra* note 1, on the gendered nature of crimes occurred in Uganda, and pp. 493–94, on the investigative approach and challenges.

[62] Charges of rape and of persecution as crime against humanity through sexual violence are part of warrants of arrests, see ICC, *Prosecutor v. Ahmad Muhammad Harun ("Ahmad Harun") and Ali Muhammad Ali Abd-Al-Rahman ("Ali Kushayb")*, Pre-Trial Chamber, Warrant of Arrest for Ali Kushayb, ICC-02/05-01/07-3, 27 April 2007 (http://www.legal-tools.org/doc/cfa830/): rape: counts 13, 14, 42, 43 (pp. 8–9, 14–15), persecution: count 10 (p. 8), count 39 (p. 14); ICC, *Prosecutor v. Ahmad Muhammad Harun ("Ahmad Harun") and Ali Muhammad Ali Abd-Al-Rahman ("Ali Kushayb")*, Pre-Trial Chamber, Warrant of Arrest for Ahmad Harun, ICC-02/05-01/07-2, 27 April 2007 (http://www.legal-tools.org/doc/7276ad/): rape: count 13, 14, 42, 43 (pp. 8–9, 13–14), persecution: count 10 (p. 8), count 39 (p. 13); ICC, *Prosecutor v. Omar Hassan Ahmad Al Bashir*, Pre-Trial Chamber, Warrant of Arrest for Omar Hassan Ahmad Al Bashir, ICC-02/05-01/09-1, 4 March 2009, p. 6 ("thousands of rapes") and p. 8, para. vii (http://www.legal-tools.org/doc/e26cf4/).

[63] The ICC's summons to appear against Muthaura, Kenyatta und Ali include rape allegations: "Muthaura and Kenyatta are criminally responsible as indirect co-perpetrators in accordance with article 25(3)(a) of the Rome Statute for the crimes against humanity of murder, forcible transfer, rape, persecution and other inhumane acts". Cf. ICC, "Pre-Trial Chamber II Delivers Six Summonses to Appear in the Situation in the Republic of Kenya", Press Release, 9 March 2011, ICC-CPI-20110309-PR637.

[64] As one point among several activities, the ICC prosecutor reported to the UN Security Council to investigate rape allegations: ICC, Statement to the United Nations Security Council on the Situation in the Libyan Arab Jamahiriya, pursuant to UNSCR 1970 (2011), 4 May 2011, para. 12.

---

all, least of all acts of sexual violence.[65] In such a context, a full-fledged investigation of alleged acts of sexual violence is hampered. Moreover, sexual violence, its consequences and the specific harms caused,[66] call for further exploration and more profound understanding.[67] In other words, the actual meaning of sexual violence for the victims and their relatives and friends may not yet be fully revealed at the moment of a criminal investigation or trial – it may need more time to find out the complete truth with all its consequences.

If one adds to this the fact, already mentioned above, that sex crimes are (more) difficult to prove, it is clear that their investigation is of a complexity that makes specialisation indispensable. Various authors complain that rape prosecutions have failed because of insufficiently skilled and trained investigators and inappropriate interview techniques.[68]

---

[65] For example, in some societies any conversation about sexual behaviour is considered completely taboo. In other societies, to speak about rape may be taboo given the violation of the dignity and honour of the people involved (of either the victim, his or her marriage partner, family, clan and/or tribe); see *infra* note 68 and "Crimes of Sexual Violence: Overcoming Taboos, Ending Stigmatization, Fighting Impunity", International Federation for Human Rights, The Hague, 29 October 2007.

[66] Critically as to whether international criminal accountability duly reflects women's subjective experiences and harms, see Ní Aoláin *et al.*, 2011, pp. 428 ff., *supra* note 6.

[67] See *supra* note 7 and text; *ibid.*, p. 428.

[68] Franklin, 2008, pp. 210, see *supra* note 3, arguing that the effective realisation of interviews with the witness and victims requires that they feel safe and comfortable to share their experience. There is need of highly skilled expert interviewers otherwise the sexual violence might be ignored as it was in the past, when some investigators ignored rape entirely because of an assumption that "African women don't want to talk about rape"; Nowrojee, 2005, p. 9, see *supra* note 35: "A shortage in investigators, budget difficulties and the lack of training for investigators all contributed to spotty investigations. Additionally, inappropriate interviewing methodology and the absence of an organized effort precluded the office from effectively obtaining many rape testimonies"; and p. 12: "Often investigators come from backgrounds where they have not had any experience with this issue, or they believe this is not a crime that deserves serious attention. Many investigators, though fully equipped with the necessary skills to investigate cases, lack training and direction on how to elicit information about sexual violence from witnesses". van Schaack, 2009, p. 369, see *supra* note 24: investigators need to be specifically trained to elicit sensitive information; SáCouto and Clearly, 2009, pp. 353 ff., see *supra* note 6, p. 358: "Thus, without a thorough investigation, significant expertise, and intensive analysis of evidence relating to these crimes-including the broader context which makes clear that the sexual violence is an integral part of the organized war effort rather than mere 'incidental' or 'opportunistic' incidents-these cases are unlikely to be pursued or successfully prosecuted". See also Stephanie K. Wood, "A Woman Scorned for the Least Condemned War Crime", in *Columbia Journal of Gender and Law*, 2004, vol. 13, no. 2, pp.

The former ICTY/ICTR chief prosecutor, Louise Arbour, recalls that because of the difficulty of investigating sex crimes, it was debated whether her Office should "continue to use a team that is particularly trained and sensitive to the special need of this kind of an investigation, one that will ensure that these investigations are not neglected?"[69]

Thus, clearly, specialised (especially psychological) skills for investigation, in particular for properly interviewing rape victims and witnesses are required.[70] Also, specialised experience in prosecution and litigation is necessary, especially with regard to the presentation of hearsay and circumstantial evidence.

13.3.2.2. Great Interest and Concern of the International Community

A series of UN Security Council resolutions has been issued in recent years, which shows the awareness of the international community as to the use of sexual violence as a 'tactic of war' and the risks that this implies for national and regional peace and security.[71] At the same time,

---

304–05: "Some prosecutors come to the Tribunal with domestic experience in investigating and prosecuting local murders and homicides. When these individuals investigate in the field, they may ask leading questions that do not allow survivors to paint a full picture of the suffering they endured" (fn. omitted).

[69] Arbour, 2003, p. 203, see *supra* note 9.

[70] The highly required expertise in sexual violence investigations has been convincingly demonstrated by Xabier Agirre Aranburu, "Sexual Violence beyond Reasonable Doubt: Using Pattern Evidence and Analysis for International Cases", in *Leiden Journal of International Law*, 2010, vol. 23, no. 4, pp. 609 ff.

[71] UN Security Council, Resolution 1820, UN Doc. S/RES/1820 (2008), 19 June 2008, para. 1 (http://www.legal-tools.org/doc/298f16/):

> [...] that sexual violence, when used or commissioned as a tactic of war in order to deliberately target civilians or as a part of a widespread or systematic attack against civilian populations, can significantly exacerbate situations of armed conflict and may impede the restoration of international peace and security, affirms in this regard that effective steps to prevent and respond to such acts of sexual violence can significantly contribute to the maintenance of international peace and security.

See also UN Security Council, Resolution 1960, UN Doc. S/RES/1960 (2010), 16 December 2010, Preamble, para. 11 (http://www.legal-tools.org/doc/e1de8f/): "[...] noting that such mechanisms can promote not only individual responsibility for serious crimes, but also peace, truth, reconciliation and the rights of the victims".

---

these resolutions show a considerable trust in criminal justice as a means of not only to end impunity but also to achieve "sustainable peace, justice, truth, and national reconciliation".[72] The ICC Statute does not only criminalise certain sexual acts as crimes against humanity (Article 7(1)(g)) and war crimes (Article 8(2)(b)(xxii) and (e)(vi)) but also draws particular attention to sexual violence in other provisions, for example in Article 54(1)(b).[73] In the same vein, Regulation 34(2) of the Office of the Prosecutor Regulations explicitly refers to sexual violence,[74] and the ICC's Rules of Procedure and Evidence include a special provision on the Principles of Evidence in cases of sexual violence.[75]

Thus, thematic investigations may also be demanded by the emerging international law on the matter and in light of the increasing concern of international policymakers. Such investigations may further reinforce the international commitment to fight sexual violence as a means of war, and may help to refute still existing perceptions, which continue to underestimate the destructive potential of sexual violence in armed conflicts.[76]

---

[72] *Ibid.*, para. 4: "[...] the importance of ending impunity for such acts as part of a comprehensive approach to seeking sustainable peace, justice, truth, and national reconciliation." Similarly, UN Security Council, Resolution 1888, UN Doc. S/RES/1888 (2009), 30 September 2009, Preamble, para. 8 (http://www.legal-tools.org/doc/874a1a/).

[73] ICC Statute, Article 54(1)(b), see *supra* note 41, provides that the prosecutor shall "take appropriate measures to ensure the effective investigation and prosecution of crimes within the jurisdiction of the Court, and in doing so, [...] take into account the nature of the crime, in particular where it involves sexual violence, gender violence or violence against children".

[74] ICC, Regulations of the Office of the Prosecutor, ICC-BD/05-01-09, entry into force 23 April 2009, Regulation 34(2) (http://www.legal-tools.org/doc/a97226/) reads:

> In each provisional case hypothesis, the joint team shall aim to select incidents reflective of the most serious crimes and the main types of victimisation – including sexual and gender violence and violence against children – and which are the most representative of the scale and impact of the crimes.

[75] ICC, Rules of Procedure and Evidence, *supra* note 20. Cf. also ICTY, Rules of Procedure and Evidence, Rule 96, see *supra* note 20.

[76] For example, Ní Aoláin *et al.*, 2011, p. 428, see *supra* note 6, identifies an "ongoing intellectual and legal resistance to accepting the extensive empirical evidence that women's bodies have been specifically targeted to further military-political objectives".

13.3.2.3. Specialised Prosecution Better Reinforces the Validity of the Norm

Recourse to the purposes of punishment is always of doubtful argumentative force in criminal law theory for the simple fact that available theories are of a normative, value-based nature and, as such, fraught with ambiguities. This has been demonstrated in our Cape Town seminar by the emphasis laid on purposes by some,[77] and the relativisation of these theories by others.[78] To name but a few arguments: such prosecutions may restore the dignity and integrity of the victim[79] or even the (international) order;[80] the establishment of international standards against sexual violence may possibly have a 'knock-on effect' on domestic criminal proceedings.[81] Reviewing all these approaches, in my view, it is most convincing, in line with the theory of positive general prevention or – how it is now labelled – 'expressivism',[82] to argue that thematic prosecutions compellingly reinforce and confirm the norms prohibiting sexual violence, actually breached by the commission of these crimes. Clearly the existence of thematic prosecutions carried out by specialised prosecution authorities or

---

[77] See, for a feminist's approach, Margaret M. deGuzman's chapter in this volume (Chapter 2); see also Margaret M. deGuzman, "Giving Priority to Sex Crime Prosecutions at International Courts: The Philosophical Foundations of a Feminist Agenda", in *International Criminal Law Review*, 2011, vol. 11, pp. 515 ff., arguing that priority to sex crimes in favour of killing crimes may better advance the goals of international justice. On the other hand, calling for limitations and warning of potential costs of international criminal prosecution of sexual violence as an feminist goal: Doris Buss, "Performing Legal Order: Some Feminist Thoughts on International Criminal Law", in *International Criminal Law Review*, 2011, vol. 11, no. 3, p. 423.

[78] Hence Neha Jain's caveat with regard to retribution, during her seminar presentation; cf. summary in Morten Bergsmo, "International Sex Crimes as a Criminal Justice Theme", FICHL Policy Brief Series No. 4, 2011, p. 3 (http://www.toaep.org/pbs-pdf/4-bergsmo) and her chapter in this volume, Chapter 10.

[79] Ní Aoláin *et al.*, 2011, p. 440, see *supra* note 6.

[80] Buss, 2011, p. 422, see *supra* note 77.

[81] Ní Aoláin *et al.*, 2011, p. 443, see *supra* note 6. Ramji-Nogales, 2011, p. 475, see *supra* note 16, connects this possible effect with the concept of "positive complementarity".

[82] For Mark A. Drumbl, *Atrocity, Punishment, and International Law*, Cambridge University Press, Cambridge, 2007, pp. 173 ff. expressivism means that the purpose of punishment is to strengthen faith in rule of law among the general public and the pedagogical dissemination to the public of historical narratives is viewed as a central goal. Comparing expressivism and the much older theory of positive general prevention it becomes clear that both theories are based on the same concept: strengthening confidence in the rule of law by punishing.

---

units gives this kind of crime a much higher visibility in the public domain and thus better reinforces the perception that these crimes are especially serious and the respective prohibitions will be strictly enforced.

13.3.2.4. Specialised Prosecutions are More Efficient

The setting up of highly specialised teams within a prosecutorial authority may enhance the efficiency of the entire institution. It may entail a concentration of resources, and this may also increase the efficiency of the institution as a whole. As to sexual violence, a thematic and focused approach may improve the quality of the charges brought forward, and thus increase the chances for convictions.[83] The ICC Office of the Prosecutor's approach of providing specialised assistance and advice through the GCU, ensuring that the members of investigation teams have the necessary specialised knowledge and that witness interviews are conducted accordingly,[84] is certainly to be welcomed in this regard.

Obviously, there is a flip side to this. Given the limited resources of international criminal justice, a concentration of resources in one area would only be possible at the expense of investigation and prosecution in other areas.[85]

13.4. Conclusion

Thematic investigations and prosecutions in the sense of focused, but not exclusive, prosecutions of sex crimes are a useful tool to increase awareness of and reinforce the norms prohibiting and criminalising acts of sexual violence. They may help not only to draw attention to the sexual violence, but also to clarify the broader context in which such sexual vio-

---

[83] See, for example, Luping, 2009, p. 434, *supra* note 1:

> In this context, it is crucial that investigations and prosecutions are focused to be effective. Careful selections need to be made regarding the scope and focus of any investigation or prosecution in a case. A focused approach to sexual and gender-based violent crimes must be taken from the outset, during the pre-analysis phase and before any decision is made to initiate an investigation in any country.

[84] *Ibid.*, pp. 489 ff.

[85] Given the limited resources, Mouthaan, 2011, p. 802, see *supra* note 6, calls for a "good dialogue between the ICC and the expanding community of victims about what is achievable within the constraints of its limited resources".

lence takes place. They may enable prosecutions in an area where the otherwise high degree of traumatisation of the surviving victims often hampers serious investigations in the first place. Clearly, such focused investigations and prosecutions require specialised knowledge, which is not always easy to get hold of and may involve additional costs. As recent experience shows, however, such knowledge can be made available by specialised units or especially skilled advisers without negatively affecting investigative or prosecutorial capacities regarding other crimes. As this experience also shows, albeit complex, "if done properly, investigating crimes of sexual violence need not be overly burdensome or difficult".[86]

---

[86] Linda Bianchi, "The Investigation and Presentation of Evidence Relating to Sexual Violence", Paper presented at a Roundtable on Cooperation between the International Criminal Tribunals and National Prosecuting Authorities, Arusha, 26–28 November 2008.

14

United Nations Military Peacekeeper Complicity in Sexual Abuse: The International Criminal Court or a Tri-hybrid Court

Róisín Burke[*]

> We condemn publicly the abuses committed by international peacekeeping personnel, abuses that include the crimes of rape, the trafficking of human beings and illicit narcotics, but we remain tight-lipped when it is our own peacekeepers who commit them.[1]

Rape, prostitution and other forms of sexual abuse and exploitation have featured in military environments throughout the ages. The quintessential example of this was the abuse of 'comfort women' by the Japanese military or the German brothels during the Second World War.[2] As has been revealed in numerous reports by prominent non-governmental organisations ('NGOs') and the United Nations ('UN') itself since the 1990s, such activity is present even in the context of UN peacekeeping operations, with incidents of rape, forced prostitution and even more significantly sexual abuse of children, child pornography, trafficking and other forms of sexual violence, abuse and exploitation being perpetrated by a minority of UN peacekeepers.[3] This activity not only undermines the credibility of

---

[*] **Róisín Burke** is a Senior Lecturer at the College of Business and Law, University of Canterbury, New Zealand. At the time of writing, she was a Teaching Fellow and Ph.D. candidate at the Asia Pacific Centre for Military Law, University of Melbourne Law School, Australia. She has since obtained her Ph.D.

[1] Prince Zeid Ra'ad al-Hussein, "For Love of Country and International Criminal Law", in *American University International Law Review*, 2009, vol. 24, no. 4, pp. 647–50.

[2] H. Patricia Hynes, "On the Battlefield of Women's Bodies: An Overview of the Harm of War to Women", in *Women's Studies International Forum*, 2004, vol. 27, nos. 5/6, pp. 431–45.

[3] Francis Elliott and Ruth Elkins, "UN Shame Over Sex Scandal", in *The Independent* (UK), 20 January 2007. Between 6,000 to 10,000 women and girls were trafficked into Bosnia, and kept captive at brothels patronised by the International Police Task Force ('IPTF'), the UN civilian police. Olivera Simic, "Accountability of UN Civilian Police Involved in Trafficking of Women in Bosnia and Herzegovina", in *University for Peace and Conflict Monitor*, 16 November 2004; US House of Representatives Subcommittee on International

---

the UN missions, but it can also have a seriously detrimental effect on local populations and on the promotion of the rule of law. It is therefore pertinent that this behaviour is not tolerated and that justice be assured to victims.

In the late 1990s, NBC's Dateline investigated UN peacekeeper complicity in acts of violence, including rape and torture. NBC's reporter Lea Thompson recounted that Canadian peacekeepers beat a Somali child to death after first raping him with a baton, and burning his feet and genitals with cigarettes'.[4] Allegations of sexual abuse and exploitation have been made against peacekeepers on UN operations in Bosnia and Herzegovina, Sudan, Liberia,[5] Sierra Leone,[6] Cambodia,[7] Kosovo, the Democratic Republic of Congo ('DRC'), Somalia,[8] Côte d'Ivoire, Burundi,[9] Guinea[10] and Haiti.[11] A report issued in May 2008 by Save the Children in the United Kingdom, examining sexual abuse perpetrated by UN peacekeepers in Côte d'Ivoire, southern Sudan and Haiti, highlighted the fact

---

Operations and Human Rights, "The U.N. and the Sex Slave Trade in Bosnia: Isolated Case or Larger Problem in the U.N. System?", Testimony of Ambassador Nancy Ely-Raphael, 24 April 2002, Serial No. 107-85. See also "Hopes Betrayed: Trafficking of Women and Girls to Post-Conflict Bosnia and Herzegovina", in *Human Rights Watch Report*, vol. 14, no. 9(D), 26 November 2002, p. 14; Isabelle Talleyrand, "Military Prosecution: How the Authorities Worldwide Aid and Abet International Trafficking in Women", in *Syracuse Journal of International Law and Commerce*, 2000, vol. 27, no. 1, p. 166.

4   UNWIRE, "TV Show Investigates Alleged Acts of Violence", United Nations Foundation, 1999.

5   IRIN News, "UNIMIL Investigating Alleged Sexual Misconduct by Peacekeepers in Four Incidents", 3 May 2005.

6   Bojana Stoparic, "Report Says Abuse by U.N.'s Blue Helmets Persists", in *We News*, 18 October 2005.

7   During the UN mission in Cambodia, prostitution rose from 6,000 to 25,000. See Angela Mackay, "Sex and the Peacekeeping Soldier: The New UN Resolution", in *Peace News*, no. 2443, June–August 2001.

8   In the1990s, photographs were released of Italian soldiers raping a Somali girl. Elliott and Elkins, 2007, see *supra* note 3.

9   BBC News, "UN Sex Abuse Sackings in Burundi", 19 July 2005.

10   Tanonoka Joseph Whande, "Peacekeepers as Predators: UN Sex Crimes", in *Sunday Standard* (Gaborone), 29 January 2007.

11   Kate Holt and Sarah Hughes, "UN Staff Accused of Raping Children in Sudan", in *Daily Telegraph*, 4 January 2007; Kate Holt and Sarah Hughes, "Sex and the UN: When Peacemakers Become Predators", in *The Independent* (UK), 11 January 2005; Colum Lynch, "UN Faces More Accusations of Sexual Misconduct", in *Washington Post*, 13 March 2005, A22.

---

that sexual abuse and exploitation is disproportionately perpetrated against children and young girls.[12]

UN Standards of Conduct do explicitly prohibit sexual abuse and exploitation, in particular of children, as set out in "The Ten Rules: Code of Personal Conduct for Blue Helmets, We Are United Nations Peacekeepers", [13] and the secretary-general's 2003 bulletin on "Special measures for protection from sexual exploitation and sexual abuse".[14] However, until recently these rules were only termed 'guidelines'[15] and their implementation varies across missions. Furthermore, the 2003 bulletin does not directly apply to military contingents, although as of 2007 its content for the most part was incorporated into the revised Model Agreement between the United Nations and the Member States Contributing Personnel and Equipment to the United Nations Peacekeeping Operations ('Memorandum of Understanding'),[16] which is binding on states, but it is

---

[12] Corinna Csáky, "No One to Turn To: The Under-Reporting of Child Sexual Exploitation and Abuse by Aid Workers and Peacekeepers", Save the Children, 2008, p. 5. In 2003, Italian, Danish and Slovak peacekeepers were repatriated for having sex with minors. See Elise Barth, "The United Nations Mission in Eritrea/Ethiopia: Gender(ed) Effects", in L. Olsson *et al.* (eds.), *Gender Aspects of Conflict Interventions: Intended and Unintended Consequences*, International Peace Research Institute, Oslo, 2004, p. 9. In January 2007, it was reported that in a town in Sudan, a 12-year-old girl were systematically forced to have sex with at least four Bangladeshi peacekeepers for an 18-month period; see Elliot and Elkins, 2007, *supra* note 3. For the most recent statistics complied by the United Nations Conduct and Discipline Unit ('UNCDU') on incidents of sexual exploitation and abuse, their type and form, and the status of allegations, see https://conduct.unmissions.org/sea-data-introduction.

[13] United Nations ('UN'), "The Ten Rules: Code of Personal Conduct for Blue Helmets, We Are United Nations Peacekeepers", United Nations, New York, 1998.

[14] UN Secretariat, Secretary-General's Bulletin: Special Measures for the Protection from sexual exploitation and sexual abuse, UN Doc. ST/SGB/2003/13, 9 October 2003 ('Secretary-General's Bulletin').

[15] Elizabeth Defeis, "UN Peacekeepers and Sexual Abuse and Exploitation: An End to Impunity", in *Washington University Global Studies Law Review*, 2008, vol. 7, no. 2, pp. 185, 196.

[16] United Nations General Assembly, Model Agreement between the United Nations and the Member States Contributing Personnel and Equipment to the United Nations Peace-keeping Operations: Report of the Secretary-General, UN Doc. A/46/185 (1991), 23 May 1991 ('Model Agreement'). For the text of the revised Memorandum of Understanding, see United Nations General Assembly, Manual on Policies and Procedures Concerning the Reimbursement and Control of Contingent-Owned Equipment of Troop/Police Contributors Participating in Peacekeeping Missions (COE Manual), UN Doc. A/C.5/63/18, 29 January 2009, ch. 9, pp. 161–224 ('Manual on Policies and Procedures').

---

difficult to see how it can be enforced. Criminal prosecution for sexual abuse and exploitation perpetrated by UN peacekeepers is rare, given immunities granted by a plethora of legal instruments.[17] In general, they are at most subject to disciplinary measures such as repatriation or summary dismissal.

Recently the question of whether or not UN peacekeepers, civilian or military, could be subject to the jurisdiction of the International Criminal Court ('ICC') has been the subject of debate.[18] This chapter criticises some of the arguments put forward with respect to UN military personnel. It addresses, in brief, whether the prosecution of such personnel by the ICC, where troop-contributing countries prove unwilling or unable to do so, is plausible or justifiable. Given that the rules and immunities applicable to various categories of UN personnel differ substantially, the focus is limited to incidents of sexual abuse and exploitation by UN military personnel, as distinct from UN officials and experts on mission.[19]

The chapter proceeds in two parts. Part one focuses on the potentialities and limitations of the ICC as an avenue for holding UN military peacekeepers complicit in sexual abuse and exploitation to account. Part two examines, as an alternative, the possible establishment of a hybrid/tri-hybrid justice mechanism.

Arguably serious incidents of sexual abuse and exploitation could fall within the *actus reus* not only of specific gender-based crimes enumerated in the ICC Statute, but also other acts constituting war crimes and crimes against humanity.

---

[17] See generally, Róisín Burke, "Status of Forces Deployed on UN Peacekeeping Operations: Jurisdictional Immunity", in *Journal of Conflict and Security Law*, 2011, vol. 16, no. 1, pp. 63–104.

[18] Noëlle Quénivet, "The Role of the International Criminal Court in the Prosecution of Peacekeepers for Sexual Offenses", in Roberta Arnold (ed.), *Law Enforcement within the Framework of Peace Support Operations*, Martinus Nijhoff Publishers, Leiden, 2008, p. 414; Roy S. K. Lee, "An Assessment of the ICC Statute", in *Fordham International Law Journal*, 2002, vol. 25, no. 1, pp. 760–61. Melanie O'Brien suggests that Article 28 of the ICC Statute could be used as a basis for the prosecution of commanders and superiors on UN operations: Melanie O'Brien, "The Ascension of Blue Beret Accountability: International Criminal Court Command and Superior Responsibility", in *Journal of Conflict and Security Law*, 2010, vol. 15, no. 3, pp. 533–55; Max du Plessis and Stephen Pete, "Who Guards the Guards", in *African Security Review*, 2004, vol. 13, no. 4, p. 5.

[19] See further Burke, 2011, pp. 63–104, *supra* note 17.

That stated, in sections 14.1.1. and 14.1.2., it is argued that the high thresholds set by the *chapeau* elements of war crimes and crimes against humanity would be difficult to overcome and serve as barriers to prosecuting UN military personnel before the ICC for sexual offences. When serious sexual violence or abuse occurs as part of an overall 'systematic' plan or policy to destroy the overall fabric of a societal group, it may amount to genocide under the ICC Statute.[20] A *dolus specialis* requirement is embedded within Article 6, namely the intent to destroy a national, ethnic, racial or religious group in whole or in part.[21] It seems implausible that sexual abuse and exploitation by UN peacekeepers are ever likely to be committed with genocidal intent or pursuant to any policy or plan. Therefore genocide will not be considered.

Section 14.1.3. examines in brief the possible difficulties posed by other provisions of the ICC Statute for any possible prosecution of UN military personnel by the ICC, including the mechanisms for triggering the ICC's jurisdiction, and Articles 16 and 98. Article 16 of the ICC Statute enables the Security Council to request a deferral of prosecution by the ICC for a perpetually renewable period of 12 months in the interests of maintaining international peace and security.[22] Article 98 provides that the ICC cannot request the surrender of those suspected of egregious crimes under the Statute, where a bilateral agreement exists that would be violated on surrender. The nature of crimes dealt with by the ICC is limited to the "most serious crimes of concern to the international community".[23] It is unlikely, save in the gravest cases, that crimes of sexual abuse

---

[20] According to the International Criminal Tribunal for Rwanda ('ICTR') Trial Chamber in *Akayesu*, "sexual violence was a step in the process of destruction of the Tutsi group – destruction of the spirit, of the will to live, and of life itself"; ICTR, *Prosecutor v. Jean-Paul Akayesu*, Trial Chamber, Judgment, ICTR-96-4-T, 2 September 1998, para. 732 ('*Akayesu* Trial Judgment') (http://www.legal-tools.org/doc/b8d7bd/); Kelly D. Askin, "Prosecuting Wartime Rape and Other Gender Related Crimes under International Law; Extraordinary Advances, Enduring Obstacles", in *Berkeley Journal of International Law*, 2003, vol. 21, no. 2, p. 316.

[21] UN General Assembly, Convention on the Prevention and Punishment of the Crime of Genocide, 9 December 1948, entered into force 12 January 1951, Article 2 (http://www.legal-tools.org/doc/498c38/).

[22] Geert-Jan G.J. Knoops, *The Prosecution and Defense of Peacekeepers Under International Criminal Law*, Martinus Nijhoff Publishers, Leiden, 2004, p. 299.

[23] Rome Statute of the International Criminal Court, 17 July 1998, in force 1 July 2002, Article 5 ('ICC Statute') (http://www.legal-tools.org/doc/7b9af9/).

---

and exploitation by UN peacekeepers would attract the attention of the court.

Sections 14.1.4. and 14.1.5. address gravity and prosecutorial discretion and the possible implications these factors may have on the ICC exercising jurisdiction over UN military personnel. The principle of complementarity, the foundational principle of the ICC Statute, provides that national courts have primary jurisdiction, even if an act constitutes a crime under the ICC Statute, and that the ICC may only assume jurisdiction when states are unwilling or unable to prosecute.

Section 14.1.6. examines complementarity in light of any potential prosecution of peacekeepers by the Court. Complementarity is returned to in Section 14.1.7., albeit from a slightly different perspective, through the lens of positive complementarity, namely the ability of the ICC to assist and encourage national prosecution of core crimes.

Section 14.2. examines the promise of hybrid courts as an alternative avenue for prosecution of UN military peacekeepers, where the troop-contributing country proves unwilling or unable to exercise jurisdiction over their soldiers. This examination is made in light of a suggestion by a UN group of legal experts for the establishment of a hybrid justice mechanism to hold UN officials and experts on mission to account for serious sexual abuse and exploitation. I consider the advantages and disadvantages of such a mechanism, in light of its potential application to serious misconduct by UN military peacekeepers. While the group of legal experts favoured host state primary jurisdiction, with the UN exercising partial or shared jurisdiction where the host state's justice system proves inadequate, I argue that primary jurisdiction should rather rest with the troop-contributing country. I propose alternatively the possible establishment of a tri-hybrid court, which requires input from troop-contributing countries, host states and international personnel. In doing so, I suggest that the ICC could possibly play a supportive role through positive complementarity, should the crimes committed also amount to crimes under the ICC Statute. Finally, I consider the possible value of punishment of UN military peacekeepers who are complicit in sexual abuse and exploitation at an international or hybrid level.

14.1. Prosecution of UN Military Peacekeepers for Sexual Abuse and Exploitation before the ICC

International law in recent years has seen massive developments in the recognition of gender crimes, sexual violence and rape as prosecutable offences.[24] The *ad hoc* tribunals have prosecuted sexual violence as forms of genocide, crimes against humanity, war crimes, torture, persecution and enslavement.[25] It is increasingly recognised that sexual violence in armed conflict is a violation of customary international law.[26] The ICC Statute now codifies many of the advancements made, through the specific codification of gender-based crimes.

Sexual abuse under the secretary-general's 2003 bulletin is defined as "actual or threatened physical intrusion of a sexual nature, whether by force or under unequal or coercive conditions". Sexual exploitation is defined as "any actual or attempted abuse of a position of vulnerability, differential power, or trust, for sexual purposes, including, but not limited to, profiting monetarily".[27] Sexual abuse and exploitation as defined by the bulletin is nowhere defined in international law, yet certain acts fitting

---

[24] On the historical development of international law as it relates to gender crimes, see further Askin, 2003, p. 288, *supra* note 20. See for example, ICTY, *Prosecutor v. Duško Tadić et al.*, Trial Chamber, Sentencing Judgment, IT-94-1-T, 14 July 1997 ('*Tadić* Trial Judgment') (http://www.legal-tools.org/doc/af6f8c/); ICTY, *Prosecutor v. Zdravko Mucić, Hazim Delić, Esad Landžo and Zejnil Delalić*, Trial Chamber, Judgment, IT-96-21, 16 November 1998 (http://www.legal-tools.org/doc/6b4a33/); ICTY, *Prosecutor v. Anto Furundžija*, Trial Chamber, Judgment, IT-95-17/1, 10 December 1998 (http://www.legal-tools.org/doc/e6081b/); ICTY, *Prosecutor v. Dragoljub Kunarać, Radomir Kovač, Zoran Vuković*, Trial Chamber, Judgment, IT-96-23-T and 96-23/I, 22 February 2001 ('*Kunarać* Trial Judgment') (http://www.legal-tools.org/doc/fd881d/); *Akayesu* Trial Judgment, see *supra* note 20.

[25] United Nations, Statute of the International Criminal Tribunal for the former Yugoslavia, adopted 25 May 1993 by resolution 827, amended 7 July 2009, Article 7(1) ('ICTY Statute') (http://www.legal-tools.org/doc/b4f63b/); United Nations, Statute of the International Criminal Tribunal for Rwanda, adopted 8 November 1994 by resolution 955, Article 6(1) ('ICTR Statute') (http://www.legal-tools.org/doc/8732d6/). See, generally, Askin, 2003, *supra* note 20.

[26] Theodor Meron, "Rape as a Crime under International Humanitarian Law", in *American Journal of International Law*, 1993, vol. 87, no. 3, pp. 424, 427.

[27] Secretary-General's Bulletin, see *supra* note 14.

---

within this definition may nevertheless violate international criminal law.[28]

The ICC Statute contains the most extensive list of sexual offences to date in an international criminal law statute.[29] Acts such as rape, sexual slavery, enforced prostitution,[30] forced pregnancy, enforced sterilisation and "sexual violence of comparable gravity" are enumerated as prosecutable offences under both Articles 7 and 8 of the Statute.[31] Sexual offences, however, could in certain circumstances be regarded as "torture", "other inhumane acts of a similar character intentionally causing great suffering, or serious injury to body or to mental or physical health",[32] "inhumane treatment", "wilfully causing great suffering, or serious injury to body or health", and "other serious violations of international humanitarian law", namely "committing outrages upon personal dignity, in particular humiliating and degrading treatment".[33] Where the *chapeau* elements are met, such acts may constitute crimes against humanity or war crimes under Articles 7 and 8 of the ICC Statute. At stated, numerous allegations of

---

[28] On the over-inclusiveness of the term 'sexual exploitation' in particular, see Olivera Simic, "Rethinking 'Sexual Exploitation' in UN Peacekeeping Operations", in *Women's Studies International Forum*, 2009, vol. 32, no. 4, pp. 288–95.

[29] See, generally, Rana Lehr-Lehnardt, "One Small Step for Women: Female Friendly Provisions in the Rome Statute of the International Criminal Court", in *BYU Journal of Public Law*, 2002, vol. 16, no. 2, pp. 317, 321–22.

[30] Quénivet correctly notes that it is important to distinguish when it comes to UN military peacekeepers between prostitution and enforced or forced prostitution, as while both are prohibited by the Secretary-General's Bulletin, only the latter constitutes an offence under international criminal law and the ICC Statute. She argues that the former does not reach the level of coercion envisaged under the Elements of Crimes to constitute such crimes for the purpose of the ICC Statute. Quénivet, 2008, pp. 416–17, see *supra* note 18.

[31] Sexual violence as an umbrella term may catch a broad variety of behaviour, not meeting the elements of the other specific acts, such as rape, attempted rape, forced nudity, sexual exploitation and abuse; trafficking; forced pregnancy, and so on. See further, Inter-Agency Standing Committee ('IASC'), *Guidelines for Gender-based Violence Interventions in Humanitarian Settings: Focusing on Prevention and Response to Sexual Violence*, Taskforce on Gender in Humanitarian Assistance, September 2005, p. 8.

[32] ICC Statute, Articles 7 and 8, see *supra* note 23.

[33] Sexual offences may also be prosecuted under other categories of offences constituting grave breaches of international humanitarian law. The Yugoslavia Commission of Experts also refers to rape as a grave breach. UN Security Council, Final Report of the Commission of Experts established pursuant to Security Council Resolution 780 (1992), UN Doc. S/1994/674, 27 May 1994, para. 46 ('Report of the Commission of Experts') (http://www.legal-tools.org/doc/4eb957/). See generally, Meron, 1993, pp. 424–28, *supra* note 26.

---

rape and other forms of sexual abuse and exploitation have been made against UN military peacekeepers, some of which could be regarded as coming under the *actus reus* of one or more of these crimes.

Sexual abuse and exploitation by UN military peacekeepers raises issues of the unequal power dynamics between peacekeepers and victims, particularly when the perpetrators are in military attire or bear weapons. This will particularly be the case in conflict and post-conflict environments.[34] It also raises issues of victims' vulnerability due to socio-economic factors and the capacity of peacekeepers to exchange sexual favours for food, services, protection, money and so on.[35] Reports and statistics show that many of the victims of sexual abuse and exploitation by UN peacekeepers are in fact children or young girls.[36] Sexual interactions with children irrefutably constitute sexual violence, as they are incapable of genuine consent to sexual intercourse. This obviously may depend on the legal age of consent under the troop-contributing country and host Statute laws, despite the fact that the secretary-general's 2003 bulletin prohibits sexual activity with children under the age of 18.[37]

---

[34] "Abuse of power", "taking advantage of a coercive environment" and "natural, induced or age-related incapacity" are identified in the ICC's Elements of Crimes as factors which may be considered as obviating consent to certain sexual interactions, in certain circumstances. UN, Report of the Preparatory Commission for the International Criminal Court, Addendum, Part II, finalised draft text of the Elements of Crimes, UN Doc. PCNICC/2000/1/Add.2, approved by Assembly of State Parties at first meeting, 3–10 September 2002, fn. 15 and 51. ICC, Elements of Crimes, ICC-ASP/1/3, 11 June 2010 (http://www.legal-tools.org/doc/3c0e2d/). As stated by the Trial Chamber in *Akayesu*, "coercion may be inherent in certain circumstances such as armed conflict or the military presence": *Akayesu* Trial Judgment, para. 688, see *supra* note 20.

[35] Csáky, 2008, p. 5, see *supra* note 12; Wolfgang Schomburg and Ines Peterson note that even in domestic criminal law many states criminalise sexual conduct between those in unequal positions of power, as taking advantage of such may render consent irrelevant: Wolfgang Schomburg and Ines Peterson, "Genuine Consent to Sexual Violence under International Criminal Law", in *American Journal of International Law*, 2007, vol. 101, no. 1, pp. 121, 138.

[36] For data on sexual abuse allegations see UN Conduct and Discipline Unit (https://conduct.unmissions.org/sea-data-introduction).

[37] Secretary-General's Bulletin, Section 3, see *supra* note 14.

14.1.1. *Chapeau* Elements of Crimes against Humanity

Article 7 of the ICC Statute, which covers crimes against humanity, specifically prohibits forced pregnancy, enslavement, rape, sexual slavery, and enforced prostitution "when *committed as part of* a *widespread* or *systematic* attack directed against a civilian population, *with knowledge* of that attack".[38] As noted, sexual offences may also be prosecuted under other categories of crimes under Article 7. Article 7 requires that in order for a crime to reach the threshold of a crime against humanity it must satisfy a number of chapeau elements. Acts must: 1) fit within the definition of a crime covered by Article 7; 2) be committed as part of a widespread of systematic attack; 3) the attack must be directed against a civilian population; and 4) the perpetrator must have "knowledge" of that attack and intend his acts to further this attack.[39] There is no requirement for a nexus with an armed conflict under Article 7.[40] Nor is there a need for a discriminatory motive *per se*. However, there must be a sufficient link between the acts of the perpetrator and the overall attack. Attack does not require that armed force be used for the purposes of crimes against humanity.[41] "Widespread" or "systematic" under Article 7(1) are phrased in the alternative.

14.1.1.1. Systematic

The term 'systematic' suggests the need for some form of state or organisational plan or policy to attack a civilian population, and that the accused's act can be linked to this. This requirement is not found in the Statutes of the International Criminal Tribunal for the Former Yugoslavia ('ICTY') or International Criminal Tribunal for Rwanda ('ICTR'), nor the Nuremburg Charter, Tokyo Charter or Control Council Law No. 10, and

---

[38] ICC Statute, Article 7, see *supra* note 23 (emphasis added).

[39] See further, Michael P. Scharf and Nigel Rodley, "International Law Principles on Accountability", in M. Cherif Bassiouni (ed.), *Post-Conflict Justice*, Transnational Publishers, Ardsley, NY, 2002, p. 94; Darryl Robinson, "Defining 'Crimes Against Humanity' at the Rome Conference", in *American Journal of International Law*, 1999, vol. 93, no. 1, pp. 43, 45.

[40] Christine Byron, *War Crimes and Crimes against Humanity in the Rome Statute of the International Criminal Court*, Manchester University Press, Manchester, 2009, pp. 100–01.

[41] *Ibid.*, pp. 104–05.

its necessity is disputed.[42] Domestic courts or hybrid courts prosecuting core international crimes would not necessarily need to follow the approach set out in the ICC Statute.

According to the ICTY in *Kunarać et al.*:

> ['systematic'] signifies the organised nature of the acts of violence and the improbability of their random occurrence. Patterns of crimes – that is the non-accidental repetition of similar criminal conduct on a regular basis [...].[43]

Article 7(2) of the ICC Statute seems to support this interpretation, defining 'attack' as "course of conduct involving the multiple commission of acts referred to in [Article 7(1)] pursuant to or in furtherance of a *State or organizational policy* to commit such attack".[44] The policy element need not, however, be formalised, rather it "can be deduced from the way in which the acts occur".[45] Gerhard Werle suggests that such evidence could be deduced from "actual event, political platforms of writings, public statements or propaganda programs" and so on.[46] There is, however, no

---

42   *Ibid.*, p. 112; Gerhard Werle, *Principles of International Criminal Law*, TMC Asser Press, The Hague, 2005, pp. 229–30; *Kunarać* Trial Judgment, para. 98, see *supra* note 24; Antonio Cassese, "Areas Where Article 7 Is Narrower than Customary International Law", in Antonio Cassese, Paola Gaeta and John R. W. D. Jones (eds.), *The Rome Statute of the International Criminal Court: A Commentary*, vol. 1, Oxford University Press, Oxford, 2002, p. 375; William Schabas, *An Introduction to the International Criminal Court*, 2nd ed., Cambridge University Press, 2004, p. 46. The need for such a plan or policy for crimes against humanity was specifically rejected in ICTY, *Prosecutor v. Dragoljub Kunarać, Radomir Kovač, Zoran Vuković*, Appeals Chamber, Judgment, IT-96-23-T and 96-23/I, 12 June 2002, para. 98 ('*Kunarać* Appeals Judgment') (http://www.legal-tools.org/doc/029a09/); Scharf and Rodley, 2002, see *supra* note 39.

43   *Kunarać* Appeals Judgment, para. 429, see *supra* note 42; Kevin Jon Heller, "Situational Gravity under the Rome Statute", in Carsten Stahn and Larissa van den Herik (eds.), *Future Perspectives on International Criminal Justice*, TMC Asser Press, The Hague, 2010, p. 229.

44   ICC Statute, Article 7(2), see *supra* note 23.

45   *Tadić* Trial Judgment, para. 653, see *supra* note 24. The ICTR in *Akayesu* stated that "[t]here is no requirement that this policy must be adopted formally as the policy of a state. There must however be some kind of preconceived plan or policy": *Akayesu* Trial Judgment, para. 580, see *supra* note 20; Werle, 2005, p. 227, see *supra* note 42.

46   *Akayesu* Trial Judgment, p. 228, see *supra* note 20.

---

requirement that the perpetrator be involved in the organising or planning of the attack overall or multiple commission of attacks.[47]

The Elements of Crimes provide that a "policy to commit such attack" requires that the state or organisation actively promote or encourage such an attack against a civilian population.[48] Authorities have also pointed to use of resources, planning, political motivation and the continuous nature of acts as indicative elements of an attack being 'systematic'.[49] According to the Elements of Crimes, state omission could in exceptional circumstances alter crimes to crimes against humanity, through "deliberate failure to take action, which is consciously aimed at encouraging such attacks".[50] This stance has also been taken by a number of international authorities, and in the literature.[51] The Elements of Crimes elaborate, however, that "[t]he existence of such a policy cannot be inferred solely from the absence of governmental or organizational action".[52] Therefore what is required is something more than mere acquiescence.[53]

14.1.1.2. Widespread

Alternatively, the attack must be 'widespread' to constitute a crime against humanity. 'Widespread' appears to denote either the large-scale nature of attacks; the scale of the geographic area in which they occur; or the multiplicity of victims.[54] The Trial Chamber in *Akayesu* defined

---

[47] Timothy L.H. McCormack, "Crimes Against Humanity", in Dominic McGoldrick, Peter Rowe and Eric Donnelly (eds.), *The Permanent International Criminal Court*, Hart Publishing, Oxford, 2004, pp. 179, 189.

[48] ICC, Elements of Crimes, see *supra* note 34.

[49] Robert Cryer *et al.*, *An Introduction to International Criminal Law and Procedure*, 2nd ed., Cambridge University Press, Cambridge, 2010, p. 237.

[50] ICC, Elements of Crimes, see *supra* note 34.

[51] See ICTY, *Prosecutor v. Duško Tadić et al.*, Appeals Chamber, Judgment, IT-94-1-T, 15 July 1999, para. 14 ('*Tadić* Appeals Judgment') (http://www.legal-tools.org/doc/8efc3a/); Report of the Commission of Experts, 1994, p. 8, see *supra* note 33; Kai Ambos, "The Current Law of Crimes Against Humanity: An Analysis of UNTAET Regulation 15/2000", in *Criminal Law Forum*, 2002, vol. 13, no. 1, pp. 1, 31–33.

[52] ICC, Elements of Crimes, Article 7(3), fn. 6, see *supra* note 34.

[53] Quénivet, 2008, p. 422, see *supra* note 18.

[54] ICC, Pre-Trial Chamber, Warrant of Arrest for Omar Hassan Ahmad Al Bashir, ICC-02/05-01/09-1, 4 March 2009, para. 81 ('*Al Bashir* Arrest Warrant') (http://www.legal-tools.org/doc/814cca/); Cryer *et al.*, 2010, p. 236, see *supra* note 49.

'widespread' as "massive, frequent, large scale action, carried out collectively with considerable seriousness and directed against a multiplicity of victims".[55] However, it further stated that the widespread element may be satisfied by "the cumulative of a serious of inhumane acts or the singular effect of an inhumane act of extraordinary magnitude".[56] Crimes against humanity in essence entail an element of group victimisation and criminality.[57] Part of the offence is that it does not only impact the victim, but also the broader international community.

What is required is that the overall attack be widespread, not the individual's action. The consequence of the conduct must form part of the widespread attack, even if the conduct is otherwise singular in nature.[58]

While 'systematic' and 'widespread' are phrased in the alternative under Article 7(1), Article 7(2), in setting out the context in which the attack must occur, qualifies that:

> Attack directed against any civilian population' means a course of conduct involving the *multiple commission* of acts [...] pursuant to or in furtherance of a State or organizational policy to commit such attack.[59]

The requirement for the attack to form part of the "multiple commission of acts" does not mean that the perpetrator must carry out multiple acts, so long as the act can be linked to the overall attack. Some authors question the extent that Article 7(2) affects the disjunctive reading of "widespread *or* systematic".[60] Article 7(2) was largely a response to opposition during the drafting phase to 'widespread' and 'systematic' being read disjunc-

---

[55] *Akayesu* Trial Judgment, para. 580, see *supra* note 20. The ICTY in *Blaškić* held that "widespread refers to the scale of acts perpetrated and to the number of victims": ICTY, *Prosecutor v. Tihomir Blaškić*, Trial Chamber, Judgment, ICTY-95-14-T, 3 March 2000, para. 206 ('*Blaškić* Judgment') (http://www.legal-tools.org/doc/e1ae55/). Byron, 2009, p. 103, see *supra* note 40 argues that the ICC would likely require hundreds or thousands of victims for an attack to be considered 'widespread'.

[56] *Blaškić* Judgment, para. 206, see *supra* note 55; ICTY, *Prosecutor v. Dario Kordić and Mario Čerkez*, Trial Chamber, Judgment, IT-95-14/2-T, 26 February 2001, para. 179 ('*Kordić and Čerkez* Trial Judgment') (http://www.legal-tools.org/doc/d4fedd/).

[57] Allison Marston Danner, "Constructing a Hierarchy of Crimes in International Criminal Law Sentencing", in *Virginia Law Review*, 2001, vol. 87, no. 3, pp. 474–77.

[58] Byron, 2009, p. 105, see *supra* note 40.

[59] ICC Statute, Article 7(2), see *supra* note 23.

[60] McCormack, 2004, p. 187, see *supra* note 47; Cryer *et al.*, 2010, p. 236, see *supra* note 49.

---

tively, the concern being that random criminal acts would then be within the remit of crimes against humanity.[61] Timothy McCormack notes that this means that even if a plan to commit an attack exists, there must be multiple victims.[62] The use of the term "directed against a civilian population" denotes some level of scale, thereby excluding isolated and unrelated acts.[63] Nevertheless, this threshold is lower than widespread.[64] According to the Trial Chamber in *Tadić*, 'systematic' is a higher threshold than 'directed' as direction might not be formal but "deduced from the way in which the acts occur".[65] So arguably, the chapeau of 'widespread' or 'systematic' are not entirely disjunctive, but rather represent a middle ground.

14.1.1.3. *Mens Rea*

Article 7(1) of the ICC Statute requires that the perpetrator has knowledge of the attack against the civilian population, however he or she does not have to have been involved in the planning of the attack.[66] In addition to knowledge of the context, the Elements of Crimes require that "[t]he perpetrator *knew* that the conduct was part of or intended the conduct to be part of a widespread or systematic attack directed against a civilian population".[67] That stated, it qualifies that this

> element should not be interpreted as requiring proof that the perpetrator had knowledge of all characteristics of the attack or the precise details of the plan or policy of the State or organization. In the case of an emerging widespread or systematic attack against a civilian population, the intent clause

---

[61] Cryer *et al.*, 2010, p. 238, see *supra* note 49.

[62] McCormack, 2004, pp. 187–88, see *supra* note 47.

[63] *Al Bashir* Arrest Warrant, para. 81, see *supra* note 54; *Kunarać* Trial Judgment, paras. 422, 427, see *supra* note 24.

[64] Robinson, 1999, pp. 43, 48, see *supra* note 39; Phyllis Hwang, "Defining Crimes Against Humanity in the Rome Statute of the International Criminal Court", in *Fordham International Law Journal*, 1998, vol. 22, no. 2, pp. 457, 503.

[65] *Tadić* Trial Judgment, para. 653, see *supra* note 24.

[66] Robinson, 1999, pp. 51–52, *supra* note 39.

[67] ICC, Elements of Crimes, *supra* note 34. The *Blaškić* Trial Chamber stated that the required *mens rea* is that the accused had "knowledge of the context" and that he "knowingly participated in that context": *Blaškić* Judgment, paras. 247–57, see *supra* note 55.

---

of the last element indicates that this mental element is satisfied if the perpetrator intended to further such an attack.[68]

Therefore, the perpetrator must be aware of the greater context in
which he commits the crime and that the crime furthers the attack.[69] The
ICTY Trial Chamber in *Tadić* held knowledge could be imputed from the
circumstances. It elaborated that 'while there may also be personal motives' for conduct "motives ought not to be solely personal".[70] The latter
part was overruled by the Appeals Chamber, which found that nothing in
the ICTY Statute indicated that the existence of a personal motive would
prevent it from being a crime against humanity.[71] It seems under the Elements of Crimes, personnel motive might co-exist if the perpetrator also
has knowledge of the attack and intends to further it. An otherwise isolated incident may constitute a crime against humanity if it can be sufficiently linked to the collective attack on the civilian population.[72]

14.1.1.4. Application to UN Military Peacekeepers Complicit in Sexual Offences

While certain serious sexual crimes by UN military peacekeepers may fall
within the remit of enumerated acts coming under Article 7 of the ICC
Statute, for a UN peacekeeper to be prosecuted for a crime against humanity it would have to be proven that his or her crimes were committed
as part of a widespread or systematic attack by a group and that he or she
intended his or her actions to further this attack.[73] Although in certain host

---

[68] ICC, Elements of Crimes, Article 7(2), see *supra* note 34. See also *Kunarac* Trial Judgment, para. 418, *supra* note 24; *Tadić* Appeals Judgment, paras. 248, 251, 271, *supra* note 51.

[69] *Al Bashir* Arrest Warrant, para. 87, see *supra* note 54; *Tadić* Appeals Judgment, para. 271, see *supra* note 51: "[t]o convict an accused of crimes against humanity, it must be proved that the crimes were related to the attack on a civilian population, and that the accused knew that his crimes were so related".

[70] *Tadić* Trial Judgment, para. 657, see *supra* note 24.

[71] *Ibid.*, paras. 657–59; *Tadić* Appeals Judgment, paras. 248, 250, see *supra* note 51. For criti-
cism of this view, see further Marco Sassòli and Laura Olson, "The Judgment of the ICTY
Appeals Chamber on the Merits in the Tadić Case", in *International Review of the Red
Cross*, 2000, vol. 82, no. 839, p. 733.

[72] *Tadić* Trial Judgment, para. 649, see *supra* note 24; Schomburg and Peterson, 2007, p. 130,
see *supra* note 35.

[73] Jennifer Murray, "Who Will Police the Peace-Builders? The Failure to Establish Accountability for the Participation of United Nations Civilian Police in the Trafficking of Women

---

states, such as the DRC, sexual offences have allegedly been perpetrated by UN military peacekeepers with relatively high frequency, the link between these acts and a widespread attack on the civilian population would be extremely difficult to establish. Given their ordinarily isolated nature they are unlikely to be considered by themselves as a widespread attack. However, if such acts can be linked to the broader context in which they occur, namely the acts of other perpetrators in the host state, the nature of these acts might constitute crimes against humanity.[74]

Equally, sexual crimes by UN military peacekeepers are unlikely to be perpetrated pursuant to a plan or policy of either the UN or troop-contributing countries to commit an attack on a civilian population. Rather it is more probable that they are opportunistic acts, taking advantage of a coercive environment and differential power dynamics. Sexual crimes in this context are likely to be carried out primarily for personal motives. Yet the existence of a plan or policy need not necessarily be that of the UN or troop-contributing country, or even a group of peacekeepers, arguably the act might further an attack pursuant to a plan or policy of other entities within an area. What appears to be the key is that the peacekeeper is aware of this attack, commits the offence within this context, and intends to further the attack. The ICTY Trial Chamber in *Blaškić* stated that the perpetrator need not even identify "with the ideology, policy or plan in whose name mass crimes were perpetrated nor even that he supported it. It suffices that he knowingly took the risk of participating in the implementation of the ideology, policy or plan".[75]

Knowledge of attack and how a peacekeeper might be aware of his part in it might be difficult to prove.[76] Marten Zwanenburg argues that knowledge of circumstances, given the *ad hoc* nature of UN peacekeeping operations and unclear command and control structures, may be difficult

---

in Post-Conflict Bosnia and Herzegovina", in *Columbia Human Rights Law Review*, 2003, vol. 34, pp. 475, 512.

[74] Du Plessis and Pete, 2004, p. 11, see *supra* note 18.

[75] *Blaškić* Judgment, para. 257, see *supra* note 55; *Kunarać* Appeals Judgment, para. 103, see *supra* note 42; ICTY, *Prosecutor v. Dario Kordić and Mario Čerkez*, Appeals Chamber, Judgment, IT-95-14/2-T, 17 December 2004, para. 99 ('*Kordić and* Čerkez Appeals Judgment')

[76] Du Plessis and Pete, 2004, pp. 10–11, see *supra* note 18; Marten Zwanenburg, "The Statute for an International Criminal Court and the United States: Peacekeepers under Fire", in *European Journal of International Law*, 1999, vol. 10, no. 1, p. 134.

to impute to individuals soldiers.[77] That stated, soldiers are briefed prior to deployment to UN peacekeeping operations. An ongoing attack may be quite obvious on the ground. However, the real difficulty rests in connecting sexual abuse and exploitation by peacekeepers to the attack. That stated, when it comes to complicity in crimes of an organised nature, which take advantage of, and arguably further the attack, such as trafficking, such crimes might meet the *chapeau* elements crimes against humanity. It seems unlikely, however, that most incidents of sexual abuse and exploitation by UN peacekeepers would meet the threshold set by the chapeau elements of crimes against humanity under the ICC Statute, save in the most exceptional of circumstances.

14.1.2. War Crimes

The 1949 Geneva Conventions and their Additional Protocols of 1977 and 1978, in addition to the Hague Conventions, govern what is labelled the laws and customs of war or international humanitarian law.[78] Serious violations of the provisions of these Conventions constitute war crimes. The Geneva Conventions distinguish between grave breaches and other breaches of the laws and customs of war. Crimes constituting "grave breaches" are set out in Article 50 of Geneva Convention I, Article 51 of Geneva Convention II, Article 130 of Geneva Convention III and Article 147 of Geneva Convention IV. Article 147 of Geneva Convention IV enumerates "graves breaches" as "willful killing, torture or inhuman treatment including biological experiments, wilfully causing great suffering or serious injury to body or health, unlawful deportation or unlawful confinement of a protected person".[79] Article 8 of the ICC Statute deals

---

[77] Zwanenburg, 1999, pp. 134–135, see *supra* note 76.

[78] See Jackson Nyamuya Maogoto, "Watching the Watchdogs: Holding the UN Accountable for Violations of International Humanitarian Law by the 'Blue Helmets'", in *Deakin Law Review*, 2000, vol. 5, p. 59.

[79] Convention (I) for the Amelioration of the Conditions of the Wounded and Sick in Armed Forces in the Field, 12 August 1949, 6 UST 3114, 75 UNTS 31 ('Geneva Convention I') (http://www.legal-tools.org/doc/baf8e7/); Convention (II) for the Amelioration of the Conditions of the Wounded, Sick and Shipwrecked Members of the Armed Forces at Sea, 12 August 1949, 6 UST 3217, 75 UNTS 85 ('Geneva Convention II') (http://www.legal-tools.org/doc/0d0216/); Convention (III) Relative to the Treatment of Prisoners of War, 12 August 1949, 6 UST 6616, 75 UNTS 135 ('Geneva Convention III') (http://www.legal-tools.org/doc/365095/); Convention (IV) Relative to the Protection of Civilian Persons in Time of War, 12 August 1949, 6 UST 3516, 75 UNTS 287 ('Geneva Convention IV')

---

with war crimes committed in international and non-international armed conflict. Article 8(2)(a) prohibits grave breaches of the Geneva Conventions, which drawing on the language of the Conventions, include possible acts under which sexual abuse and exploitation could fall, namely: torture or inhuman treatment, and "wilfully causing great suffering or serious injury to body or health". "Grave breaches" of the Geneva Conventions have acquired *jus cogens* status, obliging all states to prosecute or extradite those who violate these norms.[80] Article 8(2)(b) enumerates "other serious violations of the laws and customs of war" applicable to international armed conflict.

There has been considerable debate in the literature as to whether international humanitarian law applies to UN military peacekeepers.[81] The difficulty revolves around the fact that only states can become parties to international treaties, and not the UN.[82] The debate has been somewhat resolved with the issuance of the secretary-general's 1999 bulletin "Ob-

---

(http://www.legal-tools.org/doc/d5e260/); Protocol (I) Additional to the Geneva Conventions of 12 August 1949, and Relating to the Protection of Victims of International Armed Conflicts, 8 June 1977, 1125 UNTS 3, 37, 16 ILM 1391, 1423 ('Additional Protocol I') (http://www.legal-tools.org/doc/d9328a/); Protocol (II) Additional to the Geneva Conventions of 12 August 1949, and Relating to the Protection of Victims of Non-International Armed Conflicts, 7 December 1978, UNTS 17513, vol. 1125, p. 609 ('Additional Protocol II') (http://www.legal-tools.org/doc/fd14c4/).

[80] Theodor Meron notes, however, that this does not mean that other breaches of the GCs should be punished by States. Theodor Meron, "International Criminalization of Internal Atrocities", in *American Journal of International Law*, 1995, vol. 89, no. 3, pp. 554, 569.

[81] On review of the literature, and state and organisational practice, it appears largely accepted that international humanitarian law is applicable to state led forces authorised by the UN, but there is greater disagreement with regard to its applicability to UN-led, commanded and controlled forces. See Keiichiro Okimoto, "Violations of International Humanitarian Law by United Nations Forces and their Legal Consequences", in *Yearbook of International Humanitarian law*, 2003, vol. 6. pp. 199, 204.

[82] Marten Zwanenburg, *Accountability of Peace Support Operations*, Martinus Nijhoff Publishers, Leiden, 2005, p. 174; In relation to the Bihać incident, where UN peacekeepers felt it was their duty to protect a hospital, the UN Office of Legal Affairs took the position that UN peacekeepers are bound only by the Security Council mission mandate, therefore given their international purpose, they were not required to adhere to the provisions of the Geneva Conventions. Furthermore, it could be argued that on the basis of Article 103 of the UN Charter, Security Council resolutions take precedence over any other international treaties or agreements. See Statement by S. Katz, UN Office of Legal Affairs official, cited in Roy Gutman, "United Nations and the Geneva Conventions", in Roy Gutman and David Rieff (eds.), *Crimes of War: What the Public Should Know*, W. W. Norton, New York, 2007, p. 361.

---

servance by United Nations Forces of International Humanitarian Law",
which affirms that international humanitarian law is applicable to its forces where they are actively engaged in hostilities, or at least certain provisions thereof.[83] I will proceed on the assumption that international humanitarian law does apply and thereby that it is plausible that UN peacekeepers can commit war crimes as defined under the ICC Statute, when engaged as combatants.[84]

Article 8(2)(c) of the ICC Statute prohibits serious violations of
Common Article 3 of the Geneva Conventions and Article 8(2)(e) "other
serious violations of the laws and customs of war" applicable in non-
international armed conflict.[85] Where peacekeepers engage as belligerents
in a conflict that is otherwise a non-international armed conflict, in my
view it internationalises that conflict, if only insofar as it relates to their
conduct, rendering the full corpus of the Geneva Conventions applicable.
I will proceed on the assumption that UN engagement in an armed conflict renders the whole corpus of the Geneva Conventions applicable. Fo-

---

[83] However, the bulletin contains only minimal international humanitarian law rules and sets a
high threshold for their application. UN Secretariat, Secretary-General's Bulletin: Ob-
servance by United Nations Forces of International Humanitarian Law, UN Doc.
ST/SGB/1999/13, 6 August 1999. See also Daphna Shraga, "UN Peacekeeping Operations: Applicability of International Humanitarian Law and Responsibility for Operations-
Related Damage", in *American Journal of International Law*, 2000, vol. 94, no. 2, p. 406.

[84] Indeed the Convention on the Safety of United Nations and Associated Personnel, 2051
UNTS 363, 9 December 1994, entered into force 15 January 1999, Article 2(2) suggests
that the full corpus of international humanitarian law should apply to UN operations authorised by the Security Council under Chapter VII of UN Charter as an enforcement action
"in which any of the personnel are engaged as combatants against organized armed forces".

[85] Common Article 3 may be applicable in far as it constitutes a mandatory minimum threshold of protection of civilians in an armed conflict, constituting customary international
law. See further Ray Murphy, "United Nations Military Operations and International Humanitarian Law: What Rules Apply to Peacekeepers", in *Criminal Law Forum*, 2003, vol.
14, no. 2, pp. 153–94; Okimoto, 2003, p. 199, see *supra* note 81; ICTY, *Prosecutor v.
Duško Tadić et al.*, Appeals Chamber, Decision on the Defence Motion for Interlocutory
Appeal on Jurisdiction, IT-94-1, 2 October 1995, paras. 87–98 ('*Tadić* Appeal Decision')
(http://www.legal-tools.org/doc/866e17/); Hilarie McCoubrey, *International Humanitarian
Law: Modern Developments in the Limitation Of Warfare*, Ashgate, Dartmouth, 1998, p. 282.
In the *Nicaragua* case, the International Court of Justice ('ICJ') stipulated that "Article 3 [...]
constitutes a minimum yardstick [...] rules which in the court's opinion reflect what the court
in 1949 called 'elementary considerations of humanity'": ICJ, *Nicaragua v. United States
(Case Concerning Military and Paramilitary Activities in and against Nicaragua)*, Judgment,
Merits, 1986, 27 June 1986 (http://www.legal-tools.org/doc/046698/).

cus will therefore be placed on Articles 8(2)(a) and 8(2)(b) of the ICC Statute, which apply to war crimes in an international armed conflict.[86]

Sexual violence and rape when committed in the context of armed conflict have been recognised as grave breaches of the Geneva Conventions and prosecuted as torture, and inhumane treatments as war crimes by the *ad hoc* and hybrid tribunals.[87] Article 8 of the ICC Statute specifically enumerates a series of sexual offences as other violations of the laws and customs of war, including rape, sexual slavery, enforced prostitution, forced pregnancy, enforced sterilisation and other forms of sexual violence.[88] However, in order for an act to constitute a war crime under the ICC Statute it will need to meet certain *chapeau* elements.

14.1.2.1. *Chapeau* Elements

The *chapeau* for Article 8 of the ICC Statute provides that the ICC shall have jurisdiction "*in particular* when committed as part of a plan or policy *or* as part of a large-scale commission of such crimes".[89] The term 'in particular' suggests that it is not a prerequisite that the commission of war crimes necessarily be large scale or perpetrated as part of plan or policy but that the existence of these additional elements may go towards an assessment of gravity.[90] That stated, the words 'in particular' would not have been used if the ICC must reject every case that is not part of a plan or policy or large-scale commission. Therefore, in theory a single serious act of sexual violence could constitute a war crime. Nevertheless, what it

---

[86] ICC Statute, Article 8(2)(d) and (f), see *supra* note 23.

[87] *Akayesu* Trial Judgment, see *supra* note 20. Sexual violence, in particular rape has been prosecuted as a violation of Common Article 3, for instance in ICTY, *Prosecutor v. Radovan Karadžić*, Trial Chamber, Review of Indictments, IT-95-5, 25 July 1995, at Count 4 (outrages upon personal dignity) (http://www.legal-tools.org/doc/792bb3/); ICTY, *Prosecutor v. Duško Sikirica et al.*, Indictment, IT-95-8, 21 July 1995, at Count 19 (cruel treatment) (http://www.legal-tools.org/doc/3eda3a/); ICTY, *Prosecutor v. Blagoje Simić et al.*, Indictment, IT-95-9, 21 July 1995, at Counts 37, 52 (humiliating and degrading treatment) (http://www.legal-tools.org/doc/8edc06/). See also Meron, 1993, pp. 426, *supra* note 26; Judith Gardam, "Women, Human Rights and International Humanitarian Law", in *International Review of the Red Cross*, 1998, no. 324, pp. 421–32.

[88] ICC Statute, Article 8(b), see *supra* note 23.

[89] *Ibid.*, Article 8 (emphasis added).

[90] Peter Rowe, "War Crimes", in Dominic McGoldrick, Peter Rowe and Eric Donnelly (eds.), *The Permanent International Criminal Court*, Hart Publishing, Oxford, 2004, pp. 203, 205.

---

does suggest is that less significant violations should not be dealt with by the ICC. The problem is that this appears to create what some authors have dubbed a "non-threshold threshold" requirement.[91] The insertion of this "non-threshold" in Article 8 was the result of compromise at the negotiating phase, given that some advocates wanted the jurisdiction of the ICC to be restricted to large-scale and systematic crimes, but others were of the view that this would undermine the Court's deterrent effect.[92] With respect to this added non-threshold requirement, the ICC Appeals Chamber has stated:

> First, with regard to war crimes, the requirement of large-scale commission under the Statute is alternative to the requirement of commission as part of a policy. Second, the statutory requirement of either large-scale commission or part of a policy is not absolute but qualified by the expression "in particular". Third, the requirement of "systematic" commission of crime is not contained in Article 8 but only Article 7 on crimes against humanity.[93]

For a crime to constitute a war crime, there has to be a nexus with armed conflict. Article 8 provides that the offence is committed "in the context of *and* was associated with an international armed conflict". Therefore in order for a sexual offence by a UN military peacekeeper to constitute a war crime, it would not be sufficient for the conduct only to occur "in the context of" an armed conflict, it must also be proven that it is "closely related" to it. In essence the context of the armed conflict ought to be what enables the perpetrator to commit the offence. As stated by the ICTY in *Kunarać et al.*:

> [C]ivilians were killed, raped or otherwise abused as a direct result of the armed conflict and because the armed conflict apparently offered blanket impunity to perpetrators.[94]

---

[91] Du Plessis and Pete, 2004, p. 12, see *supra* note 18.

[92] See further Herman von Hebel and Darryl Robinson, "Crimes within the Jurisdiction of the Court", in Roy S. Lee (ed.), *The International Criminal Court: The Making of the Rome Statute: Issues, Negotiations, Results*, Kluwer Law International, The Hague, 1999, pp. 107–08.

[93] ICC, Appeals Chamber, Situation in the Democratic Republic of the Congo, Judgment on the Prosecutor's appeal against the decision of Pre-Trial Chamber I entitled "Decision on the Prosecutor's Application for Warrants of Arrest, Article 58", ICC-01-04-169, 13 July 2006, para. 70 ('ICC, Situation in the DRC, Judgment') (http://www.legal-tools.org/doc/8c20eb/).

[94] *Kunarać* Trial Judgment, para. 568, see *supra* note 24.

A crime could be "closely related", according the ICTY in *Kunarać et al.*, even if "crimes are committed in the aftermath of the fighting [...] and are committed in furtherance *or* take advantage of the situation created by the fighting".[95] Accordingly, what distinguishes a domestic criminal offence from a war crime is that that the crime

> is shaped by or dependent upon the environment – the armed conflict – in which it is committed [...] The armed conflict need not have been causal to the commission of the crime, but the existence of an armed conflict must, at a minimum, have played a substantial part in the perpetrator's ability to commit it, his decision to commit it, the manner in which it was committed or the purpose for which it was committed.[96]

If the ICC were to follow this approach it could have interesting consequences for UN military peacekeepers complicit in serious sexual offences where an armed conflict is ongoing, assuming all other requirements had been met. Taking the DRC for instance, it could be argued that the ongoing conflict in the state has created an environment wherein it is much easier to commit sexual offences with relative impunity. Peacekeepers engaging in such abuse are taking advantage of this environment. This is particularly so given unequal power dynamics between civilians and peacekeepers in soldiers' attire and carrying arms. This might render their conduct sufficiently associated with the conflict. That is assuming in the circumstances international humanitarian law applies to peacekeepers.

However, Wolfgang Schomburg and Ines Peterson explain the mere existence of an armed conflict is not by itself a sufficient nexus, and that it cannot be presumed that relationships between members of foreign armed forces and the local civilian population are inherently coercive.[97] Additional factors would need to be shown, which might include: 1) the perpetrator's status; 2) status of the victim; 3) "circumstances in which offence committed"; 4) assistance of parties to the conflict in the commission of the offence; and 5) a link between conduct and official duties, and so on.[98]

---

[95] *Ibid.*

[96] *Kunarać* Appeals Judgment, para. 58, see *supra* note 42.

[97] Schomburg and Peterson, 2007, pp. 130–31, see *supra* note 35.

[98] *Ibid.*, p. 131.

In this author's view if the nexus with armed conflict is proven then consent to sexual interactions may be negated.[99]

The general consensus is that for conduct to be associated with armed conflict it is not necessarily required to take place within the same geographic area as where fighting is occurring, as Article 8 applies to the territory as a whole.[100] Under the Elements of Crimes for Article 8, the perpetrator must have both knowledge of the armed conflict and intend to commit the offence. The Elements of Crimes provide that he or she must be aware of factual circumstances that established the existence of an armed conflict that is implicit in the terms "took place in the context of and was associated with".[101] However, there is no requirement that the perpetrator make a legal evaluation as to the existence of an armed conflict or even be aware of facts that establish the nature of the conflict, all that is required is that he be aware of factual circumstances that establish that an armed conflict exists.[102]

14.1.2.2. Conclusion

In limited circumstances where international humanitarian law might be deemed to apply to UN military peacekeepers, the prospect of being prosecuted for war crimes before the ICC appears more plausible than for crimes against humanity. Sexual abuse and exploitation could certainly come within the remit of the *actus reus* of war crimes. Isolated acts may constitute a war crime if they take place in and are somehow connected to

---

[99] *Ibid.* The ICTY Appeals Chamber in *Kunarać* provided a non-exhaustive list of factors that might be considered in determining whether an act was sufficiently related to an armed conflict, including "the fact that the perpetrator is a combatant; the fact that the victim is a non-combatant; the fact that the victim is a member of the opposing party; the fact that the act may be said to serve the ultimate goal of a military campaign; and the fact that the crime is committed as part of or in the context of the perpetrator's official duties": *Kunarać* Appeals Judgment, para. 59, see *supra* note 42.

[100] Rowe, 2004, p. 208, see *supra* note 90. The Appeals Chamber in *Kunarać*, affirming the Trial Chamber's position, stated, "the requirement that the acts of the accused must be closely related to the armed conflict would not be negated if the crimes were temporally and geographically remote from the actual fighting": *Kunarać* Appeals Judgment, para. 57, see *supra* note 42. See also *Tadić* Trial Judgment, para. 573, *supra* note 24. It stated that there is no requirement that "armed conflict was occurring at the exact time and place of the proscribed acts".

[101] See ICC, Elements of Crimes, introduction to Article 8, *supra* note 34.

[102] *Ibid.*, p. 14.

---

an armed conflict. At least in some incidents when sexual abuse and exploitation is perpetrated by UN military personnel, they are taking advantage of the victims' vulnerability and the coercive environment. That stated, while there is no explicit requirement that such acts enumerated in Article 8 of the ICC Statute be carried out in both a widespread or systematic manner, this may well go to assessments of gravity, and impact on case selection. This means it is unlikely that single acts will be considered of sufficient gravity, save in exceptional circumstances. At present sexual abuse and exploitation by UN peacekeepers is unlikely to be prosecuted by as a war crime, unless it can be linked to the wider attack.[103]

14.1.3. Further Restrictions in the ICC Statute

14.1.3.1. Triggering Mechanisms

Even if exceptionally incidents of sexual abuse and exploitation by UN military personnel could be deemed to meet the *chapeau* of war crimes or crimes against humanity under the ICC Statute, the fact remains that a number of major troop-contributing countries are not party to the Statute.[104] This obviously has implications for any possible prosecution of UN peacekeepers by the ICC. In order for the ICC to exercise its jurisdiction over sexual abuse and exploitation by UN peacekeepers, either the state in which the conduct occurred or the state of nationality of the perpetrator would have to either be a state party or, if a non-state party, have accepted the ICC's jurisdiction.[105] The prosecutor may also initiate an investigation *propio motu* with respect to state parties.[106]

---

[103] Naomi Cahn, "Beyond Retribution and Impunity: Responding to War Crimes of Sexual Violence", in *Stanford Journal of Civil Rights and Civil Liberties*, 2005, vol. 1, p. 240.

[104] Major troop-contributing countries that have not yet ratified the ICC Statute include Pakistan and India. For statistics on troop and police contributors, see http://www.un.org/en/peacekeeping/resources/statistics/contributors.shtml.

[105] ICC Statute, Articles 12(2) and (3) and Articles 13(1) and (3), see *supra* note 23, where for the Prosecutor to use its *proprio motu* powers, the Pre-trial Chamber must "authorise" an investigation.

[106] See, for example, ICC, Situation in the Republic of Kenya, Pre-Trial Chamber, Decision Pursuant to Article 15 of the Rome Statute on the Authorization of an Investigation into the Situation in the Republic of Kenya, ICC-01/09, 31 March 2010 (http://www.legal-tools.org/doc/338a6f/).

UN operations consist of military personnel from numerous different states, who may or may not be party to the ICC Statute.[107] Are we to subject peacekeepers complicit in sexual abuse and exploitation to different standards? It appears that the only way possibly around this issue is if the Security Council, acting under Chapter VII of the UN Charter, refers a situation pursuant to Article 13(b), wherein states possibly could be compelled to co-operate with the ICC.[108] The Security Council could do so irrespective of whether the conduct occurred in or relates to the conduct of a national of a state party.[109] The problem is that it is improbable that the Security Council would ever refer UN military peacekeepers complicit in sexual abuse and exploitation, particularly given veto powers and the potential impact on troop contributions. Nevertheless, it might refer a situation to the ICC, within the framework of which the prosecutor could pursue UN military peacekeeper abuse as a case within a broader situation – for instance, if such abuse occurred in Darfur, a situation already referred by the Security Council. Equally, state parties are unlikely to refer a situation to the court on the basis of UN peacekeeper complicity in sexual abuse and exploitation, in particular due to political considerations, yet such crimes might be connected to a broader situation that might be referred to the Court, and the prosecutor could pursue such a case.

14.1.3.2. Other Restrictions

It is generally considered that under customary international law there can be no immunity for crimes against humanity, aggression, genocide and war crimes.[110] Article 27 of the ICC Statute provides that official capacity "shall in no case exempt a person from criminal responsibility under the Statute". As per Article 27(2), no immunities provided for on either na-

---

[107] There are currently 16 UN peacekeeping operations deployed in four continents (http://www.un.org/en/peacekeeping/resources/statistics/factsheet.shtml).

[108] Elizabeth Wilmshurst, "The International Criminal Court: The Role of the Security Council", in Mauro Politi and Giuseppe Nesi (eds.), *The Rome Statute of the International Criminal Court: A Challenge to Impunity*, Ashgate, Aldershot, 2001, p. 40.

[109] ICC Statute, Article 13, see *supra* note 23. In the case of either Security Council or a state party referral, the prosecutor must go ahead with an investigation unless he determines that "there is no reasonable basis to proceed". *Ibid*, Article 15(4).

[110] Claus Kress and Kimberly Prost, "Article 98", in Otto Triffterer (ed.), *Commentary on the Rome Statute of the International Criminal Court: Observers' Notes, Article by Article*, Hart Publishing, Oxford, 2008, pp. 1603, 1609.

tional or international law debar the jurisdiction of the ICC.[111] That stated, this bar on immunity seems to be somewhat contradicted by Articles 16 and 98 Of the ICC Statute. While it is beyond the scope of this chapter to discuss the debate surrounding both articles in any detail, a number of points need to be made, given their implications for any possible prosecution of UN military peacekeepers before the ICC.

Article 16 of the ICC Statute provides that the Security Council can pass a resolution, acting under Chapter VII of the UN Charter, requesting the ICC to defer a case for a perpetually renewable period of 12 months.[112] Chapter VII authorises the Security Council to act where it believes there is a threat to international peace and security.[113] Largely under US pressure, in 2002 the Security Council passed resolution 1422 on the basis of Article 16. This exempted UN peacekeeping troops from non-state parties from ICC jurisdiction for a period of 12 months, renewable annually.[114] The resolution was renewed by Security Council resolution 1487 in 2003; however, further attempts at renewal failed in 2004 after the Abu Ghraib scandal. Security Council resolution 1497 in 2003 also contained a broad exemption of forces deployed as part of a multinational force in Liberia from the ICCs jurisdiction.[115] More recently, resolution

---

[111] ICC Statute, Article 27, see *supra* note 23.

[112] *Ibid.*, Article 16. See further, Linda Keller, "The False Dichotomy of Peace versus Justice and the International Criminal Court", in *Hague Justice Journal*, 2008, vol. 3, no. 1, pp. 12, 17. The ability of the Security Council to defer a case was hotly contested at the negotiating phase of the ICC Statute: See Philippe Kirsch and John T. Holmes, "Developments in International Criminal Law", in *American Journal of International Law*, 1999, vol. 93, pp. 1, 8.

[113] Charter of the United Nations, 26 June 1945, entered into force 24 October 1945 ('UN Charter') (http://www.legal-tools.org/doc/6b3cd5/).

[114] UN Security Council, Resolution 1422, UN Doc. S/RES/1422 (2002), 12 July 2002 (http://www.legal-tools.org/doc/1701d5/). Carsten Stahn, "The Ambiguities of Security Council Resolution 1422", in *European Journal of International Law,* 2003, vol. 14, no. 1, pp. 85–105. The fear that states' military forces, including peacekeeping forces, could be brought before the ICC was evident in some states' reactions to the Court's establishment. See, for example, David J. Scheffer, "International Criminal Court: The Challenge of Jurisdiction", Ambassador at Large for War Crimes Issues, US Department of State, Address at the Annual Meeting of American Society of International Law, Washington, 26 March 1999; David J. Scheffer, "The United States and the International Criminal Court", in *American Journal of International Law*, 1999, vol. 93, no. 1, pp. 12, 18–19; see generally Zwanenburg, 1999, p. 124, *supra* note 76.

[115] UN Security Council, Resolution 1487, UN Doc. S/RES/1487 (2003), 12 June 2003 (http://www.legal-tools.org/doc/20e269/); UN Security Council, Resolution 1497, UN Doc. S/RES/1497 (2003), 1 August 2003 (http://www.legal-tools.org/doc/43299a/).

1970, in which the Security Council refers the situation in Libya to the ICC, contained a paragraph shielding nationals of non-state parties operating in Libya from the jurisdiction of the ICC, unless that state waives its jurisdiction.[116] It does not stretch the imagination that the Security Council might consider prosecution of UN troops by the ICC as a threat to international peace and security, and that it might well request deferral. Such prosecutions could have a seriously negative effect on troop contributions and therefore could undermine current peacekeeping efforts.

Article 98(2) of the ICC Statute might serve as another impediment to prosecution of UN peacekeepers before the ICC. It provides that the ICC cannot request the surrender of those suspected of crimes under the Statute, where a bilateral agreement exists that would be violated on surrender, unless the other state consents.[117] Article 98 was the result of a compromise in the debate around peacekeeper immunities and the jurisdiction of the ICC.[118] Article 98(2) has been used extensively by the United States, in negotiating Article 98 agreements or bilateral non-surrender agreements, to shield its citizens and peacekeepers from the jurisdiction of the ICC.[119] While it is not within the scope of the present chapter to discuss the debate, the propriety of such agreements under international law is contentious.[120] Suffice to state that the ramifications of these Article

---

[116] UN Security Council, Resolution 1970, UN Doc. S/RES/1970 (2011), 26 February, para. 6. 2011 (http://www.legal-tools.org/doc/00a45e/).

[117] ICC Statute, Article 98(2), see *supra* note 23.

[118] Knoops, 2004, p. 299, see *supra* note 22. It is unclear, however, whether this provision was intended to apply solely to pre-existing agreements or also to ones drawn up at a later date. The object and purpose of the treaty lends support to the prior interpretation. Markus Benzing, "U.S. Bilateral Non-Surrender Agreements and Article 98 of the Statute of the International Criminal Court: An Exercise in the Law of Treaties", in *Max Planck Yearbook of United Nations Law*, 2004, vol. 8, no. 1, pp. 214–19. Article 98(2) seems to have been drafted with Status of Forces Agreements in mind. Kress and Kimberly Prost, 2008, p. 1603, see *supra* note 110; Status of Forces Agreements are made between states deploying troops, or in the case of UN peacekeeping operations, the UN, and the state hosting those troops. Status of Forces Agreements govern the legal status of those troops in the host state. With respect to UN operations Status of Forces Agreements cover all categories of personnel deployed by the UN. See further Burke, 2011, pp. 63–104, *supra* note 17.

[119] See generally, Benzing, 2004, p. 199, *supra* note 118.

[120] Dieter Fleck, "Are Foreign Military Personnel Exempt from International Criminal Jurisdiction under SOFAs?", in *Journal of International Criminal Justice*, 2003, vol. 1, no. 3, p. 651; Kress and Prost, 2008, p. 1603, see *supra* note 110; Dapo Akande, "International Law Im-

98(2) agreements are multifold. They conflict with the object and purpose of the ICC Statute, as set out in its Preamble,[121] and arguably contravene Article 18 of the Vienna Convention on the Law of Treaties.[122] They also arguably contradict Article 27 of the ICC Statute.[123] Furthermore, Article 86 of the ICC Statute requires state parties to co-operate fully with the Court. Numerous states have taken the position that these agreements are inconsistent with state obligations under the ICC Statute.[124] That stated, it is not difficult to foresee a proliferation in the use of Article 98(2) in this manner by states were the ICC to start prosecuting military contingents deployed on UN operations.[125]

14.1.4. Gravity Threshold

The Preamble of the ICC Statute stipulates that the ICC has jurisdiction only over "the most serious crimes of concern to the international com-

---

munities and the International Criminal Court", in *American Journal of International Law*, 2004, vol. 98, no. 3, pp. 407, 426.

[121] See generally, Steffen Wirth, "Immunities, Related Problems, and Article 98 of the Rome Statute", in *Criminal Law Forum*, 2001, vol. 12, no. 4, p. 429.

[122] UN, Vienna Convention on the Law of Treaties, 23 May 1969, entered into force 27 January 1980 (http://www.legal-tools.org/doc/6bfcd4/).

[123] However, ICC Statute, Article 27 provides that no one shall be immune from the Court's jurisdiction, whereas Article 98 relates rather to the surrender of individuals to the Court.

[124] The Council of Europe stated that these agreements may be inconsistent with states' other international law obligations. The European Parliament stated that not alone do these agreements contravene states obligations under the ICC Statute, they may even be incompatible with membership of the European Union. Many African, Caribbean and Pacific states have taken a similar position on their validity. Council of the European Union, Draft Council Conclusions on the International Criminal Court, 30 September 2002, cited in Chet J. Tan, Jr., "The Proliferation of Bilateral Non-Surrender Agreements Among Non-Ratifiers of the Rome Statute of the International Criminal Court", in *American University International Law Review*, 2004, vol. 19, no. 5, pp. 1115, 1128; see also Benzing, 2004, pp. 182, 193–95, *supra* note 118.

[125] It is worth noting again the US reaction to the ICC in passing the American Servicemembers' Protection Act. The Act provides that countries ratifying the ICC Statute will have US military assistance withdrawn, unless waived by the US president. Additionally, the Act provides that the United States may use military force to free any US or allies' citizens held by the ICC. Coupled with this, the Act also restricts US participation in UN peacekeeping missions save where guaranteed immunity from any prosecution should a crime be committed by a citizen deployed. Few US troops have been deployed on UN peacekeeping operations since 1998. See American Servicemembers' Protection Act, Title II of Public Law 107–206, 2 August 2002.

---

munity as a whole". This is reiterated in Articles 1 and 5 of the Statute.[126] The ICC will step in only in cases involving those most responsible for the gravest of crimes of international concern.[127] A key question therefore is what constitutes the most serious crimes of international concern and can sexual abuse and exploitation by UN military personnel ever fall within this? While gravity is mentioned in several places in the ICC Statute, no definition is provided. This has led to considerable debate on the required gravity of a crime to enable the ICC to exercise jurisdiction.[128] This section examines the ICC prosecutor's and the Pre-Trial Chambers' approach to gravity to date, and the impact this may have on the prosecuting of UN military peacekeepers for sexual offences before the ICC.

The ICC prosecutor has highlighted that gravity is both an integral factor in assessing the nature of crimes and their admissibility.[129] Gravity is central to the selection of situations and cases by the prosecutor. It is also a key consideration for the Pre-Trial Chamber in determining admissibility. The Pre-Trial Chamber serves as a check and balance on prosecutorial discretion in making gravity assessments.[130] Ignaz Stegmiller states that the gravity assessment may be separated into two categories under the ICC Statute, namely 'legal' (Article 53(1)(b) and 17(1)(d)) and 'discretionary' (Article 53(1)(c)). 'Legal' is linked to admissibility, and 'discretionary' (alternatively 'relative' gravity) is premised on prosecutorial discretion.[131] The discretionary element relates to the prosecutor's role in weighing the relative gravity of situations, and cases within situations, when selecting situations and cases. Stegmiller notes that contextually the

---

[126] ICC Statute, Article 5, see *supra* note 23 provides: "The jurisdiction of the Court shall be limited to the most serious crimes of concern to the international community as a whole […]". See further Mohamed M. El Zeidy, "The Gravity Threshold under the Statute of the International Criminal Court", in *Criminal Law Forum*, 2008, vol. 19, no. 1, pp. 35–36.

[127] ICC, Statement by Luis Moreno-Ocampo, Prosecutor of the International Criminal Court, Informal meeting of Legal Advisors of Ministries of Foreign Affairs, New York, 24 October 2005, pp. 5–6 ('Ocampo Statement').

[128] For example Ray Murphy, "Gravity Issues and the International Criminal Court", in *Criminal Law Forum*, 2006, vol. 17, no. 3, p. 282; Margaret M. deGuzman, "Gravity and Legitimacy of the International Criminal Court", in *Fordham International Law Journal*, 2009, vol. 32, no. 5, p. 1400.

[129] Ocampo Statement, pp. 8–9, see *supra* note 127.

[130] That stated, the prosecutor and Pre-Trial Chamber are not obligated to follow each other's approaches to gravity.

[131] See further deGuzman, 2009, pp. 1400, 1405–06, *supra* note 128.

question of gravity arises at two stages: 1) on commencing an investigation; and 2) when an actual case must be assessed for gravity.[132] Admissibility is in turn made up of gravity and complementarity, the latter concept will be addressed presently.[133]

'Gravity' first appears in Article 17(1)(d) which relates to admissibility, providing that a case must be of sufficient gravity to justify further action by the ICC.[134] The use of the terminology "shall consider" in Article 17(1)(d) means that the Pre-Trial Chamber is required to consider gravity in assessing admissibility of a case. The Pre-Trial Chamber in the *Lubanga* case, however, noted that an assessment of gravity at the admissibility phase can occur at two separate stages: first, in relation to the gravity of a particular situation, and secondly, with respect to the gravity of a particular case within that situation.[135]

Gravity must also be assessed before the initiation of an investigation or prosecution. Article 15(1) provides that the prosecutor "may initiate investigations *propio motu* on the basis of information on crimes within the jurisdiction of the Court". Article 15(2) requires the prosecutor to assess this information for its seriousness when determining whether to initiate an investigation *propio motu*.[136] If on the basis of this analysis, and of any additional information received on request,[137] the prosecutor

---

[132] Ignaz Stegmiller, "The Gravity Threshold under the ICC Statute: Gravity Back and Forth in *Lubanga* and *Ntaganda*", in *International Criminal Law Review*, 2009, vol. 9, no. 3, pp. 547, 550.

[133] *Ibid.*, pp. 547–48.

[134] ICC Statute, Article 17(1), see *supra* note 23.

[135] ICC, *Prosecutor v. Thomas Lubanga Dyilo*, Pre-Trial Chamber I, Decision on the Prosecutor's Application for a warrant of arrest under Article 58, ICC-01/04-01/06-8-Corr, 10 February 2006 (unsealed 17 March 2006) ('*Lubanga* Decision') (http://www.legal-tools.org/doc/8db08a/).

[136] ICC Statute, Article 15(2), see *supra* note 23. For a discussion of Article 15, see Morten Bergsmo and Jelena Pejić, "Article 15", in Otto Triffterer (ed.), *Commentary on the Rome Statute of the International Criminal Court: Observers' Notes, Article by Article*, Hart Publishing, Oxford, 2008, pp. 581–93.

[137] At either the investigative phase or even the prosecution stage the prosecutor may receive information from various states, intergovernmental, non-governmental and other sources. ICC, Rules of Procedure and Evidence, 9 September 2002, Rule 104 (http://www.legal-tools.org/doc/8bcf6f/) permits the prosecutor to "seek additional information from States, organs of the United Nations, intergovernmental and non-governmental organizations, or other reliable resources".

determines that there is a "reasonable basis to proceed with an investiga-tion" he must request "authorisation" from the Pre-Trial Chamber.[138] If the prosecutor was to pursue incidents of sexual violence by UN military peacekeeper this might include any material gathered by UN investigative facilities, such as the Conduct and Discipline Unit or Teams and the Office of Internal Oversight Services.[139]

Article 15 is linked to Article 53(1)(c) insofar as the latter requires the prosecutor, prior to the initiation of an investigation, to consider whether, "taking into account the *gravity* of the crime and the interests of victims, there are nonetheless substantial reasons to believe that an investigation would not serve the interests of justice".[140] However, Article 53(1)(c) appears to have broader application as it applies to the initiation of all investigations, not solely those initiated *proprio motu*.[141] Article 53(2)(c) refers to the decision to prosecute, and also allows the prosecutor to exercise his discretion in deciding not to proceed where

> [a] prosecution is not in the interests of justice, taking into account all the circumstances, including the *gravity* of the crime, the interests of victims and the age or infirmity of the alleged perpetrator, and his or her role in the alleged crime.[142]

---

[138] ICC Statute, Article 15(2) and (3), see *supra* note 23. Pursuant to Article 15(4) the Pre-Trial Chamber must first authorise an investigation by the prosecutor where he or she acts *propio motu*. Under Article 15(4), if the Pre-Trial Chamber "considers that there is a reasonable basis to proceed with an investigation, and that the case appears to fall within the jurisdiction of the Court, it shall authorize the commencement of the investigation, without prejudice to subsequent determinations by the Court with regard to the jurisdiction and admissibility of a case".

[139] Co-operation, where appropriate, and exchange of information's in relation to cases between the ICC and the UN is envisaged by the Negotiated Relationship Agreement between the International Criminal Court and the United Nations, 4 October 2004, Articles 3, 5, 15 and 18 (http://www.legal-tools.org/doc/9432c6/).

[140] ICC Statute, Article 53(1), see *supra* note 23.

[141] Some authors have pointed to the lack of clarity between the two provisions: See deGuzman, 2009, p. 1410, *supra* note 128; Héctor Olásolo, *The Triggering Procedure of the International Criminal Court*, Martinus Nijhoff Publishers, Leiden, 2005, pp. 70–71.

[142] This discretionary power of the prosecutor is not unqualified, he or she must inform the Pre-Trial Chamber and the referring state, or the Security Council if it referred the situation, of any decision not to proceed with an investigation or prosecution, if the decision is made on basis of Article 53(1)(c) or 53(2)(c), who may in turn request the prosecutor to reconsider.

Stegmiller refers to this as a 'discretionary' assessment of the gravity threshold, distinguishing it from the required legal assessment of gravity required by Articles 53(1)(b) and 17(1)(d).[143]

Article 53(1)(c) seems to require the prosecutor, in exercising his discretion, to balance the 'interests of justice' with 'gravity' and the 'interests of victims'. Similarly, Article 53(2)(c) requires the prosecutor again to make such a discretionary assessment in deciding not to prosecute, adding to the aforementioned consideration the "age or infirmity of the alleged perpetrator, and his or her role in the alleged crime".[144] Prosecutorial discretion with respect to the 'interests of justice' will be returned to presently.

As a preliminary it is important to distinguish between the gravity of 'situations' and gravity of 'cases' within a situation. According to the prosecutor, a 'case' is defined as

> [c]omprising one or more alleged suspects and one or more alleged crimes within the Court's jurisdiction, while "situation" is a broader concept referring to a territorial and temporal context in which such crimes have allegedly been committed.[145]

In assessing gravity when it comes to sexual offences by UN military personnel, we first need to ask are we looking at a particular 'situation', which may require the choosing of a particular geographic area, or are we referring to 'cases' within a situation that has or may in the future be referred to the ICC or where the prosecutor may act *proprio motu*?

14.1.4.1. Quantitative

The prosecutor's approach to gravity in the selection of situations and cases appears to have been hinged to date primarily on a quantitative assessment of numbers of victims.[146] This approach has been criticised by

---

[143] Stegmiller, 2009, p. 550, see *supra* note 132.

[144] ICC Statute, Article 53(2)(c), see *supra* note 23.

[145] ICC, Office of the Prosecutor, Draft for Discussion: Criteria for Selection of Situations and Cases, 1 June 2006, quoted in deGuzman, 2009, p. 1409, fn. 35, see *supra* note 128.

[146] See, for example, ICC, Statement by Luis Moreno-Ocampo, Prosecutor of the International Criminal Court, Fourth Session of the Assembly of States Parties, The Hague, 28 November 2005.

numerous legal commentators.[147] That stated, the prosecutor's approach to attacks on peacekeepers has taken a different trajectory. In his response to the communication received on crimes within the jurisdiction of the court allegedly committed by British forces in Iraq, the prosecutor took a quantitative approach. He stated that while the crimes committed could reasonably be believed to fall with the ICC's jurisdiction, the "estimated 4 to 12 victims of wilful killing and a limited number of victims of inhuman treatment, totalling in all less than 20 persons" was an insufficient basis to proceed.[148] The prosecutor stipulated that

> [t]he Statute requires an additional threshold of gravity even where the subject-matter jurisdiction is satisfied [...] as the Court is faced with multiple situations involving hundreds or thousands of crimes [...].[149]

It was noted that a key factor to be considered in assessing gravity is the number of victims. The prosecutor proceeded to compare the number of victims of crimes by British forces in Iraq, which in his view were simply not comparable to the hundreds or thousands of victims of serious crimes in other situations under investigation by the Office of the Prosecutor, including northern Uganda, the DRC and Darfur.[150]

He did not consider the overall situation in Iraq, but only the conduct of British troops, bearing in mind Britain is a state party to the ICC Statute and Iraq is not.[151] Other factors that might feed into the gravity of particular conduct were not assessed, such as 'social alarm' – manner in which offences were committed; the impact of the crimes and other potentially aggravating factors.[152]

---

[147] William A. Schabas, "Prosecutorial Discretion v. Judicial Activism at the International Criminal Court", in *Journal of International Criminal Justice*, 2008, vol. 6, no. 4, pp. 731, 743; Heller, 2010, see *supra* note 43.

[148] ICC, Office of the Prosecutor, Communication Concerning the Situation in Iraq, 9 February 2006, p. 8 ('ICC, Iraq Communication').

[149] *Ibid.*

[150] *Ibid.*

[151] Note that Iraq was not a state party, and unless it accepted the ICC's jurisdiction or the Secruity Council had referred the situation, the prosecutor could only look at the situation insofar as it related to British troops, or other states parties to the ICC Statute deployed in Iraq.

[152] The sentencing judgments of the *ad hoc* tribunals may provide some guidance as to what factors might render conduct more or less "grave".

The prosecutor has been criticised for placing too much emphasis on the quantity of victims in assessing gravity, and for inconsistency in doing so. William A. Schabas argues that the prosecutor's comparison of the situation of British forces in the Iraq to the DRC and Uganda is questionable in so far as quantitatively the number of deaths was possibly much higher in Iraq since the war commenced. He argues that a comparison of 'situations' would have revealed as much.[153] Margaret deGuzman posits that what is required by the text of the ICC Statute is some form of gravity threshold (that is, "not of *sufficient* gravity to justify further action") rather than a comparison of situations.[154]

With respect to war crimes, in responding to the Iraq communication, the prosecutor expressed the contention that the terms "*in particular* when committed as part of a plan or policy or as part of a large-scale commission of such crimes*" in Article 8(1) of the ICC Statute, while not an element of the crime, provide guidance to the types of situations that ought to be examined by the ICC.[155] The ICC Appeals Chamber has since held that such a position fails to distinguish between war crimes and crimes against humanity.[156]

Even if the prosecutor takes a quantitative approach in assessing the gravity of situations it is plausible that a case involving serious sexual offences by UN military peacekeepers could arise within a current or future situation. The prosecutor could exercise his discretionary powers in making a relative assessment of gravity within a situation.[157] For instance, 132 sexual abuse and exploitation allegations involving United Nations Organization Stabilization Mission in the Democratic Republic of the Congo ('MONUSCO') military personnel, including military observers, have

---

[153] See Schabas, 2008, p. 747, *supra* note 147.

[154] DeGuzman, 2009, p. 1432, see *supra* note 128.

[155] ICC, Iraq Communication, p. 8, see *supra* note 148. Beyond the quantitative dimension, the prosecutor might also consider the geographic and temporal scope crimes, which is also suggested by the terms 'in particular'. ICC, Office of the Prosecutor, Policy Paper on Preliminary Examinations, 1 November 2013, pp. 13–14 (http://www.legal-tools.org/doc/acb906/). See also deGuzman, 2009, p. 1451, *supra* note 128.

[156] ICC, Situation in the DRC, Judgment, para. 70, see *supra* note 93.

[157] DeGuzman argues that this is distinct from an assessment of gravity under admissibility as the case may be of sufficient gravity to be admissible, but that the prosecutor may choose to prioritise cases within the situation on the basis of relative gravity to other cases within that same situation: DeGuzman, 2009, pp. 1432–35, see *supra* note 128.

been made since 2007.[158] One hundred and eight incidents of sexual abuse and exploitation have been substantiated by the UN since 2007 with respect to this mission alone. Since 2008 at least 75 of these allegations have involved minors.[159] There is little further information on the actual action that was taken by troop-contributing countries or detail as to the exact nature of the allegations.[160] Nevertheless, it could be argued, in the context of the DRC situation at least, that sexual abuse and exploitation by UN military peacekeepers is quantitatively high. That stated, the question remains whether – even if many of these acts could be consider war crimes or crimes against humanity – they of sufficient gravity to warrant investigation and/or prosecution by the ICC, considering the fact that thousands of Congolese women and children are raped every year.[161] It is this author's contention that if the ICC prosecutor and/or Pre-Trial Chamber focus on quantity of victims, sexual violence by UN peacekeepers is unlikely to be considered to be of sufficient gravity to warrant investigation or prosecution by the ICC.

Kevin Jon Heller notes comparisons of the seriousness of crimes are frequently made in domestic criminal law systems and international tribunals.[162] He argues that it is more logical to take a "category-based" as opposed to a quantitative approach, as "[a]n approach to gravity that focuses solely on enumerated acts thus fails to capture the specific factor that transforms an 'ordinary' domestic crime into a more serious international crime".[163] This approach has also been suggested by a number of legal commentators.[164] If the prosecutor were to take this approach it might al-

---

[158] There is no further data on the categories of such personnel and the actual types of offences involved.

[159] Numerous other investigations are pending. With respect to allegations across all UN missions since 2007, the UN has issued 330 *notes verbales* to troop-contributing countries, but has only received a total of 86 responses. Prior to 2008 statistics on the age of victims was not consolidated.

[160] See Conduct in UN Field Missions web site (https://conduct.unmissions.org/).

[161] Some studies suggesting that the figure could be as great as 1,150 women between 15 and 49 years being raped every day. Amber Peterman, Tia Palermo and Caryn Bredenkamp, "Estimates and Determinants of Sexual Violence Against Women in the Democratic Republic of the Congo", in *American Journal of Public Health*, 2011, vol. 101, no. 6, pp. 1060, 1064.

[162] Heller, 2010, p. 230, see *supra* note 43.

[163] *Ibid.*, p. 231.

[164] Katy Glassborow, "Sexual Violence in DRC: ICC Investigative Strategy Under Fire", Institute for War and Peace Reporting, 17 October 2008.

---

low greater focus to be placed on serious sexual offences committed by UN military peacekeepers.

14.1.4.2. Social Alarm

'Social alarm' has been highlighted by a number of legal commentators as a factor that might be taken into account in assessing gravity.[165] Heller posits that "social alarm is a function of how widely a crime is committed; the more global the crime, the greater the social alarm it creates in the international community".[166] The *Lubanga* Pre-Trial Chamber first introduced the notion of 'social alarm'.[167] It stated that in making a gravity assessment at the admissibility phase the Court will look at whether the conduct is either systematic or widespread; the most senior leaders in the situation; the individual's role; and the 'social alarm' caused to the international community.[168] It then stated that the enlistment of children, under 15 years, into armed groups causes such 'social alarm'.[169] However, it did not elaborate on why 'social alarm' should be taken into account.[170]

The Appeals Chamber in a 2006 decision concerning *Bosco Ntaganda*, rejected the notion of 'social alarm' as a factor that should be considered in assessing gravity given that it does not appear in the ICC Statute, and that such an assessment is subjective.[171] That stated, the Preamble of the ICC Statute does provide that "the most serious crimes of concern to the international community as a whole must not go unpunished" and refers to "atrocities that deeply shock the conscience of humanity".[172] According to the Oxford English Dictionary 'alarm' is defined as to "make

---

[165] See, generally, Heller, 2010, p. 227, *supra* note 43.

[166] *Lubanga* Decision, para. 46, see *supra* note 135.

[167] *Ibid.*

[168] *Ibid.*, para. 64.

[169] *Ibid.*, paras. 65–66.

[170] See contrary opinion in the Lubanga Appeals Chamber. The Appeals Chamber was of the view that the PTC was incorrect in its application of Article 17(1)(d): ICC, Situation in the DRC, Judgment, para. 3, *supra* note 93. El Zeidy describes 'social alarm' as a "weird novelty" of the PTC: See Mohamed M. El Zeidy, *The Principle of Complementarity in International Criminal Law: Origin, Development and Practice*, Martinus Nijhoff Publishers, Leiden, 2008, p. 45.

[171] ICC, Situation in the DRC, Judgment, para. 72, see *supra* note 93.

[172] ICC Statute, Articles 1 and 5, *supra* note 23.

(someone) feel frightened, disturbed, or in danger".[173] 'Concern' is defined as to "make (someone) anxious or worried".[174] The idea of causing anxiety or fear in the international community as a whole or shocking "the conscience of humanity" therefore arguably is suggested by the Preamble.

'Social alarm' as a category is interesting for our purposes, as it gives rise to the question: does the international community consider UN peacekeeper complicity in rape, sex trafficking, sex with children, and other forms serious sexual abuse "alarming"? Does it cause "concern to the international community as a whole"? And does such conduct "deeply shock the conscience of humanity"? Presumably the enlisting of children into armed groups alarms or concerns the international community because of their age, but so too should sex with children under the age of 15. In the Special Court for Sierra Leone's ('SCSL') view children under the age of 15 are particularly vulnerable and age adds to gravity of offences.[175] That said, the prioritisation by the prosecutor of recruitment of child soldiers over what many Congolese locals considered graver atrocities occurring in the DRC caused considerable discontent in the local population.[176]

14.1.4.3. Perpetrator's Seniority and Role in Crime

The Pre-Trial Chamber in *Lubanga* also stated that in assessing gravity focus ought to be placed on the "most senior leaders" in a situation. In its view the greatest deterrent value of the Court is in focusing on those best placed to prevent systematic or large-scale crime.[177] The prosecutor in 2003 and 2006 policy papers stipulated that he or she will "focus its investigative and prosecutorial efforts and resources on those who bear the greatest responsibility, such as leaders of the State or organisation alleg-

---

[173] Oxford English Dictionary.

[174] *Ibid.*

[175] Special Court for Sierra Leone ('SCSL'), *Prosecutor v. Issa Hassan Sesay, Morris Kallon and Augustine Gbao*, Trial Chamber, Sentencing Judgment, SCSL-04-15-T, 8 April 2009, paras. 172–188, 204 (http://www.legal-tools.org/doc/f7fbfc/).

[176] On basis of interview conducted by author with the UN Public Information and Outreach Office based in the DRC. Elena Baylis, "Reassessing the Role of International Criminal Law: Rebuilding National Courts through Transnational Networks", in *Boston College Law Review*, 2009, vol. 50, no. 1, pp. 1, 21.

[177] ICC, Situation in the DRC, Judgment, paras. 54–55, see *supra* note 93.

edly responsible or those crimes".[178] However, the ICC Statute requires the Court to concentrate on the "most serious crimes of concern to the international community". This does not necessarily equate to the "most senior leaders".[179] The ICC Appeals Chamber criticised the Pre-Trial Chamber's approach. In its view "the deterrent effect of the Court is highest if no category of perpetrators is *per se* is excluded from potentially being brought before the Court".[180] Furthermore, it stated that focusing only on the most senior leaders would achieve neither retribution nor prevention.[181] In essence it would prevent it from looking at lower-level perpetrators.[182]

In a 2005 statement, the prosecutor highlighted the need to prosecute "those who bear the greatest responsibility for the most serious crimes" as "[i]t is not feasible to bring charges against all apparent perpetrators".[183] However, in its 2003 policy paper the prosecutor noted that sometimes "[t]he focus of an investigation [...] may go wider than high-ranking officers if, for example, investigation of certain types of crimes or those officers lower down the chain of command is necessary for the whole case".[184] DeGuzman correctly observes that factors feeding into the gravity assessment that relate to the perpetrator can logically only relate to the selection of cases, and not situations.[185]

If the perpetrator's role in the commission of a crime is only marginal it is unlikely that he or she would be brought before the ICC.[186] Article 53(1)(c) supports this contention in so far as the prosecutor may find

---

[178] ICC, Office of the Prosecutor, Paper on Some Policy Issues before the Office of the Prosecutor, 5 September 2003, p. 7 ('ICC, Office of the Prosecutor, Policy Issues') (http://www.legal-tools.org/doc/f53870/).

[179] The Pre-Trial Chamber has been subject to criticism for focus on senior leaders for setting too high a threshold. See, for example, Stegmiller, 2009, pp. 547, 551, *supra* note 132.

[180] ICC, Situation in the DRC, Judgment, paras. 73, 76, see *supra* note 93.

[181] *Ibid.*, para. 74.

[182] The Appeals Chamber further criticised the *Lubanga* Pre-Trial Chamber for drawing on the practice of the ICTY and Rule 11*bis* in justifying this approach, while ignoring the fact the ICTY's approach occurred within the context of its completion strategy. *Ibid.*, paras. 54–55; Schabas, 2008, p. 746, see *supra* note 147; Stegmiller, 2009, p. 552, see *supra* note 132.

[183] Ocampo Statement, p. 5, see *supra* note 127.

[184] ICC, Office of the Prosecutor, Policy Issues, see *supra* note 178.

[185] DeGuzman, 2009, p. 1451, see *supra* note 128.

[186] *Ibid.*, p. 1454.

it not in the 'interests of justice' to proceed with the prosecution of such an individual.[187]

The UN contingent commanders are unlikely to ever order the commission of sexual offences by their troops. A commander could not realistically be held to be among those most responsible for failure to discipline crimes by troops that are not related to official duties, given that only contingent commanders or the troop-contributing country can exercise any criminal or disciplinary control over troops. It could be argued that a contingent commander's failure to hold perpetrators to account could lead to some level of responsibility, but it seems unlikely that such a failure would warrant him being brought before the ICC. The seniority and role of the perpetrator with respect to sexual violence committed by peacekeepers might perhaps be more relevant in situations such as trafficking or sexual slavery, or where individuals act in concert.

14.1.4.4. Impact of Crimes

The nature of crimes and their impact on victims and the greater community might also feed into an assessment of gravity.[188] Regulation 29(2) of the Office of the Prosecutor's 2009 Regulations provides that:

> [i]n order to assess the gravity of the crimes allegedly committed in the *situation* the Office shall consider various factors including their scale, nature, manner of commission, and impact.[189]

---

[187] ICC Statute, Article 53(1)(c), see *supra* note 23; Morten Bergsmo and Pieter Kruger, "Investigation and Prosecution", in Otto Triffterer (ed.), *Commentary on the Rome Statute of the International Criminal Court: Observers' Notes, Article by Article*, Hart Publishing, Oxford, 2008, pp. 1065, 1073.

[188] Luis Moreno-Ocampo, "Keynote Address: Integrating the Work of the ICC into Local Justice Initiatives", in *American University International Law Review*, vol. 21, no. 4, 2006, pp. 497, 498.

[189] ICC, Regulations of the Office of the Prosecutor, ICC-BD/05-01-09, 23 April 2009 (http://www.legal-tools.org/doc/a97226/). Rod Rastan states that factors the prosecutor is likely to take into account when assessing gravity include "severity; scale; systematicity; impact; and particularly aggravating aspects": Rod Rastan, "The Power of the Prosecutor in Initiating Investigations", Paper at Symposium on the International Criminal Court, Beijing, 3–4 February 2007.

These factors are recognised as being equally applicable to both situations and cases.[190] The Office of the Prosecutor has stated that it will not attempt any prioritisation of these factors when assessing gravity.[191] The prosecutor on a number of occasions has noted that consideration will be given to the "impact of crimes on the community and on regional peace and security".[192] Additional factors that might feed into impact include "crimes committed with the aim or consequence of increasing the vulnerability of civilians' or to spread terror".[193] According to the prosecutor "[t]his factor includes attacks on persons involved in humanitarian assistance and peacekeeping missions".[194]

It remains to be seen how impact will be interpreted.[195] Stegmiller posits that 'impact' could be understood in two ways: 1) "community-related" impact; and 2) "victim-orientated impact".[196] If impact is to be understood as "community-related", sexual offences by UN peacekeepers may well undermine international peace and security, and UN mission mandates given the effect such can have on relationships with local populations. Furthermore, such abuse can undermine efforts to re-establish the rule of law in conflict and post-conflict states. On the other hand, if impact is "victim-orientated" then sexual abuse and exploitation can have a profound psychological, physical and social impact on victims, and cause further fear and distrust in their communities. The prosecutor, in a statement to the Security Council, appeared to link impact with deterrence, stating that in assessing gravity amongst the factors it will take into ac-

---

[190] ICC, Office of the Prosecutor, ICC Prosecutorial Strategy 2009–2012, 1 February 2010, p. 20 (http://www.legal-tools.org/doc/6ed914/); Kai Ambos, *The Colombian Peace Process and the Principle of Complementarity of the International Criminal Court*, Springer, Heidelberg, 2010, p. 45.

[191] ICC, Office of the Prosecutor, Criteria for Selection of Situations and Cases 4–5 (Draft for Discussion), June 2006 ('Draft Criteria for Selection'), cited in Schabas, 2008, pp. 736–48, see *supra* note 147.

[192] *Ibid.* cited in Ambos, 2010, p. 46, see *supra* note 190; Ocampo Statement, p. 6, see *supra* note 127.

[193] ICC, Office of the Prosecutor, Policy Paper on Preliminary Examinations, p. 15, see *supra* note 155.

[194] Draft Criteria for Selection, p. 742, see *supra* note 191; Ocampo Statement, p. 6, see *supra* note 127.

[195] Ambos notes that there is some resemblance between 'impact' and 'social alarm'. Ambos, 2010, p. 46, see *supra* note 190.

[196] Stegmiller, 2009, p. 561, see *supra* note 132.

count is "the impact of ICC investigations and prosecutions in the prevention of further crimes".[197] Impact has been linked to the seriousness of
attacks on peacekeepers as they are mandated to protect civilians and that
such attacks could affect millions under the protection of such personnel.[198] Sexual abuse and exploitation could also undermine the security of
UN missions and their ability to achieve mission mandates.

14.1.4.5. Manner of Commission

Finally, manner of commission of crimes is a factor that may feed into
gravity. In the 2010 draft Policy Paper on Preliminary Examinations the
Office of the Prosecutor noted a number of factors relevant to the "manner
of commission" of a crime, including:

> the means employed to execute the crime, the degree of par-
> ticipation and intent in its commission, the extent to which
> the crimes were systematic or result from a plan or organized
> policy or otherwise resulted from the abuse of power or offi-
> cial capacity, and elements of particular cruelty, including
> the vulnerability of the victims, any motives involving dis-
> crimination, or the use of rape and sexual violence as a
> means of destroying communities.[199]

Probably the most relevant aspects to sexual abuse and exploitation by
UN military peacekeepers are the elements of "abuse of power or official
capacity", in addition to the "vulnerability of the victims". This has been
addressed previously.[200]

14.1.4.6. Conclusion

What renders sexual offences by UN peacekeeping personnel particularly
grave is that it violates the relationship of trust between the UN and the

---

[197] UN, Security Council, Reports of the Secretary-General on the Sudan, UN Doc. S/PV.5459,
14 June 2006, p. 2.

[198] ICC, Statement by Mr. Luis Moreno Ocampo, Prosecutor of the International Criminal Court,
to the United Nations Security Council pursuant to UNSCR 1593 (2005), 5 June 2006, p. 2.

[199] ICC, Office of the Prosecutor, Policy Paper on Preliminary Examinations, p. 14, see *supra*
note 155. The prosecutor, in the 2006 Policy Paper, noted that abuse of power might be relevant to gravity; Draft Criteria for Selection, p. 5, cited in deGuzman, 2009, p. 1453, see *supra*
note 128; Schabas, 2008, p. 742, see *supra* note 147.

[200] *Ibid.*, pp. 7–8.

local civilian population. The gravity of crimes by peacekeepers, akin to the gravity of crimes against peacekeepers, rests in their special role as protectors of international peace and security. They are often specifically mandated to protect civilian populations and promote respect for human rights.[201]

It is worth noting that the ICC charged two rebel leaders, Abdallah Banda Abkaer Nourain and Saleh Mohammed Jerbo Jamus, with war crimes for attacks on African Union peacekeepers in Darfur, which resulted in the deaths of 12 and the injuring of eight peacekeepers.[202] It found that

> the consequences of the alleged attack on MGS Haskanita were grave both for the direct victims of it [...] and for the local population, in light or the initial suspension and ultimate reduction of AMIS activities in the area as a result [...].[203]

Similarly, not only do sexual abuse and exploitation by UN military peacekeepers violate the victim directly it also undermines the broader mission mandate. Whole contingents have had to be repatriated due to sexual abuse and exploitation allegations. To ignore the seriousness of these crimes, ignores not only the abhorrent nature of these offences but also undermines international peace and security, and puts the physical security of other peacekeepers at risk.[204]

---

[201] See also UN security Council, Report of the Secretary General on the United Nations Interim Administration in Kosovo, UN Doc. S/1999/779, 12 July 1999, para. 35; David B. Hodgkinson *et al.*, "Human Rights Training to Law Enforcement Agents: A Key to PSO Success", in Roberta Arnold (ed.), *Law Enforcement in the Framework of Peace Support Operations*, Martinus Nijhoff Publishers, Leiden, 2008, p. 317. The promotion and encouragement of respect for international human rights law is also embedded in the Preamble and Articles 1(4), 55(c) of the UN Charter, see *supra* note 113.

[202] ICC, *Prosecutor v. Abdallah Banda Abkaer Nourain and Saleh Mohammed Jerbo Jamus*, Pre-Trial Chamber, Decision on the Confirmation of Charges, 02/05-03/09, 7 March 2011 (http://www.legal-tools.org/doc/5ac9eb/).

[203] *Ibid.*, para. 27.

[204] UN General Assembly, Criminal Accountability of United Nations Officials and Experts on Mission: Note by the Secretariat, UN Doc. A/62/329, 11 September 2007, paras. 11–12 ('Criminal Accountability Note'); see also ICC, Office of the Prosecutor, Eighth Report Security Council to the Security Council pursuant to UNSCR 1593 (2005), 3 December 2008, para. 9, pp. 55–56.

That stated, it must be borne in mind that the prosecutor was grant-ed discretion in the selection of situations and cases in recognition of the fact that it is not feasible for the ICC to investigate and prosecute each and every incident coming within the jurisdiction of the Court.[205] The prose-cutor receives hundreds of communications each year. Presently, the ICC has only six situations and 10 cases before it. One of the primary ration-ales for the insertion of gravity, as an additional element to be considered, was to avoid overburdening the Court with cases.[206] While sexual abuse and exploitation by UN peacekeepers are abhorrent, it seems that the prosecutor is unlikely to consider such cases of sufficient gravity, in par-ticular should it focus on the quantity of victims or solely senior leaders. Arguably 'social alarm' and 'impact of crimes' might leave greater scope for the Court to pursue such cases, as might a category-based approach. It is this author's contention, however, that even were such an approach tak-en cases of sexual abuse and exploitation by UN peacekeepers are likely to overcome the gravity threshold.

14.1.5. Prosecutorial Discretion: Other Considerations

In addition to considerations of gravity as an element of prosecutorial dis-cretion several other factors come into play. As the prosecutor has noted, other considerations that might feed into selecting situations or cases may include: legal, budgetary, strategic, the ability to take the suspect into cus-tody,[207] the likelihood of state co-operation, the ability to gather evidence, and so on.[208] Political considerations may well influence the workings of

---

[205] Matthew R. Brubacher, "Prosecutorial Discretion within the International Criminal Court", in *Journal of International Criminal Law*, 2004, vol. 2, no. 1, pp. 71, 75.

[206] See further, Susana SáCouto and Katherine Cleary, "The Gravity Threshold of the Interna-tional Criminal Court", in *American University International Law Review*, 2008, vol. 23, no. 5, p. 807.

[207] There is a suggestion that this was a factor that played into the decision to charge Lubanga. See further James Goldston, "More Candour about Criteria: The Exercise of Discretion by the Prosecutor of the International Criminal Court", in *Journal of International Criminal Jus-tice*, 2010, vol. 8, no. 2, pp. 383, 394–95.

[208] This list is merely illustrative. See further SáCouto and Cleary, 2008, *supra* note 206; Darryl Robinson, "Serving the Interests of Justice: Amnesties, Truth Commissions and the Interna-tional Criminal Court", in *European Journal of International Law*, 2003, vol. 14, no. 3, p. 488.

the Court, in particular given its reliance on state co-operation.[209] As stated by Luis Moreno-Ocampo:

> there seems to be a paradox: the ICC is independent and interdependent at the same time. It cannot act alone. It will achieve efficiency only if it works closely with other members of the international community.[210]

It is not hard to imagine that these factors would feature heavily were the prosecutor to decide pursue a case against UN military personnel for complicity in sexual abuse and exploitation.

Article 53 (1) and (2) of the ICC Statute also permits the prosecutor to exercise his or her discretion not to proceed with an investigation on the basis of the 'interests of justice'.[211] When making a decision to investigate the prosecutor, under Article 53(1)(c), must take "into account the gravity of the crime and the interests of victims". Under Article 53(2)(c) when deciding not to proceed with a prosecution, on the basis of the 'interests of justice', the prosecutor must weigh this against the "gravity of the crime, the interests of victims and the age or infirmity of the alleged perpetrator, and his or her role in the alleged crime".[212]

The ICC Statute does not define what the 'interests of justice' mean. The Office of the Prosecutor has noted that a clear definition is not appropriate as situations differ.[213] The OTP stated that the exercise of prosecutorial discretion with respect to the 'interests of justice' is excep-

---

[209] ICC Statute, Articles 86 and 99(1), 57(3)(d), see *supra* note 23.

[210] ICC, Office of the Prosecutor, Statement by Mr. Luis Moreno-Ocampo, Ceremony for the Solemn Undertaking of the Chief Prosecutor of the International Criminal Court, The Hague, 16 June 2003 ('Moreno-Ocampo Statement, 16 June 2003').

[211] ICC Statute, Article 53(1) and (2), see *supra* note 23.

[212] The Pre-Trial Chamber, however, may review decisions made solely on the basis of the 'interests of justice'. Pursuant to Article 53(3)(a) a referring state can request the Pre-Trial Chamber to review a decision made the prosecutor not to proceed with an investigation or prosecution and may ask it to reconsider. The Pre-Trial Chamber may also do so on its initiative if the prosecutor's decision is based solely on the 'interests of justice'. See ICC Statute, Article 53(3)(b), *supra* note 23. See also ICC, Office of the Prosecutor, Policy Paper on the Interests of Justice, September 2007, pp. 6–9 ('Policy Paper on the Interests of Justice') (http://www.legal-tools.org/doc/bb02e5/).

[213] Policy Paper on the Interests of Justice, p. 1, see *supra* note 212. See also Héctor Olásolo, "The Prosecutor of the ICC before the Initiation of Investigations: A Quasi-Judicial or a Political Body", in *International Criminal Law Review*, 2003, vol. 3, no. 2, pp. 87, 141 (http://www.legal-tools.org/doc/68494b/).

tional, and that it will be guided in making such decisions by the objectives and purposes of the ICC Statute. It highlighted that in its view there is a distinction between the 'interests of justice' and the 'interests of peace', and that it must only consider the former.[214] Conversely, Schabas argues that the drafting history of the ICC Statute shows no evidence that the 'interests of justice' was supposed to be distinct from the 'interests of peace'.[215] Taking Schabas's approach the Prosecutor would have to consider whether prosecution of UN peacekeeping personnel is in the 'interests of justice', in particular given the broader implications it could have on peace and security.[216] As stated, the reaction of troop-contributing countries could be to refuse to contribute troops to future UN peacekeeping operations.[217] The 'interests of justice' could therefore serve as an additional impediment to prosecution of peacekeepers for sexual abuse and exploitation by the ICC.

14.1.6. Complementarity and Its Implications

A foundational principle of the ICC is that it is to operate on the basis of complementarity, wherein states have primary jurisdiction over crimes under its jurisdiction. Complementarity is not a new concept, unique to the ICC.[218] It appears to be derived from two streams of thought, the principles of *aut dedere aut judicare*,[219] and subsidiarity in European Union

---

[214] Policy Paper on the Interests of Justice, pp. 1, 3, 4, see *supra* note 212.

[215] Schabas, 2008, p. 749, see *supra* note 147.

[216] Brubacher argues that the 'interests of justice' "requires the Prosecutor to take account of the broader interests of the international community, including the potential political ramifications of an investigation on the political environment of the state over which he is exercising jurisdiction": Brubacher, 2004, see *supra* note 205.

[217] Any decision of the prosecutor to proceed in such circumstances could however be counterbalanced by UN Security Council powers to defer case under ICC Statute, Article 16.

[218] On the history of the principle of complementarity and its development, see Mohamed M. El Zeidy, "The Principle of Complementarity: A New Machinery to Implement International Criminal Law", in *Michigan Journal of International Law*, 2002, vol. 23, no. 4, p. 870; El Zeidy, 2008, *supra* note 170.

[219] M. Cherif Bassiouni, *Introduction to International Criminal Law*, Transnational Publishers, Ardsley, NY, 2003, p. 314; William Burke-White, "Implementing a Policy of Positive Complementarity in the Rome System of Justice", in *Criminal Law Forum*, 2008, vol. 19, no. 1, pp. 59, 62, 65–66; Geert-Jan G.J. Knoops, *Surrendering to the International Criminal Courts: Contemporary Practice and Procedure*, Transnational Publishers, Ardsley, NY, 2002, p. 314.

---

law.[220] The principle of complementarity is primarily set out in Article 17 of the ICC Statute. However, the actual term 'complementarity' does not appear in the Statute itself. Article 17 provides that a case must be determined to be inadmissible where:[221]

> (a) The case is being investigated or prosecuted by a State which has jurisdiction over it, unless the State is *unwilling* or *unable genuinely* to carry out the investigation or prosecution;
>
> (b) The case has been investigated by a state which has jurisdiction over it and the State has decided not to prosecute the person concerned, unless the decision resulted from the *unwillingness* or *inability* of the State *genuinely* to prosecute.

Complementarity protects the sovereign prerogative of states to prosecute crimes over which they have jurisdiction.[222] Criminal jurisdiction over military personnel is inextricably linked to notions of national sovereignty. The exercise of criminal jurisdiction by the ICC is exceptional.

Under the principle of complementarity, for a case to be admissible before the ICC, a state with jurisdiction must not be investigating or prosecuting the case, or have already investigated and decided not to prosecute, unless deemed unwilling or unable genuinely to carry out such an investigation or prosecution.[223] Any national proceedings must cover both the accused and the conduct.[224] In the context of UN peacekeeping opera-

---

[220] Subsidiarity in European Union law essentially relates to idea that the EU will step in areas where states are incapable of achieving the end on their own. It is not the scope of this chapter to deal with the relationship between these principles and complementarity. See further Nidal Nabil Jurdi, *The International Criminal Court and National Courts: A Contentious Relationship*, Ashgate, Aldershot, 2011.

[221] ICC Statute, Article 17, see *supra* note 23.

[222] *Tadić* Appeal Decision, para. 58, see *supra* note 85.

[223] Note that the revised memorandum of understanding similarly provides that the UN may commence an investigation into alleged incidents of sexual exploitation and abuse by UN military peacekeepers where the troop-contributing country proves "unwilling or unable" to do so. Such an investigation however is a preliminary, fact-finding exercise, in order to preserve evidence. The authority to prosecute remains with the troop-contributing country. For the text of the revised memorandum of understanding, see Manual on Policies and Procedures, *supra* note 16.

[224] ICC, *Prosecutor v. Bosco Ntaganda*, Pre-Trial Chamber, Annex 2 to "Decision on the Prosecutor's application for Warrants of Arrest, Article 58", ICC-01/04-02/06, 10 February 2006, para. 38 (http://www.legal-tools.org/doc/d68b07/).

tions troop-contributing countries, under UN Status of Forces Agreements, are granted exclusive criminal jurisdiction over their military personnel. Where a Status of Forces Agreement exists the host state is debarred from exercising its jurisdiction over UN military personnel.[225] Therefore any assessment of willingness and ability of a state to investigate or prosecute will relate to the troop-contributing country. A case will also be inadmissible under Article 17(1)(c) if "[t]he person concerned has already been tried for conduct which is the subject of the complaint".[226] Article 17(1)(d) provides that the case will be inadmissible if "not of sufficient gravity". This section focuses on the principle of complementarity set out in Article 17(1)(a) and (b).

Article 17 covers 'inaction', 'unwillingness' and 'inability'. Where there is 'inaction' no further analysis of willingness or ability is required for the case to be admissible.[227] When a state party refers a case to the ICC, or where the prosecutor acts *propio motu*, Article 18 of the ICC Statute requires that the prosecutor notify state parties and states that would normally exercise jurisdiction.[228] A state that ordinarily exercises jurisdiction then has one month to inform the Court that it has or is investigating. If there is no response then the adverse inference is the absence

---

[225] UN General Assembly, Model Status-of-Forces Agreement between the United Nations and Host Countries, UN Doc. A/45/594, 9 October 1990.

[226] ICC Statute, Article 17(1)(c), see *supra* note 23.

[227] ICC, Office of the Prosecutor, Informal Expert Paper on Complementarity, 2003, p. 7; ICC, *Prosecutor v. Germain Katanga and Mathieu Ngudjolo Chui*, Appeals Chamber, Judgment on the Appeal of Mr. Germain Katanga against the Oral Decision of Trial Chamber II of 12 June 2009 on the Admissibility of the Case, ICC-01/04-01/07, 25 September 2009, paras. 78–79 (http://www.legal-tools.org/doc/ba82b5/); William W. Burke-White and Scott Kaplan, "Shaping the Contours of Domestic Justice: The International Criminal Court and an Admissibility Challenge in the Ugandan Situation", in *Journal of International Criminal Justice*, 2009, vol. 7, no. 2, pp. 257, 260; Jann K. Kleffner, *Complementarity in the Rome Statute and National Criminal Jurisdictions*, Oxford University Press, Oxford, 2008, p. 103. As stated by the prosecutor in relation to Sudan, "I determined that there are cases that would be admissible in relation to the Darfur situation. This decision does not represent a determination on the Sudanese legal system as such, but is essentially a result of the absence of criminal proceedings related to the cases on which I focus"; ICC, Statement of the Prosecutor of the International Criminal Court Mr. Luis Moreno Ocampo to the Security Council pursuant to UNSCR 1593, 29 June 2005.

[228] While notification is not required when Security Council refers case presumably that process will lead to notification in practice anyway. Michael Newton, "Comparative Complementarity: Domestic Jurisdiction Consistent with the Rome Statute of the International Criminal Court", in *Military Law Review*, 2001, vol. 167, pp. 20, 55.

---

of national proceedings.[229] If the state does respond and requests the prosecutor to defer to its investigation, the prosecutor shall defer, save where the Pre-Trial Chamber nevertheless authorises an investigation. The state's proceedings are then subject to review by the prosecutor within six months or at such other time as deemed necessary.[230]

If a crime by a UN peacekeeper came under the jurisdiction of the Court the troop-contributing country would then have the opportunity to inform the Court that it is taking action and request that any investigation be deferred. Article 18 operates in a sense as an additional complementarity provision, wherein informing states gives them yet another opportunity to exert their primary jurisdiction.[231] Troop-contributing countries are required under the revised memorandum of understanding to inform the UN of any action taken against troops, yet such responses have often not been forthcoming.[232] Threat of an investigation by the ICC might well provide a greater incentive to respond.

---

[229] Informal Expert Paper on Complementarity, p. 18, see *supra* note 227. The term 'proceedings' relates to both investigations and prosecutions. ICC, Office of the Prosecutor, Update on Communication Received by the Prosecutor, Iraq Response, 9 February 2006; ICC, Office of the Prosecutor, Update on Communication Received by the Prosecutor, Venezuela Response, 9 February 2006. Jo Stigen, *The Relationship between the International Criminal Court and National Jurisdictions: The Principle of Complementarity*, Martinus Nijhoff, Leiden, 2008, p. 186. The Pre-Trial Chamber in *Lubanga* stated:

> [c]oncerning the first part of the admissibility test, [...] no State with jurisdiction over the case against Mr. Thomas Lubanga Dyilo is acting, or has acted, in relation to such case. Accordingly, in the absence of any acting State, the Chamber need not make any analysis of unwillingness or inability.

Lubanga Decision, para. 40, see *supra* note 135.

[230] ICC Statute, Article 18, see *supra* note 23.

[231] Gregory S. Gordon, "Complementarity and Alternative Justice", in *Oregon Law Review*, 2009, vol. 88, no. 3, pp. 621, 630. The requirement to inform states where it involves a Security Council referral is less apparent, although in all probability the prosecutor would nevertheless inform these states.

[232] Revised Model Memorandum of Understanding, in Manual on Policies and Procedures, see *supra* note 16. See also UN General Assembly, Manual on Policies and Procedures Concerning the Reimbursement and Control of Contingent-Owned Equipment of Troop/Police Contributors Participating in Peacekeeping Missions (COE Manual), UN Doc. A/C.5/60/26, 11 January 2006; UN General Assembly, Comprehensive Review of a Strategy to Eliminate Future Sexual Exploitation and Abuse in United Nations Peacekeeping Operations, UN Doc. A/C.4/61/L.21, 28 June 2007. While troop-contributing countries are supposed to provide feedback to the UN on action taken against those complicit in sex-

---

Article 20(3) of the ICC Statute provides that the ICC cannot prosecute if an individual has already been tried by another court, unless the prior trial was conducted for the purpose of "shielding" the perpetrator from criminal responsibility or

> [o]therwise was not conducted independently or impartially [...] and were conducted in a manner which, in the circumstances, was inconsistent with the intent to bring the person concerned to justice.[233]

This is incorporated into the admissibility criteria under Article 17(3).[234]

14.1.6.1. 'Genuinely' Investigate and Prosecute

Article 17 requires the state to conduct an investigation or prosecution 'genuinely'.[235] The question arises as to how the genuineness of an investigation or prosecution is to be assessed. The Oxford English Dictionary definition of 'genuine' is "having the supposed character, not a sham or feigned".[236] Some authors argue that the term is analogous to the concept of good faith.[237] The term 'genuine' was favoured over 'effective' or 'efficient' by the drafters of the ICC Statute, given that it was less specific.[238] It was intended to allow for a degree of flexibility.[239] According to an informal expert paper on complementarity, the term 'genuinely' should be applied both to 'unwillingness' and 'inability'. So either the state is

---

ual exploitation and abuse, responses have only been forthcoming in a minority of incidents. See further, UN General Assembly, Revised draft model memorandum of understanding between the United Nations and [participating State] contributing resources to [the United Nations Peacekeeping Operation], Note by the Secretary-General, UN Doc. A/61/494, 3 October 2006, pp. 14–15.

[233] ICC Statute, Articles 20(3)(a) and (b), see *supra* note 23.

[234] While this rule is contained in a number of treaties and domestic laws, it constitutes customary international law only with respect to being tried within one state or jurisdiction. Stigen, 2008, pp. 207–08, see *supra* note 229, argues that the ICC could be regarded as a "prolongation of the states parties' jurisdictions", complementing national jurisdiction.

[235] Informal Expert Paper on Complementarity, p. 8, see *supra* note 227.

[236] Oxford English Dictionary.

[237] See further El Zeidy, 2008, pp. 164–65, *supra* note 170.

[238] Xavier Philippe, "The Principles of Universal Jurisdiction and Complementarity: How Do the Two Principles Intermesh?", in *International Review of the Red Cross*, 2008, vol. 88, no. 862, pp. 375, 382.

[239] Newton, 2001, p. 54, see *supra* note 228.

genuinely unwilling or genuinely unable. 'Genuinely' has both objective and subjective elements. As Kai Ambos notes, it was intended to make the meaning of 'unwilling' or 'unable' more objective, however it nevertheless requires an assessment of whether a state acts in good faith.[240]

'Genuinely' unwilling or unable refers to the national criminal justice process as opposed to the outcome of proceedings.[241] So a state can decide not to prosecute so long as it is a result of genuineness.[242] The burden of proof in demonstrating that proceedings were not genuine will generally be on the prosecutor.[243] Proving that investigations or prosecutions by troop-contributing countries in the context of their troops' complicity in sexual abuse and exploitation are not 'genuine' would likely prove notoriously difficulty and highly politically sensitive.[244]

14.1.6.2. Unwillingness

Article 17(2) provides some clarification on when a state might be deemed 'unwilling':

    (a) The proceedings were or are being undertaken or the national decision was made for the *purpose of shielding* the person concerned from criminal responsibility for crimes within the jurisdiction of the Court referred to in Article 5;

    (b) There has been an *unjustified delay* in the proceedings which *in the circumstances is inconsistent with an intent to bring a person to justice*;

    (c) The proceedings were not or are not being *conducted independently* or *impartially*, and they were or are being conducted in a manner which, in the circumstances, is inconsistent with an *intent* to bring the person concerned to justice.

---

[240] Ambos, 2010, pp. 64–65, see *supra* note 190.

[241] Stigen, 2008, pp. 216–17, see *supra* note 256.

[242] *Ibid.*, p. 217. See also El Zeidy, 2008, p. 166, *supra* note 170.

[243] Informal Expert Paper on Complementarity, p. 17, see *supra* note 227.

[244] Sharon Williams and William Schabas, "Article 17", in Otto Triffterer (ed.), *Commentary on the Rome Statute of the International Criminal Court: Observers' Notes, Article by Article*, Hart Publishing, Oxford, 2008, pp. 605, 617.

'Unwillingness' according to the Oxford Dictionary means "not intending, purposing, or desiring (to do a particular thing)".[245] Making a determination of 'unwillingness' will obviously be politically sensitive, and will involve at least some subjectivity. It requires an assessment of the 'intent' of the state and the concept of 'good faith' and the 'purpose' of national decisions.[246] The elements of "unjustified delay" and "independently or impartially" require a more objective assessment.[247]

14.1.6.2.1. Shielding

Article 17(2)(a) provides that the Court shall consider whether proceedings were only conducted for the "purpose of shielding the person concerned from criminal responsibility". The question arises whether prosecuting an individual for a lesser offence can be considered as shielding.[248] In the context of UN peacekeepers and sexual abuse and exploitation, if a crime for instance meets the threshold of a war crime, and the state prosecutes the individual for a disciplinary offence, for example "conduct unbecoming of an officer and a gentleman", can this amount to shielding?[249] This would require an assessment of proceedings taken against peacekeepers by troop-contributing countries.[250] With respect to UN military peacekeeper complicity in sexual abuse and exploitation and other serious offences, investigations have often proved to be lacking, and in the past there has been evidence of efforts to frustrate proceedings and cover up evidence.[251] Such scenarios leave open the question of proceedings being conducted with the sole purpose of shielding the perpetrator from justice.

---

[245] Oxford English Dictionary.

[246] Jessica Gavron, "Amnesties in Light of Developments in International Law and the Establishment of the International Criminal Court", in *International and Comparative Law Quarterly*, 2002, vol. 51, no. 1, p. 111; Jurdi, 2011, p. 38, see *supra* note 220.

[247] Benjamin Perrin, "Making Sense of Complementarity: The Relationship between the International Criminal Court and National Jurisdictions", in *Sri Lanka Journal of International Law*, 2006, vol. 18, no. 2, pp. 301, 306.

[248] Stigen, 2008, p. 260, see *supra* note 229.

[249] United States, Uniform Code of Military Justice, 10 UCMJ 832, Article 133 ('UCMJ').

[250] Kleffner, 2008, p. 135, see *supra* note 227.

[251] UN General Assembly, Investigation by the Office of Internal Oversight into allegations of sexual exploitation and abuse in the United Nations Organisation Mission in the Democratic Republic of the Congo, UN Doc. A/59/661, 5 January 2005. This issue was highlighted, for instance, in an early 1990s inquiry into serious human rights abuses, including

The 'purpose' element is, however, difficult to prove as it involves an assessment of the state's intent. The purposive element might be demonstrated where there is written or testimonial evidence. However, it is more likely that reliance will have to be placed on circumstantial evidence. Jo Stigen suggests a list of factors that might be indicative of shielding.[252] Some of these factors might include:

1. Few if any successful investigations and prosecutions (prosecution by troop-contributing countries of sexual abuse and exploitation by UN military personnel is rare).

2. Shared purpose between the state and the suspect. It may well not either be in the interests of the troop-contributing country or the perpetrator for a prosecution to go ahead, in particular given the reluctance of states to be named and shamed.

3. Inadequate legislation. The troop-contributing country may simply not have adequate legislation covering the particular offence or ability to act extraterritorially.

4. Inadequate allocation of resources. The troop-contributing country may not have allocated sufficient resources to conduct what could prove to be costly investigations and prosecutions extraterritorially, in particular given the security environment in some mission host states.

5. Access and security of investigators, and the intimidation of actors in the proceedings.

---

the rape and torturing to death of a teenage boy, committed by Canadian UN peacekeepers deployed in Somalia. See Sherene H. Razack, *Dark Threats and White Knights: The Somalia Affair, Peacekeeping and the New Imperialism*, University of Toronto Press, Toronto, 2004.

[252] See further, Stigen, 2008, pp. 262–68, *supra* note 229. See UN General Assembly, A Comprehensive Strategy to Eliminate Future Sexual Exploitation and Abuse in United Nations Peacekeeping Operations, UN Doc. A/59/710, 24 March 2005 ('Comprehensive Strategy'). On the basis of analysis of international human rights law, El Zeidy identifies a number of other factors that might suggest an individual is being shielded by the state concerned, such as: lack of an effective or serious investigation; lack of records on the investigation; investigation of conduct of armed forces by the same armed forces; hiding reports; cover-ups; manipulation of evidence, and so on: El Zeidy, 2008, pp. 175–180, see *supra* note 170; European Court of Human Rights ('ECtHR'), *Case of Nachova and Others v. Bulgaria*, Judgment, Applications nos. 43577/98 and 43579/98, 6 July 2005, para. 113 (http://www.legal-tools.org/doc/c583fc/).

---

6. Failure to take essential investigative steps. Troop-contributing countries sometimes have failed to take any investigative steps with respect to serious crimes committed extraterritorially by their troops.

7. Inadequate collection and use of evidence. An obvious problem is that when troop-contributing countries fail to send experts on national criminal or military law and procedures any evidence gathered by UN investigative bodies. This may not meet evidentiary requirements to be admissible in troop-contributing country courts.

It has been suggested that the language of Article 17(2)(a) encompasses the situations envisaged by (b) and (c), namely "unjustified delay", "inconsistent with intent to bring the person to justice" and lack of "independence and impartiality", these merely being illustrative of might be determined an exercise in shielding.[253]

14.1.6.2.2. Unjustified Delay Inconsistent with Intent to Bring to Justice

Article 17(2)(b) provides that a state may be deemed 'unwilling' when there is an *"unjustified delay* [...] which in the circumstances is inconsistent with an *intent* to bring the person concerned to justice" (emphasis added).[254] There are three elements to this provision. First, the Court must determine that there is a delay; second, such delay must be unjustified; and third, it must be "inconsistent with the intent to bring the person concerned to justice" in the particular circumstances. The term 'unjustified' suggests that the state must be granted the opportunity to justify the delay. The term, however, is not further elaborated on in the Statute.[255] Mohamed M. El Zeidy argues that 'unjustified delay' in the context of the ICC Statute refers to the whole criminal justice process.[256] The approach of the various international human rights law bodies is that persons should be tried without 'undue delay' and 'within a reasonable time', which ought to be assessed on a case-by-case basis.[257]

---

[253] El Zeidy, 2008, p. 170, see *supra* note 170; Stigen, 2008, pp. 256–57, see *supra* note 229.

[254] ICC Statute, Article 17(2)(b), see *supra* note 23.

[255] *Ibid.*

[256] El Zeidy, 2008, pp. 183–84, see *supra* note 170.

[257] Council of Europe, European Convention for the Protection of Human Rights and Fundamental Freedoms as amended by Protocols Nos. 11 and 14, supplemented by Protocols Nos.

The difficulty with delays in proceedings, in particular when it comes to sexual offences, is that it may render witnesses or evidence unavailable. El Zeidy identifies a number of factors that might be taken into account in assessing whether a delay can be justified, namely: 1) the complexity of the case; 2) the nature of the applicants conduct during proceedings; and 3) the conduct of relevant authorities.[258] Other factors might include the size of the case and the number of victims and witnesses, or the distance between the investigative and prosecuting bodies and the witnesses and evidence, and so on. A comparative approach might be used in assessing whether delay can be justified by comparing the length of time of other national proceedings dealing with similar crimes.[259]

The use of the terms 'in the circumstances' means that the Court needs to consider the surrounding circumstances in order to ascertain the intent of the state in 'unjustifiably' delaying proceedings.[260] This relates to all parts of the proceedings. In the context of sexual abuse and exploitation by UN military peacekeepers, a certain degree of delay seems inevitable given the need to make arrangements for the investigation and prosecution of offences occurring extraterritorially, often in environments with little infrastructure, collapsed or partially collapsed criminal justice systems, and so on. Added to this, any investigation or prosecution activities occurring in the host state requires obtaining the consent of the host state. Furthermore, given the security situation, societal factors, and the nature of sexual offences, victims may be unwilling to give evidence. When delay becomes 'unjustified' in such circumstances would be difficult to demonstrate.

1, 4, 6, 7, 12 and 13, 4 November 1950, Article 6(1) ('European Convention on Human Rights') (http://www.legal-tools.org/doc/8267cb/); Organization of American States, American Convention on Human Rights, 22 November 1969, Article 8(1) (http://www.legal-tools.org/doc/1152cf/); African Union, African Charter on Human and Peoples' Rights, 1 October 1986, Article 7(1)(d) (http://www.legal-tools.org/doc/f0db44/). See further, El Zeidy, 2002, pp. 184–85, *supra* note 218; Kleffner, 2008, p. 139, *supra* note 227. ICC Statute, Article 21(3), see *supra* note 23, requires that the Statute be interpreted in line with international human rights law.

[258] El Zeidy, 2008, see *supra* note 170.

[259] *Ibid.*, p. 194.

[260] Kleffner, 2008, p. 139, see *supra* note 227.

14.1.6.2.3. Independence and Impartiality

Article 17(2)(c) deals with situations where "*proceedings* were not or are not being conducted *independently* or *impartially*". The terms 'independently or impartially' may relate to the due process rights of the accused,[261] but it seems in the context of Article 17 they have broader application, given that the lack of independence and impartiality may have the diametrically opposed result of actually working to the advantage of the accused.[262]

'Independence' generally denotes a separation of powers of investigation, prosecution and adjudication, roles which ought to be free from executive interference.[263] According to the European Court of Human Rights ('ECtHR'), 'impartiality' implies "lack of prejudice or bias".[264] 'Independence' and 'impartiality' appear to have a broader meaning under the ICC Statute than in international human rights law, as they relate to the whole of the 'proceedings', including investigative organs.[265] There is ample reference to what might constitute sufficient independence and impartiality in the context of judicial proceedings by the various international human rights law monitoring bodies and *ad hoc* criminal tribunals. El Zeidy notes that elements that might feed into an assessment of impartiality and independence might include, the independence of an adjudicating body from the executive, and "guarantees against outside pressure".[266]

---

[261] ICC Statute, Article 17, see *supra* note 23 (emphasis added). European Convention on Human Rights, Article 6(1), see *supra* note 257; American Convention on Human Rights, Article 8(1), see *supra* note 257; UN General Assembly, International Covenant on Civil and Political Rights, UN Doc. A/6316 (1966), entry into force 23 March 1976, Article 14(1), ('ICCPR') (http://www.legal-tools.org/doc/2838f3/); African Charter on Human and Peoples' Rights, Article 7(1), see *supra* note 257. See further Kevin Jon Heller, "The Shadow Side of Complementarity: The Effect of Article 17 of the Rome Statute on National Due Process", in *Criminal Law Forum*, 2006, vol. 17, p. 255.

[262] For a detailed discussion of what independence and impartiality might entail, in particular in light of the jurisprudence of the various international human rights law monitoring bodies, see El Zeidy, 2002, pp. 196–203, *supra* note 218; Kleffner, 2008, p. 130, *supra* note 227.

[263] Stigen, 2008, pp. 300–01, see *supra* note 229.

[264] ECtHR, *Case of Piersack v. Belgium*, Judgment, Series no. 53, 26 October 1984, cited in William A. Schabas, "The Rights to a Fair Trail", in Flavia Lattanzi and William A. Schabas (eds.), *Essays on the Rome Statute of the International Criminal Court*, vol. 2, Editrice il Sirente, Ripa di Fagnano Alto, 2003, pp. 90, 276.

[265] Stigen, 2008, p. 300, see *supra* note 229.

[266] El Zeidy, 2002, pp. 202–03, see *supra* note 218.

Military courts have been widely criticised for their lack of independence and impartiality.[267] The ECtHR noted on a number of occasions that independence includes "[n]ot only a lack of hierarchical or institutional connection but also practical independence".[268] Military disciplinary proceedings or courts martial may give rise to questions of impartiality and independence given the hierarchical structure under which such proceedings tend to operate. This is relevant for our purposes as many UN military peacekeepers complicit in sexual offences may be subject to such proceedings.[269]

14.1.6.2.4. Conclusion

The ICC's Rules of Procedure and Evidence lend some interpretative guidance as to when a state may be deemed 'unwilling'. States may provide the ICC with information on the national justice system and processes, which can feed into an assessment of 'unwilling' or 'unable'.[270] Evaluations of 'unwillingness' with respect to the investigation and prosecution of UN military peacekeepers would have to be made on a case-by-

---

[267] John McKenzie, "A Fair and Public Trial", in Eugene R. Fidell and Dwight H. Sullivan (eds.), *Evolving Military Justice*, Naval Institute Press, Annapolis, 2002, p. 230; UN Commission on Human Rights, Report of the Special Rapporteur on the Independence of Lawyers and Judges, Report of Mission to Columbia, UN Doc. E/CN.4/1998/39/Add.2, 30 March 1998. The Human Rights Committee, in its Concluding Observations on Guatemala, highlighted that the wide jurisdiction of the military court there "to hear all cases involving the trial of military personnel and their powers to decide cases that belong to the ordinary courts contribute to the impunity enjoyed by such personnel and prevent their punishment for serious human rights violations": UN Human Rights Committee, Concluding Observations of the Human Rights Committee, Republic of Guatemala, CCPR/CO/72/GTM, 27 August 2001, para. 20, cited in Stigen, 2008, p. 308, see *supra* note 229.

[268] In the *Hugh Jordan* case before the ECtHR, the Court found that there was lack of insufficient impartiality given the hierarchal link between those police officers under investigation and those conducting it, and those instituting disciplinary or criminal proceedings: ECtHR, *Hugh Jordan v. United Kingdom*, Judgment, Application no. 24746/94, 4 May 2001, para. 120. See also ECtHR, *Finucane v. United Kingdom*, Judgment (Merits and Just Satisfaction), Application no. 29178/95, 4 May 2003, para. 68; ECtHR, *Hugh Jordan v. United Kingdom*, Judgment, Application no. 24746/94, 4 May 2001, para. 120.

[269] Others may be tried before civilian courts for serious criminal offences committed abroad, depending on the laws on the particular troop-contributing country.

[270] Such information should show "that its Courts meet internationally recognized norms and standards for the independent and impartial prosecution of similar conduct". ICC, Rules of Procedure and Evidence, Rule 51, see *supra* note 137.

---

case basis. This could prove complex, in particular given the extraterritorial nature of these offences and the environments in which they are committed. The granting of immunity under the terms of the Status of Forces Agreement from host state jurisdiction could also be deemed a form of unwillingness on the part of the host state. Assessment would need to focus of the troop-contributing country's proceedings or lack thereof. Different parts of a state make-up may display a greater or lesser degree of willingness.[271] For instance, while a state's judiciary might be willing to investigate and prosecute, the military may attempt to hinder the investigation through refusal to co-operate.

14.1.6.3. Inability

Article 17(3) of the ICC Statute relates to a state's inability to bring a perpetrator to justice, wherein, "due to a *total or substantial collapse* or *unavailability* of its national judicial system, the state is unable to obtain the accused or the necessary evidence and testimony or otherwise unable to carry out its proceedings".[272] This sets forth two scenarios amounting to inability, which are phrased in the alternative. First, a state may be unable due to its judicial system being in a state of "total or substantial collapse", rendering it either "unable to obtain the accused or the necessary evidence and testimony *or* otherwise unable to carry out its proceedings". The second scenario is where a state's judicial system is 'unavailable', rendering it either "unable to obtain the accused or the necessary evidence and testimony *or* otherwise unable to carry out its proceedings".

Inability, at first sight, appears more straightforward than unwillingness, as an assessment of inability is more objective. It is significant that Article 17(3) refers to 'collapse' or 'unavailability'. It may entail inability to obtain the accused or evidence and witness testimony or there may be some other factor causing inability. This provision is of particular relevance to cases of sexual abuse and exploitation by UN military peacekeepers. First, the host state may be unable to exercise its jurisdiction due to the exclusive criminal jurisdiction of the troop-contributing country granted under the Status of Forces Agreement. Second, in environments where UN peacekeeping missions are deployed the host state judicial sys-

---

[271] Informal Expert Paper on Complementarity, p. 14, see *supra* note 227.

[272] ICC Statute, Article 17(3), see *supra* note 23 (emphasis added).

tem may be in a state of "total or substantial" collapse. The troop-contributing country's judicial system, however, is unlikely to be in a state of "total or substantial" collapse.

That said, while troop-contributing countries will generally have a functioning judicial system at the national level, they may nevertheless be unable to render this fully operative in the host state. Therein "*or* unavailability" may apply. A number of factors may feed into this. First, lack of infrastructure in addition to broad geographic areas may make it difficult or impossible to locate victims, witnesses and evidence. Second, host state co-operation and consent is necessary for any part of criminal proceedings to take place in its territory. Third, with respect to conducting criminal proceedings in the host state, many troop-contributing countries may not have the capacity or the necessary domestic legislation to conduct on-site courts martial or other proceedings, and distance may render prosecution in the troop-contributing country ineffective, or at least extremely difficult.[273] Fourth, conducting criminal investigations abroad, in particular in conflict or post-conflict environments, may prove extremely costly. Fifth, the troop-contributing country may lack expertise in prosecuting offences, in particular offences that violate international law, occurring extraterritorially, and expertise in dealing with sexual offences against women and children. Other barriers may include lack of cultural awareness, victim and witness protection, evidentiary requirements, or the ability to use evidence gathered by host state authorities or by the UN Conduct and Discipline or Office of Internal Oversight Services, and obvious linguistic issues. This list could go on.

One of the difficulties with complementarity is that it may require a detailed examination, and certainly knowledge, of states' legal systems.[274] That stated admissibility may only necessitate an assessment of a state's legal system insofar as it relates to specific misconduct by military personnel deployed overseas.

The Office of the Prosecutor's report on complementarity listed the following factors as indicative of 'inability':

> lack of necessary personnel, judges, investigators, prosecutor; lack of judicial infrastructure; lack of substantive or pro-

---

[273] Comprehensive Strategy, see *supra* note 252.

[274] Stegmiller, 2009, p. 548, see *supra* note 132.

cedural penal legislation rendering system "unavailable";
lack of access rendering system "unavailable"; obstruction
by uncontrolled elements rendering system unavailable; amnesties, immunities rendering system "unavailable".[275]

Some authors suggest that the inadequacy of domestic laws in reflecting
crimes under the ICC Statute could arguably amount to 'inability', as this
might result in an otherwise international criminal law offence being
prosecuted as a lesser offence.[276] This raises the question of whether a
case can be deemed admissible if prosecuted as a lesser offence under national law, for example as rape instead of a war crime.[277] The special rapporteur on rape, sexual slavery and slave-like practices in armed conflict
stated:

> [I]n evaluating the competence of national judicial systems
> to adjudicate international crimes is the extent to which the
> national system in question protects the rights of women. In
> particular the existence of gender biases in municipal laws of
> procedures must be taken into account when assessing the
> general competence of domestic courts.[278]

The principle of legality or *nullum crimen, nulla poena sine lege*
may mean that domestic courts in such scenarios are unable to prosecute,
at least for the relevant international law offence.[279] However, the ICC

---

[275] Informal Expert Paper on Complementarity, p. 15, see *supra* note 227.

[276] Kleffner, 2008, p. 130, see *supra* note 227; El Zeidy, 2002, p. 228, see *supra* note 218. See
Dawn Sedman, "Should the Prosecution of ordinary crimes in Domestic Jurisdictions Satisfy
the Complementarity Principle?", in Carsten Stahn and Larissa van den Herik (eds.), *Future
Perspectives on International Criminal Justice*, TMC Asser Press, The Hague, 2010; Markus
Benzing, "The Complementarity Regime of the International Criminal Court: International
Criminal Justice between State Sovereignty and the Fight against Impunity", in *Max Planck
Yearbook of United Nations Law*, 2003, vol. 7, p. 59; Katherine L. Doherty and Timothy L.H.
McCormack, "'Complementarity' as a Catalyst for Comprehensive Domestic Penal Legisla-
tion", in *UC Davis Journal of International Law and Policy*, 1999, vol. 5 p. 147.

[277] Note that the *ne bis in idem* principle set out under Article 20(3) of the ICC Statute focuses
on trying a person for the same conduct twice; Schabas, 2004, p. 88, see *supra* note 42. Sedman argues that what matters is that the same conduct is not prosecuted, but does not preclude prosecution for a separate offence that does not involve the same conduct: Sedman,
2010, pp. 259, 262, see *supra* note 276.

[278] UN Commission on Human Rights, Systematic Rape, Slavery and Slave-like Practices During Armed Conflict: Update to the Final Report Submitted by Ms. Gay J. McDougall, UN
Doc. E/CN.4/Sub.2/2000/21, 6 June 2000, para. 42.

[279] Kleffner, 2008, p. 130, see *supra* note 227.

Statute refers to unavailability of domestic judicial systems as opposed to domestic legislation.[280] Under Article 88, states are not required to adopt legislation implementing Statute crimes at the national level, but rather legislation enabling them to co-operate with the Court.[281] Benjamin Perrin suggests, however, that it is plausible that the prosecutor could argue that the crime under the ICC Statute had not actually been prosecuted.[282]

14.1.6.4. Conclusion

While the principle of complementarity at first glance might suggest that the ICC works as system of 'proxy justice' for international criminal law offences where states prove unwilling or unable to act, this goes too far, romanticising the institution and its capabilities.[283] When it comes to sexual abuse and exploitation by UN peacekeepers it seems possible that complementarity could in exceptional circumstances be overcome, but it would likely prove extremely contentious. This, added to the other barriers mentioned above, makes prosecution by the ICC extremely improbable, save in the most exceptional of circumstances, and even in such cases it is questionable whether it would even be desirable for it to do so. Having said that, I would like to address a related question: how else might the ICC play a role in encouraging the enforcement of international criminal law either through domestic of hybrid courts?

Perrin argues that complementarity under the ICC Statute is best understood in terms of six separate roles to be played by the ICC, namely: "a safety net", where no state takes action; a "catalyst"; a "monitor" of a state's willingness or ability; "a passive standard setter"; an "intervener", where it proceeds to investigate and prosecute; and a "burden sharer"

---

[280] On possible inadequacy of some states' domestic laws to prosecute crimes under the ICC Statute, see Perrin, 2006, p. 310, *supra* note 247.

[281] ICC Statute, Article 88, see *supra* note 23. On state obligations to prosecute or extradite pursuant to the ICC Statute, see Payam Akhavan, "Whither National Courts? The Rome Statute's Missing Half", in *Journal of International Criminal Justice*, 2010, vol. 8, no. 5, pp. 1245–66.

[282] Perrin, 2006, p. 310, see *supra* note 247.

[283] Robert Sloane, "The Expressive Capacity of International Punishment: The Limits of the National Law Analogy and the Potential of International Criminal Law", in *Stanford Journal of International Law*, 2007, vol. 43, no. 1, pp. 39, 50.

where a division of labour is agreed between the ICC and a state.[284] The possible catalyst function refers to the potential for the prosecutor to encourage states to exercise their jurisdiction, for instance through using the notification requirement as a method by which to pressurise states.[285] It is solely to this possible role of the ICC as a catalyst that we will turn to in the next section, in the context of positive complementarity.

14.1.7. Positive Complementarity

The Preamble of the ICC Statute emphasises "that it is the duty of every state to exercise criminal jurisdiction over those responsible for international crimes".[286] It further provides

> that the most serious crimes of concern to the international community as a whole must not go unpunished and that their effective prosecution must be ensured by taking measures at the national level and by enhancing international cooperation.[287]

Therefore the primary obligation to prosecute international crimes rests with states.[288] It is widely accepted that international and/or internationalised courts should only exercise jurisdiction over serious international

---

[284] A 'safety net' refers to the ability of the ICC to step in where no state with jurisdiction takes action against the perpetrator. The 'monitor' role most clearly arises when the ICC defers to state jurisdiction under Article 18. However, it might also arise when examining the 'inability' or 'unwillingness' of a state to investigate or prosecute. The monitoring of national proceedings may well encourage states to ensure such proceedings are effective. The 'passive standard setter' role is reflected by the mere existence of the ICC and threat of ICC intervention, which has pushed many states to implement the crimes set out in the ICC Statute domestically. The role of 'intervener' is when the ICC proceeds to investigate and prosecute alleged crimes. Finally, the 'burden sharer' role, while also involving ICC intervention, works in co-operation with the state, wherein the ICC takes on certain cases that may be difficult for the state to pursue, yet the state proceeds with cases against other perpetrators within the situation. Perrin, 2006, pp. 301–2, see *supra* note 247. In relation to the possible division of labour between the ICC and the DRC, see ICC, Office of the Prosecutor, Statement of the Prosecutor Luis Moreno Ocampo to Diplomatic Corps, The Hague, 12 February 2004 ('Moreno-Ocampo Diplomatic Corps Statement').

[285] Perrin, 2006, p. 312, see *supra* note 247.

[286] ICC Statute, Preamble, see *supra* note 23.

[287] *Ibid.*

[288] Jurdi, 2011, pp. 1, 3, see *supra* note 220.

---

crimes where national courts prove unable or unwilling.[289] One of the primary objectives of complementarity is "[t]o serve as a mechanism to encourage and facilitate the compliance of states with their primary responsibility to investigate and prosecute core crimes".[290] Alternatively this might be referred to as a 'catalyst' function of the ICC, acting indirectly to encourage states to meet their international law obligations to prosecute those responsible for core international crimes.[291] The Prosecutor stated that the ICC should be measured not on the number of cases that come before it, but the absence of trials coming before the Court "as a consequence of the regular functioning of national institutions".[292]

Bearing in the mind that the ICC has limited resources, even if a case could be deemed admissible, how many UN military peacekeepers complicit in sexual abuse and exploitation could realistically be brought before the ICC? It is worth noting that offences which may be grave in nature but which do not meet the stringent jurisdictional requirements, or other barriers posed by the ICC Statute, may be easier to prosecute under a domestic or other legal framework which also cover lesser offences. The encouragement of prosecutions at a national or hybrid level may produce more effective outcomes, both in terms of deterrence and the expressive value of prosecution of such personnel.[293] I will return to this presently. Here it will be argued that the ICC may nevertheless have an important residual role to play, which is best expressed through positive complementarity, through acting as a catalyst for prosecutions at the troop-contributing country or failing this a hybrid court level. The Office of the Prosecutor has stated that while it will concentrate on those most responsible for international crimes it will "encourage national prosecutions,

---

[289] See for example, Report of the Secretary-General, The Rule of Law and Transitional Justice in Conflict and Post-conflict Societies, UN Doc. S/2004/616, 23 August 2004, para. 40.

[290] Informal Expert Paper on Complementarity, ICC-OTP, 2003, p. 3.

[291] Individual criminal responsibility and State responsibility and even international organisation responsibility might be regarded as component parts of international responsibility. André Nollkaemper, "Concurrence between individual criminal responsibility and state responsibility in international law", in *International Criminal Law Quarterly*, 2003, vol. 52, p. 615.

[292] Moreno-Ocampo Statement, 16 June 2003, see *supra* note 210.

[293] Lisa Laplante, "The Domestication of International Criminal Law: A Proposal for Expanding the International Criminal Court's Sphere of Influence", in *John Marshall Law Review*, 2010, vol. 43, no. 3, pp. 635, 645–46.

where possible, for the lower-ranking perpetrators, or work with the international community to ensure that the offenders are brought to justice by some other means".[294]

'Positive complementarity' is the idea that the ICC should use its position to encourage national prosecutions and to increase avenues for criminal justice to be delivered.[295] According to the Office of the Prosecutor, in taking a positive approach to complementarity, it encourages national proceedings where possible, relies on national and international networks, and participates in a system of international co-operation.[296] Lisa Laplante refers to this idea as envisaging the ICC as a 'catalyst', encouraging states to realise their own pre-existing obligations under international law.[297] The mere threat of ICC investigations may encourage states to exercise their primary jurisdiction.[298] The Office of the Prosecutor notifies states with jurisdiction very early on of any action that might be taken.[299] This is one mechanism that can be used to promote national prosecutions, wherein states may wish to avoid adverse political reaction and 'naming and shaming'. Allison Marston Danner identifies a number of levels at which the ICC prosecutor interacts with national systems, including: "with states' executives (through requests for co-operation), with states' legislatures (by seeking legislation enabling co-operation between the state and the Court), and, indirectly, with states' judiciaries (by monitoring whether domestic proceedings fulfil the requirements of the admissibility regime)".[300] These interactions can be used for encouraging domestic prosecutions, as might provisions in the ICC Statute requiring state

---

[294] ICC, Office of the Prosecutor, Policy Issues, see *supra* note 178.

[295] Laplante, 2010, pp. 635, 646, see *supra* note 293. See further William W. Burke-White, "Proactive Complementarity: The International Criminal Court and National Courts in the Rome System of International Justice", in *Harvard International Law Journal*, 2008, vol. 49, no. 1, pp. 53–54.

[296] Moreno-Ocampo Statement, 16 June 2003, see *supra* note 210; Moreno-Ocampo Diplomatic Corps Statement, see *supra* note 284.

[297] Laplante, 2010, p. 648, see *supra* note 293.

[298] Burke-White, 2008, p. 73, see *supra* note 295; Heller, 2010, p. 248, see *supra* note 43.

[299] ICC, Office of the Prosecutor, Policy Issues, Annex, Referrals and Communications, para. I(B), see *supra* note 178.

[300] Danner, 2001, pp. 474–77, see *supra* note 57.

parties to co-operate with the ICC.[301] The ICC might also serve as a catalyst for domestic justice sector reform.[302] Where genuine investigations and prosecutions can be encouraged by the prosecutor it is clearly more resource effective for the state to prosecute than the ICC.[303]

While positive complementarity is not provided for in the ICC Statute, William Burke-White puts forward three justifications for a role for the prosecutor through positive complementarity: 1) it is not prohibited by the ICC Statute; 2) the prosecutor's express powers could allow him to employ this tactic; and (3) as do the prosecutor's inherent powers.[304] Articles 15, 18 and 53, as discussed above, allow for a series of communications between the prosecutor and states, and continued monitoring of national proceedings when the prosecutor defers to state jurisdiction.[305] Arguably these communications can be used as a conduit through which to encourage, advise and perhaps even lend some support to genuine national level investigations and prosecutions.[306] Moreover, Article 54(3) specifically allows the prosecutor to enter into co-operation agreements with states.[307] Burke-White suggests that the prosecutor may also have inherent powers to advance the principle of positive complementarity given the object and purpose of the Statute is to eradicate impunity for the core crimes set out therein.[308]

According to an informal expert paper produced by the Office of the Prosecutor, "partnership" and "vigilance" are key "guiding principles"

---

[301] Under ICC Statute, Article 86, see *supra* note 23, state parties are required to co-operate with ICC investigations and prosecutions. Article 88 requires states to adopt laws allowing them to co-operate with Court. Under Article 87, non-state parties whose personnel deployed on UN operations commit serious offences under the jurisdiction of the Court are not obliged to co-operate, unless they voluntarily enter into an agreement with the ICC to do so. Under Article 54(3) the prosecutor can enter into co-operation arrangements with states and international organisations in order to facilitate investigations.

[302] William W. Burke-White, "Complementarity in Practice: The International Criminal Court as Part of a System of Multi-level Global Governance in the Democratic Republic of the Congo", in *Leiden Journal of International Law*, 2005, vol. 18, no. 3, pp. 557, 568–74.

[303] Burke-White, 2008, p. 62, see *supra* note 219.

[304] *Ibid.*, p. 63.

[305] ICC Statute, Articles 15, 18 and 53, see *supra* note 23.

[306] See further Burke-White, 2008, pp. 67–68, *supra* note 219.

[307] ICC Statute, Article 54(3), see *supra* note 23; *ibid.*, p. 68.

[308] Burke-White, 2008, pp. 68–69, see *supra* note 219.

of complementarity.[309] It further envisages enhancing the impact of the ICC in part through "encouragement and co-operation"; "through the prospect of the ICC exercising jurisdiction"; "through its own exemplary and standard-setting proceedings"; and "through its moral presence".[310] Article 93(10) of the ICC Statute contemplates this:

> The Court may, upon request, cooperate with and provide assistance to a State Party conducting an investigation into or trial in respect of conduct which constitutes a crime within the jurisdiction of the Court or which constitutes a serious crime under the national law of the requesting State.[311]

This may include requests for assistance also from non-state parties,[312] expanding its potential field of influence. Assistance might include statements, documents and other forms of evidence, or potentially even technical assistance, training and brokering assistance between states.[313]

The Office of the Prosecutor could potentially provide technical support to national judiciaries through the Office's outreach programme. Various legal experts have suggested mechanisms for doing so including: legislative and technical assistance, capacity-building, "assistance with construction of physical infrastructure",[314] assistance with investigations, training, resources,[315] and dissemination of codes of best practices for domestic prosecutions.[316]

The Office of the Prosecutor's Jurisdiction, Complementarity, and Co-operation Division is already working on establishing networks for international co-operation, not only through engagement with states but also with other stakeholders.[317] It is possible that such networks could be developed to include transnational networks, which could through mutual

---

[309] Informal Expert Paper on Complementarity, pp. 3–4, see *supra* note 227.

[310] *Ibid.*, pp. 4–5.

[311] ICC Statute, see *supra* note 23.

[312] *Ibid.*, Article 98(10)(c).

[313] Informal Expert Paper on Complementarity, p. 6, see *supra* note 227.

[314] That is, courts, detention facilities, and so on. ICC, Assembly of States Parties, Report of the Bureau on Stocktaking: Complementarity, ICC-ASP/8/51, 22–25 March 2010, pp. 4–5, para. 17.

[315] Burke-White, 2008, pp. 92–93, see *supra* note 295.

[316] *Ibid.*, p. 93.

[317] See ICC, Office of the Prosecutor (https://www.icc-cpi.int/about/otp).

agreements be used to exert ICC influence over effective national-level prosecutions. Such networks might incorporate bodies already involved in rule of law capacity-building efforts in many peacekeeping mission states. The ICC has also made available legal tools, including a case matrix, an elements digest, a proceedings digest and a means of proof digest, which provide some basic guidance for domestic-level prosecutions.[318]

Laplante notes that an obvious difficulty with positive complementarity is that it may give rise to disparities between national criminal legislation and the ICC Statute.[319] A number of authors are sceptical of the ICC's capacity to assist or support national courts in the prosecution of international crimes given resource constraints.[320] Just how much of a role the ICC can play through positive complementarity is uncertain, in particular given that it could divert resources from actual prosecutions by the Court. However, if the ICC were to work on the basis of positive complementarity this could also be a mechanism by which to encourage national level prosecutions of UN military peacekeepers if they are complicit in crimes under the Court's jurisdiction. It might also support any alternative mechanism to hold such persons to account, such as a hybrid or tri-hybrid justice mechanism, when troop-contributing countries prove unwilling or unable to exercise their primary jurisdiction, which is explored next.

14.2. Alternative Justice Mechanisms

First, it seems best to view the ICC as one of a number of bodies that could plausibly feed into the overall responsibility framework for sexual abuse and exploitation by UN military personnel, but one that cannot even begin to resolve the issue of responsibility for sexual abuse and exploitation. As discussed in section 14.1., practical and legal limitations make it unlikely and perhaps unjustifiable for the ICC to prosecute UN military personnel for sexual abuse and exploitation, save in exceptional circumstances. Furthermore, the ICC is obviously incapacitated to a large extent

---

[318] The ICC Case Matrix is aimed at judges, investigators, prosecutors, defence, NGOs and victim representatives. These tools are designed to be adaptable to various national criminal justice systems to assist in the management of complex legal case involving elements of international criminal law (https://www.casematrixnetwork.org/purpose/).

[319] Laplante, 2010, pp. 660–61, see *supra* note 293.

[320] Baylis, 2009, p. 25, see *supra* note 176; Burke-White, 2008, p. 98, see *supra* note 295.

by resource constraints.[321] Many acts of sexual abuse and exploitation may not even constitute war crimes or crimes against humanity, in particular as set out under the ICC Statute. This is not to say that sexual abuse and exploitation committed by UN peacekeeping personnel are not of a serious nature or are simply ordinary criminal offences. Peacekeepers have a duty of care and a duty to protect civilian populations.[322] Sexual abuse and exploitation breaches the special relationship of trust between the UN and local populations. The position taken by the UN Secretariat on this issue is that such crimes

> should not be viewed as merely domestic crimes. The fact that alleged offenders are individuals who have been placed in a position of trust in the host State to serve the international community, as well as the impact that crimes have on the image and credibility of the international mandate, warrants the establishment of jurisdiction on an extradite or prosecute basis.[323]

It is further noted that the Convention on the Safety of United Nations and Associated Personnel provides this basis for jurisdiction for crimes committed against peacekeeping personnel given their special status, and that a similar rationale should apply when these persons commit serious offences against the civilians that they have been sent to protect.[324] To ignore the seriousness of these crimes disregards not only their abhorrent nature, but also how they undermine UN mission mandates and thereby international peace and security.[325] To date, troop-contributing countries have not proven the most successful avenue for holding such personnel to account, therefore some alternative form of institutionalised mechanism appears warranted.

---

[321] Gabriel Bottini, "Universal Jurisdiction After the Creation of the International Criminal Court", in *New York University Journal of International Law and Politics*, 2004, vol. 36, pp. 503, 547.

[322] According to the secretary-general, sexual abuse and exploitation by UN military personnel is "a violation of the fundamental duty of care that all United Nations peacekeeping personnel owe to the local population that they are sent to serve": Comprehensive Strategy, "Introduction", see *supra* note 252.

[323] Criminal Accountability Note, para. 32, see *supra* note 204.

[324] *Ibid.*, paras. 32–33.

[325] *Ibid.*, paras. 11–12.

Pursuant to Resolution 59/300, a group of legal experts was established by the secretary-general to examine the legal aspects of criminal accountability of UN officials and experts on mission.[326] In 2006, the group of legal experts issued a report, which included a sample draft Convention on Criminal Accountability of UN Officials and Experts on Mission.[327] The group correctly noted that sexual abuse and exploitation may well fall somewhere in between an ordinary criminal offence and an international crime, and suggested that balance is best sought through an "extradite or prosecute" approach, underpinned by a treaty.[328] One of the possibilities briefly explored in the group of legal experts' report was the creation of a separate institutionalised hybrid justice mechanism at the international level to address criminal offences, albeit solely with respect to those committed by UN officials and experts on mission. UN military personnel are a distinct category of personnel.[329] The report and suggestions made therein are currently under consideration by the UN.[330]

The group of legal experts was not mandated to examine accountability of UN military contingents.[331] They did not therefore consider the inclusion of UN military peacekeepers within the remit of their proposals,

---

[326] See UN, Ad Hoc Committee on the Criminal Accountability of United Nations Officials and Experts on Mission (http://legal.un.org/committees/criminal_accountability/).

[327] The draft Convention on Criminal Accountability of UN Officials and Experts on Mission was designed solely to illustrate what such a convention might resemble. UN General Assembly, Report of the Group of Legal Experts Ensuring the Accountability of United Nations Staff and Experts on Mission with Respect to Criminal Acts Committed in Peacekeeping Operations, UN Doc. A/60/980, 16 August 2006 ('Group of Legal Experts Report'). See further Marco Odello, "Tackling Criminal Acts in Peacekeeping Operations: The Accountability of Peacekeepers", in *Journal of Conflict and Security Law*, 2010, vol. 15, no. 2, pp. 347, 354; Melanie O'Brien, "Issues of the Draft Convention on Criminal Accountability of United Nations Officials and Experts on Mission", in Noëlle Quénivet and Shilan Shah-Davis (eds.), *International Law and Armed Conflict: Challenges in the 21st Century*, TMC Asser Press, The Hague, 2010, pp. 57–75.

[328] Group of Legal Experts Report, para. 58, see *supra* note 327.

[329] See further Burke, 2011, pp. 63–104, *supra* note 17.

[330] Another working group is envisaged in 2018, see *supra* note 326.

[331] I refer here solely to UN military personnel and not to military observers who generally come under the category of "experts on mission". It was also not mandated to consider issues of vicarious liability of the UN or member states; Group of Legal Experts Report, fn. 3, see *supra* note 327.

---

in part due to its terms of reference.[332] It was felt that unlike UN officials and experts on mission, military contingents are already subject to troop-contributing country criminal/military justice systems, so no jurisdiction gap arises. Separately, but in parallel, the issue of accountability of UN military contingents was studied by another expert group.[333] Steps were taken to revise the model memorandum of agreement between the UN and troop-contributing countries in order to require the latter to ensure their military personnel are held to account; however, there is little in the way of enforcement.[334] The problem is that while military personnel might not necessarily fall within a jurisdictional gap, impunity nevertheless is evident given the reluctance of troop-contributing countries to hold soldiers

---

[332] UN General Assembly, Report of the Ad Hoc Committee on Criminal Accountability of United Nations Officials and Experts on Mission, UN Doc. A/62/54, 9–13 April 2007, para. 21 ('Report on Criminal Accountability'). The UN Secretariat has stated that any convention, if drawn up, should apply equally to Chapter VI and Chapter VII operations. See Criminal Accountability Note, para. 36, *supra* note 204. While not applicable to UN military contingents, the General Assembly has passed a number of resolutions in which it strongly urges or encourages states to take action to combat sexual exploitation and abuse, including through clarifying and/or extending their extraterritorial jurisdiction over nationals on UN operations and through co-operation with other states and the UN. UN General Assembly, Resolution 64/110 Criminal Accountability of United Nations Officials and Experts on Mission, UN Doc. A/RES/64/110, 15 January 2010 (http://www.legal-tools.org/doc/24efa2/); UN General Assembly, Resolution 62/63 Criminal Accountability of United Nations Officials and Experts on Mission, UN Doc. A/RES/62/63, 8 January 2008 (http://www.legal-tools.org/doc/57d021/); UN General Assembly, Resolution 63/119 Criminal Accountability of United Nations Officials and Experts on Mission, UN Doc. A/RES/63/119, 11 December 2008 (http://www.legal-tools.org/doc/7a2ad8/); UN General Assembly, Resolution 65/20 Criminal Accountability of United Nations Officials and Experts on Mission, UN Doc. A/RES/65/20, 10 January 2011 (http://www.legal-tools.org/doc/97d1fb/). See also UN General Assembly, Criminal Accountability of United Nations Officials and Experts on Mission, Report of the Sixth Committee, UN Doc. A/62/448, 21 November 2007; and UN General Assembly, Criminal Accountability of United Nations Officials and Experts on Mission, Report of the Sixth Committee, UN Doc. A/63/437, 17 November 2008.

[333] See UN General Assembly, Report of the Group of Legal Experts on Making the Standards Contained in the Secretary-General's Bulletin Binding on Contingent Members and Standardizing the Norms of Conduct so that They Are Applicable to all Categories of Peacekeeping Personnel", UN Doc. A/61/645, 18 December 2006.

[334] For a copy of the revised memorandum of understanding, see Manual on Policies and Procedures, *supra* note 16. For discussion of the revisions made to the memorandum of understanding, see generally, Zsuzsanna Deen-Racsmány, "The Amended UN Model Memorandum of Understanding: A New Incentive for States to Discipline and Prosecute Military Members of National Peacekeeping Contingents?", in *Journal of Conflict and Security Law*, 2011, vol. 16, no. 2, pp. 1–35.

---

to account. It is not within the scope of this chapter to analyse revisions to the memorandum of agreement.[335] Nor will I examine the possible advantages of a convention on criminal accountability, and its extended application to UN military personnel.[336]

The group of legal experts highlighted the need for primacy of host state jurisdiction over UN officials and experts on mission,[337] for reasons among which is respect for sovereignty, and to allow easier access to witnesses and evidence.[338] It correctly observed that host state prosecution would be in line with the requirement that peacekeepers respect local laws.[339] It suggested that where the host state criminal justice system proves inadequate, it might be possible to locate partial or shared jurisdiction with other states in the various phases of proceedings.[340] It proposed that a hybrid mechanism could, if necessary, be established, incorporating international personnel to bolster the host state's criminal justice sys-

---

[335] Suffice to say that the revisions reaffirm troop-contributing country exclusive criminal jurisdiction over UN military contingents; they detail investigative procedures which, while somewhat weakening UN investigative capacity, strengthen the possible admissibility of evidence in troop-contributing country courts; and to some extent the revisions clarify applicable rules and standards of conduct. See, generally, Deen-Racsmány, 2011, pp. 1–35, *supra* note 334.

[336] There has been some debate on the exclusion of military contingents from the remit of any proposed convention by the first group of legal experts. UN Summary Records of the Sixth Committee, Statements, Mr. Bichet (Switzerland), UN Doc. A/C.6/62/SR.6, 6 November 2007; Mr. Kanyimbue (DRC), UN Doc. A/C.6/64/SR.7, 10 November 2009, paras. 19 and 41; Mr. Saripudin (Indonesia), UN Doc. A/C.6/63/3R.5, para. 52 ('Sixth Committee Statements'). For further discussion of the draft convention, see generally O'Brien, 2010, *supra* note 18; see also Deen-Racsmány, 2011, pp. 32–34, *supra* note 334. The adoption of a convention could add weight to the prohibition of sexual exploitation and abuse, clarify what types of conduct are considered sexual exploitive or abusive, provide for the protection of victims and witnesses, in addition to providing for a more robust legal framework in which states and the UN could better co-operate. Furthermore, such a convention might cater better towards the unique environment in which these offences take place.

[337] Group of Legal Experts Report, para. 44(a), see *supra* note 327.

[338] It noted that the major advantage of criminal trials being conducted in the host State is that it would, "avoid the cost, delays and inconvenience of witnesses having to travel overseas and evidence having to be transmitted abroad". *Ibid.*, para. 27(b).

[339] *Ibid.*, para. 27 (c)(d).

[340] *Ibid.*, paras. 40–44. See further, Noëlle Quénivet, "The Dissonance between the United Nations Zero-tolerance Policy and the Criminalisation of Sexual Offences on the International Level", in *International Criminal Law Review*, 2007, vol. 7, no. 4, pp. 657, 666.

---

tem.[341] Such tribunals could have an investigative, judicial, prosecutorial and administrative component.[342] For the purpose of this chapter, I focus primarily on this singular aspect of the group of legal experts' report, namely, the establishment of hybrid courts, in view of their possible application to UN military peacekeepers.

This section questions what the advantages and disadvantages of such an institutionalised mechanism might be. I argue that a hybrid or tri-hybrid justice mechanism may provide for an appropriate alternative forum in which to prosecute UN military personnel.[343] That stated, the make-up of the group of legal experts' hybrid model, which foresees locating jurisdiction in the host state, I contend, is not suited to the prosecution of UN military personnel. Instead I put forward some tentative suggestions for the establishment of some form of a tri-hybrid system with at least partial jurisdiction remaining located in the troop-contributing country legal system. It is argued that a tri-hybrid justice mechanism might allow for partial or shared jurisdiction at multiple levels: the UN, the troop-contributing country and the host state. I do not contend that the establishment of a hybrid justice would not be met with significant practical and legal difficulties, not least troop-contributing country resistance to any external interference in prosecution of their soldiers. Finally, I touch on some possible justifications for punishment of UN military peacekeepers complicit in sexual abuse and exploitation at an international or internationalised level. Focusing solely on deterrence and norm expression, I posit that these goals might be better met by a hybrid or tri-hybrid justice mechanism than in the forum of the ICC.

14.2.1. Hybrid Justice Mechanism

Hybrid courts emerged largely as a response to what were perceived as failures or limitations of international courts, such as the ICTY and ICTR, not least on account of the slow pace of trials and costs involved.[344] A hy-

---

[341] Group of Legal Experts Report, paras. 29–33, see *supra* note 327.

[342] *Ibid.*, paras. 33–37.

[343] See also Sixth Committee Statements, Bichet, para. 19; Kanyimbue, para. 41, *supra* note 336.

[344] Ralph Zacklin, "The Failings of Ad Hoc International Tribunals", in *Journal of International Criminal Justice*, 2004, vol. 2, no. 2, pp. 541–45; Rosanna Lipscomb, "Restructur-

brid court is not an international tribunal but rather an 'internationalised' national court; internationalised in terms of both the law applied and personnel involved in the investigative and trial process. The practice of applying an amalgamation of domestic and international law, and using domestic and international staff has precedence, such as courts created in Sierra Leone, East Timor, Cambodia and Kosovo.[345] The East Timor hybrid tribunal, the Special Panels for Serious Crimes of the District Court of Dili, for instance, had two international and one East Timorese judge on each panel. The panels were charged with jurisdiction over a mixture of international and domestic crimes, including crimes against humanity, war crimes, murder, sexual offences, genocide and torture.[346] Prosecutors and investigators also were drawn from a mix of international and domestic personnel.[347] The hybrid justice system created in Sierra Leone was treaty-based and also had mixed jurisdiction.[348] While not operating under the national criminal justice system, it nevertheless applied both domestic and international law, and involved both international and national personnel.[349] It also had a mix of domestic and international judges, with a slight majority being international.[350] On the other hand, the Extraordinary Chambers in the Courts of Cambodia ('ECCC') was integrated into the Cambodian domestic court system and applies Cambodian law, and

---

ing the ICC Framework to Advance Transitional Justice: A Search for a Permanent Solution in Sudan", in *Columbia Law Review*, 2006, vol. 106, no. 1, pp. 182, 205.

[345] Laura A. Dickinson, "The Promise of Hybrid Courts", in *American Journal of International Law*, 2003, vol. 97, no. 2, pp. 295–98.

[346] United Nations Transitional Administration in East Timor ('UNTAET'), UN Regulation No. 2000/11 on the Organization of Courts in East Timor, Section 10(1), 6 March 2000 (http://www.legal-tools.org/doc/2bedb8/).

[347] David Cohen, "'Hybrid' Justice in East Timor, Sierra Leone and Cambodia: 'Lessons Learned' and Prospects for the Future", in *Stanford Journal of International Law*, 2007, vol. 43, no. 1, p. 8; Dickinson, 2003, pp. 298–99, see *supra* note 345.

[348] UN Security Council, Report of the Secretary-General on the Establishment of a Special Court for Sierra Leone, UN Doc. S/2000/915, 4 October 2000, para. 9 (http://www.legal-tools.org/doc/4af5d2/).

[349] Statute of the Special Court for Sierra Leone, created 14 August 2000, entry into force 16 January 2002, Article 5 ('SCSL Statute') (http://www.legal-tools.org/doc/aa0e20/) covers a range of domestic law offences, including abuse of girls under 14 years old.

[350] UN Security Council, Report of the Planning Mission on the Establishment of the Special Court for Sierra Leone, UN Doc. S/2002/246, Appendix I.

has a majority of domestic judges with a minority of international.[351] In the so-called Regulation 64 Panels in Kosovo, foreign judges and lawyers sat with their domestic counterparts to try those suspected of war crimes and other serious ethnically motivated crimes.[352] The majority of the judges were foreign. The law that was applied consisted of an amalgamation of international and domestic law.[353]

While not without their flaws, a clear benefit of hybrid courts is that they have the capacity to draw on the advantages of national and international courts, and they tend to be more adaptable. The establishment of a hybrid justice system could allow for the gradual building of expertise if granted jurisdiction to deal with particular types of offences, such as serious extraterritorial criminal conduct by UN troops, in particular sexual offences. In this context, national systems, those of both troop-contributing countries and host states, could gain expertise in dealing with such cases. Hybrid courts provide a valuable process in which domestic legal professionals, including judges, prosecutors, investigators and researchers, can learn more about international law, how to interpret it, and its implementation through day-to-day interaction with their foreign counterparts.[354] The degree of capacity-building achieved through these interactions, however, would depend largely on how well national and international staff work in collaboration with one another.[355] The Court and international staff might also engage with legal professionals outside the court itself, for instance through the provision of occasional training.[356]

However, one of the difficulties that arose, to varying degrees, with previous hybrid courts is that while international personnel are assumed to have more extensive knowledge of international law (which is not always

---

[351] Tanaz Moghadam, "Revitalizing Universal Jurisdiction: Lessons from Hybrid Tribunals Applied to the Case of Hissène Habré", in *Columbia Human Rights Law Review*, 2008, vol. 39, no. 2, pp. 471, 493.

[352] Laura A. Dickinson, "The Relationship between Hybrid Courts and International Courts: The Case of Kosovo", in *New England Law Review*, 2003, vol. 37, no. 4, pp. 1059, 1062.

[353] *Ibid.*, pp. 1063–64.

[354] Baylis notes, however, that this international law expertise has however at times been absent in previous hybrid courts: See Baylis, 2009, p. 19, *supra* note 176.

[355] Olga Martin-Ortega and Johanna Herman, *Hybrid Tribunals and the Rule of law: Notes from Bosnia and Herzegovina and Cambodia*, JAD-PbP Working Paper no. 7, May 2010, pp. 1, 19.

[356] *Ibid.* p. 16.

---

the case), they may lack awareness of national laws.[357] Added to this, there may also be cultural and linguistic difficulties. Were a hybrid court to be established to prosecute serious offences by UN military personnel, these problems would likely be intensified given the number of nationalities involved. Furthermore, were a hybrid court established it might require the application of military law, and may require knowledge of varying command and control structures. International personnel may lack expertise in the application of such law.

The presence of international personnel in a hybrid court may give an increased perception of impartiality and greater ability to ensure due process standards.[358] Practice has shown that victims or victim communities sometimes view purely international courts as foreign and illegitimate, in particular if not located in their territory.[359] Hybrid courts tend to be perceived as being more politically viable.[360] Such courts are less likely to be seen to infringe state sovereignty, if the state retains partial jurisdiction. However, as I argue, troop-contributing country partial jurisdiction over military personnel may be required. It must be borne in mind that troop-contributing countries consider criminal and disciplinary control over their troops as integral to command and control, as very much a sovereign prerogative.[361]

A number of authors have noted that distance between victim communities and international courts undermines the ability to communicate with victim communities.[362] Hybrid courts, when located in the territory where crimes take place, enable victim communities to attend trials, facili-

---

[357] Baylis, 2009, p. 18, see *supra* note 176.

[358] Jenia Iontcheva Turner, "Nationalizing International Criminal Law", in *Stanford Journal of International Law*, 2005, vol. 41, no. 1, pp. 1, 16; William W. Burke-White, "Regionalization of International Criminal Law Enforcement: A Preliminary Exploration", in *Texas International Law Journal*, 2003, vol. 38, no. 4, p. 729. Baylis notes, however, that these claims have been criticised: See Baylis, 2009, pp. 11–13, *supra* note 176.

[359] Mark A. Drumbl, "Collective Violence and Individual Punishment: The Criminality of Mass Atrocity", in *Northwestern University Law Review*, 2005, vol. 99, no. 2, pp. 539, 602–03; Turner, 2005, see *supra* note 358; Dickinson, 2003, pp. 1066–68, see *supra* note 352.

[360] Turner, 2005, p. 2, see *supra* note 358.

[361] See, for example, Kuljit Ahluwalia, *The Legal Status, Privileges and Immunities of the Specialized Agencies of the United Nations and Certain Other International Organizations*, Martinus Nijhoff Publishers, The Hague, 1964, p. 24.

[362] Cohen, 2007, p. 4, see *supra* note 347.

tating greater communication with them and would-be perpetrators.[363] This enhances the expressive and deterrent value of prosecutions.

Sexual abuse and exploitation by UN peacekeepers could plausibly amount to an international criminal law offence, a transnational crime and/or a crime against domestic laws of the host state and troop-contributing country. Unlike the ICC, a hybrid court may draw on both domestic and international law and procedure, as appropriate, to prosecute individuals.[364] If a hybrid court was established its statute could provide for broader definitions of war crimes or crimes against humanity than the ICC Statute.[365] A hybrid model could allow for the application of domestic laws, reformed in line with international standards.[366] The difficulty, however, would be in determining the applicable law for incidents of sexual violence by UN peacekeepers, given that the hybrid would have to hear cases from multiple jurisdictions. A convention might prove useful in this regard. A pre-agreed set of crimes and their elements could be relied on. Training could be provided to all peacekeepers on standards set out.

Domestic-level prosecution of international crimes is generally seen as being more economically viable and less time-consuming than international trials.[367] Nevertheless, hybrid courts, especially if they are expected to serve capacity-building roles, will still require significant funding.[368] When it comes to extraterritorial offences by UN military peacekeepers costs will undoubtedly be higher given distances between troop-contributing countries, host states, perpetrators, victims, witnesses and evidence, in addition to the fact that there may be considerable security concerns in investigating and prosecuting such crimes in host states. For

---

[363] On the problem of perceived legitimacy of international courts, see further Dickinson, 2003, pp. 232–33, *supra* note 345.

[364] *Ibid.*, pp. 294–95.

[365] While national or internationalised courts set in state parties to the ICC Statue may draw on its definitions they are not obligated to do so. It is worth reminding ourselves that the international crimes codified by the ICC Statute may be narrower than and certainly do not cover all categories of offences prohibited by international law. See further Newton, 2001, p. 31, *supra* note 228.

[366] Dickinson, 2003, p. 295, see *supra* note 345.

[367] Frédéric Mégret, "In Defense of Hybridity: Towards a Representational Theory of International Criminal Justice", in *Cornell International Law Journal*, 2005, vol. 38, no. 3, pp. 725, 731.

[368] Dickinson, 2003, p. 307, see *supra* note 345.

similar reasons such cases could prove lengthy. That stated, if a hybrid justice mechanism was established to operate on the basis of complementarity, it is likely that the majority of cases would be dealt with by the troop-contributing country.

The question arises whether the ICC would necessarily be debarred from exercising jurisdiction where some hybrid court exercised jurisdiction.[369] Jenia Iontcheva Turner suggests that the ICC should take a more versatile role, by supporting the work of hybrid courts to prosecute international crimes at the domestic level.[370] There seems to be no reason why the existence of a hybrid court could not complement the role of the ICC and domestic prosecutions.[371] A hybrid justice mechanism might prove a useful halfway house for cases in which troop-contributing countries are either unwilling or unable to prosecute but, given the limitations discussed in section 14.1., cannot be brought before the ICC. Furthermore, with respect to core international crimes, the ICC could play a residual role here through positive complementarity.

Hybrid courts have the ability to bolster domestic justice mechanisms, as opposed to substituting them, where a state may be willing to genuinely investigate and prosecute but lacks or partially lacks the capacity to do so. Moreover, they have the potential to advance the rule of law and capacity-building efforts at domestic level through the sharing of expertise.[372] In the context of crimes by UN military personnel this might operate on two levels: developing practice in dealing with these cases, and more generally a rule of law demonstrating effect[373] both within the court structure itself and the host state and troop-contributing country national criminal justice systems. Many UN peacekeeping operations already have rule of law components working alongside host states to re-establish a working criminal justice sector.[374] That stated, as demonstrated by the ef-

---

[369] Schabas, 2004, p. 88, see *supra* note 42.

[370] Turner, 2005, p. 3, see *supra* note 358.

[371] Dickinson, 2003, pp. 295–310, see *supra* note 345.

[372] Jane E. Stromseth, "Pursuing Accountability for Atrocities after Conflict: What Impact on Building the Rule of Law?", in *Georgetown Journal of International Law*, 2007, vol. 38, no. 2, p. 226.

[373] On the rule of law element, see further Martin-Ortega and Herman, 2010, p. 7, *supra* note 355.

[374] Group of Legal Experts Report, para. 38, see *supra* note 327.

forts of past hybrid courts, rule of law and capacity-building are not without difficulties and one must be realistic as to what can be achieved.[375] Re-establishing the rule of law and capacity-building are long-term goals.[376] Some of the problems with this approach are that it may not be expeditious enough to deal with sexual offences, and may have serious impacts on the right to a fair trial for the accused. Furthermore, it may divert resources from ongoing rule of law and justice sector reform initiatives in certain host states. Olga Martin-Ortega and Johanna Herman note that in the case of the War Crimes Chamber in Bosnia and Herzegovina tension arose over resources and competing jurisdiction between the hybrid court and local courts charged with the prosecution of human rights violations not falling within the War Crime Chamber's jurisdiction.[377] One can imagine that where some form of hybrid court is established to prosecute serious crimes by the UN peacekeepers, victims of serious human rights abuses (including mass rapes by local militias, armed forces and police) and local courts might feel that diverting resources away from the prosecution of the latter offenders is unjust. Such double standards might not be easily reconciled with or understood by local populations.

Capacity-building, both where a troop-contributing country is unable to prosecute, and with respect to the host state, would require some sort of capacity assessment. This could be limited to an assessment of capacity solely with respect to prosecuting the particular offence.[378] Probably one of the greatest difficulties is that many UN mission host states have highly dysfunctional justice systems, and while capacity-building is a worthwhile endeavour, as the Stimson Center puts it, "it would be like 'trying to build a ship while you are on it'".[379] If a hybrid court were set

---

[375] Authors discuss problems faced by the War Crimes Chamber in Bosnia and Herzegovina and ECCC in Cambodia: See Martin-Ortega and Herman, 2010, pp. 15–21, *supra* note 355.

[376] *Ibid.*, p. 16.

[377] The potential for the ECCC to impact on the capacity-building of the local Courts in Cambodia, given the impossibility of setting up similar procedures, and case management mechanisms as a mere 1 per cent of the ECCC budget is equivalent to the budget allocated to run 25 local courts by the Ministry of Justice. *Ibid.*, pp. 15–16.

[378] The Stimson Center suggests the Model Codes for Post-Conflict Criminal Justice might be prove useful in this regard in bringing the criminal justice system in line with acceptable international standards. See further, William J. Durch *et al.*, *Improving Criminal Accountability in United Nations Peace Operations*, Stimson Center Report no. 65, Rev. 1, June 2009.

[379] Group of Legal Experts Report, see *supra* note 327.

up, rule of law and capacity-building efforts would require interaction between the troop-contributing country and international personnel and their counterparts in the host state criminal justice sector. Such efforts would need to be accompanied by the willingness of state authorities to pursue this goal.

The establishment of a hybrid justice mechanism to deal with serious criminal offences by UN peacekeepers, in particular sexual ones, would create precedence and practice in dealing with such crimes. Trials could be made accessible electronically.[380]

One of the problems with hybrid courts is that any treaty negotiation may prove lengthy.[381] Furthermore, the establishment of a hybrid tribunal that could exercise jurisdiction over UN military personnel would require both host state[382] and troop-contributing country consent. This might be dealt with under the Status of Forces Agreement and memorandum of understanding. Alternatively, Articles 25 and 29 of the UN Charter could arguably be used as a basis for the establishment of a hybrid justice mechanism, given that it permits the Security Council to establish such other bodies as necessary for the performance of its functions, and that states are obliged to accept and carry out Security Council decisions.[383]

14.2.2. Transnational Legal Networks

A number of authors argue that the use of transnational legal networks to bolster a hybrid system should not be excluded.[384] Laura A. Dickinson posits that hybrid Courts can foster such networks, allowing for the transnationalisation of legal processes, which in turn may result in "internationalisation and interpenetration of norms".[385] Drawing on Elena Baylis's analysis of transnational legal networks and their influence on national

---

[380] Jenia Iontcheva Turner, "Transnational Networks and International Criminal Justice", in *Michigan Law Review*, 2007, vol. 105, no. 5, pp. 985, 1020.

[381] Lipscomb, 2006, p. 208, see *supra* note 344.

[382] Group of Legal Experts Report, para. 35, see *supra* note 327.

[383] UN Charter, Articles 25 and 29, see *supra* note 113.

[384] A number of authors suggest this in the context of interactions between the ICC and national courts. Burke-White, 2008, p. 98, see *supra* note 295; Turner, 2005, p. 32, see *supra* note 358; Baylis, 2009, p. 24, see *supra* note 176.

[385] Dickinson, 2003, p. 304, see *supra* note 345.

justice systems, I would like to turn to what she terms their "functional hybrid character", while locating "formal authority and effective control" in the domestic system.[386] This differs from hybrid courts as it locates authority and control solely with domestic actors, with the role of international personnel being to support and facilitate domestic criminal justice reform efforts and trials.[387] International personnel would not sit as judges, prosecutors, investigators and so on, but rather provide assistance, training and technical support to national counterparts, where required. Some scholars posit that states are more likely to comply with their international obligations through assistance and encouragement, and that transnational networks can assist in this role. Furthermore, they could bolster domestic systems in areas where they come up short.[388] Such networks already are developing among investigators, prosecutors and judges.[389] One of the primary advantages of the use of transnational legal networks to support domestic prosecutions is flexibility, namely their ability to adapt to different legal and political environments.[390] Involvement of international legal networks may well reduce any political interference with criminal proceedings involving soldiers,[391] such as through trial monitoring. Such networks could work alongside any hybrid courts, or should troop-contributing countries prove unwilling to implement a hybrid system to hold peacekeepers to account, they might be a viable, albeit weaker, alternative, provided the UN puts appropriate support structures in place.

A number of Congolese military court trials have drawn on the ICC Statute for the definition of crimes, procedure and due process standards,[392] irrespective of implementing legislation. The ICC Statute's definitions of sexual offences were considerably broader than under Congolese

---

[386] See Baylis, 2009, p. 7, *supra* note 176. On transnational legal networks, see also Turner, 2007, p. 985, *supra* note 380.

[387] See Baylis, 2009, p. 80, *supra* note 176.

[388] Kal Raustiala, "The Architecture of International Cooperation: Transgovernmental Networks and the Future of International Law", in *Virginia Journal of International Law*, 2002, vol. 43, no. 1, pp. 78–79.

[389] For a detailed discussion of these networks and their influence in the realm of international criminal law, see Turner, 2007, p. 985, *supra* note 380.

[390] *Ibid.*

[391] *Ibid.*, p. 999.

[392] Baylis, 2009, pp. 33–34, 37, 45, see *supra* note 176.

law.[393] Baylis puts this advancement down to the efforts not only of national military courts, but also given the influence of transnational networks through both advocacy for such prosecutions and through actual
support and assistance.[394] Indeed if some sort of hybrid justice mechanism
were established, it could also attract the interest and assistance of international legal networks and funding, should it play a dual role of host state
capacity-building.

14.2.3. Tri-hybrid

There seems to be considerable merit in proposals for the establishment of
a hybrid court for dealing with incidents of sexual abuse and exploitation
by UN peacekeepers, where troop-contributing countries fail to exercise
jurisdiction. As mentioned, the group of legal experts suggested locating
such courts in the host state legal system.[395] While at first glance this
might appear an ideal model, in this author's view it speaks more to rhetoric than to realism. Many host states may simply not be institutionally
equipped to deal with crimes by peacekeepers, in particular in host states
where such abuse is most prevalent. That is not to state that where it is
feasible that the host state should not play a key role in a hybrid system.

I contend that at least partial jurisdiction over military contingents
needs to remain with the troop-contributing country. There are two primary reasons for this. States will not be willing to' expose their soldiers to
host state criminal justice systems over which they have no control and
where their rights might be violated. Should the troop-contributing country be required to do so this could well result in a massive fall in troop-
contributions and prove seriously detrimental to UN peacekeeping. Secondly, given the particular nature of militaries, national military law experts need to be present on anybody prosecuting such personnel.

As an alternative, I propose the troop-contributing country retaining
primary jurisdiction. However, should a troop-contributing country prove

---

[393] *Ibid.*, pp. 37, 43.

[394] Baylis notes that United Nations Organisation Mission in the Democratic Republic of Congo
('MONUC', now United Nations Organisation Stabilisation Mission in the Democratic Republic of the Congo, 'MONUSCO') and the European Union provided briefings on legal issues or legal materials or other resource and legal materials to those involved in conducting at
least some of the trials. *Ibid.*, pp. 43–44, 48.

[395] Group of Legal Experts Report, para. 33, see *supra* note 327.

unwilling or unable to investigate or prosecute, a secondary tri-hybrid mechanism, with input from the UN, sending and host states, could exercise jurisdiction. As the group of legal experts noted:[396]

> Jurisdiction is not an indivisible concept and the host State and other States may be involved in different but mutually supportive aspects of the overall exercise of criminal jurisdiction.

This is particularly relevant to extraterritorial criminal acts committed by UN military peacekeepers given that such acts may give rise to nationality and territorially based jurisdiction.[397] A tri-hybrid justice model would allow for the apportionment of jurisdiction between both the troop-contributing country and host states and the tribunal. It would also assist in countering perceptions at the local level that UN peacekeepers are immune from the law, which have the possible dual purpose of enhancing the rule of law. However, the central feature would be that the international component is on permanent standby, so that it is rapidly deployable. This might help create some consistency in dealing with incidents of sexual abuse and exploitation or other serious crimes by UN peacekeepers. It could have permanent offices in larger mission states, such as the DRC, along with a headquarters in New York. Such a mechanism would require host state consent, and draw on state jurisdiction, whether territorial or nationality based, unless established under Chapter VII of the UN Charter or underpinned by a treaty.

The immunity of military personnel could be qualified, wherein the troop-contributing country could retain exclusive jurisdiction over on-duty offences, and offences that only affect the force itself.[398] The hybrid model court has subject matter jurisdiction over a set of pre-agreed serious offences. The system could operate on the basis of complementarity, whereby it would be a court of last resort, exercising jurisdiction only where the troop-contributing country is unwilling or unable to prosecute,

---

[396] Group of Legal Experts Report, p. 2, see *supra* note 327.

[397] Although in practice UN military contingents are immune from host state jurisdiction under UN Status of Forces Agreements as they stand.

[398] This follows the framework set out in the NATO Status of Forces Agreement, which provides for concurrent jurisdiction. Agreement between the Parties to the North Atlantic Treaty regarding the Status of their Forces, 4 UST 1972, TIAS 2846, 199 UNTS 67, 19 June 1951, entered into force 23 August 1953.

such as: 1) where prosecution is essentially conducted to shield the perpetrator; 2) proceedings are not being conducted in an independent or impartial manner; or 3) the state lacks the ability to adequately investigate and/or prosecute abroad.

The tri-hybrid model would comprise a mix of international and domestic personnel at all levels of the proceedings from investigation to prosecution and adjudication. International personnel could be drawn from a permanent component of this model, which includes a roster of appropriately qualified personnel. All troop-contributing countries and host states (where there are suitably trained personnel) could maintain a roster of appropriately trained personnel that could be deployed should serious allegations arise. Troop-contributing country personnel should have military law expertise when dealing with crimes by military contingents.

A difficulty, however, is that under the present model Status of Forces Agreement and model memorandum of understanding troop-contributing countries are granted exclusive criminal jurisdiction over their troops, and host states are debarred from exercising any jurisdiction over UN military contingents. As I have argued elsewhere, these documents could be amended to allow for a broader approach to jurisdiction. It is my contention that troop-contributing country exclusive criminal jurisdiction is too broad, and perhaps not required for the independent functioning of UN operations. In my view, the Status of Forces Agreement, memorandum of understanding and any convention that might eventually emerge on this issue should provide for concurrent or complementary jurisdiction over military contingents by an international or hybrid court, if the troop-contributing country proves unwilling or unable to exercise jurisdiction.[399] Status of Forces Agreements and memoranda of understanding could possibly provide for a system by which immunity could be waived, where a tri-hybrid court is to conduct proceedings.

The Statute of the SCSL contains a unique provision insofar as the Courts' jurisdiction covers crimes committed by peacekeepers in certain circumstances.[400] Article 1 specifically provides for the primacy of troop-

---

[399] See further Burke, 2011, pp. 63–104, *supra* note 17.

[400] SCSL Statute, Article 1, see *supra* note 349.

contributing country jurisdiction over peacekeeping personnel, in accordance with the Status of Mission Agreement.[401] It further provides:[402]

> 2. Any transgressions by peacekeepers and related personnel present in Sierra Leone pursuant to the Status of Mission Agreement in force between the United Nations and the Government of Sierra Leone or agreements between Sierra Leone and other Governments or regional organizations, or, in the absence of such agreement, provided that the peacekeeping operations were undertaken with the consent of the Government of Sierra Leone, shall be within the primary jurisdiction of the sending State.
>
> 3. In the event the sending State is unwilling or unable genuinely to carry out an investigation or prosecution, the Court may, if authorized by the Security Council on the proposal of any State, exercise jurisdiction over such persons.

The provision contemplates the possibility of the SCSL exercising secondary jurisdiction, akin to the principle of complementarity, when the troop-contributing country proves "unwilling or unable genuinely" to investigate or prosecute peacekeepers. In such circumstances a state would have to propose that the SCSL exercise jurisdiction over such personnel and it could only do so if authorised by the Security Council, both of which are unlikely. Nevertheless, the insertion of such a provision, albeit more broadly worded, providing for possible partial relinquishment of jurisdiction over UN military personnel, through the exercise of secondary jurisdiction by a hybrid court, may make troop-contributing countries more open to it.[403]

Even if a more limited form of immunity from host state jurisdiction is not provided for, host state co-operation would still be required, in

---

[401] On Status of Forces and Status of Mission Agreements and jurisdictional implications, see Burke, 2011, pp. 63–104, *supra* note 17.

[402] SCSL Statute, Articles 2 and 3, see *supra* note 349.

[403] It is also interesting that the provision seems to contemplate that the hybrid court could exercise jurisdiction over peacekeepers where a Status of Mission Agreement is not in place granting the troop-contributing country exclusive criminal jurisdiction and where such personnel are present in the absence of consent of the government of Sierra Leone. On the significance of host state consent to the legal status of UN forces deployed in that state, in the absence of a Status of Mission Agreement, see Burke, 2011, pp. 63–104, *supra* note 17.

particular through assisting investigations, the gathering of evidence and so on. Involvement of host state personnel is important, not only given that it can contribute to capacity-building in the host state, but also given that they will have a better understanding of local customs, language, the security situation on the ground, and other issues that may be encountered in the host state. This may be particularly important when dealing with rape victims and children. Furthermore, the host state would be more likely to consent to various phases of the proceedings being conducted in its territory if it is involved. A number of authors have also pointed towards a supportive role that the ICC could play in its interactions with hybrid and national courts.[404]

Apart from the possible impediments already mentioned, a real difficulty I foresee with a hybrid or tri-hybrid justice mechanism is getting judges, whether international or from the troop-contributing country, to travel to a conflict or post-conflict state, in addition to other personnel necessary for the investigation and prosecution. Existing UN bodies, the Office of Internal Oversight Services and Conduct and Discipline Unit and Teams, already involved in receiving complaints and the administration of serious offences by peacekeepers, including sexual abuse and exploitation, could help bolster the latter part of any given system, in conjunction with host states' authorities.[405] Furthermore, evidence gathered appropriately by the Office of Internal Oversight Services could be used for prosecution purposes,[406] and the assistance and expertise of these bodies in operating in a conflict or post-conflict environment could be drawn upon.

Some of the already established networks for dealing with sexual abuse and exploitation by peacekeepers could tie into the overall system of which the hybrid justice mechanism could form a part. This might in-

---

[404] Turner, 2005, p. 1, see *supra* note 358; Baylis, 2009, p. 1, see *supra* note 176; Burke-White, 2008, p. 53, see *supra* note 295.

[405] The Conduct and Discipline Unit and Teams are the first to receive allegations of sexual exploitation and abuse in the field. See further UN General Assembly, Comprehensive Report of Conduct and Discipline including Full Justification of All Posts, Report of the Secretary-General, UN Doc. A/62/758, 20 March 2008.

[406] Note, however, that the difficulty with Office of Internal Oversight Services/UN investigation is that they are administrative in nature, and the troop-contributing country may not accept such evidence as a basis for criminal prosecution. Report on Criminal Accountability, para. 27, see *supra* note 332.

clude the UN's strategy for providing assistance and support to victims of sexual abuse and exploitation by UN staff and related personnel,[407] which provides certain medical, legal, social and psychological support through the use of existing programmes and services.[408]

It is my contention that, where possible, the prosecution of UN peacekeepers needs to occur and be seen to occur in host states. Local communities need to see justice being done.[409] A tri-hybrid court might also draw on the mobility of the recent Congolese mobile military/gender justice courts.[410] In the DRC, mobile court trials are often conducted outdoors or in private homes where other infrastructure in unavailable.[411] These are already operating in the DRC with UN support and assistance, in addition to that of transnational legal networks.[412] Mobility would add to the capacity to hold trials in remote communities, and thereby better promote the rule of law.[413]

14.2.4. Justifications for Prosecution of UN Military Personnel by an International or Internationalised Justice Mechanism

At this juncture, it is important to reflect briefly on whether the prosecution of UN peacekeepers is an appropriate role for the international community. One of the primary reasons for punishing crimes by peacekeepers at an internationalised level is the international dimension of such offences, and their effect on values of the international community and interna-

---

[407] The General Assembly has now adopted Resolution 62/214: UN General Assembly, United Nations Comprehensive Strategy on Assistance and Support to Victim Exploitation and Abuse by United Nations Staff and Related Personnel, UN Doc. A/RES/62/214, 7 March 2008.

[408] *Ibid.*, paras. 6–7; UN General Assembly, Implementation of the United Nations Comprehensive Strategy on Assistance and Support to Victims of Sexual Exploitation and Abuse by United Nations Staff and Related Personnel, Report of Secretary-General, UN Doc. A/64/176, 27 July 2009, para. 6.

[409] The Comprehensive Strategy to deal with sexual exploitation and abuse by UN peacekeepers recommended conducting on-site courts martial, see *supra* note 252.

[410] See further Eric A. Witte, *Putting Complementarity into Practice: Domestic Justice for International Crimes in DRC, Uganda and Kenya*, Open Society Foundations, New York, 2011, pp. 53–58.

[411] *Ibid.*, pp. 52–53.

[412] For instance, prosecution support cells are already deployed to MONUSCO in the DRC to provide training to investigators and so on. *Ibid.*, p. 55.

[413] *Ibid.*, pp. 52–53.

---

tional peace and security as a whole. It must be borne in mind that the ICC has limited capacity to prosecute perpetrators of serious international criminal law offences even when they come within the jurisdiction of the Court. While sexual offences committed by UN military peacekeepers are abhorrent, can we justify their prosecution at an international level? That is, where troop-contributing countries prove unwilling or unable to prosecute members of their military contingents, are the ICC or hybrid/tri-hybrid courts favourable alternatives?

In determining the appropriate forum for holding UN military peacekeepers complicit in sexual abuse and exploitation to account, the objectives of such prosecutions ought to be considered. Is the primary goal to deter either specifically the perpetrator or more generally UN military personnel, or is the goal to deter sexual offences more broadly in the host state by demonstrating that nobody is outside the law? Alternatively, does the importance of ensuring the prosecution of UN peacekeepers for serious crimes, in particular sexual offences, rest in its expressive or pedagogical value, within the host state, the troop-contributing country, military in general, and the broader international community? Indeed each of these objectives may play a part, but just how far these goals can be achieved would seem to depend on the forum. There may also be other justifications for punishment including rehabilitation, restoration, retribution, incapacitation and reconciliation. However, these are outside the scope of the current discussion.[414] Concentrating solely on deterrence and expressive theory, I suggest that localised hybrid/tri-hybrid tribunals might better serve these ends than prosecution of peacekeepers by the ICC.

14.2.4.1. Deterrence

Deterrence is frequently cited as a primary objective of punishment for criminal offences both in the domestic and international sphere. The Preamble of the ICC Statute suggests that the drafters had deterrence in mind in punishing perpetrators of serious violations of international criminal law, wherein it provides that the ICC is "[d]etermined to put an end to

---

[414] There is considerable debate on the capacity of the ICC or any international court to serve any of these purposes and the utility of transposing domestic criminal law theory to the international context.

impunity for the perpetrators of these crimes and thus to contribute to the prevention of such crimes".[415] The essence of deterrence is that potential violators of the law fear the consequences of the law,[416] through threats of punishment.[417] Mark A. Drumbl posits that there is a "utilitarian and consequentialist effect of that punishment: namely, reducing recidivism".[418] Deterrence in effect operates at two levels: 1) "specific", namely aimed at the author of the impugned conduct; and 2) "general", aimed at the broader community.[419] Punishment is not only to prevent repetition of the impugned conduct by the perpetrator but also at deterring would-be perpetrators of similar offences.[420]

Johannes Andenæs contends that general deterrence is also about the "moral or socio-pedagogical influence of punishment".[421] As noted by the ICTY in the *Rutanga* case, punishment has the power to deter by "showing them that the international community shall not tolerate the serious violations of international humanitarian law and human rights".[422] The ICC in *Lubanga* stated that deterrence is a key objective of the ICC and that "any retributory effect of the activities of the Court must be subordinate to the higher purpose of prevention".[423]

However, the deterrent value of punishment is problematic to assess even in the domestic context, given the difficulty in measuring its effect

---

[415] ICC Statute, Preamble, see *supra* note 23; Keller, 2008, p. 41, see *supra* note 112.

[416] See further Richard A. Posner, "An Economic Theory of the Criminal Law", in *Columbia Law Review*, 1985, vol. 85, no. 6, p. 1193.

[417] Payam Akhavan states: "sanctions are most important because the help instil voluntary of 'good faith' respect for just conduct by discrediting inhumane or unjust conduct, the cumulative effect of which encourages habitual or subliminal conformity with the law". Payam Akhavan, "Justice in the Hague, Peace in the Former Yugoslavia? A Commentary on the United Nations War Crimes Tribunal", in *Human Rights Quarterly*, 1998, vol. 20, no. 4, pp. 737, 741.

[418] Drumbl, 2005, p. 560, see *supra* note 359. See also Keller, 2008, p. 41, *supra* note 112.

[419] Keller, 2008, p. 41, see *supra* note 112.

[420] Sloane, 2007, p. 43, see *supra* note 283.

[421] Johannes Andenæs, *Punishment and Deterrence*, University of Michigan Press, Ann Arbor, 1974, pp. 34–35, cited in Akhavan, 1998, p. 746, see *supra* note 417.

[422] ICTR, *Prosecutor v. Georges Rutaganda*, Trial Chamber, Judgment and Sentence, ICTR-96-3-A, 26 May 2003 (http://www.legal-tools.org/doc/f0dbbb/).

[423] *Lubanga* Decision, para. 48, see *supra* note 135.

on the perceptions of potential perpetrators.[424] This difficulty is more acute when it comes to punishment by international courts.[425] This is primarily due to the lack of empirical data on the issue.[426] There is substantial cynicism on the actual ability of the ICC to deter crimes under its jurisdiction.[427] In order for deterrence to function fear of punishment must be realistic and properly communicated to potential perpetrators. Given the ICC's limited resources and capacity only to take a few situations and cases at any one time, when contrasted with the thousands of potential defendants that could be bought before the ICC, any deterrent value the Court is likely to be limited. Robert Sloane notes that the rational actor model of deterrence, based on a cost-benefit calculus, simply does not work effectively in the international context, given the context in which many international criminal law offences occur.[428] Deterrence theory assumes that potential perpetrators of international criminal law offences are rational actors, but other authors contend that such persons are unlikely to be rational actors who calculate the risk of their actions.[429] When it comes to crimes perpetrated by UN military peacekeepers deployed in conflict or post-conflict environments, the ability to act rationally is further thrown into flux. The total or partial collapse of the rule of law in many host states enables actors to commit crimes with little real fear of prosecution that they likely would never commit in the troop-contributing country.

Let us take, for instance, the situation in the DRC. The DRC has been in the midst of an armed conflict almost non-stop since the mid-

---

[424] Margaret M. deGuzman, "Choosing to Prosecute: Expressive Selection at the International Criminal Court", in *Michigan Journal of International Law*, 2012, vol. 33, no. 2, p. 305; see also Margaret M. deGuzman's chapter in the present volume; Paul H. Robinson and John M. Darley, "The Role of Deterrence in the Formulation of Criminal Law Rules: At its Worst When Doing Its Best", in *Georgetown Law Journal*, 2003, vol. 91, no. 5, p. 949.

[425] Eric D. Blumenson, "A Challenge of a Global Standard of Justice: Peace, Pluralism, and Punishment at the International Criminal Court", in *Columbia Journal of Transnational Law*, 2006, vol. 44, no. 3, pp. 798, 827–82.

[426] *Ibid.*, p. 828, fn. 84.

[427] See, for example, David Wippman, "Atrocities, Deterrence, and the Limits of International Justice", in *Fordham International Law Journal*, 1999, vol. 23, no. 2, p. 473; Julian Ku, "How System Criminality Could Exacerbate the Weaknesses of International Criminal Law", in *Santa Clara Journal of International Law*, 2010, vol. 8, p. 36.

[428] Sloane, 2007, see *supra* note 283.

[429] Drumbl comments on the ability of actor to act rationally in situations of mass violence and societal collapse: Drumbl, 2005, p. 590, see *supra* note 359.

1990s.[430] Sexual violence and rape at the hands of the Congolese armed forces, police and militia groups are widespread. According to a study, approximately 420,000 women and girls are raped in the DRC every year.[431] Accountability for such crimes is virtually non-existent, save for some recent advances by mobile gender courts.[432] In such circumstances the deterrent value of a few international prosecutions is likely to be weak. It may have greater impact on the level of senior leaders than on lower-level perpetrators. [433] The DRC is spread across an area of 2,345,408 square kilometres, with little infrastructure connecting regions, and there is considerable risk in travelling. Sexual abuse and exploitation by UN military personnel have been rampant in the DRC, yet thus far there has little accountability for such. This is partially due to the afore-mentioned difficulties, but also due to their immunity from criminal juris-diction in the host state, and the lack of political will or perhaps the inabil-ity of troop-contributing countries to effectively exercise their jurisdic-tion. One can imagine the difficulties that would be faced by the ICC or a troop-contributing country in exercising jurisdiction over these troops for incongruous extraterritorial conduct, in particular conduct which is sexual in nature, given the difficulties of investigating and gathering evidence, in addition to the possible resistance of the armed forces to such investiga-tions. This leaves us to question whether these personnel would perceive themselves as being genuinely at risk of prosecution by the ICC or any other body? Given the extent of violence perpetrated by other armed groups in the DRC, which quantitatively outweighs that by UN peace-keepers, can they realistically feel threatened? Ongoing sexual abuse and exploitation suggest that these personnel do not at present perceive them-selves as being at risk of prosecution by the ICC, or even by their home state.

Conversely, Payam Akhavan contends that prosecution of a large number of persons is not necessary in order to serve the goal of deter-

---

[430] The civil war in the DRC has been classed as Africa's war, the worst since the Second World War: The Economist, "Making Africa Smile", 17 January 2004.

[431] Peterman *et al.*, 2011, p. 1064, see *supra* note 161.

[432] See, for example, PeaceWomen, "DR Congo Court Convicts Nine Police of Rape", 8 November 2010.

[433] Payam Akhavan, "Beyond Impunity: Can International Criminal Justice Deter Future Atrocities?", in *American Journal of International Law*, 2001, vol. 95, no. 1, p. 7; Sloane, 2007, pp. 42–43, see *supra* note 283.

rence, but rather that a few exemplary prosecutions might suffice to deter other members of the community. He argues that punishment deters through internalisation of norms of conduct, wherein individual criminal accountability is expected for violating these norms.[434] Logically it does seem, however, that the deterrent value of any court or tribunal is linked to the perceived likelihood of punishment. There must be a realistic threat of punishment.[435] As stated by Michael Smidt, the likelihood of being brought before the ICC is about equal to winning the lottery.[436] Arguably, the establishment of a tri-hybrid court where troop-contributing countries prove unwilling or unable to prosecute, which has the ability and resources to prosecute substantial numbers of personnel, could increase the deterrent value of punishment, given the increased likelihood of been held to account. A number of authors argue that the ICC might better serve the goals of deterrence through positive complementarity, which is aimed at encouraging states to enforce international criminal law.[437] It is this author's contention that both bodies could complement one another in serving such goals, where appropriate.

14.2.4.2. Expressive Value

Theorists increasingly argue that a primary objective of the ICC in selecting cases for prosecution ought to be to express global norms.[438] As noted by the Office of the United Nations High Commissioner for Human Rights ('OHCHR'), in approaching the issue of prosecution of serious human rights violations, policymakers need to have an informed view on what they hope to achieve from prosecution at the international level. Deterrence is difficult to achieve and therefore may create unrealistic expectations. Retribution, on the other hand, may create conditions that can encourage vengeance. In the OHCHR's view a better approach is that the

---

[434] Akhavan, 1998, p. 751, see *supra* note 417. In essence deterrence has a norm-reinforcing role, see Blumenson, 2006, p. 819, *supra* note 425.

[435] Laplante, 2010, p. 641, see *supra* note 293.

[436] Michael L. Smidt, "The International Criminal Court: An Effective Means of Deterrence?", in *Military Law Review*, 2001, vol. 167, pp. 156, 188.

[437] Laplante, 2010, p. 635, see *supra* note 293.

[438] DeGuzman, 2012, p. 36, *supra* note 424.

---

ultimate goal of prosecution is disapproval.[439] Expressive theory is the idea that prosecution and punishment can be used as a vehicle to express certain values when particular actors reject them.[440] Punishment by the ICC arguably serves to reaffirm faith in the rule of law,[441] through communicating that certain acts violate social norms. Punishment may serve a moral educative value.[442]

DeGuzman argues that prosecution for the recruitment of child soldiers by the ICC has an expressive value in reinforcing a norm that has otherwise been underprosecuted and under-recognised. A similar rationale might be applied to the prosecution of attacks on UN peacekeepers.[443] As discussed, Heller suggests a possible "category-based" approach in the prioritisation of cases.[444] This could arguably allow for the selection of cases on the basis that they fall within a particular category, which is perhaps underprosecuted, and the gravity of which needs to be emphasised. Indeed particular emphasis does appear to be placed gender-based crimes and crimes against children by the ICC Statute.[445] Punishment at the international level can be seen as condemnation of such abhorrent con-

---

[439] Office of the United Nations High Commissioner for Human Rights ('OHCHR'), *Rule-of-Law Tools for Post-Conflict States: Prosecution Initiatives*, New York, United Nations, 2006, p. 4.

[440] Dan M. Kahan, "Two Liberal Fallacies in the Hate Crimes Debate", in *Law and Philosophy*, 2001, vol. 20, no. 2, p. 175.

[441] Mark A. Drumbl, "The Expressive Value of Prosecuting and Punishing Terrorists: *Hamdan, the Geneva Conventions, and International Criminal Law*", in *George Washington Law Review*, 2007, vol. 75, nos. 5/6, pp. 1165, 1182.

[442] Drumbl posits that "[s]ince expressivism is concerned with the narrative and messaging function of law, it places considerable import on the methodology of how individuals are convicted and punished and, thereby, has come to value due process and legalism": *Ibid.*, p. 1184.

[443] DeGuzman, 2012, p. 50, see *supra* note 424.

[444] See section 14.1.4.

[445] Susana SáCouto and Katherine Cleary, "Importance of Effective Investigation of Sexual Violence and Gender-Based Crimes at the International Criminal Court", in *American University Journal of Gender, Social Policy and the Law*, 2009, vol. 17, no. 2, p. 337.

---

duct.[446] It sends a moral message that this conduct is perceived as wrongful.[447] As Sloane aptly notes:

> International criminal tribunals can contribute most effectively to world public order as self-consciously expressive penal institutions: publically condemning acts deplored by international law, acting as an engine of jurisprudential development at the local level, and encouraging the legal and normative internalization of international human rights law and humanitarian law.[448]

Serious sexual offences must be seen to be condemned by the international community, in particular when involving UN peacekeepers. It is difficult to see how the UN and international community can preach about the need to establish the rule of law and yet allow impunity for peacekeepers who violate the standards that they seek to promote.[449] Yet whether the ICC is the appropriate venue to express indignation is questionable. As addressed in section 14.1., even if crimes by UN peacekeepers meet the *chapeau* elements of war crimes or crimes against humanity under the ICC Statute, it seems unlikely that sexual crimes committed by UN military peacekeepers would be prosecuted by the ICC given gravity, prosecutorial discretion, the need to select and prioritise cases and so on. Yet if a pedagogical function is to be served, the prosecution of such cases at an internationalised or hybrid level appears warranted. Not only would it reinforce norms on sexual violence against women and children, it would demonstrate that no person is above the law. As Jean Hampton notes:

> [a] decision not to punish wrongdoers such as the rapist is also expressive: it communicates to the victim and to the wider society the idea that such treatment, and the status it attributes to the victim, are appropriate, and thus, in the case of

---

[446] Matthew Alder, "Expressive Theories of Law: A Skeptical Overview", in *University of Pennsylvania Law Review*, 2001, vol. 148, no. 5, p. 1363; Dan M. Kahan, "What Do Alternative Sanctions Mean?", in *University of Chicago Law Review*, vol. 63, no. 2, 1996, p. 591.

[447] See further Stephen P. Garvey, "Restorative Justice, Punishment, and Atonement", in *Utah Law Review*, 2003, vol. 203, no. 1, pp. 303, 308; Jean Hampton, "The Moral Education Theory of Punishment", in *Philosophy and Public* Affairs, 1981, vol. 13, no. 3, p. 209.

[448] Sloane, 2007, p. 43, see *supra* note 283.

[449] OHCHR, 2006, p. 41, see *supra* note 439.

> the rape victim, reinforces the idea that women are objects to
> be possessed and are there for the taking.[450]

The ICC does appear to be having a subtle impact on armies all over the world in how they perceive and engage with international law. The establishment of the institution is leaving military commanders to question whether the actions of their troops could result in their being held criminally liable. As noted by ICC chief prosecutor: "Armies, all over the world, are adjusting their operational standards, training and rules of engagement to the Rome Statute".[451] The fact is that states do not generally desire their troops ever being brought before an international court for serious violations of international criminal law. Moreno-Ocampo elaborated:

> This is what we call the 'shadow' of the Court [...] the concept of the shadow explains how one court ruling in an individual case can affect a multiplicity of other cases, resulting in agreements being made and disputes being settled without further judicial intervention: they are solved under the 'shadow of the law'.[452]

However, as stated, the ICC is not necessarily the only or most appropriate avenue for pursing prosecutions of UN military peacekeepers for sexual violence. An internationalised hybrid/tri-hybrid court arguably could better achieve the expressive and pedagogical function of punishing peacekeepers complicit in serious sexual abuse and exploitation. Given greater proximity to military peacekeepers and victims and integration with domestic justice sectors, it would be better suited to communicate condemnation at a local level and to reaffirm the rule of law.

Past investigations into sexual abuse and exploitation by military personnel on the MONUSCO operation revealed a culture of solidarity and secrecy regarding such abuses. Military officials deliberately frustrated UN investigations, shielding perpetrators.[453] Condemnation of sexual

---

[450] Jean Hampton, "Correcting Harms versus Righting Wrongs: The Goal of Retribution", in *UCLA Law Review*, 1992, vol. 39, no. 6, pp. 1659, 1684.

[451] ICC, Office of the Prosecutor, Luis Moreno-Ocampo, Keynote Address, Council on Foreign Relations, Washington, 4 February 2010, para. 2.

[452] Luis Moreno-Ocampo, "The International Criminal Court: Some Reflections", in *Yearbook of International Humanitarian Law*, 2009, vol. 12, pp. 3, 9.

[453] UN General Assembly, Investigation by the Office of Internal Oversight into Allegations of Sexual Exploitation and abuse in the United Nations Organisation Mission in the Democratic

violence through prosecution and punishment by a tri-hybrid court may well help bring about behavioural change among would-be perpetrators. It could also have the dual value of expressing the seriousness of sexual offences and the international community's indignation at such conduct and the need to enforce universal values and the rule of law not only among troop-contributing countries and their military contingents, but also at the level of the host state. Furthermore, it would demonstrate that nobody is immune from the law.

14.2.4.3. Conclusion

It is my contention that when it comes to sexual abuse and exploitation by UN military peacekeepers, a tri-hybrid model may well have greater deterrent and expressive value than purely international prosecutions. A possible advantage of adding the international element to prosecutions is that it may highlight the gravity of the crime, the international community's condemnation, and the fact that it affects more than one nation.[454] The presence of international personnel in a tri-hybrid court would garner greater international attention, and therefore would likely have greater deterrent effect on would-be perpetrators of sexual abuse and exploitation, not only UN troops but possibly other potential perpetrators. Additionally, a tri-hybrid justice mechanism might have the ability to exert influence over troop-contributing countries' military and civilian laws dealing with sexual offences by the military, and to reinforce the UN's current zero-tolerance policy.

14.2.5. Overall Observations and Conclusion

Sexual abuse and exploitation by UN military peacekeepers are not an ephemeral or passing concern and serious action needs to be taken to counter the current culture of impunity that still appears to lie within UN

Republic of the Congo, UN Doc. A/59/661, 5 January 2005. Sarah Martin argues that a "hyper-masculine culture that encourages sexual exploitation and abuse and a tradition of silence have evolved within (peacekeeping missions)": Sarah Martin, *Must Boys Be Boys? Ending Sexual Exploitation & Abuse in UN Peacekeeping*, Refugees International, Washington, DC, October 2005, p. ii; the attitude that seems to prevail is one of "boys will be boys". Colum Lynch, "U.N. Faces More Accusations of Sexual Misconduct", in *Washington Post*, 12 March 2005, A22.

[454] Mégret, 2005, p. 737, see *supra* note 367.

operations. While domestic jurisdiction ought to be the first port of call for holding UN military peacekeepers to account for sexual abuse and exploitation, the criminal prosecution of such persons by troop-contributing countries is rare. Serious incidents of sexual abuse and exploitation by UN military peacekeepers cannot be regarded as simply ordinary criminal offences. That stated, most such offences are unlikely to meet the high thresholds and other barriers set by the ICC Statute to be prosecuted before the Court. It is this author's contention that we need to be prudent in advocating the prosecution of UN military peacekeepers before the ICC, save in the most exceptional circumstances. As Akhavan cautioned with respect to the ICTY, it is not "befitting to subscribe to the judicial romanticism of some circles that views the ICTY as a panacea for all the ills of the former Yugoslavia".[455] A similar argument may be made of the ICC and the ills of the world. It simply cannot adequately achieve all the goals that the international community might desire of it. Yet adding an international element appears warranted when the troop-contributing country proves unwilling or unable to prosecute soldiers who sexually abuse the civilians they have been mandated to protect. Frédéric Mégret notes the difference between the utility of international and domestic criminal processes lies in their expressive value or message.[456] Sexual abuse and exploitation, when perpetrated by UN peacekeepers, not only offends the victim, but the broader international community and "the dignity of mankind".[457]

The establishment of a tri-hybrid justice mechanism, when it comes to serious international criminal law offences, may provide a viable alternative. Such a solution would be in line with the principle of complementarity as it locates jurisdiction in national courts. Indeed the ICC could still play a residual role through positive complementarity, where appropriate. Transnational legal networks might also feed into a system through the support of troop-contributing country and tri-hybrid court proceedings. A system which increases the possibility of been held to account for sexual abuse and exploitation would likely serve to deter would-be perpetrators.

---

[455] Akhavan, 1998, p. 740, see *supra* note 417.

[456] *Ibid.*; Mégret, 2005, p. 743, see *supra* note 367.

[457] Mégret, 2005, p. 744, see *supra* note 367.

Whichever approach is taken to addressing sexual abuse and exploitation by UN military peacekeepers, a word of caution seems warranted. While the rebuilding of national justice systems is really important for states in conflict and post-conflict states, we need to step carefully so as not to make UN military peacekeepers the "sacrificial lambs" for goals that are better achieved elsewhere. Adequate safeguards would need to be in place to protect the rights of the accused.

To conclude with a quote from Prince Zeid, whose report was instrumental in bringing the problem of sexual abuse and exploitation by UN peacekeepers to the limelight:

> I was left feeling numb by the extent to which people can be made to suffer. The young women of Bunia, in the Democratic Republic of the Congo, had survived the most gruesome wartime experiences-massacres, multiple rapes, disease and hunger – only to then find themselves tormented by the very people who were sent in to save them. [... I]f the victims of UN abuse were properly treated today, the negotiators at the United Nations, representing all our countries, would by now have agreed to the mandatory holding of all court-martials in the territorial or host state, whenever the accused came from a military contingent. They would have allowed for joint United Nations-member state investigations of alleged criminal offenses [...]. For lawyers from the world's respective defense establishments and various ministries to think only of securing and defending the rights of their own soldiers, of their own nationals, with little regard to the victims thereof begs the rather obvious question: if not them, then who?[458]

---

[458] Al-Hussein, 2009, pp. 654–55, *supra* note 1.

15

The Impact of Prosecutorial Strategy
on the Investigation and Prosecution of Sexual
Violence at International Criminal Tribunals

Niamh Hayes[*]

15.1. Introduction

Prosecuting violations of international criminal law is no easy task. In a national criminal jurisdiction, prosecuting authorities bear the responsibility of constructing a comprehensive case against an accused person for violations of the applicable domestic laws, but do so in co-operation with a police force with a mandate to gather the necessary physical evidence, identify relevant witnesses and arrest and interview potential suspects. Police and prosecutors know the locality, the language and the law,[1] and have a career's worth of formative experience in investigating and prosecuting crimes. They are acutely aware of the vagaries of national criminal procedure and evidentiary rules, and they carry out their duties on behalf of the state, and, by implication, the society against whom the crime in question was committed. In an international criminal context, prosecuting authorities from a wide array of different legal systems are responsible for the identification, investigation and prosecution of individuals who are suspected of having committed violations of international criminal and international humanitarian law in another state. The state in question may be still experiencing open hostilities or may have entered an uneasy post-conflict atmosphere, but is likely to be politically and socially unstable and lacking a functioning police force or judiciary. Field investigations

---

[*] **Niamh Hayes** is a Ph.D. candidate at the Irish Centre for Human Rights, National University of Ireland, Galway, researching the prosecution of sexual violence by international criminal tribunals. She previously worked as a consultant for the Institute for International Criminal Investigations and as a legal consultant for Women's Initiatives for Gender Justice, an international women's rights organisation based in The Hague. The author would like to thank Joe Powderly and John Ralston for their comments on an earlier draft of this piece. All views expressed are the author's own.

[1] As the (unattributed) saying goes, "a good lawyer knows the law, a great lawyer knows the judge".

---

will have to be carried out under significant security constraints, most likely via interpreters (assuming appropriately trained personnel can be found), by staff of varying experiences, who come from a variety of jurisdictional backgrounds, and who are very unlikely to be able to operate unobtrusively. The crimes in question may have been committed months if not years previously, so physical evidence will have degraded, and witnesses may have suffered severe trauma, have had to leave their homes, or have been killed in the intervening period. International tribunals may not have the power to compel evidence, and the lack of an international police force means that such courts are dependent on states to enforce their arrest warrants, which may (and frequently does) take years. International criminal prosecutors operate in a legal system entirely alien to their own, applying a hybrid of common and civil law rules of procedure and evidence, and acting on an occasionally amorphous mandate from the international community which may not be supported or even recognised by the affected communities in the state in question.

Prosecuting any international crime under these circumstances is not an easy task, but prosecuting sexual violence – a category of crime which is perceived as notoriously difficult to prove even within domestic criminal systems – is a challenge of another magnitude altogether. If we take the jurisdictions of England and Wales, Sweden or Ireland as examples of states where national prosecuting authorities operate in relatively idyllic conditions by comparison to international criminal prosecutors, one may be shocked or simply disheartened to learn that domestic conviction rates in rape cases are derisory: according to a 2003 study of attrition rates in sexual violence cases, only 8 per cent of reported rapes in England and Wales resulted in a conviction, 7 per cent in Sweden and a truly pathetic 1 per cent in Ireland.[2] If this is the prognosis in states with a relatively high degree of social equality, political stability and a functioning criminal justice system, then the scale of the task facing international prosecutors – exacerbated by cultural stigmatisation of rape, precarious security conditions and the logistical difficulties inherent in all interna-

---

[2] Linda Regan and Liz Kelly, "Rape: Still a Forgotten Issue", in *Rape Crisis Network Europe*, 2003, p. 13. The figure for conviction rates in England and Wales dropped to 5.3 per cent in 2004/2005. See further Jennifer Temkin and Barbara Krahé, *Sexual Assault and the Justice Gap: A Question of Attitude*, Hart Publishing, Oxford, 2008, p. 20; and Office for Criminal Justice Reform, "Convicting Rapists and Protecting Victims – Justice for Victims of Rape", 2006, p. 8.

tional criminal investigations – seems almost overwhelming. Experience from Rwanda and the former Yugoslavia has shown that it is beyond the capacity of most post-conflict state or transitional justice mechanisms to comprehensively address sexual and gender-based violence,[3] which places an even more onerous burden on international criminal tribunals to provide some (if not the only) semblance of a judicial response to sexual and gender-based violence committed during conflict.

Thankfully, some of the normal evidentiary requirements attached to prosecutions for rape and sexual violence in a national criminal system have been mitigated in international criminal proceedings, to reflect the unique challenges faced by international investigators and prosecutors. The Rules of Procedure and Evidence of the International Criminal Tribunal for the former Yugoslavia ('ICTY'), International Criminal Tribunal for Rwanda ('ICTR'), Special Court for Sierra Leone ('SCSL') and International Criminal Court ('ICC') all include specific provisions relating to evidence in cases of sexual violence.[4] These rules permit the exclusion of evidence relating to the prior sexual conduct of the victim,[5] the elimination of consent as a defence in cases where the victim was subject to threats, coercion or violence,[6] and the explicit waiver of any requirement

---

3   See, for example, African Rights and Redress, "Survivors and Post-Genocide Justice in Rwanda: Their Experiences, Perspectives and Hopes", 2008; and Amnesty International, "'Whose Justice?' The Women of Bosnia and Herzegovina Are Still Waiting", 2009.

4   International Criminal Tribunal for the Former Yugoslavia ('ICTY'), Rules of Procedure and Evidence, adopted 11 February 1994, as amended 8 December 2010, IT/32/Rev.45, Rule 96 (http://www.legal-tools.org/doc/950cb6/); International Criminal Tribunal for Rwanda ('ICTR'), Rules of Procedure and Evidence, adopted 29 June 1995, as amended 1 October 2009, Rule 96 (http://www.legal-tools.org/doc/c6a7c6/); Special Court for Sierra Leone ('SCSL'), Rules of Procedure and Evidence, 16 January 202, amended 28 May 2010, Rule 96 (http://www.legal-tools.org/doc/b36b82/); International Criminal Court ('ICC'), Rules of Procedure and Evidence, adopted 9 September 2002, ICC-ASP/1/3, Rules 70 and 71 (http://www.legal-tools.org/doc/8bcf6f/). Of course, the inclusion of these rules at the ICTY and ICTR was intended to facilitate a progressive approach to the adjudication of sexual violence, as well as merely to counteract practical investigatory issues. See further Fionnuala Ní Aoláin, "Radical Rules: The Effects of Evidential and Procedural Rules on the Regulation of Sexual Violence in War", in *Albany Law Review*, 1996–1997, vol. 60, no. 3, p. 883.

5   ICTY, Rules of Procedure and Evidence, Rule 96(iv), see *supra* note 4; ICTR, Rules of Procedure and Evidence, Rule 96(iv), see *supra* note 4; SCSL, Rules of Procedure and Evidence, Rule 96(iv), see *supra* note 4; ICC, Rules of Procedure and Evidence, Rule 70(d) and Rule 71, see *supra* note 4.

6   ICTY, Rules of Procedure and Evidence, Rule 96(ii), see *supra* note 4; ICTR, Rules of Procedure and Evidence, Rule 96(ii), see *supra* note 4; SCSL, Rules of Procedure and Evidence,

---

of corroboration of the victim's testimony.[7] Despite these concessions, the record of international criminal tribunals to date in prosecuting sexual violence remains patchy at best. This can be best comprehended (and indeed avoided) as a question of prosecutorial strategy, rather than as an inherently problematic combination of practical hurdles and definitional or evidentiary obstacles. An examination of both the successes and failures of international criminal tribunals in this regard shows that unless a specific effort is made to prioritise and strategise the investigation of sexual violence from the earliest possible stage in the international criminal process, it will not be adequately addressed in the prosecution's case or duly reflected in the judgment of the court. The avoidance of this outcome is not merely a preference – it is a responsibility incumbent on international criminal tribunals if they are to live up to their stated aims of ending impunity and prosecuting the most serious crimes of concern to the international community.[8] However, prior experience from international tribunals also shows that some strategies are more effective than others, and certain specific practical efforts can have a significant impact on the success rates of international prosecutions for sexual violence. These will be discussed throughout the chapter.

Prosecutorial strategy, in the sense that it is referred to throughout this chapter, encompasses both the investigation phase of a case and trial proceedings. It includes issues such as the selection of defendants, pursuance of thematic or geographical investigations, characterisation of facts and charges, treatment of victims and witnesses, assignment of personnel and existence of a coherent gender policy. This chapter will examine these issues by reference to the past experience of international criminal tribu-

---

Rule 96(i)–(iii), see *supra* note 4; ICC, Rules of Procedure and Evidence, Rule 70(a)–(c), see *supra* note 4.

[7] ICTY, Rules of Procedure and Evidence, Rule 96(i), see *supra* note 4; ICTR, Rules of Procedure and Evidence, Rule 96(i), see *supra* note 4; SCSL, Rules of Procedure and Evidence, Rule 96(i)–(iii), see *supra* note 4; ICC, Rules of Procedure and Evidence, Rule 63(4), see *supra* note 4.

[8] See, for example, Rome Statute of the International Criminal Court, 17 July 1998, in force 1 July 2002, Preamble ('ICC Statute') (http://www.legal-tools.org/doc/7b9af9/):

> Affirming that the most serious crimes of concern to the international community as a whole must not go unpunished and that their effective prosecution must be ensured [...]. Determined to put an end to impunity for the perpetrators of these crimes and thus to contribute to the prevention of such crimes.

nals to assess the foundational importance of a coherent, systematic prosecutorial strategy for the successful investigation and prosecution of sexual crimes in international criminal law. Despite its reputation as a difficult
crime to achieve a conviction for, or some of the received wisdom about
victims being unwilling to come forward, and despite the hesitancy, even
squeamishness, of some investigators and prosecutors to address it, sexual
and gender-based violence is not impossible to uncover or prove when it
is prioritised and normalised from the outset. If it is addressed consciously, thoroughly, deliberately and tactically, sexual and gender-based violence – even if committed in conflict and prosecuted from afar – need not
continue to be synonymous with impunity. International criminal law, despite its legal and practical challenges, provides an opportunity; prosecutorial strategy provides the means of realising it.

15.2. Prosecutorial Strategy at the Investigation Phase

In international criminal tribunals, investigations are a sub-division of the
Office of the Prosecutor. The head of investigations occupies a senior
management position and will co-ordinate strategy with the chief prosecutor, deputy prosecutor and other heads of divisions within the Office of
the Prosecutor, such as prosecutions, appeals, complementarity or legal
affairs. For the ICTY, ICTR and SCSL, the geographical scope of the tribunals' jurisdictions was set in their establishing Statutes, and therefore,
the initial priority for the Offices of the Prosecutor was to identify potential defendants according to prosecutorial strategy. For example, the Office of the Prosecutor at the ICTY initially took what was referred to as a
"pyramidal approach" in its earlier investigations, otherwise known as a
"bottom-up" strategy, to address lower-level perpetrators first, establish a
crime base, and gradually follow the evidence higher up the chain to military and political leaders who ordered, planned or instigated the crimes.[9]

---

[9]   See ICTY, "Investigations" (http://www.icty.org/sid/97):

> The OTP decided to follow what has been called a pyramidal inves-
> tigation strategy, starting from the bottom, in other words, with
> crime base evidence and lower-ranking persons who actually com-
> mitted or ordered the crimes. Investigations began in refugee centres
> throughout the world, where victims and witnesses were able to
> provide evidence implicating the persons who had physically com-
> mitted the crimes, such as, for example, the persons in the camps
> where they were detained or the camp commanders. As the evidence

This approach quickly became more complex and multi-layered. Within a few months, the ICTY had developed an investigative strategy which concentrated on four inter-related elements: 1) senior political and military leaders; 2) sexual and gender-based violence; 3) notorious offenders; and 4) notorious events.[10] Prosecutors at SCSL took a more holistic approach and pursued a limited number of cases against what were seen as the main actors in the conflict: the Armed Forces Revolutionary Council ('AFRC'), the Revolutionary United Front ('RUF'), the Civil Defence Forces ('CDF') and Charles Taylor, former president of neighbouring Liberia. At the ICC, by comparison, the Court's jurisdiction potentially encompasses more than 100 states, so even the selection of countries for investigation necessitates prosecutorial discretion. Once the Court's jurisdiction has been triggered in relation to a particular state or "situation", the Office of the Prosecutor must assess whether there is a reasonable basis to believe that crimes within the jurisdiction of the Court have been committed, make an assessment of gravity and admissibility, and then decide whether to apply for authorisation from the Pre-Trial Chamber to officially open an investigation into that situation.

Once an investigation is authorised at the ICC, the Office of the Prosecutor will begin conducting its investigations and the process of identifying potential cases and defendants, although it is somewhat constrained in its autonomous pursuit of this task by the statutory framework of the Court, which emphasises the principle of gravity.[11] This has been interpreted by the ICC prosecutor to require a focus on senior perpetrators, within a political or military hierarchy, as "those who bear the greatest responsibility for the most serious crimes".[12] This means that the ICC

---

grew, investigators began working up the pyramid to the persons who could be regarded as most responsible for the crimes.

[10] According to John Ralston, former chief of investigations at the ICTY, interview on file with author.

[11] ICC Statute, Articles 53 and 54, see *supra* note 8.

[12] ICC, Office of the Prosecutor, Prosecutorial Strategy 2009–2012, 1 February 2010, pp. 5–6 (http://www.legal-tools.org/doc/6ed914/):

In accordance with this statutory scheme, the Office consolidated a *policy of focused investigations and prosecutions*, meaning it will investigate and prosecute those who bear the greatest responsibility for the most serious crimes, based on the evidence that emerges in the course of an investigation. Thus, the Office will select for prosecution those situated at the highest echelons of responsibility, in-is unlikely to prosecute the lower-level direct perpetrators of crimes, as occurred in the initial years of the ICTY and ICTR. The ICC prosecutor has also chosen to pursue a policy of "focused investigations", wherein "incidents are selected to provide a sample that is reflective of the gravest incidents and the main types of victimisation".[13] This is an acknowledgment of the finite resources available to the Court, and of the importance of selecting cases and crimes that are representative of broader patterns within the conflict. Article 54 of the ICC Statute also requires the prosecutor to ensure the effective investigation and prosecution of crimes within the jurisdiction of the Court, explicitly including sexual and gender-based violence as categories of crimes necessitating particular consideration.[14] Likewise, Regulation 34 of the Regulations of the Office of the Prosecutor stipulates that, when developing a case hypothesis, the joint investigation team should aim to select incidents which reflect the most serious crimes and the main types of victimisation, in particular, sexual and gender violence and violence against children.[15] It is clear that for the ICC at least, the statutory and procedural framework of the Court explicitly requires the prosecutor to prioritise sexual and gender-based violence in its investigative and prosecutorial strategy.

Dianne Luping, who has worked as both an investigator and trial lawyer at the ICC, has argued that a focused approach to sexual and gender-based violence must be implemented "from the outset, during the pre-analysis phase and before any decision is made to initiate an investigation in any country".[16] Patricia Viseur Sellers, former legal adviser for gender in the Office of the Prosecutor at the ICTY and ICTR, has similarly argued that "gender strategy is not a luxury. Its absence is an absurdity".[17] However, it is easy to talk about "focused investigations" or "gender

---

cluding those who ordered, financed, or otherwise organized the alleged crimes. (emphasis added)

[13] *Ibid.*, p. 6.

[14] ICC Statute, Article 54(1)(b), see *supra* note 8.

[15] ICC, Regulations of the Office of the Prosecutor, ICC-BD/05-01-09, entry into force 23 April 2009, Regulation 34(2) (http://www.legal-tools.org/doc/a97226/).

[16] Dianne Luping, "Investigation and Prosecution of Sexual and Gender-Based Crimes Before the International Criminal Court", in *American University Journal of Gender, Social Policy and Law*, 2009, vol. 17, no. 2, pp. 431, 434.

[17] Patricia Viseur Sellers, "Gender Strategy is Not a Luxury for International Courts", in *American University Journal of Gender, Social Policy and Law*, 2009, vol. 17, no. 2, pp. 301, 325.

strategy", but it is often much harder, particularly in academic literature, to pin down what this actually entails and how it is achieved. One primary and fundamental issue is personnel. Prosecution and investigation teams need to have both a healthy gender balance and a strong degree of aware-ness and competence in dealing with sexual and gender-based violence. Richard Goldstone, the first chief prosecutor of the ICTY and ICTR, has spoken openly about the "gender bias" among investigative staff in the initial years at the tribunals, and has shown a remarkable degree of tact simply to say that "[t]heir culture was not such as to make them con-cerned about gender-related crime".[18] As he describes, when the majority of the staff were ex-army or police, very few senior investigators were women, and a "locker-room mentality" prevailed. The importance of staff attitudes was obvious even in the infancy of the tribunals:

> I became convinced that if we did not have an appropriate gender policy in the Office of the Prosecutor, we would have little chance of getting it right outside of the office.[19]

This was not just an issue of team dynamics but one of "smoulder-ing sexism";[20] not only were female staff members uncomfortable in their work environment, but some (although certainly not all) male staff mem-bers were actively resentful of attempts to emphasise the importance of gender balance within the investigations division. Sellers recalls one occa-sion where, as legal adviser for gender, she organised a meeting between a psychologist and a particularly testosterone-heavy investigations team to discuss the importance of including both male and female team members in investigative activities. Immediately following the meeting, she was subject to a spurious and petty disciplinary complaint from the chief of investigations, deputy chief of investigations and the leader of the team in question, ostensibly for having revealed the internal workings of an inves-tigation team to an outside expert.[21] The "gender atmosphere" problem within the Office of the Prosecutor was more insidious than merely creat-ing a boorish work environment. The attitude of some male staff members towards sexual crimes was dismissive at best, antediluvian at worst: Peg-

---

[18] Richard J. Goldstone, "Prosecuting Rape as a War Crime", in *Case Western Reserve Journal of International Law*, 2002, vol. 34, no. 3, pp. 277, 280.

[19] *Ibid.*

[20] Sellers, 2009, p. 312, see *supra* note 17.

[21] *Ibid.*

gy Kuo recalls encountering resistance from (admittedly overworked) male colleagues, who frequently minimised the gravity of sexual violence by making comments such as "So a bunch of guys got riled up after a day of war, what's the big deal?".[22] Another former ICTY staff member recalled the senior trial attorney in a case refusing to contemplate including sexual violence in the indictment by saying "I have enough on my plate, I don't need a bunch of hysterical women in my courtroom".[23]

Thankfully, gender parity and gender attitudes have improved since then across all international criminal tribunals, although Women's Initiatives for Gender Justice has consistently highlighted the gender disparity in senior management positions at the ICC.[24] As recently as 2007, of 13 individuals appointed to the list of professional investigators at the ICC, only one was a woman.[25] That is not to say that men should be barred from involvement in sexual violence investigations or that exclusively female investigation teams would automatically produce miraculous results; the ideal investigation team would include a mixture of genders and ages but also a consistent standard of expertise and competence at investigating sexual and gender-based violence. True, some female victims may not be comfortable discussing their rape or sexual assault with a male investigator, but by the same token a male victim may feel humiliated discussing his experience of sexual violence with an investigator who reminds him of one of his daughters. The most important component is choice. Based on her experience as part of an ICC investigation team in Uganda, Luping concluded:

> The lesson learned in that situation is that a victim should be provided the choice of a male or female interviewer, wherever possible, to ensure that they feel most comfortable sharing their experiences of sexual violence. Accordingly, it was important that all investigators, male and female, were

---

22 Peggy Kuo, "Prosecuting Crimes of Sexual Violence in an International Tribunal", in *Case Western Reserve Journal of International Law*, 2002, vol. 34, no. 3, pp. 305, 311.

23 Interview on file with author.

24 See, for example, Women's Initiatives for Gender Justice, "Gender Report Card on the International Criminal Court 2010", November 2010, pp. 12–23.

25 *Ibid.*, p. 24.

---

trained to conduct sexual violence interviews with both male and female victims.[26]

According to Sellers:

[i]n other words, investigations could field all male team members, or all female team members or mixed-gendered teams depending on what configuration would be more likely to obtain a witness's evidence.[27]

Another crucial personnel component for an effective prosecutorial strategy on sexual violence is the appointment of a gender adviser within the Office of the Prosecutor, something that the majority of international tribunals have failed to do. Sellers occupied the position of legal adviser for gender in the ICTY from 1994 until 2007, and unsurprisingly that tribunal has the strongest record by far of any international criminal tribunal in prosecuting sexual violence. She also held the same position within the Office of the Prosecutor at the ICTR from 1995 until 1999, but with the exception of two abortive short-term appointments in the immediate aftermath, the position has not been filled since then, and the ICTR has been harshly criticised for its abysmal record of prosecutions for sexual violence. The position of legal adviser for gender at the ICTY has (officially at least) remained vacant since 2007, while the SCSL has never had a legal adviser for gender. Despite years of sustained advocacy and an explicit statutory requirement,[28] the ICC prosecutor did not appoint a special adviser on gender crimes until 2008.[29] Unfortunately, Catharine MacKinnon's other commitments have meant that the appointment is relatively symbolic:

---

[26]   Luping, 2009, p. 493, see *supra* note 16.

[27]   Sellers, 2009, p. 311, see *supra* note 17.

[28]   ICC Statute, Article 42(9), see *supra* note 8, states: "The Prosecutor shall appoint advisers with legal expertise on specific issues, including, but not limited to, sexual and gender violence and violence against children." In 2008, Women's Initiatives for Gender Justice recommended the prosecutor to urgently appoint a gender legal adviser, noting that the wrongful dismissal fine imposed by the International Labour Organisation on the ICC that same year would amount to over two years salary for a gender adviser: Women's Initiatives for Gender Justice, "Gender Report Card on the International Criminal Court 2008", December 2008, p. 29.

[29]   ICC, "ICC Prosecutor Appoints Prof. Catharine A. MacKinnon as Special Adviser on Gender Crimes", Press Release, ICC-OTP-20081126-PR377, 26 November 2008 (http://www.legal-tools.org/doc/866eda/).

> [A]s it is a part-time position based outside The Hague, the
> ability of the post to influence and advise on the day-to-day
> decisions regarding investigation priorities, the selection of
> incidents and the construction of an overarching gender
> strategy will be extremely limited.[30]

In the absence of a dedicated in-house gender legal adviser,[31] the
then deputy prosecutor, Fatou Bensouda, acted as the focal point for sexual and gender-based violence within the ICC.[32] Sellers has stressed the
importance not only of the appointment of a competent gender adviser but
also the level of appointment, noting that within the United Nations
('UN') system only P-5 or higher staff positions are considered senior
management and therefore are able to set policy.[33] Anyone who has ever
been an employee in a large organisation can appreciate that the seniority
of a person's position has an exponential impact on their capacity to be
effective in that position, and also exerts a significant influence on recep-
tiveness and co-operation from other staff members, both superiors and
subordinates. Although, as Beth van Schaack has pointed out, no gender
adviser at the *ad hoc* tribunals has ever been appointed above a P-4 position,[34] specific efforts on the part of Richard Goldstone and Louise Arbour ensured that Patricia Sellers was included in senior management
meetings.[35] Obviously, for a gender adviser to be effective – which entails
both monitoring and influencing prosecutorial policy on sexual and gender-based violence – they must be integrally involved in senior levels of
decision-making, rather than simply being responsible for pointing out the
gender failings of policies which have already been set by higher management, and they must have a very close involvement with investigation
and prosecution teams (both at the trial and appeals stage), in order to
identify, react to or avoid procedural or substantive errors. This will be

---

30 Women's Initiatives for Gender Justice, 2008, p. 21, see *supra* note 28.

31 The Office of the Prosecutor does include a Gender and Children Unit, but it is not structured
or staffed to provide an equivalent function to a legal adviser on gender.

32 Luping, 2009, pp. 435, 489, see *supra* note 16.

33 Sellers, 2009, p. 308, fn. 17, see *supra* note 17.

34 Beth van Schaack, "Obstacles on the Road to Gender Justice: The International Criminal
Tribunal for Rwanda as Object Lesson", in *American University Journal of Gender, Social
Policy and Law*, 2009, vol. 17, no. 2, pp. 361, 366, fn. 16.

35 Sellers, 2009, p. 308, fn. 17, see *supra* note 17.

examined further in the discussion of prosecutorial strategy at the trial phase.

Another major component of gender strategy at the investigation phase involves the development of a case hypothesis. In order to ensure that potential patterns of sexual violence are not overlooked, it is essential for investigation teams to conduct a detailed overview of the conflict or region in order to identify the best possible investigative strategy. International criminal prosecutions ordinarily fall into one of two categories: geographic or thematic investigations. Geographic investigations will pursue evidence of all potential crimes committed within a specific region, such as the siege of Sarajevo or the campaign of genocide in Butare province, and the results of the investigation may be used in a number of subsequent prosecutions. If conducted thoroughly, there is no reason why geographic investigations should not be able to produce compelling evidence of patterns of sexual violence, albeit only those committed in the region in question. Thematic investigations, on the other hand, focus on a specific aspect of the conflict. This may relate to the category of crimes involved (sexual violence being one common example), a particular group of defendants (the military and government cases at the ICTR, for example), or a specific military campaign (such as Operation Storm in Croatia). Although both categories of investigation can be and have been employed in sexual violence prosecutions, it is futile to insist that a tribunal should exclusively follow one in preference to the other. According to John Ralston, former chief of investigations at the ICTY and executive director of the Institute for International Criminal Investigations, it is not possible to choose either strategy in the abstract without conducting comprehensive background research into the conflict.[36] Also, there is nothing to say that the two categories are mutually exclusive. Although the *Kunarać et al.* case at the ICTY is frequently trumpeted as the classic or original example of thematic investigations of sexual violence, as it was the first indictment from the ICTY to deal exclusively with sexual crimes, it actually originated out of a geographic investigation of crimes committed in the Foča municipality in 1992 and 1993.[37] Although Foča is a small town, its strategic location and significant Muslim population made it the site of significant atrocities during the Bosnian conflict. The 1991 census record-

---

[36] Interview on file with author.
[37] Kuo, 2002, p. 310, see *supra* note 22.

ed approximately 20,000 Muslim inhabitants in Foča, roughly half of the town's population; at the end of the war, 10 remained.[38] The *Kunarać et al.* case represents the female experience of mass rape and sexual enslavement,[39] while the *Krnojelac* case addressed the killings and beatings of male residents of Foča at the KP Dom detention camp.[40]

Conducting a comprehensive overview of a conflict not only allows investigators to select the most appropriate investigative strategy, it will also help to identify potential patterns of sexual violence at an early stage. Not every conflict will feature systematic sexual violence – despite its entrenched and intractable nature, the Israel/Palestine conflict is a good example of this[41] – but, even in those that do, it can take many different forms: it may be ethnically motivated, a deliberate military tactic, part of a genocidal campaign, a means of torturing or punishing political opponents, or simply opportunistic, all of which will have implications for charging and modes of liability, which are discussed later in the chapter. Moreover, sexual violence should not only be seen as a stand-alone crime; it may also be a feature or expression of the gendered nature of the conflict. The scale of sexual and gender-based violence committed in a conflict will vary and will have significant implications for prosecutorial and investigative policy; when rape is committed on a mass scale, as occurred during the Rwandan genocide, its token inclusion in a handful of international criminal indictments constitutes an abject failure to adequately address the reality of the crimes committed and victimisation perpetrated during that conflict.[42] Although sexual violence is predominantly committed against women and girls, it is also frequently committed against men

---

[38] ICTY, "Facts About *Foča*", p. 1 (on file with the author).

[39] ICTY, *Prosecutor v. Dragoljub Kunarać, Radomir Kovač*, and *Zoran Vuković*, Trial Chamber, Judgment, IT-96-23/1, 22 February 2001 (http://www.legal-tools.org/doc/fd881d/).

[40] ICTY, *Prosecutor v. Milorad Krnojelac*, Trial Chamber, Judgment, IT-97-25, 15 March 2002 (http://www.legal-tools.org/doc/1a994b/).

[41] See Elisabeth Wood, "Variation in Sexual Violence During War", in *Politics and Society*, 2006, vol. 34, no. 3, pp. 307, 314.

[42] For example, one study of all available information and statistics for rape victimisation in the Rwandan genocide concluded that, at a conservative estimate, more than 350,000 women were raped during the conflict – half the number of victims who were killed. See Catrien Bijleveld, Aafke Morssinkhof and Alette Smeulers, "Counting the Countless: Rape Victimization During the Rwandan Genocide", in *International Criminal Justice Review*, 2009, vol. 19, no. 2, p. 208.

and boys,[43] a fact which has historically been neglected or overlooked in international criminal prosecutions, with the notable exception of the IC-TY.[44] Ralston notes that certain factual scenarios will raise red flags for experienced investigators as *indicia* of an increased likelihood of sexual and gender-based violence, such as detention camps (for both male and female victims), the use of child soldiers, or concentration of populations in refugee or internally displaced persons' camps.[45] Identifying the presence or absence of these factors at a very early point in the investigation permits the development of a clear strategy, to target investigations and prepare investigators prior to their deployment to the field.

Before investigators are deployed, they need to understand the cultural context of a country, if they are to have the best possible chance of creating a rapport with a victim or witness and obtaining valuable, credible information. A pre-deployment gender analysis can assist in this task; for example, understanding the cultural and ethnic context in Rwanda, where Tutsi women were both prized and resented for their beauty and where a heavy stigma attaches to victims of rape, would help investigators to be aware of whether the person they were interviewing was likely to have been a target of sexual violence, and whether they were likely to be unwilling or uncomfortable in volunteering such information. In order to conduct a successful interview, specific cultural information may also be vital. For example, an investigator from Europe or North America may suspect that an interviewee is being evasive if they avert their gaze or refuse to maintain eye contact, not realising that this is a mark of respect or deference to a person of authority. Shaking hands with a person of the opposite gender when introduced may seem like basic courtesy, but it has the potential to be highly inappropriate in certain cultures, while seeming-

---

[43] For example, in one empirical public health survey conducted in eastern Democratic Republic of Congo ('DRC'), 75 per cent of women and 65 per cent of men reported experience conflict-related sexual violence. See Kirsten Johnson, Jennifer Scott, Bigy Rughita, Michael Kisielewski, Jana Asher, Ricardo Ong and Lynn Lawry, "Association of Sexual Violence and Human Rights Violations with Physical and Mental Health in Territories of the Eastern Democratic Republic of the Congo", in *Journal of the American Medical Association*, 2010, vol. 304, no. 5, p. 553.

[44] See Dustin A. Lewis, "Unrecognized Victims: Sexual Violence Against Men in Conflict Settings Under International Law", in *Wisconsin International Law Journal*, 2009, vol. 27, no. 1, p. 1.

[45] Interview on file with author.

ly innocuous actions such as sitting cross-legged can also be considered offensive. Cultural awareness also extends to the use of language. For example, while working in one situation country, Ralston discussed the use of safe houses in the context of witness protection measures, not realising that the phrase 'safe house' was used to refer to the buildings in which people are detained and tortured by the intelligence services.[46] Words and actions which may be intended to be respectful or comforting have the potential to be construed as offensive or frightening, so extensive preparation and cultural awareness are vital. Likewise, recognising the oblique meaning behind an interviewee's use of language is also critical, particularly in relation to sexual violence. A person may refer to an incident which happened to a 'friend' or 'neighbour' to avoid revealing that they were themselves the victims, or may use euphemistic language to refer to rape or sexual violence, such as "he lay with me", "he disrespected me" or "he made me his wife", rather than providing explicit anatomical details of the assault. Investigators must be very careful in situations such as this to ensure that they do not overlook evidence of sexual violence which is raised indirectly or in the third person, or to wrongly assume that a witness whose prior statements make no reference to sexual violence has no relevant information in relation to it.

As mentioned earlier, most international criminal investigators will not speak the local language fluently, and will therefore be reliant on interpreters to communicate with victims and witnesses. Conducting interviews through interpreters presents a barrage of challenges, most of which can be overcome with concerted preparation prior to the interview and sufficient patience during the interview. An investigator needs to understand that not everything they or the interviewee say will have a direct word-for-word translation and that certain styles of question (particularly rhetorical questions or long, barrister-style conditional questions) are particularly difficult to convey to an interviewee. The interpreter, however, needs to understand that it is the investigator, not them, who is conducting the interview. The relationship between an investigator and interpreter is crucial, and lots of planning and preparation before the interview will be necessary, to ensure that the interview is conducted in a manner that meets the required evidence-gathering standards and produces accurate

---

[46] Interview on file with author.

and credible information. For example, the interpreter should present both the question and the response in the first person (that is, "How old were you?" and not "He wants to know how old you are"), and should ask clarifying questions when necessary, so as to ensure that they do not paraphrase or substitute their own interpretation of a person's meaning where a direct translation is not possible.[47] Despite the presence of the interpreter, the investigator should make sure they do not lose their rapport with the interviewee, and should understand that the interviewee will need to trust both the interpreter and the investigator if they are to reveal particularly sensitive information. The investigator and interpreter should also be particularly careful in identifying and correcting any mistakes or inaccuracies in the witness statement before the interview ends, as errors which are discovered at a later point in proceedings may be taken as evidence of unreliability in the interviewee's version of events.

Planning and preparation also extends to the selection of the location for the interview with a victim or witness. Obviously, in ideal circumstances, the interview would take place in a quiet, private, comfortable room with a table and chairs. However, in practice, such a location may not be available. Investigators have a responsibility to ensure the security, privacy and confidentiality of interviewees,[48] which applies just as much to an assessment of the potential risks an individual may be exposed to for co-operating with the investigation as it does to an investigator's efforts to identify a suitable interview setting; as Ralston puts it, there must be a 'do no harm' approach on the part of investigators to ensure that the victim or witness is not going to be put in a worse position by their interaction with the investigation team.[49] If the potential risks to the interviewee are too great, the investigators should not proceed with the interview. Although an ideal interview location would allow for complete privacy (auditory and visual), security and anonymity on the part of the interviewee, investigators may find themselves in a position where they

---

[47] Dermot Groome has also noted that an interpreter should be careful to resist the impulse to "improve" the responses of the interviewee to make them sound more coherent or credible. See Dermot Groome, *The Handbook of Human Rights Investigation: A Comprehensive Guide to the Investigation and Documentation of Violent Human Rights Abuses*, Human Rights Press, Northborough, 2001, p. 296.

[48] Luping, 2009, pp. 486, 491, see *supra* note 16.

[49] Interview on file with author.

cannot guarantee all of these factors and must choose the 'least worst' option. For example, the international criminal investigator Jan Pfundheller, who has conducted interviews with victims of sexual violence for the ICTY in the former Yugoslavia and for the US State Department in Darfur, recalls arranging a group interview with female Darfuri victims near a riverbed some distance away from the refugee camp to allow for some degree of privacy.[50] The criminal process for which the interview is being conducted should also be clearly explained to the interviewee. This is to ensure the interviewee can give informed consent to being interviewed, including the fact that they could be called to testify, that their name could be made public, and that a trial, if one materialises, may not take place for years. Although international tribunals allow for extensive protective measures for victims, witnesses and those put at risk on account of their interaction with the activities of the court,[51] Ralston stresses that an interviewer should never make promises to an interviewee, either of financial inducements or of any specific protective measures such as relocation.[52]

As part of a systematic investigative approach to sexual violence, investigators should make sure to avoid making prejudgments or assumptions regarding witnesses. All interviewees – male, female, young and old – should be questioned sensitively about any information they may have regarding sexual and gender-based violence.[53] Even witnesses who have not been victims of sexual violence may have relevant information regarding its commission, and the profile of those who are capable of being victimised may be a lot broader than less-experienced investigators may initially assume. There is also a common perception that victims will be reluctant to discuss their experiences of sexual violence with a stranger[54], especially in conservative cultures. Although this is true of some victims, it may also be caused by a flawed interview technique, a failure to establish rapport, or simply the lack of an opportunity to do so in response to suitably open questioning. Making any such sweeping generalisations

---

[50] See John Hagan and Wenona Rymond-Richmond, *Darfur and the Crime of Genocide*, Cambridge University Press, Cambridge, 2009, p. 9.

[51] See Anne-Marie L. M. de Brouwer, *Supranational Criminal Prosecution of Sexual Violence: The ICC and the Practice of the ICTY and the ICTR*, Intersentia, Antwerp, 2005, pp. 231–83.

[52] Interview on file with author.

[53] Luping, 2009, p. 493, see *supra* note 16.

[54] Van Schaack, 2009, p. 369, see *supra* note 34.

about victims is counter-productive, as it fails to take into account the simple fact that victims are not a homogenous group and will have very different attitudes, wishes and degrees of vulnerability. Some witnesses may be retraumatised at the prospect of testifying in front of the person responsible for their victimisation; others will feel empowered by it.[55] For an investigator, the most important thing is to sensitively and patiently facilitate the interviewee's ability to tell his or her own story. For example, the investigator could explain his or her own background to reassure the interviewee that they have dealt with very serious cases in the past. Investigators will also need to be trained and be capable of dealing with traumatised witnesses.[56] Trauma may cause an interviewee to present a disjointed narrative of events, become distressed at reliving certain incidents or become triggered by aspects of their environment, such as a closed or locked door for victims of forcible detention or the presence of people in uniform for victims of sexual violence at the hands of police or military authorities. Investigators must be sure to provide plenty of breaks for a vulnerable witness, be empathetic and non-judgmental, and even allow for the presence of a support person (whether a friend, relative or psychologist) if the witness requests it.

The identification of potential interviewees, victims or witnesses will sometimes take place through the use of an intermediary; thankfully, we have come a long way from the crass victim identification techniques recounted by war correspondent Edward Behr, where refugees from Stanleyville in the Congo in the mid-1960s were greeted by a television journalist shouting "Anyone here been raped and speaks English?".[57] Intermediaries can come in many different forms – fixers, psychologists or members of support organisations, police contacts – but should be carefully vetted, just as one would with police informants in national criminal jurisdictions.[58] The ICC has produced both positive and negative examples of the use of intermediaries in international criminal investigations.

---

[55] Kuo, 2002, p. 317, see *supra* note 22.

[56] See Anthony Forde, "Identifying Victims of Sexual Violence in the Absence of Forensic Evidence Using Investigative Interview Strategies", Paper presented at Conference on Human Rights and Forensic Science, NUI Galway, 24–25 April 2009.

[57] Edward Behr, *Anyone Here Been Raped and Speaks English?*, New English Library, London, 1985.

[58] John Ralston, interview on file with author.

For example, in the ICC's investigation of sexual and gender-based violence committed in the Central African Republic, they secured the cooperation of a local victims' organisation known as the Organisation for Compassion and Development for Families in Distress, set up by a former schoolteacher who had herself been raped and widowed in the conflict, which helped the investigators to identify individuals (male and female) who had been subject to sexual crimes and would be willing to speak about them.[59] In the *Lubanga* case in the Democratic Republic of Congo ('DRC') situation, however, the first prosecution witness to take the stand dramatically recanted his testimony, claiming he had been coached by an intermediary to provide false testimony of having been forcibly conscripted as a child soldier,[60] while subsequent similar allegations and the prosecutor's refusal to reveal the identity of one specific intermediary who had come under suspicion ultimately led to the Trial Chamber temporarily imposing a stay of proceedings against Lubanga, on the grounds that he could not receive a fair trial under the circumstances.[61] Although intermediaries can be a valuable and at times irreplaceable asset to an investigation team, their activities should be carefully supervised to ensure that they do not conduct themselves in a way which has the potential to damage the investigation or the evidence obtained in the course of the process.

Of course, many of the recommendations above relate to interviews with victims and witnesses who have direct experience of sexual violence, often referred to as "crime base witnesses". However, international criminal investigators have a complex task to fulfil to obtain evidence not only

---

[59] See Marlies Glasius, "Global Justice Meets Local Civil Society: The International Criminal Court's Investigation in the Central African Republic", in *Alternatives: Global, Local, Political*, 2008, vol. 33, no. 4, p. 413.

[60] See Rachel Irwin, "Witness Says He Lied, Was Coached", Summary from Thomas Lubanga at the International Criminal Court, in *International Justice Monitor*, 28 January 2009, although the witness later retracted the retraction and testified under oath; see Rachel Irwin, "Witness Admits to False Statement", Summary from Thomas Lubanga at the International Criminal Court, in *International Justice Monitor*, 19 June 2009, and "Lubanga Witness Says He Was Paid US$200 to Tell Lies", Summary from Thomas Lubanga at the International Criminal Court, in *International Justice Monitor*, 8 February 2010.

[61] ICC, *Prosecutor v. Thomas Lubanga Dyilo*, Trial Chamber, Decision on the Prosecution's Urgent Request for Variation of the Time-Limit to Disclose the Identity of Intermediary 143 or Alternatively to Stay Proceedings Pending Further Consultation with the VWU, ICC-01/04-01/06, 8 July 2010 (http://www.legal-tools.org/doc/cd4f10/). See also Women's Initiatives for Gender Justice, 2010, pp. 147–56, *supra* note 24.

---

of the commission of crimes such as sexual violence, torture or murder, but also the background context to the conflict, military and political chains of command, existence of specific *chapeau* elements for crimes against humanity, war crimes or genocide charges, and evidence in relation to persons who ordered, instigated or directed the commission of the crimes in question. This will necessarily require a broader spectrum of potential witnesses, including expert witnesses,[62] overview witnesses – who can testify to patterns of fact (such as a doctor or psychologist testifying about the number of conflict-related sexual violence victims they have treated), and 'linkage' or insider witnesses – who can provide evidence of the involvement or criminal responsibility of state authorities, military groups or specific defendants in relation to the crimes charged.[63]

Investigators and prosecutors also work with teams of analysts, whose job is to assess and categorise the evidence produced by investigators, to tailor the evidence to specific aspects of the prosecution case. Analysts can fall into many different categories – military experts, historians, demographers – but their contribution to the investigation will be vital to correctly identify patterns of criminal conduct and responsibility so as to compile a coherent prosecution case from the evidence collected by investigators. Their involvement is another crucial component of investigative strategy on sexual violence in order to piece together a strong enough case to proceed with a prosecution for specific crimes. For example, the work of prosecution analysts is vital in identifying responsible military commanders on the basis of troop movements and established chains of command during periods of intense sexual violence, or providing analysis of the ethnic breakdown of victims, to establish whether the sexual violence was carried out as a form of persecution on ethnic

---

[62] For example, the special representative to the UN secretary-general for children and armed conflict, Radhika Coomaraswamy, submitted an *amicus curiae* brief to the Trial Chamber in the *Lubanga* trial arguing that the sexual victimisation of male and female child soldiers constituted an inherent element of the crime of using them to "actively participate in hostilities". See ICC, *Prosecutor v. Thomas Lubanga Dyilo*, Submission of the Observations of the Special Representative of the Secretary General of the United Nations for Children and Armed Conflict pursuant to Rule 103 of the Rules of Procedure and Evidence, ICC-01/04-01/06, 18 March 2008 (http://www.legal-tools.org/doc/35097b/).

[63] See further Morten Bergsmo and William H. Wiley, "Human Rights Professionals and the Criminal Investigation and Prosecution of Core International Crimes", in *Manual on Human Rights Monitoring: An Introduction for Human Rights Field Officers*, Norwegian Centre for Human Rights, Oslo, 2008.

---

grounds or as part of a genocidal ideology.[64] Xabier Agirre Aranburu, who has worked as an analyst at the ICTY and ICC, has also noted the potential of using pattern evidence to prove charges of sexual violence.[65]

Ensuring that a focused strategy, to identify patterns of sexual and gender-based violence and implement best practice for obtaining evidence is put in place at the investigation stage, will pre-empt and avoid many of the mistakes which have plagued previous international criminal prosecutions for sexual crimes. It is significantly easier to follow the procedures outlined above from the outset than it is to retroactively address investigative flaws that become obvious only at a later stage in the proceedings. Likewise, prosecutors should work cooperatively with investigators and be willing to follow the patterns of evidence they unearth, rather than follow the example of the first trial at the ICC, where investigators in the DRC initially discovered preliminary evidence of a range of crimes – including rape, torture, pillage and enslavement – but were told by the Office of the Prosecutor to focus only on evidence relating to the conscription and use of child soldiers.[66] Thorough and competent investigations are the foundation of any successful international criminal prosecution; however, as will be seen in the following discussion, errors made at the investigation stage will give rise to serious and recurring ramifications for prosecutors throughout the trial phase.

15.3. Prosecutorial Strategy at the Trial Phase

If one needs a microcosm for the functioning of prosecutorial strategy on sexual and gender-based violence in the early years of the *ad hoc* international criminal tribunals (both positive and negative), one need look no further than the *Akayesu* case at the ICTR. The judgment in the *Akayesu* case[67] is held up as a watershed in international criminal jurisprudence

---

[64]   John Ralston, interview on file with author.

[65]   Xabier Agirre Aranburu, "Sexual Violence beyond Reasonable Doubt: Using Pattern Evidence and Analysis for International Cases", in *Leiden Journal of International* Law, 2010, vol. 23, no. 4, p. 609.

[66]   See Katy Glassborow, "Sexual Violence in DRC: ICC Investigative Strategy Under Fire", Institute for War and Peace Reporting, 17 October 2008.

[67]   ICTR, *Prosecutor v. Jean-Paul Akayesu*, Trial Chamber, Judgment, ICTR-96-4-T, 2 September 1998 ('*Akayesu* Trial Judgment') (http://www.legal-tools.org/doc/b8d7bd/).

---

and one of the central achievements of the Rwanda tribunal,[68] which is hardly an exaggeration given that it was the first conviction at that tribunal,[69] the first conviction for genocide by an international criminal tribunal since the adoption of the Genocide Convention in 1948, the first international criminal conviction for rape as a crime against humanity, and the first time an international tribunal had acknowledged that sexual violence could be considered a constituent element of the crime of genocide. However, it is a little less inspiring to recall that, at the beginning of what would turn out to be one of the flagship international criminal prosecutions of this crime, there were no sexual violence charges included in the indictment. It was only after the spontaneous testimony regarding acts of rape from a number of witnesses – including the gang rape of the six-year-old daughter of one witness – and sustained questioning from the judges, one of whom was subsequently the UN high commissioner for human rights, Navi Pillay, that the trial was adjourned to permit the prosecution to conduct further investigations and amend the indictment to include charges of rape, other inhumane acts and outrages on personal dignity.[70] One of the most important precedents in all of international criminal jurisprudence on sexual violence almost never was. However, the *Akayesu* case is also a sterling example of the immense importance and precedence that an international criminal conviction for sexual violence can generate, however precarious its origins.

---

[68] See, for example, Diane Amann, "Prosecutor v. Akayesu. Case ICTR-96-4-T", in *American Journal of International Law*, 1999, vol. 93, no. 1, p. 195; Catherine MacKinnon, "The ICTR's Legacy on Sexual Violence", in *New England Journal of International and Comparative Law*, 2008, vol. 14, no. 2, p. 101; Niamh Hayes, "Creating a Definition of Rape in International Law: The Contribution of the International Criminal Tribunals", in Shane Darcy and Joseph Powderly (eds.), *Judicial Creativity at the International Criminal Tribunals*, Oxford University Press, Oxford, 2010, p. 129.

[69] Although Jean Kambanda had already pleaded guilty, his conviction and sentence were not handed down until 4 September 1998, two days after the issuance of the judgment in *Akayesu*. See ICTR, *Prosecutor v. Jean Kambanda*, Trial Chamber, Judgment and Sentence, ICTR-97-23-S, 4 September 1998 (https://www.legal-tools.org/doc/49a299/pdf/).

[70] See Beth van Schaack, "Engendering Genocide: The *Akayesu* Case Before the International Criminal Tribunal for Rwanda", Santa Clara University School of Law, Legal Studies Research Paper Series, Working Paper no. 08-55, 2008.

Kelly Askin once described the prosecution of gender-based crimes as "fraught with inherent difficulties and gratuitous obstacles".[71] As discussed above, international criminal investigations have all but cornered the market in inherent difficulties; it is at the prosecution stage that the truly gratuitous obstacles have to be navigated, particularly when so many of them are self-imposed. No less than at the investigation stage, it is possible to pursue a predetermined and comprehensive sexual violence strategy throughout the prosecution phase of a case, to avoid the more obvious pitfalls, and contribute to a significantly higher standard of prosecution for such crimes than has often been the case. However, it is all but impossible to achieve a successful prosecution for sexual and gender-based crimes by happy accident and without deliberate care, attention and effort. Again, an examination of the past practice of international criminal tribunals produces some signal examples of what to do and, equally, what not to do.

When developing a case hypothesis, and again when assessing the evidence produced from the investigation stage of proceedings, prosecutors need to consider two crucial issues before drafting the indictment or application for a warrant of arrest: the most appropriate mode of individual criminal liability, and the most effective characterisation of facts as specific charges. Choosing the most suitable mode of liability is not just a matter of correctly identifying and categorising a potential defendant's contribution to the commission of crimes; it may also be the difference between an acquittal and a conviction.[72] As mentioned above, in the initial years of the *ad hoc* tribunals, the majority of accused (in custody at least) were on a relatively low rung in the political or military hierarchy, which made the determination of the mode of liability less problematic as they could be charged either with principal responsibility as a direct perpetrator, or some form of accessorial liability for ordering, planning, instigating, or aiding and abetting the commission of the crimes. Obtaining sufficient evidence to prove these forms of individual criminal responsibility is

---

[71] Kelly D. Askin, "Prosecuting Wartime Rape and Other Gender-Related Crimes Under International Law: Extraordinary Advances, Enduring Obstacles", in *Berkeley Journal of International Law*, 2003, vol. 21, no. 2, pp. 288, 318.

[72] See Gerhard Werle, *Principles of International Criminal Law*, 2nd ed., TMC Asser Press, The Hague, 2009, p. 168: "Modes of participation have also gained increasing importance in the areas of sentencing and cumulative convictions."

---

significantly less problematic than the two other main forms of liability: command responsibility and joint criminal enterprise or "common purpose" liability. Proving the requisite elements of command responsibility in relation to sexual violence – the existence of a superior–subordinate relationship, that the superior knew or had reason to know of his subordinates' crimes, and a failure by the superior to prevent or punish their commission – can be extremely problematic, predominantly in relation to establishing adequate notice (actual, constructive or imputed) on the part of the superior that such crimes were being committed,[73] although some noteworthy convictions have been achieved through this form of liability.[74]

To a certain extent, the difficulty in achieving a conviction for command responsibility in relation to sexual violence may be attributable to the bench rather than to the prosecution; Judge Arlette Ramaroson drafted a palpably frustrated dissent in the *Kajelijeli* case at the ICTR bemoaning the unwillingness of the other judges to convict for sexual violence on the basis of command responsibility when they had no qualms doing so in analogous factual circumstances in relation to the crime of murder.[75] Prosecuting sexual violence under the rubric of joint criminal enterprise or common purpose liability, on the other hand, allows prosecutors to focus on the foreseeability of the commission of sexual and gender-based violence as part of a common plan rather than an individual de-

---

[73] See, for example, ICTR, *Prosecutor v. Alfred Musema*, Trial Chamber, Judgment and Sentence, ICTR-96-13-T, 27 January 2000 (http://www.legal-tools.org/doc/1fc6ed/); ICTR, *Prosecutor v. Tharcisse Muvunyi*, Trial Chamber, Judgment and Sentence, ICTR-00-55A-T, 12 September 2006 (http://www.legal-tools.org/doc/fa02aa/); and ICTR, *Prosecutor v. Eliezer Niyitegeka*, Trial Chamber, Judgment, ICTR-96-14-T, 16 May 2003 (http://www.legal-tools.org/doc/325567/). See further Patricia Viseur Sellers and Kaoru Okuizumi, "Intentional Prosecutions of Sexual Assaults", in *Transnational Law and Contemporary Problems*, 1997, vol. 7, no. 1, pp. 45, 66–67; Nicola LaViolette, "Commanding Rape: Sexual Violence, Command Responsibility, and the Prosecution of Superiors by the International Criminal Tribunals for the Former Yugoslavia and Rwanda", in *Canadian Yearbook of International Law*, 1998, vol. 36, p. 93.

[74] See, for example, ICTY, *Prosecutor v. Zdravko Mucić, Hazim Delić, Esad Landžo and Zejnil Delalić*, Trial Chamber, Judgment, IT-96-21-T, 16 November 1998 (*'Delić et al.* Trial Judgment') (http://www.legal-tools.org/doc/6b4a33/).

[75] ICTR, *Prosecutor v. Juvénal Kajelijeli*, Trial Chamber, Dissenting Opinion of Judge Arlette Ramaroson, ICTR-98-44A-T, 1 December 2003 (http://www.legal-tools.org/doc/e4797f/). See further MacKinnon, 2008, pp. 101, 104–05, *supra* note 68.

---

fendant's notice of the commission of specific incidents of sexual violence.[76] As Patricia Viseur Sellers has argued:

> [i]t is almost impossible for an accused to participate in
> criminal activity that concomitantly generates sexual vio-
> lence, and not be cogent that the sexual violence was reason-
> ably foreseeable.[77]

However, a note of caution should be sounded in relation to the
ICC. Although the majority of charges for sexual violence at the ICC do
not involve direct physical perpetration,[78] and only one case to date is
based on command responsibility for sexual violence,[79] the prosecutor's
difficulties in achieving the inclusion of genocide charges for rape and
sexual violence in the arrest warrant against Omar al-Bashir is a worrying
development.[80] Although the Appeals Chamber found that the Pre-Trial
Chamber had erred by applying a higher standard of proof than is required
for the issuance of an arrest warrant,[81] it does not bode well for the Office
of the Prosecutor's ability to obtain sufficient linkage evidence, to prove
beyond a reasonable doubt the responsibility of senior political leaders for
sexual violence crimes which require specific intent.

---

[76] See further Rebecca L. Haffajee, "Prosecuting Crimes of Rape and Sexual Violence at the
ICTR: The Application of Joint Criminal Enterprise Theory", in *Harvard Journal of Law and
Gender*, 2006, vol. 29, no. 1, p. 201; and Allison Marston Danner and Jenny S. Martinez,
"Guilty Associations: Joint Criminal Enterprise, Command Responsibility and the Develop-
ment of International Criminal Law", in *California Law Review*, 2005, vol. 93, no. 1, p. 75.

[77] Sellers, 2009, p. 314, see *supra* note 17.

[78] In the Darfur situation, Ali Kushayb was charged as a co-perpetrator under Article 25(3)(a) in
relation to one count of outrages on personal dignity. See ICC, *Prosecutor v. Ahmad Muhammad Harun ("Ahmad Harun") and Ali Muhammad Ali Abd-Al-Rahman ("Ali
Kushayb")*, Pre-Trial Chamber, Warrant of Arrest for Ali Kushayb, ICC-02/05-01/07-3, 27
April 2007 (http://www.legal-tools.org/doc/cfa830/).

[79] See ICC, *Prosecutor v. Jean-Pierre Bemba*, Pre-Trial Chamber, Decision Pursuant to Article 61(7)(a) and (b) of the Rome Statute on the Charges of the Prosecutor Against Jean-Pierre
Bemba Gombo, ICC-01/05-01/08-424, 15 June 2009 (http://www.legal-
tools.org/doc/07965c/).

[80] See Women's Initiatives for Gender Justice, "Gender Report Card on the International Criminal Court 2009", October 2009, pp. 59–61; and Women's Initiatives for Gender Justice,
2010, pp. 106–09, see *supra* note 24.

[81] ICC, *Prosecutor v. Omar Hassan Ahmad Al Bashir*, Appeals Chamber, Judgment on the
Appeal of the Prosecutor Against the "Decision on the Prosecution's Application for a Warrant of Arrest Against Omar Hassan Ahmad Al Bashir", ICC-02/05-01/09-73, 3 February
2010 (http://www.legal-tools.org/doc/9ada8e/).

The second major preparatory issue in a prosecution case, and one of the most crucial steps in relation to sexual and gender-based violence, is the selection of charges. Obviously, the standard and breadth of evidence obtained at the investigation stage will be crucial in this regard, particularly if (as in the *Akayesu* case) such evidence is initially overlooked, as this can have a ruinous impact on the prosecution's ability to amend the indictment in sufficient time to have the charges included at trial. Unfortunately, the experience in the *Akayesu* case is exceptional in this regard; the normal consequence of a failure to identify or include sexual violence evidence at a sufficiently early point in proceedings is the exclusion of charges for sexual crimes. One of the most striking failures in this regard comes from the *Lukić* case at the ICTY. As with many other cases at the ICTY, the initial indictment against the Lukić brothers was drafted in 1998, several years before their arrest and transfer to the tribunal.[82] Although the involvement of both defendants in rapes and sexual violence committed in Višegrad was well-known, then prosecutor Carla Del Ponte took the mystifying decision not to amend the indictment to add sexual violence charges on the basis that it would unduly lengthen the trial and thereby fall foul of the UN Security Council completion strategy for the tribunal.[83] When her successor Serge Brammertz applied to have the indictment amended to include charges of rape and sexual slavery, the Trial Chamber refused, as the deadline for amending the indictment had already passed. The Trial Chamber also held that adding new charges so close to the commencement of trial would be in violation of the fair trial rights of the accused.[84] The outrageous result of this abject failure of prosecutorial strategy was that evidence of sexual violence was admitted only to undermine the accused's defence of alibi; one witness testified that, at the time Milan Lukić claimed to have been in another location, he was in fact

---

[82] ICTY, *Prosecutor v. Milan Lukić and Sredoje Lukić*, Indictment, IT-98-32/1, 26 October 1998 (http://www.legal-tools.org/doc/cdf403/).

[83] See ICTY, *Prosecutor v. Milan Lukić and Sredoje Lukić*, Trial Chamber, Decision on Prosecution Motion Seeking Leave to Amend the Second Amended Indictment and on Prosecution Motion to Include UN Security Council Resolution 1820 (2008) as Additional Supporting Material to Proposed Third Amended Indictment as well as on Milan Lukić's Request for Reconsideration on Certification of the Pre-Trial Judges Order of 19 June 2008, IT-98-32/1-PT, 8 July 2008 ('*Lukić* Decision') (http://www.legal-tools.org/doc/8f755c/); and Simon Jennings, "Lukic Trial Ruling Provokes Outcry", Institute for War and Peace Reporting, 15 August 2008.

[84] *Lukić* Decision, see *supra* note 83.

raping her in Višegrad.[85] Likewise, judges at the SCSL refused prosecutors permission to amend the indictment in the *CDF* case to add charges of sexual violence as it was too close to the start of trial, although the unfortunate impact in that case was the exclusion of all witness testimony regarding sexual violence, a source of great distress to the witnesses in question.[86]

Assuming that sexual violence evidence has been identified early and included from the beginning of the preparations of the prosecution case, it is still vital for prosecutors to choose the correct characterisation of facts to ensure that all elements of the crime in question can be met on the evidence. This is particularly important at the ICC, where judges in the Pre-Trial Chambers have not one but two opportunities – at the issuance of an arrest warrant phase and again at the confirmation of charges phase – to exclude charges for insufficient evidence or incorrect characterisation of facts. The experience of the Court to date has shown that charges of sexual or gender-based crimes have been particularly vulnerable to attrition at the earlier stages in the proceedings.[87] Prosecutorial strategy at this stage should also include a conscious effort to make full use of the expansive range of sexual violence offences included in the

---

[85] Dermot Groome, quoted in Jennings, 2008, see *supra* note 83.

[86] See Institute for War and Peace Reporting, "International Justice Failing Rape Victims", 15 February 2010; Sara Kendall and Michelle Staggs, "Silencing Sexual Violence: Recent Developments in the CDF Case at the Special Court for Sierra Leone", UC Berkeley War Crimes Studies Centre, 28 June 2005; Michelle Staggs Kelsall and Shanee Stepakoff, "'When We Wanted to Talk About Rape': Silencing Sexual Violence at the Special Court for Sierra Leone", in *International Journal of Transitional Justice*, 2007, vol. 1, no. 3, p. 355.

[87] Although this has sometimes been a matter of insufficient prosecution evidence (such as the shrinking of the geographic scope of the rape charges in the *Muthaura* case), it has also frequently been caused by an incorrect interpretation of the law by the judges – for example, the exclusion of other forms of sexual violence in the arrest warrant in the *Bemba* case on the grounds that forcible public nudity did not meet the threshold for "other forms of sexual violence of comparable gravity", despite the fact that when the crime of other forms of sexual violence was first identified in the *Akayesu* case, the archetypal example given was forcing women to undress and parade in public. See ICC, *Prosecutor v. Francis Kirimi Muthaura, Uhuru Muigai Kenyatta and Mohammed Hussein Ali*, Pre-Trial Chamber, Decision on the Prosecutor's Application for Summonses to Appear for Francis Kirimi Muthaura, Uhuru Muigai Kenyatta and Mohammed Hussein Ali, ICC-01/09-02/11-01, 8 March 2011 (http://www.legal-tools.org/doc/df8391/); ICC, *Prosecutor v. Jean-Pierre Bemba*, Warrant of Arrest for Jean-Pierre Bemba Gombo Replacing the Warrant of Arrest Issued on 23 May 2008, ICC-01/05-01/08-15-tENG, 10 June 2008 (http://www.legal-tools.org/doc/fb80c6/); Akayesu Trial Judgment, para. 688, see *supra* note 67.

ICC Statute,[88] as well as the incorporation of evidence of sexual violence, to illustrate the gendered nature of other crimes within the jurisdiction of the Court. International judges to date have shown willingness to consider evidence of sexual violence as a constituent factor in the commission of a wide range of offences beyond explicitly sexual or gender-based crimes, including genocide, extermination, enslavement, torture, persecution, other inhumane acts, grave breaches, outrages on personal dignity and cruel treatment. Prosecutors may be inclined to err on the side of caution in their characterisation of charges, but in doing so may miss a valuable opportunity to create an important precedent in international criminal law. For example, in the *Delalić* case at the ICTY, prosecutors sought charges only of inhuman treatment and cruel treatment in relation to an incident where two male detainees were forced to perform fellatio on each other. However, in the trial judgment, the judges noted that they would have been willing to convict the detainees for rape on the facts if they had been charged as such.[89] It is vital to adopt an open-minded and progressive approach to gender in the selection of charges; international criminal trials have already inverted some preconceptions by hearing testimonies of sexual violence from male victims, and convicting a woman for the perpetuation of sexual violence.[90]

Although international criminal trials are a costly and time-consuming business, there are certain concessions prosecutors should not make in exchange for a guilty plea, if they conflict with prosecutorial

---

[88] This includes rape, sexual slavery, enforced prostitution, forced pregnancy, enforced sterilisation and other forms of sexual violence: ICC Statute, Articles 7(g), 8(b)(xxii) and 8(c)(vi), see *supra* note 8.

[89] *Delić et al.* Trial Judgment, paras. 1056–66, see *supra* note 74.

[90] As mentioned above, the ICTY has by far the best record in relation to the prosecution of sexual violence committed against men, but more recently, a male rape victim testified in the *Bemba* case at the ICC, which is an encouraging development. See Women's Initiatives for Gender Justice, "Legal Eye on the ICC", March 2011. In June 2011, Pauline Nyiramasuhuko became the first woman to be convicted of rape by an international criminal tribunal for her role in the Rwandan genocide. See ICTR, *Prosecutor v. Pauline Nyiramasuhuko et al.*, Trial Chamber, Judgment and Sentence, ICTR-98-42-T, 24 June 2011 (http://www.legal-tools.org/doc/e2c881/); Stephanie Nieuwoudt, "Arusha Trial Challenges Gender Stereotypes", in *Institute for War and Peace Reporting*, 21 August 2006; Stephanie K. Wood, "A Woman Scorned for the 'Least Condemned' War Crime: Precedent and Problems With Prosecuting Rape as a Serious War Crime in the International Criminal Tribunal for Rwanda", in *Columbia Journal of Gender and Law*, 2004, vol. 13, no. 2, p. 274.

strategy. It is interesting to compare the practice of the ICTY and ICTR in relation to sexual violence charges and guilty pleas. At the Rwanda tribunal, sexual violence charges were dropped entirely in exchange for a guilty plea in no fewer than four cases.[91] Although the defendants pleaded guilty to a lesser charge relating to killings perpetrated in pursuit of the genocidal policy, charges of rape and sexual violence which were initially included in the indictments were removed without any corresponding manifestation in the ultimate conviction, weakening the already paltry prosecution record of that tribunal in relation to sexual crimes. At the Yugoslavia tribunal, by comparison, prosecutors succeeded in obtaining a guilty plea on sexual violence charges in six separate cases,[92] thereby proving that sexual and gender-based crimes need not be jettisoned in subservience to quick, efficient convictions. International criminal tribunals will not be judged on conviction rates alone; excessive eagerness on the part of prosecutors to sacrifice any reflection of a defendant's criminal responsibility for a serious and widespread crime, such as sexual violence in the final judgment of a case, shows a failure to appreciate the didactic importance of international criminal prosecutions.

When dealing with sexual and gender-based crimes at trial, prosecutors need to include a consideration of the needs of victims and witnesses in their prosecutorial strategy. The practice of witness proofing is a valuable means of preparing a vulnerable witness for the experience of testifying, and can have the added advantage of removing the potential for

---

[91] ICTR, *Prosecutor v. Paul Bisengimana*, Trial Chamber, Judgment and Sentence, ICTR-00-60, 13 April 2006 (http://www.legal-tools.org/doc/694dd8/); ICTR, *Prosecutor v. Joseph Nzabirinda*, Trial Chamber, Sentencing Judgment, ICTR-2001-77, 23 February 2007 (http://www.legal-tools.org/doc/e6069d/); ICTR, *Prosecutor v. Juvenal Rugambarara*, Trial Chamber, Sentencing Judgment, ICTR-00-59, 16 November 2007 (http://www.legal-tools.org/doc/37e659/); and ICTR, *Prosecutor v. Omar Serushago*, Trial Chamber, Sentence, ICTR-98-39-S, 5 February 1999 (http://www.legal-tools.org/doc/e2dddb/).

[92] ICTY, *Prosecutor v. Ranko Cesić*, Trial Chamber, Sentencing Judgment, IT-95-10/1, 11 March 2004 (http://www.legal-tools.org/doc/c86c07/); ICTY, *Prosecutor v. Dragan Nikolić*, Trial Chamber, Sentencing Judgment, IT-94-2, 18 December 2003 (http://www.legal-tools.org/doc/f8722c/); ICTY, *Prosecutor v. Ivica Rajić*, Trial Chamber, Sentencing Judgment, IT-95-12-S, 8 May 2006 (http://www.legal-tools.org/doc/b50857/); ICTY, *Prosecutor v. Milan Simić*, Trial Chamber, Sentencing Judgment, IT-95-9/2-S, 17 October 2002 (http://www.legal-tools.org/doc/fa0575/); ICTY, *Prosecutor v. Stevan Todorović*, Trial Chamber, Sentencing Judgment, IT-95/1, 31 July 2001 (http://www.legal-tools.org/doc/0cd4b3/); and ICTY, *Prosecutor v. Zelenović et al.*, Trial Chamber, Sentencing Judgment, IT-96-23/2, 4 April 2007 (http://www.legal-tools.org/doc/2a9e0b/).

an appearance of unreliability in a witness who may have given their initial statement to investigators years earlier.[93] Obviously, the trauma of reliving the experience of sexual violence in a courtroom will not be an easy experience for any witness, and can be particularly distressing for victims suffering from post-traumatic stress disorder. Thankfully, the ICTY has held in the *Furundžija* case that "there is no reason why a person with PTSD cannot be a perfectly reliable witness", although the other decisions taken in that case in relation to the disclosure of a traumatised witness's psychological and medical records were significantly less encouraging.[94] Where necessary, prosecutors should also co-operate with the Victims and Witnesses Unit to take full advantage of the in-court and out of court protective measures available to vulnerable witnesses, including face and voice distortion, testifying under a pseudonym, redaction of identifying information, the presence of a resource person or psychologist from the Victims and Witnesses Unit in the courtroom, and even (if strictly necessary) testimony in closed session.[95] Ultimately, however, the highest form of consideration that prosecutors can show to victims of sexual violence is to ensure that every layer of their investigative and prosecutorial strategy is designed to ensure the most effective and comprehensive prosecutions of sexual and gender-based violence possible.

15.4. Conclusion

Although there have undoubtedly been errors over the last two decades of modern international criminal prosecutions, it would be churlish not to acknowledge the incredible significance of the body of law on sexual and gender-based crimes which has been developed, and the hard work and

---

[93] Witness proofing is not technically permitted at the ICC; however, the practice of 'witness familiarisation' is broadly analogous for this purpose. See further Sergey Vasiliev, "Proofing the Ban on 'Witness Proofing': Did the ICC Get it Right?", in *Criminal Law Forum*, 2009, vol. 20, no. 2, p. 193; Christine Schön, "Telling Their Stories in Their Own Words: Witness Familiarisation at the International Criminal Court", in *Revue Internationale de Droit Pénal*, 2010, vol. 81, no. 1, p. 189.

[94] ICTY, *Prosecutor v. Anto Furundžija*, Trial Chamber, Judgment, IT-95-17/1, 10 December 1998, para. 105 (http://www.legal-tools.org/doc/e6081b/). See further Kelly D. Askin, "Sexual Violence in Decisions and Indictments of the Yugoslav and Rwandan Tribunals: Current Status", in *American Journal of International Law*, 1999, vol. 93, no. 1, pp. 97, 110–13.

[95] See further de Brouwer, 2005, pp. 231–83, *supra* note 51.

dedication of the many talented and committed people who have made such concerted efforts to pursue these prosecutions. However, the very scale of the normative and interpretative precedents set by the limited roster of international criminal convictions for sexual violence imposes an even more onerous requirement on prosecutors, to ensure that they prosecute these crimes to the fullest possible extent. Nothing raises expectations like success. It would be a mistake to allow the perception of sexual and gender-based violence as a problematic or difficult crime to prosecute, to be used as an excuse to relegate such crimes to an afterthought or a handful of token allegations scattered across the case files. Prosecuting sexual violence effectively at the international criminal level is not easy, but nor is it impossible. As has been seen throughout this chapter, if sexual crimes are to be dealt with in a sufficiently thorough manner, they must be prioritised at all levels in the work of the investigation and prosecution teams. The result will not only better reflect the reality of the underlying conflicts and the experience of victims (both male and female), but will enable international tribunals to live up to their mandates and to continue to contribute vital precedents to the growing body of international criminal jurisprudence.

16

Prosecuting Wartime Sexual Violence Committed against Men: Where Did It All Go Wrong?

Fletch Williams[*]

16.1. Introduction

When innovations regarding international and wartime sex crimes entered the legal arena at the International Criminal Tribunal for the former Yugoslavia ('ICTY') and International Criminal Tribunal for Rwanda ('ICTR') there was a significant opportunity to engage with preconceptions and attitudes about international sex crimes. In many ways, and in some cases, prosecutors and judges took that opportunity. However, in other ways they did not. This chapter seeks to examine some of the barriers to equal legal protection concerning international sex crimes for male and female victims, and the harms that instigates.

It is important to recognise that the statutes concerning sex crimes committed in conflict do not reference sex or gender. This rather obvious point sits in contrast to the gendered application of those statutes, including the Rome Statute of the International Criminal Court ('ICC Statute'),[1] the Convention against Torture,[2] the Convention on the Prevention and Punishment of Crimes of Genocide,[3] and the Statutes of *ad hoc* tribunals such as the ICTY[4] and ICTR.[5] Unfortunately, a disparity is appearing:

---

[*] **Fletch Williams** is a Doctoral Candidate at the Department of Law, London School of Economics, United Kingdom; and a Member of the Research School of Peace and Conflict, Peace Research Institute Oslo. She previously served as a Policy Advisor at the Mission of Ireland to the United Nations.

[1] Rome Statute of the International Criminal Court, 17 July 1998, in force 1 July 2002 ('ICC Statute') (http://www.legal-tools.org/doc/7b9af9/).

[2] United Nations General Assembly, Convention against Torture and Other Cruel, Inhuman or Degrading Treatment or Punishment, 10 December 1984 (http://www.legal-tools.org/doc/713f11/).

[3] United Nations General Assembly, Convention on the Prevention and Punishment of the Crime of Genocide, 9 December 1948, UN Doc. A/Res/3/260 (http://www.legal-tools.org/doc/498c38/).

[4] Statute of the International Tribunal for the former Yugoslavia, adopted 25 May 1993, amended 7 July 2009 (https://www.legal-tools.org/doc/b4f63b/).

---

while the perpetrators of rape against women face the increasing likelihood of prosecution,[6] those who perpetrate the rape of men in war do not. The result is relative impunity based on the gender of the victim. This chapter focuses on the treatment that male victims receive. (The problems that female victims experience are referenced, but they are not the specific focus of the discussion.)

What is most bewildering about the distinction drawn between male and female victims is that it undermines the ICC's and international community's own definitions of justice, as stated in Article 21(3) of the ICC Statute.[7] Furthermore, there is scope within the current legal apparatus for this not to be a problem. Thus the question that needs to be asked is: what does it mean when male victims are left out of key prosecutions? This chapter focuses on the following: 1) the gender neutrality of written legislation on sex crimes committed during war; 2) the implicit understandings of, and attitudes towards, sexual violence; and 3) the problems that arise when international sex crimes committed against men are not considered in a gender-neutral manner. The chapter goes on to highlight some sex crimes cases which were not gender neutral, particularly those concerning both male and female victims. Some comparative analysis is offered in order to examine the attitudes and considerations given to each gender when prosecuting international sex crimes.

16.2. International Law Regarding Sex Crimes and Gender Neutrality

It is a fact that current *statutes* that concern sex crimes are written in a gender-neutral manner. That is not true of many United Nations ('UN') and European Union resolutions that concern sexual violence. To further

---

5   Statute of the International Tribunal for Rwanda, adopted 8 November 1994, (http://www.legal-tools.org/doc/8732d6/).

6   Hilmi M. Zawati, "Impunity or Immunity: Wartime Male Rape and Sexual Torture as a Crime Against Humanity", in *Torture*, 2007, vol. 17, no. 1, p. 27.

7   ICC Statute, Article 21(3), see *supra* note 1:

> The application and interpretation of law pursuant to this article must be consistent with internationally recognized human rights, and be without any adverse distinction founded on grounds such as gender as defined in article 7, paragraph 3, age, race, colour, language, religion or belief, political or other opinion, national, ethnic to social origin, wealth, birth or other status.

---

facilitate prosecutions, many of the articles pertaining to sex crimes list the types of acts that can be considered as wartime sexual violence, but clearly state that those lists are not exhaustive.[8] As already noted, this does not mean that they are implemented in that way. Nonetheless, the gender-neutral construction of the laws of war is a concession to the principle that the harms incurred by any individual should be considered as equal. Realising equal protection under international law is vital in order to achieve wider principles of justice. It also demonstrates the intent and ability of the international community to prosecute acts they deem to be unacceptable even in times of war. Put simply, acts of sexual and gender-based violence are considered to be unacceptable acts. Practically, by entering the legal process, it becomes easier for victims to access rehabilitation facilities, psychological support and social assistance due to the acknowledgment of their situation. The prosecution of international sex crimes is accompanied by a rise in advocacy and activism on behalf of victims' needs. When men are not seen to be legally legitimate victims of international sex crimes, through a lack of prosecution, they lose out on these opportunities (to a greater or lesser extent), which are ultimately designed to alleviate the suffering experienced by victims.

It is possible to consider the increasing legitimacy of international law concerning sex crimes to be linked with, and be complementary to, the greater presence of human rights within the consciousness of people, organisations and states. Specific efforts to focus the application of the principle of non-discrimination, "including 'sex' discrimination is enshrined throughout all human rights instruments and recognized as the most fundamental principle of human rights law".[9] However, the number of cases about sex crimes committed against men that reach international tribunals can be counted on the fingers of one hand. This is at odds with the rather large number of well-known and documented cases.[10] When

---

[8]   ICC Statute, Article 7(1)(k): "other inhumane acts of similar character", thus leaving the list outlined in the article open-ended, see *supra* note 1.

[9]   Kelly D. Askin, "Prosecuting Wartime Rape and Other Gender-Related Crimes Under International Law: Extraordinary Advances, Enduring Obstacles", in *Berkeley Journal of International Law*, 2003, vol. 21, no. 2, p. 3.

[10] For details on the lack of cases of sexual violence committed during wartime against men, and those which were brought to the ICC's and international tribunals' attention, see Zawati, 2007, pp. 27–47, *supra* note 6; Kelly D. Askin, "A Decade of the Development of Gender Crimes in International Courts and Tribunals: 1993 to 2003", in *Human Rights Debrief*,

laws are not applied evenly to all victims and situations, wherever possible, actors necessarily obtain impunity for the actions they commit.[11] This is particularly so when done in a manner akin to discrimination, because it contributes to an international narrative of (perhaps wilful) ignorance about the sexual violence committed against men in wartime. Not only does that discourse further hinder possible prosecutions, but at a local level it can impact negatively on the level of services male victims can access, degrees of social ostracism (and the ability of aid workers to engage with that), and even the ability of male victims to be cognisant of the events they have experienced. Because male victims face the problem of medical workers denying the possibility that men can be sexually tortured, assaulted and raped, war contributes significantly to the difficulties outlined above and also creates a barrier to the collection of data, evidence and formation of policy.[12]

When there is a thematic prosecution of international sex crimes, there may be a (subconscious) attempt to actively identify victims of those crimes as a tool to help boost the attention a conflict receives from the international community. A vicious circle can be seen regarding the problem of policy formation. While medical aid workers do not acknowledge the existence of male victims of sex crimes then there is no apparent need for policy to be created. However, without the policy being created, the perceptions and attitudes of medical aid workers are not challenged in or-

---

2004, vol. 11, no. 3, pp. 16–19; Karen Engle, "Feminism and Its (Dis)contents: Criminalizing Wartime Rape in Bosnia and Herzegovina", in *American Journal of International Law*, 2005, vol. 99, no. 4, pp. 778–816; Pauline Oosterhoff, Prisca Zwanikken and Evert Ketting, "Sexual Torture of Men in Croatia and Other Conflict Situations: An Open Secret" in *Reproductive Health Matters*, 2004, vol. 12, no. 23, pp. 68–77.

[11] Oosterhoff *et al.*, 2004, p. 70, see *supra* note 10.

[12] The problem of collecting data and offering medical services for male victims of sexual violence in war was noted in an interview with a therapist at the International Rehabilitation Council for Torture. The therapist said that "she had not believed that men could be raped until one night a man was brought in naked and bleeding from the anus". That such attitudes exist among frontline care-givers might further problematise the ability for male victims to come forward. Furthermore, the UN has issued expert reports pointing out that there have been instances where medical workers have been unwilling to acknowledge that a male victim of rape has presented themselves to the relevant services. See UN Security Council, Final Report of the United Nations Commission of Experts, Annex IX, A, Sexual Assault Investigations, UN Doc. S/1994/674/Add.2, vol. V, 28 December 1994 ('UN Commission of Experts Final Report'); Oosterhoff *et al.*, 2004, p. 74, see *supra* note 10.

der for male victims to be recognised. All of this amounts to sexual discrimination.

The current trend of thematically prosecuting international sex crimes presents an opportunity to engage with and overcome these problematic areas of international law. The argument presented above, and throughout this chapter, is for the most part not new. It is the same as the argument put forward as to why sex crimes had to be prosecuted in the first place. It is an oversight that many of the proponents of this argument have omitted male victims from their purview, considering the non-mutual exclusivity of the needs and generalised aims of the victims of international sex crimes. This is ironic, given that the omission of male victims demonstrates the need for them to be included in the very policies and laws that they have been excluded from. It is only reasonable to acknowledge that under certain circumstances there will be a lack of evidence and other factors that prevent prosecution (evidentiary burdens are discussed below). Those situations are unfortunate and it is regretful that they occur. However, even within known and demonstrable cases of international sex crimes in war, comparable crimes committed against men and women are approached and evaluated differently.

Various justifications have been offered for this. One, which is implicit in most arguments, is that the international community's concern should lie with female victims, as they are more numerous. Further, women may be in a more vulnerable position in society, be subject to greater backlash or, as they are more likely to be non-combatants, should be afforded special legal protections under crimes against humanity. Variants of this line of argument also point out that women have been historically subjugated and are therefore (arguably) the predominant victims of masculinity-driven power dynamics.[13] The conclusion drawn from this is that female victims need to be prioritised.

There are several flaws with this line of reasoning. First, current data show that female victims do outnumber male victims. However, as is true with all statistics on rape, it is acknowledged that there are many victims who do not come forward and report crimes. Male victims face the additional challenge of medical workers not even considering that rape

---

[13]   James R. McHenry, "The Prosecution of Rape Under International Law: Justice that is Long Overdue", in *Vanderbilt Journal of Transnational Law*, 2002, vol. 35, pp. 1274, 1280, 1282.

and sexual violence can happen to them.[14] The United Nations High Commissioner for Refugees only issued its guidelines on how to protect male rape victims on 8 October 2012.[15] This indicates the significant lag in acknowledging the needs of male victims.

Second, just because there are more female victims, it does not automatically make male victims less deserving of legal attention, particularly when it is mutually advantageous to assist both groups simultaneously. It is debatable as to whether victims should be considered separate groups at all. Male victims are known to suffer just as much backlash from their communities, many being ostracised and shamed. It is worth pointing out a strange linguistic hierarchy when discussing the effects of sex crimes upon the individual: men are 'emasculated' (become feminine) whereas women are 'dehumanised'. By combining the interests of male and female rape victims within political and legal discourse, rather than considering male and female victims as competing groups, these unhelpful gendered distinctions may fall into disuse faster and the level of protection that female victims are currently afforded can be extended to include more victims.

The idea that male and female victims experience different harms can be considered further. The harms that victims experience are very much dependent on individual perception, situation(s), as well as other factors, and border on the incomprehensible in the minds of others. This is true of most crimes considered in international tribunals. It is not the purpose of the ICC or other international tribunals to quantitatively assess the harms incurred to the individual, a community or society, especially in comparison to others. Rather, surely it is appropriate to assess the behaviour of those who committed and instigated the crimes.[16] When and where the comparative assessment of harms is done, there is the risk of 'crime ranking', that is, crimes against humanity are considered to be more serious than war crimes.[17] The constructive purpose and role of this activity have yet to be concretely argued. What crime ranking does allow for is a

---

[14] UN Commission of Experts Final Report, see *supra* note 12.

[15] Fatoumata Lejeune-Kaba, "UNHCR Issues Guidelines on Protection of Male Rape Victims", United Nations High Commissioner for Refugees, 8 October 2012.

[16] Engle, 2005, pp. 781–84, see *supra* note 10.

[17] The idea of prioritising, or creating a crime hierarchy, is discussed in other chapters of this book.

prioritisation of some over others. Where there is a lack of resources the temptation to do this is understandable, but caution should be taken, as some crimes may be permanently 'demoted'.

In short, the personal harms experienced are impactful, but should not be crucial to prosecution. Importantly, it is possible to do this while also acknowledging that actions committed are atrocities. However, it worth acknowledging that it is challenging to do this while deploying a policy of thematic prosecution.

It is not that there have been no prosecutions that concern male victims, nor that other sex crime judgments could not be used as jurisprudence for future cases concerning men. The *Čelebići*[18] and *Tadić*[19] judgments of the ICTY concerned both male and female victims. The *Akayesu* judgment[20] at the ICTR was liberal enough not to reference genitalia, and therefore could be used as a basis for constructing the legal reasoning for a plethora of potential cases; the fact that it has been referenced in other judgments demonstrates this. So the potential for a liberal interpretation of international law concerning sex crimes has been used in some cases, but notably less so when it comes to male victims trying to prosecute. When there is no distinction in law, then the alternative source for this divide is those who enact the law. The justification given for decisions is indicative of this being the case.

In order to confront these ideas more fully, and in the context of the practical application of international legislation, the next section first engages with the recent decision of the confirmation of charges regarding the case of the *Prosecutor v. Muthaura, Kenyatta and Hussein Ali*,[21] and then with two historical cases concerning the sex crimes committed

---

[18] International Criminal Tribunal for the former Yugoslavia ('ICTY'), *Prosecutor v. Zdravko Mucić et al.*, Trial Chamber, Judgment, IT-96-21-T, 16 November 1998 ('*Čelebići* Judgment') (http://www.legal-tools.org/doc/6b4a33/).

[19] ICTY, *Prosecutor v. Duško Tadić et al.*, Trial Chamber, Judgment, IT-94-1-T, 7 May 1997 ('*Tadić* Trial Judgment') (http://www.legal-tools.org/doc/a0948e/).

[20] International Criminal Tribunal for Rwanda ('ICTR'), *Prosecutor v. Jean-Paul Akayesu*, Trial Chamber, Judgment, ICTR-96-4-T, 2 September 1998 (http://www.legal-tools.org/doc/b8d7bd/).

[21] International Criminal Court ('ICC'), *Prosecutor v. Francis Kirimi Muthaura, Uhuru Muigai Kenyatta and Mohammed Hussein Ali*, Pre-Trial Chamber, Decision on the Confirmation of Charges Pursuant to Article 61(7)(a) and (b) of the Rome Statute, ICC-01/09-02/11, 23 January 2012, paras. 257–66 ('*Muthaura* Decision') (http://www.legal-tools.org/doc/4972c0/).

against men and women, namely those of *Čelebići* and *Tadić*. This analysis aims to demonstrate the distinctions drawn between male and female victims of international wartime sex crimes.

16.3. 'Legal' Interpretations of Male Rape

16.3.1. The Decision of the Confirmation of Charges of the Case of the *Prosecutor v. Muthaura and Others*: Epitomising a Problem

In the decision of the confirmation of charges regarding the case of the *Prosecutor v. Muthaura and Others*, the presiding judges had to consider the issue of forced circumcision and penile amputation committed against Luo men by Mungiki attackers.[22] The prosecutor reported four cases of forced circumcision (reports by human rights organisations found more[23]), and it was noted that many cases had gone unreported due to the trauma and societal stigma caused by the crimes. Those that were reported were witnessed by doctors, who spoke of the forced circumcision of Luo men by the use of *pangas* (a kind of machete) and broken bottles. In some cases there was partial or total removal of the penis. Relevant to this discussion, the reports of forced circumcision were considered alongside those of Luo women being raped, also by the Mungiki, during the same two-day period of violence. Both were brought forward as potential charges of crimes against humanity, pursuant to Article 7(1)(g) of the ICC Statute.[24]

---

[22] The Mungiki are an offshoot of a religious sect in Kenya that consists mainly of youth from the country's largest tribe, the Kikuyu. Its size is unknown. The police describe it as Kenya's version of the mafia; it uses a politically militant tone and has been described as using Mau Mau-style fear tactics. See Reuters, "FACTBOX: Key Facts about Kenya's Mungiki Gang", 6 March 2009.

[23] Reporting organisations included the Commission of Inquiry into the Post-Election Violence, Human Rights Watch and Kenya National Commission on Human Rights.

[24] ICC Statute, Article 7 categorises crimes against humanity, and 7(1)(g) reads:

> "crime against humanity" means any of the following acts when committed as part of a widespread attack directed against any civilian population, with knowledge of the attack: [...]
>
> g) Rape, sexual slavery, enforced prostitution, forced pregnancy, enforced sterilization, or any other form of sexual violence of comparable gravity

See *supra* note 1.

Regarding the female victims, the decision found that the evidence threshold for rape was found, without detailing what the presiding judges considered that threshold to be. The decision took into consideration a witness statement which said that the perpetrators of the crime were of Kikuyu ethnicity (most Mungiki are Kikuyu).[25] The result of this decision meant that prosecution could proceed. Three brief paragraphs were provided for this section of the decision. There was no theoretical questioning regarding the issue of rape. It may be considered by some that the simplicity of the consideration of these charges demonstrates how far attempts to prosecute international sex crimes have advanced.

The reports of forced circumcision were not considered in the same style. There was theoretical questioning and the consideration of potential charges was not simple. Paragraph 265 'discusses' whether forced penile circumcision constitutes a violation of Article 7(1)(g) of the ICC Statute. The decision reads:

> The Chamber is of the view that not every act of violence which targets parts of the body commonly associated with sexuality should be considered an act of sexual violence. In this respect, the chamber considered that the determination of whether an act is of a sexual nature is inherently a question of fact.

It is not unreasonable to consider the possibility that an act of violence committed against the sexual organs may be committed without the intent to sexually target the victim. The question of the connection between the sex organs, sexuality and identity should be, and is, asked constantly within academia and by other interested parties. Using it with little justification to 'denote'[26] an act that can be considered to be sexual violence under previous jurisprudence to "acts causing severe physical injury" is a step backwards from landmark judgments like *Akayesu* and *Musema*[27] that took a liberal understanding of rape.[28] What the presiding

---

[25]   *Muthaura* Decision, para. 258, see *supra* note 21.

[26]   'Denote' is used here because of the generally accepted view of crime ranking.

[27]   ICTR, *Prosecutor v. Alfred Musema*, Trial Chamber, Judgment, ICTR-96-13-T, 27 January 2000 (http://www.legal-tools.org/doc/1fc6ed/).

[28]   The *Akayesu* judgment described rapes as "a form of aggression and that the central elements of the crime of rape cannot be captured in a mechanical description of objects and body parts", and goes on to state that rape is "a physical invasion of a sexual nature committed on a person under circumstances which are coercive". Similarly, the same Tribunal defined sexual

judges of the *Muthaura and Others* decision did was to bluntly draw a line between attacking identity by attacking the sexual organs and sexual violence. No such line was drawn for the female victims. This line was drawn in paragraph 266, where the judges observed that "the acts were motivated by ethnic prejudice and intended to demonstrate cultural superiority of one tribe over the other".[29]

Article 7(1)(g) of the ICC Statute forbids "rape, sexual slavery, enforced prostitution, forced pregnancy, enforced sterilization, or any other form of *sexual violence of comparable gravity*" as part of a "widespread or systematic attack directed against any civilian population".[30] Many may consider the forced removal of all or part of the penis to be an act of comparable gravity, and definitely an issue that concerns human dignity relevant to crimes against humanity. The presiding judges did not challenge the content of the violence, but the basis. What was emphasised was that the men were Luo. Presumably it was considered that being Luo was the only *reason* they were attacked, and not their Luo masculinity that *was* attacked. The organs that were attacked appear to be coincidental, and not integral, to the attack. As such, this example of violence did not qualify as "other forms of sexual violence" relevant to Article 7(1)(g), but solely as a form of ethnic violence.

The mutual exclusivity of a masculine identity, ethnicity and sexual attack against Luo men is not broached in the decision. Instead, it seems to have been thought out in a very shallow way, particularly bearing in mind that the evidence brought forward by witnesses and NGOs was fair-

---

violence as "any act of [a] sexual nature which is committed on a person under circumstances which are coercive" (para. 598), see *supra* note 20. The *Musema* judgment carries on in this vein, expressing the view that "the essence of rape is not the particular details of the body parts and objects involved, but rather the aggression that is expressed in a sexual manner under conditions of coercion" (para. 226), see *supra* note 27. Both the definitions provided by the *Akayesu* and *Musema* judgments are broadly similar in nature. They provide the understanding that rape is not merely a man using his penis to penetrate a woman. Rather, it is far more complex and involves intent to demonstrate power over an individual. However, the *Akayesu* judgment does restrict rape to the following elements:

a) a physical invasion of sexual nature;
b) to be committed against and on a person (importantly, male or female);
c) under circumstances which are coercive (that is, against the victim's will or without their consent).

[29] *Muthaura* Decision, para. 266, see *supra* note 21.
[30] ICC Statute, Article 7(1)(g), see *supra* note 1 (emphasis added).

---

ly similar. The basis on which the evidence (the content of which was the same) was considered for victims of each gender was different. The potential charges concerning female victims were not challenged with the same theoretically invasive questions as those of the male victims. No justification was given for the alternative lines of enquiry. Both lines of reasoning offered by the presiding judges regarding the potential charges of sexual violence against male and female victims were interchangeable.

The logic applied to the example of the female victims may be attributed (at least in part) to the increasing amount of *repeated* jurisprudence that finds that 'feminine' identity and female sexual organs are intrinsically linked, as the sexual organs are the most demonstrable physical manifestation of any feminine identity, and are therefore the locus of attack. There seems to be little reason to see why this same logic could not apply to male victims. More of a justification needs to be given if it is not. The crux of the issue is that the judges demanded a different burden of evidence for the different victims even though witnesses described the motivations and attributes of the violence to be the same.

Part of the legal usefulness of crimes against humanity, rather than crimes of genocide (similar acts fall under both categories), is that the prosecutor is not faced with the same burden to prove an intent to a particular end. What the judges have then requested from this consideration is that the prosecutor attains more than the usual legal burden to reach the evidence threshold. This does not amount to legal parity, and appears to undermine principles of non-discrimination. It is additionally problematic to deploy this line of justification in a legal context, as future prosecutors are then required to prove more than just the facts of an event, but also to extrapolate and prove something that is all too often a matter of personal interpretation. There thus arises the need for legal consistency, which is so difficult to establish within the newly fledged area in international law concerning sex crimes.

Not since the jurisprudence of the ICTY and ICTR has the question of the connection between sexual organs and sexual violence been raised when the prosecutor brings forward reports of sexual violence committed against women. Comparable cases of the coerced mutilation of the women's bodies were considered to be rape, both by the ICTY and ICTR.[31]

---

[31] McHenry, 2002, pp. 1285–95, see *supra* note 13.

That judges are able to make such strong statements about the sexuality of men, and how that relates to their anatomy, can have prominent effects on the consideration of these crimes at a policy creation and implementation level. One effect is that the longer men are kept on the sidelines of prosecutions of, and decisions about, international sex crimes the harder it will be to include them, due to the snowballing effect of jurisprudence.

Although there are still many obstacles for female rape victims to overcome within the international legal environment, they benefit from having a relatively more stable base when it comes to the jurisprudence from which prosecutors may build a case. Male victims have repeatedly suffered from the assumptions held by the international legal community about the connection between physicality and identity, and how that relationship impacts on the cause of a crime. Those assumptions are demonstrated clearly by the example provided above. However, distinctions can also be seen in earlier cases of the ICTY.

16.3.2. The *Čelebići* Judgment and Gendered Approaches to Torture

The *Čelebići* case demonstrates the problem of distinguishing between the nature of sexual crimes committed against male and female victims. In this case, comparable violent acts happened to male and female victims, in the same situation and environment. The judgment demonstrated a subtle but distinct difference in how the crime of sexual torture was considered, and therefore how they were prosecuted. The case concerned actions that were taken in the Čelebići Camp by Zejnil Delalić,[32] Zdravko Mucić and Hazim Delić.[33] Mucić was convicted for sexual violence committed against male detainees in the camp, whereas Delić was prosecuted for sexual violence committed against female detainees.[34] The comparison between the treatment of male and female victims by the courts was something that the Trial Chamber was aware of; this awareness may be in part because the Trial Chamber's judgment was made only 10 weeks after the *Akayesu* judgment. Many in the international community welcomed

---

[32] Delalić was initially indicted for and charged with individual or superior responsibility for sex crimes. He was acquitted by the Trial Chamber due to lack of evidence.

[33] A fourth accused was also involved in this case, but he was not charged with responsibility for, involvement in, or facilitation of sex crimes.

[34] *Čelebići* Judgment, para. 394, see *supra* note 18.

the liberality of the *Akayesu* judgment on wartime sexual violence and those interested were watching how it would be received.

Mucić was held to be responsible for subordinates forcing two brothers to perform fellatio on one another as well as tying a burning fuse cord around the genitalia of another male detainee. The prosecution brought this forward to the Trial Chamber on counts of cruel treatment, inhumane treatment and wilfully causing great suffering.[35] These are contributory elements of torture, and were prosecuted under war crimes legislation as mandated by the ICTY Statute. Mucić was found guilty on these bases.

Delić was also found guilty of torture. He was convicted of raping two women for the purposes of obtaining information, coercion, intimidation, and as a form of punishment because they reported previous abuse that they suffered in the Čelebići Camp. These actions were considered to be a form of sex discrimination by the Trial Chamber as well as a mechanism deployed by the accused to create an atmosphere of powerlessness and fear within the camp.[36] Due to this additionally proven element, Delić was also convicted of cruel and inhumane treatment, tantamount to crimes against humanity as defined by the ICC Statute.

Both prosecutions against Mucić and Delić, upheld by the Appeals Chamber, were fundamental in solidifying what were then new legal principles of accountability and responsibility. Within the 500-page judgment justification, the Trial Chamber greatly developed the principle of command responsibility, including responsibility for gender-based crimes.[37] It also explicitly stated that the rape of women *and* men were a form of torture;[38] this was the first judgment justification to do so. The Trial Cham-

---

[35] Kelly D. Askin, "Sexual Violence in Decisions and Indictments of the Yugoslav and Rwandan Tribunals: Current Status", in *American Journal of International Law*, 1999, vol. 93, no. 1, p. 105.

[36] *Čelebići* Judgment, para. 425, see *supra* note 18.

[37] *Ibid.*, paras. 334–56.

[38] Some current legal positivists have enquired about whether it would be more sensible to simply have a broad law against torture, rather than categorising forms of torture. The claim would then be that by having a broad anti-torture law the difficulties of prosecutory categories, gender disparities and other issues that problematise prosecutions would be removed. The question asked is: why add sex and gender into prosecutory practice when it only further confuses the issue? Although there are concerns about this approach, given current prosecutory discrepancies, this appears a fair question to ask.

ber acknowledged that there was the ability for the crimes committed against the male detainees to also fall under crimes against humanity legislation.[39] It also emphasised that there was scope for the forced oral sex prosecuted in the case to have been charged as rape. Yet, it was not.

As it was the presiding judges who pointed out this new legal possibility, one should not hold them responsible for not interpreting the law in a gender-neutral way, as it was with other examples. Rather, questions have to be asked as to why the prosecution did not try to protect the victims that they were representing within the full allowance of the law as it stood. These questions become all the more pertinent considering the legal attention that the *Akayesu* judgment had had.[40] Regardless of whether the implicitly accepted narrower understanding of rape that the prosecution lawyers approached this case with in reference to the male victims was conscious or not, it had the effect of those victims being afforded a lower level of justice than what international law acknowledges they deserve. They were therefore afforded a degree of benefit due to this understanding of rape and sexual abuses. But even the presiding judge pointed out that they would have been afforded more benefit by a broader definition of rape. The presiding judge in question was Judge Elizabeth Odio Benito, who has considerable expertise in sexual violence and gender crimes, particularly within international law. It is likely that it was her personal expertise that impacted upon this being made explicit in the judgment justification. Again, this is indicative of the importance, role and function of attitudes and understandings of sex crimes. When international law currently plays an important role as an attitude changing mechanism, surely the attitudes that it perpetrates must be held up to scrutiny.

All the examples so far provided demonstrate that cases concerning male victims of sexual violence are extremely vulnerable to the personal inclinations of the judge and lawyers. The result that victims may experience then depends upon who is allocated their case. Leaving such serious cases to the whim of happenstance is unsatisfactory, especially when those cases can have a direct effect on the outcome of future cases, the development of current policy that numerous victims depend upon for

---

[39] Askin, 2003, pp. 23–24, see *supra* note 9.

[40] Askin, 1999, p. 114, see *supra* note 35.

personal and social rehabilitation, and the legal development practices deployed in communities to reduce the stigma faced by victims.

What this comparison shows particularly effectively is that even when both men and women are considered to be victims of sexual torture within the same case, the starting point of analysis (and therefore understanding) appears to be different for men and women. The assumption seems to be made by the prosecutor that men are primarily tortured, and that torture can take the form of sexual assault. For women, the assumption appears to be that they are first sexually assaulted, and that assault takes the form of torture. This slight nuance may not seem relevant. However, it has a significant impact, as can be seen by the *Čelebići* case, since it then allows for the differentiation of the same act into different legal and criminal categories. When crime categories appear to function within the psyches of onlookers, this in turn affects the perceptions held about the seriousness of certain crimes. Furthermore, it has freed up scope for discussion about the sexual organ/sexual violence question used in the decision on the confirmation of charges in the case of *Muthaura*. In reality, it is likely these crimes can be prosecuted as torture under war crimes and crimes against humanity for both men and women. Failure to prosecute on all counts is the responsibility of the prosecutor. Apart from personal bias and prosecutorial discretion, there is little to indicate why this discriminatory phenomenon occurs.

16.3.3. The *Tadić* Judgment and Evidentiary Burdens

Problems surrounding the establishment of where the evidence threshold lies for sex crimes also appeared in previous judgments. The *Tadić* case at the ICTY saw medical workers providing evidence about sexual violence committed against men and women. Put simply, it is easier to accept that a woman has had act of sexual violence committed against her than a man. To believe that a man has been sexually attacked more of a justification must be given; a judge needs to be *more* persuaded.

Tadić was indicted for a number of sex crimes including personal involvement in gang rapes, sexual assaults and partaking in a campaign of terror. One specific instance concerned his forcing two male prisoners to perform fellatio upon a third prisoner and genitally mutilate him by biting off one testicle.[41] This was done in front of an audience. A medical worker provided the following testimony about sex crimes in the *Tadić* case:

> The very act of rape, in my opinion – I spoke to these people, I observed their reactions – it had a terrible effect on them. They could, perhaps, explain it to themselves when somebody steals something from them, or even beatings or even some killings. Somehow they sort of accepted it in some way, but when the rapes started they lost all hope. Until then they had hope that this war could pass, that everything would quiet down. When the rapes started, everybody lost hope, everybody in the camp, men and women. There was such fear, horrible.[42]

This testimony was given to contextualise the environment of fear in which many crimes were carried out. It concerned both men and women. However, this testimony was provided only as evidence to the suffering of women and girls in the camp. Female detainees in the camp were also forced to perform fellatio, experienced public sexual humiliation and the coerced mutilation of the genitalia. References to rapes were not made gender specific by the medical worker in question. This is true of most of the evidence given in this case. However, while the actions committed against female prisoners were considered to be rape (and not torture), those committed against male prisoners were considered to be torture. It is particularly bizarre that gendered inferences were made in the *Tadić* case considering that a significant proportion of it was about the sexual assault of men, and the relative liberality with which male victims saw the perpetrators of their crimes prosecuted. The form that the gender distinction took in the *Tadić* case was not that men could not be sexually assaulted; it was the difficulty in being able to recognise sexual violence as torture, instead of two distinct entities. Similarly, that barrier prevented female victims from being able to have their rapes recognised as torture. That same conceptual barrier can be seen in the *Muthaura* decision.

---

41   *Tadić* Trial Judgment, see *supra* note 19.

42   ICTY, *Prosecutor v. Duško Tadić et al.*, Trial Chamber, Opinion and Judgment, IT-94-1, 7 May 1997, para. 175 ('*Tadić* Opinion and Judgment') (http://www.legal-tools.org/doc/0a90ae/).

This criticism of the *Tadić* case is clearly put forward in an ICC policy document that clarifies definitions of gender in law. That criticism takes the following form:

> Take the example of the Tadić incident described above: the prosecutors recognized that the biting off of the male victim's testicle constituted both sexual violence and torture and therefore included this in the indictment. However, despite the fact that the women prisoners at the Omarska Camp were viciously raped as a way to torture them, the prosecutors did not understand the torture aspect of the rapes and therefore failed to include torture in the indictment relating to the rape of the women.[43]

This criticism is correct in pointing out that the sexual violence against women should have been recognised as torture. It is not that the crimes committed against women were down played, but rather their complexity was not fully understood – a failing indeed. However, a comparable failing is to not understand that male rape victims, such as Fikret Harambašić, suffered at the hands of the same campaign. That there were even testimonies provided to that end makes this omission unforgivable. Still, on the ICTY website the *Tadić* case is hailed as a landmark for prosecuting sexual crimes committed against men.[44] And while it is a landmark case in that it was the first such case, and remains better than most, it fell painfully short of prosecuting the case under the fullness of the law that was available to it.

Simply put, the Trial Chamber levied different burdens of evidence towards the prosecution for the same crimes committed against different genders. It appears to have been ignorant of its own inequity, partially because it failed to address it of its own accord, to provide the same burden of evidence to crimes committed against either gender, or to recognise that equivalent crimes were committed against individuals of different gender and thus invite the prosecution to expand their allegations accordingly. This is tantamount to discrimination on the basis of gender. It is something that the same laws under which *Tadić* was prosecuted, as well as other legislation that the international tribunals are bound by, legislated

---

[43] Women's Initiatives for Gender Justice, "Clarification of Term 'Gender'" (http://www.iccwomen.org/resources/gender.html).

[44] See ICTY, "Landmark Cases" (http://www.icty.org/sid/10314).

against. Additionally, the Trial Chamber praised itself in providing a higher level of justice to victims than national courts do by stating that the ICTY "accords to the testimony of a victim of sexual assault the same presumption of reliability as the testimony of victims of other crimes, something long denied to victims of sexual assault by the common law".[45] However, this is false praise. Although the burdens of evidence for sexual crimes at national level are often considered to be problematic,[46] just because the *ad hoc* international tribunals had a lower standard of evidence and better procedures for victims does not mean that those standards and procedures are or were *good* or the best they could be. The fact that witnesses (including male witnesses) in the *Tadić* case failed to produce evidence out of fear, and charges had to be withdrawn because of that, suggests there were significant failings on the part of the ICTY to care for victims.[47] Many years later, as the decision on the confirmation of charges in *Muthaura* shows, not much has changed.

16.4. Effects of Legal Decision-Making and Problematic Perceptions

That international legislation, at least in theory, allows the equal access of justice for both male and female victims of wartime rape is a massive triumph, considering the relatively short amount of time in which it has actively operated. However, significant issues with how laws are applied practically via jurisprudence demonstrates that the full scope of the law is not applied in these cases. It has been noted here that differing definitions of rape and sexual violence in war have created a barrier to justice for many victims, particularly males. Prosecutors also do not appear to press for charges on all counts of crimes, but lean towards wanting to prosecute for war crimes when the victims are male, and crimes against humanity when the victims are female. That could be understandable when one victim is a combatant and another is a civilian, which may indeed differentiate them. However, the *Mucić* and *Delić* cases offer a direct comparison

---

[45] *Tadić* Trial Judgment, paras. 536 and 256, see *supra* note 19. The trial chamber specifically determined that this rule also applied outside the context of sexual assault testimony.

[46] Kim Thuy Seelinger, Helene Silverberg and Robin Mejia, *The Investigation and Prosecution of Sexual Violence: Sexual Violence and Accountability Project*, Human Rights Centre, University of California, Berkeley, 2011, pp. 9, 18, 21, 50.

[47] Askin, 1999, p. 101, see *supra* note 35.

of that pursuit of justice down one avenue of crimes (or another), and still suggest that there is gender bias.

Further problems can arise from the perceptions of other involved parties. The UN special rapporteur on torture, Nigel Rodley, is an example of this bias in perception, which should be not apparent before the law. He submitted a report to the UN Commission on Human Rights on the issue of torture and other cruel, inhuman or degrading treatment or punishment. In the report he stated that he received abundant information regarding the practice of rape and sexual abuse as a weapon to punish, intimidate and humiliate the victims, who were mostly women. He added that rape and other forms of sexual abuse were apparently associated with other methods of torture used upon men.[48] This analytical order of 'rape-then-torture' for women and 'torture-then-rape' has been rejected by some cases, but maintained in others. This 'instability' in the jurisprudence allows those involved to play to their preferred interpretations, and inhibits the possibility of a consistently justifiable level of protection to be afforded to victims (and therefore a lack of impunity to perpetrators).

Occasionally the question is raised as to why sexual crimes need a special category within crimes of torture, crimes against humanity, war crimes and crimes of genocide. The answer to that question arises out of what has been discussed above. Without specific mention of acts of sexual violence, it is possible for these crimes to be overlooked. Historically, and for a variety of reasons, this has been true. Unfortunately, it remains so, with male victims consistently losing out on the level of protection that the law affords them. Without specific mention, victims are left vulnerable to human mistakes. This has particularly harmed women in the past, and so the emphasis placed on female victims is understandable; as noted, every policy document about rape until 8 October 2012 explicitly mentioned only female and child victims of sexual crimes. This has resulted in male victims, as a significant victim group, being excluded from accessing the assistance they need.

There remains potential in the ability of international law and the parties involved to ensure equal opportunity to the law for male and fe-

---

[48] See UN Commission on Human Rights, Report of Special Rapporteur on Torture, Cruel, Inhuman or Degrading Treatment or Punishment, UN Doc. E/CN.4/1994/31, 6 January 1994, paras. 431–32.

male victims of sexual violence, though problems will continue as long as there is no explicit engagement with the lack of equality between the consideration of cases concerning male and female victims. In turn, this would facilitate a more stable jurisprudential environment which can influence current policy, future cases and the interpretation of sex crimes.

17

Case Selection and Complementarity at the International Criminal Court: Exposing the Vulnerability of Sexual and Gender-Based Violence Crimes in the Admissibility Test

Dieneke de Vos[*]

Laying down criteria for the prioritisation and selection of cases by the International Criminal Court ('ICC' or 'the Court') is important for many reasons. Clear criteria contribute to the perceived legitimacy of proceedings among victims and affected communities,[1] guide investigators and help to disprove alleged politicisation of prosecutions. It has also been argued that carefully selected prosecutions of international crimes may reinforce broader transitional justice processes domestically, specifically by contributing to national reconciliation.[2] Finally, limited resources necessitate clear charging strategies and priorities.[3] Criteria for selection and prioritisation are especially important for countries transitioning out of

---

[*] **Dieneke de Vos** received her Ph.D. from the European University Institute, Florence, Italy, where she researched interactions between the International Criminal Court ('ICC') and national accountability processes for sexual violence crimes in Colombia and the Democratic Republic of Congo. She has previously worked for the Women's Initiatives for Gender Justice and the International Criminal Court; and as a consultant for the International Federation for Human Rights. All views expressed are the author's own.

[1] Morten Bergsmo, "The Theme of Selection and Prioritization and Why It Is Relevant", in Morten Bergsmo (ed.), *Criteria for Prioritizing and Selecting Core International Crimes Cases*, Torkel Opsahl Academic EPublisher, Brussels, 2010, p. 9; Allison Marston Danner, "Enhancing the Legitimacy and Accountability of Prosecutorial Discretion at the International Criminal Court", in *American Journal of International Law*, 2010, vol. 97, no. 3, p. 542.

[2] Hassan B. Jallow, "Prosecutorial Discretion and International Criminal Justice", in *Journal of International Criminal Justice*, 2005, vol. 3, no. 1, p. 154.

[3] Matthew R. Brubacher, "Prosecutorial Discretion within the International Criminal Court", in *Journal of International Criminal Justice*, 2004, vol. 2, no. 1, p. 76; Jo Stigen, *The Relationship between the International Criminal Court and National Jurisdictions: The Principle of Complementarity*, Martinus Nijhoff Publishers, Leiden, 2008, p. 343.

---

conflict given the vast number of crimes often committed and the complex nature of those crimes.[4]

It is perhaps unsurprising, then, that scholars have devoted much attention to critically assessing the ICC Office of the Prosecutor's charging strategies and their broader impact on international criminal justice.[5] This chapter joins this discussion by focusing on one particular aspect: the principle of complementarity and its relationship with case selection criteria, in particular as it relates to accountability for crimes of sexual and gender-based violence. Complementarity – the principle that the ICC shall complement, not supersede, domestic jurisdictions – constitutes a key

---

[4] Rolf Einer Fife, "Criteria for Prosecution of International Crimes: The Importance for States and the Importance for States and the International Community of the Quality of the Criminal Justice Process for Atrocities, in Particular the Exercise of Fundamental Discretion by Key Justice Actors", in Morten Bergsmo (ed.), *Criteria for Prioritizing and Selecting Core International Crimes Cases*, Torkel Opsahl Academic EPublisher, Brussels, 2010, p. 19; Ilia Utmelidze, "The Time and Resources Required by Criminal Justice for Atrocities and *de facto* Capacity to Process Large Backlogs of Core International Crimes Cases: The Limits of Prosecutorial Discretion and Independence", in Morten Bergsmo (ed.), *Criteria for Prioritizing and Selecting Core International Crimes Cases*, Torkel Opsahl Academic EPublisher, Brussels, 2010, p. 189.

[5] See, for example, Brubacher, 2004, pp. 71–95, *supra* note 3; Daniel D. Ntanda Nsereko, "Prosecutorial Discretion before National Courts and International Tribunals", in *Journal of International Criminal Justice*, 2005, vol. 3, no. 1, pp. 124–44; Luc Côté, "Reflections on the Exercise of Prosecutorial Discretion in International Criminal Law", in *Journal of International Criminal Justice*, 2005, vol. 3, no. 1, pp. 163–86; Jallow, 2005, pp. 71–95, see *supra* note 2; Phil Clark, "Law, Politics and Pragmatism: The ICC and Case Selection in the Democratic Republic of Congo and Uganda", in Nicholas Waddell and Phil Clark (eds.), *Courting Conflict: Justice, Peace and the ICC in Africa*, Royal African Society, London, 2008, pp. 37–44; William A. Schabas, "Prosecutorial Discretion v. Judicial Activism at the International Criminal Court", in *Journal of International Criminal Justice*, 2008, vol. 6, no. 4, pp. 731–61; Carla Ferstman, "Limited Charges and Limited Judgments by the International Criminal Court – Who Bears the Greatest Responsibility?", in *International Journal of Human Rights*, 2010, vol. 16, no. 5, pp. 796–813; Phil Clark, "Chasing Cases: The ICC and the Politics of State Referral in the Democratic Republic of the Congo and Uganda", in Carsten Stahn and Mohamed M. El Zeidy (eds.), *The International Criminal Court and Complementarity: From Theory to Practice*, vol. 2, Cambridge University Press, Cambridge, 2011, pp. 1180–203; Margaret M. deGuzman, "Choosing to Prosecute: Expressive Selection at the International Criminal Court", in *Michigan Journal of International Law*, 2012, vol. 33, pp. 265–320; Kai Ambos and Ignaz Stegmiller, "Prosecuting International Crimes at the International Criminal Court: Is There a Coherent and Comprehensive Prosecution Strategy?", in *Crime, Law and Social Change*, 2013, vol. 59, no. 4, pp. 415–37.

---

consideration when selecting and prioritising cases, both for the ICC[6] and for domestic courts. In particular, this chapter underscores that complementarity is grounded in what has been called the ICC Statute's "expressive" function:[7] what the Office of the Prosecutor focuses on sends a message about which crimes it deems important and how it conceives its mandate. Through the legal test for admissibility, what the ICC focuses on determines (in part) what states will focus on in their domestic proceedings if they wish to avoid ICC interference.[8]

Complementarity is often considered fundamental to the work of the ICC. However, as Louise Chappell *et al.* argue, there is a "gender justice shadow" to complementarity: the disconnect between the complementarity framework and the ICC Statute's gender justice provisions "undermines the Court's ability to extend gender justice measures at the domestic level".[9] Given the ICC Statute's emphasis on the prosecution and investigation of sexual and gender-based violence crimes, it is important to connect complementarity with the ICC Statute's gender inclusiveness. As this chapter illustrates, ensuring that complementarity is gender inclusive depends not only on the Office of the Prosecutor's assessment of admissibility but also on judicial interpretations of the ICC Statute's admissibility provisions.

This chapter starts with a brief overview of the ICC Statute's gender justice provisions. It then sets out in more detail the complementary relationship between the ICC and domestic jurisdictions, distinguishing between notions of 'legal' complementarity (the test for admissibility) and

---

[6] In September 2016 the Office of the Prosecutor adopted its policy paper on case selection and prioritisation. The policy paper confirms the centrality of admissibility and complementarity for case selection and prioritisation at the ICC: See ICC, Office of the Prosecutor, "Policy Paper on Case Selection and Prioritisation", 15 September 2016.

[7] On the ICC Statute's expressive function, see Margaret M. deGuzman, "An Expressive Rationale for the Thematic Prosecution of Sex Crimes", 2017, in this volume; deGuzman, 2012, see *supra* note 5.

[8] Amrita Kapur, "Complementarity at Work in Unwilling States: Raising the Threshold of Accountability for Gender-Based International Crimes", Paper presented at Justice for All? The International Criminal Court: A Conference: 10 Year Review of the ICC, University of New South Wales, Sydney, Australia, 15 February 2012.

[9] Louise Chappell, Rosemary Grey and Emily Waller, "The Gender Justice Shadow of Complementarity: Lessons from the International Criminal Court's Preliminary Examinations in Guinea and Colombia", in *International Journal of Transitional Justice*, 2013, vol. 7, no. 3, p. 457.

'broad' complementarity. The section that follows delineates in more detail the admissibility test as interpreted by the judges. It illustrates that there are potential gender biases in this test which may adversely affect the domestic prosecution of sexual and gender-based violence crimes or, at a minimum, leave them vulnerable to exclusion.

17.1. The ICC Statute's Gender Provisions

In recognition of the historical barriers facing the prosecution and investigation of sexual and gender-based violence crimes in domestic and international courts,[10] and following successful lobbying by women's rights activists,[11] the drafters of the ICC Statute adopted a broad range of gender-sensitive provisions. The innovative provisions break ground already trodden by previous international tribunals, in relation to the Court's substantive jurisdiction, the Office of the Prosecutor's investigative and prosecutorial powers and obligations, and the Court's institutional set-up.

---

[10] DeGuzman, 2017, p. 14, see *supra* note 7. See also, more generally, Kelly D. Askin, *War Crimes against Women: Prosecution in International War Crimes Tribunals*, Kluwer Law International, The Hague, 1997; Kelly D. Askin, "Prosecuting Wartime Rape and Other Gender-Related Crimes under International Law: Extraordinary Advances, Enduring Obstacles", in *Berkeley Journal of International Law*, 2003, vol. 21, no. 3, pp. 288–349; Kelly D. Askin, "Treatment of Sexual Violence in Armed Conflicts: A Historical Perspective and the Way Forward", in Anne-Marie de Brouwer *et al.* (eds.), *Sexual Violence as an International Crime: Interdisciplinary Approaches*, Intersentia, Antwerp, 2013, pp. 19–55; Susana SáCouto, "Investigation and Prosecution of Sexual and Gender-Based Violence by the International Criminal Court: Mandate, Good Policy or Both?", Gender Jurisprudence and International Criminal Law Project, 2012; Hilary Charlesworth and Christine Chinkin, *The Boundaries of International Law: A Feminist Analysis*, Manchester University Press, Manchester, 2000; Rhonda Copelon, "Gender Crimes as War Crimes: Integrating Crimes Against Women into International Criminal Law", in *McGill Law Journal*, 2000, vol. 46, pp. 217–40.

[11] For an overview of women's rights activists' lobbying around the drafting of the ICC Statute, see, for example, Brigid Inder, "Partners for Gender Justice", in Anne-Marie de Brouwer *et al.* (eds.), *Sexual Violence as an International Crime: Interdisciplinary Approaches*, Intersentia, Antwerp, 2013, p. 320; Barbara Bedont and Katherine Hall Martinez, "Ending Impunity for Gender Crimes under the International Criminal Court", in *Brown Journal of World Affairs*, 1999, vol. 6, no. 1, pp. 65–85; Marlies Glasius, "Who Is the Real Civil Society? Women's Groups versus Pro-Family Groups at the International Criminal Court Negotiations", in Jude Howell and Diane Mulligan (eds.), *Gender and Civil Society: Transcending Boundaries*, Routledge, London, 2005, pp. 222–41.

First, the ICC Statute contains the most advanced articulation of sexual and gender-based violence crimes of the international tribunals,[12] and thus provides a broad basis for their prosecution. Second, it specifically mandates the Office of the Prosecutor to prioritise the investigation and prosecution of sexual and gender-based violence crimes. Most notably, Article 54(1)(b) provides that the Office of the Prosecutor shall "[t]ake appropriate measures to ensure the effective investigation and prosecution of crimes within the jurisdiction of the Court, […] and take into account the nature of the crime, in particular where it involves sexual violence, gender violence or violence against children". As some have argued, this does not just provide the Office with a mandate to prosecute such crimes, but establishes an obligation to do so.[13] Third, the ICC Statute requires the recruitment of staff and election of judges with specific expertise on (victims of) gender-based violence,[14] and provides protective measures for witnesses, in particular victims of gender-based violence.[15] Finally, Article 21(3) confers a broad obligation on the Court to apply and interpret the law in a manner that is non-discriminatory, including on grounds of gender.[16]

---

[12] The ICC Statute includes rape, sexual slavery, enforced prostitution, forced pregnancy, enforced sterilisation, gender-based persecution, trafficking and other forms of sexual violence as war crimes, crimes against humanity and, in some circumstances, genocide. See Women's Initiatives for Gender Justice, "Gender Report Card on the International Criminal Court 2013", March 2014, p. 7; Louise Chappell, "Nested Newness and Institutional Innovation: Expanding Gender Justice in the International Criminal Court", in Mona Lena Krook and Fiona MacKay (eds.), *Gender, Politics and Institutions: Towards a Feminist Institutionalism*, Palgrave Macmillan, London, 2011, p. 163; Inder, 2013, p. 320, see *supra* note 11.

[13] See also SáCouto, 2012, *supra* note 10: "the Rome Statute and its drafting history suggest that the Court should not only prioritize sexual and gender-based crimes, but also ensure that allegations regarding such crimes feature prominently in the Prosecutor's investigation and charging strategy from the outset."

[14] See, for example, Rome Statute of the International Criminal Court, 17 July 1998, in force 1 July 2002, Article 42(9) and Article 36(8)(b) ('ICC Statute') (http://www.legal-tools.org/doc/7b9af9/). The latter requires judges with expertise on 'violence against women' rather than the broader category of 'gender-based violence'.

[15] *Ibid.*, Article 68(1).

[16] *Ibid.*, Article 21 deals with the applicable law that the Court must apply. As Patricia Viseur Sellers underscores, the use of the word 'Court' in Article 21 means that this obligation falls on *all* organs and units of the Court. Patricia Viseur Sellers, "Gender Strategy Is Not Luxury for International Courts: Prosecuting Sexual and Gender-Based Crimes before International/ized Criminal Courts", in *American University Journal of Gender, Social Policy and the Law*, 2009, vol. 17, no. 2, p. 341.

Taken together, these provisions indicate that the ICC must focus on the prosecution of sexual and gender-based violence crimes; the drafters of the ICC Statute specifically included this prioritisation "to ensure that gender-based crimes [were] not side-lined or ignored".[17] Because of the procedural and substantive gender justice emphasis enshrined in the ICC Statute, and given the centrality of the principle of complementarity, the Statute arguably created a larger international criminal justice project that is, or should be, gender inclusive. It is thus surprising that few scholars have linked complementarity to the ICC Statute's gender justice provisions.[18]

17.2. Complementarity and Case Selection

The principle of complementarity, found in Article 1 and the Preamble of the ICC Statute,[19] dictates that the ICC shall complement – not supersede – domestic jurisdictions, subject to certain conditions. This suggests that domestic jurisdictions are accorded a primary role (and corresponding duty[20]) in investigating and prosecuting crimes within the ICC's jurisdic-

---

[17] Valerie Oosterveld, "The Definition of 'Gender' in the Rome Statute of the International Criminal Court: A Step Forward or Back for International Criminal Justice?", in *Harvard Human Rights Journal*, 2005, vol. 18, p. 81. See also SáCouto, 2012, *supra* note 10; Cate Steains, "Gender Issues", in Roy S.K. Lee (ed.), *The International Criminal Court: The Making of the Rome Statute: Issues, Negotiations, Results*, Kluwer Law International, The Hague, 2009, pp. 357–90.

[18] For a preliminary analysis linking complementarity to the ICC Statute's gender justice provisions, see Chappell *et al.*, 2013, *supra* note 9; Kapur, 2012, *supra* note 8; Milli Lake, "Ending Impunity for Sexual and Gender-Based Crimes: The International Criminal Court and Complementarity in the Democratic Republic of Congo", in *African Conflict and Peacebuilding Review*, 2014, vol. 4, no. 1, pp. 1–32. See also, to a more limited extent, Sellers, 2009, *supra* note 16; Inder, 2013, *supra* note 11; Susana SáCouto and Katherine Cleary, "The Importance of Effective Investigation of Sexual Violence and Gender-Based Crimes at the International Criminal Court", in *American University Journal of Gender, Social Policy and the Law*, 2009, vol. 17, pp. 337–59; Amrita Kapur, "The Value of International-National Interactions and Norm Interpretations in Catalysing National Prosecutions of Sexual Violence", in *Oñati Socio-legal Studies*, 2016, vol. 6, no. 1, pp. 62–90.

[19] Article 1 and the tenth preambular paragraph of the ICC Statute provide that the ICC "shall be complementary to domestic criminal jurisdictions", see *supra* note 14.

[20] Mauro Politi argues that the ICC Statute establishes a *substantive* duty on states to carry out investigations and prosecutions, not just a mere formal duty: Mauro Politi, "Reflections on Complementarity at the Rome Conference and beyond", in Carsten Stahn and Mohamed M. El Zeidy (eds.), *The International Criminal Court and Complementarity: From Theory to Practice*, vol. 1, Cambridge University Press, Cambridge, 2011, p. 145.

tion. In that respect, the Statute's preamble recalls that "*it is the duty of every State* to exercise its criminal jurisdiction over those responsible for international crimes" and that "the most serious crimes of concern to the international community as a whole must not go unpunished and that their effective prosecution must be ensured *by taking measures at the national level* and by enhancing international cooperation".[21] Complementarity, some argue, strikes a careful balance between state sovereignty and the necessity for international criminal jurisdiction, exercised by the ICC, in certain situations.[22]

---

[21] ICC Statute, preambular paragraphs 6 and 4, respectively, see *supra* note 14 (emphasis added).

[22] See, for example, Markus Benzing, "Complementarity of the ICC – International Criminal Justice between State Sovereignty and the Fight against Impunity", in *Max Planck Yearbook of United Nations Law*, 2003, vol. 7, pp. 595, 597; Xavier Philippe, "The Principle of Universal Jurisdiction and Complementarity: How Do the Two Principles Intermesh?", in *International Review of the Red Cross*, 2006, vol. 88, no. 862, p. 381; Carsten Stahn, "Complementarity: A Tale of Two Notions", in *Criminal Law Forum*, 2007, vol. 19, p. 88; Stigen, 2008, p. 17, see *supra* note 3; Mark S. Ellis, "International Justice and the Rule of Law: Strengthening the ICC through Domestic Prosecutions", in *Hague Journal on the Rule of Law*, 2009, vol. 1, p. 81; Politi, 2009, p. 144, see *supra* note 20; Nidal Nabil Jurdi, "The Prosecutorial Interpretation of the Complementarity Principle: Does It Really Contribute to Ending Impunity on the National Level?", in *International Criminal Law Review*, 2010, vol. 10, no. 1, pp. 73–74; Olympia Bekou, "In the Hands of the State: Implementing Legislation and Complementarity", in Carsten Stahn and Mohamed M. El Zeidy (eds.), *The International Criminal Court and Complementarity: From Theory to Practice*, vol. 1, Cambridge University Press, Cambridge, 2011, pp. 830–31. See ICC, *Prosecutor v. Germain Katanga*, Appeals Chamber, Judgment on the Appeal of Mr. Germain Katanga against the Oral Decision of Trial Chamber II of 12 June 2009 on the Admissibility of the Case, ICC-01/04-01/07, 25 September 2009, para. 85 (http://www.legal-tools.org/doc/ba82b5/) underscoring "the complementarity principle, as enshrined in the Statute, strikes a balance between safeguarding the primacy of domestic proceedings vis-à-vis the International Criminal Court on the one hand, and the goal of the Rome Statute to 'put an end to impunity' on the other hand"; ICC, *Prosecutor v. Germain Katanga*, Appeals Chamber, Judgment on the Appeal of Mr Germain Katanga against the Oral Decision of Trial Chamber II of 12 June 2009 on the Admissibility of the Case, ICC-01/04-01/07-1497, 25 September 2009, para. 85 ('*Katanga* Admissibility Decision') (http://www.legal-tools.org/doc/ba82b5/). See also ICC, *Prosecutor v. Joseph Kony, Vincent Otti, Okot Odhiambo, Dominic Ongwen*, Pre-Trial Chamber II, Decision on the admissibility of the case under article 19(1) of the Statute, ICC-02/04-01/05-377, 10 March 2009, para. 34 (http://www.legal-tools.org/doc/44f5b3/); ICC, *Prosecutor v. Saif Al-Islam Gaddafi and Abdullah Al-Senussi*, Pre-Trial Chamber I, Public redacted Decision on the admissibility of the case against Saif Al-Islam Gaddafi, ICC-01/11-01/11-344-Red 31 May 2013, para. 52 ('*Saif Al-Islam Gaddafi* Admissibility Decision') (http://www.legal-tools.org/doc/339ee2/).

The principle of complementarity was at the heart of each stage of the ICC Statute's drafting process. States feared an interventionist court and for that reason made the ICC complementary to national jurisdictions, rather than giving it primary jurisdiction. Yet – and this is perhaps not emphasised often enough – this structure confers significant obligations on national systems. The threat of intervention by the Court spurring domestic action may thus be an important aspect of complementarity – what some scholars have termed the "catalyst" effect of complementarity.[23] Others have argued that, rather than constituting a threat, complementarity provides a powerful "incentive" for states to initiate domestic proceedings and enact domestic implementing legislation.[24]

Complementarity is often construed as a strict legal test, which may present a "barrier to [ICC] jurisdiction".[25] This view of complementarity is called "narrow", "procedural" or "classical" complementarity.[26] However, beyond this legal understanding, complementarity is increasingly understood as being of a dual nature, what Sarah Nouwen terms a "legal life" and a "big idea life".[27] In this model, complementarity is seen as the cornerstone of a broader ICC Statute system, in which domestic courts

---

[23] Robert Cryer, *Prosecuting International Crimes: Selectivity and the International Criminal Law Regime*, Cambridge University Press, Cambridge, 2005, p. 171; Jann K. Kleffner, *Complementarity in the Rome Statute and National Criminal Jurisdictions*, Oxford University Press, Oxford, 2008; Stigen, 2008, p. 473, see *supra* note 3; Morten Bergsmo, Olympia Bekou and Annika Jones, "Complementarity after Kampala: Capacity Building and the ICC's Legal Tools", in *Goettingen Journal of International Law*, 2010, vol. 2, no. 2, p. 795; Sarah Nouwen, *Complementarity in the Line of Fire: The Catalysing Effect of the International Criminal Court in Uganda and Sudan*, Cambridge University Press, Cambridge, 2013.

[24] Stahn, 2007, p. 92, see *supra* note 22; Lake, 2014, p. 5, see *supra* note 18; Fionnuala Ní Aoláin, "Gendered Harms and their Interface with International Criminal Law: Norms, Challenges and Domestication", in *University of Minnesota Law School: Legal Studies Research Paper Series*, 2013, nos. 13–19.

[25] Benzing, 2003, p. 595, see *supra* note 22.

[26] Kleffner, 2008, p. 3, see *supra* note 23; Benzing, 2003, p. 600, see *supra* note 22; Chappell *et al.*, 2013, p. 459, see *supra* note 9; Stahn, 2007, see *supra* note 22.

[27] Nouwen, 2013, see *supra* note 23. In a similar vein, Chappell *et al.*, 2013, see *supra* note 9 refer to the "narrow" and "broad" conceptions of complementarity. Likewise, Stahn refers to the "dual foundation of complementarity": the institutional versus the systemic conception of complementarity, or the classical (negative) versus the positive concepts of complementarity. To him, the classical conception of complementarity focuses on balancing state sovereignty and ICC jurisdiction, and provides a remedy for shortcomings of domestic jurisdictions through admissibility criteria. Positive complementarity, on the other hand, is a "forum for managerial interaction between the Court and states": Stahn, 2007, p. 88, see *supra* note 22.

---

and the ICC together create a web of accountability for perpetrators of international crimes, and where complementarity affects various dimensions of state and ICC practice.[28] While there are interesting and important questions to analyse around such broader notions of complementarity and their interaction with the ICC Statute's provisions on the prosecution of sexual and gender-based violence crimes, those are beyond the scope of this chapter. This chapter is primarily concerned with the legal dimension of complementarity: the admissibility test.[29]

According to the ICC Statute's admissibility provisions, the ICC may only exercise its jurisdiction when a state that would normally have jurisdiction is not taking action domestically, or, when it is taking action, where that state is unable or unwilling genuinely to investigate or prosecute.[30] The ICC must also declare a case inadmissible when national authorities have investigated the case, but those authorities decided not to proceed, provided those proceedings were genuine.[31] Further, a person may not be tried twice for the same conduct.[32] Cases that are "not of sufficient gravity to justify further action by the Court" are also inadmissi-

---

[28] See, for example, Bekou, 2011, *supra* note 22; Stahn, 2007, *supra* note 22; Carsten Stahn, "Introduction: Bridge over Troubled Waters? Complementarity Themes and Debates in Context", in Carsten Stahn and Mohamed M. El Zeidy (eds.), *The International Criminal Court and Complementarity: From Theory to Practice*, vol. 1, Cambridge University Press, Cambridge, 2011, p. 1; Morten Bergsmo, Olympia Bekou and Annika Jones, "Complementarity and the Construction of National Ability" in Carsten Stahn and Mohamed M. El Zeidy (eds.), *The International Criminal Court and Complementarity: From Theory to Practice*, vol. 2, Cambridge University Press, Cambridge, 2011; Clark, 2011, p. 1183, see *supra* note 5; Sylvia Fernandez de Gurmendi, "Foreword", in Carsten Stahn and Mohamed M. El Zeidy (eds.), *The International Criminal Court and Complementarity: From Theory to Practice*, vol. 1, Cambridge University Press, Cambridge, 2011, p. xx; Bergsmo *et al.*, 2010, p. 796, see *supra* note 23.

[29] The Appeals Chamber in the *Al-Senussi* case underscored that the question of the admissibility of a case is "primarily a question of forum – the relationship between States and the Court is the principal issue in these proceedings". ICC, *Prosecutor v. Saif Al-Islam Gaddafi and Abdullah Al-Senussi*, Judgment on the appeal of Mr Abdullah Al-Senussi against the decision of Pre-Trial Chamber I of 11 October 2013 entitled "Decision on the admissibility of the case against Abdullah Al-Senussi", ICC-01/11-01/11-565, 24 July 2014, para. 169, see also para. 215 ('*Al-Senussi* Appeals Judgment') (http://www.legal-tools.org/doc/ef20c7/).

[30] ICC Statute, Article 17(1)(a), see *supra* note 14.

[31] *Ibid.*, Article 17(1)(b).

[32] *Ibid.*, Article 17(1)(c); Article 20(3).

---

ble.[33] These admissibility boundaries thus circumscribe the prosecutor's ability to freely select cases and situations.

Beyond establishing boundaries for case selection, legal complementarity/admissibility also constitutes an important criterion in the selection of cases. Pursuant to Article 53 of the ICC Statute, the prosecutor shall consider a number of factors in the initiation of an investigation and the subsequent selection of cases arising from that investigation. First, the prosecutor must be satisfied that there is a "reasonable basis to believe" crimes within the jurisdiction of the Court are being or have been committed.[34] Second, the case must be admissible before the Court.[35] Finally, he or she must evaluate whether, "taking into account the gravity of the crime and the interests of victims, there are nonetheless substantial reasons to believe that an investigation would not serve the interests of justice".[36] The final criterion is a countervailing factor against the investigation or prosecution of a case, employed only in "exceptional circumstances".[37]

The Office of the Prosecutor's ability to bring cases is not only circumscribed by requirements of complementarity and admissibility but is also subject to judicial review at different stages of proceedings.[38] For instance, the opening of investigations on the prosecutor's own initiative pursuant to Article 15 is subject to approval by a Pre-Trial Chamber, which will assess whether there is a reasonable basis to believe crimes within the jurisdiction of the Court have been committed.[39] Further, regardless of whether an investigation was opened on her own initiative, or pursuant to a state or Security Council referral, the prosecutor must apply to the Pre-Trial Chamber for the issuance of arrest warrants and/or summonses to appear. The Pre-Trial Chamber will issue an arrest warrant or

---

33 *Ibid.*, Article 17(1)(d).

34 *Ibid.*, Article 53(1)(a).

35 *Ibid.*, Article 53(1)(b).

36 *Ibid.*, Article 53(1)(c).

37 ICC, Office of the Prosecutor, Policy Paper, "The Interests of Justice", September 2007, pp. 1, 3, 9.

38 On the topic of judicial review of prosecutorial discretion more broadly, see deGuzman, 2012, pp. 274–75, *supra* note 5; Brubacher, 2004, p. 72, see *supra* note 3; Côté, 2005, see *supra* note 5; Danner, 2010, see *supra* note 1; Schabas, 2008, see *supra* note 5.

39 ICC Statute, Article 15(4), see *supra* note 14.

summons to appear when it is satisfied that there are reasonable grounds to believe the person is responsible for the alleged crimes.[40] Following the arrest and surrender of a suspect to the Court, the prosecutor's evidence undergoes another level of judicial scrutiny before trial: the confirmation of charges proceedings. A suspect will only stand trial for those charges for which – in the Pre-Trial Chamber's assessment – the prosecutor brings evidence establishing substantial grounds to believe he or she is responsible.[41]

17.3. Legal Complementarity: Admissibility

As discussed, the ICC is complementary to national criminal jurisdiction, meaning national courts have the primary duty and responsibility to carry out investigations and prosecutions for ICC Statute crimes. This legal dimension of complementarity as a jurisdictional restriction can be found in the ICC Statute's provisions on the admissibility of cases in Article 17. While the Office of the Prosecutor carries out the majority of admissibility assessments, ensuring these assessments are gender inclusive is not exclusively the Office's domain.[42] This section describes the admissibility test as set out by the judges, and illustrates that pronouncements by ICC Chambers warrant caution in relation to the admissibility test from a gender perspective.

The Pre-Trial Chamber interpreted Article 17 (the admissibility test) for the first time when it issued an arrest warrant for Thomas Lubanga Dyilo in 2006.[43] In that decision, the Chamber held that the admissibil-

---

[40] *Ibid.*, Article 58(1)(b), (7).

[41] *Ibid.*, Article 61(7).

[42] Commenting on the role of the ICC judges, the Women's Initiatives for Gender Justice has illustrated that "the roles of both the Prosecution and the Pre-Trial Chambers are significant in determining the success of charges for gender-based crimes": Women's Initiatives for Gender Justice, 2014, p. 66, see *supra* note 12. See also Niamh Hayes, "Sisyphus Wept: Prosecuting Sexual Violence at the International Criminal Court", in Niamh Hayes, Yvonne McDermott and William A. Schabas (eds.), *The Ashgate Research Companion to International Criminal Law*, Ashgate, Aldershot, 2013, pp. 7–43.

[43] Thomas Lubanga Dyilo was charged with crimes related to the enlistment, conscription and use of child soldiers. His case was the first in the Situation in the Democratic Republic of the Congo, and the first trial to be completed at the ICC. ICC, *Prosecutor v. Thomas Lubanga Dyilo*, Pre-Trial Chamber I, Decision on the Prosecutor's Application for a warrant of arrest under Article 58, ICC-01/04-01/06-8-Corr, 10 February 2006 (unsealed 17 March 2006) ('*Lubanga* Decision') (http://www.legal-tools.org/doc/8db08a/).

---

ity assessment consists of two components: 1) the existence of genuine investigations and/or prosecutions (that is, complementarity); and 2) gravity.[44] The admissibility test essentially poses three (sets of) questions. First, are there domestic proceedings; do they relate to the same case that is the subject of proceedings at the ICC; and have such proceedings been completed, or was a decision made not to pursue the case? Second, is or was the state genuinely able and willing to carry out those proceedings? Third, is the case of sufficient gravity to justify action by the ICC? In other words, the ICC's jurisdiction is pre-empted when a state is undertaking or undertook prosecutions, or where a state has carried out an investigation but decided not to proceed in relation to the same case as that before the ICC. Where a state is carrying out domestic proceedings, the ICC will assess whether the domestic authorities are undertaking concrete, tangible and progressive steps in relation to that case.[45] Relinquishing jurisdiction to the ICC, and surrendering a suspect to the Court, would not qualify as a "decision not to prosecute" under Article 17.[46] The Appeals Chamber in 2009 confirmed that the assessment of genuine ability or willingness is

---

[44] *Ibid.*, para. 29.

[45] *Saif Al-Islam Gaddafi* Admissibility Decision, paras. 54, 55, 73, see *supra* note 22; ICC, *Prosecutor v. Francis Kirimi Muthaura, Uhuru Muigai Kenyatta and Mohammed Hussein Ali*, Appeals Chamber, Judgment on the appeal of the Republic of Kenya against the decision of Pre-Trial Chamber II of 30 May 2011 entitled "Decision on the Application by the Government of Kenya Challenging the Admissibility of the Case Pursuant to Article 19(2)(b) of the Statute", ICC-01/09-02/11-274, 30 August 2011, para. 1 ('*Muthaura, Kenyatta and Ali* Admissibility Decision') (http://www.legal-tools.org/doc/c21f06/); ICC, *Prosecutor v. Saif Al-Islam Gaddafi and Abdullah Al-Senussi*, Pre-Trial Chamber I, Decision requesting further submissions on issues related to the admissibility of the case against Saif Al-Islam Gaddafi, ICC-01/11-01/11-239, 7 December 2012, para. 11 (http://www.legal-tools.org/doc/f8a7cf/).

[46] In 2009, defence counsel for Germain Katanga alleged the Democratic Republic of Congo ('DRC') authorities had investigated Katanga for the same case before the ICC, but had decided not to proceed. Defence counsel for Jean-Pierre Bemba Gombo presented similar arguments in relation to alleged investigations against Bemba in the Central African Republic ('CAR') in 2010. However, in both instances, the national authorities in the DRC and the CAR, respectively, had made such decisions to relinquish jurisdiction to the ICC. The Appeals Chamber confirmed: "a 'decision not to prosecute' in terms of Article 17(1)(b) of the Statute does not cover decisions of a State to close judicial proceedings against a suspect because of his or her surrender to the ICC". *Katanga* Admissibility Decision, para. 83, see *supra* note 22; ICC, *Prosecutor v. Jean-Pierre Bemba Gombo*, Appeals Chamber, Judgment on the appeal of Mr Jean-Pierre Bemba Gombo against the decision of Trial Chamber III of 24 June 2010 entitled "Decision on the Admissibility and Abuse of Process Challenges", ICC-01/05-01/08-962, 19 October 2010, para. 74 ('*Bemba* Admissibility Appeals Judgment') (http://www.legal-tools.org/doc/47a9e4/).

---

required only where there is or has been action by the state.[47] Inaction by domestic jurisdictions therefore renders a case automatically admissible before the ICC, provided it is of sufficient gravity.

The assessment of admissibility can thus be reduced to three distinct elements: a test of sameness, a test of genuineness (tied to the ability or willingness of a state) and a test of gravity. This third limb is arguably of a different nature to the first two, as it does not relate specifically to proceedings in domestic systems. While it is an important criterion affecting the selection and prioritisation of cases by the Office of the Prosecutor,[48] given the emphasis of this chapter on (legal) complementarity, this section will focus on the first two limbs of the admissibility test only.

Emilie Hunter has illustrated that "admissibility proof" justice at a national level requires far lower adherence to these admissibility standards than some have argued: the legal standards that have emerged from the Court's case law on admissibility set a very low norm that domestic proceedings must satisfy in order to pre-empt the ICC's intervention.[49] From a gender perspective, the question that arises is whether those standards are interpreted in a gender-neutral manner. The remainder of this section applies such a gender lens to the two tests of sameness and genuineness of ability and willingness. This analysis illustrates that the interpretation of admissibility contains potential gender biases (or what Michelle Jarvis and Kate Vigneswaran call "pressure points"[50]): there is a risk that specific concerns around sexual and gender-

---

[47] *Katanga* Admissibility Decision, paras. 1–2, 75–79, see *supra* note 22; see also *Lubanga* Decision, para. 40, *supra* note 43.

[48] On gravity, see, for example, Margaret M. deGuzman, "Gravity and the Legitimacy of the International Criminal Court", in *Fordham International Law Journal*, 2008, vol. 32, pp. 1400–65; Ray Murphy, "Gravity Issues and the International Criminal Court", in *Criminal Law Forum*, 2006, vol. 17, pp. 281–315. See also ICC, Office of the Prosecutor, 2016, *supra* note 6.

[49] Emilie Hunter, "The International Criminal Court and Positive Complementarity: The Impact of the ICC's Admissibility Law and Practice on Domestic Jurisdictions", Ph.D. thesis, European University Institute, 2014.

[50] Michelle Jarvis and Kate Vigneswaran, "Facing Challenges in Sexual Violence Cases", in Serge Brammertz and Michelle Jarvis (eds.), *Prosecuting Conflict-Related Sexual Violence at the ICTY*, Oxford University Press, Oxford, 2016, p. 35.

---

based violence crimes will be overlooked and remain unaddressed within admissibility assessments, thus perpetuating impunity for these crimes.[51]

17.3.1. First Limb: Domestic Proceedings for the "Same Case"

Whether a domestic system is successful in challenging admissibility firstly depends on whether that state's (genuine) proceedings cover the *same case*. The Court has determined that for domestic proceedings to be considered the same case as that before the ICC, they must cover "the same person" and "substantially the same conduct".[52] Hence, the essential characteristics of a 'case' for the purposes of admissibility challenges are both the *person* and the *conduct*,[53] which can be deduced from the arrest warrant or summons to appear issued by the Pre-Trial Chamber under Article 58 or the charges confirmed by the Pre-Trial Chamber under Article 61.[54] While the meaning of the "same person" criterion is clear, the inter-

---

[51] Chappell *et al.*, 2013, p. 467, see *supra* note 9, similarly argue that "the bar for assessing complementarity appears to have been set very low, leaving significant impunity gaps for sexual violence crimes".

[52] ICC, *Prosecutor v. William Samoei Ruto, Henry Kiprono Kosgey and Joshua Arap Sang*, Appeals Chamber, Judgment on the appeal of the Republic of Kenya against the decision of Pre-Trial Chamber II of 30 May 2011 entitled "Decision on the Application by the Government of Kenya Challenging the Admissibility of the Case Pursuant to Article 19(2)(b) of the Statute", ICC-01/09-01/11-307, 30 August 2011, para. 40 (*'Ruto, Kosgey and Sang* Admissibility Decision') (http://www.legal-tools.org/doc/ac5d46/); *Muthaura, Kenyatta and Ali* Admissibility Decision, para. 39, see *supra* note 45.

[53] *Saif Al-Islam Gaddafi* Admissibility Decision, paras. 61, 76, see *supra* note 22; ICC, *Prosecutor v. Saif Al-Islam Gaddafi and Abdullah Al-Senussi*, Pre-Trial Chamber I, Decision on the admissibility of the case against Abdullah Al-Senussi, ICC-01/11-01/11-466-Red, 11 October 2013, para. 66 (*'Al-Senussi* Admissibility Decision') (http://www.legal-tools.org/doc/af6104/).

[54] *Ruto, Kosgey and Sang* Admissibility Decision, para. 40, see *supra* note 52; Muthaura, Kenyatta and Ali Admissibility Decision, para. 39, see *supra* note 45. In 2014, the Pre-Trial Chamber dismissed Côte d'Ivoire's admissibility challenge in the case against Simone Gbagbo because Côte d'Ivoire had not submitted sufficient evidence to attest to concrete, tangible and progressive investigative steps in the domestic case against her. This made it impossible for the Chamber to determine the factual parameters of the domestic case, and as such, enter into a comparative analysis for the purposes of the "same conduct" test. It held: "If a State is unable to clearly indicate the contours of its national investigation, the State cannot assert that there exists a conflict of jurisdictions with the Court." ICC, *Prosecutor v. Simone Gbagbo*, Pre-Trial Chamber I, Decision on Côte d'Ivoire's challenge to the admissibility of the case against Simone Gbagbo, ICC-02/11-01/12-47-Red, 11 December 2014, para. 76 (http://www.legal-tools.org/doc/ef697a/). The decision was confirmed by the Appeals Chamber; ICC, *Prosecutor v. Simone Gbagbo*, Appeals Chamber, Judgment on the appeal of

pretation of what constitutes "substantially the same conduct" remains more ambiguous. The use of the word "conduct", rather than "crime" or "charge", suggests that the Court envisages some degree of flexibility for domestic authorities. What constitutes "substantially the same conduct", particularly when a domestic case is *substantially* the same, will depend on the facts and circumstances of a particular case, and therefore must be assessed on a case-by-case basis.[55]

Issuing its decision on the admissibility of the two cases in the Libya situation,[56] Pre-Trial Chamber I stressed that in assessing the conduct that is the subject of domestic proceedings the focus must be on the crimes, not their legal characterisation.[57] In particular, the Pre-Trial Chamber found it unnecessary for domestic courts to characterise relevant conduct as "international crimes", so long as the *underlying conduct* is

---

Côte d'Ivoire against the decision of Pre-Trial Chamber I of 11 December 2014 entitled "Decision on Côte d'Ivoire's challenge to the admissibility of the case against Simone Gbagbo", ICC-02/11-01/12-75-Red, 27 May 2015 (http://www.legal-tools.org/doc/cfc2de/).

[55] *Saif Al-Islam Gaddafi* Admissibility Decision, para. 77, see *supra* note 22; Al-Senussi Admissibility Decision, para. 74, see *supra* note 53; ICC, *Prosecutor v. Saif Al-Islam Gaddafi and Abdullah Al-Senussi,* Appeals Chamber, Judgment on the appeal of Libya against the decision of Pre-Trial Chamber I of 31 May 2013 entitled "Decision on the admissibility of the case against Saif Al-Islam Gaddafi", ICC-01/11-01/11-547-Red, 21 May 2014, paras. 62, 71 ('*Saif Al-Islam Gaddafi* Appeals Judgment') (http://www.legal-tools.org/doc/0499fd/); *Al-Senussi* Appeals Judgment 2014, paras. 99–100, see *supra* note 29. It must be noted that Judge Ušacka, in her dissenting opinion to the Gaddafi and Al-Senussi admissibility appeals, held that "'conduct' should be understood much more broadly than the current test". ICC, *Prosecutor v. Saif Al-Islam Gaddafi and Abdullah Al-Senussi*, Appeals Chamber, Dissenting Opinion of Judge Anita Ušacka (Gaddafi), ICC-01/11-01/11-547-Anx2, 21 May 2014, para. 58 (http://www.legal-tools.org/doc/b1cc88/); ICC, *Prosecutor v. Saif Al-Islam Gaddafi and Abdullah Al-Senussi*, Appeals Chamber, Separate Opinion of Judge Anita Ušacka (Al-Senussi), ICC-01/11-01/11-565-Anx2, 24 July 2014, para. 5 (http://www.legal-tools.org/doc/441633/).

[56] Pre-Trial Chamber I issued two decisions, one on the admissibility of the case against Saif Al-Islam Gaddafi, and one in the case against Al-Senussi. Both decisions have been appealed. The Appeals Chamber issued its decision the admissibility of the *Gaddafi* case on 21 May 2014, and on the *Al-Senussi* case on 24 July 2014, confirming the Pre-Trial Chamber's decisions. The case against Gaddafi was held admissible, whereas the case against Al-Senussi was deemed inadmissible.

[57] *Saif Al-Islam Gaddafi* Admissibility Decision, para. 85, see *supra* note 22; *Al-Senussi* Admissibility Decision, para. 66, see *supra* note 53.

---

covered by the charges.[58] The Appeals Chamber confirmed this interpretation.[59] Under this rationale, an act of murder as a war crime may be prosecuted domestically as an ordinary crime of murder, or an act of rape as a crime against humanity as 'ordinary' rape – such ordinary charges would not necessarily render a case admissible before the ICC. To substantiate its findings, the Pre-Trial Chamber relied upon Article 20(3), which does not permit the ICC to prosecute if a person has already been tried for that same conduct (*ne bis in idem*).[60] Similar provisions in the Statutes of the *ad hoc* tribunals for Yugoslavia and Rwanda explicitly allowed these courts to assert jurisdiction over persons who had been charged only with ordinary crimes domestically.[61] The absence of such a provision in the ICC Statute in the Chamber's view suggested that the classification of crimes *as international crimes* is of no consequence to admissibility.[62]

---

[58] *Saif Al-Islam Gaddafi* Admissibility Decision, paras. 85, 88, see *supra* note 22. This finding by the Pre-Trial Chamber was not one of the grounds of appeal, and, as such, the Appeals Chamber has not ruled on the correctness of these findings.

[59] *Al-Senussi* Appeals Judgment, para. 119, see *supra* note 29.

[60] *Saif Al-Islam Gaddafi* Admissibility Decision, para. 86, fn. 136, see *supra* note 22.

[61] United Nations, Statute of the International Criminal Tribunal for the former Yugoslavia, adopted 25 May 1993 by resolution 827, amended 7 July 2009, Article 10(2)(a) ('ICTY Statute') (http://www.legal-tools.org/doc/b4f63b/); United Nations, Statute of the International Criminal Tribunal for Rwanda, adopted 8 November 1994 by resolution 955, Article 9(2)(a) provides: "A person who has been tried by a national court for acts constituting serious violations of international humanitarian law may be subsequently tried by the International Tribunal only if: (a) the act for which he or she was tried was characterized as an ordinary crime [...]" ('ICTR Statute') (http://www.legal-tools.org/doc/8732d6/).

[62] The discussion on international versus ordinary crimes prosecutions under the ICC Statute's admissibility provisions remains a contested issue among scholars. For instance, Kevin Jon Heller argues that the legal classification of crimes is of no importance at all, because a reference to "ordinary crimes" in Article 20(3) was explicitly taken out of the ICC Statute at the drafting stage: Kevin Jon Heller, "A Sentenced-Based Theory of Complementarity", in *Harvard International Law Journal*, 2012, vol. 53, no. 1, pp. 91–93. By contrast, according to Benzing, "it may be argued that a more flexible approach is called for than merely stating that the prosecution of such acts as 'ordinary crimes' automatically and without further requirement entails an exception to the rule of double jeopardy": Benzing, 2003, p. 616, see *supra* note 22. See also Charles C. Jalloh, "Kenya v. the ICC Prosecutor", in *Harvard International Law Journal*, 2012, vol. 53, pp. 227–43; Linda E. Carter, "The Principle of Complementarity and the International Criminal Court: The Role of *Ne Bis in Idem*", in *Santa Clara Journal of International Law*, 2010, vol. 8, no. 1, pp. 165–98; Carsten Stahn, "Libya, the International Criminal Court and Complementarity: A Test for 'Shared Responsibility'", in *Journal of International Criminal Justice*, 2012, vol. 10, no. 2, p. 339; Spencer Thomas, "A Complementarity Conundrum: International Criminal Enforcement in the Mexican Drug War", in *Van-*

Applying a gender lens to this illustrates the first pressure point for sexual and gender-based violence crimes. The still prevalent idea that sexual violence in conflict is incidental or opportunistic (overlooking the broader context of criminality in which they are embedded) means these crimes (if charged at all) are much more likely to be charged as ordinary crimes, rather than as crimes against humanity or war crimes,[63] which does not adequately represent the "scope, scale and gravity of the conduct".[64] While it could be said that the ICC Statute includes no obligation on states to implement its provisions into domestic criminal laws *verbatim*, doing so would greatly contribute to states' apparent ability and willingness to prosecute international crimes.[65] Limited domestic legal frameworks may not be able to capture the full extent of criminality – domestic definitions of sexual and gender-based violence crimes, where they exist, often fall short of those included in the ICC Statute. As a result, "nuances in the definitions of sexual violence crimes are obscured in the application of the 'same person, same conduct' test".[66] Further, prosecuting sexual and gender-based violence crimes as ordinary crimes fails to recognise the context and meaning of these crimes.[67] This is particularly worrisome in relation to sexual and gender-based violence crimes be-

---

derbilt Journal of Transnational Law, 2012, vol. 45, no. 2, pp. 604, 624–28, arguing that prosecuting as ordinary crimes "trivializ[es] the crime and aid[s] impunity".

[63] Jarvis and Vigneswaran, 2016, p. 39, see *supra* note 50.

[64] Bergsmo *et al.*, 2010, p. 801, see *supra* note 23. See also Chappell *et al.*, 2013, p. 464, *supra* note 9; Heller, 2012, p. 132, *supra* note 62; Louise Chappell, *The Politics of Gender Justice at the International Criminal Court: Legacies and Legitimacy*, Oxford University Press, Oxford, 2015, p. 184.

[65] Benzing, 2003, p. 616, see *supra* note 23: "Where the charge chosen by national authorities does not reflect and adequately capture the severity of the perpetrator's conduct, or where the national legal system provides for excessively broad defences or statutes of limitation, this may be seen as conflicting with an intent to bring the perpetrator to justice or even to shield him or her from criminal responsibility and thus falls under one of the exceptions of article 20(3)(a) and (b)." See also Marta Bo, "The Situation in Libya and the ICC's Understanding of Complementarity in the Context of UNSC-Referred Cases", in *Criminal Law Forum*, 2014, vol. 25, no. 3, pp. 505–40.

[66] Chappell *et al.*, 2013, p. 463, see *supra* note 9.

[67] *Ibid.* See also, for example, Bergsmo *et al.*, 2010, p. 801, see *supra* note 23: "prosecuting core crimes as murder or rape, rather than their international equivalents, is not desirable since ordinary crimes do not represent the scope, scale and gravity of the conduct"; Heller, 2012, p. 132, see *supra* note 62: "there is no question that expressive value is lost when a state prosecutes an international crime as an ordinary crime."

cause, as Chappell *et al.* illustrate, such crimes have "historically been seen as separate to broader political conflicts when in fact they are often instrumental to those conflicts".[68] In other words, there is a disproportionate risk that sexual and gender-based violence crimes remain overlooked and disconnected from the broader context in which ICC Statute crimes are committed in this admissibility context that places almost no emphasis on a crime's legal characterisation.

In order to qualify as the same case, ICC case law has determined that national proceedings do not have to cover all features of the ICC's case. There has to be a certain degree of 'sameness' but it does not have to be identical. Notably, the domestic proceedings do not necessarily have to cover all the same alleged incidents.[69] For instance, when the Office of the Prosecutor has charged murder or rape in locations X, Y and Z on specific dates, a domestic case would not necessarily need to cover those exact same incidents. It would be sufficient for it to cover acts of similar conduct and/or only some of those incidents. So long as the domestic charges cover the same general "temporal, geographic and material parameters" of the ICC's charges, the first limb of the admissibility test will be met.[70] While not critical, the specific incidents alleged against the suspect do, however, "play a central role" in the comparison between the ICC's case and that before the national court.[71]

In some circumstances, specific incidents of a certain crime charged *do* have to be explicitly covered by the domestic case in order to successfully challenge admissibility. In this respect, the Appeals Chamber envisages a scale of overlap, running from identical cases before the ICC and the domestic court, at the one end, and a domestic case that does not cover any of the same incidents investigated by the ICC, at the other. The Appeals Chamber underscored that it is not possible to lay down a "hard and fast rule" to be followed for this "degree of overlap",[72] but that this re-

---

[68] Chappell *et al.*, 2013, p. 462, see *supra* note 9.

[69] The Appeals Chamber defined 'incidents' as: "a historical event, defined in time and place, in the course of which crimes within the jurisdiction of the Court were allegedly committed by one or more direct perpetrators"; *Saif Al-Islam Gaddafi* Appeals Judgment, para. 62, see *supra* note 55.

[70] *Saif Al-Islam Gaddafi* Admissibility Decision, para. 75, see *supra* note 22; *Al-Senussi* Admissibility Decision, paras. 75, 77, see *supra* note 53.

[71] *Al-Senussi* Appeals Judgment, paras. 101, 105, see *supra* note 29.

[72] *Saif Al-Islam Gaddafi* Appeals Judgment, para 72, see *supra* note 55. Emphasis added.

quires a case-by-case analysis as to whether or not the domestic case "sufficiently mirrors" that of the ICC prosecutor.[73]

In other words, the *substance* of the overlap appears to be significant for the determination of sameness. Where the incidents included in the ICC's arrest warrant are "illustrative", "non-exhaustive", do not represent "unique manifestations of [the suspect's] alleged criminal conduct",[74] or are "very minor when compared with the case as a whole",[75] the domestic case is not required to cover these exact same incidents. However, when the incidents or events in the arrest warrant are considered to be "particularly violent", appear to be "significantly representative of the [suspect's] conduct",[76] or "form the crux of the Prosecutor's case and/or represent the most serious aspects of the case",[77] they must be included in the domestic case to warrant a finding of non-admissibility. Their absence may lead to a conclusion that the domestic proceedings do not cover 'substantially the same conduct', and that, as such, it does not involve the 'same case' for the purposes of the admissibility test.

Essentially, the Chamber incorporated a test of seriousness into the sameness determination. Yet, how is this test of 'seriousness' interpreted? When are crimes considered 'significantly representative' versus only 'minor' crimes? As extensively discussed elsewhere,[78] sexual violence crimes have long been held (and often continue to be seen as) less serious than other crimes, and as a result have been deprioritised in post-conflict

---

[73] *Ibid.*, paras. 71–73. See also *Al-Senussi* Appeals Judgment, paras. 105, 119, *supra* note 29. Judge Song issued a separate opinion to the Appeals Chamber decision on this issue, writing that: "overlap between the incidents is not a relevant factor for the purposes of determining whether the national investigation covers the same conduct". ICC, *Prosecutor v. Saif Al-Islam Gaddafi and Abdullah Al-Senussi*, Appeals Chamber, Separate Opinion of Judge Sang-Hyun Song, ICC-01/11-01/11-547-Anx1, 21 May 2014, para. 6 ('Separate Opinion of Judge Song in Gaddafi case') (http://www.legal-tools.org/doc/67bf29/); ICC, *Prosecutor v. Saif Al-Islam Gaddafi and Abdullah Al-Senussi*, Appeals Chamber, Separate Opinion of Judge Sang-Hyun Song, ICC-01/11-01/11-565-Anx1, 24 July 2014, para. 2 ('Separate Opinion of Judge Song in *Al-Senussi* case') (http://www.legal-tools.org/doc/67bf29/).

[74] *Saif Al-Islam Gaddafi* Admissibility Decision, paras. 81–82, see *supra* note 22. See similar findings in *Al-Senussi* Admissibility Decision, para. 76, *supra* note 53.

[75] *Saif Al-Islam Gaddafi* Appeals Judgment, para. 72, see *supra* note 55.

[76] *Al-Senussi* Admissibility Decision, para. 79, see *supra* note 53.

[77] *Saif Al-Islam Gaddafi* Appeals Judgment, para. 72, see *supra* note 55.

[78] See, for example, Serge Brammertz and Michelle Jarvis (eds.), *Prosecuting Conflict-Related Sexual Violence at the ICTY*, Oxford University Press, Oxford, 2016.

---

justice efforts. In this respect, one particular aspect of the Pre-Trial Chamber's decision in the *Al-Senussi* case needs to be mentioned. The acts of persecution in the case against Al-Senussi were qualified by the ICC prosecutor as having been committed against certain individuals "because of [their] political opposition (whether actual or perceived) to Gaddafi's regime".[79] Despite finding that this "factual aspect"[80] of the charges against Al-Senussi did *not* form part of the charges with which Libya intended to charge him domestically – in fact no charges for persecutory conduct exist in Libyan criminal law – the Pre-Trial Chamber held that this did not render the case admissible before the ICC. It observed that these aspects would be taken into account by the Libyan court as aggravating factors at the sentencing stage only (were Al-Senussi to be convicted by the Libyan court). For the Chamber, this "sufficiently capture[d] Mr Al-Senussi's conduct".[81]

This finding is problematic from a gender perspective for two reasons. As mentioned, domestic criminal law frameworks often do not criminalise or inadequately criminalise sexual and gender-based violence. For instance, in two-thirds of the world's countries, criminal law only recognises female victims of rape and 67 countries criminalise men who report sexual violence due to domestic prohibitions on what may be deemed or assumed to be "homosexual acts".[82] Faced with legal impossibilities to charging such conduct *at all*, domestic cases will not include specific charges for such conduct. Yet, following the Chamber's reasoning, this

---

[79] ICC, Pre-Trial Chamber I, *Prosecutor v. Saif Al-Islam Gaddafi and Abdullah Al-Senussi*, Warrant of Arrest for Abdullah Al-Senussi, ICC-01/11-15 and ICC-01/11-01/11-4, 27 June 2011, p. 5 (http://www.legal-tools.org/doc/c8d796/); ICC, Pre-Trial Chamber I, *Prosecutor v. Saif Al-Islam Gaddafi and Abdullah Al-Senussi*, Decision on the "Prosecutor's Application Pursuant to Article 58 as to Muammar Mohammed Abu Minyar Gaddafi, Saif Al-Islam Gaddafi and Abdullah Al-Senussi", ICC-01/11-12, 27 June 2011, para. 65 (http://www.legal-tools.org/doc/094165/).

[80] *Al-Senussi* Admissibility Decision, para. 166, see *supra* note 53.

[81] *Ibid.*, para. 166. This finding by the Pre-Trial Chamber was one of the grounds of appeal by the defence for Al-Senussi. The Appeals Chamber confirmed this finding. Al-Senussi Admissibility Appeals Judgment, paras. 118–22, see *supra* note 29: "the Appeals Chamber concludes that the conduct underlying the crime of persecution is sufficiently covered in the Libyan proceedings so that the conduct being investigated is substantially the same as that alleged before the Court".

[82] Chris Dolan, "Into the Mainstream: Addressing Sexual Violence against Men and Boys in Conflict", Refugee Law Project, 2014, p. 6.

---

would not necessarily lead to a finding of admissibility and as such may allow the domestic case to proceed without any attention to such sexual violence charges. Concretely, Chappell *et al.* found that some of the crimes identified by the Office of the Prosecutor as part of its preliminary examinations, such as sexual slavery in Guinea and forced pregnancy in Colombia, could not be prosecuted domestically "because they are not included in the domestic penal codes".[83] Nonetheless, the Office of the Prosecutor appears not to have considered these factors in its admissibility assessment.[84]

Second, this finding fails to appreciate one of the specific identifying characteristics of such acts. The discriminatory nature of acts of persecution, for example targeting individuals because of their political affiliation, is what distinguishes such acts from other crimes. The persecutory nature of a particular act, whether it is murder or rape, is a constitutive aspect of that crime, and, for reasons of fair labelling,[85] should be acknowledged as such. The discriminatory intent of these acts is "the underlying conduct" that makes it *persecution*.[86] It is problematic that the Chambers evaluate such a key aspect of a crime as outside the scope of 'the same case'. Even if we accept that international crimes may be charged as ordinary offences at the domestic level, at the very least, "these

---

[83] Chappell *et al.*, 2013, p. 474, see *supra* note 9. At the time of their writing, Colombian penal law was quite restrictive in recognising sexual and gender-based violence. In June 2014, however, the Colombian Penal Code was amended to include, among others, the crime of forced pregnancy within its ambit. República de Colombia, Ley 1719 de 2014 por la cual se modifican algunos artículos de las leyes 599 de 200, 906 de 2004 y se adoptan medidas para garantizar el acceso a la justicia de las víctimas de violencia sexual, en especial la violencia sexual con ocasión del conflicto armado, y se dictan otras disposiciones, Diario Official Edición 49.186, 18 June 2014.

[84] *Ibid.*

[85] The principle of fair labelling, "is to see that widely felt distinctions between kinds of offences and degrees of wrongdoing are respected and signalled by the law, and that offences are subdivided and labelled so as to represent fairly the nature and magnitude of the lawbreaking": Andrew Ashworth, *Principles of Criminal Law*, Oxford University Press, Oxford, 1995, p. 86. See also James Chalmers and Fiona Leverick, "Fair Labelling in Criminal Law", in *Modern Law Review*, 2008, vol. 71, no. 2, p. 219. While there is much to say about the principle of fair labelling, this is beyond the scope of this chapter.

[86] ICC, *Prosecutor v. Saif Al-Islam Gaddafi and Abdullah Al-Senussi*, Defence for Al Senussi, 'Document in Support of Appeal on behalf of Abdullah Al-Senussi against Pre-Trial Chamber I's "Decision on the admissibility of the case against Abdullah Al-Senussi"', ICC-01/11-01/11-474, 4 November 2013, para. 177 (http://www.legal-tools.org/doc/c61c02/).

---

ordinary crimes must be *capable* of covering the same conduct as before the ICC".[87] According to the Pre-Trial and Appeals Chambers, the domestic prosecution does not have to cover the specific persecutory intent for it to qualify as the same case. In fact, following the Pre-Trial Chamber's reasoning, the domestic legal system does not even have to include the *possibility* to charge such conduct. By not requiring Libya to acknowledge the discriminatory motives underlying these acts in the domestic prosecution, the Chamber in effect allows domestic systems to apply legal frameworks that significantly alter the recognition of the harm suffered, and holds that this may not be an obstacle to successfully challenging admissibility.

Like persecution, sexual and gender-based violence crimes "virtually always convey[s] a message of discrimination".[88] They are committed against a person because of their gender, and because it relies on underlying inequalities and conceptions of masculinities and femininities. This discriminatory element of sexual and gender-based violence crimes, and the specific "nature, effect and rationale of these offences",[89] would be lost if it were charged as a different, more generic, offence. Similarly, as Laurie Green argues, recognising the gender specificity of crimes is "critical to the process of empowering victims, marginalising perpetrators, recognising the severity and gravity of sexual violence, eliminating the historic misunderstanding of rape and sexual violence, and contributing to the elimination of sexual violence altogether".[90] The Chamber's insistence on the 'underlying conduct' requirement suggests that appropriate labelling of crimes is not taken into account. Characterising conduct as inhumane treatment rather than as sexual violence changes the perception and recognition of the harm suffered.[91] For instance, when a victim was re-

---

[87] *Ibid.*, para. 181. Emphasis added.

[88] DeGuzman, 2017, pp. 35–36 of this volume.

[89] Ní Aoláin, 2013, p. 5, see *supra* note 24.

[90] Laurie Green, "First-Class Crimes, Second-Class Justice: Cumulative Charges for Gender-Based Crimes at the International Criminal Court", in *International Criminal Law Review*, 2011, vol. 11, no. 3, p. 531.

[91] *Ibid.*, pp. 531, 541: "by identifying an act of sexual violence as rape, torture or an outrage upon personal dignity society attributes specific meanings to the act and deems it morally and socially reprehensible in addition to acknowledging the spectrum of harms suffered" and "charging the perpetrators of such heinous atrocities for the full range of their crimes is an important and necessary step in changing societal attitudes that perpetuate sexual and

peatedly raped and died from those rapes, this crime could be prosecuted as an act of murder. While such prosecutions may (erroneously) be deemed easier or less complicated, this does not capture the full extent of the harm, or the gendered particularities of the crime.[92] As Fionnuala Ní Aoláin reasons, such non-gender specific charges are "insufficient normatively".[93] Yet, following the 'underlying conduct' rationale set out by the judges to determine whether a national proceeding relates to 'the same case', this would not be considered.

In other words, in adopting a seriousness perspective (which it interpreted loosely), the Chamber has weakened the interpretation of 'sameness' from a gender perspective. More concretely, under this part of the admissibility test, in a situation where the ICC charges an individual with murder, rape, torture and pillaging, and the domestic system prosecutes that same individual only for the acts of murder, torture and pillaging, this could qualify as 'substantially' the same conduct. If that same domestic system were found able and willing genuinely to prosecute that conduct, this would result in a finding of inadmissibility – the case would be left to the national court. The resulting impunity for sexual and gender-based violence crimes in this situation is clear. This is not to say that, when faced with a situation where a domestic case has not charged rape as an international crime, or even as a domestic sexual violence crime, the ICC would necessarily rule the case inadmissible. However, it illustrates the need for caution in the application of this part of the admissibility test if we take that as a standard to which we hold domestic authorities from a positive complementarity perspective. In short, the interpretation of the

---

[gender-based violence]". See also Sandesh Sivakumaran, "Sexual Violence against Men in Armed Conflict", in *European Journal of International Law*, 2007, vol. 18, no. 2, p. 257: "An accurate classification of abuse is important not just to give victims a voice, not only to break down stereotypes and not merely to accurately record the picture".

[92] Chappell *et al.*, 2013, p. 462, see *supra* note 9: "While ordinary sexual violence crimes may be easier to prove from an evidentiary point of view, they do not necessarily locate the violence in its political context".

[93] Ní Aoláin, 2013, p. 5, see *supra* note 24. See also Chappell, 2015, p. 184, *supra* note 64; Daniela Kravetz, "Promoting Domestic Accountability for Conflict-related Sexual Violence: The Cases of Guatemala, Peru and Colombia", in *American University International Law Review*, 2017, vol. 32, no. 2, p. 735.

---

sameness requirement of admissibility "potentially reinforces gender mis-recognition and misrepresentation" at a national level.[94]

17.3.2. Second Limb: Unwillingness or Inability Genuinely to Carry Out Proceedings

Once a Chamber finds that the domestic proceedings cover the same case as that before the ICC, the second limb of the admissibility test demands an assessment of the state's genuine *willingness* and *ability* to carry them out. In contrast to the factors relevant for the first limb of the admissibility test, the ICC Statute sets out specific factors to be taken into account to assess unwillingness or inability.[95] Nonetheless, the exact terms remain open to interpretation. The *travaux préparatoires* suggest that the drafters purposely left their interpretation to the Court.[96] In comparison to the first limb of the admissibility test, however, much less has been said by Chambers about the factors that are relevant for an assessment of genuine ability and willingness. This is partly because most admissibility challenges were dismissed because there were either no domestic proceedings, or those alleged proceedings did not cover the same case as that before the

---

[94] Chappell, 2015, p. 170, see *supra* note 64.

[95] See ICC Statute, Article 17(2) and (3), *supra* note 14.

[96] During the negotiations in the preparatory committee, many states indicated that qualifications such as "not well-founded" or "ineffective" national proceedings to trigger ICC jurisdiction, as had been suggested by the International Law Commission and *ad hoc* committee, were too subjective. Other suggestions such as "good faith", "diligently" or "sufficient grounds" were also rejected for leaving too much discretion to the Court. States eventually settled for the somewhat ambiguous term "genuine", which proved "the least objectionable" term, and was able to "achieve broad consensus", despite its ambiguity. See John T. Holmes, "The Principle of Complementarity", in Roy S. K. Lee (ed.), *The International Criminal Court: The Making of the Rome Statute. Issues, Negotiations, Results*, Kluwer Law International, The Hague, 1999, pp. 48–50; John T. Holmes, "Complementarity: National Courts versus the ICC", in Antonio Cassese, Paola Gaeta and John R. W. D. Jones (eds.), *The Rome Statute of the International Criminal Court: A Commentary*, vol. 1, Oxford University Press, Oxford, 2002, p. 674; Mohamed M. El Zeidy, *The Principle of Complementarity in International Criminal Law: Origins, Development, and Practice*, Martinus Nijhoff Publishers, Leiden, 2008, p. 129; United Nations, Report of the Preparatory Committee on the Establishment of an International Criminal Court – Annex Complementarity: Compilation of Concrete Proposals, Proceedings of the Preparatory Committee during 25 March–12 April 1996, 8 April 1996, UN Doc. A/AC.249/CRP.9/Add.1, paras. 164–69.

ICC.[97] In line with Appeals Chamber jurisprudence, where states failed the first part of the test, Chambers did not enter into an assessment of the other parts of the test. As such, only limited observations can be made about the second limb of the admissibility test as interpreted by the judges.

Regarding unwillingness, Article 17(2) provides that a state is unwilling to carry out proceedings when: 1) those proceedings were carried out with a view to shield the accused from justice; 2) there were unjustified delays; or 3) those proceedings were not carried out independently or impartially, and were inconsistent with an intent to bring the person to justice. The exact elements to satisfy any of these remain, however, less clear. Chappell *et al.* argue that the admissibility analysis must evaluate any rules or regulations that may discriminate against victims of sexual and gender-based violence crimes, including, but not limited to the absence of laws criminalising these crimes; the absence of protective measures for victims and witnesses of such crimes; and discriminatory evidentiary requirements. Such gender biases in domestic legal systems impeding access to justice for these victims must be seen as evidence of a state's inaction and its unwillingness or inability to carry out proceedings.[98] Similarly, observing the widespread scale of sexual and gender-based violence in conflict, and the fact that such crimes remain largely unaddressed, Amrita Kapur concludes: "[i]f there is any type of crime the OTP can focus on to assess unwillingness, it is this category".[99] Patricia Sellers similarly argues that cases should be declared admissible by the ICC if there are procedural or substantive obstacles for women to access justice in their national jurisdictions, or if women "are subjected to gender 'sham' trials".[100]

However, the Appeals Chamber stated that this provision "should generally be understood as referring to proceedings which will lead to a suspect evading justice, in the sense of not appropriately being tried genuinely to establish his or her criminal responsibility, in the equivalent of

---

[97] The only case in which the judges entered into a substantive discussion on a state's alleged willingness and ability to carry out proceedings genuinely is that of *Al-Senussi*.

[98] Chappell *et al.*, 2013, see *supra* note 9. See also Inder, 2013, p. 322, *supra* note 11; Chappell, 2015, p. 160–89, *supra* note 64.

[99] Kapur, 2012, see *supra* note 8.

[100] Sellers, 2009, p. 22, see *supra* note 16.

sham proceedings that are concerned with that person's protection".[101] In other words, this suggests that only where proceedings are carried out with complete disregard for procedural requirements or the rights of accused persons or victims would a case be deemed inadmissible pursuant to Article 17(2)(a) . This suggests the threshold for demonstrating the requirement of "evading criminal responsibility" is high, and it remains questionable to what extent inadequate gender justice procedures or other obstacles to accountability for sexual and gender-based violence could, following the Chamber's view, lead to a finding of "evading criminal responsibility".

Emphasising the ICC Statute's gender inclusiveness, Susana SáCouto and Katherine Cleary argue that even when a state seems willing and able to prosecute *some* perpetrators for *some* crimes that would fall under the ICC's jurisdiction, the ICC prosecutor must "dig deeper".[102] In their view, the assessment of legal complementarity should extend beyond a mere evaluation of a state's willingness and ability to prosecute international crimes in general, for instance by evaluating domestic procedures and the extent to which these negatively affect accountability for sexual and gender-based violence. Such relevant procedures could include rules concerning the admissibility of evidence, the nature and type of evidence required, the classification of crimes of sufficient gravity to prioritise their investigations, or the protection of witnesses. Kapur gives the following example: "a failure to allocate resources to gender-sensitive training of interviewers of women victims of sexual violence or recruitment of female law enforcement officers may result in the constructive unavailability of the judicial system with respect to these crimes, resulting in an inability to prosecute them",[103] or to obtain the necessary evidence or testimony.

However, the relevant provisions of genuine ability or willingness, Article 17(2) and (3), indicate that the Court shall not consider a domestic system's *general* ability or willingness to carry out proceedings in evaluating a case's admissibility: it concerns an assessment of unwillingness or

---

[101] *Al-Senussi* Appeals Judgment, para. 230, see *supra* note 29.

[102] SáCouto and Cleary, 2009, p. 344, see *supra* note 18.

[103] Kapur, 2016, p. 78, see *supra* note 18.

inability "in a particular case".[104] In other words, the assessment must be limited to an evaluation of a state's willingness and/or ability to carry out the proceedings in the case that is the subject of the admissibility challenge.[105] Nonetheless, the Pre-Trial Chamber, in assessing Libya's ability and willingness to carry out proceedings against Al-Senussi, held that this "must be assessed in light of the relevant law and procedures applicable to domestic proceedings in Libya".[106] As such, the general legal framework according to which proceedings are carried out forms a limited part of the admissibility test, and can provide important contextual information to assess genuine ability and willingness in a particular case. Similarly, assessing the admissibility of the *Bemba* case in 2010, the Trial Chamber concluded that the judicial system in the Central African Republic was "unavailable" under Article 17 due to its limited judicial and investigative capacity, which it linked to insufficient human resources, the large backlog of cases pending before national courts, and a shortage of judges in the country.[107]

This latter finding has not, however, been confirmed by the Appeals Chamber,[108] and subsequent jurisprudence suggests it may in fact rule such factors pertaining to the general system irrelevant to assess admissibility in a specific case. For instance, when asked to rule on the adequacy of general witness security to prove lack of independence or impartiality

---

[104] The chapeau of ICC Statute, Article 17(2) provides: "In order to determine unwillingness *in a particular case*, the Court shall consider, having regard to the principles of due process recognized by international law, whether one or more of the following exist, as applicable [...]." Likewise, Article 17(3) reads, in relevant part: "In order to determine inability *in a particular case*, the Court shall consider [...]" (emphasis added), see *supra* note 14.

[105] The Pre-Trial Chamber in Al-Senussi advanced a similar reading of the ICC Statute. *Al-Senussi* Admissibility Decision, para. 202, see *supra* note 53.

[106] *Ibid.*, para. 203. See also para. 223, where the Chamber noted: "the determination of whether there has been any such unjustified delay must be made not against an abstract ideal of 'justice', but against the specific circumstances surrounding the investigation concerned".

[107] ICC, *Prosecutor v. Jean-Pierre Bemba Gombo*, Trial Chamber III, Decision on the Admissibility and Abuse of Process Challenges, ICC-01/05-01/08-802, 24 June 2010, paras. 245–46 (http://www.legal-tools.org/doc/a5de24/).

[108] While this finding was one of the grounds of appeal of the defence, the Appeals Chamber declined to rule of the correctness of this finding, as it held there had not been a decision not to proceed in the case. In line with prior jurisprudence, the Appeals Chamber stressed that the question of unwillingness or inability does not arise if the answer to the first question of the test (sameness) is negative. *Bemba* Admissibility Appeals Judgment, para. 106, see *supra* note 46.

---

of the Libyan system, the Appeals Chamber ruled that only situations where witnesses would "*deliberately* be exposed to, or *intentionally* left unprotected from, security threats" would render a case admissible under Article 17(2)(c).[109] This finding suggests that general conditions leading to inadequate witness protection during trial that are outside the direct control of the authorities are not relevant for the admissibility assessment. This may prove particularly problematic from a gender perspective given the difficulties victims of sexual and gender-based violence crimes often face during court proceedings and the inadequacy of many domestic systems to protect these witnesses. These inadequacies often do not stem from a deliberate or intentional policy to negatively position victims of these crimes, but result from structural and institutional biases (sometimes overtly, other times unconsciously) that affect sexual and gender-based violence in particular.

For inability, under Article 17(3), the Appeals Chamber confirmed that "the Court must be satisfied that there is *both* a 'total or substantial collapse or unavailability' of the national judicial system *and* that, as a result, 'the State is unable to obtain the accused or the necessary evidence and testimony or otherwise unable to carry out its proceedings'".[110] In this respect, Judge Song, in his separate opinion in the Gaddafi admissibility appeal, held that "unavailability" includes a situation where "the national system is incapable of being used, which incorporates the notion of being inaccessible".[111] It remains unclear what degree of collapse or unavailability would qualify as "substantial", as this has not yet been the subject of judicial assessment. The *travaux préparatoires* illustrate that states replaced the original suggestion of "partial" collapse with "substantial" collapse, which "seemingly avoided the situation where part of a State's judicial apparatus was incapacitated but significant portions remained intact".[112] This suggests that the threshold for satisfying the "substantial collapse or unavailability" requirement to demonstrate inability is high.

---

[109] *Al-Senussi* Admissibility Appeals Judgment, para. 244(i), see *supra* note 29; *Al-Senussi* Admissibility Decision, para. 288, see *supra* note 53.

[110] *Al-Senussi* Appeals Judgment, para. 265, see *supra* note 29 (emphasis in original).

[111] Separate Opinion of Judge Song, *Gaddafi* case, para. 25, see *supra* note 73.

[112] Holmes, 1999, p. 55, see *supra* note 96; Holmes, 2002, p. 677, see *supra* note 96. See the proposal made by Mexico in this respect: United Nations, Summary Records of the Plenary Meetings and of the Meetings of the Committee of the Whole, UN Diplomatic Conference of

In short, the analysis provided here suggests that the threshold for satisfying the requirements to demonstrate a state's inaction on the same case, or its inability or unwillingness is high, which risks overlooking, reducing or eliminating accountability for sexual violence.

17.4. Conclusion: The Vulnerability of Sexual and Gender-based Violence Crimes

Those who have examined complementarity from a gender perspective have mostly focused on the Office of the Prosecutor's assessment of the admissibility test at the preliminary examination stage of proceedings, which is the first time admissibility is assessed. However, ensuring the admissibility test is gender sensitive is not only the domain of the Office of the Prosecutor. Judges also have an important role to play in admissibility assessments. Notably, the test as laid down by ICC Chambers has a direct bearing on admissibility assessments subsequently carried out by the Office of the Prosecutor during preliminary examinations and investigations. Similarly, the Chambers' decisions set standards around the admissibility of cases; states wishing to pre-empt the ICC's jurisdiction need to satisfy *this* test.

This chapter illustrates that, from a gender perspective, the judges appear to have set a relatively low standard for domestic proceedings. National authorities must investigate the same person for substantially the same conduct as the ICC for the Court to relinquish jurisdiction to the national court. The charges brought before the national courts do not have to match the charges before the ICC. In fact, the judges have deemed the legal characterisation of crimes largely irrelevant for admissibility assessments. This has resulted in potential gender biases that may adversely affect the domestic recognition and prosecution of sexual and gender-based violence crimes or, at a minimum, leave them vulnerable to exclusion. There is a risk such crimes may simply be left out of prosecutions in a setting where most other criminal conduct is charged. The resulting impunity for sexual and gender-based violence crimes in such a situation is

Plenipotentiaries on the Establishment of an International Criminal Court (Rome 15 June–17 July 1998), 2002, vol. II, UN Doc. A/CONF.183/13, p. 317; and UN Doc. A/CON.183/C.1/L.14/REV.1 in United Nations, Reports and other Documents, UN Diplomatic Conference of Plenipotentiaries on the Establishment of an International Criminal Court (Rome 15 June–17 July 1998), 2002, vol. III, UN Doc. A/CONF.183/13.

clear. Further, the admissibility test leaves such crimes vulnerable because there is a risk that such crimes may be charged in ways that insufficiently reflect the gendered specificity of the crimes. Although these specific questions have not yet arisen before the judges in relation to specific admissibility proceedings,[113] this may become an issue in the future, given the "paucity of charging gender-based crimes in domestic settings",[114] and what Niamh Hayes describes as ICC Chambers "extreme reticence to progressively interpret the law on sexual and gender-based crimes".[115]

ICC Chambers have at times adopted restrictive interpretations of the ICC Statute's gender justice provisions, which suggest a tendency to misunderstand the complexities of these types of crimes. For instance, the Pre-Trial Chamber held that penile amputation and forced circumcision committed against Luo men during the post-election violence in Kenya in 2007–2008, charged by the prosecutor as "other forms of sexual violence", did not constitute sexual violence,[116] and recharacterised the charges as "other inhumane acts".[117] While the Pre-Trial Chamber does

---

[113] Nonetheless, as Chappell *et al.* demonstrate, a similar situation has arisen in relation to the Office of the Prosecutor's preliminary examination of Guinea. They argue: "Guinean authorities have taken some action to investigate and to prosecute some of those responsible for the [2009 Conakry] massacre. However, it appears that until May 2013, no charges had been brought for the sexual violence crimes documented by the OTP or the UN. This information suggests that the OTP overlooked sexual violence crimes when it concluded that the 'same person, same conduct' test was satisfied in November 2012". See Chappell *et al.*, 2013, p. 468, *supra* note 9.

[114] Ní Aoláin, 2013, p. 11, see *supra* note 24.

[115] Hayes, 2013, p. 39, see *supra* note 42.

[116] The Chamber held, without substantiating its findings, that these acts "cannot be considered acts of a 'sexual nature'": ICC, *Prosecutor v. Kirimi Muthaura, Uhuru Muigai Kenyatta and Mohammed Hussein Ali*, Pre-Trial Chamber II, Decision on the Prosecutor's Application for Summonses to Appear for Francis Kirimi Muthaura, Uhuru Muigai Kenyatta and Mohammed Hussein Ali, ICC-01/09-01/11-01, 8 March 2011, para. 27 (http://www.legal-tools.org/doc/df8391/). See also ICC, *Prosecutor v. Francis Kirimi Muthaura, Uhuru Muigai Kenyatta and Mohammed Hussein Ali*, Pre-Trial Chamber II, Decision on the Confirmation of Charges Pursuant to Article 61(7)(a) and (b) of the ICC Statute, ICC-01/09-02/11-382-Red, 23 January 2012, paras. 264–66 (http://www.legal-tools.org/doc/4972c0/).

[117] This is a trend that is not unique to the ICC. As Sandesh Sivakumaran illustrates, while the international criminal law framework is adequate to prosecute sexual violence regardless of the gender of its victims, in practice male sexual violence is often characterised as other (non-sexual) categories of crimes. Sandesh Sivakumaran, "Prosecuting Sexual Violence against Men and Boys", in Anne-Marie de Brouwer Charlotte Ku, Renée G. Römkens and Larissa van den Herik (eds.), *Sexual Violence as an International Crime: Interdisciplinary Ap-*

---

not divulge into a detailed discussion of its findings, the decision appears to be grounded in a particular understanding of what it means for an act to be 'sexual' – that it has a *sexual intent*. Forced circumcision and penile amputation, acts against men's sexual organs, for the Pre-Trial Chamber did not have any such sexual intent; the perpetrator derived no sexual pleasure or gratification out of the act. However, it is important to understand "the non-sexual intent behind what appear to be sexual acts".[118] Sexual violence in conflict, due to its stigmatising effect, is committed on both male and female victims because of the meaning of gender in a society, because of what the act communicates to the victim about their gender and that of the perpetrator, and is embedded in gendered structures of power. Sexual violence often has nothing to do with sex.

In this decision, the Pre-Trial Chamber failed to understand the power relations between ethnic groups and the meaning of circumcision in Kenyan society.[119] It is the context that makes these crimes gendered – they were committed because of their impact on conceptions of masculinities for the two main ethnic groups in Kenya. In this decision, gendered norms or assumptions operate to invisibilise male victims of sexual violence through the inaccurate labelling (or misrecognition) of their harm. In fact, this decision is emblematic of the general disregard in international criminal law for sexual violence committed against men.[120]

Another such example is the confirmation decision in the *Bemba* case,[121] in which the Pre-Trial Chamber held that charges of torture and

---

proaches, Intersentia, Antwerp, 2013, p. 97; Sivakumaran, 2007, pp. 256–57, see *supra* note 101.

[118] Refugee Law Project, "Comments on the ICC Draft Policy Paper on Sexual and Gender Based Crimes", 23 February 2014, para 36. See also Fionnuala Ní Aoláin, Dina Francesca Haynes and Naomi R. Cahn, "Criminal Justice for Gendered Violence and Beyond", in *International Criminal Law Review*, 2011, vol. 11, no. 3, p. 429: "Perpetrators understand (as do the victims) that public sexual violence is a form of communication and power, and not only a sexual act."

[119] IRIN News, "Kenya: Plea to ICC over Forced Male Circumcision", 25 April 2011; Women's Initiatives for Gender Justice, "Gender Report Card on the International Criminal Court 2011", November 2011, pp. 180–81; Women's Initiatives for Gender Justice, "Gender Report Card on the International Criminal Court 2012", November 2012, p. 108.

[120] Refugee Law Project, 2014, para 23, see *supra* note 118.

[121] Jean-Pierre Bemba Gombo, who is Congolese, is charged in relation to the Situation in the CAR. He faces charges of murder, rape and pillaging for his alleged responsibility as superior

---

outrages upon personal dignity in relation to victims forced to watch the rape of their family members were "fully subsumed by the count of rape".[122] It declined to confirm these charges, which would have addressed the different aspects of the crimes and acknowledged the harm inflicted upon the victims by the public nature of the crimes.[123] By failing to acknowledge the different dimensions of the crimes, the Pre-Trial Chamber conflated distinct gendered harms and reinforced the often-held conception that rape is the only type of gender-based violence committed in conflict.[124] It can be expected that these Pre-Trial Chambers, if faced with a domestic system that is not prosecuting these different elements of crimes committed, may accept the domestic system's limited case. An outcome such as this would conform to Chambers' history of misconceiving sexual and gender-based violence crimes, and would contribute to continued impunity for such crimes.

The exclusion of sexual and gender-based violence crimes charges is not simply theoretical. Given the widespread nature of sexual and gender-based violence crimes in conflict, one would expect such crimes to feature prominently in accountability processes. However, these crimes remain vulnerable in both domestic and international prosecutions – in fact, they are "the most vulnerable category of crimes" at the ICC.[125] Similarly, sexual and gender-based violence crimes are more likely to be ex-

---

commander of a militia group that entered the CAR in 2002–2003 to assist then-President Ange-Félix Patassé to fight an attempted coup in that country.

[122] ICC, *Prosecutor v. Jean-Pierre Bemba Gombo*, Pre-Trial Chamber II, Decision Pursuant to Article 61(7)(a) and (b) of the Rome Statute on the Charges of the Prosecutor Against Jean-Pierre Bemba Gombo, ICC-01/05-01/08-424, 15 June 2009, paras. 204–5 (http://www.legal-tools.org/doc/07965c/).

[123] On this point, see generally Green, 2011, *supra* note 90.

[124] *Ibid.*, pp. 535–38.

[125] Women's Initiatives for Gender Justice, 2011, p. 122, see *supra* note 119. Patricia Wildermuth and Petra Kneuer, "Addressing the Challenges to Prosecution of Sexual Violence Crimes before International Tribunals and Courts", in Morten Bergsmo, Alf Butenschøn Skre and Elisabeth Jean Wood (eds.), *Understanding and Proving International Sex Crimes*, Torkel Opsahl Academic EPublisher, Brussels, 2012, pp. 67, 105. Others have demonstrated that gender-based crimes are also vulnerable at other international courts, including the ICTY, ICTR and Special Court for Sierra Leone: See Sellers, 2009, p. 17, *supra* note 16; Askin, 2013, p. 52, *supra* note 10. Gender-based crimes have been among the first charges to be dropped in plea bargains at the *ad hoc* tribunals. As Sita Balthazar states, "[r]ape charges seem to be the first to go": See Sita Balthazar, "Gender Crimes and the International Criminal Tribunals", in *Gonzaga Journal of International Law*, 2006, vol. 10, p. 48.

cluded from domestic prosecutions than other types of crimes. This is not always due to a conscious decision to exclude such crimes,[126] but more often results from misconceptions and limited legal frameworks. Therefore, the low standard for domestic proceedings set by the judges sits uncomfortably with the reluctance of many states to prosecute sexual and gender-based violence crimes.

As demonstrated by Xabier Agirre Aranburu, resistance to the prosecution and investigation of sexual and gender-based violence crimes originates in a "lack of awareness and sensitivity in teams usually led by senior male officers, and a certain taboo or embarrassment when dealing with intimate aspects of our bodies and minds".[127] While he made these observations in relation to international prosecutions, they apply equally to the domestic level. While difficulties surrounding the investigation and prosecution of large-scale violence affect all types of crimes, these difficulties are exacerbated in relation to sexual and gender-based violence crimes.[128] Further, these crimes face unique difficulties, originating in sexist attitudes of police officers, investigators, prosecutors or judges.[129]

---

[126] Although an example given by Xabier Agirre Aranburu is telling in this respect: "When drafting an indictment for an international tribunal in the late 1990s my modest attempt to include a reference to sexual violence under the chapeau of 'persecutions' (a crime against humanity) was stopped by two attorneys senior to me because in their view 'there was no sufficient evidence'. Later I discussed the issue with one of them and was puzzled when he explained that in his country as a prosecutor he always avoided sexual violence because it was 'very annoying and difficult to prove'". See Xabier Agirre Aranburu, "Beyond Dogma and Taboo: Criteria for Effective Investigation of Sexual Violence", in Morten Bergsmo, Alf Butenschøn Skre and Elisabeth Jean Wood (eds.), *Understanding and Proving International Sex Crimes*, Torkel Opsahl Academic EPublisher, Brussels, 2012, p. 269.

[127] *Ibid*, p. 271.

[128] Wildermuth and Kneuer, 2012, p. 67, see *supra* note 125: "The practical problems associated with bringing sexual crime perpetrators to justice are often the very same challenges that are presented in cases in which non-gender violence are charged […]. However, several of these challenges are exacerbated while other challenges emerge based on the very nature of these sexual offences."

[129] See, for example, Askin, 2013, p. 52, *supra* note 10: "sexist attitudes and ignorance surrounding sex crimes continue to be common, alongside harmful stereotypes and archaic practices." Kai Ambos, "Sexual offences in International Criminal Law: With a Special Focus on the Rome Statute of the International Criminal Court", in Morten Bergsmo, Alf Butenschøn Skre and Elisabeth Jean Wood (eds.), *Understanding and Proving International Sex Crimes*, Torkel Opsahl Academic EPublisher, Brussels, 2012, pp. 149–50: "As the respective conflicts are normally not taking place in the highly developed industrial societies, but rather in underdeveloped or developing countries (especially Sub-Saharan Africa), ICL is confronted with

This unawareness, insensitivity and general reluctance to deal with sexual and gender-based violence crimes means that many justice systems are not sufficiently able to prosecute such crimes, and will leave them out of prosecutions. Likewise, they often result in inadequate legal frameworks. For instance, Chappell *et al.* found that the Guinean Penal Code does not provide for the full range of gender-based crimes that allegedly occurred during the 28 September 2009 massacre in Conakry, nor does it provide for formal witness protection mechanisms.[130] Similarly, in Colombia it appears investigators and prosecutors have received inadequate or no training on sexual violence crimes, the protection mechanisms provided for in the legislative framework are ineffective, and the overburdened judicial system has deprioritised the prosecution of sexual and gender-based violence crimes.[131] Such biases in domestic systems, under the interpretation given to the admissibility test by the judges, would not be factors that would have to be considered. This may contribute to continued impunity for sexual and gender-based violence crimes in these contexts.

Despite the potential gender biases outlined in this chapter, however, there is room for the Court to make it explicit that the adequate prosecution of sexual and gender-based violence crimes domestically remains as much a priority for domestic courts as it is for the ICC. Indeed, in its 2014 policy paper on "Sexual and Gender-Based Crimes", the Office of the Prosecutor has indicated that gender is an important factor for its admissibility assessments.[132] However, it remains unclear whether the Office is willing (and able) to take the next step and assume jurisdiction over those crimes where states fail to prosecute. It remains unclear what would happen if a state were genuinely able and willing to prosecute and investigate crimes within the ICC's jurisdiction *except* sexual and gender-based violence crimes (the case of Colombia comes to mind).

---

highly traditional, sometimes even archaic conceptions, according to which sexual offences are primarily considered as attacks on the honor – yet not of the female victim but of her male partners." See also, generally, Brammertz and Jarvis, 2016, *supra* note 78.

[130] Chappell *et al.*, 2013, p. 468, see *supra* note 9.

[131] *Ibid.*, pp. 469–71.

[132] ICC, Office of the Prosecutor, Policy Paper, "Sexual and Gender-Based Crimes", June 2014, paras. 7, 38–47, 109–10.

Ultimately, this chapter highlights that it cannot have been the intention of the drafters to bestow upon the ICC a mandate and obligation to prosecute a broad range of sexual and gender-based violence crimes, fully integrating such crimes into the framework of international criminal law, yet allow such crimes to escape prosecution through the legal test for admissibility. By virtue of the centrality of the principle of complementarity, and given the ICC Statute's emphasis on gender sensitivity, this chapter argues that the ICC Statute establishes a larger international criminal justice project that is or should be gender inclusive. It is therefore important to connect the ICC Statute's ground-breaking gender justice provisions with the principle of complementarity. This chapter provides an attempt to do so by focusing on identifying biases in the admissibility test as set out by the judges. More work is needed to ensure the practical application of the admissibility test, and broader complementarity analyses, become fully inclusive of a gender perspective.

18

Sexual Violence as an International Crime, the Restorative Paradigm and the Possibilities of a More Just Response

Estelle Zinsstag and Virginie Busck-Nielsen Claeys[*]

18.1. Introduction

Sexual violence is widespread and affects women and men in all countries, whether peaceful, fragile[1] or undergoing armed conflicts. A common characteristic among these places and persons is the lack of a just, appropriate and consistent response after such an offence. Restorative justice, in its maximalist approach, may be able to offer a number of responses to such crime which traditional criminal justice simply does not (at least not on its own).

There are a number of definitions of sexual violence. In its broad acceptance, sexual violence includes a variety of sexually harmful behaviours involving men, women and children. These behaviours may or may not imply physical contact, criminal or civil court proceedings or even a conflict or post-conflict context. The violence may, for example, be linked to child sexual abuse, sexual assault, molestation, rape, sexual trafficking, sexual slavery, forced sterilisation, forced marriages, forced pregnancy and sexual violence perpetrated through the use of communication technology. This chapter is concerned with international sexual crimes perpetrated within an armed conflict or an authoritarian re-

---

[*]   **Estelle Zinsstag** is a Senior Researcher at the Leuven Institute of Criminology, University of Leuven, Belgium; and Managing Editor of the *International Journal of Restorative Justice*. **Virginie Busck-Nielsen Claeys** is a Ph.D. candidate at the Leuven Institute of Criminology, University of Leuven, Belgium.

1   The concept of 'fragile state' is borrowed from Catherine Burns and Kathleen Daly, "Responding to Everyday Rape in Cambodia: Rhetorics, Realities and *Somroh Somruel*", in *Restorative Justice: An International Journal*, 2014, vol. 2, no. 1, pp. 64–84. See also Wim Naudé, Amelia U. Santos-Paulino and Mark McGillivray, *Fragile States: Causes, Costs, and Responses*, Oxford University Press, Oxford, 2011.

---

gime. Victims[2] in this context have frequently suffered extreme violence which can manifest itself on a number of levels, traumatising and affecting not only them, but their families and entire communities. Furthermore, alleged perpetrators frequently continue to live within the very communities where the crime took place.[3] Whether perpetrated by government forces or rebel groups (or both), sexual violence may be part of a campaign of terror and torture intended to degrade, intimidate and target specific sectors of the population, as well as to force them to migrate.[4] In some conflicts, such as currently in eastern Democratic Republic of Congo or Nigeria, it may be used strategically as a weapon of war intended to destroy the very core of communities, families and livelihoods.[5]

A series of mechanisms, commonly referred to as 'transitional justice'[6] may assist a country in departing from its violent past.[7] These may include criminal prosecutions, reparations (material or symbolic), institutional reform (judiciary, government, security forces), and also commis-

---

[2] We acknowledge that both 'victims' and 'survivors' are used in this context; for the sake of simplicity, we use 'victims' while acknowledging that it is not always the most accurate or acceptable term.

[3] See, for example, Mark A. Drumbl, "Sclerosis: Retributive Justice and the Rwandan Genocide", in *Punishment and Society*, 2000, vol. 2, no. 3, p. 288.

[4] See, for example, Maria Eriksson Baaz and Maria Stern, *Rape as a Weapon of War*, Zed Books, London, 2013.

[5] On 19 June 2008, the United Nations Security Council passed resolution 1820, UN Doc. S/RES/1820, which addresses a wide range of harms associated with sexual violence in conflict and, crucially, recognises that sexual violence, by terrorising and destabilising entire communities is a tangible security threat and not 'just' an unfortunate consequence of conflict (http://www.legal-tools.org/doc/298f16/).

[6] The term 'transitional justice' gained prominence in the 1980s and 1990s with the fall of military regimes in South and Central America and in Eastern Europe. See generally Ruti G. Teitel, *Transitional Justice*, Oxford University Press, Oxford, 2000.

[7] The goals of transitional justice vary according to the historical and the political contexts of the conflict and the priorities of the society in transition. By and large, the goals of transitional justice are the presumed resumption or a transition to democracy, establishment of rule of law, reconstruction of the nation, psycho-social reconciliation of the people with the past and documentation of collective memory of the past to avoid repetition among others. See, for example, Teitel, 2000, *ibid.*; Naomi Roht-Arriaza and Javier Mariezcurrena (eds.), *Transitional Justice in the Twenty-First Century: Beyond Truth versus Justice*, Cambridge University Press, Cambridge, 2006.

---

sions of inquiry or truth commissions.[8] The insecure aftermath of conflict
and regime change means implementation of the latter is complex, but
there is a growing consensus that some or all these mechanisms must be
pursued simultaneously and in an integrated or blended manner for the
transition to be successful and comprehensive.[9] As such, transitional justice in itself appears to have similar objectives to 'core principles' of a
more maximalist approach to restorative justice such as healing, accountability and wrongs inflicted to a person rather than to the state.[10] Some
specific mechanisms even follow the conventional restorative justice focus on encounter, amends, reintegration, inclusion of victim and offender[11] with procedures akin to victim–offender mediation or victim–offender
dialogue.[12]

The restorative paradigm in the case of sexual violence in the context of transition is about looking into the possibilities of offering a more
comprehensive response for this particular crime, which transcends the
traditional punitive approach and its many limitations. It attempts to address the 'collective responsibility' rather than solely 'individual liability'.[13] It facilitates mechanisms for victims, offenders and communities in
order to allow a transition in which eventually some healing and rebuild-

---

[8] Report of the Secretary General, The Rule of Law and Transitional Justice in Conflict and
    Post-Conflict Societies, UN Doc. S/2004/616, 3 August 2004 (http://www.legal-
    tools.org/doc/77bebf/).

[9] See, for example, Drumbl, 2000, *supra* note 3; Charles Villa-Vicencio, "Transitional Justice,
    Restoration and Prosecution", in Dennis Sullivan and Larry Tifft (eds.), *Handbook of Restor-
    ative Justice*, Routledge, London, 2006; Estelle Zinsstag, "Sexual Violence against Women
    in Armed Conflicts: Standard Responses and New Ideas", in *Social Policy and Society*, 2006,
    vol. 5, no. 1, pp. 137–48; Estelle Zinsstag, "Sexual Violence, Transitional Justice and the
    Possibility of a 'Blended' Approach'", in Adam Czarnota and Stephan Parmentier (eds.),
    *Transitional Justice and Rule of Law: Institutional Design and the Changing Normative
    Structure of Post-Authoritarian Societies,* Intersentia, Antwerp, Cambridge, Portland, 2015.

[10] See, for example, Lode Walgrave, *Restorative Justice, Self-interest and Responsible Citizen-
    ship*, Willan, Cullompton, 2008; Howard Zehr, *Changing Lenses: A New Focus for Crime
    and Justice*, Herald Press, Scottdale, 1990.

[11] For more information see Zehr, 1990, *supra* note 10.

[12] See, for example, Susan L. Miller, *After the Crime: The Power of Restorative Justice Dia-
    logues between Victims and Violent Offenders*, New York University Press, New York, 2011.

[13] Estelle Zinsstag, "Sexual Violence against Women in Armed Conflicts and Restorative Jus-
    tice: an Exploratory Analysis", in Martha Albertson Fineman and Estelle Zinsstag (eds.),
    *Feminist Perspectives on Transitional Justice: From International and Criminal to Alterna-
    tive Forms of Justice*, Intersentia, Antwerp, 2013, pp. 189–213.

---

ing may be started and possibly some closure may be reached. Restoration encourages a more inclusive, victim-friendly and forward-looking approach to post-conflict justice. This alternative, which is characterised by a wide array of practices, cannot intend to replace but rather complement the traditional retributive response to atrocity after an armed conflict.[14] Charles Villa-Vicencio claims that the co-ordination of the two approaches is needed for a transition from a conflict-ridden country to a country with a functioning rule of law and where a human rights culture may develop to be successful.[15] Desmond Tutu also claims that:

> Retributive justice – in which an impersonal state hands down punishment with little consideration for victims and hardly any for the perpetrator – is not the only form of justice. I contend that there is another kind of justice, restorative justice [...] Here the central concern is not retribution or punishment but, in the spirit of ubuntu, the healing of breaches, the redressing of imbalances, the restoration of broken relationships. [...] Thus we would claim that justice, restorative justice, is being served when efforts are being made to work for healing, for forgiveness and for reconciliation.[16]

This chapter examines the value of this type of justice for sexual violence by exploring some of the restorative justice mechanisms that are currently available to respond to victims of sexual violence after an armed conflict or in fragile states. Therefore only restorative mechanisms that are directly relevant, or may become so, for sexual violence survivors are examined, that is to say truth commissions, the Rome Statute of the International Criminal Court ('ICC Statute') and proceedings before the ICC as well as a selection of local restorative justice mechanisms.[17]

Indeed, it is paradoxical to note that internal strife and violence are often endemic after peace has been brokered,[18] and government structures (justice, security, administration) find themselves unable to address this because of lack of means or lack of political will (violence may, for in-

---

14   *Ibid.*

15   Villa-Vicencio, 2006, p. 391, see *supra* note 9.

16   Desmond Tutu, *No Future without Forgiveness*, Random House, New York, 1999, pp. 51–52.

17   Sometimes also referred to as informal justice systems.

18   In Guatemala, Haiti and South Africa, levels were actually higher after transition than during conflict or dictatorship.

stance, implicate security forces who are still in place). Sexual violence[19] follows the same general pattern, the only difference being that during an authoritarian regime or conflict it will manifest itself in the public sphere (as a means of terror or torture),[20] whereas in a transitioning society it tends to shift to the private sphere, typically in the form of domestic violence.[21] Reasons for this are varied and complex. They sit within deeply rooted discriminations, which pre-exist a conflict or authoritarian regime. They also appear simply because of lack of punishment and implicit legitimisation.[22] This all needs to be comprehensively understood for interventions to be effective.[23]

In this chapter we first examine responses to international sexual violence (section 18.2.). Next, we discuss some of the basic ideas behind the restorative justice paradigm (section 18.3.) in order to then examine restorative mechanisms which may be appropriate for dealing with international sexual violence (section 18.4.). We conclude by considering some ideas towards a way forward (section 18.5.).

18.2. Responses to International Sexual Violences

While sexual violence in war has been condemned since time immemorial, war codes and international conventions have tried, more recently, to offer tools to strengthen safeguards against this specific form of viola-

---

[19] The present research considers sexual violence, which may or may not have resulted in criminal or civil court proceedings and may have occurred in peacetime or in a conflict/ post-conflict context. It does not, however, include domestic or any other forms of gendered violence.

[20] As already noted, the term 'transitional justice' gained prominence in the 1980s and 1990s with the fall or military regimes in South and Central America and in Eastern Europe: Naomi Roht-Arriaza, *The Pinochet Effect: Transnational Justice in the Age of Human Rights,* University of Pennsylvania Press, Philadelphia, 2006.

[21] See, for example, Sheila Meintjies, Anu Pillay and Meredith Turshen (eds.), *The Aftermath: Women in Post-Conflict Transformation,* Zed Books, London, 2001.

[22] Mary Caprioli, "Primed for Violence: The Role of Gender Inequality in Predicting Internal Conflict", in *International Studies Quarterly,* 2005, vol. 49, no. 2, pp. 161–78.

[23] Tina Sideris, "Rape in War and Peace: Social Context, Gender, Power and Identity", in Sheila Meintjies, Anu Pillay and Meredith Turshen (eds.), *The Aftermath: Women in Post-Conflict Transformation,* Zed Books, London, 2001, pp. 142–58. She explains that "differentiating between rape in war and peace carries the danger that [...] rape that is used as a tactic of ethnic cleansing evokes moral outrage, yet forced sex in the privacy of family life is accepted" (p. 146).

---

tion.[24] But there has been a dearth of actual enforcement and prosecutions. In the aftermath of the Second World War, the Nuremberg and Tokyo international military tribunals did investigate and prosecute some sexual violence crimes, but this was limited in scope and impunity for sexual violence remained pervasive until about two decades ago.[25]

It was indeed 20 years ago that the international community drove forward the need to prosecute genocide, war crimes and crimes against humanity and, with this, to emphasise the inclusion of sexual crimes within the understanding of these crimes. The gendered interpretation of these crimes is especially clear in the ICC Statute (1998), but the emphasis on the need to prosecute these crimes also appears, although with some challenges, at the International Criminal Tribunal for the former Yugoslavia ('ICTY'), the International Criminal Tribunal for Rwanda ('ICTR'), the Special Court for Sierra Leone and the Extraordinary Chambers in the Courts of Cambodia.[26] There is an argument today that genocide, war crimes and crimes against humanity are so abhorrent to humankind that they are to be applied *erga omnes* by all jurisdictions that are able to do

---

[24] Instruments have already existed for some decades. See, for example, Part I, Article 3 of the Geneva Convention relative to the Treatment of Prisoners of War, 27 July 1929, which explicitly mentions the need for protection of prisoners of war, both male and female against attacks on "their persons and honour" (http://www.legal-tools.org//1d2cfc/). Another is Control Council Law No. 10, a martial law decree issued after the Second World War, in which rapes are considered to be crimes against humanity (http://www.legal-tools.org/doc/ffda62/).

[25] See, for example, Patricia Viseur Sellers, "Foreword", in Anne-Marie de Brouwer *et al.* (eds.), *Sexual Violence as an International Crime: Interdisciplinary Approaches*, Intersentia, Antwerp, 2013, pp. vii–xii. For a historical overview, see Kelly D. Askin, "Treatment of Sexual Violence in Armed Conflicts: A Historical Perspective and the Way Forward", in de Brouwer *et al.*, 2013, pp. 19–55, *ibid.*

[26] The Genocide Convention includes sexual violence when it refers to Article 2(b) and Nazi sexual and reproductive experiments on women and men as well as Article 2(d) which refers to preventing birth for non-Aryans; United Nations General Assembly, Convention on the Prevention and Punishment of the Crime of Genocide, 9 December 1948 (http://www.legal-tools.org/doc/498c38/). The understanding is that the genocide in Rwanda and Darfur also included sexual violence. For more information, see Anne-Marie de Brouwer, *Supranational Criminal Prosecution of Sexual Violence: The ICC and the Practice of the ICTY and the ICTR*, Intersentia, Antwerp, 2005; Sarah Williams, *Hybrid and Internationalised Criminal Tribunals: Selected Jurisdictional Issues*, Hart, Oxford, 2012; Silke Studzinsky, "Neglected Crimes: The Challenge of Raising Sexual Gender-Based Crimes before the Extraordinary Chambers in the Courts of Cambodia", in Susanne Buckley-Zistel and Ruth Stanley (eds.), *Gender in Transitional Justice*, Palgrave Macmillan, London, 2012, pp. 88–112.

---

so, regardless of whether there is an international private law connection.
Some states, such as Belgium and Canada, have legislation that enshrines
this principle, referred to as 'universal jurisdiction'. Another example is
France which prosecuted a former Rwandan leader for crimes against humanity during the 1994 Rwandan genocide.[27]

One of the preliminary conclusions practitioners and academics
seem to be drawing from initial criminal prosecutions of international
sexual crimes, however, is the difficulty of dealing with this form of
crime. Both at international and domestic levels, courts face very practical
problems due of the sheer numbers of victims involved, the lack of practical means to collect and preserve forensic evidence, and the difficulty of
investigating, prosecuting and adjudicating where there is a scarcity of
staff and a high risk of bribery. There are also obvious risks associated
with victim and witness protection (particularly if alleged perpetrators are
linked to security forces) and, finally, there are practical problems in offering reparation to victims or survivors because of the limited funds
available.

These challenges are considerable but others are perhaps more decisive still in explaining why victims, particularly in cases of sexual violence, appear to favour informal or alternative justice systems over formal
courts.[28] The latter crucially tend to give victims a voice in proceedings
and offer them the opportunity, often through a familiar community figure, to express their needs and in some cases be offered some compensation.

Empirical studies themselves demonstrate that what victims want is
not necessarily more painful or stringent punishments of an offender but
the ability to receive information about proceedings of criminal acts they
are party to and to be given the possibility to participate if they so wish.[29]
Because entire communities are included in proceedings, there is also a
greater chance of reparations actually being implemented, a less than cer-

---

[27] Pascal Simbikangwu is alleged by prosecutors of France's special genocide court to have
been number three in the Rwandan Intelligence Unit during the 1994 genocide against minority Tutsis and moderate Hutus. His trial began in March 2014.

[28] See Burns and Daly, 2014, *supra* note 1.

[29] See, for example, Heather Strang, *Repair or Revenge: Victims and Restorative Justice*, Oxford University Press, Oxford, 2002.

---

tain outcome with a formal court hearing.[30] In most, if not all, societies, sexual violence carries with it heavy social implications, both for the victim and his or her community. It also has connections with underlying gender discrimination, which may pre-exist the violence. Having an informal system either on its own if formal court systems are not accessible, or in parallel to the court system,[31] may therefore be an interesting approach to addressing international sexual violence. We will therefore concentrate on an alternative or complementary approach represented by the restorative paradigm broadly defined, which may have the capacity to improve the existing responses to sexual violence in general and international sexual violence in particular.

18.3. The Restorative Paradigm

We intend to examine briefly the main characteristics of the restorative paradigm by making some theoretical and introductory remarks concerning restorative justice in order to set the ground for an examination of restorative justice mechanisms in relation to international sexual violence later in the chapter.[32]

18.3.1. Origins, Definitions and Debates

The origins and history of restorative justice have been described in a number of scholarly writings and here we only state some of the basic facts. Restorative ideals often date back as far as the ancient Greeks.[33] Some argue also that restorative justice actually originates and takes after a number of traditional forms of justice such as the ones used by the Maoris in New Zealand and the Navajos or First Nation people in North

---

[30] United Nations Development Programme ('UNDP'), *Informal Justice Systems: Charting a Course for Human Rights-Based Engagement*, United Nations Development Programme, UN Women and UNICEF, New York, 2012.

[31] See, for example, Guinea, Liberia, Sierra Leone and Uganda.

[32] For a more detailed presentation of restorative justice, see Marie Keenan and Estelle Zinsstag, "Restorative Justice and Sexual Offenses: Can 'Changing Lenses' Be Appropriate in this Case Too?", in *Monatsschrift für Kriminologie und Strafrechtsreform*, 2014, vol. 97, no. 1, pp. 93–106.

[33] See, for example, Zehr, 1990, *supra* note 10; Dan van Ness and Karen Heetderks Strong, *Restoring Justice: An Introduction to Restorative Justice*, 4th ed., Matthew Bender, New Providence, 2010; Walgrave, 2008, *supra* note 10.

America.[34] Albert Eglash was one of the first to use the term 'restorative justice' in a consistent way from the late 1950s.[35] Other authors in the 1970s, such as Nils Christie[36] and Randy Barnett,[37] have laid the foundations and influenced its development with defining pieces of writing, whose legacy still resonates strongly today. Kitchener, Ontario (Canada) is generally considered the birthplace of the modern restorative justice movement, where in 1977 a probation officer used mediation with success to deal with two juvenile offenders who, after having pleaded guilty to vandalising several properties, visited each of their victims and arranged to pay restitution.[38]

There have been many discussions and debates around a possible definition of restorative justice. However, through its flexible nature, not one definition has emerged to be able to represent the diverse views. A definition that has received much attention is that of Tony Marshall in the late 1990s: "restorative justice is a process whereby all the parties with a stake in a particular offence come together to resolve collectively how to deal with the aftermath of the offence and its implications for the future".[39]

The United Nations *Handbook on Restorative Justice Programmes* also has taken a more process-orientated approach which some prefer: restorative justice "is any process in which the victim and the offender and, where appropriate, any other individuals or community members af-

---

34 See, for example, Kathleen Daly, "Restorative Justice: The Real Story", in *Punishment and Society*, 2002, vol. 4, no. 1, pp. 55–79; Estelle Zinsstag, Marlies Teunkens and Brunilda Pali, "Conferencing: A Way Forward for Restorative Justice in Europe?", European Forum for Restorative Justice, Leuven, 2011.

35 See Shadd Maruna, "The Role of Wounded Healing in Restorative Justice: An Appreciation of Albert Eglash", in *Restorative Justice: An International Journal*, 2014, vol. 2, no. 1, pp. 9–23; van Ness and Strong, 2010, see *supra* note 33.

36 Nils Christie, "Conflicts as Property", in *British Journal of Criminology*, 1977, vol. 17, no. 1, pp. 1–26.

37 Randy Barnett, "Restitution: A New Paradigm of Criminal Justice", in *Ethics: An International Journal of Social, Political and Legal Philosophy*, 1977, vol. 87, no. 4, pp. 279–301.

38 See, for example, Zehr, 1990, *supra* note 10; Dan van Ness, Allison Morris and Gabrielle Maxwell, "Introducing Restorative Justice", in Allison Morris and Gabrielle Maxwell (eds.), *Restorative Justice for Juveniles: Conferencing, Mediation & Circles*, Hart, London, 2001, pp. 3–16.

39 Tony Marshall, "The Evolution of Restorative Justice in Britain", in *European Journal on Criminal Policy and Research*, 1996, vol. 4, no. 4, p. 37.

fected by a crime participate together actively in the resolution of matters arising from the crime, generally with the help of a facilitator".[40] Some authors such as Lode Walgrave have criticised this approach as it tends to focus more on the outcome of the process than on the process in itself.[41] The process is believed by some as needing to be the purpose itself as it may be extremely important for the stakeholders and may achieve results that neither the criminal justice system nor 'pure' restorative justice programmes can hope to achieve. As a consequence, Gordon Bazemore and Walgrave propose a very simple definition, only mentioning essential elements: "Restorative justice is every action that is primarily oriented toward doing justice by repairing the harm that has been caused by a crime".[42] This definition is the gateway to enter the purist or maximalist debate.[43]

For the purposes of this chapter and in the context of sexual violence, we believe that a maximalist approach is the most appropriate. Indeed we believe that in the case of sexual violence 'pure' restorative justice programmes and approaches may not be suitable, as they would have very little result or impact on their own (without the intervention of the criminal justice system or unaccompanied by psychosocial treatment). However, we believe, as argued elsewhere, that well-designed restorative processes to cater for the specific needs and consequences of this particular type of crime may enable a much fairer response.[44] Other debates within restorative justice worth mentioning in this context are the institutionalisation debate[45] or the 'top-down' versus 'bottom-up' approaches to

---

[40] United Nations, *Handbook on Restorative Justice Programmes*, United Nations, Office of Drugs and Crime, New York, 2006, p. 6.

[41] Walgrave, 2008, see *supra* note 10. See also, for example, Dan van Ness and Karen H. Strong, *Restoring Justice*, 2nd ed., Anderson Publishing, Cincinnati, OH, 2002 for an outcome-based restorative justice model.

[42] Gordon Bazemore and Lode Walgrave, "Restorative Juvenile Justice: In Search of Fundamentals and an Outline for Systemic Reform", in Gordon Bazemore and Lode Walgrave (eds.), *Restorative Justice for Juveniles: Repairing the Harm of Youth Crime*, Criminal Justice Press, Monsey, NY, 1999, p. 48.

[43] For more information see, for example, Walgrave, 2008, *supra* note 10; Ivo Aertsen, Tom Daems and Luc Robert (eds.), *Institutionalizing Restorative Justice*, Willan, Cullompton, 2006.

[44] See Keenan and Zinsstag, 2014, *supra* note 32.

[45] See, for more information, Aertsen *et al.*, 2006, *supra* note 43.

---

restorative justice,[46] which are both relevant in a transitional context since there is room for institutional reform and the community may be able to achieve much for victims when the state might not, or at least not yet. Furthermore, restorative justice practices may take place at any stage or level and this has also caused some discussions within the field. Some programmes may take place at a pre-sentence stage, some at a post-sentence stage, and some may take place completely outside of any court proceedings or even without police involvement[47] – and this is particularly true in some cases of sexual offences, for which there is a very low rate of reporting and even when reported the attrition rates soar.[48]

18.3.2 In Practice[49]

There are a number of different practices and programmes which can be defined as restorative. We only briefly describe a couple of types that have shown through practice to be particularly adequate in cases of sexual offences,[50] and may be more directly relevant to the transitional context, dealt with more specifically later in this chapter. We examine mediation, assisted dialogues and conferencing, which can be considered as 'traditional' or 'fully' restorative justice programmes.

There are several conditions which need to be fulfilled in order for a restorative justice programme to be able to be set in motion. One is that the offender must recognise his or her guilt prior to the initiative, or at least not deny it. A second is that participation by both parties should be

---

[46] See, for more information, John Braithwaite, "Setting Standards for Restorative Justice", in *British Journal of Criminology*, 2002, vol. 42, no. 3, pp. 563–77.

[47] Daly, 2002, see *supra* note 34.

[48] See, for example, C. Quince Hopkins and Mary Koss, "Incorporating Feminist Theory and Insights into a Restorative Justice Response to Sex Offences", in *Violence Against Women*, 2005, vol. 11, no. 5, pp. 693–723; Kathleen Daly and Sarah Curtis-Fawley, "Restorative Justice for Victims of Sexual Assault", in Karen Heimer and Candace Kruttschnitt (eds.), *Gender and Crime: Patterns of Victimization and Offending*, New York University Press, New York, 2006, pp. 230–65.

[49] Some of the ideas, facts and findings discussed in this section come from a European Commission-funded project entitled "Developing integrated responses to sexual violence: An interdisciplinary research project on the potential of restorative justice" (Daphne project JUST/2011/DAP/3350) which was co-ordinated by the University of Leuven (Belgium) and in which both authors were actively involved.

[50] See Keenan and Zinsstag, 2014, *supra* note 32.

completely voluntary. The programme may take place within or without the involvement of the court. Indeed it is clear that today many such initiatives happen informally, organised by rape crisis centres, hospitals, within prisons and mediation services.[51] In some cases they take place through self-referrals rather than referrals generated by the criminal justice system or other official referring mechanisms. One of the main keys to any such programmes is a careful preparation of all parties prior to a meeting, facilitated dialogue, conference or circle. It has become clear that the outcome of the process often depends on the quality of the preparation.

Mediation or assisted dialogues are the most widespread restorative justice programmes regarding sexual violence. The main reason is that due to the specific characteristics and nature of and traditionally held views on sexual violence (some victims experience feelings of shame or guilt), the main stakeholders tend to favour not involving others when meeting with the mediator(s). That said, in some cases therapists or other support persons may also be present. Victim–offender mediation, which is the most common programme is described in Estelle Zinsstag *et al.* as a "one-to-one meeting between the crime victim and the offender [...] generally facilitated by a mediator who helps the parties to achieve a new perception of their relationship and of the harm caused".[52] The victim and the offender may decide to meet face-to-face or indirectly, in which case it is possible to use video links, telephone facilities or surrogates for either of the main protagonists. The exchange of letters may also be a way of establishing a dialogue.[53] In the case of sexual violence, mediation, when practised in a safe environment, has been considered by some as favouring feelings of empowerment and autonomy.[54]

Conferencing, also often called family group conferencing, started in its current form in New Zealand when the Children, Young Persons and

---

[51] For examples of possibilities in a peaceful setting, see Brunilda Pali and Karin Sten Madsen, "Dangerous Liaisons? A Feminist and Restorative Approach to Sexual Assault", in *Temida*, 2011, vol. 14, no. 1, pp. 40–65; Clare McGlynn, Nicola Westmarland and Nikki Godden, "'I just wanted him to hear me': Sexual Violence and the Possibilities of Restorative Justice", in *Journal of Law and Society*, 2012, vol. 39, no. 2, pp. 213–40.

[52] Zinsstag *et al.*, 2011, p. 44, see *supra* note 34.

[53] Miller, 2011, see *supra* note 12.

[54] Karin Sten Madsen, "Mediation as a Way of Empowering Women Exposed to Sexual Coercion", in *Nordic Journal of Feminist and Gender Research*, 2004, vol. 12, no. 1, pp. 58–61.

Families Act was passed in 1989 and in Australia in the early 1990s.[55] The main difference when compared to other restorative justice programmes is the active participation of the family or close friends, also called the 'community of care'. All the parties affected by an offence will therefore be involved in the process and the decisions about the outcome, under the supervision of a facilitator and with the participation of a number of other relevant actors depending on the type of conferences, for example a police officer, a social worker, a community or legal representative.[56]

Both of those types of programmes could be introduced under one form or another in a transitional context, especially since these are ideal times to implement deep-rooted institutional and judicial reforms.[57] These programmes are flexible and can be adapted whether within or outside the criminal justice system for all types of crime.

18.4. Restorative Responses to International Sexual Crimes

As previously mentioned, victims of sexual violence, even in the context of a society that is transitioning away from conflict, appear to seek mechanisms of redress outside the formal courts because they provide them with a central role in proceedings, allow them to express their lived experience of a crime, their needs and how they envisage their future. Since the 1970s, this emphasis on harm to individuals rather than to an abstract society is gaining ground in the domestic law of non-transitional societies as well as in international law. Until recently, the primacy of victims' needs had been considered non-existent in criminal law since the twelfth to thirteenth centuries. For more than 800 years, crime was seen as inflict-

---

[55] For more details see, for example, Estelle Zinsstag, "Conferencing: A Developing Practice of Restorative Justice", in Estelle Zinsstag and Inge Vanfraechem (eds.), *Conferencing and Restorative Justice: International Practices and Perspectives*, Oxford University Press, Oxford, 2012, pp. 11–32.

[56] Zinsstag *et al.*, 2011, see *supra* note 34.

[57] See the case of Northern Ireland where, in the transitional period a couple of years after the peace agreement, restorative justice has been introduced through legislation and is now implemented systematically in cases of juvenile crime. See Estelle Zinsstag and Tim Chapman, "Conferencing in Northern Ireland: Implementing Restorative Justice at the Core of the Criminal Justice System", in Estelle Zinsstag and Inge Vanfraechem (eds.), *Conferencing and Restorative Justice: International Practices and Perspectives*, Oxford University Press, Oxford, 2012, pp. 173–88.

---

ing harm to society rather than to an individual, and the only possible outcome was an adversarial proceeding in which the victim appeared only as a witness.[58] The result of proceedings could only be an acquittal or a custodial sentence for the offender.[59]

18.4.1. International Responses: ICC Statute, a Combination of Retributive and Restorative Justice?

In international law, the ICC Statute is the first international instrument that explicitly states that crime inflicts harm firstly to an individual and, hence, that the court must imperatively ask the individual what his or her needs are, both in terms of 'looking back' at the crime committed and 'looking forward' towards the future. When one considers statements of victims of international sexual crime,[60] these needs are reiterated. For victims or survivors, 'looking back' entails the search for factual truth, his or her version of the truth, and accountability of the offender for the crime. In societies emerging from dictatorship or conflict, truth-telling plays a critical role in acknowledging the wrongs suffered by victims, encourages individual and community healing, and may identify necessary reforms to prevent such violations from happening again.[61]

At the same time, 'looking forward' for victims entails an active participation in proceedings and providing some means of partially restoring his or her life. Yet the ICC Statute is heavily criticised by the very victims it is intended to assist. Although it purports to combine retribution

---

[58] The reparative justice theory emerged because of the marginalisation of the interests and needs of victims when addressing the harm inflicted by a crime.

[59] Rome Statute of the International Criminal Court, 17 July 1998, in force 1 July 2002 ('ICC Statute') (http://www.legal-tools.org/doc/7b9af9/). Article 75 expressly focuses on the needs of victims and requires the award reparations tailored to these needs.

[60] See UN Office of the High Commissioner for Human Rights ('OHCHR'), "Report of the Panel on Remedies and Reparations for Victims of Sexual Violence in the Democratic Republic of Congo to the High Commissioner for Human Rights", March 2011.

[61] OHCHR, Human Rights Resolution 2005/66: Right to the Truth, UN Doc. E/CN.4/RES/2005/66, 20 April 2005; and International Center for Transitional Justice ('ICTJ') Briefing, "Confronting the Past: Truth Telling and Reconciliation in Uganda", ICTJ Uganda, September 2012. In a study on the reoccurrence of conflict in post-conflict societies in Africa, Paul Collier found that societies emerging from conflict stood a 40 per cent risk of renewed conflict within five years of a peace agreement or cessation of violence. See Paul Collier, *Economic Causes of Civil Conflict and their Implications for Policy*, Oxford University Press, Oxford, 2000.

---

and restoration by focusing on victims as well as on punishment, the reality is that the ICC's proceedings are so stringently based on traditional criminal proceedings that victims' voices, and general participation of offenders and community, cannot be conducted in accordance with a restorative justice paradigm. Efforts have clearly been made by the Court to try at least to capture victims' views – such as appointing special guidance to legal representatives of victims and having a Victims Participation and Reparation Section – but the outcomes remains limited.

Another problem linked to the restorative justice paradigm and the ICC Statute is the inability, in practice, of its institutions to reach out to a majority of victims, including victims of sexual violence. In the first ICC trial (*Thomas Lubanga Dyilo*) thousands of victims, including sexual violence victims, have, for practical reasons or reasons of opportunity in the prosecutor's indictment, not been included in proceedings.[62] The second trial (*Germain Katanga*) did include sexual violence, but the defendant saw his involvement 'downgraded' to accessory to the crimes in the indictment.[63] These are still early days in the ICC's history, but this issue has already caused serious misgivings about the Court on the ground. Of particular concern is the absence, so far, of cumulative charging by Chambers, thereby rejecting the fact that sexual violence results in an array of harmful behaviours (torture, persecution, trafficking, sexual slavery, for instance, as well as rape).

ICC institutions are acutely aware of these problems, and considerable efforts are undeniably been made to allow the ICC, the Office of the Prosecutor and the Registry to address specific needs of victims involved in proceedings before the Court, especially for the victims of sexual and gender-based violence.[64] As with ordinary domestic courts, however,

---

[62] ICC, *Prosecutor v. Thomas Lubanga Dyilo*, Trial Chamber, Judgment pursuant to Article 74 of the Statute, ICC-01/04-01/06, 14 March 2012 (http://www.legal-tools.org/doc/677866/); ICC, *Prosecutor v. Thomas Lubanga Dyilo*, Appeals Chamber, Judgment on the appeal of Mr Thomas Lubanga Dyilo against his conviction, ICC-01/04-01/06, 1 December 2014 (http://www.legal-tools.org/doc/585c75/).

[63] ICC, *Prosecutor v. Germain Katanga*, Trial Chamber, Judgment pursuant to Article 74 of the Statute, ICC-01/04-01/07, 7 March 2014 (http://www.legal-tools.org/doc/f74b4f/).

[64] Measures include the repeated focus of the chief prosecutor, Fatou Bensouda (elected in 2011), to prioritise sexual and gender-based violence at all stages of proceedings. ICC, Office of the Prosecutor, "Policy Paper on Sexual and Gender-Based Crimes", June 2014 (http://www.legal-tools.org/doc/7ede6c/) has been drafted by her Office and been widely

limitations will always appear because of the formal and rigid procedures of a traditional criminal justice system. These challenges come to the fore with even greater prominence in the context of crimes committed on a massive scale in the context of conflict. Dealing with extreme violence, massive numbers of victims and complex societies with frequent inherent discriminations requires flexible systems capable of adapting to multiple needs.

18.4.2. Domestic Responses to International Sexual Crimes: Truth Commissions and Other Local Restorative Practices

Given the limitations of the traditional criminal justice system in dealing with international sexual crimes, this section highlights mechanisms that do not involve court systems (or at least not on their own). It focuses on truth commissions[65] and a selection of other local restorative practices, often founded on customary or religious traditions that pre-date the crimes they are brought to address. These approaches have a restorative value on multiple levels (individual, interpersonal and also societal, as most involve local communities).[66] Some involve dialogue with all parties (with a facilitator or a mediator); others consider the needs of one party only (generally victims). Some systems emphasise the importance of process, others of outcome (such as reparations or apologies). Many, however, focus on giving parties a voice and allowing them to relate their version of the past.

These processes may seem very different from conventional restorative justice mechanisms in a non-transitional setting. Their difference may also stem from the fact that they do not necessarily include all parties to a crime (victim, offender and community). In this sense they are not 'full' or 'pure' restorative justice, but they do all emphasise overarching

---

distributed for consultations among non-governmental organisations and victims groups Specialised offices have been set up within the Registry to assist victims and their counsel (legal, psychological assistance).

[65] This terminology is used to mean both truth commissions and truth and reconciliation commissions.

[66] David Androff, "Reconciliation in a Community-Based Restorative Justice Intervention", in *Journal of Sociology & Social Welfare*, 2012, vol. 39, no. 4, pp. 73–96. Official truth-telling mechanisms can also be fact-finding missions, *ad hoc* parliamentary committee hearings, documentation, exhumation processes, as well as criminal justice processes.

restorative justice principles of healing, accountability and wrongs inflicted to a person rather than on an abstract state.[67] There is, therefore, an argument to include these systems within a wider restorative justice response to crime.

In some cases, these practices may include the victim and offender as active participants in proceedings,[68] thereby contributing to them taking responsibility for the harm inflicted and adhering even more closely to the classic objectives of restorative justice (to allow "encounter, amends, reintegration, inclusion" for all parties affected by crime sometimes[69]).[70] In a context of transitional societies, this approach seems especially fitting. Situations are frequently so complex and dangerous that there are rarely obvious victims or perpetrators. Victims may have been complicit in the violation of the rights of others at one point and, similarly, perpetrators may themselves have been victimised at another.[71]

At present, the fundamental structure of criminal justice and the gendered operation of the adversarial system make it a highly problematic forum for addressing sexual crime.[72] Increasing awareness of the inadequacies of criminal justice in meeting the needs of victims motivates a growing movement to use alternative, more informal forms of instituting justice for victims, offenders and communities affected by sexual vio-

---

[67] See generally Marian Liebmann, *Restorative Justice: How It Works*, Jessica Kingsley, London, 2007; Kay Pranis, "Restorative Values", in Gerry Johnstone and Daniel van Ness (eds.), *Handbook of Restorative Justice*, Routledge, London, 2007; Walgrave, 2008, *supra* note 10; Howard Zehr and Harry Mika, *Fundamental Concepts of Restorative Justice*, Pennsylvania Mennonite Central Committee, Akron, 1997.

[68] Generally, the alleged offender does not usually appear voluntarily at the ICC (a notable exception is the case of *Bosco Ntaganda*, ICC-01/04-02/06) and is remanded in custody. There may be a dialogue between the victim and alleged offender, but within a formal court setting.

[69] Zehr, 1990, see *supra* note 10.

[70] The ICC and truth and reconciliation commissions do follow the overall spirit of restorative justice, or 'core principles', of healing, accountability and wrongs inflicted to a person rather than to the state.

[71] David Gray, "An Excuse-Centered Approach to Transitional Justice", in *Fordham Law Review*, 2006, vol. 74, pp. 2621–93.

[72] Bronwyn Naylor, "Effective Justice for Victims of Sexual Assault: Taking Up the Debates on Alternative Pathways", in *University of New South Wales Law Journal*, 2010, vol. 33, no. 3, pp. 662–84.

---

lence.[73] Nonetheless, Mary Koss notes that within jurisprudence scholarship the consensus is that restorative methods must be approached cautiously in cases of sexual violence.[74]

Using restorative justice approaches for serious crimes such as sexual violence is indeed not exempt from controversy, whether in a transitional justice setting or in peacetime. Some concerns relate to the lack of certainty on the rules applied as they depend on the parties and the process. To these concerns we respond that legislation is still applicable to the process so that upper limits in terms of sanctions and human rights standards do apply. Of greater concern, however, are objections based on the inherent unequal bargaining position of the victim, the lack of security of the parties, and the risk of appearing to trivialise the crime. These concerns must indeed be considered in the context of international human rights standards and particularly so in a post-conflict or post-authoritarian society where there are frequent issues of structural violence and deep-rooted discriminations. We should also recognise that victims of sexual violence themselves are using restorative justice mechanisms, even when formal courts are able to function. This may be because they offer creative, complementary and relevant responses to multiple layers of trauma.

Rather than rejecting these practices for sexual violence outright, there is an argument to say that, with appropriate support on human rights issues (including with regard to women), they may offer an interesting and practical means of dealing with international sexual violence.

18.4.2.1. Truth Commissions

Truth commissions, sometimes also referred to as commissions of inquiry, are temporary, non-judicial fact-finding bodies, which are authorised by the state, generally further to international impetus and with a suggested framework. Since the late 1990s and early 2000s, new truth commissions have learned from other truth commission experiences and adapted their

---

[73] Katherine van Wormer, "Restorative Justice as Social Justice for Victims of Gendered Violence: A Standpoint Feminist Perspective", in *Social Work*, 2009, vol. 54, no. 2, pp. 107–16.

[74] See Mary Koss, "Restorative Justice for Acquaintance Rape and Misdemeanor Sex Crimes", in James Ptacek (ed.), *Restorative Justice and Violence against Women*, Oxford University Press, Oxford, 2010, pp. 218–38.

mandate to their specific needs.[75] Truth commissions and commissions of
inquiry focus on human rights abuses that occurred during a specified
time, address the needs of victims and recommend measures to prevent
the repetition of abuses.[76] Typically, commissions of inquiry have a mandate that is more limited in time and scope. Truth commissions and commissions of inquiry have been implemented officially since the 1970s.

There is some debate over what bodies can constitute a truth commission or commission of inquiry *per se*.[77] Some authors, such as Priscilla
Hayner,[78] do not even offer a strong distinction between these two bodies.
Overall, however, the objective is always the same: to allow parties to tell
their story or 'truth', to receive acknowledgement and to begin restoring
their lives. For ease of reading, this chapter refers to both systems as truth
commissions.

18.4.2.1.1. Search for the Truth

The right to truth, an evolving legal concept in international law,[79] has its
historical roots in the struggle of families of the disappeared in Latin

---

[75] See Truth Commission of Peru (Comisión de la Verdad y Reconciliación, CVR), Final Report, 28 August 2008.

[76] Priscilla Hayner, *Unspeakable Truths: Transitional Justice and the Challenge of Truth
Commissions*, 2nd ed., Routledge, London, 2010.

[77] This debate explains discrepancies in the numbers of truth commissions cited: 33 cited by the
United States Institute of Peace, for instance, whereas Olsen, Payne and Reiter list 53 truth
commissions, see *ibid*.

[78] *Ibid.*

[79] The right to truth is enshrined in a number of international instruments and resolutions. UN,
Economic and Social Council, Updated Set of Principles for the Protection and Promotion of
Human Rights through Action to Combat Impunity, 8 February 2005, UN Doc.
E/CN.4/2005/Add.1. Principle 2 states: "Every people has the inalienable right to know the
truth about past events concerning the perpetration of heinous crimes and about the circumstances and reasons that led, through massive or systematic violations, to the perpetration of
those crimes". OHCHR resolution 2005/66, see *supra* note 61, "recognizes the importance of
respecting and ensuring the right to the truth so as to contribute to ending impunity and to
promote and protect human rights". UN General Assembly, Basic Principles and Guidelines
on the Right to a Remedy and Reparation for Victims of Gross Violations of International
Human Rights and Serious Violations of Humanitarian Law, Resolution 60/147, UN Doc.
A/RES/60/147, 16 December 2005 ('UN Basic Principles'). Principle 24 provides that the
right to reparations of the victim includes "verification of the facts and full and public disclosure of the truth". At the regional level, the Inter-American Commission has held that the
right to truth is found in the right to a fair trial, the right to freedom of expression, and the

---

America who tried to force authorities to disclose information about the fate of their relatives. The search for the truth is seen as key element for a society to address its past, honour its victims and put in place measures that will allow for individual and societal reconstruction.

Truth commissions usually pursue their mandate, as the term indicates, to search for the truth. To do this, they conduct detailed research and hold public and *in camera* hearings into atrocities, including abuses of power and economic crimes. Unlike criminal trials, truth commissions enjoy a wider mandate that enables them to delve into the underlying causes of the conflict and look to the future.[80] Because of this, some groups, which may have traditionally been discriminated against, have seen them as an opportunity to highlight neglected abuses, provide a forum for victims and recommend reparations to redress injustices. In the case of women, for instance, although many may feel they have not always been as supportive as they could have been, they have recognised that truth commissions can provide an extraordinary window of opportunity that is responsive to women's history and quest for reform.[81] Similarly, pervasive discrimination against other groups, such as indigenous Andean populations in Peru, can also be addressed by truth commissions.

An interesting point made by some scholars, including the Canadian writer Michael Ignatieff, is that a truth commission actually has to address different types of truths (factual, personal, social truths and healing or restorative truths in the sense of acknowledgement of what happened).[82] The flexibility of a commission is interesting because it is able to address these multiple layers of truths while adapting to local beliefs, needs and even to local mechanisms of dispute resolution.[83]

To some, truth commissions may appear the only option in the search for truth. This may be the case where amnesty has been granted (as

---

right to judicial protections. The African Convention on Human and People's Rights includes the right to truth under the right to an "effective remedy".

[80] ICTJ, 2012, see *supra* note 61.

[81] Vasuki Nesiah, "Gender and Truth Commission Mandates", Presentation at Open Society Institute Forum: Gender and Transitional Justice: Pursuing Justice and Accountability in Post-Conflict Situations, New York, 7 February 2006.

[82] Michael Ignatieff, "Overview: Articles of Faith", in *Index on Censorship*, 1996, vol. 25, no. 5, pp. 110–22.

[83] Roht-Arriaza, 2006, see *supra* note 20.

in Sierra Leone) or where effective prosecution is difficult (those responsible may still be in power or perpetrators cannot be brought to trial). To most, however, they complement the formal judicial system. Trials indeed have their own shortcomings in establishing the truth, particularly for vulnerable victims such as women and children for whom the formal procedures of the court induce a high risk of secondary victimisation. Overall, the flexibility of truth commissions appears well-suited to establishing and enforcing what the UN special rapporteur Louis Joinet calls the "inalienable right to truth".[84]

18.4.2.1.2. Forms of Truth-Seeking

In some cases (South Africa, Timor-Leste and Sierra Leone), truth commissions involve hearings where victims[85] and perpetrators[86] are brought together[87] in a dialogue format. When a dialogue between the parties ex-

---

[84] UN, Economic and Social Council, Question of the Impunity of Perpetrators of Human Rights Violations (Civil and Political), Final Report Prepared by Mr Joinet pursuant to Sub-Commission decision 1996/119, 26 June 1997, UN Doc. E/CN.4/Sub.2/1997/20, para. 17.

[85] In international law, a person is a 'victim' where, as a result of acts or omissions that constitute a violation of international human rights and humanitarian law norms, that person, individually or collectively, suffered harm, including physical or mental injury, emotional suffering, economic loss, or impairment of that person's fundamental legal rights. A 'victim' may also be a dependant or a member of the immediate family or household of the direct victim as well as a person who, in intervening to assist a victim or prevent the occurrence of further violations, has suffered physical, mental or economic harm. UN, Economic and Social Council, The Right to Restitution, Compensation and Rehabilitation for Victims of Gross Violations of Human Rights and Fundamental Freedoms, Final report of the Special Rapporteur, Mr. M. Cherif Bassiouni, submitted in accordance with Commission Resolution 1999/33, 18 January 2000, UN Doc. E/CN.4/2000/62, para. 8.

[86] The term 'perpetrator' is widely used in international human rights law to describe individuals who are responsible for violations of human rights and international humanitarian law. Accordingly, the United Nation's Sub-Commission on the Protection and Promotion of Human Rights mandated Louis Joinet in 1997 to examine the question of impunity. A distinction is made here with the state itself, which is also responsible for human rights violations under international law. Historically, human rights law addressed itself essentially to violations committed by the state. The development of the concept of 'perpetrators' indicates a desire to focus on individuals who bear personal responsibility for human rights violations and abuses. See José Zalaquett, "Balancing Ethical Imperatives and Political Constraints: The Dilemma of New Democracies Confronting Past Human Rights Violations", in *Hastings Law Journal*, 1992, vol. 43, no. 6, pp. 1425–38.

[87] This is not always the case and victims may, as in the truth commissions of Peru or Sierra Leone, simply relate their story to the commission *in camera*.

---

ists, each may go back and forth on the 'facts' and, out of this process, a vision of the truth may emerge that can enable participants to deal with the past and, perhaps, put it behind them. In time, this truth-telling process is intended to allow communities to have a common understanding of the past and to begin to reconcile (some truth commissions, such as those of Sierra Leone or South Africa, are indeed called 'truth and reconciliation commissions'). Reconciliation is sometimes misunderstood to refer to social harmony, which has led to expectations of friendly relationships between parties in conflict.[88] In a post-conflict and post-dictatorship setting, reconciliation definitions usually involve communication and mutual tolerance between opposing groups.[89] Reconciliation does not necessarily entail forgiveness. As in a conventional restorative justice process, forgiveness in a transitional context is often criticised as unrealistic.[90] This 'healing and restorative truth' provides the foundation for the second aim of most truth commissions, which is reconciliation. As in conventional restorative justice processes, however, the latter may not always be possible, or indeed desirable.

Women's experiences of conflict were often cast aside in initial truth commissions (such as in Chile or Argentina) under the rhetoric of a 'gender-neutral' approach. As Kimberly Theidon notes, however, this meant that men's perspectives and experiences were privileged thereby weakening the truth commissions' ability to understand and reform societies in transition.[91] Such criticisms explain why subsequent commissions, such as those of Guatemala, Peru, South Africa and later Haiti, Timor-Leste and Sierra Leone actively sought the testimony of women. Another milestone in specifically including women in truth-seeking procedures of

---

[88] Krishna Kumar, "Promoting Social Reconciliation in Post-conflict Societies: Selected Lessons from USAID's Experiences", USAID Program and Operations Assessment Report No. 24, US Agency for International Development, 1999; Eric Stover and Harvey Weinstein (eds.), *My Neighbour, My Enemy: Justice and Community in the Aftermath of Mass Atrocity*, Cambridge University Press, Cambridge, 2004; Androff, 2012, see *supra* note 66.

[89] See, for example, Martha Minow, *Between Vengeance and Forgiveness: Facing History after Genocide and Mass Violence*, Beacon Press, Boston, 1998.

[90] See Kumar, 1999, *supra* note 88; Minow, 1998, *supra* note 89; Tutu, 1999, *supra* note 16; Androff, 2012, *supra* note 66.

[91] Kimberly Theidon, "Gender in Transition: Common Sense, Women, and War", in *Journal of Human Rights*, 2007, vol. 6, no. 4, pp. 453–78. See also Fionnuala Ní Aoláin and Eilish Rooney, "Underenforcement and Intersectionality: Gendered Aspects of Transition for Women", in *International Journal of Transitional Justice*, 2007, vol. 1, no. 3, pp. 338–54.

---

truth commissions was the criminalisation of sexual violence in international criminal tribunals. This first occurred with the ICTR in the landmark *Akayesu* case,[92] then the ICTY, and then finally in the ICC Statute where sexual violence can constitute genocide, crimes against humanity or a war crime.

18.4.2.1.3. Truth Commissions and the Formal Judiciary

The use of these alternative restorative mechanisms in societies in transition may first stem from the absence of a functioning court and security system. Often transitioning societies will indeed no longer have sufficient judges, lawyers and security staff to ensure the functioning of a formal judiciary. In many cases, however, courts are not effective (due to corruption or lack of capacity) or too difficult or costly to access. Interestingly, some countries do have a functioning court system but victims, including of sexual violence, appear to prefer alternative, community-based, mechanisms. The choice may be linked to the inclusion of the victim, offender, community elders and hence a restorative approach, which is absent from the formal courts. In addition, because reparation is decided by the parties and the community, they tend to have a much greater chance of being implemented than those awarded by the courts.[93]

When truth commissions are set up, it is possible they are organised to collaborate with an existing formal court system, if it exists, just as it is able to do so with local restorative mechanisms (or informal justice systems). For Martha Minow, these systems can coexist and, with careful planning, they may even complement each other with truth commissions establishing accountability for widespread human rights abuses and, hence, augmenting the work of prosecutions.[94]

In some cases, a dual justice system (formal and informal justice system) exists in a transitioning society, such as in Liberia, Sierra Leone and Uganda. In others – for example, Rwanda with the *gacaca* courts (until May 2012) – legislation enacts how rights and procedures are shared

---

[92] ICTR, *Prosecutor v. Jean-Paul Akayesu*, Trial Chamber, Judgment, ICTR-96-4-T, 2 September 2001 (http://www.legal-tools.org/doc/b8d7bd); ICTR, *Prosecutor v. Jean-Paul Akayesu*, Appeals Chamber, Judgment, ICTR-96-4-T, 1 June 2001 (http://www.legal-tools.org/doc/c62d06/).

[93] For example, in Cambodia, see Burns and Daly, 2014, *supra* note 1.

[94] Minow, 1998, see *supra* note 89.

between them. The links between the truth commissions and the formal judiciary are sometimes very apparent, for example in Argentina, Chad and Sri Lanka where information collected for the truth commissions eventually led to prosecutions. In other cases, truth commissions themselves have the ability to grant amnesties (as in South Africa or Kenya) and therefore to halt prosecutions.

Most practitioners today would admit that restorative justice is not to be opposed to retributive justice. There is indeed a form of retribution within restorative justice, even if there are clear differences such as victims having a central role, procedures being more informal, and a negotiated process that includes lay and professional actors. Experience in transitional societies in particular demonstrate what Kathleen Daly has observed, namely that "informal (and non-discriminatory, non-stigmatising) processes of social control, coupled with the use of dialogue and persuasion, should form a larger share of justice system activity".[95]

18.4.2.1.4. Restoration and Reconciliation

Truth-telling in itself is essential to restore people's shattered lives, but it is not necessarily sufficient. Reconciliation, although pursued by many truth commissions, is in itself a step further, which cannot be equated with truth-telling or even forgiveness.

Whether reconciliation occurs on an individual and community level depends on how a person responds to the truths revealed. This, in turn, generally depends on the level of psychological support offered, which, in most resource-strapped truth commissions, is unfortunately limited. Beyond the factor of individual and collective trauma, for a truth commission to have a restorative impact, let alone the possibility of achieving reconciliation, it will also require a combination of tangible variables: credibility and perceived fairness of proceedings, reparations for victims, and access to resources (political and financial) to ensure that its recommendations are implemented.

A truth commission needs credibility and legitimacy. This requires the involvement of all stakeholders, including civil society, to determine

---

[95] Kathleen Daly, "Revisiting the Relationship Between Retributive and Restorative Justice", in Heather Strang and John Braithwaite (eds.), *Restorative Justice: Philosophy to Practice*, Ashgate, Aldershot, 2000, pp. 33–54.

the truth-seeking mandate, the periods to be covered and the types of violations to be investigated. The truth commission must also remain independent and immune from political manipulation. The latter is not always
easy given most transitioning societies continue to have at least some of
the same leaders in the realm of power after transition has begun. Finally,
the objectives and realistic outcomes of the truth commission need to be
clearly explained from the outset, particularly to victims who may otherwise run the risk of being retraumatised.

Civil society in Sierra Leone, for instance, was involved in many
aspects of the truth commission from its inception, including organising
consultations on the draft legislation, taking statements, providing support
to victims, giving input into the final recommendations, publicising the
final report, and creating awareness on its findings and recommendations.
The strong involvement of civil society ensured that certain crimes, such
as sexual violence, remained high on the agenda throughout the commission's work.

A truth commission must have perceived fairness of its proceedings. A regular concern over truth commissions is the need for them to
abide by procedural fairness, particularly when recommendations include
traditional dispute resolution mechanisms. Such concerns were clear for
the Liberian truth commission, for instance, but also in Timor-Leste's
reconciliation commission, which referred to ancestral dispute resolution
mechanisms through shamans.[96] Similarly, these issues have come up in
the Ugandan debate over the use of traditional religious ceremonies (including 'matu oput') to facilitate reconciliation between victims and perpetrators in Acholiland in northern Uganda. Concerns are especially vocal
for vulnerable groups, such as women and children, who may suffer from
societal discrimination. These informal restorative practices are considered further in the next section of this chapter.

Although conventional restorative justice mechanisms (in a non-
transitioning context) do not necessarily involve reparations, a majority of
victims involved in a truth commission tend to see these as essential to
their healing process and their ability to look forward. As the International
Center for Transitional Justice suggests, truth-telling without reparation
may be perceived by victims to be an incomplete process as they reveal

---

[96] Androff, 2012, see *supra* note 66.

their pain and suffering without any mechanism being put in place to deal with the consequences of this pain. Similarly, reparations without truth-telling could be perceived by the beneficiaries as an attempt to buy their silence.

Reparation may take a variety of forms (such as compensation, guarantees of non-repetition, rehabilitation, restitution or satisfaction),[97] but monetary compensation remains essential in a transitional context. As a consequence of mass violence, people often find themselves living in abject poverty, some having to endure the loss of limbs and others shunned because of their personal experiences such as rape and sexual slavery. For many victims, economic dependency and social exclusion are constant reminders of the suffering they have endured. A reparations programme with monetary measures may assist in a creating a context in which they may come to terms with the past and look forward.[98] In contrast to conventional restorative justice mechanisms, reparations recommended by truth commissions will frequently be of a collective nature (in whole or in part). In many cases, the sheer numbers of victims may mean it is not feasible to consider individual reparations. In cases of collective harm, collective reparations may also make sense to the community and encourage a sense of solidarity.

In all cases of reparations for mass atrocities, the primary duty to provide reparations lies with the state, either as instigator of the violence or because it failed in its task to provide adequate protection to its citizens. As Pablo De Greiff says, a clear commitment of the state, for example through a national reparations fund, leads to the restoration of civic trust.[99] However, in many cases, truth commission recommendations on reparations are only partly implemented, and sometimes not at all (consider recommendations in Sierra Leone, Liberia, Uganda, El Salvador, Guatemala, Peru and Paraguay, to name but a few). This is not to say the entire process is flawed and unhelpful. As truth commissions are mainly

---

[97] See UN Basic Principles, 2005, *supra* note 79.

[98] Sierra Leone Truth and Reconciliation Commission, *Final Report: Witness to Truth*, vol. 1, ch. 3, "Concepts", 2004, p. 84 ('SLTRC, Final Report').

[99] Pablo de Greiff, "Repairing the Past: Compensation for Victims of Human Rights Violations", in Pablo de Greiff (ed.), *The Handbook of Reparations*, Oxford University Press, Oxford, 2006, pp. 1–20.

process-driven mechanisms,[100] it can be argued that the process of truth-telling, in itself, may have a restorative value for victims and their communities (possibly perpetrators when they are involved).

If this is the case, non-governmental organisations ('NGOs') and other justice mechanisms then tend to intervene. Some also advocate development programmes as a possible means of offering reparations, although this brings about the difficulty of addressing vicarious liability. It also runs the risk of confusion among victims as to what part of the programme relates to their reparation and what part simply targets an entire population facing difficulties post-dictatorship or post-conflict. Reparations and truth-telling mechanisms, which are not supported by the state, are briefly considered hereafter in recommendations of the Sierra Leone truth commission, under "alternative restorative justice mechanisms".

18.4.2.2. Sexual Violence and Truth Commissions

When truth commissions are set up in the aftermath of an authoritarian regime, the sexual violence they confront is mostly committed by government forces. Rebuilding in the context of sexual violence is difficult on a personal and societal level, but some truth commissions have chosen to address this openly. In doing so, many have referred to local alternative restorative justice mechanisms with a view to ensuring healing is both meaningful for victims and perpetrators and to avoid the process being held up by lack of political will.

In Latin America, for example, several truth commissions mention sexual violence specifically: Ecuador (2007), Haiti (1995–1996), Paraguay (2008) and Peru (2001–2003). In Africa, Liberia (2003) and Sierra Leone (1999) focus extensively on the issue. The Democratic Republic of Congo Truth and Reconciliation Commission does so too, although this was not done comprehensively and lacked credibility. Timor-Leste's Truth Commission (through the Serious Crimes Panels and the Reconciliation Commission) also focused on sexual violence. In the latter case, this was considered in relation to women, sometimes with regard to children, and more rarely with regard to men.

---

[100] For some truth commissions there is a greater focus on outcome (such as reparations recommendations in Sierra Leone) and others on truth-telling and process (such as in Peru).

A number of truth commissions have decided to include key issues on the agenda from the moment the commission is designed, so that substantial attention can be awarded to them throughout the truth commissions process (fact-finding, hearings, report and recommendations). This has been the case notably for the Sierra Leone and Timor-Leste truth commissions. Elsewhere, such as Peru, Guatemala and the Solomon Islands, the truth commissions did not have sexual violence in their mandate at the outset but have chosen to address this in their final reports and recommendations.

If the process is done in close consultation with local leaders and associations, and if it is done with a clear focus on fair trial standards, it may be a flexible and appropriate mechanism to deal with sexual violence cases. As women victims of sexual violence themselves indicated in the truth commission consultations in Liberia, victims appeared to prefer alternative restorative justice mechanisms to the formal judiciary to assist them in coming to terms with their past.

It is interesting to note the variety of ways in which sexual violence has been addressed in the context of truth commissions. Some, such as early commissions in Latin American (Argentina and Chile) do not necessarily include it as a critical aspect of truth-telling and reconciliation. Others (such as Peru, Guatemala and South Africa) do not specifically mention sexual violence, or indeed gender violence, in their original mandate but have come to focus on it in their hearings and final reports. This is especially the case for the Peru Truth and Reconciliation Commission which dedicates two entire chapters to women and sexual violence. Reforms and awareness campaigns have followed the work of this commission, which, in turn, broke the silence on the daily sexual abuse women are suffering in their homes and in the streets.[101]

It Haiti, Sierra Leone and Timor-Leste, on the other hand, there was always a strong emphasis on sexual violence (and gendered violence generally) as this was seen as an essential component of the truth and reconciliation process. Regrettably, this did not lead to recommendations in the

---

[101] Julissa Mantilla Falcón, "The Peruvian Truth and Reconciliation Commission's Treatment of Sexual Violence against Women", Human Rights Brief, Centre for Human Rights and Humanitarian Law, American University Washington College of Law, 2005. See also Final Report of the Peru Truth Commission (Comisión de la Verdad y Reconciliación, CVR), 28 August 2008.

final reports that are specific or creative. The Sierra Leone final report, while it does focus on sexual violence, offers only general recommendations. Nevertheless, the process of truth-telling, the attention on the plight of certain groups during conflict and also within the wider community outside conflict, seems to have had an important impact on victim recognition and on their renewed sense of citizenship. It may also have practical repercussions, such as legislative changes for certain groups victimised during a conflict or authoritarian regime (women and certain indigenous groups in Peru, such as those in the Ayacucho region) or changes in relation to sexual violence. The work of the Truth and Reconciliation Commission of the Solomon Islands, for instance, demonstrated that this form of violence was prevalent against men as well as women during civil conflict. As a consequence, changes were made in the Penal Code so as to extend sexual violence to include men as well. Similarly, the Equity and Reconciliation Commission of Morocco advised changes in the criminal laws and procedures so as to include sexual violence, and the Chilean National Commission for Truth and Reconciliation recommended that national laws be brought in line with international human rights standards and led to the creation of a Human Rights Institute[102]

18.4.3. Other Alternative Restorative Justice Mechanisms

In societies transitioning away from conflict or authoritarian regimes, pre-existing systems of dispute resolution (often referred to as informal justice systems) may emerge as an alternative means of offering restorative justice. These mechanisms generally use traditional systems and ceremonies that may or may not be religious. Village elders or religious leaders, such as shamans, frequently play the role of mediators or facilitators and, most often, processes involve victims, offenders and the wider community. There is generally a strong emphasis on making amends and rehabilitation of parties to a crime. Victim participation and victims' needs are key, although it is recognised that some groups (notably women and children) may not actually benefit from full and free participation. Some practition-

---

[102] Final Report of the Chilean National Commission for Truth and Reconciliation (Comisión de Verdad y Reconciliación), also known as the 'Retting Report' in February 1991. More than two decades later, the Chilean Congress passed Law No. 20.405 (November 2009) creating the Institute for Human Rights and reopened the qualification of victims entitled to reparations.

ers indeed feel the risk of discrimination for these victims is too high in the context of informal justice systems and hence they feel they should never deal with sexual violence.[103]

Although reservations about these systems are understandable, especially for vulnerable groups, it is difficult to dismiss them outright, even in the delicate context of sexual violence. Victims and their families do refer to them,[104] and they seem to offer adaptability to local traditions, an implication of the local community and a better likelihood that reparations will be implemented because of the community involvement in devising them. Some may argue that, with appropriate support in abiding with human rights standards, these systems may, in the context of transition, offer considerable benefits to parties to a crime even in cases of sexual violence. In the latter cases, the use of informal justice systems may even have some influence on societal beliefs in relation to this form of violence and to its victims.

Truth commissions themselves often consider that sexual violence victims and perpetrators may best achieve resolution through informal justice systems rather than the formal judiciary (Peru or Haiti, Liberia, Sierra Leone and Timor-Leste, for instance). Some recommend the use of local religious groups or women's groups (Peru and Haiti); others refer to traditional mechanisms (Liberia, Sierra Leone and Timor-Leste). In Liberia, the truth commission recommended extending the use of the traditional dispute resolution mechanisms called 'palava hut'.[105] The latter have, until now, been part of the customary law system (formal and informal justice systems coexist in a dual justice system) and, traditionally, they have not resolved serious crimes such as sexual violence or rape. It is unclear at this stage how well the adaptation has worked. Other reconciliation mechanisms were also encouraged by the Liberian Truth and Reconciliation Commission, including the use of traditional leaders, especially

---

[103] UNDP, 2012, see *supra* note 30.

[104] See Truth and Reconciliation Commission of Liberia, *Final Report*, vol. 3, title 1, 58, June 2009.

[105] The definition of '*palava hut*' as adopted by the Liberia truth commission refers to a gathering place in a town or village, generally a thatched hut, where disputes are settled, usually through a process akin to mediation with a respected member of the community.

female traditional leaders, to facilitate reconciliation and influence community reconstruction.[106]

In Sierra Leone, the truth commission recommended extending reconciliation activities of the district reconciliation committees established in partnership with the Inter-Religious Council of Sierra Leone. The latter has had a wide variety of reconciliation activities, including reconciliation ceremonies where victim and perpetrator are brought together, sometimes with their respective communities. Traditional dances, theatre, traditional hunting, cleansing ceremonies (sometimes referred to as 'cleansing of the bush') may facilitate these processes. Specific categories of victims, including sexual violence victims, were awarded reparations in the form of free healthcare and free education for their children if the injury took place between 23 March 1991 and 1 March 2001. In contrast to the South African Truth and Reconciliation Commission, reparations are not reserved only to those who partake in commission proceedings.[107] There is some discussion about linking reparations to social assistance, since the latter is an obligation from the state to all its citizens. It may be acceptable if reparation is clearly labelled as such for specific categories of people.

The Sierra Leone truth commission also recommended that the government look into harmonising common law and customary law practices so that the latter abide by human rights standards. The truth commission had specific reservations about customary laws in relation to rape and sexual violence where, in the case of young girls, it was felt these were too often settled between perpetrator and the victims' family through monetary compensation and without the victim having any actual say in the matter. In addition, it was noted that, under customary law, consent of a minor for sexual relations is not required. The truth commission recommended that UNIFEM and the Ministry of Social Welfare and Gender Affairs raise awareness about the culture of silence that surrounds rape and sexual violence.

In Timor-Leste, the truth commission strongly referred to reconciliatory justice systems, which existed well before colonisation. The latter coexisted with formal courts as a dual system when the Timor-Leste conflict began in 1999. The system involves a community-led shaming of of-

---

[106] See SLTRC, Final Report, vol. 3, title I, p. 90, *supra* note 98.

[107] *Ibid.*, vol. 2, chapter 3, October 2004.

fenders and then exchanges of forgiveness and apology between perpetrators and victims. In some cases, these processes are facilitated by shamans or by village priests (95 per cent of the Timorese population are Roman Catholic). Critics have pointed out the risk of such systems leading to mob justice, although links with the formal truth commission, and hence international human rights standards, can mitigate these concerns to a degree.

In societies where truth commissions have not been installed, or only partially, informal justice systems have sometimes attempted to deal with the past and push for reconciliation through other means. In Uganda, two successive truth commissions have failed abysmally and, although a 2001 law has tried to foster peace through an amnesty programme aimed at ex-Lord's Resistance Army combatants in northern Uganda, most victims feel this should have been accompanied by measures of accountability and reparations.[108] For some, traditional dispute resolution mechanisms, such as cleansing and purification rites of the Acholi people, of which the '*matu oput*' is well known, were most suited to operationalise reconciliation. According to the Acholi moral code, parties in conflict must be reconciled and cleansed before being reintegrated into the community. In the *matu oput* ceremony, both perpetrator and victim must drink from the same cup and an Acholi leader, who has considerable influence in the community, facilitates the ceremony. Many in Uganda feel this may be an interesting approach, particularly given the perception that most perpetrators, particularly among former child soldiers, were in fact victims themselves. There are, however, reservations about this system, including the fact that there is no central quest for the truth about the past and that there is no apparent mechanism to ask victims what their needs are. As practitioners themselves indicate, there are multiple levels of truths and multiple levels of reconciliation that must be addressed in a context of a society in transition in order for peace to be sustainable.[109]

In the context of Rwanda, a National Unity and Reconciliation Commission was set up in 1999, but it considered only issues related to education and the causes of the Rwandan genocide of 1994. The use of

---

[108] ICTJ, 2012, see *supra* note 61.

[109] Chris Mburu, "Etude de cas: Ouganda", in *La Justice Transitionnelle dans le Monde Francophone*, Département Suisse des Affaires Etrangères, DFAE, Conference Paper, 2007, no. 2.

the well-known local courts, the *gacaca*,[110] was established through legislation.[111] They have no longer been in use since 4 May 2012, but the system is original and merits mentioning in the context of restorative justice
and sexual violence in societies in transition. According to legislation,
category one crimes (including those responsible for planning the genocide, and those responsible for rape and sexual violence) were not transferred to *gacaca* courts but to the formal justice system where victims
benefited from anonymity and procedures *in camera*. However, if a suspect confessed to crimes early on in proceedings, before his or her name
was included on the register of those suspected of genocide, he or she
could confess and see the crime downgraded from a category one to a category two crime. The case would then benefit from a *gacaca* or local
court procedure with a local judge and the local community. Rwanda and
its legislation must abide by international human rights standards and,
hence, so must *gacaca* courts. Even so, while *gacaca* courts did favour
community participation and procedures familiar to the local population,
there were misgivings. These included a general climate not conducive to
openness and tolerance,[112] and judges who were not properly trained and
who were not paid.

Alternative restorative justice systems in societies in transition of
course go beyond informal justice systems to include more conventional
restorative justice systems, such as mediation and conciliation, through
NGOs or other civil society groups. Criticisms of these systems in relation
to sexual violence are the same as for all restorative justice measures and
sexual violence. A report of the Inter-American Commission on Human
Rights, for instance, voiced classic concerns over victim protection and
actual freedom of the victim (it especially referred to mediation and conciliation) although, as it pointed out, many jurisdictions do seem to revert

---

[110] *Gacaca* refers to 'grass', and by extension to 'justice on the grass', in Kinyarwanda. This
form of local justice was used after the Rwandan genocide to assist the overburdened courts.

[111] Law No. 08/96, 30 August 1996 as amended by Law No. 16/04, 19 June 2004.

[112] On *gacaca* see Anne-Marie de Brouwer and Sandra Ka Hon Chu (eds.), *The Men Who Killed
Me: Rwandan Survivors of Sexual Violence*, Douglas and McIntyre, Vancouver, 2009. See
also Anne-Marie de Brouwer and Sandra Ka Hon Chu, "Gacaca Courts in Rwanda: 18 Years
after the Genocide, Is There Justice and Reconciliation for Survivors of Sexual Violence?", in
IntLawGrrls, 7 April 2012.

to restorative justice for sexual violence.[113] In Nicaragua, sexual violence cases have been settled through mediation,[114] and in Guatemala, the law allows the use of "victim's forgiveness" as a result of conciliation proceedings in cases of sexual violence.[115] In Honduras, statutory rape, incest, forcible abduction and "criminal sexual contact" may be subject to conciliation if the victim is over 14 years old.[116] El Salvador also appears to allow reconciliation mechanisms outside the courtroom in cases of sexual violence.[117]

Restorative justice measures undertaken by NGOs and civil society in cases of sexual violence go beyond conventional processes such as mediation or conciliation. As in the context of truth commissions, they include investigating systematic human rights abuses, giving a voice to victims and securing the greater involvement of civil society. They can undertake interviews, document human rights abuses (including sexual violence cases), publish reports, hold community meetings, and pursue community-led memorials such as those held annually to commemorate massacres or disappearances. Similarly, human rights groups and leaders may decide to set up an alternative non-governmental commission to investigate abuses. This was the case in Honduras where the Argentine Nobel Prize winner Adolfo Pérez Esquivel created such a commission to investigate abuses leading to and following the 28 June 2009 coup against President Manuel Zelaya. Others still may use public hearings where there is shaming, repentance and forgiveness.[118] The latter seems to be most used in societies with a strong Christian tradition, such as in Peru, South Africa and Timor-Leste. Sometimes, other truth-telling mechanisms have

---

[113] Inter-American Commission on Human Rights ('IACHR'), *Access to Justice for Women Victims of Sexual Violence in Mesoamerica*, Organization of American States, OEA Ser.L/V/II. Doc.63, 2011, pp. 75–76.

[114] Supreme Court of Justice of Nicaragua and the Spanish Agency for International Cooperation, legal analysis of verdicts delivered in cases involving intra-family and domestic violence and civil suits in family law, in *ibid.*, p. 74.

[115] Familiares y Mujeres Sobre Vivientes de la Violencia, "Análisis Sobre la Situación de Violencia en contra de la Mujer en Guatemala" [Analysis of Violence against Women in Guatemala], in *ibid.*, p. 53.

[116] Response to a questionnaire presented by Eduardo Montes Manzano, in *ibid.*, p. 74.

[117] Observatorio de la Violencia de Género contra las Mujeres (Observatory on Gender Violence Against Women), Organización de mujeres salvadoreñas por la Paz, in *ibid.*, p. 75.

[118] See John Braithwaite, *Crime, Shame and Reintegration*, Cambridge University Press, Cambridge, 1989.

appeared in parallel to an internationalised court because the latter did not sufficiently respond to victims' needs (consider the truth-telling groups for victims which were organised by NGOs on the fringes of the Extraordinary Chambers in the Courts of Cambodia).

18.5. Concluding Thoughts: Sexual Violence as a Core International Crime and the Way Forward

The responses to international sexual crimes have changed over the last decade, focusing more closely on the needs of all the parties to the crime, particularly on victims. This may better address the specific and difficult needs that result from extreme violence on a massive scale, especially in societies with inherent tensions and discriminations. This approach may allow for individual healing, accountability, acknowledgement and real involvement in proceedings. This amounts to restorative justice. This chapter has analysed some characteristics and strengths of restorative justice, and considered reasons why an application of this justice paradigm to the theme of international sexual crimes may be warranted.

Some attempts are being made to combine a restorative justice approach to international sexual crimes and retributive justice. Although these are not theoretically incompatible, they are difficult to combine in practice due to the stringent and formal procedures of traditional criminal justice. The ICC Statute continuously tries to overcome this challenge, but with limited success so far.

Alternative restorative justice systems – whether they be truth commissions or informal justice systems – have an essential role to play in offering some form of redress to victims of international sexual violence which makes sense to them and which is thus more likely to be abided by, as well as ensuring that international standards are respected. There are clearly noteworthy concerns over fair trial standards, especially for vulnerable victims such as those of sexual violence. This must be considered carefully and each restorative system must, evidently, be appreciated and its own merits and understood as being only one measure among many in addressing sexual violence.

Although research in this field should proceed further, it appears that the complexity of international sexual crimes in conflict may be best accommodated if local restorative practices are able to connect with more formal systems of justice, both in order to have better assurances for human rights standards, but also to ensure that multiple needs (individual, interpersonal and community) can be addressed holistically. Restorative practices in societies in transition – particularly so in societies emerging from conflict where limited sources of justice are available – demonstrate considerable practical creativity. As such, they constitute an invaluable resource for considering new restorative justice approaches to sexual violence, both in transitioning societies and indeed in societies at peace.

INDEX

A

Abney, Mark, 287
accountability, 3, 8-9, 21, 45, 49, 58-59,
    71-81, 120-124, 128, 136-139, 146,
    166-168, 173, 176, 195, 211-213, 220,
    229-231, 244, 253, 295-298, 311, 384,
    405, 457, 466, 473, 490-496, 503, 514-
    517, 523, 532-535
Adjami, Mima, 132
admissibility, 149, 345-352, 364-365, 374,
    379, 386, 418, 467, 471-493, 498-499
Aertsen, Ivo, 510
Africa, 62, 67-73, 77, 504, 514, 527
African Charter on Human and Peoples'
    Rights, 370-371, 520
African Charter on the Rights and Welfare
    of the Child, 143
African Commission on Human and
    Peoples' Rights
    Principles and Guidelines on the Right
        to a Fair Trial and Legal Assistance
        in Africa, 132
African Union, 132, 225, 358, 370
Agirre Aranburu, Xabier, 21, 57, 206,
    208, 312, 433, 497
Ahluwalia, Kuljit, 390
Ahmed, Anees, 232
Akande, Dapo, 61, 343
Akhavan, Payam, 18, 27, 51-55, 128, 222,
    227, 376, 403-406, 411
Aldana-Pindell, Raquel, 234
Alder, Matthew, 408
Alexander, James F., 27
al-Hussein, Zeid Ra'ad, 317, 412
Alliot-Marie, Michèle, 243
Alston, Philip, 22
Altman, Andrew, 153
Amann, Diana Marie, 18-20, 32, 35, 118,
    434
Ambos, Kai, 9, 87, 156, 293-297, 309,
    328, 356, 366, 466, 497, 559
American Bar Association, 302

American Convention on Human Rights,
    88, 92, 94, 105, 370-371
Amnesty International, 65, 119-122, 241,
    415
Anderson, Elizabeth S., 33
Andrews, Katherine N., 393
Androff, David, 516, 522-525
Angermaier, Claudia, 47, 169, 559
Antoniadis, Antonis, 241
Arbour, Louise, 47, 169, 296, 312, 423
Arendt, Hannah, 53
Argentina, 45, 50-52, 90, 96-105, 140,
    182-185, 189, 522-524, 528
    amnesty laws, 184
    Arsenales Case, 185
    Fernandez Juarez Case, 186
    Gregorio Rafael Molina Case, 105-
        108, 185
    Horacio Américo Barcos Case, 105
    Miara et al. Case, 105-108, 185
    Santiago Omar Riveros et al. Case,
        106
    Tepedino Case, 186
Arieff, Alexis, 113
Arnold, Roberta, 320, 358
Arsanjani, Mahnoush A., 221-222
Asher, Jana, 426
Ashworth, Andrew, 234, 485
Asian Development Bank, 231
Askin, Kelly D., 59, 120, 131, 180, 194-
    195, 265, 273, 294, 321-323, 435, 442,
    447, 457-462, 468, 497, 506
attack
    context, 329
    definition, 327
    knowledge, 332
    requirements, 328, 329
Aukerman, Miriam, 31
Australia, 30, 238, 513
Austria, 238
aut dedere aut judicare, principle of, 361
Avocats Sans Frontières, 131, 282, 283
Aydelott, Danise, 122, 123
Ayiera, Eve, 114

failure of norm enforcement, 38
harm against women, 24
lack of attention, 231
prioritisation. *See* prioritisation of sex
    crimes
re-victimisation, 164
scope, 16
Special Court for Sierra Leone, 24
victimisation, 163
sex difference, theories of, 8
sex-based biology, 275
sex-specific agendas, 271, 278-279, 288
sexual abuse
    definition, 323
sexual exploitation
    definition, 323
sexual slavery, 16, 57, 113, 129, 145, 151-
    162, 171-172, 180, 193, 203, 256, 295,
    307-309, 324-326, 336, 355, 375, 438-
    440, 452-454, 469, 485, 501, 515, 526
sexual torture, 107
sexual violence
    allegations against UN Peacekeepers,
        318
    command responsibility, 436
    concept of gender, 196
    consideration as torture, 101
    core of degrading practices, 107
    discrimination, 195
    efforts for international recognition,
        262
    feminist theory, 199
    gender perspective analysis, 183
    recognition as grave violation of
        human rights, 95
Shah-Davis, Shilan, 384
Shamir, Hila, 262, 272
Shearer, David, 66
Shinoda, Hideaki, 228
Shoamanesh, Sam Sasan, 126-127
Sideris, Tina, 505
Sierra Leone, 6, 17, 25, 40-41, 57, 61-85,
    145, 150, 167, 173, 194, 318, 388,
    415, 508, 521-530
    Armed Forces Revolutionary Council,
        418
    Civil Defence Forces, 418
    Lomé amnesty, 70

Revolutionary United Front, 64, 202,
    418
Truth and Reconciliation Commission,
    65, 526, 531
Silverberg, Helene, 120, 462
Simonovic, Ivan, 122
Simpson, Gerry J., 79, 238
Singer, P.W., 65
Sivakumaran, Sandesh, 124, 195, 487,
    494
Skelsbaek, Inger, 319
Skjeie, Hege, 3
Skjelsbæk, Inger, 3
Skre, Alf Butenschøn, 294, 496-497, 559,
    563
Sloane, Robert D., 17-18, 27-29, 35, 89,
    222, 376, 403-408
Sluiter, Göran, 46, 115, 122, 163
Smeulers, Alette, 138, 425
Smidt, Michael L., 406
Society for Women's Health Research,
    257, 267, 275-278
Solís, María Eugenia, 188
Solomon Islands
    Truth and Reconciliation Commission,
        529
South Africa, 45, 521-524, 528-534
    Truth and Reconciliation Commission,
        531
Spain, 104, 182-183, 188-189, 238-241
Special Court for Sierra Leone, 6, 56, 62,
    75-81, 145-147, 157-162, 169-174,
    180, 194, 198, 305, 353, 388, 399,
    415-418, 422, 439, 496, 506
    Prosecutor v. Brima et al., 42, 171
    Prosecutor v. Fofana et al., 80, 146,
        158-159, 198
    Prosecutor v. Sesay et al., 22, 81, 157,
        158, 180, 194, 202-203, 353
    Prosecutor v. Sesay, Kallon and Gbao,
        81
    Prosecutor v. Taylor, 64, 68, 73, 171
    Statute, 74-75, 168
    Witness and Victims Section, 81
specialised *ad hoc* arrangements
    advantages, 8, 242, 251
    benefits, 8
    disadvantages, 8, 246, 252
    judges, 250

Vincent, Robin, 76-77
Vinck, Patrick, 230
von Hebel, Herman, 337
von Hirsch, Andrew, 20, 224, 234

W

Waddell, Nicholas, 466
Waite, Emily, 21
Wald, Patricia, 39
Walgrave, Lode, 503, 508-510, 517
Waller, Emily, 467
Wallstorm, Margot, 131
war crimes
  conscripting, 2
  enlisting, 2
  using child soldiers, 2
Ward, Jeanne, 113, 164, 168
Warr, Mark, 21
Weed, Matthew C., 393
Weigend, Thomas, 49
Weiner, Tim, 68-71
Weinstein, Harvey, 31, 167, 229, 522
Weisman, Carole S., 260
Weiss, Lauren A., 287
Wellman, Christopher Heath, 153
Werle, Gerhard, 327, 435
Werner, Alain, 233
West, Robin, 19, 24
Westad, Odd Arne, 213
Westmarland, Nicola, 512
Whande, Tanonoka Joseph, 318
widespread
  definition, 328
Wilde, Alexander, 229
Wildermuth, Patricia, 496-497

Willard, Huntington, 285
Williams, Fletch, 3, 9, 445
Williams, Sarah, 506
Wilmshurst, Elizabeth, 328, 341
Wing, Adrien Katherine, 24
Wippman, David, 18, 27, 404
Wirth, Steffen, 344
witnesses
  crime base, 431
  overview and linkage, 432
Witte, Eric A., 401
Women's Initiatives for Gender Justice,
  41, 130, 282, 421-423, 431, 437, 440,
  461, 469, 475, 495-496
Women's Link Worldwide, 7, 183-187
Wood, Elisabeth J., 122, 137-138, 227,
  294, 425, 496-497, 563
Woods, Ngaire, 63, 82
Working Group on Children and Armed
  Conflict, 143
World Bank, 231
Wormington, Jim, 131

Z

Zacklin, Ralph, 387
Žagovec, Gorana, 13, 561
Zahar, Alexander, 122
Zalaquett, José, 521
Zawati, Hilmi M., 446
Zehr, Howard, 503, 508-509, 517
Zelaya, Manuel, 534
Zinsstag, Estelle, 3, 9, 501-503, 508-513
Zwanenburg, Marten, 332-334, 342
Zwanikken, Prisca, 448

TOAEP TEAM

Editors

Mr. Antonio Angotti, Editor
Professor Olympia Bekou, Editor
Mr. Mats Benestad, Editor
Professor Morten Bergsmo, Editor-in-Chief
Mr. Alf Butenschøn Skre, Senior Executive Editor
Ms. Eleni Chaitidou, Editor
Mr. CHAN Ho Shing Icarus, Editor
Assistant Professor CHEAH Wui Ling, Editor
Dr. FAN Yuwen, Editor
Ms. Manek Minhas, Editor
Mr. Gareth Richards, Senior Editor
Mr. Nikolaus Scheffel, Editor
Mr. SIN Ngok Shek, Editor
Ms. SONG Tianying, Editor
Mr. Moritz Thörner, Editor
Ms. ZHANG Yueyao, Editor

Editorial Assistants

Ms. Pauline Brosch
Ms. Marquise Lee Houle
Ms. Genevieve Zingg

Law of the Future Series Co-Editors

Dr. Alexander (Sam) Muller
Professor Larry Cata Backer
Professor Stavros Zouridis

Nuremberg Academy Series Editor

Dr. Viviane Dittrich, Deputy Director, International Nuremberg Principles Academy

Scientific Advisers

Professor Danesh Sarooshi, Principal Scientific Adviser for International Law
Professor Andreas Zimmermann, Principal Scientific Adviser for Public International Law
Professor Kai Ambos, Principal Scientific Adviser for International Criminal Law
Dr.h.c. Asbjørn Eide, Principal Scientific Adviser for International Human Rights Law

Editorial Board

Dr. Xabier Agirre, International Criminal Court
Dr. Claudia Angermaier, Austrian judiciary
Ms. Neela Badami, Narasappa, Doraswamy and Raja
Dr. Markus Benzing, Freshfields Bruckhaus Deringer, Frankfurt

OTHER VOLUMES IN THE
PUBLICATION SERIES

Morten Bergsmo, Mads Harlem and Nobuo Hayashi (editors):
Importing Core International Crimes into National Law
Torkel Opsahl Academic EPublisher
Oslo, 2010
FICHL Publication Series No. 1 (Second Edition, 2010)
ISBN: 978-82-93081-00-5

Nobuo Hayashi (editor):
National Military Manuals on the Law of Armed Conflict
Torkel Opsahl Academic EPublisher
Oslo, 2010
FICHL Publication Series No. 2 (Second Edition, 2010)
ISBN: 978-82-93081-02-9

Morten Bergsmo, Kjetil Helvig, Ilia Utmelidze and Gorana Žagovec:
The Backlog of Core International Crimes Case Files in Bosnia and Herzegovina
Torkel Opsahl Academic EPublisher
Oslo, 2010
FICHL Publication Series No. 3 (Second Edition, 2010)
ISBN: 978-82-93081-04-3

Morten Bergsmo (editor):
Criteria for Prioritizing and Selecting Core International Crimes Cases
Torkel Opsahl Academic EPublisher
Oslo, 2010
FICHL Publication Series No. 4 (Second Edition, 2010)
ISBN: 978-82-93081-06-7

Morten Bergsmo and Pablo Kalmanovitz (editors):
Law in Peace Negotiations
Torkel Opsahl Academic EPublisher
Oslo, 2010
FICHL Publication Series No. 5 (Second Edition, 2010)
ISBN: 978-82-93081-08-1

Morten Bergsmo, César Rodríguez Garavito, Pablo Kalmanovitz and Maria Paula Saffon (editors):

Distributive Justice in Transitions
Torkel Opsahl Academic EPublisher
Oslo, 2010
FICHL Publication Series No. 6 (2010)
ISBN: 978-82-93081-12-8

Morten Bergsmo, César Rodriguez-Garavito, Pablo Kalmanovitz and Maria Paula
Saffon (editors):
Justicia Distributiva en Sociedades en Transición
Torkel Opsahl Academic EPublisher
Oslo, 2012
FICHL Publication Series No. 6 (2012)
ISBN: 978-82-93081-10-4

Morten Bergsmo (editor):
*Complementarity and the Exercise of Universal Jurisdiction for Core International
Crimes*
Torkel Opsahl Academic EPublisher
Oslo, 2010
FICHL Publication Series No. 7 (2010)
ISBN: 978-82-93081-14-2

Morten Bergsmo (editor):
Active Complementarity: Legal Information Transfer
Torkel Opsahl Academic EPublisher
Oslo, 2011
FICHL Publication Series No. 8 (2011)
ISBN print: 978-82-93081-56-2
ISBN e-book: 978-82-93081-55-5

Morten Bergsmo (editor):
Abbreviated Criminal Procedures for Core International Crimes
Torkel Opsahl Academic EPublisher
Brussels, 2017
FICHL Publication Series No. 9 (2018)
ISBN print: 978-82-93081-20-3
ISBN e-book: 978-82-8348-104-4

Sam Muller, Stavros Zouridis, Morly Frishman and Laura Kistemaker (editors):
The Law of the Future and the Future of Law
Torkel Opsahl Academic EPublisher
Oslo, 2010
FICHL Publication Series No. 11 (2011)
ISBN: 978-82-93081-27-2

Morten Bergsmo, Alf Butenschøn Skre and Elisabeth J. Wood (editors):
Understanding and Proving International Sex Crimes
Torkel Opsahl Academic EPublisher
Beijing, 2012
FICHL Publication Series No. 12 (2012)
ISBN: 978-82-93081-29-6

Morten Bergsmo (editor):
Thematic Prosecution of International Sex Crimes
Torkel Opsahl Academic EPublisher
Beijing, 2012
FICHL Publication Series No. 13 (2012)
ISBN: 978-82-93081-31-9

Terje Einarsen:
The Concept of Universal Crimes in International Law
Torkel Opsahl Academic EPublisher
Oslo, 2012
FICHL Publication Series No. 14 (2012)
ISBN: 978-82-93081-33-3

莫滕·伯格斯默 凌岩(主编):
国家主权与国际刑法
Torkel Opsahl Academic EPublisher
Beijing, 2012
FICHL Publication Series No. 15 (2012)
ISBN: 978-82-93081-58-6

Morten Bergsmo and LING Yan (editors):
State Sovereignty and International Criminal Law
Torkel Opsahl Academic EPublisher
Beijing, 2012
FICHL Publication Series No. 15 (2012)
ISBN: 978-82-93081-35-7

Morten Bergsmo and CHEAH Wui Ling (editors):
Old Evidence and Core International Crimes
Torkel Opsahl Academic EPublisher
Beijing, 2012
FICHL Publication Series No. 16 (2012)
ISBN: 978-82-93081-60-9

YI Ping:
戦争と平和の間――発足期日本国際法学における「正しい戦争」の観念とその帰結
Torkel Opsahl Academic EPublisher
Beijing, 2013
FICHL Publication Series No. 17 (2013)
ISBN: 978-82-93081-66-1

Morten Bergsmo and SONG Tianying (editors):
On the Proposed Crimes Against Humanity Convention
Torkel Opsahl Academic EPublisher
Brussels, 2014
FICHL Publication Series No. 18 (2014)
ISBN: 978-82-93081-96-8

Morten Bergsmo (editor):
Quality Control in Fact-Finding
Torkel Opsahl Academic EPublisher
Florence, 2013
FICHL Publication Series No. 19 (2013)
ISBN: 978-82-93081-78-4

Morten Bergsmo, CHEAH Wui Ling and YI Ping (editors):
Historical Origins of International Criminal Law: Volume 1
Torkel Opsahl Academic EPublisher
Brussels, 2014
FICHL Publication Series No. 20 (2014)
ISBN: 978-82-93081-11-1

Morten Bergsmo, CHEAH Wui Ling and YI Ping (editors):
Historical Origins of International Criminal Law: Volume 2
Torkel Opsahl Academic EPublisher
Brussels, 2014
FICHL Publication Series No. 21 (2014)
ISBN: 978-82-93081-13-5

Morten Bergsmo, CHEAH Wui Ling, SONG Tianying and YI Ping (editors):
Historical Origins of International Criminal Law: Volume 3
Torkel Opsahl Academic EPublisher
Brussels, 2015
FICHL Publication Series No. 22 (2015)
ISBN print: 978-82-8348-015-3
ISBN e-book: 978-82-8348-014-6

Morten Bergsmo, CHEAH Wui Ling, SONG Tianying and YI Ping (editors):
Historical Origins of International Criminal Law: Volume 4
Torkel Opsahl Academic EPublisher
Brussels, 2015
FICHL Publication Series No. 23 (2015)
ISBN print: 978-82-8348-017-7
ISBN e-book: 978-82-8348-016-0

Morten Bergsmo, Klaus Rackwitz and SONG Tianying (editors):
Historical Origins of International Criminal Law: Volume 5
Torkel Opsahl Academic EPublisher
Brussels, 2017
FICHL Publication Series No. 24 (2017)
ISBN print: 978-82-8348-106-8
ISBN e-book: 978-82-8348-107-5

Morten Bergsmo and SONG Tianying (editors):
Military Self-Interest in Accountability for Core International Crimes
First Edition
Torkel Opsahl Academic EPublisher
Brussels, 2015
FICHL Publication Series No. 25 (2015)
ISBN print: 978-82-93081-61-6
ISBN e-book: 978-82-93081-81-4

Wolfgang Kaleck:
Double Standards: International Criminal Law and the West
Torkel Opsahl Academic EPublisher
Brussels, 2015
FICHL Publication Series No. 26 (2015)
ISBN print: 978-82-93081-67-8
ISBN e-book: 978-82-93081-83-8

LIU Daqun and ZHANG Binxin (editors):
Historical War Crimes Trials in Asia
Torkel Opsahl Academic EPublisher
Brussels, 2016
FICHL Publication Series No. 27 (2015)
ISBN print: 978-82-8348-055-9
ISBN e-book: 978-82-8348-056-6

Mark Klamberg (editor):
Commentary on the Law of the International Criminal Court
Torkel Opsahl Academic EPublisher

Brussels, 2017
FICHL Publication Series No. 29 (2017)
ISBN print: 978-82-8348-100-6
ISBN e-book: 978-82-8348-101-3

All volumes are freely available online at http://www.toaep.org/ps/. For printed copies, see http://toaep.org/about/distribution/. For reviews of earlier books in this Series in academic journals and yearbooks, see http://toaep.org/reviews/.

www.ingramcontent.com/pod-product-compliance
Lightning Source LLC
Chambersburg PA
CBHW050529190326
41458CB00045B/6764/J